Encyclopedia of Capital Punishments in the World

Editor
Nelly Deaton

Scribbles

Year of Publication 2018

ISBN : 9789352979707

Book Published by

Scribbles

(An Imprint of Alpha Editions)

email - alphaedis@gmail.com

Produced by: PediaPress GmbH
Limburg an der Lahn
Germany
http://pediapress.com/

The content within this book was generated collaboratively by volunteers. Please be advised that nothing found here has necessarily been reviewed by people with the expertise required to provide you with complete, accurate or reliable information. Some information in this book may be misleading or simply wrong. Alpha Editions and PediaPress does not guarantee the validity of the information found here. If you need specific advice (for example, medical, legal, financial, or risk management) please seek a professional who is licensed or knowledgeable in that area.

Sources, licenses and contributors of the articles and images are listed in the section entitled "References". Parts of the books may be licensed under the GNU Free Documentation License. A copy of this license is included in the section entitled "GNU Free Documentation License"

The views and characters expressed in the book are those of the contributors and his/her imagination and do not represent the views of the Publisher.

Contents

Articles 1

Introduction 1
   Capital punishment 1

Current methods 37
   Hanging 37
   Execution by shooting 67
   Lethal injection 71
   Electric chair 92
   Gas chamber 104
   Decapitation 111

Ancient methods 135
   Execution by elephant 135
   Blowing from a gun 145
   Blood eagle 160
   Death by boiling 163
   Brazen bull 167
   Breaking wheel 171
   Premature burial 187
   Death by burning 200
   Crucifixion 250
   Crushing (execution) 275

Disembowelment	279
Dismemberment	286
Hanged, drawn and quartered	298
Falling (execution)	316
Flaying	318
Garrote	325
Gibbeting	330
Immurement	340
Impalement	364
Keelhauling	391
Poena cullei	394
Poisoning	410
Pendulum	411
Death by sawing	452
Scaphism	474
Lingchi	476
Suffocation in ash	486
Stoning	487
Strangling	512

Appendix 517

References	517
Article Sources and Contributors	571
Image Sources, Licenses and Contributors	576

Article Licenses 583

Index 585

Contents

Articles 1

Introduction 1
    Capital punishment 1

Current methods 37
    Hanging 37
    Execution by shooting 67
    Lethal injection 71
    Electric chair 92
    Gas chamber 104
    Decapitation 111

Ancient methods 135
    Execution by elephant 135
    Blowing from a gun 145
    Blood eagle 160
    Death by boiling 163
    Brazen bull 167
    Breaking wheel 171
    Premature burial 187
    Death by burning 200
    Crucifixion 250
    Crushing (execution) 275

Disembowelment 279

Dismemberment 286

Hanged, drawn and quartered 298

Falling (execution) 316

Flaying 318

Garrote 325

Gibbeting 330

Immurement 340

Impalement 364

Keelhauling 391

Poena cullei 394

Poisoning 410

Pendulum 411

Death by sawing 452

Scaphism 474

Lingchi 476

Suffocation in ash 486

Stoning 487

Strangling 512

Appendix   517

References 517

Article Sources and Contributors 571

Image Sources, Licenses and Contributors 576

Article Licenses   583

Index   585

Introduction

Capital punishment

Criminal procedure
Criminal trials and convictions
Rights of the accused
<ul><li>Fair trial</li><li>Pre-trial</li><li>Speedy trial</li><li>Jury trial</li><li>Counsel</li><li>Presumption of innocence</li><li>Exclusionary rule[1]</li><li>Self-incrimination</li><li>Double jeopardy[2]</li></ul>
Verdict
<ul><li>Conviction</li><li>Acquittal</li><li>Not proven[3]</li><li>Directed verdict</li></ul>
Sentencing
<ul><li>Mandatory</li><li>Suspended</li><li>Custodial</li><li>Discharge</li><li>Guidelines</li><li>Totality[5, 6]</li><li>Dangerous offender[4, 5]</li><li>Capital punishment</li><li>Execution warrant</li><li>Cruel and unusual punishment</li><li>Imprisonment</li><li>Life imprisonment</li><li>Indefinite imprisonment</li></ul>
Post-sentencing

- Parole
- Probation
- Tariff [6]
- Life licence[6]
- Miscarriage of justice
- Exoneration
- Pardon
- Sex offender registration
- Sexually violent predator legislation[1]

Related areas of law

- Criminal defenses
- Criminal law
- Evidence
- Civil procedure

Portals

- Law
- Criminal justice

- [1] US courts
- [2] Not in English/Welsh courts
- [3] Scottish courts
- [4] English/Welsh courts
- [5] Canadian courts
- [6] UK courts

- v
- t
- e[1]

Capital punishment, also known as the **death penalty**, is a government-sanctioned practice whereby a person is killed by the state as a punishment for a crime. The sentence that someone be punished in such a manner is referred to as a **death sentence**, whereas the act of carrying out the sentence is known as an **execution**. Crimes that are punishable by death are known as **capital crimes** or **capital offences**, and they commonly include offences such as murder, treason, espionage, war crimes, crimes against humanity and genocide. Etymologically, the term *capital* (lit. "of the head", derived via the Latin *capitalis* from *caput*, "head") in this context alluded to execution by beheading.

Fifty-six countries retain capital punishment, 103 countries have completely abolished it *de jure* for all crimes, six have abolished it for ordinary crimes (while maintaining it for special circumstances such as war crimes), and 30 are abolitionist in practice.

Capital punishment is a matter of active controversy in several countries and states, and positions can vary within a single political ideology or cultural region. In the European Union, Article 2 of the Charter of Fundamental Rights of the European Union prohibits the use of capital punishment. The Council of Europe, which has 47 member states, has sought to abolish the use of the

Figure 1: *Anarchist Auguste Vaillant guillotined in France in 1894*

death penalty by its members absolutely, through Protocol 13 of the European Convention on Human Rights. However, this only affects those member states which have signed and ratified it, and they do not include Armenia, Russia, and Azerbaijan.

The United Nations General Assembly has adopted, in 2007, 2008, 2010, 2012 and 2014, non-binding resolutions calling for a global moratorium on executions, with a view to eventual abolition. Although most nations have abolished capital punishment, over 60% of the world's population live in countries where the death penalty is retained, such as China, India, the United States, Indonesia, Pakistan, Bangladesh, Japan and Sri Lanka.

History

Execution of criminals has been used by nearly all societies since the beginning of civilizations on Earth. Until the nineteenth century, without developed prison systems, there was frequently no workable alternative to insure deterrence and incapacitation of criminals. The executions themselves often involved torture with cruel methods such as the breaking wheel.

The use of formal execution extends to the beginning of recorded history. Most historical records and various primitive tribal practices indicate that the death penalty was a part of their justice system. Communal punishment for wrongdoing generally included compensation by the wrongdoer, corporal punishment, shunning, banishment and execution. Usually, compensation and shunning were enough as a form of justice.[2] The response to crime committed by neighbouring tribes or communities included a formal apology, compensation or blood feuds.

A blood feud or vendetta occurs when arbitration between families or tribes fails or an arbitration system is non-existent. This form of justice was common before the emergence of an arbitration system based on state or organized religion. It may result from crime, land disputes or a code of honour. "Acts of retaliation underscore the ability of the social collective to defend itself and demonstrate to enemies (as well as potential allies) that injury to property, rights, or the person will not go unpunished."[3] However, in practice, it is often difficult to distinguish between a war of vendetta and one of conquest.

In most countries that practise capital punishment it is now reserved for murder, terrorism, war crimes, espionage, treason, or as part of military justice. In some countries sexual crimes, such as rape, fornication, adultery, incest and sodomy, carry the death penalty, as do religious crimes such as Hudud and Qisas crimes, such as apostasy (formal renunciation of the state religion), blasphemy, moharebeh, hirabah, Fasad, Mofsed-e-filarz and witchcraft. In many countries that use the death penalty, drug trafficking is also a capital offence. In China, human trafficking and serious cases of corruption and financial crimes are punished by the death penalty. In militaries around the world courts-martial have imposed death sentences for offences such as cowardice, desertion, insubordination, and mutiny.

Ancient history

Elaborations of tribal arbitration of feuds included peace settlements often done in a religious context and compensation system. Compensation was based on the principle of *substitution* which might include material (for example, cattle, slave) compensation, exchange of brides or grooms, or payment of the blood debt. Settlement rules could allow for animal blood to replace human blood, or transfers of property or blood money or in some case an offer of a person for execution. The person offered for execution did not have to be an original perpetrator of the crime because the system was based on tribes, not individuals. Blood feuds could be regulated at meetings, such as the Norsemen *things*.[4] Systems deriving from blood feuds may survive alongside more advanced legal systems or be given recognition by courts (for example, trial by combat). One of the more modern refinements of the blood feud is the duel.

Figure 2: *The Christian Martyrs' Last Prayer, by Jean-Léon Gérôme (1883). Roman Colosseum.*

In certain parts of the world, nations in the form of ancient republics, monarchies or tribal oligarchies emerged. These nations were often united by common linguistic, religious or family ties. Moreover, expansion of these nations often occurred by conquest of neighbouring tribes or nations. Consequently, various classes of royalty, nobility, various commoners and slave emerged. Accordingly, the systems of tribal arbitration were submerged into a more unified system of justice which formalized the relation between the different "classes" rather than "tribes". The earliest and most famous example is Code of Hammurabi which set the different punishment and compensation, according to the different class/group of victims and perpetrators. The Torah (Jewish Law), also known as the Pentateuch (the first five books of the Christian Old Testament), lays down the death penalty for murder, kidnapping, magic, violation of the Sabbath, blasphemy, and a wide range of sexual crimes, although evidence suggests that actual executions were rare.

A further example comes from Ancient Greece, where the Athenian legal system was first written down by Draco in about 621 BC: the death penalty was applied for a particularly wide range of crimes, though Solon later repealed Draco's code and published new laws, retaining only Draco's homicide statutes. The word draconian derives from Draco's laws. The Romans also used death penalty for a wide range of offences.

Figure 3: *Ling Chi – execution by slow slicing –* was a form of torture and execution used in China from roughly AD 900 (Tang era) until it was banned in 1905.

Tang dynasty

Although many are executed in the People's Republic of China each year in the present day, there was a time in the Tang dynasty (618–907) when the death penalty was abolished.[5] This was in the year 747, enacted by Emperor Xuanzong of Tang (r. 712–756). When abolishing the death penalty Xuanzong ordered his officials to refer to the nearest regulation by analogy when sentencing those found guilty of crimes for which the prescribed punishment was execution. Thus depending on the severity of the crime a punishment of severe scourging with the thick rod or of exile to the remote Lingnan region might take the place of capital punishment. However, the death penalty was restored only 12 years later in 759 in response to the An Lushan Rebellion.[6] At this time in the Tang dynasty only the emperor had the authority to sentence criminals to execution. Under Xuanzong capital punishment was relatively infrequent, with only 24 executions in the year 730 and 58 executions in the year 736.

The two most common forms of execution in the Tang dynasty were strangulation and decapitation, which were the prescribed methods of execution for 144 and 89 offences respectively. Strangulation was the prescribed sentence for lodging an accusation against one's parents or grandparents with a magistrate, scheming to kidnap a person and sell them into slavery and opening a coffin while desecrating a tomb. Decapitation was the method of execution prescribed for more serious crimes such as treason and sedition. Despite the great discomfort involved, most of the Tang Chinese preferred strangulation to decapitation, as a result of the traditional Tang Chinese belief that the body is a gift from the parents and that it is, therefore, disrespectful to one's ancestors to die without returning one's body to the grave intact.

Some further forms of capital punishment were practised in the Tang dynasty, of which the first two that follow at least were extralegal.Wikipedia:Please clarify The first of these was scourging to death with the thick rodWikipedia:Please clarify which was common throughout the Tang dynasty especially in cases of gross corruption. The second was truncation, in which the convicted person was cut in two at the waist with a fodder knife and then left to bleed to death.[7] A further form of execution called Ling Chi (slow slicing), or death by/of a thousand cuts, was used from the close of the Tang dynasty (around 900) to its abolition in 1905.

When a minister of the fifth grade or above received a death sentence the emperor might grant him a special dispensation allowing him to commit suicide in lieu of execution. Even when this privilege was not granted, the law required that the condemned minister be provided with food and ale by his keepers and transported to the execution ground in a cart rather than having to walk there.

Nearly all executions under the Tang dynasty took place in public as a warning to the population. The heads of the executed were displayed on poles or spears. When local authorities decapitated a convicted criminal, the head was boxed and sent to the capital as proof of identity and that the execution had taken place.

Middle Ages

In medieval and early modern Europe, before the development of modern prison systems, the death penalty was also used as a generalized form of punishment. During the reign of Henry VIII of England, as many as 72,000 people are estimated to have been executed.

In early modern Europe, a massive moral panic regarding witchcraft swept across Europe and later the European colonies in North America. During this period, there were widespread claims that malevolent Satanic witches were operating as an organized threat to Christendom. As a result, tens of thousands of women were prosecuted for witchcraft and executed through the witch trials of the early modern period (between the 15th and 18th centuries).

Figure 4: *The burning of Jakob Rohrbach, a leader of the peasants during the German Peasants' War.*

Figure 5: *The breaking wheel was used during the Middle Ages and was still in use into the 19th century.*

Capital punishment

Figure 6: *Antiporta of Dei delitti e delle pene (On Crimes and Punishments), 1766 ed.*

The death penalty also targeted sexual offences such as sodomy. In England, the Buggery Act 1533 stipulated hanging as punishment for "buggery". James Pratt and John Smith were the last two Englishmen to be executed for sodomy in 1835.

Despite the wide use of the death penalty, calls for reform were not unknown. The 12th century Jewish legal scholar, Moses Maimonides, wrote, "It is better and more satisfactory to acquit a thousand guilty persons than to put a single innocent man to death." He argued that executing an accused criminal on anything less than absolute certainty would lead to a slippery slope of decreasing burdens of proof, until we would be convicting merely "according to the judge's caprice". Maimonides's concern was maintaining popular respect for law, and he saw errors of commission as much more threatening than errors of omission.[8]

The Abbasid Caliphs in Baghdad, such as Al-Mu'tadid, were often cruel in their punishments.[9]Wikipedia:Citing sources

Modern era

In the last several centuries, with the emergence of modern nation states, justice came to be increasingly associated with the concept of natural and legal

Figure 7: *Mexican execution by firing squad, 1916*

rights. The period saw an increase in standing police forces and permanent penitential institutions. Rational choice theory, a utilitarian approach to criminology which justifies punishment as a form of deterrence as opposed to retribution, can be traced back to Cesare Beccaria, whose influential treatise *On Crimes and Punishments* (1764) was the first detailed analysis of capital punishment to demand the abolition of the death penalty. Jeremy Bentham, regarded as the founder of modern utilitarianism, also called for the abolition of the death penalty. Beccaria, and later Charles Dickens and Karl Marx noted the incidence of increased violent criminality at the times and places of executions. Official recognition of this phenomenon led to executions being carried out inside prisons, away from public view.

In England in the 18th century, when there was no police force, there was a large increase in the number of capital offences to more than 200. These were mainly property offences, for example cutting down a cherry tree in an orchard. In 1820, there were 160, including crimes such as shoplifting, petty theft or stealing cattle.[10] The severity of the so-called Bloody Code was often tempered by juries who refused to convict, or judges, in the case of petty theft, who arbitrarily set the value stolen at below the statutory level for a capital crime.[11]

20th century

In Nazi Germany there were three types of capital punishment; hanging, decapitation and death by shooting. Also, modern military organisations employed capital punishment as a means of maintaining military discipline. In

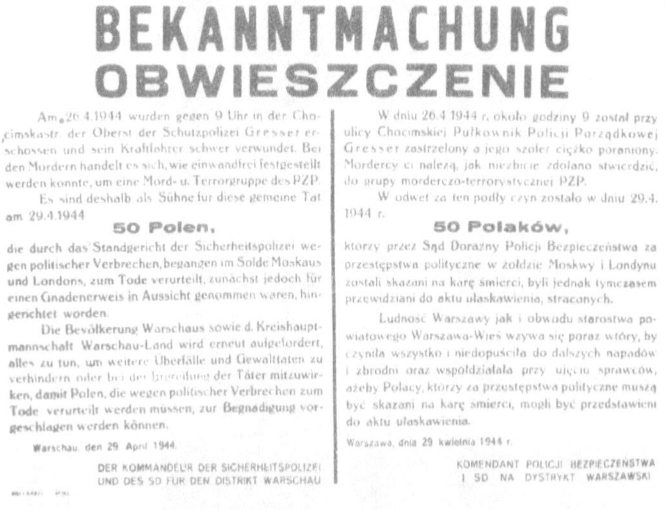

BEKANNTMACHUNG
OBWIESZCZENIE

Am 26.4.1944 wurden gegen 9 Uhr in der Chocimskastr. der Oberst der Schutzpolizei Gresser erschossen und sein Kraftfahrer schwer verwundet. Bei den Mördern handelt es sich, wie einwandfrei festgestellt werden konnte, um eine Mord- u. Terrorgruppe des PZP.

Es sind deshalb als Sühne für diese gemeine Tat am 29.4.1944

50 Polen,

die durch das Standgericht der Sicherheitspolizei wegen politischer Verbrechen, begangen im Solde Moskaus und Londons, zum Tode verurteilt, zunächst jedoch für einen Gnadenerweis in Aussicht genommen waren, hingerichtet worden.

Die Bevölkerung Warschaus sowie d. Kreishauptmannschaft Warschau-Land wird erneut aufgefordert, alles zu tun, um weitere Überfälle und Gewalttaten zu verhindern oder bei der Ergreifung der Täter mitzuwirken, damit Polen, die wegen politischer Verbrechen zum Tode verurteilt werden müssen, zur Begnadigung vorgeschlagen werden können.

Warschau, den 29. April 1944.

DER KOMMANDEUR DER SICHERHEITSPOLIZEI
UND DES SD FÜR DEN DISTRIKT WARSCHAU

W dniu 26.4.1944 r. około godziny 9 został przy ulicy Chocimskiej Pułkownik Policji Porządkowej Gresser zastrzelony a jego szofer ciężko poraniony. Mordercy ci należą, jak niezbicie zdołano stwierdzić, do grupy morderczo-terrorystycznej PZP.

W odwet za ten podły czyn zostało w dniu 29.4.1944 r.

50 Polaków,

którzy przez Sąd Doraźny Policji Bezpieczeństwa za przestępstwa polityczne w żołdzie Moskwy i Londynu zostali skazani na karę śmierci, byli jednak tymczasem przewidziani do aktu ułaskawienia, straconych.

Ludność Warszawy jak i obwodu starostwa powiatowego Warszawa-Wieś wzywa się poraz wtóry, by czyniła wszystko i niedopuściła do dalszych napadów i zbrodni oraz współdziałała przy ujęciu sprawców, ażeby Polacy, którzy za przestępstwa polityczne muszą być skazani na karę śmierci, mogli być przedstawieni do aktu ułaskawienia.

Warszawa, dnia 29 kwietnia 1944 r.

KOMENDANT POLICJI BEZPIECZEŃSTWA
I SD NA DYSTRYKT WARSZAWSKI

Figure 8: *50 Poles tried and sentenced to death by a Standgericht in retaliation for the assassination of 1 German policeman in Nazi-occupied Poland, 1944*

the past, cowardice, absence without leave, desertion, insubordination, looting, shirking under enemy fire and disobeying orders were often crimes punishable by death (see decimation and running the gauntlet). One method of execution, since firearms came into common use, has also been firing squad, although some countries use execution with a single shot to the head or neck.

Various authoritarian states—for example those with fascist or Communist governments—employed the death penalty as a potent means of political oppression. According to Robert Conquest, the leading expert on Joseph Stalin's purges, more than one million Soviet citizens were executed during the Great Terror of 1937–38, almost all by a bullet to the back of the head.[12] Mao Zedong publicly stated that "800,000" people had been executed in China during the Cultural Revolution (1966-1976). Partly as a response to such excesses, civil rights organizations started to place increasing emphasis on the concept of human rights and an abolition of the death penalty.

Figure 9: *Lithuanian President Antanas Smetona's regime was the first in Europe to sentence Nazis and Communists to death; both were seen as a threat to the Independence of Lithuania.*

Contemporary era

Among countries around the world, all European (except Belarus) and many Oceanic states (including Australia, New Zealand and East Timor), and Canada have abolished capital punishment. In Latin America, most states have completely abolished the use of capital punishment, while some countries such as Brazil and Guatemala allow for capital punishment only in exceptional situations, such as treason committed during wartime. The United States (the federal government and 31 of the states), some Caribbean countries and the majority of countries in Asia (for example, Japan and India) retain capital punishment. In Africa, less than half of countries retain it, for example Botswana and Zambia. South Africa abolished the death penalty in 1995.

Abolition was often adopted due to political change, as when countries shifted from authoritarianism to democracy, or when it became an entry condition for the European Union. The United States is a notable exception: some states have had bans on capital punishment for decades, the earliest being Michigan where it was abolished in 1846, while other states still actively use it today. The death penalty in the United States remains a contentious issue which is hotly debated.

In retentionist countries, the debate is sometimes revived when a miscarriage of justice has occurred though this tends to cause legislative efforts to improve the judicial process rather than to abolish the death penalty. In abolitionist countries, the debate is sometimes revived by particularly brutal murders though few countries have brought it back after abolishing it. However, a spike in serious, violent crimes, such as murders or terrorist attacks, has prompted some countries to effectively end the moratorium on the death penalty. One notable example is Pakistan which in December 2014 lifted a six-year moratorium on executions after the Peshawar school massacre during which 132 students and 9 members of staff of the Army Public School and Degree College Peshawar were killed by Taliban terrorists. Since then, Pakistan has executed over 400 convicts.

In 2017 two major countries, Turkey and the Philippines, saw their executives making moves to reinstate the death penalty. As of March 2017[13], passage of the law in the Philippines awaits the Senate's approval.

Modern-day public opinion

The public opinion on the death penalty varies considerably by country and by the crime in question. Countries where a majority of people are against execution include Norway where only 25 percent are in favour. Most French, Finns and Italians also oppose the death penalty. A 2016 Gallup poll shows that 60% of Americans support the death penalty, down from 64% in 2010 65% in 2006 and 68% in 2001. A 2010 poll found that 61% of Americans would choose a penalty other than the death sentence for murder.

The support and sentencing of capital punishment has been growing in India in the 2010s due to anger over several recent brutal cases of rape even-though actual executions are comparatively rare. While support for the death penalty for murder is still high in China, executions have dropped precipitously, with 3,000 executed in 2012 versus 12,000 in 2002. A poll in South Africa found that 76 percent of millennium generation South Africans support re-introduction of the death penalty, which is abolished in South Africa. A 2017 poll found younger Mexicans are more likely to support capital punishment than older ones. 57% of Brazilians support the death penalty. The age group that shows the greatest support for execution of those condemned is the 25 to 34-year-old category, in which 61% say they are in favor.

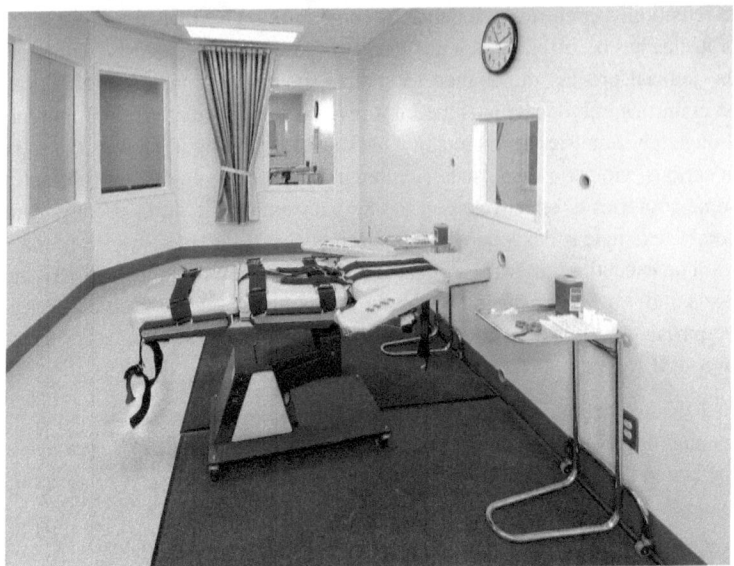

Figure 10: *A gurney at San Quentin State Prison in California used for executions by lethal injection*

Movements towards non-painful execution

Trends in most of the world have long been to move to private and less painful executions. France developed the guillotine for this reason in the final years of the 18th century, while Britain banned drawing and quartering in the early 19th century. Hanging by turning the victim off a ladder or by kicking a stool or a bucket, which causes death by suffocation, was replaced by long drop "hanging" where the subject is dropped a longer distance to dislocate the neck and sever the spinal cord. Mozaffar ad-Din Shah Qajar, Shah of Persia (1896-1907) introduced throat-cutting and blowing from a gun (close-range cannon fire) as quick and relatively painless alternatives to more torturous methods of executions used at that time. In the United States, electrocution and gas inhalation were introduced as more humane alternatives to hanging, but have been almost entirely superseded by lethal injection. A small number of countries still employ slow hanging methods and stoning.

A study of executions carried out in the United States between 1977 and 2001 indicated that at least 34 of the 749 executions, or 4.5%, involved "unanticipated problems or delays that caused, at least arguably, unnecessary agony for the prisoner or that reflect gross incompetence of the executioner". The rate of these "botched executions" remained steady over the period of the study.[14]

Figure 11: *Peter Leopold II, Grand Duke of Tuscany, by Joseph Hickel, 1769*

A separate study published in *The Lancet* in 2005 found that in 43% of cases of lethal injection, the blood level of hypnotics was insufficient to guarantee unconsciousness.[15] However, the U.S. Supreme Court ruled in 2008 (*Baze v. Rees*) and again in 2015 (*Glossip v. Gross*) that lethal injection does not constitute cruel and unusual punishment.[16]

Abolition of capital punishment

Many countries have abolished capital punishment either in law or in practice. Since World War II there has been a trend toward abolishing capital punishment. Capital punishment has been completely abolished by 102 countries, a further six have done so for all offences except under special circumstances and 32 more have abolished it in practice because they have not used it for at least 10 years and are believed to have a policy or established practice against carrying out executions.

The death penalty was banned in China between 747 and 759. In Japan, Emperor Saga abolished the death penalty in 818 under the influence of Shinto and it lasted until 1156.

In England, a public statement of opposition was included in The Twelve Conclusions of the Lollards, written in 1395. Sir Thomas More's *Utopia*, published in 1516, debated the benefits of the death penalty in dialogue form, coming to no firm conclusion. More was himself executed for treason in 1535. More recent opposition to the death penalty stemmed from the book of the Italian Cesare Beccaria *Dei Delitti e Delle Pene* ("On Crimes and Punishments"), published in 1764. In this book, Beccaria aimed to demonstrate not only the injustice, but even the futility from the point of view of social welfare, of torture and the death penalty. Influenced by the book, Grand Duke Leopold II of Habsburg, the future Emperor of Austria, abolished the death penalty in the then-independent Grand Duchy of Tuscany, the first permanent abolition in modern times. On 30 November 1786, after having *de facto* blocked executions (the last was in 1769), Leopold promulgated the reform of the penal code that abolished the death penalty and ordered the destruction of all the instruments for capital execution in his land. In 2000, Tuscany's regional authorities instituted an annual holiday on 30 November to commemorate the event. The event is commemorated on this day by 300 cities around the world celebrating Cities for Life Day.

The Roman Republic banned capital punishment in 1849. Venezuela followed suit and abolished the death penalty in 1863[17] and San Marino did so in 1865. The last execution in San Marino had taken place in 1468. In Portugal, after legislative proposals in 1852 and 1863, the death penalty was abolished in 1867. The last execution of the death penalty in Brazil was 1876, from there all the condemnations were commuted by the Emperor Pedro II until it's abolition for civil offences and military offences in peacetime in 1891. The penalty for crimes committed in peacetime was then reinstated and abolished again twice (1938–53 and 1969–78), but on those occasions it was restricted to acts of terrorism or subversion considered "internal warfare" and all sentence were commuted and were not carried out.

Abolition occurred in Canada in 1976 (except for some military offences, with complete abolition in 1998), in France in 1981, and in Australia in 1973 (although the state of Western Australia retained the penalty until 1984). In 1977, the United Nations General Assembly affirmed in a formal resolution that throughout the world, it is desirable to "progressively restrict the number of offences for which the death penalty might be imposed, with a view to the desirability of abolishing this punishment".

In the United Kingdom, it was abolished for murder (leaving only treason, piracy with violence, arson in royal dockyards and a number of wartime military offences as capital crimes) for a five-year experiment in 1965 and permanently in 1969, the last execution having taken place in 1964. It was abolished for all peacetime offences in 1998.

In the United States, Michigan was the first state to ban the death penalty, on 18 May 1846.[18] The death penalty was declared unconstitutional between 1972

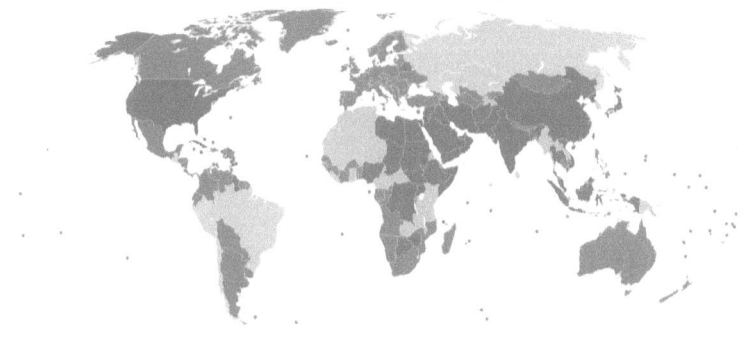

Figure 12:
World map of the use of capital punishment as of 26 March 2018
Legend
*Retentionist countries: 56
Abolitionist in practice countries (have not executed anyone during the last 10 years and are believed to have a policy or established practice of not carrying out executions): 29
Abolitionist countries except for crimes committed under exceptional circumstances (such as crimes committed in wartime): 7
Abolitionist countries: 106*

and 1976 based on the *Furman v. Georgia* case, but the 1976 *Gregg v. Georgia* case once again permitted the death penalty under certain circumstances. Further limitations were placed on the death penalty in *Atkins v. Virginia* (death penalty unconstitutional for people with an intellectual disability) and *Roper v. Simmons* (death penalty unconstitutional if defendant was under age 18 at the time the crime was committed). In the United States, 18 states and the District of Columbia ban capital punishment.

Abolitionists believe capital punishment is the worst violation of human rights, because the right to life is the most important, and capital punishment violates it without necessity and inflicts to the condemned a psychological torture. Human rights activists oppose the death penalty, calling it "cruel, inhuman, and degrading punishment". Amnesty International considers it to be "the ultimate, irreversible denial of Human Rights".

Contemporary use

Capital punishment by country

Most countries, including almost all First World nations, have abolished capital punishment either in law or in practice. Notable exceptions are the United States, China, India, Japan, and most Islamic states. The United States is the only Western country to still use the death penalty.

Since World War II, there has been a trend toward abolishing the death penalty. 58 countries retain the death penalty in active use, 102 countries have abolished capital punishment altogether, six have done so for all offences except under special circumstances, and 32 more have abolished it in practice because they have not used it for at least 10 years and are believed to have a policy or established practice against carrying out executions.

According to Amnesty International, 23 countries are known to have performed executions in 2016. There are countries which do not publish information on the use of capital punishment, most significantly China and North Korea. As per Amnesty International, around 1000 prisoners were executed in 2017.

Country	Total executed (2016)
China	1,000+
Iran	567+
Saudi Arabia	154+
Iraq	88+
Pakistan	87
Egypt	44+
United States	20
Somalia	14+
Bangladesh	10
Malaysia	9
Afghanistan	6
Belarus	4+
Indonesia	4
Singapore	4
Japan	3
Nigeria	3
Palestine	3

Sudan	2
Botswana	1
Taiwan	1
North Korea	Unknown
South Sudan	Unknown
Vietnam	Unknown

The use of the death penalty is becoming increasingly restrained in some retentionist countries including Taiwan and Singapore. Indonesia carried out no executions between November 2008 and March 2013. Singapore, Japan and the United States are the only developed countries that are classified by Amnesty International as 'retentionist' (South Korea is classified as 'abolitionist in practice'). Nearly all retentionist countries are situated in Asia, Africa and the Caribbean. The only retentionist country in Europe is Belarus. The death penalty was overwhelmingly practised in poor and authoritarian states, which often employed the death penalty as a tool of political oppression. During the 1980s, the democratisation of Latin America swelled the ranks of abolitionist countries.

This was soon followed by the fall of Communism in Europe. Many of the countries which restored democracy aspired to enter the EU. The European Union and the Council of Europe both strictly require member states not to practise the death penalty (see Capital punishment in Europe). Public support for the death penalty in the EU varies. The last execution in a member state of the present-day Council of Europe took place in 1997 in Ukraine. In contrast, the rapid industrialisation in Asia has seen an increase in the number of developed countries which are also retentionist. In these countries, the death penalty retains strong public support, and the matter receives little attention from the government or the media; in China there is a small but significant and growing movement to abolish the death penalty altogether. This trend has been followed by some African and Middle Eastern countries where support for the death penalty remains high.

Some countries have resumed practising the death penalty after having previously suspended the practice for long periods. The United States suspended executions in 1972 but resumed them in 1976; there was no execution in India between 1995 and 2004; and Sri Lanka declared an end to its moratorium on the death penalty on 20 November 2004, although it has not yet performed any further executions. The Philippines re-introduced the death penalty in 1993 after abolishing it in 1987, but again abolished it in 2006.

The United States and Japan are the only developed countries to have recently carried out executions. The U.S. federal government, the U.S. military, and 31

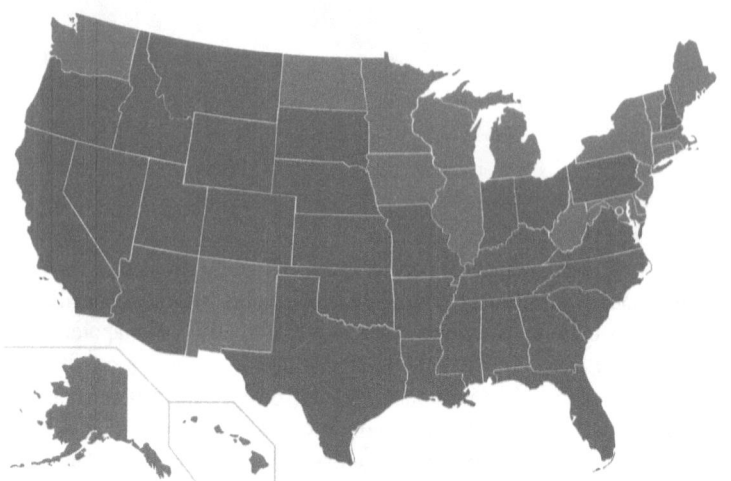

Figure 13:
A map showing the use of the death penalty in the United States by individual states. Note that the death penalty is used throughout the United States for certain federal crimes (cf. Dzhokhar Tsarnaev).
States with a valid death penalty statute
States without the death penalty

states have a valid death penalty statute, and over 1,400 executions have been carried in the United States since it reinstated the death penalty in 1976, including 28 in 2015 alone. Japan has 111 inmates with finalized death sentences as of July 26, 2018[13]; after executing Shoko Asahara and six other senior members of Aum Shinrikyo, a cult group which carried out multiple atrocities involving thousands of victims such as the Tokyo subway sarin attack, which took place on March 20, 1995, on July 6 the executions of the remaining six senior members took place on July 26.

The most recent country to abolish the death penalty was Burkina Faso in June 2018.

Juvenile offenders

The death penalty for juvenile offenders (criminals aged under 18 years at the time of their crime although the legal or accepted definition of *juvenile offender* may vary from one jurisdiction to another) has become increasingly rare. Considering the age of majority is still not 18 in some countries or has not been clearly defined in law, since 1990 ten countries have executed offenders who were considered juveniles at the time of their crimes: The People's

Republic of China (PRC), Bangladesh, Democratic Republic of Congo, Iran, Iraq, Japan, Nigeria, Pakistan, Saudi Arabia, Sudan, the United States, and Yemen. The PRC, Pakistan, the United States, Yemen and Iran have since raised the minimum age to 18. Amnesty International has recorded 61 verified executions since then, in several countries, of both juveniles and adults who had been convicted of committing their offences as juveniles. The PRC does not allow for the execution of those under 18, but child executions have reportedly taken place.

Starting in 1642 within the then British American colonies until present day, an estimated 365 juvenile offenders were executed by the British Colonial authorities and subsequently by State authorities and the federal government of the United States.[19] The United States Supreme Court abolished capital punishment for offenders under the age of 16 in *Thompson v. Oklahoma* (1988), and for all juveniles in *Roper v. Simmons* (2005).

Between 2005 and May 2008, Iran, Pakistan, Saudi Arabia, Sudan and Yemen were reported to have executed child offenders, the largest number occurring in Iran.

During Hassan Rouhani's tenure at least 3,602 death sentences carried out. This includes the executions of 34 juvenile offenders.[20,21]

The United Nations Convention on the Rights of the Child, which forbids capital punishment for juveniles under article 37(a), has been signed by all countries and subsequently ratified by all signatories with the exceptions of Somalia and the United States (despite the US Supreme Court decisions abolishing the practice).[22] The UN Sub-Commission on the Promotion and Protection of Human Rights maintains that the death penalty for juveniles has become contrary to a jus cogens of customary international law. A majority of countries are also party to the U.N. International Covenant on Civil and Political Rights (whose Article 6.5 also states that "Sentence of death shall not be imposed for crimes committed by persons below eighteen years of age...").

Iran, despite its ratification of the Convention on the Rights of the Child and International Covenant on Civil and Political Rights, was the world's largest executioner of juvenile offenders, for which it has been the subject of broad international condemnation; the country's record is the focus of the Stop Child Executions Campaign. But on 10 February 2012, Iran's parliament changed controversial laws relating to the execution of juveniles. In the new legislation the age of 18 (solar year) would be applied to accused of both genders and juvenile offenders must be sentenced pursuant to a separate law specifically dealing with juveniles. Based on the Islamic law which now seems to have been revised, girls at the age of 9 and boys at 15 of lunar year (11 days shorter than a solar year) are deemed fully responsible for their crimes. Iran accounted for two-thirds of the global total of such executions, and currently-Wikipedia:Manual of Style/Dates and numbers#Chronological items has approximately 140 people considered as juveniles awaiting execution for crimes committed (up from 71 in 2007).[23] The past executions of Mahmoud Asgari, Ayaz Marhoni and Makwan Moloudzadeh became the focus of Iran's child capital punishment policy and the judicial system that hands down such sentences.[24]

Saudi Arabia also executes criminals who were minors at the time of the offence. In 2013, Saudi Arabia was the center of an international controversy after it executed Rizana Nafeek, a Sri Lankan domestic worker, who was believed to have been 17 years old at the time of the crime.

Japan has not executed juvenile criminals after August 1997, when they executed Norio Nagayama, a spree killer who had been convicted of shooting four people dead in the late 1960s. Nagayama's case created the eponymously named *Nagayama standards*, which take into account factors such as the number of victims, brutality and social impact of the crimes. The standards have been used in determining whether to apply the death sentence in murder cases. Teruhiko Seki, convicted of murdering four members including a 4-year-old daughter and raping a 15-year-old daughter of a family in 1992, became the second inmate to be hanged for a crime committed as a minor in the first such execution in 20 years after Nagayama on December 19, 2017. Takayuki Otsuki, who was convicted of raping and strangling a 23-year-old woman and subsequently strangling her 11-month-old daughter to death on April 14, 1999, when he was 18, is another inmate sentenced to death, and his request for retrial has been rejected by the Supreme Court of Japan.

There is evidence that child executions are taking place in the parts of Somalia controlled by the Islamic Courts Union (ICU). In October 2008, a girl, Aisha Ibrahim Dhuhulow was buried up to her neck at a football stadium, then stoned to death in front of more than 1,000 people. Somalia's established Transitional Federal Government announced in November 2009 (reiterated in 2013)[25] that it plans to ratify the Convention on the Rights of the Child. This move was lauded by UNICEF as a welcome attempt to secure children's rights in the country.

Methods

The following methods of execution were used in 2015:
- Hanging (Afghanistan, Iran, Iraq, Japan, Malaysia, Pakistan, Palestinian National Authority, Yemen, Egypt, India, Myanmar, Singapore, Sri Lanka, Syria, Zimbabwe, Malawi, Liberia, Chad, Washington state in the USA)

- Shooting (the People's Republic of China, Republic of China, Vietnam, Belarus, North Korea, Indonesia, Yemen, and in the U.S. states of Oklahoma and Utah).
- Lethal injection (United States, Guatemala, Thailand, the People's Republic of China, Vietnam)
- Electrocution and gas inhalation (some U.S. states, but only if the prisoner requests it or if lethal injection is unavailable)
- Beheading (Saudi Arabia)

Public execution

A public execution is a form of capital punishment which "members of the general public may voluntarily attend". This definition excludes the presence of a small number of witnesses randomly selected to assure executive accountability. While today the great majority of the world considers public executions to be distasteful and most countries have outlawed the practice, throughout much of history executions were performed publicly as a means for the state to demonstrate "its power before those who fell under its jurisdiction be they criminals, enemies, or political opponents". Additionally, it afforded the public a chance to witness "what was considered a great spectacle".

Social historians note that beginning in the 20th century in the U.S. and western Europe death in general became increasingly shielded from public view, occurring more and more behind the closed doors of the hospital. Executions were likewise moved behind the walls of the penitentiary. The last formal public executions occurred in 1868 in Britain, in 1936 in the U.S. and in 1939 in France.

According to Amnesty International, in 2012 "public executions were known to have been carried out in Iran, North Korea, Saudi Arabia and Somalia". There have been reports of public executions carried out by state and non-state actors in Hamas-controlled Gaza, Syria, Afghanistan, and Yemen. Executions which can be classified as public were also carried out in the U.S. states of Florida and Utah as of 1992.

Figure 14: *A sign at the Taiwan Taoyuan International Airport warns arriving travelers that drug trafficking is a capital crime in the Republic of China (photo taken in 2005)*

Capital crime

Crimes against humanity

Crimes against humanity such as genocide are usually punishable by death in countries retaining capital punishment. Death sentences for such crimes were handed down and carried out during the Nuremberg Trials in 1946 and the Tokyo Trials in 1948, but the current International Criminal Court does not use capital punishment. The maximum penalty available to the International Criminal Court is life imprisonment.

Murder

Intentional homicide is punishable by death in most countries retaining capital punishment, but generally provided it involves an aggravating factor required by statute or judicial precedents.

Drug trafficking

Some countries provide the death penalty for drug trafficking and related offences, mostly in West Asia, South Asia, Southeast Asia and East Asia. Among countries who regularly execute drug offenders are China, Indonesia, Saudi Arabia, Iran and Singapore.

Other offences

Other crimes that are punishable by death in some countries include terrorism, treason, espionage, crimes against the state (most countries with the death penalty), political protests (Saudi Arabia), rape (China, India, Iran, Saudi Arabia, Brunei, etc.), economic crimes (China), kidnapping (China), separatism (China), adultery (Saudi Arabia, Iran, Qatar, Brunei, etc.), sodomy (Saudi Arabia, Iran, Brunei, etc.), and religious Hudud offences such as apostasy (Saudi Arabia, Iran, Sudan, etc.), blasphemy (Saudi Arabia, Iran, Pakistan), Moharebeh (Iran), Witchcraft and Sorcery (Saudi Arabia). and forms of aggravated robbery/hirabah, (Saudi Arabia, Kenya, Zambia).

Controversy and debate

Capital punishment is controversial. Death penalty opponents regard the death penalty as inhumane and criticize it for its irreversibility. They argue also that capital punishment lacks deterrent effect, discriminates against minorities and the poor, and that it encourages a "culture of violence". There are many organizations worldwide, such as Amnesty International, and country-specific, such as the American Civil Liberties Union (ACLU), that have abolition of the death penalty as a fundamental purpose.[26]

Advocates of the death penalty argue that it deters crime, is a good tool for police and prosecutors in plea bargaining, makes sure that convicted criminals do not offend again, and is a just penalty.[27]

Retribution

Supporters of the death penalty argued that death penalty is morally justified when applied in murder especially with aggravating elements such as for murder of police officers, child murder, torture murder, multiple homicide and mass killing such as terrorism, massacre and genocide. This argument is strongly defended by New York Law School's Professor Robert Blecker, who says that the punishment must be painful in proportion to the crime. Eighteenth-century philosopher Immanuel Kant defended a more extreme position, according to which every murderer deserves to die on the grounds that loss of life is incomparable to any jail term.

Figure 15: *Execution of a war criminal in 1946*

Some abolitionists argue that retribution is simply revenge and cannot be condoned. Others while accepting retribution as an element of criminal justice nonetheless argue that life without parole is a sufficient substitute. It is also argued that the punishing of a killing with another death is a relatively unique punishment for a violent act, because in general violent crimes are not punished by subjecting the perpetrator to a similar act (e.g. rapists are not punished by corporal punishment).

Human rights

Abolitionists believe capital punishment is the worst violation of human rights, because the right to life is the most important, and capital punishment violates it without necessity and inflicts to the condemned a psychological torture. Human rights activists oppose the death penalty, calling it "cruel, inhuman and degrading punishment". Amnesty International considers it to be "the ultimate irreversible denial of Human Rights". Albert Camus wrote in a 1956 book called *Reflections on the Guillotine, Resistance, Rebellion & Death*:

<templatestyles src="Template:Quote/styles.css"/>

> An execution is not simply death. It is just as different from the privation of life as a concentration camp is from prison. [...] For there to be an equivalency, the death penalty would have to punish a criminal who had

warned his victim of the date at which he would inflict a horrible death on him and who, from that moment onward, had confined him at his mercy for months. Such a monster is not encountered in private life.

In the classic doctrine of natural rights as expounded by for instance Locke and Blackstone, on the other hand, it is an important idea that the right to life can be forfeited.[28] As John Stuart Mill explained in a speech given in Parliament against an amendment to abolish capital punishment for murder in 1868:

<templatestyles src="Template:Quote/styles.css"/>

> And we may imagine somebody asking how we can teach people not to inflict suffering by ourselves inflicting it? But to this I should answer – all of us would answer – that to deter by suffering from inflicting suffering is not only possible, but the very purpose of penal justice. Does fining a criminal show want of respect for property, or imprisoning him, for personal freedom? Just as unreasonable is it to think that to take the life of a man who has taken that of another is to show want of regard for human life. We show, on the contrary, most emphatically our regard for it, by the adoption of a rule that he who violates that right in another forfeits it for himself, and that while no other crime that he can commit deprives him of his right to live, this shall.

Wrongful execution

It is frequently argued that capital punishment leads to miscarriage of justice through the wrongful execution of innocent persons. Many people have been proclaimed innocent victims of the death penalty.[29]

Some have claimed that as many as 39 executions have been carried out in the face of compelling evidence of innocence or serious doubt about guilt in the US from 1992 through 2004. Newly available DNA evidence prevented the pending execution of more than 15 death row inmates during the same period in the US, but DNA evidence is only available in a fraction of capital cases. As of 2017[13], 159 prisoners on death row have been exonerated by DNA or other evidence, which is seen as an indication that innocent prisoners have almost certainly been executed.[30] It is impossible to assess how many have been wrongly executed, since courts do not generally investigate the innocence of a dead defendant, and defense attorneys tend to concentrate their efforts on clients whose lives can still be saved; however, there is strong evidence of innocence in many cases.

Improper procedure may also result in unfair executions. For example, Amnesty International argues that in Singapore "the Misuse of Drugs Act contains a series of presumptions which shift the burden of proof from the prosecution to the accused. This conflicts with the universally guaranteed right to

Figure 16: *Capital punishment was abolished in the United Kingdom in part because of the case of Timothy Evans, an innocent man who was hanged in 1950 after being wrongfully convicted of two murders that had been committed by his neighbour.*

be presumed innocent until proven guilty".[31] This refers to a situation when someone is caught with drugs. In this situation, in almost any jurisdiction, the prosecution has a prima facie case.

Racial, ethnic and social class bias

Opponents of the death penalty argue that this punishment is being used more often against perpetrators from racial and ethnic minorities and from lower socioeconomic backgrounds, than against those criminals who come from a privileged background; and that the background of the victim also influences the outcome. Researchers have shown that white Americans are more likely to support the death penalty when told that it is mostly applied to African Americans, and that more stereotypically black-looking defendants are more likely to be sentenced to death if the case involves a white victim.

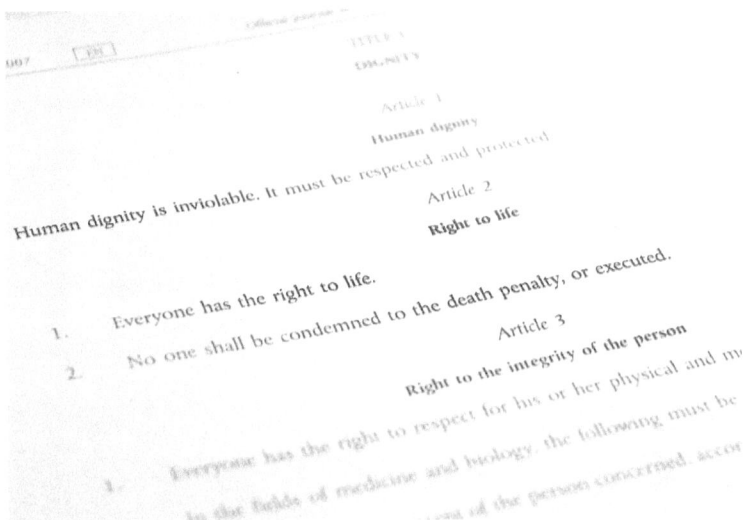

Figure 17: *Article 2 of the Charter of Fundamental Rights of the European Union affirms the prohibition on capital punishment in the EU*

International views

The United Nations introduced a resolution during the General Assembly's 62nd sessions in 2007 calling for a universal ban. The approval of a draft resolution by the Assembly's third committee, which deals with human rights issues, voted 99 to 52, with 33 abstentions, in favour of the resolution on 15 November 2007 and was put to a vote in the Assembly on 18 December.

Again in 2008, a large majority of states from all regions adopted a second resolution calling for a moratorium on the use of the death penalty in the UN General Assembly (Third Committee) on 20 November. 105 countries voted in favour of the draft resolution, 48 voted against and 31 abstained.

A range of amendments proposed by a small minority of pro-death penalty countries were overwhelmingly defeated. It had in 2007 passed a non-binding resolution (by 104 to 54, with 29 abstentions) by asking its member states for "a moratorium on executions with a view to abolishing the death penalty".

A number of regional conventions prohibit the death penalty, most notably, the Sixth Protocol (abolition in time of peace) and the 13th Protocol (abolition in all circumstances) to the European Convention on Human Rights. The same is also stated under the Second Protocol in the American Convention on Human Rights, which, however has not been ratified by all countries in the Americas,

Figure 18: *Signatories to the Second Optional Protocol to the ICCPR: parties in dark green, signatories in light green, non-members in grey*

most notably Canada and the United States. Most relevant operative international treaties do not require its prohibition for cases of serious crime, most notably, the International Covenant on Civil and Political Rights. This instead has, in common with several other treaties, an optional protocol prohibiting capital punishment and promoting its wider abolition.

Several international organizations have made the abolition of the death penalty (during time of peace) a requirement of membership, most notably the European Union (EU) and the Council of Europe. The EU and the Council of Europe are willing to accept a moratorium as an interim measure. Thus, while Russia is a member of the Council of Europe, and the death penalty remains codified in its law, it has not made use of it since becoming a member of the Council – Russia has not executed anyone since 1996. With the exception of Russia (abolitionist in practice), Kazakhstan (abolitionist for ordinary crimes only), and Belarus (retentionist), all European countries are classified as abolitionist.

Latvia abolished *de jure* the death penalty for war crimes in 2012, becoming the last EU member to do so.

The Protocol no.13[32] calls for the abolition of the death penalty in all circumstances (including for war crimes). The majority of European countries have signed and ratified it. Some European countries have not done this, but all of them except Belarus and Kazakhstan have now abolished the death penalty in all circumstances (*de jure*, and Russia *de facto*). Poland is the most recent country to ratify the protocol, on 28 August 2013.

The Protocol no.6[33] which prohibits the death penalty during peacetime has been ratified by all members of the European Council, except Russia (which has signed, but not ratified).

There are also other international abolitionist instruments, such as the Second Optional Protocol to the International Covenant on Civil and Political Rights, which has 81 parties; and the Protocol to the American Convention on Human Rights to Abolish the Death Penalty[34] (for the Americas; ratified by 13 states).

In Turkey, over 500 people were sentenced to death after the 1980 Turkish coup d'état. About 50 of them were executed, the last one 25 October 1984. Then there was a *de facto* moratorium on the death penalty in Turkey. As a move towards EU membership, Turkey made some legal changes. The death penalty was removed from peacetime law by the National Assembly in August 2002, and in May 2004 Turkey amended its constitution in order to remove capital punishment in all circumstances. It ratified Protocol no. 13 to the European Convention on Human Rights in February 2006. As a result, Europe is a continent free of the death penalty in practice, all states but Russia, which has entered a moratorium, having ratified the Sixth Protocol to the European Convention on Human Rights, with the sole exception of Belarus, which is not a member of the Council of Europe. The Parliamentary Assembly of the Council of Europe has been lobbying for Council of Europe observer states who practise the death penalty, the U.S. and Japan, to abolish it or lose their observer status. In addition to banning capital punishment for EU member states, the EU has also banned detainee transfers in cases where the receiving party may seek the death penalty.

Sub-Saharan African countries that have recently abolished the death penalty include Burundi, which abolished the death penalty for all crimes in 2009, and Gabon which did the same in 2010. On 5 July 2012, Benin became part of the Second Optional Protocol to the International Covenant on Civil and Political Rights (ICCPR), which prohibits the use of the death penalty.

The newly created South Sudan is among the 111 UN member states that supported the resolution passed by the United Nations General Assembly that called for the removal of the death penalty, therefore affirming its opposition to the practice. South Sudan, however, has not yet abolished the death penalty and stated that it must first amend its Constitution, and until that happens it will continue to use the death penalty.

Among non-governmental organizations (NGOs), Amnesty International and Human Rights Watch are noted for their opposition to capital punishment. A number of such NGOs, as well as trade unions, local councils and bar associations formed a World Coalition Against the Death Penalty in 2002.

Religious views

The world's major faiths have differing views depending on the religion, denomination, sect and/or the individual adherent. As an example, the majority of Christendom opposes the death penalty and the world's largest Christian denomination - Catholicism - opposes capital punishment in all cases, whereas both the Baha'i and Islamic faiths support capital punishment.

References

Notes

Bibliography

- Kronenwetter, Michael (2001). *Capital Punishment: A Reference Handbook* (2 ed.). ABC-CLIO. ISBN 978-1-57607-432-9.<templatestyles src="Module:Citation/CS1/styles.css"></templatestyles>
- Marian J. Borg and Michael L. Radelet. (2004). On botched executions. In: Peter Hodgkinson and William A. Schabas (eds.) Capital Punishment. pp. 143–68. [Online]. Cambridge: Cambridge University Press. Available from: Cambridge Books Online doi: 10.1017/CBO9780511489273.006[35].
- Gail A. Van Norman. (2010). Physician participation in executions. In: Gail A. Van Norman et al. (eds.) Clinical Ethics in Anesthesiology. pp. 285–91. [Online]. Cambridge: Cambridge University Press. Available from: Cambridge Books Online doi: 10.1017/CBO9780511841361.051[36].

Further reading

<templatestyles src="Template:Refbegin/styles.css" />

- Curry, Tim. " Cutting the Hangman's Noose: African Initiatives to Abolish the Death Penalty[37]." (Archive[38]) American University Washington College of Law.
- Gaie, Joseph B. R (2004). *The ethics of medical involvement in capital punishment : a philosophical discussion*[39]. Kluwer Academic. ISBN 1-4020-1764-2.<templatestyles src="Module:Citation/CS1/styles.css"></templatestyles>
- Johnson, David T.; Zimring, Franklin E. (2009). *The Next Frontier: National Development, Political Change, and the Death Penalty in Asia*[40]. Oxford University Press. ISBN 978-0-19-533740-2.<templatestyles src="Module:Citation/CS1/styles.css"></templatestyles>
- Kronenwetter, Michael (2001). *Capital punishment: a reference handbook*[41] (2nd ed.). ABC-CLIO. ISBN 1-57607-432-3.<templatestyles src="Module:Citation/CS1/styles.css"></templatestyles>
- MacLean, Colonel French L. *The Fifth Field: The Story of the 96 American Soldiers Sentenced to Death and Executed in Europe and North Africa in World War II*, 2013, Schiffer Publishing, <templatestyles src="Module:Citation/CS1/styles.css" />ISBN 9780764345777.
- McCafferty, James A (2010). *Capital Punishment*[42]. Aldine-Transaction. ISBN 978-0-202-36328-8.<templatestyles src="Module:Citation/CS1/styles.css"></templatestyles>
- Mandery, Evan J (2005). *Capital punishment: a balanced examination*[43]. Jones and Bartlett Publishers. ISBN 0-7637-3308-3.<templatestyles src="Module:Citation/CS1/styles.css"></templatestyles>
- Marzilli, Alan (2008). *Capital Punishment – Point-counterpoint*[44] (2nd ed.). Chelsea House. ISBN 978-0-7910-9796-0.<templatestyles src="Module:Citation/CS1/styles.css"></templatestyles>
- Woolf, Alex (2004). *World issues – Capital Punishment*[45]. Chrysalis Education. ISBN 1-59389-155-5.<templatestyles src="Module:Citation/CS1/styles.css"></templatestyles>
- Simon, Rita (2007). *A comparative analysis of capital punishment : statutes, policies, frequencies, and public attitudes the world over*[46]. Lexington Books. ISBN 0-7391-2091-3.<templatestyles src="Module:Citation/CS1/styles.css"></templatestyles>

External links

- About.com's Pros & Cons of the Death Penalty and Capital Punishment[47]
- Capital Punishment[48] article in the *Internet Encyclopedia of Philosophy*.
- 1000+ Death Penalty links all in one place[49]
- Updates on the death penalty generally and capital punishment law specifically[50]
- Texas Department of Criminal Justice: list of executed offenders and their last statements[51]
- Death Penalty Worldwide:[52] Academic research database on the laws, practice, and statistics of capital punishment for every death penalty country in the world.
- Answers.com entry on capital punishment[53]
- "How to Kill a Human Being"[54], BBC Horizon TV programme documentary, 2008
- U.S. and 50 State death penalty/capital punishment law and other relevant links[55] Megalaw
- Two audio documentaries covering execution in the United States: Witness to an Execution[56] The Execution Tapes[57]
- Wrongfully Convicted Citizens:[58] capital punishment of wrongfully convicted citizens in the US, 2017

In favour

- Studies showing the death penalty saves lives[59]
- Criminal Justice Legal Foundation[60]
- Keep life without parole and death penalty intact[61]
- Why the death penalty is needed[62]
- Pro Death Penalty.com[63]
- Pro Death Penalty Resource Page[64]
- 119 Pro DP Links[65]
- The Death Penalty is Constitutional[66]
- The Paradoxes of a Death Penalty Stance[67] by Charles Lane in the Washington Post
- Clark County, Indiana, Prosecutor's Page on capital punishment[68]
- In Favor of Capital Punishment[69] – Famous Quotes supporting Capital Punishment
- Studies spur new death penalty debate[70]

Opposing

- World Coalition Against the Death Penalty[71]
- Death Watch International[72] International anti-death penalty campaign group
- Campaign to End the Death Penalty[73]
- Anti-Death Penalty Information[74]: includes a monthly watchlist of upcoming executions and death penalty statistics for the United States.
- The Death Penalty Information Center[75]: Statistical information and studies
- Amnesty International – Abolish the death penalty Campaign[76]: Human Rights organisation
- European Union[77]: Information on anti-death penalty policies
- IPS Inter Press Service[78] International news on capital punishment
- Death Penalty Focus[79]: American group dedicated to abolishing the death penalty
- Reprieve.org[80]: United States-based volunteer program for foreign lawyers, students, and others to work at death penalty defense offices
- American Civil Liberties Union[81]: Demanding a Moratorium on the Death Penalty
- National Coalition to Abolish the Death Penalty[82]
- NSW Council for Civil Liberties[83]: an Australian organisation opposed to the Death Penalty in the Asian region
- Winning a war on terror: eliminating the death penalty[84]
- Electric Chair at Sing Sing[85], a 1900 photograph by William M. Vander Weyde, accompanied by a poem by Jared Carter.
- Lead prosecutor apologizes for role in sending man to death row[86] Shreveport Times, 2015

Religious views

- The Dalai Lama[87] – Message supporting the moratorium on the death penalty
- Buddhism & Capital Punishment[88] from The Engaged Zen Society
- Orthodox Union website: Rabbi Yosef Edelstein: Parshat Beha'alotcha: A Few Reflections on Capital Punishment[89]
- Priests for Life[90] – Lists several Catholic links
- The Death Penalty: Why the Church Speaks a Countercultural Message[91] by Kenneth R. Overberg, S.J., from AmericanCatholic.org[92]
- Wrestling with the Death Penalty[93] by Andy Prince, from *Youth Update* on AmericanCatholic.org[92]

- Herbermann, Charles, ed. (1913). "Capital Punishment". *Catholic Encyclopedia*. New York: Robert Appleton Company.<templatestyles src="Module:Citation/CS1/styles.css"></templatestyles>
- Catholics Against Capital Punishment[94]: offers a Catholic perspective and provides resources and links
- Kashif Shahzada 2010[95]: Why The Death Penalty Is un-Islamic?

Current methods

Hanging

Hanging is the suspension of a person by a noose or ligature around the neck.[96] The *Oxford English Dictionary* states that hanging in this sense is "specifically to put to death by suspension by the neck", though it formerly also referred to crucifixion and death by impalement in which the body would remain "hanging". Hanging has been a common method of capital punishment since medieval times, and is the primary execution method in numerous countries and regions. The first account of execution by hanging was in Homer's *Odyssey* (Book XXII). In this specialised meaning of the common word *hang*, the past and past participle is *hanged*[97] instead of *hung*.

Hanging is also a common method of suicide in which a person applies a ligature to the neck and brings about unconsciousness and then death by suspension. Partial suspension or partial weight-bearing on the ligature is sometimes used, particularly in prisons, mental hospitals or other institutions, where full suspension support is difficult to devise, because high ligature points (e.g., hooks or pipes) have been removed.

Methods of judicial hanging

There are four ways of performing a judicial hanging: suspension hanging, the short drop, the standard drop, and the long drop. A mechanised form of hanging, the upright jerker, was also experimented with in the 18th century, with a variant of it used today in Iran.

Figure 19: *The execution of Henry Wirz in 1865 near the U.S. Capitol, moments after the trap door was sprung.*

Figure 20: *Detail from a painting by Pisanello, 1436–1438*

Hanging

Figure 21: *Execution of guards and kapos of the Stutthof concentration camp on 4 July 1946 by short-drop hanging. In the foreground were the female overseers: Jenny-Wanda Barkmann, Ewa Paradies, Elisabeth Becker, Wanda Klaff, Gerda Steinhoff (left to right)*

Suspension

Suspension causes death by using the weight of the body to tighten the noose around the trachea and neck structure. Prisoners are reported to have little or no struggle before they go limp because their jugular vein and carotid arteries are blocked and blood flow to the brain is reduced. The person slowly dies of strangulation, which typically takes between ten and twenty minutes, resulting in a considerably more prolonged and painful death as compared to the standard or long drop hanging. "If the airway is constricted, and full suspension achieved (feet fully off the floor), this method, at least initially, is likely to be very painful, as the person struggles for air against the compression of the noose and against the weight of their own body, being supported entirely by the neck and jaw."

Short drop

The short drop is performed by placing the condemned prisoner on the back of a cart, horse, or other vehicle, with the noose around the neck. The object is then moved away, leaving the person dangling from the rope. A ladder was also commonly used with the condemned being forced to ascend, af-

Figure 22: *Mass execution of Serbs by Austro-Hungarian army in 1916*

ter which the noose was tied and the ladder pulled away or turned, leaving the condemned hanging. Another method involves using a stool, which the condemned is required to stand on, being kicked away. The guards from the Stutthof concentration camp who were sentenced to death were executed by short-drop hanging; they were placed in the noose while standing or sitting on a truck, and the trucks were driven away.

As with suspension hanging, the condemned prisoner slowly dies of strangulation. This typically takes between ten and twenty minutes but unconsciousness occurs already within 6–15 seconds, resulting in a considerably more prolonged and painful death as compared to the standard or long drop hanging, which is intended to kill by using the shock of the drop to fracture the spinal column at the neck. Before 1850, the short drop was the standard method for hanging, and is still common in suicides and extrajudicial hangings (such as lynchings and summary executions) which do not benefit from the specialised equipment and drop-length calculation tables used by the newer methods.

Pole method

A short drop variant is the Austro-Hungarian "pole" method, called Würgegalgen (literally: strangling gallows), in which the following steps take place:

1. The condemned is made to stand before a specialized vertical pole or pillar, approximately 10 feet (3.0 m) in height.

2. A rope is attached around the condemned's feet and routed through a pulley at the base of the pole.
3. The condemned is hoisted to the top of pole by means of a sling running across the chest and under the armpits.
4. A narrow diameter noose is looped around the prisoner's neck, then secured to a hook mounted at the top of the pole.
5. The chest sling is released, and the prisoner is rapidly jerked downward by the assistant executioners via the foot rope.
6. The executioner stands on a stepped platform approximately 4 feet (1.2 m) high beside the condemned, and guides the head downward with his hand simultaneous to the efforts of his assistants.

This method was later also adopted by the successor states, most notably by Czechoslovakia; where the "pole" method was used as the single type of execution from 1918 until the abolition of the capital punishment in 1990. Nazi war criminal Karl Hermann Frank, executed in 1946 in Prague, was among approximately 1,000 condemned people executed in this manner in Czechoslovakia.

Standard drop

The standard drop, which arrived as calculated in English units, involves a drop of between 4 and 6 feet (1.2 and 1.8 m) and came into use from 1866, when the scientific details were published by an Irish doctor, Samuel Haughton. Its use rapidly spread to English-speaking countries and those where judicial systems had an English origin. It was considered a humane improvement on the short drop because it was intended to be enough to break the person's neck, causing immediate paralysis and immobilisation (and probable immediate unconsciousness). This method was used to execute condemned Nazis under United States jurisdiction after the Nuremberg Trials including Joachim von Ribbentrop and Ernst Kaltenbrunner.[98] In the execution of Ribbentrop, historian Giles MacDonogh records that: "The hangman botched the execution and the rope throttled the former foreign minister for twenty minutes before he expired."[99] A *Life* magazine report on the execution merely says: "The trap fell open and with a sound midway between a rumble and a crash, Ribbentrop disappeared. The rope quivered for a time, then stood tautly straight."[100]

Long drop

This process, also known as the measured drop, was introduced to Britain in 1872 by William Marwood as a scientific advance on the standard drop. Instead of everyone falling the same standard distance, the person's height and weight were used to determine how much slack would be provided in the rope

Figure 23: *Sepia-tone photo from a contemporary 1901 postcard showing Tom Ketchum's decapitated body. Caption reads "Body of Black Jack after the hanging showing head snapped off."*

Figure 24: *Execution of German war criminal Franz Strasser at Landsberg Prison on 2 January 1946*

so that the distance dropped would be enough to ensure that the neck was broken, but not so much that the person was decapitated. The careful placement of the eye or knot of the noose (so that the head was jerked back as the rope tightened) contributed to breaking the neck.

Prior to 1892, the drop was between four and ten feet (about one to three metres), depending on the weight of the body, and was calculated to deliver a force of 1,260 lbf (5,600 newtons or 572 kgf), which fractured the neck at either the 2nd and 3rd or 4th and 5th cervical vertebrae. This force resulted in some decapitations, such as the infamous case of Black Jack Ketchum in New Mexico Territory in 1901, owing to a significant weight gain while in custody not having been factored into the drop calculations. Between 1892 and 1913, the length of the drop was shortened to avoid decapitation. After 1913, other factors were also taken into account, and the force delivered was reduced to about 1,000 lbf (4,400 N or 450 kgf). The decapitation of Eva Dugan during a botched hanging in 1930 led the state of Arizona to switch to the gas chamber as its primary execution method, on the grounds that it was believed more humane.[101] One of the more recent decapitations as a result of the long drop occurred when Barzan Ibrahim al-Tikriti was hanged in Iraq in 2007. Accidental decapitation also occurred during the 1962 hanging of Arthur Lucas, one of the last two people to be put to death in Canada.

Nazis executed under British jurisdiction, including Josef Kramer, Fritz Klein, Irma Grese and Elisabeth Volkenrath, were hanged by Albert Pierrepoint using the variable drop method devised by Marwood. The record speed for a British long drop hanging was 7 seconds from the executioner entering the cell to the drop. Speed was considered to be important in the British system as it reduced the condemned's mental distress.

As suicide

Hanging is a common method for suicide. The materials necessary for suicide by hanging are readily available to the average person, compared with firearms or poisons. Full suspension is not required, and for this reason, hanging is especially commonplace among suicidal prisoners (see suicide watch). A type of hanging comparable to full suspension hanging may be obtained by self-strangulation using a ligature around the neck and the partial weight of the body (partial suspension) to tighten the ligature. When a suicidal hanging involves partial suspension the deceased is found to have both feet touching the ground, e.g., they are kneeling, crouching or standing.

In Canada, hanging is the most common method of suicide, and in the U.S., hanging is the second most common method, after self-inflicted gunshot wounds. In the United Kingdom, where firearms are less easily available, in

Figure 25: *Suicide by hanging*

2001 hanging was the most common method among men and the second most commonplace among women (after poisoning).

Those who survive a suicide-via-hanging attempt, whether due to breakage of the cord or ligature point, or being discovered and cut down, face a range of serious injuries, including cerebral anoxia—which can lead to permanent brain damage, laryngeal fracture, cervical spine fracture—which may cause paralysis, tracheal fracture, pharyngeal laceration, and carotid artery injury.

As human sacrifice

There are some suggestions that the Vikings practiced hanging as human sacrifices to Odin, to honour Odin's own sacrifice of hanging himself from the Yggdrasil. In Northern Europe, it is widely speculated that the Iron Age bog bodies, many who show signs of having been hanged were examples of human sacrifice to the gods.

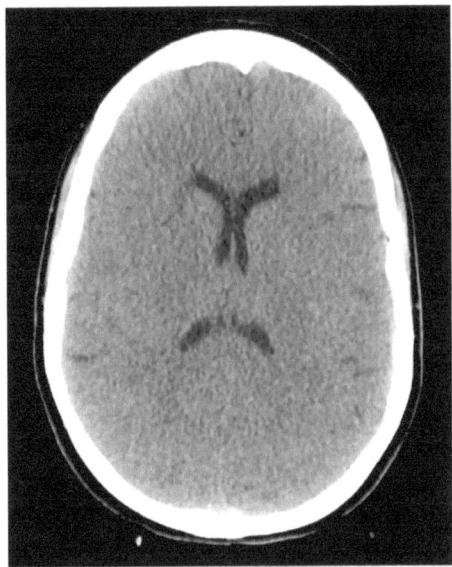

Figure 26: *Anoxic brain injury following a hanging. The loss of grey white matter differentiation and small ventricles due to brain swelling are visible.*

Medical effects

A hanging may induce one or more of the following medical conditions, some leading to death:

- Closure of carotid arteries causing cerebral hypoxia
- Closure of the jugular veins
- Induction of carotid sinus reflex death, which reduces heartbeat when the pressure in the carotid arteries is high, causing cardiac arrest
- Breaking of the neck (cervical fracture) causing traumatic spinal cord injury or even unintended decapitation
- Closure of the airway

The cause of death in hanging depends on the conditions related to the event. When the body is released from a relatively high position, the major cause of death is severe trauma to the upper cervical spine. The injuries produced are highly variable. One study showed that only a small minority of a series of judicial hangings produced fractures to the cervical spine (6 out of 34 cases studied), with half of these fractures (3 out of 34) being the classic "hangman's fracture" (bilateral fractures of the pars interarticularis of the C2 vertebra).[102] The location of the knot of the hanging rope is a major factor in determining the mechanics of cervical spine injury, with a submental knot (hangman's knot under the chin) being the only location capable of producing the sudden, straightforward hyperextension injury that causes the classic "hangman's fracture".

According to *Historical and biomechanical aspects of hangman's fracture*, the phrase in the usual execution order, *"hanged by the neck until dead,"* was necessary. By the late 19th century that methodical study enabled authorities to routinely employ hanging in ways that would predictably kill the victim quickly.

There is evidence suggesting that there might be superior alternatives if there were sufficient interest to support research into such matters. Consider in particular an event recounted in the biography of Albert Pierrepoint. Events followed a most unconventional sequence during the hanging of a particularly powerful and uncooperative German spy during World War II. Pierrepoint relates:

> *Just as I was crossing to the lever, he jumped with bound feet. The drop opened, and he plunged down, and I saw with horror that the noose was slipping. It would have come right over his head had it not caught roughly at a point halfway up the hood – it had in fact been stopped on his upper lip by the projection of his nose – and the body jerked down, then became absolutely still apart from the swinging of the rope. I went down into the pit with the prison medical officer. He examined the body and said to me: "A clean death. Instantaneous." He sounded surprised, and I did not blame him. I was surprised myself, and very relieved. On my next visit to Wandsworth the governor told me that the severance of the spinal cord had been perfect.*

Not surprisingly in retrospect, it appears that such unconventional application of forces might be particularly efficient. There is at least some evidence that some of the countries with particularly active programmes of judicial execution may have given the question of the design of efficient and reliable nooses practical attention. For example, photographs of nooses in a South African execution chamber opened to the public after abolition of the death penalty showed double nooses.[103] Presumably the upper noose held the lower one in place to ensure a perfect hangman's fracture.

The side, or subaural knot, has been shown to produce other, more complex injuries, with one thoroughly studied case producing only ligamentous injuries to the cervical spine and bilateral vertebral artery disruptions, but no major vertebral fractures or crush injuries to the spinal cord.[104] Death from a "hangman's fracture" occurs mainly when the applied force is severe enough to also cause a severe subluxation of the C2 and C3 vertebra that crushes the spinal cord and/or disrupts the vertebral arteries. Hangman's fractures from other

Figure 27: *John Ogilvie, who in 1615 was hanged and disembowelled after torture for his refusal to give up the Catholic faith and convert to Protestantism*

hyperextension injuries (the most common being unrestrained motor vehicle accidents and falls or diving injuries where the face or chin suddenly strike an immovable object) are frequently survivable if the applied force does not cause a severe subluxation of C2 on C3.

Another process that has been suggested is carotid sinus reflex death. By this theory, the mechanical stimulation of the carotid sinus in the neck brings on terminal cardiac arrest.

In the absence of fracture and dislocation, occlusion of blood vessels becomes the major cause of death, rather than asphyxiation. Obstruction of venous drainage of the brain via occlusion of the internal jugular veins leads to cerebral oedema and then cerebral ischemia. The face will typically become engorged and cyanotic (turned blue through lack of oxygen). There will be the classic sign of strangulation, petechiae, little blood marks on the face and in the eyes from burst blood capillaries. The tongue may protrude.

Compromise of the cerebral blood flow may occur by obstruction of the carotid arteries, even though their obstruction requires far more force than the obstruction of jugular veins, since they are seated deeper and they contain blood in much higher pressure compared to the jugular veins. Where death has occurred through carotid artery obstruction or cervical fracture, the face will typically

Figure 28: *La Pendaison (The Hanging), a plate from French artist Jacques Callot's 1633 series The Great Miseries of War.*

be pale in colour and not show petechiae. Many reports and pictures exist of actual short-drop hangings that seem to show that the person died quickly, while others indicate a slow and agonising death by strangulation.

When cerebral circulation is severely compromised by any mechanism, arterial or venous, death occurs over four or more minutes from cerebral hypoxia, although the heart may continue to beat for some period after the brain can no longer be resuscitated. The time of death in such cases is a matter of convention. In judicial hangings, death is pronounced at cardiac arrest, which may occur at times from several minutes up to 15 minutes or longer after hanging. During suspension, once the prisoner has lapsed into unconsciousness, rippling movements of the body and limbs may occur for some time which are usually attributed to nervous and muscular reflexes. In Britain, it was normal to leave the body suspended for an hour to ensure death.

After death, the body typically shows marks of suspension: bruising and rope marks on the neck. Sphincters will relax spontaneously and urine and faeces will be evacuated. Forensic experts may often be able to tell if hanging is suicide or homicide, as each leaves a distinctive ligature mark. One of the hints they use is the hyoid bone. If broken, it often means the person has been murdered by manual choking.

Notable references by country (political)

Hanging has been a method of capital punishment in many countries.

Australia

Capital punishment was a part of the legal system of Australia from its early days as a penal colony for the British Empire, until 1985, when Australia abolished the death penalty in all states;[105] in practice, the last execution in Australia was the hanging of Ronald Ryan on 3 February 1967, in Victoria.[106]

During the 19th century, crimes that could carry a death sentence included burglary, sheep stealing, forgery, sexual assaults, murder and manslaughter. During the 19th century, there were about 80 people hanged each year throughout Australia for these crimes.

Brazil

Death by hanging was the customary method of capital punishment in Brazil throughout its history. Some important national heroes like Tiradentes (1792) were killed by hanging. The last man executed in Brazil was the slave Francisco, in 1876. The death penalty was abolished for all crimes, except for those committed under extraordinary circumstances such as war or military law, in 1890.[107]

Bulgaria

Bulgaria's national hero, Vasil Levski, was executed by hanging by the Ottoman court in Sofia in 1873. Every year since Bulgaria's liberation, thousands come with flowers on the date of his death, 19 February, to his monument where the gallows stood. The last execution was in 1989, and the death penalty was abolished for all crimes in 1998.

Canada

Historically, hanging was the only method of execution used in Canada and was in use as possible punishment for all murders until 1961, when murders were reclassified into capital and non-capital offences. The death penalty was restricted to apply only for certain offences to the National Defence Act in 1976 and was completely abolished in 1998.[108] The last hangings in Canada took place on 11 December 1962.

Egypt

In 1955, Egypt hanged three Israelis on charges of spying. In 2004, Egypt hanged five militants on charges of trying to kill the Prime Minister.

Figure 29: *Public execution of Polish civilians by the Nazi Germans in Kraków in 1942*

Germany

In the territories occupied by Nazi Germany from 1939 to 1945, strangulation hanging was a preferred means of public execution, although more criminal executions were performed by guillotine than hanging. The most commonly sentenced were partisans and black marketeers, whose bodies were usually left hanging for long periods. There are also numerous reports of concentration camp inmates being hanged. Hanging was continued in post-war Germany in the British and US Occupation Zones under their jurisdiction, and for Nazi war criminals, until well after (western) Germany itself had abolished the death penalty by the German constitution as adopted in 1949. West Berlin was not subject to the *Grundgesetz* (Basic Law) and abolished the death penalty in 1951. The German Democratic Republic abolished the death penalty in 1987. The last execution ordered by a West German court was carried out by guillotine in Moabit prison in 1949. The last hanging in Germany was the one ordered of several war criminals in Landsberg am Lech on 7 June 1951. The last known execution in East Germany was in 1981 by a pistol shot to the neck.

Figure 30: *Soviet partisans hanged by German forces in January 1943*

Hungary

The prime minister of Hungary, during the 1956 Revolution, Imre Nagy, was secretly tried, executed by hanging, and buried unceremoniously by the new Soviet-backed Hungarian government, in 1958. Nagy was later publicly exonerated by Hungary.[109] Capital punishment was abolished for all crimes in 1990.

India

All executions in India are carried out by hanging. In 1949, Nathuram Godse, Mahatma Gandhi's assassin, was the first person to be executed by hanging in independent India.

The Supreme Court of India has suggested that capital punishment should be given only in the "rarest of rare cases".

Since 2010, three people have been executed in India. Ajmal Kasab, the lone surviving terrorist of the 2008 Mumbai attacks was executed on 21 November 2012 in Yerwada Central Jail, Pune. The Supreme Court of India had previously rejected his mercy plea, which was then rejected by the President of India. He was hanged one week later. Afzal Guru, a terrorist found guilty of conspiracy in the December 2001 attack on the Indian Parliament, was executed by hanging in Tihar Jail, Delhi on 9 February 2013. Yakub Memon was convicted over his involvement in the 1993 Bombay bombings by Special

Figure 31: *The hanging of two participants in the Indian Rebellion of 1857*

Terrorist and Disruptive Activities court on 27 July 2007. His appeals and petitions for clemency were all rejected and he was finally executed by hanging on 30 July 2015 in Nagpur jail.

Iran

Death by hanging is the primary means of capital punishment in Iran. It is legal for murder, rape, and drug trafficking unless the criminal pays diyya to the victim's family, thus attaining their forgiveness (see Sharia law). If the presiding judge deems the case to be "causing public outrage", he can order the hanging to take place in public at the spot where the crime was committed, typically from a mobile telescoping crane which hoists the condemned high into the air. On 19 July 2005, two boys, Mahmoud Asgari and Ayaz Marhoni, aged 15 and 17 respectively, who had been convicted of the rape of a 13-year-old boy, were hanged at Edalat (Justice) Square in Mashhad, on charges of homosexuality and rape. On 15 August 2004, a 16-year-old girl, Atefeh Sahaaleh (also called Atefeh Rajabi), was executed for having committed "acts incompatible with chastity".

At dawn on 27 July 2008, the Iranian government executed 29 people at Evin Prison in Tehran. On 2 December 2008, an unnamed man was hanged for murder at Kazeroun Prison, just moments after he was pardoned by the murder victim's family. He was quickly cut down and rushed to a hospital, where he was successfully revived.[110]

The conviction and hanging of Reyhaneh Jabbari caused international uproar as she was sentenced to death in 2009 and hanged on 25 October 2014 for murdering a former intelligence officer; according to Jabbari's testimony she stabbed him during an attempt at rape and then another person killed him.

Iraq

Hanging was used under the regime of Saddam Hussein, but was suspended along with capital punishment on 10 June 2003, when a coalition led by the United States invaded and overthrew the previous regime. The death penalty was reinstated on 8 August 2004.

In September 2005, three murderers were the first people to be executed since the restoration. Then on 9 March 2006, an official of Iraq's Supreme Judicial Council confirmed that Iraqi authorities had executed the first insurgents by hanging.

Saddam Hussein was sentenced to death by hanging for crimes against humanity on 5 November 2006, and was executed on 30 December 2006 at approximately 6:00 a.m. local time. During the drop, there was an audible crack indicating that his neck was broken, a successful example of a long drop hanging. A week later, another video surfaced on the Internet, which showed Saddam's body with an open wound on the left lower jaw, caused by the impact of the knot.

Barzan Ibrahim, the head of the Mukhabarat, Saddam's security agency, and Awad Hamed al-Bandar, former chief judge, were executed on 15 January 2007, also by the long drop method, but Barzan was decapitated by the rope at the end of his fall.

Former vice-president Taha Yassin Ramadan had been sentenced to life in prison on 5 November 2006, but the sentence was changed to death by hanging on 12 February 2007. He was the fourth and final man to be executed for the 1982 crimes against humanity on 20 March 2007. The execution went smoothly.

At the Anfal genocide trial, Saddam's cousin Ali Hassan al-Majid (aka Chemical Ali), former defence minister Sultan Hashim Ahmed al-Tay, and former deputy Hussein Rashid Mohammed were sentenced to hang for their role in the Al-Anfal Campaign against the Kurds on 24 June 2007.[111] Al-Majid was sentenced to death three more times: once for the 1991 suppression of a Shi'a uprising along with Abdul-Ghani Abdul Ghafur on 2 December 2008;[112] once for the 1999 crackdown in the assassination of Grand Ayatollah Mohammad al-Sadr on 2 March 2009;[113] and once on 17 January 2010 for the gassing of the Kurds in 1988;[114] he was hanged on 25 January.

On 26 October 2010, Saddam's top minister Tariq Aziz was sentenced to hang for persecuting the members of rival Shi'a political parties. His sentence was commuted to indefinite imprisonment after Iraqi president Jalal Talabani did not sign his execution order and he died in prison in 2015.

On 14 July 2011, Sultan Hashim Ahmed al-Tay and two of Saddam's half-brothers – Sabawi Ibrahim al-Tikriti and Watban Ibrahim al-Tikriti—both condemned to death on 11 March 2009 for the role in the executions of 42 traders who were accused of manipulating food prices—were handed over to the Iraqi authorities for execution.

It is alleged that Iraq's government keeps the execution rate secret, and hundreds may be carried out every year. In 2007, Amnesty International stated that 900 people were at "imminent risk" of execution in Iraq.

Israel

Although Israel has provisions in its criminal law to use the death penalty for extraordinary crimes, it has only been used twice. On 31 May 1962, Nazi leader Adolf Eichmann was executed by hanging. Meir Tobianski was summarily executed for espionage during the Israeli War of Independence, but he was later exonerated.

Japan

On 23 December 1948, Hideki Tojo, Kenji Doihara, Akira Mutō, Iwane Matsui, Seishirō Itagaki, Kōki Hirota, and Heitaro Kimura were hanged at Sugamo Prison by the U.S. occupation authorities in Ikebukuro in Allied-occupied Japan for war crimes, crimes against humanity, and crimes against peace during the Asia-Pacific theatre of World War II.

On 27 February 2004, the mastermind of the Sarin gas attack on the Tokyo subway, Shoko Asahara, was found guilty and sentenced to death by hanging. On 25 December 2006, serial killer Hiroaki Hidaka and three others were hanged in Japan. Long drop hanging is the common method of execution in capital punishment cases in Japan, as in the cases of Norio Nagayama, Mamoru Takuma, and Tsutomu Miyazaki. In 2018 Shoko Asahara and several of his cult members were hanged for committing the 1995 sarin gas attack.

Jordan

Death by hanging is the traditional method of capital punishment in Jordan. In 1993, Jordan hanged two Jordanians convicted of spying for Israel. Sajida al-Rishawi, "The 4th bomber" of the 2005 Amman bombings, was executed by hanging alongside Ziad al-Karbouly on 4 February 2015 in retribution for the immolation of Jordanian Pilot Muath Al-Kasasbeh.

Hanging

Figure 32: *The Hanging of the Harper Seven, Liberia - 16 February 1979*

Lebanon

Lebanon hanged two men in 1998 for murdering a man and his sister. However, capital punishment ended up being altogether suspended in Lebanon, as a result of staunch opposition by activists and some political factions.

Liberia

On 16 February 1979, seven men convicted of the ritual killing of the popular Kru traditional singer Moses Tweh, were publicly hanged at dawn in Harper.[115,116]

Malaysia

Hanging is the traditional method of capital punishment in Malaysia and has been used to execute people convicted of murder and drug trafficking.

Portugal

The last person executed by hanging in Portugal was Francisco Matos Lobos on 16 April 1842. Before that, it had been a common death penalty.

Pakistan

In Pakistan, hanging is the most common form of execution.

Russia

Hanging was commonly practised in the Russian Empire during the rule of the Romanov Dynasty as an alternative to impalement, which was used in the 15th and 16th centuries.

Hanging was abolished in 1868 by Alexander II after serfdom, but was restored by the time of his death and his assassins were hanged. While those sentenced to death for murder were usually pardoned and sentences commuted to life imprisonment, those guilty of high treason were usually executed. This also included the Grand Duchy of Finland and Kingdom of Poland under the Russian crown. Taavetti Lukkarinen became the last Finn to be executed this way. He was hanged for espionage and high treason in 1916.

The hanging was usually performed by short drop and in public. The gallows were usually either a stout nearby tree branch, as in case of Lukkarinen, or a makeshift gallows constructed for the purpose.

After the October Revolution in 1917, capital punishment was, on paper, abolished, but continued to be used unabated against people perceived to be enemies of the regime. Under the Bolsheviks, most executions were performed by shooting, either by firing squad or by a single firearm. The last to be hanged were Andrey Vlasov and his companions in 1946.

Singapore

In Singapore, hanging using the long-drop method is currently used as mandatory punishment for various crimes, such as drug trafficking, murder and some types of kidnapping. It has also been used for punishing those convicted of unauthorised discharging of firearms.

Syria

Syria has publicly hanged people, such as two Jews in 1952, Israeli spy Eli Cohen in 1965, and a number of Jews accused of spying in 1969.

According to a 19th-century report, members of the Alawite sect centred on Lattakia in Syria had a particular aversion towards being hanged, and the family of the condemned was willing to pay "considerable sums" to ensure its relation was impaled, instead of being hanged. As far as Burckhardt could make out, this attitude was based upon the Alawites' idea that the soul ought to leave the body through the mouth, rather than leave it in any other fashion.[117]

Figure 33: *Eli Cohen, publicly hanged by Syria on 18 May 1965*

United Kingdom

As a form of judicial execution in England, hanging is thought to date from the Anglo-Saxon period. Records of the names of British hangmen begin with Thomas de Warblynton in the 1360s;Wikipedia:Citation needed complete records extend from the 16th century to the last hangmen, Robert Leslie Stewart and Harry Allen, who conducted the last British executions in 1964.

Until 1868 hangings were performed in public. In London, the traditional site was at Tyburn, a settlement west of the City on the main road to Oxford, which was used on eight hanging days a year, though before 1865, executions had been transferred to the street outside Newgate Prison, Old Bailey, now the site of the Central Criminal Court.

Three British subjects were hanged after World War II after having been convicted of having helped Nazi Germany in its war against Britain. John Amery, the son of prominent British politician Leo Amery, became an expatriate in the 1930s, moving to France. He became involved in pre-war fascist politics, remained in what became Vichy France following France's defeat by Germany in 1940 and eventually went to Germany and later the German puppet state in Italy headed by Benito Mussolini. Captured by Italian partisans at the end of the war and handed over to British authorities, Amery was accused of having made propaganda broadcasts for the Nazis and of having attempted to recruit

British prisoners of war for a Waffen SS regiment later known as the British Free Corps. Amery pleaded guilty to treason charges on 28 November 1945 and was hanged at Wandsworth Prison on 19 December 1945. William Joyce, an American-born Irishman who had lived in Britain and possessed a British passport, had been involved in pre-war fascist politics in the UK, fled to Nazi Germany just before the war began to avoid arrest by British authorities and became a naturalised German citizen. He made propaganda broadcasts for the Nazis, becoming infamous under the nickname Lord Haw Haw. Captured by British forces in May 1945, he was tried for treason later that year. Although Joyce's defence argued that he was by birth American and thus not subject to being tried for treason, the prosecution successfully argued that Joyce's pre-war British passport meant that he was a subject of the British Crown and he was convicted. After his appeals failed, he was hanged at Wandsworth Prison on 3 January 1946. Theodore Schurch, a British soldier captured by the Nazis who then began working for the Italian and German intelligence services by acting as a spy and informer who would be placed among other British prisoners, was arrested in Rome in March 1945 and tried under the Treachery Act 1940. After his conviction, he was hanged at HM Prison Pentonville on 4 January 1946.

The Homicide Act 1957 created the new offence of capital murder, punishable by death, with all other murders being punishable by life imprisonment.

In 1965, Parliament passed the Murder (Abolition of Death Penalty) Act, temporarily abolishing capital punishment for murder for 5 years. The Act was renewed in 1969, making the abolition permanent. With the passage of the Crime and Disorder Act 1998 and the Human Rights Act 1998, the death penalty was officially abolished for all crimes in both civilian and military cases. Following its complete abolition, the gallows were removed from Wandsworth Prison, where they remained in full working order until that year.

The last woman to be hanged was Ruth Ellis on 13 July 1955, by Albert Pierrepoint who was a prominent hangman in the 20th century in England. The last hanging in Britain took place in 1964, when Peter Anthony Allen, at Walton Prison in Liverpool, and Gwynne Owen Evans, at Strangeways Prison in Manchester were executed for the murder of John Alan West.

Hanging was also the method used in many colonies and overseas territories.

Silken rope

In the UK, some felons were traditionally executed by hanging with a silken rope:

- Hereditary peers who committed capital offences,[118] as anticipated by the fictional Duke of Denver, brother of Lord Peter Wimsey. The Duke was accused of murder in the novel *Clouds of Witness*, and if convicted, this execution would have been his fate, after conviction by his peers in a trial in the House of Lords. It has been claimed that the execution of Earl Ferrers in 1760 – the only time a peer was hanged after trial by the House of Lords – was carried out with the normal hempen rope instead of a silk one. The writ of execution does not specify a silk rope be used, and The Newgate Calendar makes no mention of the use of such an item – an unusual omission given its highly sensationalist nature.
- Those who have the Freedom of the City of London.

Figure 34: *An image of suspected witches being hanged in England, published in 1655.*

Figure 35: *Balvenie Pillar, also known as Tom na Croiche (Hangman's Knoll). The pillar was erected in 1755 to commemorate the last public hanging in the Atholl region of Scotland in 1630.*

Figure 36: *Hanging noose used at public executions outside Lancaster Castle, c. 1820–1830.*

United States

Capital punishment in the U.S. varies from state to state; it is outlawed in some states but used in most others. However, the death penalty under federal law is applicable in every state.

The largest mass execution in the United States, of 38 Sioux Indians sentenced to death for engaging in massacres of American settlers, was carried out by hanging in Mankato, Minnesota in 1862. A total of 40 suspected Unionists were hanged in Gainesville, Texas in October 1862. On 7 July 1865, four people involved in the assassination of President Abraham Lincoln—Mary Surratt, Lewis Powell, David Herold, and George Atzerodt—were hanged at Fort McNair in Washington, D.C.

The last public hanging in the United States took place on 14 August 1936, in Owensboro, Kentucky. Rainey Bethea was executed for the rape and murder of 70-year-old Lischa Edwards. The execution was presided over by the first female sheriff in Kentucky, Florence Shoemaker Thompson.

In California, Clinton Duffy, who served as warden of San Quentin State Prison between 1940 and 1952, presided over ninety executions. He began to oppose the death penalty and after his retirement he wrote a memoir entitled *Eighty-Eight Men and Two Women* in support of the movement to abolish

Figure 37: *The execution of Mary Surratt, Lewis Powell, David Herold, and George Atzerodt, who were all convicted by a military tribunal for being involved in the assassination of Abraham Lincoln*

the death penalty. The book documents several hangings gone wrong and describes how they led his predecessor, Warden James B. Holohan, to persuade the California Legislature to replace hanging with the gas chamber in 1937.

Various methods of capital punishment have been replaced by lethal injection in most states and the federal government. Many states that offered hanging as an option have since eliminated the method. Condemned murderer Victor Feguer became the last inmate to be executed by hanging in the state of Iowa on 15 March 1963. Hanging was the preferred method of execution for capital murder cases in Iowa until 1965, when the death penalty was abolished and replaced with life imprisonment without parole. Barton Kay Kirkham was the last person to be hanged in Utah, preferring it over execution by firing squad. No subsequent inmate in Utah had been hanged by the time the option was replaced with lethal injection in 1980.Wikipedia:Citation needed Laws in Delaware were changed in 1986 to specify lethal injection, except for those convicted before 1986 (who were still allowed to choose hanging). If a choice was not made, or the convict refused to choose injection, then hanging would become the default method. This was the case in the 1996 execution of Billy Bailey, the most recent hanging in American history; since then, no Delaware prisoner has fitted this category, and thus the state's gallows were dismantled.

Figure 38: *Woodcut by Johann Stumpf, who witnessed this type of execution in 1553*

Only the state New Hampshire retain hanging as an option. In New Hampshire, if it is found to be "impractical" to carry out the execution by lethal injection, then the condemned is hanged.

The United States also has an extensive history of extrajudicial hangings, known as lynching. This was especially common during the Jim Crow era.

Inverted hanging, the "Jewish" punishment

A completely different principle of hanging is to hang the convicted person from his legs, rather than from his neck, either as a form of torture, or as an execution method. In late medieval Germany, this came to be primarily associated with Jewish thieves, called the "Judenstrafe". The jurist Ulrich Tengler, in his highly influential "Layenspiegel" from 1509, describes the procedure as follows, in the section "Von Juden straff":[119]

<templatestyles src="Template:Quote/styles.css"/>

> About dragging the Jew to the ordinary execution place between two mad or biting dogs. After dragging, to hung him from his feet by rope or chain at a designated gallows between the dogs, and in such inverted manner to be executed, from life to death[120]

Guido Kisch showed that originally, this type of inverted hanging between two dogs was not a punishment specifically for Jews. Esther Cohen writes:[121]

> The inverted hanging with the accompaniment of two dogs, originally reserved for traitors, was identified from the fourteenth century as the "Jewish execution", being practised in the later Middle Ages in both northern and Mediterranean Europe. The Jewish execution in Germany has been thoroughly studied by G. Kisch, who has argued convincingly that neither the inverted hanging nor the stringing up of dogs or wolves beside the victim were particularly Jewish punishments during the High Middle Ages. They first appeared as Jewish punishments in Germany only towards the end of the thirteenth century, never being recognized as exclusively Jewish penalties. In France the inverted, animal-associated hanging came to be connected with Jews by the later Middle Ages. The inverted hanging of Jews is specifically mentioned in the old customs of Burgundy in the context of animal hanging. The custom, dogs and all, was still in force in Paris shortly before the final expulsion of the Jews in 1394

In Spain 1449, during a mob attack against the Marranos (Jews nominally converted to Christianity), the Jews resisted, but lost and several of them were hanged up by the feet. The first attested German case for a Jew being hanged by the feet is from 1296, in present-day Soultzmatt. Some other historical examples of this type of hanging within the German context are one Jew in Hennegau 1326, two Jews hanged in Frankfurt 1444,[122] one in Halle in 1462,[123] one in Dortmund 1486,[124] one in Hanau 1499, one in Breslau 1505,[125] one in Württemberg 1553,[126] one in Bergen 1588, one in Öttingen 1611, one in Frankfurt 1615 and again in 1661, and one condemned to this punishment in Prussia in 1637.[127]

The details of the cases vary widely: In the 1444 Frankfurt cases and the 1499 Hanau case, the dogs were dead prior to be hanged, and in the late 1615 and 1661 cases in Frankfurt, the Jews (and dogs) were merely kept in this torture for half an hour, before being garroted from below. In the 1588 Bergen case, all three victims were left hanging till they were dead, ranging from 6 to 8 days after being hanged. In the Dortmund 1486 case, the dogs bit the Jew to death while hanging. In the 1611 Öttingen case, the Jew "Jacob the Tall" thought to blow up the "Deutsche Ordenhaus" with gunpowder after having burgled it. He was strung up between two dogs, and a large fire was made close to him, and he expired after half an hour under this torture. In the 1553 Württemberg case, the Jew chose to convert to Christianity after hanging like this for 24 hours; he was then given the mercy to be hanged in the ordinary manner, from the neck, and without the dogs beside him. In the 1462 Halle case, the Jew Abraham also converted after 24 hours hanging upside down, and a priest went up on a ladder and baptised him. For two more days, Abraham was left hanging, while the priest argued with the city council that a true Christian should not be punished in this way. On the third day, Abraham was granted a reprieve, and was taken down, but died 20 days later in the local hospital having meanwhile suffered in extreme pain. In the 1637 case, where the Jew had murdered a Christian jeweller, the appeal to the empress was successful, and out of mercy, the Jew was condemned to be merely pinched with glowing pincers, have hot lead dripped into his wounds, and then be broken alive on the wheel.

Some of the reported cases may be myths, or wandering stories. The 1326 Hennegau case, for example, deviates from the others in that the Jew was not a thief, but was suspected (even though he was a convert to Christianity) of having struck an al fresco painting of Virgin Mary, so that blood had begun to seep down the wall from the painting. Even under all degrees of judicial torture, the Jew denied performing this sacrilegious act, and was therefore exonerated. Then a brawny smith demanded from him a trial by combat, because, supposedly, in a dream the Virgin herself had besought the smith to do so. The court accepted the smith's challenge, he easily won the combat against the Jew, who was duly hanged up by the feet between two dogs. To add to the injury, one let him be slowly roasted as well as hanged. This is a very similar story to one told in *France*, in which a young Jew threw a lance at the head of a statue of the Virgin, so that blood spurted out of it. There was inadequate evidence for a normal trial, but a frail old man asked for trial by combat, and bested the young Jew. The Jew confessed his crime, and was hanged by his feet between two mastiffs.

The features of the earliest attested case, that of a Jewish thief hanged by the feet in Soultzmatt in 1296 are also rather divergent from the rest. The Jew managed, somehow, after he had been left to die to twitch his body in such a manner that he could hoist himself up on the gallows and free himself. At that time, his feet were so damaged that he was unable to escape, and when he was discovered 8 days after he had been hanged, he was strangled to death by the townspeople.

As late as in 1699 Celle, the courts were sufficiently horrified at how the Jewish leader of a robber gang (condemned to be hanged in the normal manner), declared blasphemies against Christianity, that they made a ruling on the *post mortem* treatment of Jonas Meyer. After 3 days, his corpse was cut down, his tongue cut out, and his body was hanged up again, but this time from its feet.[128]

The punishment for traitors

Guido Kisch writes that the first instance he knows where a person in Germany was hanged up by his feet between two dogs until he died occurred about 1048, some 250 years earlier than the first attested Jewish case. This was a knight called Arnold, who had murdered his lord; the story is contained in Adam of Bremens "History of the Archbishops of Hamburg-Bremen"[129] Another example of a non-Jew who suffered this punishment as a torture, in 1196 Richard, Count of Acerra, was one of those executed by Henry VI in the suppression of the rebelling Sicilians:[130]

> He [Henry VI] held a general court in Capua, at which he ordered that the count first be drawn behind a horse through the squares of Capua, and then hanged alive head downwards. The latter was still alive after two days when a certain German jester called Leather-Bag [Follis], hoping to please the emperor, tied a large stone to his neck and shamefully put him to death

A couple of centuries earlier, in France 991, a viscount Walter nominally owing his allegiance to the French King Hugh Capet chose, on instigation of his wife, to join the rebellion under Odo I, Count of Blois. When Odo found out he had to abandon Melun after all, Walter was duly hanged before the gates, whereas his *wife*, the fomentor of treason, was hanged by her feet, causing much merriment and jeers from Hugh's soldiers as her clothes fell downwards revealing her naked body, although it is not wholly clear if she *died* in that manner.

Elizabethan maritime law

During Queen Elizabeth I's reign, the following was written concerning those who stole a ship from the Royal Navy:

> If anye one practysed to steale awaye anye of her Majesty's shippes, the captaine was to cause him to be hanged by the heels untill his braines were beaten out against the shippe's sides, and then to be cutt down and lett fall intoe the sea.

Hanging by the ribs

In 1713, Juraj Jánošík, a semi-legendary Slovak outlaw and folk hero, was sentenced to be hanged from his left rib. He was left to slowly die.[131]

The German physician Gottlob Schober (1670–1739), who worked in Russia from 1712, notes that a person could hang from the ribs for about three days

Figure 39: *A Negro Hung Alive by the Ribs to a Gallows by William Blake. Originally published in Stedman's Narrative.*

prior to expiring, his primary pain being that of extreme thirst. He thought this degree of insensitivity was something peculiar to the Russian mentality.

The Dutch overlords in Suriname were also in the habit of hanging a slave from the ribs. John Gabriel Stedman stayed in South America from 1772–77 and described the method as told by a witness:[132]

> Not long ago, (continued he) I saw a black "man suspended alive from a gallows by the ribs, between which, with a knife, was first made an incision, and then clinched an iron hook with a chain: in this manner he kept alive three days, hanging with his head "and feet downwards, and catching with his tongue the "drops of water (it being in the rainy season) that were "flowing down his bloated breast. Notwithstanding all this, he never complained, and even upbraided a negro "for crying while he was flogged below the gallows, by calling out to him: "You man ?—Da boy fasy? Are you a man? you behave like a boy". Shortly after which he was knocked on the head by the commiserating sentry, who stood over him, with the butt end of his musket.

William Blake was specially commissioned to make illustrations to Stedman's narrative.[133]

Grammar

The proper, traditional past tense and past participle form of the verb "hang", in this sense, is (to be) "hanged". Some dictionaries list only "hung",[134,135] whereas others show both forms. For example, "people are hanged; meat is hung".

Further reading

- Jack Shuler, *The Thirteenth Turn: A History of the Noose*. New York: Public Affairs, 2014, <templatestyles src="Module:Citation/CS1/styles.css" />ISBN 978-1610391368

External links

- A Case Of Strangulation Fabricated As Hanging[136]
- Obliquity vs. Discontinuity of ligature mark in diagnosis of hanging – a comparative study[137]
- Death Penalty Worldwide[138] Academic research database on the laws, practice, and statistics of capital punishment for every death penalty country in the world.

Execution by shooting

Execution by shooting is a method of capital punishment in which a person is shot to death by one or more firearms. It is the most common method of execution worldwide, used in about 70 countries, with execution by firing squad being one particular form.

In most countries, execution by a firing squad has historically been considered a more honorable death and was used primarily for military personnel, though in some countries—among them Belarus, the only state in Europe today that practices the death penalty—the single-executioner shooting inherited from the Soviet past is still in use.

Figure 40: *A Batista firing squad executing a revolutionary in Cuba, 1956.*

Brazil

Although Brazil abolishes any death penalty completely, it can be executed in the occurrence of certain crimes in a period of war, such as betrayal, conspiracy, mutiny, unauthorized retreating in battles and theft of equipment or supplies in a military base. The execution method in this case is, specifically, execution by shooting.

Soviet Bloc

In 20th-century communist states, shooting was a standard form of execution of civilian and military prisoners alike, with the Soviet Union setting an example of single-executioner approach. The firing squad, with its usual solemn and lengthy ceremony was used infrequently.

The most-common method was the firing of a pistol bullet ("nine grams of lead") into the back of the head.

This method was widely used during the Great Purges of the late 1930s at locations outside the major cities, e.g. Krasny Bor near Petrozavodsk, against purportedly anti-social elements, "counter-revolutionaries" and other Enemies of the People.

It was also used in the execution of those who had committed ordinary criminal offences. On occasion, it is said, the person to be executed was led through a series of corridors, not knowing when or where the shot takes place.Wikipedia:Citation needed Even after the break up of the Soviet Union, people continued to be executed by shooting. The mass murderer Andrei Chikatilo was executed in this way in 1994, just before Russia halted use of the death penalty as part of its accession to the Council of Europe.

The phrase "execution by firing squad" is often incorrectly used to translate the Russian term *расстрел* (translit. *rasstrel*). This, in general, describes any form of shooting, regardless of method though it is more likely to refer to the single executioner who fires a bullet to the back of the head, than to a firing squad.

United Kingdom

No British citizen has ever been executed for a civilian crime by shooting. A Royal Commission on Capital Punishment considered shooting as a possible alternative to hanging, although the findings published in 1953 concluded shooting was not sufficiently effective a means of execution to justify a switch to the method from hanging.

United States

Since 1608, about 142 men have been judicially shot in the United States and its English-speaking predecessor territories, excluding executions related to the American Civil War.[139]

Asia

- Bahrain uses firing squads for execution.[140]
- In the People's Republic of China, shooting as a method of execution takes two typical formats, either a pistol shot in the back of the neck or a shot by a rifle in the back from behind. Some more recent executions have been private and carried out using lethal injection, though shooting is still used.[141] Hong Kong abolished the death penalty and Macau never had death penalty before handover, and didn't restore it when they became an autonomous territory of China.
- In India, during the Mughal rule, soldiers who committed crimes were executed by being strapped to a cannon which was then fired. This was known as blowing from a gun. This method, invented by the Mughals, was continued by the British who used it to execute native deserters and mutineers, especially after the Sepoy Mutiny of 1857.[142]
- In Indonesia, capital punishment is administered by a firing squad which aims for the heart. The number of blanks and live bullets is known. Three live bullets are used. The remaining rounds are blanks.

- In Mongolia, the method of execution before abolition in 2012 was a bullet to the neck[143] from a .38 revolver, a method inherited from Soviet legislation. (See Capital punishment in Mongolia) Earlier Mongolia was a part of China.
- Executions by shooting have occurred in Myanmar.[144]
- In North Korea, executions are carried out by firing squad in public, making North Korea one of the last four countries to perform public executions.
- Oman uses firing squads for execution.[145]
- In Taiwan, the customary method is a single shot aimed at the heart (or at the brain stem, if the prisoner consents to organ donation). Before the execution, the prisoner is injected with a strong anesthetic to leave them completely senseless (see capital punishment in Taiwan).
- In Thailand from 1934 until 19 October 2001, a single executioner would shoot the convict in the back from a mounted machine gun.[146] In 1979 a Thai woman named Ginggaew was executed only to wake up and walk. She was thus shot a second time.[147] Executions are now done by lethal injection.[148]
- Shooting is the primary method of execution in the United Arab Emirates.[149]
- Shooting is the primary method of execution in Yemen.[150]

References

- Zelitch, Judah. "Soviet Administration of Criminal Law". University of Pennsylvania Press, 1931

External links

- Method of Execution: A Stark Tradition[151] *The New York Times*, September 30, 2006

Lethal injection

Lethal injection is the practice of injecting one or more drugs into a person (typically a barbiturate, paralytic, and potassium solution) for the express purpose of causing immediate death. The main application for this procedure is capital punishment, but the term may also be applied in a broader sense to include euthanasia and suicide. The drugs cause the person to become unconscious, stops their breathing, and causes a heart arrhythmia, in that order.

First developed in the United States, it is now also a legal method of execution in China, Thailand, Guatemala, Taiwan, the Maldives, and Vietnam, though Guatemala has not conducted an execution since 2000 and the Maldives has never carried out an execution since its independence. Although Taiwan permits lethal injection as an execution method, no executions have been carried out in this manner, probably due to drug shortages. Lethal injection was also used in the Philippines until the country re-abolished the death penalty in 2006.

History

Lethal injection gained popularity in the late 20th century as a form of execution intended to supplant other methods, notably electrocution, gas inhalation, hanging and firing squad, that were considered to be less humane. It is now the most common form of execution in the United States.

Conception

Lethal injection was first proposed on January 17, 1888, by Julius Mount Bleyer, a New York doctor who praised it as being cheaper than hanging. Bleyer's idea was never used, due to a series of botched executions and the eventual rise of public disapproval in electrocutions. Nazi Germany developed the Action T4 euthanasia program as one of its methods of disposing of *Lebensunwertes Leben* ("life unworthy of life").[152] The British Royal Commission on Capital Punishment (1949–53) also considered lethal injection, but eventually ruled it out after pressure from the British Medical Association (BMA).

Implementation

On May 11, 1977, Oklahoma's state medical examiner Jay Chapman proposed a new, less painful method of execution, known as Chapman's protocol: "An intravenous saline drip shall be started in the prisoner's arm, into which shall be introduced a lethal injection consisting of an ultrashort-acting barbiturate in combination with a chemical paralytic." After the procedure was approved by anesthesiologist Stanley Deutsch, formerly Head of the Department

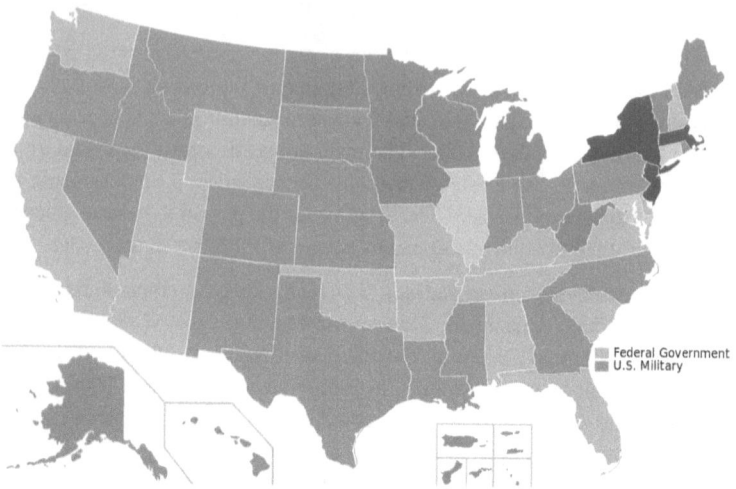

Figure 41:
*Usage of lethal injection for the death penalty in the United States.
State uses only this method.
State uses this method primarily but has other methods.
State once used this method, but does not today.
State once adopted this method, but dropped before its use.
State has never adopted this method.*
- **Federal Government**: *lethal injection as a primary method; retains secondary methods*
- **U.S. Military**: *only lethal injection*

of Anaesthesiology of the Oklahoma University Medical School, the Reverend Bill Wiseman introduced the method into the Oklahoma legislature, where it passed and was quickly adopted (Title 22, Section 1014(A)). Since then, until 2004, 37 of the 38 states using capital punishment introduced lethal injection statutes. On August 29, 1977, Texas adopted the new method of execution, switching to lethal injection from electrocution. On December 7, 1982, Texas became the first state to use lethal injection to carry out capital punishment, for the execution of Charles Brooks, Jr.

The People's Republic of China began using this method in 1997, Guatemala in 1996, the Philippines in 1999, Thailand in 2003, and Taiwan in 2005. Vietnam first used this method in 2013. The Philippines abolished the death penalty in 2006, with their last execution being in 2000. Guatemalan law still allows for the death penalty and lethal injection is the sole method allowed, but no penalties have been carried out since 2000 when the country experienced a botched, televised execution.

The export of drugs to be used for lethal injection was banned by the European Union (EU) in 2011, together with other items under the EU Torture Regulation. Since then, pentobarbital followed thiopental in the European Union's ban.

Complications of executions and cessation of supply of lethal injection drugs

By early 2014, a number of botched executions involving lethal injection, and a rising shortage of suitable drugs, had some U.S. states reconsidering lethal injection as a form of execution. Tennessee, which had previously offered inmates a choice between lethal injection and the electric chair, passed a law in May 2014 which gave the state the option to use the electric chair if lethal injection drugs are either unavailable or made unconstitutional. At the same time, Wyoming and Utah were considering the use of execution by firing squad in addition to other existing execution methods.

In 2016, Pfizer joined over 20 American and European pharmaceutical manufacturers that had previously blocked the sale of their drugs for use in lethal injections, effectively closing the open market for FDA-approved manufacturers for any potential lethal execution drug. In the execution of Carey Dean Moore on August 14, 2018, the State of Nebraska used a novel drug cocktail comprising diazepam, fentanyl, cisatracurium, and potassium chloride, over the strong objections of the German pharmaceutical company Fresenius Kabi.

Procedure

Procedure in U.S. executions

The condemned person is strapped onto a gurney; two intravenous cannulas ("IVs") are inserted, one in each arm. Only one is necessary to carry out the execution; the other is reserved as a backup in the event the primary line fails. A line leading from the IV line in an adjacent room is attached to the prisoner's IV and secured so that the line does not snap during the injections.

The arm of the condemned person is swabbed with alcohol before the cannula is inserted. The needles and equipment used are sterilized. Questions have been raised about why these precautions against infection are performed despite the purpose of the injection being death. The several explanations include: cannulae are sterilized and have their quality heavily controlled during manufacture, so using sterile ones is a routine medical procedure. Secondly, the prisoner could receive a stay of execution after the cannulae have been inserted, as happened in the case of James Autry in October 1983 (he was eventually executed on March 14, 1984). Third, use of unsterilized equipment would be a hazard to the prison personnel in case of an accidental needle stick.

Following connection of the lines, saline drips are started in both arms. This, too, is standard medical procedure: it must be ascertained that the IV lines are not blocked, ensuring the chemicals have not precipitated in the IV lines and blocked the needle, preventing the drugs from reaching the subject. A heart monitor is attached to the inmate.

In most states, the intravenous injection is a series of drugs given in a set sequence, designed to first induce unconsciousness followed by death through paralysis of respiratory muscles and/or by cardiac arrest through depolarization of cardiac muscle cells. The execution of the condemned in most states involves three separate injections (in sequential order):

1. Sodium thiopental or pentobarbital: ultrashort-action barbiturate, an anesthetic agent used at a high dose that renders the person unconscious in less than 30 seconds. Depression of respiratory activity is one of the characteristic actions of this drug. Consequently, the lethal-injection doses, as described in the Sodium Thiopental section below, will—even in the absence of the following two drugs—cause death due to lack of breathing, as happens with overdoses of opioids.
2. Pancuronium bromide: nondepolarizing muscle relaxant, which causes complete, fast, and sustained paralysis of the skeletal striated muscles, including the diaphragm and the rest of the respiratory muscles; this would eventually cause death by asphyxiation.
3. Potassium chloride: a potassium salt, which increases the blood and cardiac concentration of potassium to stop the heart via an abnormal heartbeat and thus cause death by cardiac arrest.

The drugs are not mixed externally because that can cause them to precipitate. Also, a sequential injection is key to achieve the desired effects in the appropriate order: administration of the pentobarbital essentially renders the person unconscious; the infusion of the pancuronium bromide induces complete paralysis, including that of the lungs and diaphragm rendering the person unable to breathe. If the person being executed were not already completely unconscious, the injection of a highly concentrated solution of potassium chloride could cause severe pain at the site of the IV line, as well as along the punctured vein, but it interrupts the electrical activity of the heart muscle and causes it to stop beating, bringing about the death of the person being executed.

The intravenous tubing leads to a room next to the execution chamber, usually separated from the condemned by a curtain or wall. Typically, a prison employee trained in venipuncture inserts the needle, while a second prison employee orders, prepares, and loads the drugs into the lethal injection syringes.

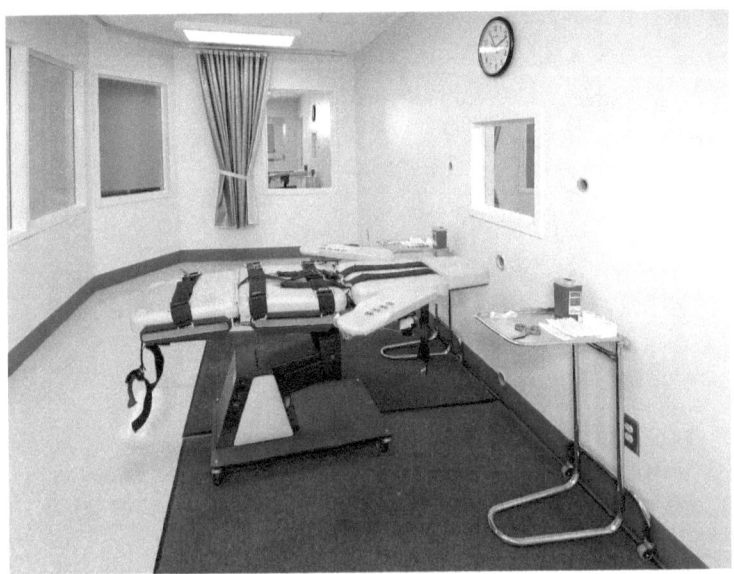

Figure 42: *Execution room in the San Quentin State Prison in California*

Two other staff members take each of the three syringes and secure them into the IVs. After the curtain is opened to allow the witnesses to see inside the chamber, the condemned person is then permitted to make a final statement. Following this, the warden signals that the execution may commence, and the executioner(s) (either prison staff or private citizens depending on the jurisdiction) then manually inject the three drugs in sequence. During the execution, the condemned's cardiac rhythm is monitored. Death is pronounced after cardiac activity stops. Death usually occurs within seven minutes, although, due to complications in finding a suitable vein, the whole procedure can take up to two hours, as was the case with the execution of Christopher Newton on May 24, 2007. According to state law, if a physician's participation in the execution is prohibited for reasons of medical ethics, then the death ruling can be made by the state medical examiner's office. After confirmation that death has occurred, a coroner signs the condemned's death certificate.

Delaware and Missouri use a lethal injection machine designed by Massachusetts-based Fred A. Leuchter consisting of two components: the delivery module and the control module. Two staff members each have a station in which the key on the machine and depress two stations' buttons to be ready in case of mechanical failure. Each person presses one station button on the console which travels to a computer which starts all three injections electronically. The computer then deletes who actually started the syringes, so the

Figure 43: *The Control Module of the lethal injection machine formerly installed in the James T. Vaughn Correctional Center, Delaware. On display in the National Museum of Crime & Punishment, Washington, D.C. (2009)*

participants are not aware if their syringe contained saline or one of the drugs necessary for execution (to assuage guilt in a manner similar to the blank cartridge in execution by firing squad). The delivery module has eight syringes. The end syringes (i.e., syringes 7 and 8) containing saline, syringes 2, 4 and 6 containing the lethal drugs for the main line and syringes 1, 3 and 5 containing the injections for the backup line. The system was used in New Jersey before the abolition of the death penalty in 2007. Illinois previously used the computer, and Missouri and Delaware use the manual injection switch on the delivery panel.Wikipedia:Citation needed

Eleven states have switched, or have stated their intention to switch, to a one-drug lethal injection protocol. A one-drug method is using the single drug sodium thiopental to execute someone. The first state to switch to this method was Ohio, on December 8, 2009.

In 2011, after pressure by activist organizations, the manufacturers of sodium thiopental and pentobarbital halted the supply of the drugs to U.S. prisons performing lethal injections and required all resellers to do the same.

Procedure in Chinese executions

In the past, the People's Republic of China executed prisoners primarily by means of shooting. In recent years, lethal injection has become more popular. The specific lethal injection procedures, including the drug or drugs used, are a state secret and not publicly known. In at least some cases, prisoners facing death by lethal injection have been sedated at a prison, then placed inside an execution van that is disguised to look like a regular police van.

Lethal injection in China was legalized in 1996. The number of shooting executions slowly decreased; and, in February 2009, the Supreme People's Court ordered the discontinuation of firing squads by the following year under the conclusion that injections were more humane to the prisoner. It has been suggested that the switch is also in response to executions being horrifying to the public. Lethal injections are less expensive than firing squads, with a single dose costing 300 yuan compared to 700 yuan for a shooting execution.

Procedure in Vietnamese executions

Just like China, executions in Vietnam were also mainly by means of shooting. The use of lethal injection method was approved by the government in June 2010, adopted in 2011 and only executed in 2013. Urges to adopt other methods as lethal injection to replace the shooting execution began earlier, in 2006, after concerns of the mental state of the firing squad members after executions.

The drugs used consist of sodium thiopental (anesthetic), pancuronium bromide (paralyzing substance) and potassium chloride (stops cardiac activity). The production of these substances, however, are low in Vietnam. This led to drug shortages, use of domestic poisons and shooting execution to be considered to be adopted back.

The first prisoner in Vietnam to be executed by lethal injection, on August 6, 2013, was the 27-year-old man Nguyen Anh Tuan, arrested for murder and robbery. Between 2013 and 2016, 429 prisoners were executed by this method in the country.

Drugs

Conventional lethal injection protocol

Typically, three drugs are used in lethal injection. Sodium thiopental is used to induce unconsciousness, pancuronium bromide (Pavulon) to cause muscle paralysis and respiratory arrest, and potassium chloride to stop the heart.

Sodium thiopental

- Lethal injection dosage: 2–5 grams

Sodium thiopental (US trade name: Sodium Pentothal) is an ultra-short acting barbiturate, often used for anesthesia induction and for medically induced coma. The typical anesthesia induction dose is 0.35 grams. Loss of consciousness is induced within 30–45 seconds at the typical dose, while a 5 gram dose (14 times the normal dose) is likely to induce unconsciousness in 10 seconds.

A full medical dose of thiopental reaches the brain in about 30 seconds. This induces an unconscious state. Five to twenty minutes after injection, approximately 15% of the drug is in the brain, with the rest in other parts of the body.

The half-life of this drug is about 11.5 hours, and the concentration in the brain remains at around 5–10% of the total dose during that time. When a 'megadose' is administered, as in state-sanctioned lethal injection, the concentration in the brain during the tail phase of the distribution remains higher than the peak concentration found in the induction dose for anesthesia, because repeated doses—or a single very high dose as in lethal injection—accumulate in high concentrations in body fat, from which the thiopental is gradually released. This is the reason why an ultra-short acting barbiturate, such as thiopental, can be used for long-term induction of medical coma.

Historically, thiopental has been one of the most commonly used and studied drugs for the induction of coma. Protocols vary for how it is given, but the typical doses are anywhere from 500 mg up to 1.5 grams. It is likely that this data was used to develop the initial protocols for state-sanctioned lethal injection, according to which one gram of thiopental was used to induce the coma. Now, most states use 5 grams to be absolutely certain the dosage is effective.

Pentobarbital was introduced at the end of 2010 due to a shortage of sodium thiopental, and has since become the primary sedative in lethal injections in the United States.

Barbiturates are the same class of drug used in medically assisted suicide. In euthanasia protocols, the typical dose of thiopental is 1.5 grams; the Dutch Euthanasia protocol indicates 1-1.5 grams or 2 grams in case of high barbiturate tolerance. The dose used for capital punishment is therefore about 3 times more than the dose used in euthanasia.

Pancuronium bromide (Pavulon)

- Lethal injection dosage: 100 milligrams

Pancuronium bromide (Trade name: Pavulon): The related drug curare, like pancuronium, is a non-depolarizing muscle relaxant (a paralytic agent) that blocks the action of acetylcholine at the motor end-plate of the neuromuscular junction. Binding of acetylcholine to receptors on the end-plate causes depolarization and contraction of the muscle fiber; non-depolarizing neuromuscular blocking agents like pancuronium stop this binding from taking place.

The typical dose for pancuronium bromide in capital punishment by lethal injection is 0.2 mg/kg and the duration of paralysis is around 4 to 8 hours. Paralysis of respiratory muscles will lead to death in a considerably shorter time.

Other drugs in use are tubocurarine chloride and succinylcholine chloride.

Pancuronium bromide is a derivative of the alkaloid malouetine from the plant *Malouetia bequaertiana*.

Potassium chloride

- Lethal injection dosage: 100 mEq (milliequivalents)

Potassium is an electrolyte, 98% of which is intracellular. The 2% remaining outside the cell has great implications for cells that generate action potentials. Doctors prescribe potassium for patients when potassium levels are insufficient, called hypokalemia, in the blood. The potassium can be given orally, which is the safest route; or it can be given intravenously, in which case strict rules and hospital protocols govern the rate at which it is given.

The usual intravenous dose is 10–20 mEq per hour and it is given slowly since it takes time for the electrolyte to equilibrate into the cells. When used in state-sanctioned lethal injection, bolus potassium injection affects the electrical conduction of heart muscle. Elevated potassium, or hyperkalemia, causes the resting electrical potential of the heart muscle cells to be lower than normal (less negative). Without this negative resting potential, cardiac cells cannot repolarize (prepare for their next contraction).

Depolarizing the muscle cell inhibits its ability to fire by reducing the available number of sodium channels (they are placed in an inactivated state). ECG changes include faster repolarization (peaked T-waves), PR interval prolongation, widening of the QRS complex, and finally, asystole. Cases of patients dying from hyperkalemia (usually secondary to renal failure) are well known in the medical community, where patients have been known to die very rapidly, having previously seemed to be normal.

New lethal injection protocols

The Ohio protocol, developed after the incomplete execution of Romell Broom, ensures the rapid and painless onset of anesthesia by only using sodium thiopental and eliminating the use of Pavulon and potassium as the second and third drugs, respectively. It also provides for a secondary fail-safe measure using intramuscular injection of midazolam and hydromorphone in the event intravenous administration of the sodium thiopental proves problematic. The first state to switch to use midazolam as the first drug in a new three-drug protocol was Florida on October 15, 2013. Then on November 14, 2013, Ohio made the same move.

- Primary: Sodium thiopental, 5 grams, intravenous
- Secondary: Midazolam, 10 mg, intramuscular, and hydromorphone, 40 mg, intramuscular

In the brief for the U.S. courts written by accessories, the State of Ohio implies that they were unable to find any physicians willing to participate in development of protocols for executions by lethal injection, as this would be a violation of medical ethics, such as the Geneva Promise, and such physicians would be thrown out of the medical community and shunned for engaging in such deeds, even if they could not lawfully be stripped of their license.

On December 8, 2009, Kenneth Biros became the first person executed using Ohio's new single-drug execution protocol. He was pronounced dead at 11:47 am EST, 10 minutes after receiving the injection. On September 10, 2010, Washington became the second state to use the single-drug Ohio protocol with the execution of Cal Coburn Brown, who was proclaimed dead within two minutes after receiving the single-drug injection of sodium thiopental. Currently, eight states (Arizona, Georgia, Idaho, Missouri, Ohio, South Dakota, Texas, and Washington) have used the single-drug execution protocol. Five additional states (Arkansas, Kentucky, Louisiana, North Carolina, and Tennessee) have announced that they are switching to a single-drug protocol but, as of April 2014, have not executed anyone since switching protocols.

After sodium thiopental began being used in executions, Hospira, the only American company that made the drug, stopped manufacturing it due to its use in executions. The subsequent nationwide shortage of sodium thiopental led states to seek other drugs to use in executions. Pentobarbital, often used for animal euthanasia, was used as part of a three-drug cocktail for the first time on December 16, 2010, when John David Duty was executed in Oklahoma. It was then used as the drug in a single-drug execution for the first time on March 10, 2011, when Johnnie Baston was executed in Ohio.

Euthanasia protocol

Lethal injection has also been used in cases of euthanasia to facilitate voluntary death in patients with terminal or chronically painful conditions. Euthanasia can be accomplished either through oral, intravenous, or intramuscular administration of drugs. In individuals who are incapable of swallowing lethal doses of medication, an intravenous route is preferred. The following is a Dutch protocol for parenteral (intravenous) administration to obtain euthanasia, with the old protocol listed first and the new protocol listed second:

> First a coma is induced by intravenous administration of 1 g sodium thiopental (Nesdonal), if necessary, 1.5-2.0 g of the product in case of strong tolerance to barbiturates. Then, 45 mg alcuronium chloride (Alloferin) or 18 mg pancuronium bromide (Pavulon) is injected. To ensure optimal availability, these agents are preferably given intravenously. However, they can also be injected intramuscularly. In severe hepatitis or cirrhosis of the liver, alcuronium is the agent of first choice.

> Intravenous administration is the most reliable and rapid way to accomplish euthanasia, so can be safely recommended. A coma is first induced by intravenous administration of 20 mg/kg sodium thiopental in a small volume (10 ml physiological saline). Then, a triple intravenous dose of a nondepolarizing neuromuscular muscle relaxant is given, such as 20 mg pancuronium bromide or 20 mg vecuronium bromide (Norcuron). The muscle relaxant should preferably be given intravenously, to ensure optimal availability. Only for pancuronium dibromide, the agent may also be given intramuscularly in a dose of 40 mg.

A euthanasia machine may allow an individual to perform the process alone.

Constitutionality in the United States

In 2006, the Supreme Court ruled in *Hill v. McDonough* that death-row inmates in the United States could challenge the constitutionality of states' lethal injection procedures through a federal civil rights lawsuit. Since then, numerous death-row inmates have brought such challenges in the lower courts, claiming that lethal injection as currently practiced violates the ban on "cruel and unusual punishment" found in the Eighth Amendment to the United States Constitution. Lower courts evaluating these challenges have reached opposing conclusions. For example, courts have found that lethal injection as practiced in California, Florida, and Tennessee is unconstitutional. Other courts have found that lethal injection as practiced in Missouri, Arizona,[153] and Oklahoma[154] is constitutionally acceptable.

As of 2014, California has nearly 750 prisoners condemned to death by lethal injection despite the moratorium imposed when in 2006 a federal court found California's lethal injection procedures to be unconstitutional. A newer lethal injection facility has been constructed at San Quentin State Prison which cost over $800,000, but it has yet to be used because a state court found that the California Department of Corrections and Rehabilitation violated the California Administrative Procedure Act by attempting to prevent public oversight when new injection procedures were being created.

On September 25, 2007, the United States Supreme Court agreed to hear a lethal-injection challenge arising from Kentucky, *Baze v. Rees*. In Baze, the Supreme Court addressed whether Kentucky's particular lethal-injection procedure comports with the Eighth Amendment and will determine the proper legal standard by which lethal-injection challenges in general should be judged, all in an effort to bring some uniformity to how these claims are handled by the lower courts. Although uncertainty over whether executions in the United States would be put on hold during the period in which the United States Supreme Court considers the constitutionality of lethal injection initially arose after the court agreed to hear Baze, no executions took place during the period between when the court agreed to hear the case and when its ruling was announced, with the exception of one lethal injection in Texas hours after the court made its announcement.

On April 16, 2008, the Supreme Court rejected *Baze v. Rees*, thereby upholding Kentucky's method of lethal injection in a majority 7–2 decision. Justices Ruth Bader Ginsburg and David Souter dissented. Several states immediately indicated plans to proceed with executions.

The U.S. Supreme Court also upheld lethal injection in the 2015 case *Glossip v. Gross*.

Ethics of lethal injection

The American Medical Association (AMA) believes that a physician's opinion on capital punishment is a personal decision. Since the AMA is founded on preserving life, they argue that a doctor "should not be a participant" in executions in any professional capacity with the exception of "certifying death, provided that the condemned has been declared dead by another person" and "relieving the acute suffering of a condemned person while awaiting execution." The AMA, however, does not have the ability to enforce its prohibition of doctors from participation in lethal injection, as it does not have the authority to revoke medical licenses, as medical licensing is handled on the state level.

Typically, most states do not require that physicians administer the drugs for lethal injection, but most states do require doctors, nurses or paramedics to prepare the substances before their application and to attest the inmate's death after it.

Some states specifically detail that participation in a lethal injection is not to be considered practicing medicine. For example, Delaware law reads "the administration of the required lethal substance or substances required by this section shall not be construed to be the practice of medicine and any pharmacist or pharmaceutical supplier is authorized to dispense drugs to the Commissioner or the Commissioner's designee, without prescription, for carrying out the provisions of this section, notwithstanding any other provision of law" (excerpt from Title 11, Chapter 42, § 4209). State law allows for the dispensing of the drugs/chemicals for lethal injection to the state's department of corrections without a prescription.

Controversy

Opposition

Opponents of lethal injection have voiced concerns that abuse, misuse and even criminal conduct is possible when there is not a proper chain of command and authority for the acquisition of death-inducing drugs.

Awareness

Opponents of lethal injection believe that it is not actually painless as practiced in the United States. Opponents argue that the thiopental is an ultrashort-acting barbiturate that may wear off (anesthesia awareness) and lead to consciousness and an uncomfortable death wherein the inmates are unable to express discomfort because they have been rendered paralyzed by the paralytic agent.

Opponents point to the fact that sodium thiopental is typically used as an induction agent and not used in the maintenance phase of surgery because of its short-acting nature. Following the administration of thiopental, pancuronium bromide is given. Opponents argue that pancuronium bromide not only dilutes the thiopental, but (since the inmate is paralyzed) also prevents the inmate from expressing pain. Additional concerns have been raised over whether inmates are administered an appropriate level of thiopental owing to the rapid redistribution of the drug out of the brain to other parts of the body.

Additionally, opponents argue that the method of administration is also flawed. They state that since the personnel administering the lethal injection lack expertise in anesthesia, the risk of failing to induce unconsciousness is greatly increased. In reference to this problem, Jay Chapman, the creator of the American method, said, "It never occurred to me when we set this up that we'd have complete idiots administering the drugs." Also, they argue that the dose of sodium thiopental must be customized to each individual patient, not restricted to a set protocol. Finally, the remote administration results in an increased risk that insufficient amounts of the lethal injection drugs enter the bloodstream.

In total, opponents argue that the effect of dilution or improper administration of thiopental is that the inmate dies an agonizing death through suffocation due to the paralytic effects of pancuronium bromide and the intense burning sensation caused by potassium chloride.

Opponents of lethal injection, as currently practiced, argue that the procedure employed is designed to create the appearance of serenity and a painless death, rather than actually providing it. More specifically, opponents object to the use of pancuronium bromide, arguing that its use in lethal injection serves no useful purpose since the inmate is physically restrained. Therefore, the default function of pancuronium bromide would be to suppress the autonomic nervous system, specifically to stop breathing.

Research

In 2005, University of Miami researchers, in cooperation with the attorney representing death-row inmates from Virginia, published a research letter in the medical journal *The Lancet*. The article presented protocol information from Texas, Virginia, and North and South Carolina, which showed that executioners had no anesthesia training, drugs were administered remotely with no monitoring for anesthesia, data were not recorded, and no peer review was done. Their analysis of toxicology reports from Arizona, Georgia, North Carolina, and South Carolina showed that *post mortem* concentrations of thiopental in the blood were lower than that required for surgery in 43 of 49 executed inmates (88%); 21 (43%) inmates had concentrations consistent with awareness. This led the authors to conclude that a substantial probability existed that some of the inmates were aware and suffered extreme pain and distress during execution. The authors attributed the risk of consciousness among inmates to the lack of training and monitoring in the process, but carefully make no recommendations on how to alter the protocol or how to improve the process. Indeed, the authors conclude, "because participation of doctors in protocol design or execution is ethically prohibited, adequate anesthesia cannot be certain. Therefore, to prevent unnecessary cruelty and suffering, cessation and public review of lethal injections is warranted."

Paid expert consultants on both sides of the lethal-injection debate have found opportunity to criticize the 2005 *Lancet* article. Subsequent to the initial publication in the *Lancet*, three letters to the editor and a response from the authors extended the analysis. The issue of contention is whether thiopental, like many lipid-soluble drugs, may be redistributed from blood into tissues after death, effectively lowering thiopental concentrations over time, or whether thiopental may distribute from tissues into the blood, effectively increasing *post mortem* blood concentrations over time. Given the near absence of scientific, peer-reviewed data on the topic of thiopental *post mortem* pharmacokinetics, the controversy continues in the lethal injection community and in consequence, many legal challenges to lethal injection have not used the *Lancet* article.

In 2007, the same group that authored the *Lancet* study extended its study of the lethal-injection process through a critical examination of the pharmacology of the barbiturate thiopental. This study – published in the online journal *PloS Medicine* – confirmed and extended the conclusions made in the article and goes further to disprove the assertion that the lethal-injection process is painless.

To date, these two studies by the University of Miami team serve as the only critical peer-reviewed examination of the pharmacology of the lethal injection process.

Single drug

According to the new lethal injection protocols section above, single-drug lethal injection is already in use, or intended, in 11 states.

The execution can be painlessly accomplished, without risk of consciousness, by the injection of a single large dose of a barbiturate. By this reasoning, the use of any other chemicals is entirely superfluous and only serves to unnecessarily increase the risk of pain during the execution. Another possibility would be I.V administration of a powerful and fast-acting opioid, such as sufentanyl, which would ensure comfort while killing via respiratory depression. When sodium pentobarbital, a barbiturate used often in single drug animal euthanasia, is administered in an overdose, it causes rapid unconsciousness followed by paralysis of the diaphragm. This drug may also kill via cardiac arrhythmia.

Cruel and unusual

On occasion, difficulties inserting the intravenous needles have also occurred, sometimes taking over half an hour to find a suitable vein. Typically, the difficulty is found in convicts with diabetes or a history of intravenous drug use. Opponents argue that the insertion of intravenous lines that take excessive amounts of time are tantamount to being cruel and unusual punishment. In addition, opponents point to instances where the intravenous line has failed, or when adverse reactions to drugs or unnecessary delays happen during the process of execution.

On December 13, 2006, Angel Nieves Diaz was not executed successfully in Florida using a standard lethal-injection dose. Diaz was 55 years old, and had been sentenced to death for murder. Diaz did not succumb to the lethal dose even after 35 minutes, necessitating a second dose of drugs to complete the execution. At first, a prison spokesman denied Diaz had suffered pain, and claimed the second dose was needed because Diaz had some sort of liver disease. After performing an autopsy, the medical examiner, Dr. William Hamilton, stated that Diaz's liver appeared normal, but that the needle had been pierced through Diaz's vein into his flesh. The deadly chemicals had subsequently been injected into soft tissue, rather than into the vein. Two days after the execution, then-Governor Jeb Bush suspended all executions in the state and appointed a commission "to consider the humanity and constitutionality of lethal injections." The ban was lifted by Governor Charlie Crist when he signed the death warrant for Mark Dean Schwab on July 18, 2007. On November 1, 2007, the Florida Supreme Court unanimously upheld the state's lethal injection procedures.

A study published in 2007 in the peer-reviewed journal *PLoS Medicine* suggested that "the conventional view of lethal injection leading to an invariably peaceful and painless death is questionable".

The execution of Romell Broom was abandoned in Ohio on September 15, 2009, after prison officials failed to find a vein after 2 hours of trying on his arms, legs, hands, and ankle. This has stirred up intense debate in the United States about lethal injection.

Dennis McGuire was executed in Lucasville, Ohio, on January 17, 2014. According to reporters, the execution of McGuire took more than 20 minutes and McGuire was gasping for air for 10 to 13 minutes. It was the first use of a new drug combination which was introduced in Ohio after the European Union banned sodium thiopental exports. This renewed criticism on the conventional three-drug method.

Clayton Lockett died of a heart attack during a failed execution attempt on April 29, 2014, at Oklahoma State Penitentiary in McAlester, Oklahoma. Lockett was administered an untested mixture of drugs that had not previously been used for executions in the U.S., and survived for 43 minutes before being pronounced dead. Lockett convulsed and spoke during the process, and attempted to rise from the execution table 14 minutes into the procedure, despite having been declared unconscious.

European Union export ban

Due to its use for executions in the US, the UK introduced a ban on the export of sodium thiopental in December 2010, after it was established that no European supplies to the US were being used for any other purpose. The restrictions were based on "the European Union Torture Regulation (including licensing of drugs used in execution by lethal injection)". From December 21, 2011, the European Union extended trade restrictions to prevent the export of certain medicinal products for capital punishment, stating, "The Union disapproves of capital punishment in all circumstances and works towards its universal abolition".

Support

Commonality

The combination of a barbiturate induction agent and a nondepolarizing paralytic agent is used in thousands of anesthetics every day. Supporters of the death penalty argue that unless anesthesiologists have been wrong for the last 40 years, the use of pentothal and pancuronium is safe and effective. In fact, potassium is given in heart bypass surgery to induce cardioplegia. Therefore, the combination of these three drugs is still in use today. Supporters of the death penalty speculate that the designers of the lethal-injection protocols intentionally used the same drugs as used in everyday surgery to avoid controversy. The only modification is that a massive coma-inducing dose of barbiturates is given. In addition, similar protocols have been used in countries that support euthanasia or physician-assisted suicide.

Anesthesia awareness

Thiopental is a rapid and effective drug for inducing unconsciousness, since it causes loss of consciousness upon a single circulation through the brain due to its high lipophilicity. Only a few other drugs, such as methohexital, etomidate, or propofol, have the capability to induce anesthesia so rapidly. (Narcotics such as fentanyl are inadequate as induction agents for anesthesia.) Supporters argue that since the thiopental is given at a much higher dose than for medically induced coma protocols, it is effectively impossible for the condemned to wake up.

Anesthesia awareness occurs when general anesthesia is inadequately maintained, for a number of reasons. Typically, anesthesia is 'induced' with an intravenous drug, but 'maintained' with an inhaled anesthetic given by the anesthesiologist (note that there are several other methods for safely and effectively maintaining anesthesia). Barbiturates are used only for induction of anesthesia and these drugs rapidly and reliably induce anesthesia, but wear off quickly.

A neuromuscular blocking drug may then be given to cause paralysis which facilitates intubation, although this is not always required. The anesthesiologist has the responsibility to ensure that the maintenance technique (typically inhalational) is started soon after induction to prevent the patient from waking up.

General anesthesia is not maintained with barbiturate drugs. An induction dose of thiopental wears off after a few minutes because the thiopental redistributes from the brain to the rest of the body very quickly. However, it has a long half-life, which means that a long time is needed for the drug to be eliminated from the body. If a very large initial dose is given, little or no redistribution takes place (since the body is saturated with the drug), which means that recovery of consciousness requires the drug to be eliminated from the body, which is not only slow (taking many hours or days), but unpredictable in duration, making barbiturates very unsatisfactory for maintenance of anesthesia.

Thiopental has a half-life around 11.5 hours (but the action of a single dose is terminated within a few minutes by redistribution of the drug from the brain to peripheral tissues) and the long-acting barbiturate phenobarbital has a half-life around 4–5 days. It contrasts towards the inhaled anesthetics have extremely short half-lives and allow the patient to wake up rapidly and predictably after surgery.

The average time to death once a lethal injection protocol has been started is about 7 to 11 minutes. Since it only takes about 30 seconds for the thiopental to induce anesthesia, 30–45 seconds for the pancuronium to cause paralysis, and about 30 seconds for the potassium to stop the heart, death can theoretically be attained in as little as 90 seconds. Given that it takes time to administer the drug, time for the line to flush itself, time for the change of the drug being administered, and time to ensure that death has occurred, the whole procedure takes about 7–11 minutes. Procedural aspects in pronouncing death also contribute to delay, so the condemned is usually pronounced dead within 10 to 20 minutes of starting the drugs. Supporters of the death penalty say that a huge dose of thiopental, which is between 14 and 20 times the anesthetic induction dose and which has the potential to induce a medical coma lasting 60 hours, could never wear off in only 10 to 20 minutes.

Dilution effect

Death penalty supporters state that the claim that pancuronium dilutes the sodium thiopental dose is erroneous. Supporters argue that pancuronium and thiopental are commonly used together in surgery every day and if there were a dilution effect, it would be a known drug interaction.

Drug interactions are a complex topic. Some drug interactions can be simplistically classified as either synergistic or inhibitory interactions. In addition, drug interactions can occur directly at the site of action, through common pathways or indirectly through metabolism of the drug in the liver or through elimination in the kidney. Pancuronium and thiopental have different sites of action, one in the brain and one at the neuromuscular junction. Since the half-life of thiopental is 11.5 hours, the metabolism of the drugs is not an issue when dealing with the short time frame in lethal injections. The only other plausible interpretation would be a direct one, or one in which the two compounds interact with each other. Supporters of the death penalty argue that this theory does not hold true. They state that even if the 100 mg of pancuronium directly prevented 500 mg of thiopental from working, sufficient thiopental to induce coma would be present for 50 hours. In addition, if this interaction did occur, then the pancuronium would be incapable of causing paralysis.Wikipedia:Citation needed

Supporters of the death penalty state that the claim that the pancuronium prevents the thiopental from working, yet is still capable of causing paralysis, is not based on any scientific evidence and is a drug interaction that has never before been documented for any other drugs.Wikipedia:Citation needed

Single drug

Amnesty International, Human Rights Watch, Death Penalty Information Center, Reprieve, and other anti-death-penalty groups have not proposed a lethal-injection protocol which they believe is less painful. SupportersWikipedia:Manual of Style/Words to watch#Unsupported attributions of the death penalty argue that the lack of an alternative proposed protocol is a testament to the fact that the pain felt during the lethal injection protocol is not the issue. Instead, supportersWikipedia:Manual of Style/Words to watch#Unsupported attributions argue that the issue is the continued existence of the death penalty, since if the only issue were the painfulness of the procedure, then Amnesty International, HRW, or the DPIC should have already proposed a less painful method.

Regardless of an alternative protocol, some death-penalty opponents have claimed that execution can be less painful by the administration of a single lethal dose of barbiturate.Wikipedia:Citation needed SupportersWikipedia:Manual of Style/Words to watch#Unsupported attributions of the death penalty, however, state that the single-drug theory is a flawed concept.Wikipedia:Citation needed Terminally ill patients in Oregon who have requested physician-assisted suicide have received lethal doses of barbiturates. The protocol has been highly effective in producing a painless death, but the time to cause death can be prolonged. Some patients have taken days to die, and a few patients have actually survived the process and have regained consciousness up to three days after taking the lethal dose. In a California legal proceeding addressing the issue of the lethal injection cocktail being "cruel and unusual," state authorities said that the time to death following a single injection of a barbiturate could be as much as 45 minutes.

Scientifically, this is readily explained. Barbiturate overdoses typically cause death by depression of the respiratory center, but the effect is variable.Wikipedia:Citation needed Some patients may have complete cessation of respiratory drive, whereas others may only have depression of respiratory function.Wikipedia:Citation needed In addition, cardiac activity can last for a long time after cessation of respiration. Since death is pronounced after asystole and given that the expectation is for a rapid death in lethal injection, multiple drugs are required, specifically potassium chloride to stop the heart. In fact, in the case of Clarence Ray Allen, a second dose of potassium chloride was required to attain asystole. The position of most death-penalty supporters is that death should be attained in a reasonable amount of time.

SupportersWikipedia:Manual of Style/Words to watch#Unsupported attributions of the death penalty agree that the use of pancuronium bromide is not absolutely necessary in the lethal injection protocol. Some supporters believe that the drug may decrease muscular fasciculations when the potassium is given, but this has yet to be proven.Wikipedia:Citation needed

Stockpiling of drugs

A 2017 study found that four U.S. states that allow capital punishment are stockpiling lethal injection drugs that are in short supply and are needed for life-saving medical procedures.

References

Additional references

- Bean, Matt (June 8, 2001). "Lethal injection—the humane alternative?"[155]. *Court TV*. Archived from the original[156] on June 25, 2001.<templatestyles src="Module:Citation/CS1/styles.css"></templatestyles>
- Bonsor, Kevin (May 3, 2001). "How Lethal Injection Works"[157]. *HowStuffWorks.com*.<templatestyles src="Module:Citation/CS1/styles.css"></templatestyles>
- Greenmeier, Larry (October 27, 2010). "Cruel and Usual?: Is Capital Punishment by Lethal Injection Quick and Painless?"[158]. *Scientific American*.<templatestyles src="Module:Citation/CS1/styles.css"></templatestyles>

- Heath, Mark (2007). "The Medicalization of Execution: Lethal Injection in the United States". *Public Health Behind Bars: From Prisons to Communities*. Springer. pp. 88–99. doi: 10.1007/978-0-387-71695-4_7[159].<templatestyles src="Module:Citation/CS1/styles.css"></templatestyles>
- Koniaris, Leonidas G.; et al. (2005). "Inadequate anesthesia in lethal injection for execution". *The Lancet*. **365** (9468): 1412–1414. doi: 10.1016/S0140-6736(05)66377-5[160]. PMID 15836890[161].<templatestyles src="Module:Citation/CS1/styles.css"></templatestyles>
- Liptak, Adam (October 7, 2003). "Critics Say Execution Drug May Hide Suffering"[162]. *The New York Times*.<templatestyles src="Module:Citation/CS1/styles.css"></templatestyles>
- Vassallo, Susi (June 2008). "Thiopental in Lethal Injection"[163] (PDF). *Fordham Urban Law Journal*. **35** (4): 957–968. Archived from the original[164] (PDF) on March 20, 2016.<templatestyles src="Module:Citation/CS1/styles.css"></templatestyles>
- "Principles of Medical Ethics"[165]. American Medical Association. June 2001.<templatestyles src="Module:Citation/CS1/styles.css"></templatestyles>
- "Prisoners 'aware' in executions"[166]. *BBC News*. April 14, 2005.<templatestyles src="Module:Citation/CS1/styles.css"></templatestyles>

External links

- Death Penalty Worldwide[167], by Cornell Law School - Academic database on every death penalty country in the world
- Lethalinjection.org[168], by UC Berkeley School of Law - Web-based information clearinghouse on lethal injection

Electric chair

Execution by electrocution, performed using an **electric chair**, is a method of execution originating in the United States in which the condemned person is strapped to a specially built wooden chair and electrocuted through electrodes fastened on the head and left ankle. This execution method, conceived in 1881 by a Buffalo, New York, dentist named Alfred P. Southwick, was developed throughout the 1880s as a "humane alternative" to hanging, and first used in 1890. This execution method has been used in the United States and, for a period of several decades,[169] in the Philippines.

Historically, once the condemned person was attached to the chair, various cycles (differing in voltage and duration) of alternating current would be passed through the individual's body, in order to cause fatal damage to the internal organs (including the brain). The first, more powerful jolt of electric current is intended to pass through the head and cause immediate unconsciousness[170] and brain death.[171] The second, less powerful jolt is intended to cause fatal damage to the vital organs. Death may also be caused by electrical overstimulation of the heart. The condemned is thought to lose consciousness in 1/240th of a second, faster than the body can register pain; some doctors believe that electrocution instantly 'scrambles' the brain and central nervous system.[172]

Although the electric chair has long been a symbol of the death penalty in the United States, its use is in decline due to the rise of lethal injection, which is widely believed to be a more humane method of execution. While some states still maintain electrocution as a method of execution, today it is only maintained as a secondary method that may be chosen over lethal injection at the request of the prisoner, except in Tennessee, where it may be used if the drugs for lethal injection are not available, without input from the prisoner.[173] As of 2014, electrocution is an optional form of execution in the states of Alabama, Florida, South Carolina, and Virginia, all of which allow the prisoner to choose lethal injection as an alternative method. In the state of Kentucky, the electric chair has been retired, except for those whose capital crimes were committed prior to March 31, 1998, and who choose electrocution; inmates who do not choose electrocution and inmates who committed their crimes after the designated date are executed by lethal injection. Electrocution is also authorized in Kentucky in the event that lethal injection is found unconstitutional by a court. In the state of Tennessee, the electric chair is available for use if lethal injection drugs are unavailable, or otherwise, if the inmate so chooses and if their capital crime was committed before 1999. The electric chair is an alternate form of execution approved for potential use in Arkansas, Mississippi, and Oklahoma if other forms of execution are found unconstitutional in the state at the time of execution.

Figure 44: *Electric chair at the Florida State Prison*

On February 8, 2008, the Nebraska Supreme Court determined that execution by electric chair was a "cruel and unusual punishment" under the state's constitution. This brought executions of this type to an end in Nebraska, the only remaining state to retain electrocution as its sole method of execution.

Invention

In the late 1870s to early 1880s, the spread of arc lighting, a type of brilliant outdoor street lighting that required high voltages in the range of 3000-6000 volts, was followed by one story after another in newspapers about how the high voltages used were killing people, usually unwary linemen, a strange new phenomenon that seemed to instantaneously strike a victim dead without leaving a mark.[174] One of these accidents, in Buffalo, New York, on August 7, 1881, led to the inception of the electric chair.[175] That evening a drunken dock worker, looking for the thrill of a tingling sensation he had noticed before, managed to sneak his way into a Brush Electric Company arc lighting power house and grabbed the brush and ground of a large electric dynamo. He died instantly. The coroner who investigated the case brought it up at a local Buffalo scientific society. Another member, Alfred P. Southwick, a dentist who had a technical background, thought some application could be found for the curious phenomenon.[176]

Southwick, local physician George E. Fell, and the head of the Buffalo ASPCA performed a series of experiments electrocuting hundreds of stray dogs, experimenting with animals in water, out of water, electrode types and placement, and conductive material until they came up with a repeatable method to euthanize animals using electricity.[177] Southwick went on in the early 1880s to advocate that this method be used as a more humane replacement for hanging in capital cases, coming to national attention when he published his ideas in scientific journals in 1882 and 1883. He worked out calculations based on the dog experiments, trying to develop a scaled-up method that would work on humans. Early on in his designs he adopted a modified version of the dental chair as a way to restrain the condemned, a device that from then on would be called the *electric chair*.[178]

The Gerry Commission

After a series of botched hangings in the United States, there was mounting criticism of this form of capital punishment and the death penalty in general. In 1886, newly elected New York State governor David B. Hill set up a three-member death penalty commission, which was chaired by the human rights advocate and reformer Elbridge Thomas Gerry and included New York lawyer and politician Matthew Hale and Southwick, to investigate a more humane means of execution.[179]

The commission members surveyed the history of execution and sent out a fact-finding questionnaire to government officials, lawyers, and medical experts all around the state asking for their opinion.[180] The questionnaires were a bit skewed because they pushed forward electrocution and did not include the choice of abolishing the death penalty, but, despite that, a slight majority of respondents recommended hanging over electrocution, and a few recommended the abolition of capital punishment. The commission also contacted electrical experts, including Thomson-Houston Electric Company's Elihu Thomson (who recommended high voltage AC connected to the head and the spine) and the inventor Thomas Edison (who also recommended AC, as well as using a Westinghouse generator).[181,182,183] They also attended electrocutions of dogs by George Fell who had worked with Southwick in the early 1880s experiments. Fell was conducting further experiments, electrocuting anesthetized dissected dogs trying to discern exactly how electricity killed a subject.[184]

In 1888, the Commission recommended electrocution using Southwick's electric chair idea with metal conductors attached to the condemned person's head and feet. They further recommended that executions be handled by the state instead of the individual counties with three electric chairs set up at Auburn, Clinton, and Sing Sing prisons. A bill following these recommendations passed the legislature and was signed by Governor Hill on June 4, 1888, set to go into effect on January 1, 1889.

EXECUTION BY ELECTRICITY, SHORTLY TO BE INTRODUCED IN N. Y. STATE.

Figure 45: *A June 30, 1888 Scientific American illustration of what the electric chair suggested by the Gerry Commission might look like.*

The Medico-Legal commission

The bill itself contained no details on the type or amount of electricity that should be used and the New York Medico-Legal Society, an informal society composed of doctors and lawyers, was given the task of determining these factors. In September 1888, a committee was formed and recommended 3000 volts, although the type of electricity, direct current (DC) or alternating current (AC), was not determined, and since tests up to that point had been done on animals smaller than a human (dogs), some members were unsure that the lethality of AC had been conclusively proven.[185]

At this point the state's efforts to design the electric chair became intermixed with what has become to be known as the War of Currents, a competition between Thomas Edison's direct current power system and George Westinghouse's alternating current based system. The two companies had been competing commercially since 1886 and a series of events had turned it into an all-out media war in 1888. The committee head, neurologist Frederick Peterson, enlisted the services of Harold P. Brown as a consultant. Brown had been on his own crusade against alternating current after the shoddy installation of pole-mounted AC arc lighting lines in New York City had caused several deaths in early 1888. Peterson had been an assistant at Brown's July

Figure 46: *Harold Brown demonstrating the killing power of AC to the New York Medico-Legal Society by electrocuting a horse at Thomas Edison's West Orange laboratory.*

1888 public electrocution of dogs with AC at Columbia College, an attempt by Brown to prove AC was more deadly than DC. Technical assistance in these demonstrations was provided by Thomas Edison's West Orange laboratory and there grew to be some form of collusion between Edison Electric and Brown.[186,187,188] Back at West Orange on December 5, 1888 Brown set up an experiment with members of the press, members of the Medico-Legal Society including Elbridge Gerry who was also chairman of the death penalty commission, and Thomas Edison looking on. Brown used alternating current for all of his tests on animals larger than a human, including 4 calves and a lame horse, all dispatched with 750 volts of AC.[189] Based on these results the Medico-Legal Society recommended the use of 1000-1500 volts of alternating current for executions and newspapers noted the AC used was half the voltage used in the power lines over the streets of American cities. Westinghouse criticized these test as a skewed self-serving demonstration designed to be a direct attack on alternating current and accused Brown of being in the employ of Edison.[190]

At the request of death penalty commission chairman Gerry, Medico-Legal Society members; electrotherapy expert Alphonse David Rockwell, Carlos Frederick MacDonald, and Columbia College professor Louis H. Laudy, were given

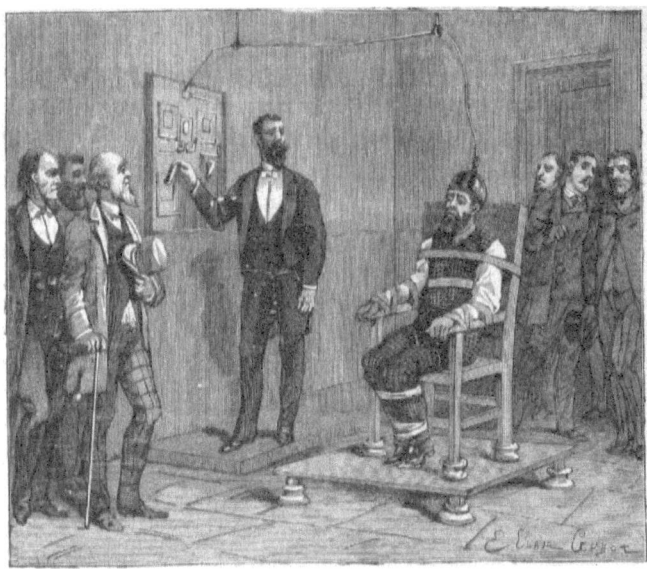

Figure 47: *The execution of William Kemmler, August 6, 1890*

the task of working out the details of electrode placement.[191,192,193] They again turned to Brown to supply the technical assistance. Brown asked Edison Electric Light to supply equipment for the tests and treasurer Francis S. Hastings (who seemed to be one of the primary movers at the company trying to portray Westinghouse as a peddler of death dealing AC current) tried to obtain a Westinghouse AC generator for the test but found none was to be had. They ended up using Edison's West Orange laboratory for the animal tests they conducted in mid-March 1889. Superintendent of Prisons Austin E. Lathrop asked Brown to design the chair, but Brown turned down the offer. Dr. George Fell drew up the final designs for a simple oak chair and went against the Medico-Legal Society recommendations, changing the position of the electrodes to the head and the middle of the back. Brown did take on the job of finding the generators needed to power the chair. He managed to surreptitiously acquire three Westinghouse AC generators that were being decommissioned with the help of Edison and Westinghouse's chief AC rival, the Thomson-Houston Electric Company, a move that made sure that Westinghouse's equipment would be associated with the first execution.[194] The electric chair was built by Edwin F. Davis, the first "state electrician" (executioner) for the State of New York.[195]

First execution

The first person in line to die under New York's new electrocution law was Joseph Chappleau, convicted for beating his neighbor to death with a sled stake, but his sentence was commuted to life imprisonment.[196] The next person scheduled to be executed was William Kemmler, convicted of murdering his wife with a hatchet. An appeal on Kemmler's behalf was made to the New York Court of Appeals on the grounds that use of electricity as a means of execution constituted a cruel and unusual punishment and was thus contrary to the constitutions of the United States and the state of New York.[197] On December 30, 1889, the writ of habeas corpus sworn out on Kemmler's behalf was denied by the court, with Judge Dwight writing in a lengthy ruling:

> We have no doubt that if the Legislature of this State should undertake to proscribe for any offense against its laws the punishment of burning at the stake, breaking at the wheel, etc., it would be the duty of the courts to pronounce upon such attempt the condemnation of the Constitution. The question now to be answered is whether the legislative act here assailed is subject to the same condemnation. Certainly, it is not so on its face, for, although the mode of death described is conceded to be unusual, there is no common knowledge or consent that it is cruel; it is a question of fact whether an electric current of sufficient intensity and skillfully applied will produce death without unnecessary suffering.[198]

Kemmler was executed in New York's Auburn Prison on August 6, 1890; the "state electrician" was Edwin F. Davis. The first 17-second passage of 1,000 volts AC of current through Kemmler caused unconsciousness, but failed to stop his heart and breathing. The attending physicians, Edward Charles Spitzka and Carlos F. MacDonald, came forward to examine Kemmler. After confirming Kemmler was still alive, Spitzka reportedly called out, "Have the current turned on again, quick, no delay." The generator needed time to re-charge, however. In the second attempt, Kemmler received a 2,000 volt AC shock. Blood vessels under the skin ruptured and bled, and the areas around the electrodes singed. The entire execution took about eight minutes. George Westinghouse later commented that, "They would have done better using an axe",[199] and a witnessing reporter claimed that it was "an awful spectacle, far worse than hanging".

Adoption

The electric chair was adopted by Ohio (1897), Massachusetts (1900), New Jersey (1906) and Virginia (1908), and soon became the prevalent method of execution in the United States, replacing hanging. Most of the states that currently use or have used the electric chair lie east of the Mississippi River. The

Electric chair

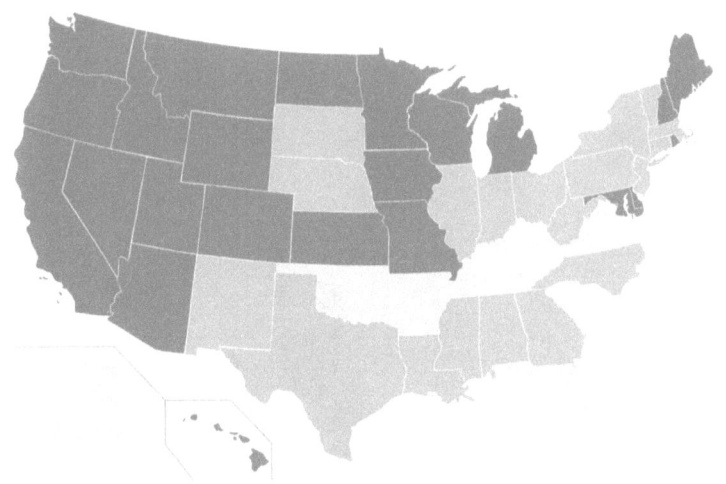

Figure 48:
Electric chair history and laws in the United States
Color key:
***Secondary** method only*
*Has **previously** used electric chair, but **does not today***
*Has **never** used electric chair*

electric chair remained the most prominent execution method until the mid-1980s when lethal injection became widely accepted for conducting judicial executions.

Other countries appear to have contemplated using the method, sometimes for special reasons. The only country other than the United States to use the electric chair was the Philippines, although the method was discontinued after 1976.

United Kingdom

The United Kingdom considered replacing hanging with the electric chair (as well as considering the gas chamber, shooting, the guillotine and lethal injection) during the Royal Commission on Capital Punishment, the findings of which were published in 1953. The Commission concluded that the electric chair had no particular advantages over hanging, and so, the electric chair was not adopted for use in the United Kingdom.

The United Kingdom performed its last execution in 1964, and abolished capital punishment for murder the following year, thereby rendering any debate over method moot.

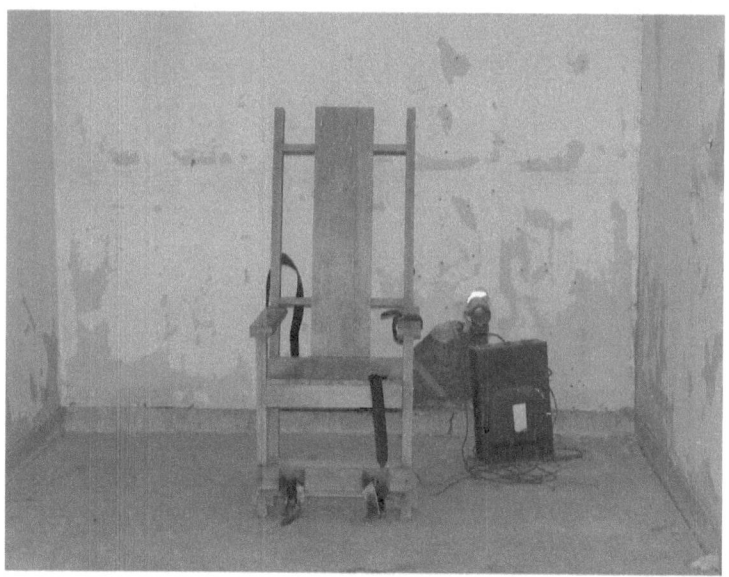

Figure 49: *The former Louisiana execution chamber at the Red Hat Cell Block in the Louisiana State Penitentiary, West Feliciana Parish. The electric chair is a replica of the original.*

Current use

A number of states still allow the condemned person to choose between electrocution and lethal injection. In all, twelve inmates nationwide – seven in Virginia, three in South Carolina, and one each in Arkansas and Tennessee – have opted for electrocution over lethal injection. The last use of the chair was on January 16, 2013, when Robert Gleason, Jr., decided to go to the electric chair in Virginia.

After 1966, electrocutions ceased for a time in the United States, but the method continued in the Philippines. A well-publicized triple execution took place in May 1972, when Jaime Jose, Basilio Pineda and Edgardo Aquino were electrocuted for the 1967 abduction and gang-rape of the young actress Maggie dela Riva.

Notable persons and events in the United States

Serial killer Lizzie Halliday was the first woman sentenced to die in the electric chair, in 1894, but governor Roswell P. Flower commuted her sentence to life in a mental institution after a medical commission declared her insane.[200] A second woman sentenced to death in 1895, Maria Barbella, was acquitted the next year.[201] Martha M. Place became the first woman to receive the deadly current in the electric chair at Sing Sing Prison on March 20, 1899, for the murder of her 17-year-old stepdaughter, Ida Place.

In a botched electrocution at Sing Sing in 1903, Fred Van Wormer was electrocuted and pronounced dead, but, upon arrival in the autopsy room, he was seen to be breathing once again. The executioner had gone home, and was called back to re-electrocute Wormer. Before the executioner returned, Wormer had died. Wikipedia:Citation needed

The electrocution of housewife Ruth Snyder at Sing Sing on the evening of January 12, 1928, for the March 1927 murder of her husband was made famous when news photographer Tom Howard, working for the *New York Daily News*, smuggled a hidden camera into the death chamber and photographed her in the electric chair as the current was turned on. The photograph was a front-page sensation the following morning, and remains one of the most famous photojournalism photographs of all time.[202]

A record was set on July 13, 1928, when seven men were executed consecutively in the electric chair at the Kentucky State Penitentiary in Eddyville. Wikipedia:Citation needed

On August 8, 1942, six German agents convicted of espionage and attempted sabotage in the Quirin case for their role in Operation Pastorius during World War II were executed by electric chair at the District of Columbia jail.

Julius and Ethel Rosenberg were executed by electric chair in 1953, after being convicted of espionage, involving sharing secrets related to the atomic bomb with the Soviet Union.

James French was executed on August 10, 1966, the last person electrocuted until 1979. French was the first person executed in Oklahoma since Richard Dare was electrocuted June 1, 1963, and the only person executed in 1966.Wikipedia:Citation needed

On May 25, 1979, John Spenkelink became the first person to be electrocuted after the *Gregg v. Georgia* decision by the Supreme Court of the United States in 1976. He was the first person to be executed in the United States in this manner since 1966. Serial murderer and rapist Ted Bundy was executed in the same electric chair in Florida on January 24, 1989.

The last person to be executed by electric chair without the choice of an alternative method was Lynda Lyon Block on May 10, 2002, in Alabama.

Decline

The use of the electric chair has declined as legislators sought what they believed to be more humane methods of execution. Lethal injection became the most widely used method, aided by media reports of botched electrocutions in the early 1980s.

The electric chair has been criticized because of several instances in which the subjects were killed only after being subjected to multiple electric shocks. This led to a call for ending of the practice, because many see it as cruel and unusual punishment. Trying to address such concerns, Nebraska introduced a new electrocution protocol in 2004, which called for administration of a 15-second-long application of electric current at a potential of 2,450 volts; after a 15-minute wait, an official then checks for signs of life. New concerns raised regarding the 2004 protocol resulted, in April 2007, in the ushering in of the current Nebraska protocol, calling for a 20-second-long application of electric current at a potential of 2,450 volts. (Prior to the 2004 protocol change, an initial eight-second application of current at 2,450 volts was administered, followed by a one-second pause, then a 22-second application at 480 volts. After a 20-second break, the cycle was repeated three more times.)

In 1946, the electric chair failed to kill Willie Francis, who reportedly shrieked, "Take it off! Let me breathe!", after the current was applied. It turned out that the portable electric chair had been improperly set up by an intoxicated prison guard and inmate.[203] A case was brought before the U.S. Supreme Court (*Louisiana ex rel. Francis v. Resweber*),[204] with lawyers for the condemned arguing that although Francis did not die, he had, in fact, been executed. The argument was rejected on the basis that re-execution did not violate the double jeopardy clause of the 5th Amendment of the United States Constitution, and Francis was returned to the electric chair and successfully executed in 1947.

Recorded incidents of botched electrocutions were prevalent after the national moratorium ended January 17, 1977; two in Alabama, three in Florida, one in Georgia, one in Indiana, and three in Virginia. All five states now have lethal injection as the default method if a choice is not made.

As of 2015[205], the only places in the world which still reserve the electric chair as an option for execution are the U.S. states of Alabama, Florida, South Carolina, Kentucky, Tennessee, and Virginia. (Arkansas and Oklahoma laws provide for its use should lethal injection ever be held to be unconstitutional.) Inmates in the other states must select either it or lethal injection. In Kentucky, only inmates sentenced before a certain date can choose to be executed by electric chair. Electrocution is also authorized in Kentucky in the event that lethal injection is found unconstitutional by a court. Tennessee was among the states that provided inmates with a choice of the electric chair or lethal injection; however, in May 2014, the state passed a law allowing the use of the electric chair if lethal injection drugs were unavailable or made unconstitutional. In the state of Florida, on July 8, 1999, Allen Lee Davis, convicted of murder, was executed in the Florida electric chair "Old Sparky". Davis' face was bloodied, and photographs were taken, which were later posted on the Internet. An investigation concluded that Davis had begun bleeding before the electricity was applied and that the chair had functioned as designed, Florida's Supreme Court ruled that the chair did not constitute cruel and unusual punishment.[206] The 1997 execution of Pedro Medina in Florida created controversy when flames burst from the inmate's head. An autopsy found that Medina had died instantly when the first surge of electricity had destroyed his brain and brain stem, and a judge ruled that Florida's electric chair was in 'excellent condition'.[207] Lethal injection has been the primary method of execution in the state of Florida since 2000. On February 15, 2008, the Nebraska Supreme Court declared execution by electrocution to be "cruel and unusual punishment" prohibited by the Nebraska Constitution.

Robert Gleason, executed in the electric chair at Greensville Correctional Center, Virginia, on January 16, 2013, is the most recent individual to choose electrocution over lethal injection.

External links

- "Kemmler's Death by Torture"[208], *New York Herald,* August 7, 1890.
- Death Penalty Worldwide[209] Academic research database on the laws, practice, and statistics of capital punishment for every death penalty country in the world.

Gas chamber

 </indicator>

A **gas chamber** is an apparatus for killing humans or other animals with gas, consisting of a sealed chamber into which a poisonous or asphyxiant gas is introduced. The most commonly used poisonous agent is hydrogen cyanide; carbon dioxide and carbon monoxide have also been used. Gas chambers were used as a method of execution for condemned prisoners in the United States beginning in the 1920s and continue to be a legal execution method in three states. During the Holocaust, large-scale gas chambers designed for mass killing were used by Nazi Germany as part of their genocide program. The use of gas chambers in North Korea has also been reported.

Nazi Germany

Nazi Germany made extensive use of various types of gas chamber for mass killing.

Beginning in 1939, gas chambers were used as part of the Nazi euthanasia program aimed at eliminating physically and intellectually disabled people. Experiments in the gassing of patients were conducted in October 1939 in occupied Posen in Poland. Hundreds of prisoners were killed by carbon monoxide poisoning in an improvised gas chamber. In 1940 gas chambers using bottled pure carbon monoxide were established at six euthanasia centres in Germany. In addition to persons with disabilities, these centres were also used to kill prisoners transferred from concentration camps in Germany, Austria, and Poland. Killings of concentration camp inmates continued after the euthanasia program was officially shut down in 1941.

During the invasion of Russia, mass executions by exhaust gas were performed by *Einsatzgruppen* using gas vans, trucks modified to divert engine exhaust into a sealed interior gas chamber.

Starting in 1941, gas chambers were used at extermination camps in Poland for the mass killing of Jews, Roma, and other victims of the Holocaust. Gas vans were used at the Chełmno extermination camp. The Operation Reinhard extermination camps at Bełżec, Sobibór, and Treblinka used exhaust fumes from stationary diesel engines. In search of more efficient killing methods, the Nazis experimented with using the hydrogen cyanide-based fumigant Zyklon B at the Auschwitz concentration camp. This method was adopted for mass killings at the Auschwitz and Majdanek camps. Up to 6000 victims were gassed with Zyklon-B each day at Auschwitz.

Figure 50: *Interior of Majdanek gas chamber, showing Prussian blue residue*

Most extermination camp gas chambers were dismantled or destroyed in the last months of the World War II as Soviet troops approached, except for those at Dachau, Sachsenhausen and Majdanek. One destroyed gas chamber at Auschwitz was reconstructed after the war to stand as a memorial.

Lithuania

In 1937–1940, Lithuania operated a gas chamber in Aleksotas within the First Fort of the Kaunas Fortress. Before, the executions were carried out by hanging or by shooting. However, these methods were viewed as brutal and in January 1937, the criminal code was amended to provide execution by gas which at the time was viewed as more civilized and humane. Lithuania considered and rejected execution by poison. The first execution was carried on July 27, 1937: Bronius Pogužinskas, age 37, convicted of murder of five people from a Jewish family. Historian Sigita Černevičiūtė counted at least nine executions in the gas chamber, though records are incomplete and fragmentary. Of the nine, eight were convicted of murder. One, Aleksandras Maurušaitis, was in addition convicted of anti-government actions during the 1935 Suvalkija strike. The last known execution took place on May 19, 1940 for robbery. The fate of the gas chamber after the occupation by the Soviet Union in June 1940 is unclear.

North Korea

Kwon Hyok, a former head of security at Camp 22, described laboratories equipped with gas chambers for suffocation gas experiments, in which three or four people, normally a family, are the experimental subjects.[210] After undergoing medical checks, the chambers are sealed and poison is injected through a tube, while scientists observe from above through glass. In a report reminiscent of an earlier account of a family of seven, Kwon claims to have watched one family of two parents, a son and a daughter die from suffocating gas, with the parents trying to save the children using mouth-to-mouth resuscitation for as long as they had the strength. Kwon's testimony was supported by documents from Camp 22 describing the transfer of prisoners designated for the experiments. The documents were identified as genuine by Kim Sang Hun, a London-based expert on Korea and human rights activist. A press conference in Pyongyang, organized by North Korean authorities, denounced this.[211]

Soviet Union

The original invention of mobile gas chambers based on adapted vans with the storage compartment sealed and exhaust redirected inside are attributed to Soviet NKVD commander Isay Berg. These vans were used by NKVD from 1936 under disguise of bread vans (Russian: душегубка).

United States

Gas chambers have been used for capital punishment in the United States to execute death row inmates. The first person to be executed in the United States by lethal gas was Gee Jon, on February 8, 1924. An unsuccessful attempt to pump poison gas directly into his cell at Nevada State Prison led to the development of the first makeshift gas chamber to carry out Gee's death sentence.

On December 3, 1948, Miran Thompson and Sam Shockley were executed in the gas chamber at San Quentin State Prison for their role in the Battle of Alcatraz.

In 1957, Burton Abbott was executed as the governor of California, Goodwin J. Knight, was on the telephone to stay the execution. Since the restoration of the death penalty in the United States in 1976, eleven executions by gas chamber have been conducted. By the 1980s, reports of suffering during gas chamber executions had led to controversy over the use of this method.

At the September 2, 1983, execution of Jimmy Lee Gray in Mississippi, officials cleared the viewing room after eight minutes while Gray was still alive and gasping for air. The decision to clear the room while he was still alive

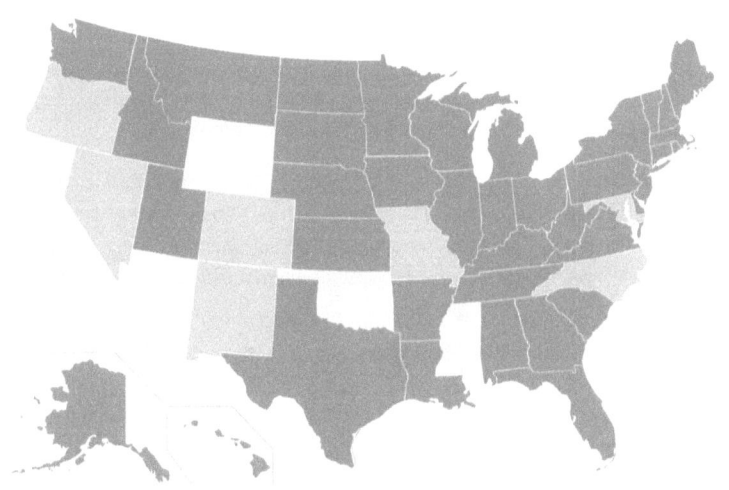

Figure 51:
Gas chamber usage in the United States.
Secondary *method only*
Previously *used, but* **not presently**
Never *used gas chamber*

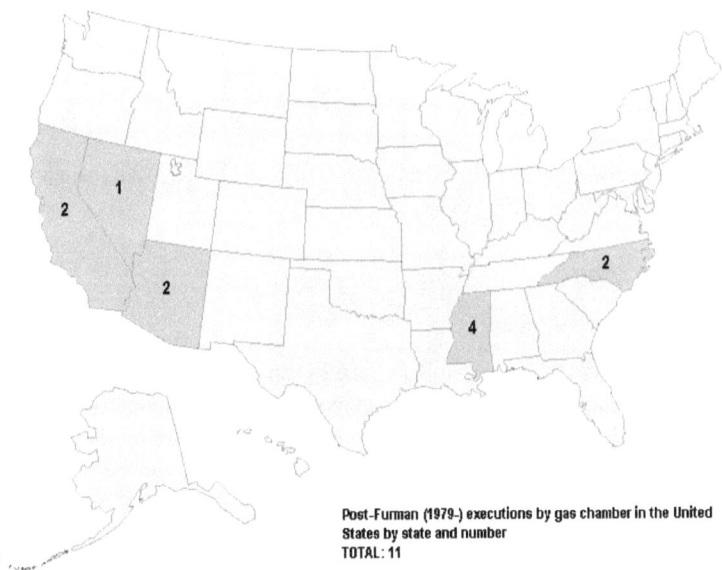

Post-Furman (1979-) executions by gas chamber in the United States by state and number
TOTAL: 11

Figure 52: *Post-Furman uses by state and numbers*

was criticized by his attorney. David Bruck, an attorney specializing in death penalty cases, said, "Jimmy Lee Gray died banging his head against a steel pole in the gas chamber while reporters counted his moans." Gray was convicted for the murder of three-year-old Deressa Jean Scales in 1976, after kidnapping and anally raping her.[212]

During the April 6, 1992, execution of Donald Harding in Arizona, it took 11 minutes for death to occur. The prison warden stated that he would quit if required to conduct another gas chamber execution. Following Harding's execution, Arizona voted that all persons condemned after November 1992 would be executed by lethal injection.

Following the execution of Robert Alton Harris, a federal court declared that "execution by lethal gas under the California protocol is unconstitutionally cruel and unusual." By the late 20th century, most states had switched to methods considered to be more humane, such as lethal injection. California's gas chamber at San Quentin State Prison was converted to an execution chamber for lethal injection.

As of 2010, the last person to be executed in the gas chamber was German national Walter LaGrand, sentenced to death before 1992, who was executed in Arizona on March 3, 1999. The U.S. Court of Appeals for the Ninth Circuit had ruled that he could not be executed by gas chamber, but the decision was overturned by the United States Supreme Court. The gas chamber was formerly used in Colorado, Nevada, New Mexico, North Carolina and Oregon. Six states, Arizona, California, Maryland, Mississippi, Missouri and Wyoming, authorize lethal gas if lethal injection cannot be administered, the condemned committed their crime before a certain date, or the condemned chooses to die in the gas chamber. In October 2010, Governor of New York David Paterson signed a bill rendering gas chambers illegal for use by humane societies and other animal shelters.

Method of use

Using hydrogen cyanide

As implemented in the United States, the gas chamber is considered to be the most dangerous, most complicated, and most expensive method of administering the death penalty.[213,214,215] The condemned person is strapped into a chair within an airtight chamber, which is then sealed. The executioner activates a mechanism which drops potassium cyanide (or sodium cyanide[216]) pellets into a bath of sulfuric acid beneath the chair; the ensuing chemical reaction generates lethal hydrogen cyanide gas. Because hydrogen cyanide gas condenses at approximately 78 °F (26 °C), the temperature in the chamber (when it is in use) is maintained at a minimum of 80 °F (27 °C).[217]

Figure 53: *The former gas chamber at New Mexico State Penitentiary, used only once in 1960 and later replaced by lethal injection.*

The gas is visible to the condemned, who is advised to take several deep breaths to speed unconsciousness. Nonetheless, there are often convulsions and excessive drooling. There may also be urinating, defecating, and vomiting.[218,219]

Following the execution the chamber is purged with air, and any remnant gas is neutralized with anhydrous ammonia, after which the body can be removed (with great caution, as pockets of gas can be trapped in the victim's clothing). Sometimes, as a safety precaution, the clothing worn by the executed person is destroyed by incineration.[220] The undertaker who handles the body wears rubber gloves for protection against any trace amounts of cyanide that might still be present on or in the body.

Excluding all oxygen

Nitrogen gas or oxygen-depleted air has been considered for human execution, as it can induce nitrogen asphyxiation. The victim detects little abnormal sensation as the oxygen level falls. This leads to asphyxiation (death from lack of oxygen) without the painful and traumatic feeling of suffocation, or the side effects of poisoning.

In April 2015, Oklahoma Governor Mary Fallin approved a bill allowing nitrogen asphyxiation as an execution method. On March 14, 2018, Oklahoma

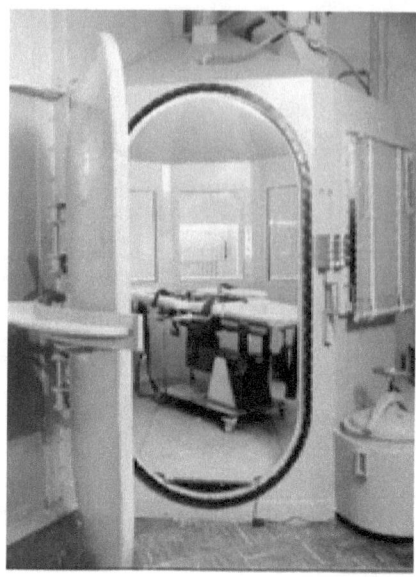

Figure 54: *Executions in California were carried out in the gas chamber at San Quentin State Prison. It was modified for the use of lethal injection, but has been returned to its original designated purpose, with the creation of a new chamber specifically for lethal injection.*

Attorney General Mike Hunter and Corrections Director Joe M. Allbaugh announced a switch to nitrogen gas as the primary method of execution.

Livestock

Gas chambers have also been used for animal euthanasia, using carbon monoxide as the lethal agent. Sometimes a box filled with anesthetic gas is used to anesthetize small animals for surgery or euthanasia. Wikipedia:Citation needed

External links

Decapitation

The Beheading of Saint Paul. Painting by Enrique Simonet in 1887, Malaga Cathedral

Decapitation is the complete separation of the head from the body. Such an injury is fatal to humans and most animals, since it deprives all other organs of the involuntary functions that are needed for the body to function, while the brain is deprived of oxygenated blood and blood pressure.

The term **beheading** refers to the act of deliberately decapitating a person, either as a means of murder or execution; it may be accomplished with an axe, sword, knife, or by mechanical means such as a guillotine. An executioner who carries out executions by beheading is called a headsman. Accidental decapitation can be the result of an explosion, car or industrial accident,[221] improperly administered execution by hanging or other violent injury. Suicide by decapitation is rare but not unknown. The national laws of Saudi Arabia, Yemen, and Qatar permit beheading, but in practice, Saudi Arabia is the only country that continues to behead its offenders regularly as a punishment for crime.

Less commonly, decapitation can also refer to the removal of the head from a body that is already dead. This might be done to take the head as a trophy, for public display, to make the deceased more difficult to identify, for cryonics, or for other, more esoteric reasons.[222]

Figure 55: *Beheadings in a painting from Froissart's Chronicles, beginning of the 15th century – the execution Guillaume Sans and his secretary on the orders of Thomas Felton*

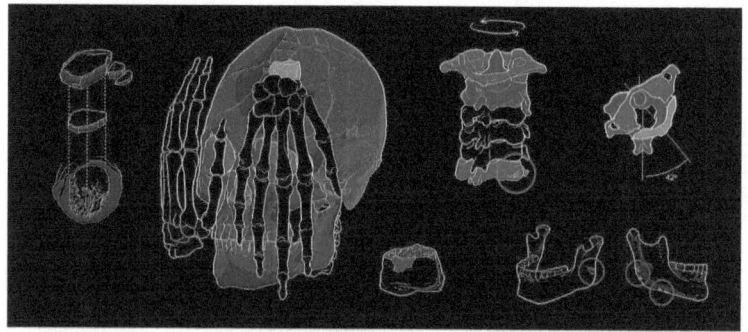

Figure 56: *The oldest decapitation in the New World (10,000 years ago).*

Figure 57: *Depiction of an Ethiopian Emperor executing a number of people, 18th century*

Etymology

The word decapitation has its roots in the Late Latin word *decapitare*. The meaning of the word *decapitare* can be discerned from its morphemes *de-* (down, from) + *capit-* (head). The past participle of *decapitare* is *decapitatus* which was used to create *decapitationem*, the noun form of *decapitatus* in Medieval Latin. From the Medieval Latin form, *decapitationem*, the French word *décapitation* was produced.

History

Execution by beheading has been used as a form of capital punishment for millennia. The Narmer Palette (c. 3000 B.C.) shows the first known depiction of decapitated corpses. The terms "capital offence", "capital crime", "capital punishment," derive from the Latin *caput*, "head", referring to the punishment for serious offences involving the forfeiture of the head; *i.e.*, death by beheading.[223] In some cultures, such as ancient Rome and Greece, decapitation was regarded as the most honorable form of death. The extension of the "privilege" of beheading to criminals of ordinary birth was among the symbolic changes brought about by the French Revolution. In other cases, such as the use of

Figure 58: *Beheading — facsimile of a miniature on wood in the Cosmographia of Sebastian Münster (1488–1552), Basel, Switzerland, 1552*

Figure 59: *Anne Boleyn in the Tower of London waiting to be executed by beheading, by Édouard Cibot (1799–1877)*

beheading by Japanese troops during World War II, its use was considered a form of contempt. In recent times, it has become associated with terrorism.

Physiological aspects

Pain

If the headsman's axe or sword was sharp and his aim was precise, decapitation was quick and was presumed to be a relatively painless form of death. If the instrument was blunt or the executioner was clumsy, multiple strokes might be required to sever the head resulting in a prolonged and more painful death. The person to be executed was therefore advised to give a gold coin to the headsman to ensure that he did his job with care. Robert Devereux, 2nd Earl of Essex, and Mary, Queen of Scots, required three strikes at their respective executions. The same could be said for the execution of Johann Friedrich Struensee, favorite of the Danish queen Caroline Matilda.[224,225] Margaret Pole, 8th Countess of Salisbury, is said to have required up to ten strokes before decapitation was achieved.[226] This particular story may, however, be apocryphal since highly divergent accounts exist. Historian and philosopher David Hume, for example, relates the following about her death:[227] <templatestyles src="Template:Quote/styles.css"/>

> She refused to lay her head on the block, or submit to a sentence where she had received no trial. She told the executioner, that if he would have her head, he must win it the best way he could: and thus, shaking her venerable grey locks, she ran about the scaffold; and the executioner followed her with his ax, aiming many fruitless blows at her neck before he was able to give the fatal stroke.

To ensure that the blow would be fatal, executioners' swords usually were blade-heavy two-handed swords. Likewise, if an axe was used, it almost invariably was wielded with both hands. In England a bearded axe was used for beheading, with the blade's edge extending downwards from the tip of the shaft.Wikipedia:Citation needed

Finland's official beheading axe resides today at the Museum of Crime in Vantaa. It is a broad-bladed two-handed axe. It was last used when murderer Tahvo Putkonen was executed in 1825, the last execution in peacetime in Finland.

Figure 60: *The Beheading of Cosmas and Damian, by Fra Angelico*

Physiology of death by decapitation

Decapitation is quickly fatal to humans and most animals. Unconsciousness occurs within 10 seconds without circulating oxygenated blood (brain ischemia). Cell death and irreversible brain damage occurs after 3–6 minutes with no oxygen due to excitotoxicity. Some anecdotes suggest more extended persistence of human consciousness after decapitation: <templatestyles src="Template:Quote/styles.css"/>

> *I consider it essential for you to know that Languille displayed an extraordinary sang-froid and even courage from the moment when he was told, that his last hour had come, until the moment when he walked firmly to the scaffold. It may well be, in fact, that the conditions for observation, and consequently the phenomena, differ greatly according to whether the condemned persons retain all their sang-froid and are fully in control of themselves, or whether they are in such state of physical and mental prostration that they have to be carried to the place of execution, and are already half-dead, and as though paralysed by the appalling anguish of the fatal instant.*
>
> *The head fell on the severed surface of the neck and I did not therefore have to take it up in my hands, as all the newspapers have vied with each other*

in repeating; I was not obliged even to touch it in order to set it upright. Chance served me well for the observation, which I wished to make.

Here, then, is what I was able to note immediately after the decapitation: the eyelids and lips of the guillotined man worked in irregularly rhythmic contractions for about five or six seconds. This phenomenon has been remarked by all those finding themselves in the same conditions as myself for observing what happens after the severing of the neck...

I waited for several seconds. The spasmodic movements ceased. The face relaxed, the lids half closed on the eyeballs, leaving only the white of the conjunctiva visible, exactly as in the dying whom we have occasion to see every day in the exercise of our profession, or as in those just dead. It was then that I called in a strong, sharp voice: "Languille!" I saw the eyelids slowly lift up, without any spasmodic contractions — I insist advisedly on this peculiarity — but with an even movement, quite distinct and normal, such as happens in everyday life, with people awakened or torn from their thoughts.

Next Languille's eyes very definitely fixed themselves on mine and the pupils focused themselves. I was not, then, dealing with the sort of vague dull look without any expression, that can be observed any day in dying people to whom one speaks: I was dealing with undeniably living eyes which were looking at me. After several seconds, the eyelids closed again, slowly and evenly, and the head took on the same appearance as it had had before I called out.

It was at that point that I called out again and, once more, without any spasm, slowly, the eyelids lifted and undeniably living eyes fixed themselves on mine with perhaps even more penetration than the first time. Then there was a further closing of the eyelids, but now less complete. I attempted the effect of a third call; there was no further movement -- and the eyes took on the glazed look which they have in the dead.

I have just recounted to you with rigorous exactness what I was able to observe. The whole thing had lasted twenty-five to thirty seconds.

—Gabriel Beaurieux[228]

But most doctors consider this unlikely and consider such accounts to be misapprehensions of reflexive twitching rather than deliberate movement, since deprivation of oxygen must cause nearly immediate coma and death ("[Consciousness is] probably lost within 2–3 seconds, due to a rapid fall of intracranial perfusion of blood.").[229]

Some animals (such as cockroaches) can survive decapitation, and die not because of the loss of the head directly, but rather because of starvation. A number of other animals, including chickens, turtles and snakes have also been

Figure 61: *Aristocratic heads on pikes — a cartoon from the French Revolution*

known to survive for some time after being decapitated, as they have a slower metabolism and their nervous systems can continue to function at some capacity for a limited time even after connection to the brain is lost, responding to any nearby stimulus.

Although head transplantation by the reattachment of blood vessels has been successful with animals, a fully functional reattachment of a severed human head (including repair of the spinal cord, muscles, and other critically important tissues) has not yet been achieved.

Technology

Guillotine

Early versions of the guillotine included the Halifax Gibbet, which was used in Halifax, England, from 1286 until the 17th century, and the "Maiden", employed in Edinburgh from the 16th through the 18th centuries.

The modern form of the guillotine was invented shortly before the French Revolution with the aim of creating a quick and painless method of execution requiring little skill on the part of the operator. Decapitation by guillotine became a common mechanically assisted form of execution.

There is dubious evidence from contemporary accounts that the severed head could remain conscious for up to ten seconds. Furthermore, the observations of Dr. Beaurieux, who witnessed the decapitation of a convict named Languille in 1905, may imply that the severed head also briefly retained the sense of sight.[230]

The French observed a strict code of etiquette surrounding such executions. For example, a man named Legros, one of the assistants at the execution of Charlotte Corday, was imprisoned for three months and dismissed for slapping the face of the victim after the blade had fallen in order to see whether any flicker of life remained.[231] The guillotine was used in France during the French Revolution and remained the normal judicial method in both peacetime and wartime into the 1970s, although the firing squad was used in certain cases. France abolished the death penalty in 1981.

The guillotine was also used in Algeria before the French relinquished control of it, as shown in Gillo Pontecorvo's film *The Battle of Algiers*.

Another guillotine existed in Vatican City until recent years.Wikipedia:Citation needed It had been brought in by Napoleon's forces during the early 19th century; and, as of 1870, the pope still claimed the authority to use it.Wikipedia:Citation needed The Holy See has since abolished capital punishment within its own jurisdiction, and recent popes have condemned capital punishment wherever it is still practised.

German Fallbeil

Many German states had used a guillotine-like device known as a *Fallbeil* ("falling axe") since the 17th and 18th centuries, and decapitation by guillotine was the usual means of execution in Germany until the abolition of the death penalty in West Germany in 1949.

In Nazi Germany, the *Fallbeil* was reserved for common criminals and people convicted of political crimes, including treason. Members of the White Rose resistance movement, a group of students in Munich that included siblings Sophie and Hans Scholl, were famously executed by decapitation.

Contrary to popular myth, executions were generally not conducted face up, and chief executioner Johann Reichhart was insistent on maintaining "professional" protocol throughout the era, having administered the death penalty during the earlier Weimar Republic. Nonetheless, it is estimated that some 16,500 persons were guillotined in Germany and Austria between 1933 and 1945, a number that includes resistance fighters both within Germany itself and in countries occupied by Nazi forces. As these resistance fighters were not part of any regular army, they were considered common criminals

Figure 62: *French anarchist Auguste Vaillant just before being guillotined in 1894*

and were in many cases transported to Germany for execution. Decapitation was considered a "dishonorable" death, in contrast to execution by firing squad.Wikipedia:Citation needed

The *Fallbeil* was used for the last time in West Germany in 1949 and in East Germany in 1966.

Historical practices by nation

Africa

Congo

In the Democratic Republic of Congo, the conflict and ethnic massacre between local army and Kamuina Nsapu rebels has caused several deaths and atrocities like rape and mutilation. One of them is decapitation, which is a fearsome way to intimidate their victims, but it also depicts some ritualistic elements. According to an UN report from Congolese refugees, they believed the Bana Mura and Kamuina Nsapu militias have "magical powers" as consecuence of drinking the blood of decapitated victims that would make them invincible. According to some reports, they indeed feed the blood from their victims' heads to younger members as baptism rite, then they often burn the

Figure 63: *A fresco by Ambrogio Lorenzetti*

remains into the fire or sometimes they consume the human remains, committing cannibalism. Besides the massive decapitations (like the beheading of 40 members of the State Police), a notorious case of worldwide impact happened in March 2017 to Swedish politician Zaida Catalán and American UN expert Michael Sharp, who were kidnapped and executed during a mission near the village Ngombe in the Kasai Province. The UN was reportedly horrified when video footage of the execution of the two experts surfaced in April that same year, where some grisly details led to assume ritual components of the beheading: the perpetrators proceeded to cut the hair of both victims first, and then one of them beheaded Catalan only, because it would "increase his power",[232] which may be linked to the fact that Congolese militians are particularly brutal in their acts of violence toward women and children. In the trial that followed the investigation after the bodies were discovered, and according to a testimony of a primary school teacher from Bunkonde, near the village of Moyo Musuila where the execution took place, he witnessed a teenage militian carrying the young woman's head, but despite the efforts of the investigation, the head was never found.

Figure 64: *Ranked beheaded bodies on the ground, in Caishikou, Beijing, China, 1905*

Asia

Azerbaijan

Kyaram Sloyan was killed during the 2016 Armenian–Azerbaijani clashes and beheaded by soldiers of Azerbaijani Armed Forces, with videos and pictures of his severed head posted on social media networks.

China

In traditional China, decapitation was considered a more severe form of punishment than strangulation, although strangulation caused more prolonged suffering. This was because in Confucian tradition, bodies were gifts from their parents, and so it was therefore disrespectful to their ancestors to return their bodies to the grave dismembered. The Chinese however had other punishments, such as dismembering the body into multiple pieces (similar to English quartering). In addition, there was also a practice of cutting the body at the waist, which was a common method of execution before being abolished in the early Qing dynasty due to the lingering death it caused. In some tales, people did not die immediately after decapitation.[233]

Figure 65: *Japanese illustration depicting the beheading of Chinese captives. Sino-Japanese War of 1894–5*

India

The British officer John Masters recorded in his autobiography that Pathans in British India during the Anglo-Afghan Wars would behead enemy soldiers who were captured, such as British and Sikh soldiers.

Pakistan

Pakistan's government employs death by hanging for capital punishment. Since 2007, militants from Tehrek-e-Taliban Pakistan have used beheadings as a form of punishment for opponents, criminals and spies in the north west region of Pakistan. Severed heads of opponents or government officials in Swat were left on popular street corners in order to terrorize local population. The beheadings have stopped in Swat since the military incursion and sweep-up that began in May 2009 and ended in June 2009. Three Sikhs were beheaded by the Taliban in Pakistan in 2010. Daniel Pearl was beheaded by his captors in the city of Karachi.

Despite official condemnation from the state itself, such beheading continues to flourish in the Taliban strongholds of Baluchistan and Khyber-PakhtunkhwaWikipedia:Citation needed and are often jarred and unprofessionalWikipedia:Citation needed resulting in increased pain for the victim.

Japan

In Japan, decapitation was a common punishment, sometimes for minor offences. Samurai were often allowed to decapitate soldiers who had fled from battle, as it was considered cowardly. Decapitation was historically performed

Figure 66: *An Australian POW captured in New Guinea, Sgt. Leonard Siffleet, about to be beheaded by a Japanese soldier with a shin guntō sword, 1943*

as the second step in seppuku (ritual suicide by disembowelment). After the victim had sliced his own abdomen open, another warrior would strike his head off from behind with a katana to hasten death and to reduce the suffering. The blow was expected to be precise enough to leave intact a small strip of skin at the front of the neck—to spare invited and honored guests the indelicacy of witnessing a severed head rolling about, or towards them; such an occurrence would have been considered inelegant and in bad taste. The sword was expected to be used upon the slightest sign that the practitioner might yield to pain and cry out—avoiding dishonor to him and to all partaking in the privilege of observing an honorable demise. As skill was involved, only the most trusted warrior was honored by taking part. In the late Sengoku period, decapitation was performed as soon as the person chosen to carry out seppuku had made the slightest wound to his abdomen.

Decapitation (without seppuku) was also considered a very severe and degrading form of punishment. One of the most brutal decapitations was that of Sugitani Zenjubō (杉谷善住坊), who attempted to assassinate Oda Nobunaga, a prominent *daimyō*, in 1570. After being caught, Zenjubō was buried alive in the ground with only his head out, and the head was slowly sawn off with a bamboo saw by passers-by for several days (punishment by sawing; *nokogiribiki* (鋸挽き)).[234] These unusual punishments were abolished in the early

Meiji era. This horrific scene is described in the last page of James Clavell's book *Shogun*.

Korea

Historically, decapitation had been the most common method of execution in Korea, until it was replaced by hanging in 1896. Professional executioners were called *mangnani* (망나니) and they were volunteered from deathrows.Wikipedia:Citation needed

Europe

Bosnia and Herzegovina

During the war in Bosnia and Herzegovina (1992–1995) there were a number of ritual beheadings of Serbs and Croats who were taken as prisoners of war by mujahedin members of the Bosnian Army. At least one case is documented and proven in court by the ICTY where mujahedin, members of 3rd Corps of Army BiH, beheaded Bosnian Serb Dragan Popović.[235]

British

The British empire used beheading and display of severed heads and other body parts on pikes, etc., as a method to support conquest, territorial expansion, pillage and looting. Heads were displayed to terrify various peoples into submission, such as enslaved Africans, Tasmanians, Chinese, and Celts.

Historically, beheading was typically used for noblemen, while commoners would be hanged; eventually, hanging was adopted as the standard means of non-military executions. The last actual execution by beheading was of Simon Fraser, 11th Lord Lovat on 9 April 1747, while a number of convicts (typically traitors sentenced to drawing and quartering, a method which had already been discontinued) were beheaded posthumously up to the early 19th century. Beheading was degraded to a secondary means of execution, including for treason, with the abolition of drawing and quartering in 1870 and finally abolished by at the monarch's discretion in 1973.

Celts

The Celts of western Europe long pursued a "cult of the severed head", as evidenced by both Classical literary descriptions and archaeological contexts.[236] This cult played a central role in their temples and religious practices and earned them a reputation as head hunters among the Mediterranean peoples. Diodorus Siculus, in his 1st-century *History* had this to say about Celtic headhunting: <templatestyles src="Template:Quote/styles.css"/>

> *They cut off the heads of enemies slain in battle and attach them to the necks of their horses. The blood-stained spoils they hand over to their attendants and striking up a paean and singing a song of victory; and they nail up these first fruits upon their houses, just as do those who lay low wild animals in certain kinds of hunting. They embalm in cedar oil the heads of the most distinguished enemies, and preserve them carefully in a chest, and display them with pride to strangers, saying that for this head one of their ancestors, or his father, or the man himself, refused the offer of a large sum of money. They say that some of them boast that they refused the weight of the head in gold.*

Both the Greeks and Romans found the Celtic decapitation practices shocking and the latter put an end to them when Celtic regions came under their control. However, Greeks and Romans both employed decapitation and other horrific tortures, highlighting a tendency to view practices as more shocking when carried out by an outside group, even if the practices are essentially similar.[237]

According to Paul Jacobsthal, "Amongst the Celts the human head was venerated above all else, since the head was to the Celt the soul, centre of the emotions as well as of life itself, a symbol of divinity and of the powers of the other-world."[238] Arguments for a Celtic cult of the severed head include the many sculptured representations of severed heads in La Tène carvings, and the surviving Celtic mythology, which is full of stories of the severed heads of heroes and the saints who carry their own severed heads, right down to *Sir Gawain and the Green Knight*, where the Green Knight picks up his own severed head after Gawain has struck it off, just as St. Denis carried his head to the top of Montmartre.

A further example of this regeneration after beheading lies in the tales of Connemara's St. Feichin, who after being beheaded by Viking pirates carried his head to the Holy Well on Omey Island and on dipping the head into the well placed it back upon his neck and was restored to full health.

Classical antiquity

<templatestyles src="Template:Quote_box/styles.css" />

Pothinus matched Mark Antony in crime:
They slew the noblest Romans of their time.
The helpless victims they decapitated,
An act of infamy with shame related.
One head was Pompey's, who brought triumphs home,
The other Cicero's, the voice of Rome.

— Martial, *Epigram* I:60 (Trans. by Garry Wills)

The ancient Greeks and Romans regarded decapitation as a comparatively honorable form of execution for criminals. The traditional procedure, however, included first being tied to a stake and whipped with rods. Axes were used by the Romans, and later swords, which were considered a more honorable instrument of death. Those who could verify that they were Roman citizens were to be beheaded, rather than undergoing the much more horrific experience of crucifixion. In the Roman Republic of the early 1st century BC, it became the tradition for the severed heads of public enemies—such as the political opponents of Marius and Sulla, for example—to be publicly displayed on the Rostra in the Forum Romanum after execution. Perhaps the most famous such victim was Cicero who, on instructions from Mark Antony, had his hands (which had penned the *Philippicae* against Antony) and his head cut off and nailed up for display in this manner.

Germany

- Fritz Haarmann, a serial killer from Hannover who was sentenced to death for killing 27 young men, was decapitated in April 1925. He was nicknamed "The Butcher from Hanover" and was rumored to have sold his victims' flesh to his neighbor's restaurant.
- In July 1931, notorious serial killer Peter Kürten, known as "The Vampire of Düsseldorf", was executed on the guillotine in Cologne.
- On 1 August 1933, in Altona, Bruno Tesch and three others were beheaded. These were the first executions in the Third Reich. The executions concerned the Altona Bloody Sunday (*Altonaer Blutsonntag*) riot, an SA march on 17 July 1932 that turned violent and led to 18 people being shot dead.
- Marinus van der Lubbe by guillotine in 1934 after a show trial in which he was found guilty of starting the Reichstag fire.

- In February 1935 Benita von Falkenhayn and Renate von Natzmer were beheaded with the axe and block in Berlin for espionage for Poland. Axe beheading was the only method of execution in Berlin until 1938, when it was decreed that all civil executions would henceforth be carried out by guillotine. However, the practice was continued in rare cases such as that of Olga Bancic and Werner Seelenbinder in 1944. Beheading by guillotine survived in West Germany until 1949 and in East Germany until 1966.
- A group of three Catholic clergymen, Johannes Prassek, Eduard Müller and Hermann Lange, and an Evangelical Lutheran pastor, Karl Friedrich Stellbrink, were arrested following the bombing of Lübeck, tried by the People's Court in 1943 and sentenced to death by decapitation; all were beheaded on 10 November 1943, in the Hamburg prison at Holstenglacis. Stellbrink had explained the raid next morning in his Palm Sunday sermon as a "trial by ordeal", which the Nazi authorities interpreted to be an attack on their system of government and as such undermined morale and aided the enemy.
- In October 1944, Werner Seelenbinder was executed by manual beheading, the last legal use of the method (other than by guillotine) in Europe. Earlier the same year, Olga Bancic had been executed by the same means.
- In February 1943, American academic Mildred Harnack and the university students Hans Scholl, Sophie Scholl, and Christoph Probst of the White Rose protest movement, were all beheaded by the Nazi State. Four other members of the White Rose, an anti-Nazi group, were also executed by the People's Court later that same year. The anti-Nazi Helmuth Hübener was also decapitated by People's Court order.Wikipedia:Citation needed
- In 1966, former Auschwitz doctor Horst Fischer was executed by the German Democratic Republic by guillotine, the last executed by this method outside France. Beheading was subsequently replaced by shooting in the neck.Wikipedia:Citation needed

France

In France, until the abolition of capital punishment in 1981, the main method of execution had been by beheading by means of the guillotine. Other than a small number of military casesWikipedia:Avoid weasel words where a firing squad was used (including that of Jean Bastien-Thiry) the guillotine was the only legal method of execution from 1791, when it was introduced by the Legislative Assembly during the last days of the kingdom French Revolution, until 1981. Before the revolution, beheading had typically been reserved to noblemen and carried out manually. In 1981, President François Mitterrand

Figure 67: *The execution of the Duke of Somerset after the battle of Tewkesbury in 1471*

abolished capital punishment and issued commutations for those whose sentences had not been executed.

The first person executed by the guillotine (in France) was highwayman Nicolas Jacques Pelletier in April 1792. The last execution was of murderer Hamida Djandoubi, in Marseilles, in 1977.[239] Djandoubi's execution was the last judicial use of the guillotine in the world.Wikipedia:Citation needed Throughout its extensive overseas colonies and dependencies, the device was also used, including on St Pierre in 1889 and on Martinique as late as 1965.[240]

Nordic countries

In Nordic countries, decapitation was the usual means of carrying out capital punishment. Noblemen were beheaded with a sword, and commoners with an axe. The last executions by decapitation in Finland in 1825, Norway in 1876, Faroe Islands in 1609, and in Iceland in 1830 were carried out with axes. The same was the case in Denmark in 1892. Sweden continued the practice for a few decades, executing its second to last criminal – mass murderer Johan Filip Nordlund – by ax in 1900. It was replaced by the guillotine, which was used for the first and only time on Johan Alfred Ander in 1910.

Figure 68: *Panel showing ballplayer being beheaded, Classic Veracruz culture, Mexico*

Nordlund's execution was the last (legal) manual beheading in the Western world except for in Germany, where it prevailed until the days of World War II (see above).

The official beheading axe of Finland resides today in the Museum of Crime, Vantaa.

Spain

In Spain executions were carried out by various methods including strangulation by the garrotte. In the 16th and 17th centuries, noblemen were sometimes executed by means of beheading. Examples include Anthony van Stralen, Lord of Merksem, Lamoral, Count of Egmont and Philip de Montmorency, Count of Horn. They were tied to a chair on a scaffold. The executioner used a knife to cut the head from the body. It was considered to be a more honourable death if the executioner started with cutting the throat.[241]

North America

Mexico

Miguel Hidalgo y Costilla, Ignacio Allende, José Mariano Jiménez and Juan Aldama were tried for treason, executed by firing squad and beheaded during

Figure 69: *King of Dahomey cuts off 127 heads to complete the ornament of his wall. 1793*

the Mexican independence in 1811. Their heads were on display on the four corners of the Alhóndiga de Granaditas, in Guanajuato.

During the Mexican Drug War, some Mexican drug cartels turned to decapitation and beheading of rival cartel members as a method of intimidation.

United States

Beheading was used in mutilations of the dead, particularly of black people like Nat Turner, who led a rebellion against slavery. When caught, he was publicly hanged, flayed, and beheaded. This was a technique used by many enslavers to discourage the "frequent bloody uprisings" that were carried out by "kidnapped Africans". While bodily dismemberment of various kinds was employed to instill terror, Dr. Erasmus D. Fenner noted postmortem decapitation was particularly effective.

The heads[242] of executed dissidents were sometimes displayed on pikes on the grounds of American slave labor camps.

US soldiers have committed decapitations in various invasions and/or conquests, including of the Native Americans, the Philippines, Korea, and Vietnam.

Regarding Vietnam, correspondent Michael Herr notes "thousands" of photoalbums made by US soldiers "all seemed to contain the same pictures": "the severed head shot, the head often resting on the chest of the dead man or being held up by a smiling Marine, or a lot of the heads, arranged in a row, with a burning cigarette in each of the mouths, the eyes open". Some of the victims were "very young".

General George S. Patton III, son of the famous WWII general, was known for keeping "macabre souvenirs", such as "a Vietnamese skull that sat on his desk." Other Americans "hacked the heads off Vietnamese to keep, trade, or exchange for prizes offered by commanders."

As a terror tactic, "some American troops hacked the heads off... dead [Vietnamese] and mounted them on pikes or poles".

Although the Utah Territory permitted a person sentenced to death to choose beheading as a means of execution, no person chose that option, and it was dropped when Utah became a state.

Middle East

Saudi Arabia

Saudi Arabia is a country that currently carries out beheadings. They are commonly performed outside of mosques in major cities after prayer services on Friday, the Muslim holy day. The punishment derives from the country's Islamic religious laws of Shariah. Crimes such as rape, murder, apostasy, and sorcery. are punishable by beheading.

According to Amnesty International, at least 79 people were executed in the kingdom in 2013. Foreigners are not exempt, accounting for "almost half" of executions in 2013.

Iraq

Though not officially sanctioned, legal beheadings were carried out against at least 50 prostitutes and pimps under Saddam Hussein as late as 2000.

Beheadings have emerged as another terror tactic especially in Iraq since 2003. Civilians have borne the brunt of the beheadings, although U.S. and Iraqi military personnel have also been targeted. After kidnapping the victim, the kidnappers typically make some sort of demand of the government of the hostage's nation and give a time limit for the demand to be carried out, often 72 hours. Beheading is often threatened if the government fails to heed the wishes of the hostage takers. Sometimes, the beheadings are videotaped and made available on the Internet. One of the most publicized of such executions was that of Nick Berg.

Judicial execution is practiced in Iraq, but is generally carried out by hanging.

Figure 70: *Assyrian military campaign in southern Mesopotamia, beheaded enemies, 7th century BC, from Nineveh, Iraq. The British Museum*

Syria

The Syrian Government employs hanging as its method of capital punishment. However, the terrorist organisation known as the Islamic State of Iraq and the Levant, which controlled territory in much of eastern Syria, had regularly carried out beheadings of people. "Rebels" and/or terrorists known to be part of the "US-vetted alliance" of armed militias attempting to overthrow the Syrian government have also[243] been implicated in beheadings.

References

※ This article incorporates text from a publication now in the public domain: Chambers, Ephraim, ed. (1728). "article name needed". *Cyclopædia, or an Universal Dictionary of Arts and Sciences* (first ed.). James and John Knapton, et al.<templatestyles src="Module:Citation/CS1/styles.css"></templatestyles>

- Media related to Decapitation at Wikimedia Commons
- Crime Library[245]
- CapitalPunishmentUK.org[246]

Ancient methods

Execution by elephant

Execution by elephant was a common method of capital punishment in South and Southeast Asia, particularly in India, where Asian elephants were used to crush, dismember or torture captives in public executions. The animals were trained and versatile, able to kill victims immediately or to torture them slowly over a prolonged period. Most commonly employed by royalty, the elephants were used to signify both the ruler's absolute power and his ability to control wild animals.

The sight of elephants executing captives both horrified and attracted the interest of European travellers and was recorded in numerous contemporary journals and accounts of life in Asia. The practice was eventually suppressed by the European empires that colonised the region in the 18th and 19th centuries. While primarily confined to Asia, the practice was occasionally adopted by Western powers, such as Ancient Rome and Carthage, particularly to deal with mutinous soldiers.

Cultural aspects

The intelligence, domesticability and versatility of the elephant gave it considerable advantages over other wild animals such as lions and bears used as executioners by the Romans. Elephants are more tractable than horses: while a horse can be trained to charge into battle, it will not willingly trample an enemy soldier, and will instead step over him. Elephants will trample their enemies, hence the popularity of war elephants with generals such as Hannibal. Elephants can be trained to execute prisoners in a variety of ways, and can be taught to prolong the agony of the victim by inflicting a slow death by torture or to kill the condemned quickly by stepping on the head.

Historically, the elephants were under the constant control of a driver or *mahout*, thus enabling a ruler to grant a last-minute reprieve and display merciful

Figure 71: *Illustration from the Akbarnama, the official chronicle of the reign of Akbar, the third Mughal emperor*

qualities.[247] Several such exercises of mercy are recorded in various Asian kingdoms. The kings of Siam trained their elephants to roll the convicted person "about the ground rather slowly so that he is not badly hurt". The Mughal Emperor Akbar the Great is said to have "used this technique to chastise 'rebels' and then in the end the prisoners, presumably much chastened, were given their lives". On one occasion, Akbar was recorded to have had a man thrown to the elephants to suffer five days of such treatment before pardoning him.[248] Elephants were occasionally used in trial by ordeal in which the condemned prisoner was released if he managed to fend off the elephant.

The use of elephants in such fashion went beyond the common royal power to dispense life and death. Elephants have long been used as symbols of royal authority (and still are in some places, such as Thailand, where white elephants are held in reverence). Their use as instruments of state power sent the message that the ruler was able to preside over very powerful creatures who were under total command. The ruler was thus seen as maintaining a moral and spiritual domination over wild beasts, adding to their authority and mystique among subjects.

Figure 72: *Geographical scope of executions by elephant*

Geographical scope

Execution by elephant has been done in many parts of the world, by both Western and Eastern empires. The earliest records of such executions date back to the classical period. However, the practice was already well established by that time and continued well into the 19th century. While African elephants are significantly larger than Asian elephants, African powers were not known to make as much use of the animals in warfare or ceremonial affairs compared to their Asian counterparts.

Asian powers

Southeast Asia

Elephants are widely reported to have been used to carry out executions in Southeast Asia, and were used in Burma and Malaysia from the earliest historical times[249] as well as in the kingdom of Champa on the other side of the Indochinese Peninsula.[250] In Siam, elephants were trained to throw the condemned into the air before trampling them to death. Alexander Hamilton provides the following account from Siam:

<templatestyles src="Template:Quote/styles.css"/>

> *For Treason and Murder, the Elephant is the Executioner. The condemned Person is made fast to a Stake driven into the Ground for the Purpose, and*

> *the Elephant is brought to view him, and goes twice or thrice round him, and when the Elephant's Keeper speaks to the monstrous Executioner, he twines his Trunk round the Person and Stake, and pulling the Stake from the Ground with great Violence, tosses the Man and the Stake into the Air, and in coming down, receives him on his Teeth, and making him off again, puts one of his fore Feet on the Carcase, and squeezes it flat.*

The journal of John Crawfurd records another method of execution by elephant in the kingdom of Cochinchina (modern south Vietnam), where he served as a British envoy in 1821. Crawfurd recalls an event where "the criminal is tied to a stake, and [Excellency's favourite] elephant runs down upon him and crushes him to death."[251]

South Asia

India

Elephants were used as executioners of choice in India for many centuries. Hindu and Muslim rulers executed tax evaders, rebels and enemy soldiers alike "under the feet of elephants". The Hindu *Manu Smriti* or Laws of Manu, written down around AD 200, prescribed execution by elephants for a number of offences. If property was stolen, for instance, "the king should have any thieves caught in connection with its disappearance executed by an elephant."[252] For example, in 1305, the sultan of Delhi turned the deaths of Mongol prisoners into public entertainment by having them crushed by elephants.[253]

During the Mughal era, "it was a common mode of execution in those days to have the offender trampled underfoot by an elephant."[254] Captain Alexander Hamilton, writing in 1727, described how the Mughal ruler Shah Jahan ordered an offending military commander to be carried "to the Elephant Garden, and there to be executed by an Elephant, which is reckoned to be a shameful and terrible Death".[255] The Mughal Emperor Humayun ordered the crushing by elephant of an imam he mistakenly believed to be critical of his reign.[256] Some monarchs also adopted this form of execution for their own entertainment. Another Mughal ruler, the emperor Jahangir, is said to have ordered a huge number of criminals to be crushed for his amusement. The French traveler François Bernier, who witnessed such executions, recorded his dismay at the pleasure that the emperor derived from this cruel punishment. Nor was crushing the only method used by the Mughals' execution elephants; in the Mughal sultanate of Delhi, elephants were trained to slice prisoners to pieces "with pointed blades fitted to their tusks". The Muslim traveler Ibn Battuta, visiting Delhi in the 1330s, has left the following eyewitness account of this particular type of execution by elephants:[257]

<templatestyles src="Template:Quote/styles.css"/>

> *Upon a certain day, when I myself was present, some men were brought out who had been accused of having attempted the life of the Vizier. They were ordered, accordingly, to be thrown to the elephants, which had been taught to cut their victims to pieces. Their hoofs were cased with sharp iron instruments, and the extremities of these were like knives. On such occasions the elephant-driver rode upon them: and, when a man was thrown to them, they would wrap the trunk about him and toss him up, then take him with the teeth and throw him between their fore feet upon the breast, and do just as the driver should bid them, and according to the orders of the Emperor. If the order was to cut him to pieces, the elephant would do so with his irons, and then throw the pieces among the assembled multitude: but if the order was to leave him, he would be left lying before the Emperor, until the skin should be taken off, and stuffed with hay, and the flesh given to the dogs.*

Other Indian polities also carried out executions by elephant. The Maratha Chatrapati Sambhaji ordered this form of death for a number of conspirators, including the Maratha official Anaji Datto in the late seventeenth century.[258] Another Maratha leader, the general Santaji, inflicted the punishment for breaches in military discipline. The contemporary historian Khafi Khan reported that "for a trifling offense he [Santaji] would cast a man under the feet of an elephant."[259]

The early 19th century writer Robert Kerr relates how the king of Goa "keeps certain elephants for the execution of malefactors. When one of these is brought forth to dispatch a criminal, if his keeper desires that the offender be destroyed speedily, this vast creature will instantly crush him to atoms under his foot; but if desired to torture him, will break his limbs successively, as men are broken on the wheel."[260] The naturalist Georges-Louis Leclerc, Comte de Buffon cited this flexibility of purpose as evidence that elephants were capable of "human reasoning, [rather] than a simple, natural instinct".[261]

Such executions were often held in public as a warning to any who may transgress. To that end, many of the elephants were especially large, often weighing in excess of nine tons. The executions were intended to be gruesome and often were. They were sometimes preceded by torture publicly inflicted by the same elephant used for the execution. An account of one such torture-and-execution at Baroda in 1814 has been preserved in *The Percy Anecdotes*:

<templatestyles src="Template:Quote/styles.css"/>

> *The man was a slave, and two days before had murdered his master, brother to a native chieftain, called Ameer Sahib. About eleven o'clock the elephant was brought out, with only the driver on his back, surrounded by natives with bamboos in their hands. The criminal was placed three yards*

Figure 73: *Louis Rousselet described this execution in Le Tour du Monde in 1868.*

behind on the ground, his legs tied by three ropes, which were fastened to a ring on the right hind leg of the animal. At every step the elephant took, it jerked him forward, and every eight or ten steps must have dislocated another limb, for they were loose and broken when the elephant had proceeded five hundred yards. The man, though covered in mud, showed every sign of life, and seemed to be in the most excruciating torments. After having been tortured in this manner for about an hour, he was taken to the outside of the town, when the elephant, which is instructed for such purposes, was backed, and put his foot on the head of the criminal.[262]

The use of elephants as executioners continued well into the latter half of the 19th century. During an expedition to central India in 1868, Louis Rousselet described the execution of a criminal by an elephant. A sketch depicting the execution showed the condemned being forced to place his head upon a pedestal, and then being held there while an elephant crushed his head underfoot. The sketch was made into a woodcut and printed in "Le Tour du Monde", a widely circulated French journal of travel and adventure, as well as foreign journals such as *Harper's Weekly*.[263]

The growing power of the British Empire led to the decline and eventual end of elephant executions in India. Writing in 1914, Eleanor Maddock noted that in Kashmir, since the arrival of Europeans, "many of the old customs are disappearing – and one of these is the dreadful custom of the execution of criminals

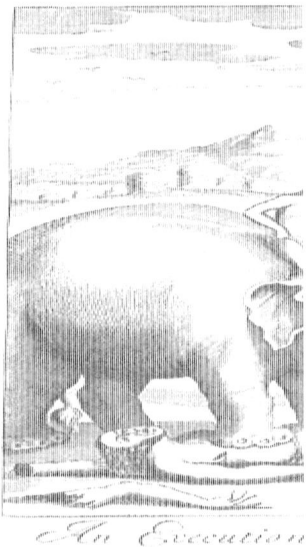

Figure 74: *A condemned prisoner being dismembered by an elephant in Ceylon. Illustration from An Historical Relation of the Island Ceylon by Robert Knox (1681).*

by an elephant trained for the purpose and which was known by the hereditary name of 'Gunga Rao'."[264]

Sri Lanka

Elephants were widely used across the Indian subcontinent and South Asia as a method of execution. The English sailor Robert Knox, writing in 1681, described a method of execution by elephant which he had witnessed while being held captive in Sri Lanka. Knox says the elephants he witnessed had their tusks fitted with "sharp Iron with a socket with three edges". After impaling the victim's body with its tusks, the elephant would "then tear it in pieces, and throw it limb from limb".[265]

The 19th century traveler James Emerson Tennent comments that "a Kandyan [Sri Lankan] chief, who was witness to such scenes, has assured us that the elephant never once applied his tusks, but, placing his foot on the prostrate victim, plucked off his limbs in succession by a sudden movement of his trunk."[266] Knox's book depicts exactly this method of execution in a famous drawing, *An Execution by an Eliphant.*

Writing in 1850, the British diplomat Henry Charles Sirr described a visit to one of the elephants that had been used by Sri Vikrama Rajasinha, the last king of Kandy, to execute criminals. Crushing by elephant had been abolished by the British after they overthrew the Kandyan kingdom in 1815 but the king's execution elephant was still alive and evidently remembered its former duties. Sirr comments:[267]

<templatestyles src="Template:Quote/styles.css"/>

> *During the native dynasty it was the practice to train elephants to put criminals to death by trampling upon them, the creatures being taught to prolong the agony of the wretched sufferers by crushing the limbs, avoiding the vital parts. With the last tyrant king of Candy, this was a favourite mode of execution and as one of the elephant executioners was at the former capital during our sojourn there we were particularly anxious to test the creature's sagacity and memory. The animal was mottled and of enormous size, and was quietly standing there with his keeper seated upon his neck; the noble who accompanied us desired the man to dismount and stand on one side.*
>
> *The chief then gave the word of command, ordering the creature to 'slay the wretch!' The elephant raised his trunk, and twined it, as if around a human being; the creature then made motions as if he were depositing the man on the earth before him, then slowly raised his back-foot, placing it alternately upon the spots where the limbs of the sufferer would have been. This he continued to do for some minutes; then, as if satisfied that the bones must be crushed, the elephant raised his trunk high upon his head and stood motionless; the chief then ordered him to 'complete his work,' and the creature immediately placed one foot, as if upon the man's abdomen, and the other upon his head, apparently using his entire strength to crush and terminate the wretch's misery.*

West Asia

During the medieval period, executions by elephants were used by several West Asian imperial powers, including the Byzantine, Sassanid, Seljuq and Timurid empires. When the Sassanid king Khosrau II, who had a harem of 3,000 wives and 12,000 female slaves, demanded as a wife Hadiqah, the daughter of the Christian Arab Na'aman, Na'aman refused to permit his Christian daughter to enter the harem of a Zoroastrian; for this refusal, he was trampled to death by an elephant.

The practice appears to have been adopted in parts of the Muslim Middle East. Rabbi Petachiah of Ratisbon, a twelfth-century Jewish traveler, reported an execution by this means during his stay in Seljuk-ruled northern Mesopotamia (modern Iraq):[268]

<templatestyles src="Template:Quote/styles.css"/>

Execution by elephant

Figure 75: *Ottoman miniature depicting the execution of prisoners of war in Nándorfehérvár*

At Nineveh there was an elephant. Its head is not protruding. It is big, eats about two wagon loads of straw at once; its mouth is in its breast, and when it wants to eat it protrudes its lip about two cubits, takes up the straw with it, and puts it in its mouth. When the sultan condemns anyone to death, they say to the elephant, "this person is guilty." It then seizes him with its lip, casts him aloft and slays him.

Western empires

The Romans, Carthaginians and ancient Macedonians occasionally used elephants for executions while also making use of war elephants for military purposes, most famously in the case of Hannibal. Deserters, prisoners of war and military criminals are recorded by ancient chroniclers to have been put to death under the foot of an elephant. Perdiccas, who became regent of Macedon on the death of Alexander the Great in 323 BC, had mutineers from the faction of Meleager thrown to the elephants to be crushed in the city of Babylon.[269] The Roman writer Quintus Curtius Rufus relates the story in his Historiae Alexandri Magni: "Perdiccas saw that they [the mutineers] were paralyzed and at his mercy. He withdrew from the main body some 300 men who had followed Meleager at the time when he burst from the first meeting held after

Alexander's death, and before the eyes of the entire army he threw them to the elephants. All were trampled to death beneath the feet of the beasts...".[270]

Similarly, the Roman writer Valerius Maximus records how the general Lucius Aemilius Paulus Macedonicus "after King Perseus was vanquished [in 167 BC], for the same fault (desertion) threw men under elephants to be trampled ... And indeed military discipline needs this kind of severe and abrupt punishment, because this is how strength of arms stands firm, which, when it falls away from the right course, will be subverted."[271]

There are fewer records of elephants being used as straightforward executioners for the civil population. One such example is mentioned by Josephus and the deuterocanonical book of 3 Maccabees in connection with the Egyptian Jews, though the story is likely apocryphal. 3 Maccabees describes an attempt by Ptolemy IV Philopator (ruled 221–204 BC) to enslave and brand Egypt's Jews with the symbol of Dionysus. When the majority of the Jews resisted, the king is said to have rounded them up and ordered them to be trampled on by elephants.[272] The mass execution was ultimately thwarted, supposedly by the intervention of angels, following which Ptolemy took an altogether more forgiving attitude towards his Jewish subjects.[273,274]

Sources

Wikimedia Commons has media related to *Execution by elephant*.

- Allsen, Thomas T. "The Royal Hunt in Eurasian History". University of Pennsylvania Press, May 2006. <templatestyles src="Module:Citation/CS1/styles.css" />ISBN 0-8122-3926-1
- Chevers, Norman. "A Manual of Medical Jurisprudence for Bengal and the Northwestern Provinces". Carbery, 1856.
- Collins, John Joseph. "Between Athens and Jerusalem: Jewish Identity in the Hellenistic Diaspora". Wm. B. Eerdmans Publishing Company, October 1999. <templatestyles src="Module:Citation/CS1/styles.css" />ISBN 0-8028-4372-7
- Eraly, Abraham. "Mughal Throne: The Saga of India's Great Emperors", Phoenix House, 2005. <templatestyles src="Module:Citation/CS1/styles.css" />ISBN 0-7538-1758-6
- Hamilton, Alexander. "A New Account of the East Indies: Being the Observations and Remarks of Capt. Alexander Hamilton, from the Year 1688 to 1723". C. Hitch and A. Millar, 1744.
- Kerr, Robert. "A General History and Collection of Voyages and Travels". W. Blackwood, 1811.

- Lee, Samuel (trans). "The Travels of Ibn Batuta". Oriental Translation Committee, 1829.
- Olivelle, Patrick (trans). "The Law Code of Manu". Oxford University Press, 2004. <templatestyles src="Module:Citation/CS1/styles.css" />ISBN 0-19-280271-2
- Schimmel, Annemarie. "The Empire of the Great Mughals: History, Art and Culture". Reaktion Books, February 2004. <templatestyles src="Module:Citation/CS1/styles.css" />ISBN 1-86189-185-7
- Tennent, Emerson James. "Ceylon: An Account of the Island Physical, Historical and Topographical". Longman, Green, Longman, and Roberts, 1860.

<indicator name="featured-star"> ★ </indicator>

Blowing from a gun

<indicator name="good-star"> ⊕ </indicator>

Blowing from a gun was a method of execution in which the victim was typically tied to the mouth of a cannon which was then fired. George Carter Stent described the process as follows:[275]

<templatestyles src="Template:Quote/styles.css"/>

> *The prisoner is generally tied to a gun with the upper part of the small of his back resting against the muzzle. When the gun is fired, his head is seen to go straight up into the air some forty or fifty feet; the arms fly off right and left, high up in the air, and fall at, perhaps, a hundred yards distance; the legs drop to the ground beneath the muzzle of the gun; and the body is literally blown away altogether, not a vestige being seen.*

Blowing from a gun was a reported means of execution as long ago as the 16th century, by the Mughal Empire, and was used until the 20th century. The method was utilized by Portuguese colonialists in the 16th and 17th centuries, from as early as 1509 across their empire from Ceylon (modern day Sri Lanka)[276] to Mozambique[277] to Brazil.[278] The Mughals used the method throughout the 17th century and into the 18th, particularly against rebels.[279]

This method of execution is most closely associated with the colonial government of the British Raj. Following the Indian Rebellion of 1857, "blowing from a gun" was a method the British used to execute rebels[280] as well as for those natives found guilty of desertion.[281] Using the methods previously practised by the Mughals, the British began implementing blowing from guns in the latter half of the 18th century.[282]

The destroying of the body and scattering the remains over a wide area had a particular religious function as a means of execution in the Indian subcontinent as it effectively prevented the necessary funeral rites of Muslims and Hindus.[283] Thus, for believers the punishment was extended beyond death. This was well understood by foreign occupiers and the practice was not generally employed by them as concurrent foreign-occupiers of Africa, Australasia or the Americas. Most recently there was an exceptional use of the practice in Afghanistan in 1930, against 11 Panjshiri rebels.[284]

Rituals

A commonly reported method of blowing a man from a gun is to tie him in front of the muzzle of the gun and then have him shot. Loading the cannon with an actual cannonball is on occasion reported; but, more commonly, the use of blank cartridge or grapeshot is attested. The following description of the manner of tying up the convicted is from Afghanistan, 7 July 1839, ordered by Shuja Shah, during the campaign against Dost Mohammad Khan:[285]

<templatestyles src="Template:Quote/styles.css"/>

> The three men were then tied with ropes to the guns, their backs against the muzzle. The rope, fastened to one of the spokes of the wheel, passed with a knot round the arms, over the muzzle of the gun, round the other arm, and then to the spoke of the opposite wheel, which kept the body fixed.

Although immobilizing a victim in front of a gun before firing the cannon is by far the most reported method, a case from Istanbul in 1596 alleges that the victim was actually put into the gun and executed in that manner.[286] Reports exist that attest that, on occasion, people were fastened to rockets and blown into the air. This is said to have been the punishment for a Brahmin during Hyder Ali's reign (1761–1782),[287] and also, in an 1800 treason case, in the Maratha Empire.[288]

Problems with the method

Things did not always work out according to plan at such executions; at a mass execution at Firozpur in 1857, there was an order that blank cartridge should be used, but some guns were loaded with grapeshot instead. Several of the spectators facing the cannons were hit by the grapeshot and some had to have limbs amputated as a result. In addition, some of the soldiers had not been withdrawn properly and sustained injuries from being hit by whizzing pieces of flesh and bone.[289] In another case, a soldier who was to be shot managed to fall down just as the shot went off, with the following result:[290]

<templatestyles src="Template:Quote/styles.css"/>
> *One wretched fellow slipped from the rope by which he was tied to the guns just before the explosion, and his arm was nearly set on fire. While hanging in his agony under the gun, a sergeant applied a pistol to his head; and three times the cap snapped, the man each time wincing from the expected shot. At last a rifle was fired into the back of his head, and the blood poured out of the nose and mouth like water from a briskly handled pump. This was the most horrible sight of all. I have seen death in all its forms, but never anything to equal this man's end.*

Others reported with shudders how birds of prey circled above the execution place and swooped down to catch pieces of human flesh in the air,[291] while others were nauseated by the dogs loitering about the place of execution and rushing to the scene to devour some of the "delicacies" spread around as a result of the execution.[292]

Mughal Empire

Blowing from a gun as a method of execution has a long and varied history on the Indian sub-continent, and many reports from the mid-18th century and onwards testify to its varied use. The execution method was used during rebellions and as punishment for a variety of crimes. Here, a focus is chosen upon the Mughal tradition of blowing from guns as a local tradition preceding, for example, the British tradition on the same sub-continent.

Several historians note that blowing people from the guns as a method of execution was an "old Mughal punishment" on the Indian sub-continent.[293] Just prior to the institution of the reign of the first Mughal emperor, Babur, his son Humayun is said to have blown from guns 100 Afghan prisoners on 6 March 1526, in one incident of his father's many struggles against the Lodi dynasty.[294] During the latter half of the 17th century, members of the Jat people in Northern India rebelled and raided against the Mughal Empire, and the emperor Aurangzeb is said in one account to have ordered one of their leaders blown from a gun.[295] Purbeel Singh, said to have been the last Hindu chief of Umga, close to Aurangabad in today's Bihar state, was reportedly taken by an unnamed Mughal emperor to Aurungabad, and blown from a gun.[296] The Sikh rebel Banda Singh Bahadur was finally vanquished in 1716 by the emperor Farrukhsiyar, and after his execution, Banda's son was ordered to be "blown to bits by a cannon".[297]

While the preceding cases are examples of rebels or military adversaries being blown from guns, the Mughal era also contained a few examples of using this form of execution for other types of perceived crime. For example, in a rather anecdotal story from the times of Jahangir (r. 1605 – 1627), the emperor had six mullahs blown from guns, for having consented to, and given approval of, the forcible abduction and marriage of a Hindu girl to a Muslim officer.[298] In 1714, thieves were a severe annoyance to a marching army; a trap was made, and two thieves caught by the concealed guards were later blown from guns. During a siege in 1719, the problem of deserters was eventually solved for the commander of the Mughal army by blowing four deserters caught in the act from guns, in the presence of his troops.[299]

Portuguese Empire

Portuguese colonialists are, in several accounts, charged with having used blowing from a gun as a form of capital punishment in many of their colonies. A short review follows:

Sri Lanka

The Portuguese explorer Francisco de Almeida is reported to have blown many individuals from guns at Ceylon, around 1509. During the Dutch siege of Colombo in 1656, the city population endured extreme famine. One nursing mother became so starved that her production of milk stopped, and her infant was dying. She chose to kill it, and eat it. Once the Portuguese general became aware of her act of cannibalism, he ordered her blown from a gun, but in this particular instance, the clergy and the principal citizens dissuaded him from carrying out the act.[300]

Mozambique

During explorer Francisco Barreto's 1569–73 campaign in Monomotapa, he at one time imprisoned some 50 Muslim individuals, and had them "impaled, blown from mortars, torn apart on tree-trunks, axed or shot". In mid-18th-century Tete, in north-western Portuguese Mozambique, the capital punishment for slaves is said to have been to be blown from guns,[301] and, in the first decade of the 19th century, it is reported that an inveterate raider chief was caught by the Portuguese and blown from a gun.[302]

Brazil

In 1618 Brazil, native resistance against the Portuguese was unshaken, although a leader of them, Amaro, was taken prisoner and blown from a gun.[303]

British-occupation of India

Before 1857

The British had a long tradition prior to the Mutiny of executing sepoys found guilty of mutiny or desertion in this manner. According to one historian, the British tradition began in 1760, when the government examined the modes of capital punishment in use. In the district of the 24 Perganas, it was found that the common military mode of capital punishment was flogging to death. Regarding blowing from a gun as an old Mughal punishment, the government opted for this technique, as being, relative to death by flogging, more deterrent, more public and more humane. Already in 1761, orders were given in Lakhipur "to fire off at the mouth of a cannon the leader of the thieves who was made prisoner, that others may be deterred".[304] Technically, in cases of court-martial, it seems that until 1857 the courts were composed of native officers rather than British, but it is added: "although they are presided over, and *generally led and ruled*, by the superintending officer, whose duty, however, is merely to transcribe the evidence, and assist the native officers with advice and counsel".[305]

In March 1764, a subedar (native officer) thought to entice his troops over to the enemy;[306] he was court-martialed and blown from a gun in front of the troops.[307] In September the same year, major Hector Munro executed 24 or 25 "ring leaders" who caused a battalion to desert (the desertion being on account of "lack of rewards", "scarcity of provisions" and problems with climate and disease). Approving of the execution, one commenter said: "no disposition to mutiny was thenceforth manifested". In 1775, the Indian soldier Muctoom Sahib (designated by the British as a "commandant") refused to embark for Mumbai when "commanded" to by foreign East India company mercenaries. Inspired by and in deference to their commander's resolve, the men under Muctoom Sahib followed suit. As a violent reprisal, the foreign-mercenaries executed Muctoom Sahib by blowing from a gun; the men under his command, demoralized, embarked to Mumbai.[308] In 1782, mutinies broke out in Bardhaman and Barrackpore. Three mutineers were sentenced to death by the court in Bardhaman, 2 of whom to be blown from a gun, the last to be hanged. In the Barrackpore trials, 4 of the 5 on trial were sentenced to be blown from a gun, while the last was to receive a thousand lashes and "to be drummed out of the cantonments with a rope around his neck".[309] During the Third Anglo-Mysore War (1789–1792), six regiments mutinied over arrears of pay and held their officers confined. When order was restored, two of the most active were blown from guns.[310] Not only mutineers were blown from guns, but also soldiers found guilty of desertion, as is shown from a few cases in 1781 and 1783.[311]

Not only sepoys were executed by being blown from a gun. In 1798, mutiny broke out in the British unit 1st battalion of the Madras artillery. One British soldier was condemned to be blown from a gun.[312] This, however, seems to have been exceptional, and one historian says that the soldier Forster is the only European on record to have been blown from a gun by the British authorities.[313]

In 1804, during a military engagement, the troops under lieutenant Birch's command refused to quit the ground of their encampment. Colonel Burn deemed harsh measures were necessary, convened a court-martial, and two of the officers involved were blown from guns and 9 others "severely flogged". With full approval of the action, the writer observes: "a measure which, there is every reason to believe, had the best effect, as the corps behaved during the subsequent siege with the greatest steadiness and propriety".[314]

In the 1806 Vellore Mutiny, beginning with a night massacre of British officers and soldiers, with many sepoys killed during the suppression, 6 individuals were sentenced to be blown from the guns.[315] In 1812, a plot was discovered at Travancore to kill the European officers; two ring leaders were blown from the guns, and several others were hanged.[316] In 1819, six deserters who had joined the ousted rajah of the annexed Kingdom of Nagpur were apprehended by the British and were blown from the guns on 7 February.[317] In 1832 Bangalore, a conspiracy allegedly designed to exterminate all Europeans was discovered. Out of some 100 implicated, 4 were sentenced to be blown from the guns, two others to be shot.[318]

Sometimes, although a person was condemned to death, he might hope for a pardon or a commuting of the punishment. In 1784, a regiment mutinied over lack of pay. Lieutenant General[319] Laing suppressed the rebels and ordered twelve to be blown from guns. The last of the twelve was very lucky, however: Bound to the cannon's mouth, he had to endure three times that the fuse burnt out. He then asked Lieutenant General Laing whether he was really destined to die in this manner, and Laing chose to pardon him.[320] In 1795 Midnapore, 5 sepoys were condemned in court-martial to be blown from guns on account of mutiny, 3 others to be hanged. Their cases were appealed, however, and their sentences were commuted to be dismissed from service instead.[321] In Barrackpore Mutiny of 1824, occasioned by the resentment of sepoys to being shipped to the front in the First Anglo-Burmese War, four days after the bloody suppression of the mutiny, one of the leaders, Bindee Tiwarree of the 47th regiment was found hiding, disguised as a faqir. In the ensuing court-martial, he was condemned to be blown from a gun, but instead he was hung in chains, and after his death his body was placed in a gibbet for a few months.[322] In 1836, a sepoy was found guilty of having fled before the enemy and abandoned

Figure 76: *Suppression of the Indian Revolt by the English*, a painting by Vasily Vereshchagin c. 1884. Note: This painting was allegedly bought by the British crown and possibly destroyed (current whereabouts unknown). It anachronistically depicts the events of 1857 with soldiers wearing (then current) uniforms of the late 19th century.

his European officers. Rungish was condemned to be blown from a gun, but the sentence was commuted into "transportation beyond the sea".[323]

The Great Rebellion

This method of execution is strongly associated with its use by British troops during the Indian Rebellion of 1857. To appreciate the scale and frequency of the executions made by the British during the 1857 insurrection, one may, for example, look at the reports of incidents given in merely a single journal, "Allen's Indian Mail", for the year 1857:

<templatestyles src="Template:Quote/styles.css"/>

> On 8 June, two sepoys from the 35th light Infantry were blown from guns. 10 June, in Ludhiana, Peshawar, some 40 from the 54th regiment were blown from guns. On 13 June, ten[324] sepoys from the 45th Regiment at Firozpur were blown from guns, two hanged. The same day, in Ambala, 10 sepoys from the 54th regiment suffered the same fate. The 26th of the same month, in Aurungabad, 1 was blown from a gun, 1 hanged, and 3 were shot. On 8 July, in Jhelum, it is assumed that captured rebels would

be blown away. On the 19th, Aurungabad, 1 was blown away, 2 shot. On 5 September, Settara, 6 were blown away. On 17 September, Multan, 1 was blown away, 121 were summarily executed. On 23 September, in Karachi, 1 was blown away, 7 were hanged and 20 deported. (The local body count on court-martialed individuals then came to 4 blown away, 14 hanged, 22 deported and 3 beheadings.) At the end of October, in Rohilkhand near Agra, 1 was blown away. On 16 November, Bombay, two sepoys from the 10th regiment were blown away.[325]

As an example of official statistics, rather than a collection of newspaper reports, in an 1859 paper to the House of Commons of the United Kingdom on the rebellion in the Peshawar Valley in the Punjab, for the period May–September 1857, 523 were recorded executed, of them 459 shot by musketry, 20 hanged (13 for desertion) and the last 44 blown from a gun. Of those 44, 4 were executed on charges of desertion, rather than mutiny.[326] Official July–November statistics for the area about Agra says that of 78 who were given capital sentences, two had their sentence commuted into imprisonment, whereas 4 were blown from guns.[327] Other official statistics, this time from Indore, state that, of 393 sepoys officially punished, 32 were executed, 21 of them by being blown from guns.[328]

The preceding cases are examples of execution after formal court martial, and do not, therefore, record deaths as occurring during battle or during informal executions or massacres.

Several British were convinced that the sepoy insurgents had blown British women from guns.[329] A specific case, mentioned by several sources, concerns that of Mr. and Mrs. Birch, Mrs. Eckford and Mrs. Defontaine,[330] all of whom were said to have been blown from guns at Fatehgarh.[331]

The skull of an Indian soldier blown from a gun was found in a British pub and is the subject of the book, "The Skull of Alum Bheg: The Life and Death of a Rebel of 1857."[332]

After 1857

The Rebellion of 1857 was not the last time that British military used blowing from a cannon as an execution method. In 1871, for example, 65 members of the Sikh sect Kukas or Namdhari were executed by the military, by being blown from guns.[333]

Afghanistan

Within Afghanistan, a tradition of using blowing from a gun as capital punishment is attested from the early nineteenth century up to 1930. Some examples are following:

Early cases

In 1802, the forces of Mahmud Shah Durrani inflicted a crushing defeat on the Ghilzai tribes, and to discourage further aggression, he ordered one leader and his two sons blown from guns, as well as building a minaret out of Ghilzai skulls.[334] In 1803, when Shah Shujah Durrani ousted his half-brother Mahmud from power, he revenged himself on an ally of Mahmud, Ashik, by blowing him from a gun for having captured by means of treachery Shujah's and Mahmud's half-brother Zaman Shah Durrani, who had been king of the Durrani Empire prior to having been ousted by Mahmud in 1800.[335]

The iron emir, 1880–1901

In 1880, Abdur Rahman Khan became emir of Afghanistan, and he swiftly gained the nickname "the iron emir" for his perceived brutality and strong rule. For example, one source estimates that, during his 20 years on the throne, an average of 5,000 executions a year took place, several by blowing from guns.[336] For example, in December 1889 alone, 24 are recorded as having been blown from guns, and many others executed in other ways.[337]

Tajik reign of terror, 1929

In January 1929, a new cycle of extreme violence broke out in Afghanistan when the Tajik Habibullāh Kalakāni became emir. The British minister Humphreys wrote: "None was safe, houses were pillaged indiscriminately, women were ravished and a reign of terror was established unprecedented in the annals of bloody Afghan history". Political opponents were often blown from guns or executed in other ways.[338] Habibullah's regime was toppled in October 1929, and then the Kuhestani Tajiks were persecuted. An article in *The New York Times* from 6 April 1930 was headlined with: "Eleven Afghans Blown from Guns at Kabul".

In fiction

In *Flashman in the Great Game*, written by George MacDonald Fraser and set during the 1857 Indian Rebellion, Harry Flashman, a British Army officer who is impersonating an Indian, is knocked unconscious and captured during a British attack on the camp of Rani Lakshmibai. Flashman is assumed to be a rebel and awakens gagged and tied over the muzzle of a gun. He narrowly manages to avoid execution and has the rebels who were to be executed alongside him freed, an uncharacteristically humane act for a character usually portrayed as a liar, a bully and a scoundrel.

The Steam House (French: *La maison à vapeur*) is an 1880 Jules Verne novel ending with Nana Sahib getting blown up with a large cannon.

In H. Beam Piper's *Lord Kalvan of Otherwhen*, Kalvan, transferred from our universe into an Alternate History, proposes that captured clergy of the corrupt "church" Styphon's House should be killed this way. He rationalizes to himself that the British had used that technique on Sepoy Mutineers, "in the reign of her enlightened Majesty, Victoria, and could you get any more respectable than that?" Kalvan also thinks this constitutes "a bad pun about cannon-ized martyrs." It's particularly appropriate because Styphon's House made its wealth as the sole source of gunpowder.

Bibliography

<templatestyles src="Template:Refbegin/styles.css" />

- Adolphus, John (1840). *The history of England*[339]. **1**. London: John Lee. Retrieved 2 May 2013.<templatestyles src="Module:Citation/CS1/styles.css"></templatestyles>
- Afsos, Scher Ali; Court, Henry (1871). *The Araish-i-mahfil*[340]. Allahabad: G.A. Savielle. Retrieved 2 May 2013.<templatestyles src="Module:Citation/CS1/styles.css"></templatestyles>
- Akbarzadeh, Shahram; Macqueen, Benjamin (2008). *Islam and Human Rights in Practice*[341]. New York: Routledge. ISBN 978-1-134-05926-3. Retrieved 2 May 2013.<templatestyles src="Module:Citation/CS1/styles.css"></templatestyles>
- Alden, Dauril (1996). *The Making of an Enterprise*[342]. Stanford University Press. ISBN 978-0-8047-2271-1. Retrieved 2 May 2013.<templatestyles src="Module:Citation/CS1/styles.css"></templatestyles>
- Allen, W.H. (1857). *ALLEN'S INDIAN MAIL*[343]. London: W.H. Allen Press. Retrieved 2 May 2013.<templatestyles src="Module:Citation/CS1/styles.css"></templatestyles>

- Almon, John (1791). *The Parliamentary Register*[344]. London: J. Debrett. Retrieved 2 May 2013.<templatestyles src="Module:Citation/CS1/styles.css"></templatestyles>
- American Peace Society (1858). *The Advocate of Peace*[345]. Boston: American Peace Society. Retrieved 2 May 2013.<templatestyles src="Module:Citation/CS1/styles.css"></templatestyles>
- Anderson, T.C. (1859). "Andersons reply in". *Notes and Queries: a medium of enter communication for literary men, artists, antiquaries, genealogists, etc*[346]. London: Bell&Daldy. Retrieved 2 May 2013.<templatestyles src="Module:Citation/CS1/styles.css"></templatestyles>
- Asiatic Journal (1837). *The Asiatic journal and monthly register*[347]. London: Allen. Retrieved 2 May 2013.<templatestyles src="Module:Citation/CS1/styles.css"></templatestyles>
- Asiatic Society of Bengal (1847). *Journal of the Asiatic Society of Bengal*[348]. **16**. Calcutta: Baptist Mission Press. Retrieved 2 May 2013.<templatestyles src="Module:Citation/CS1/styles.css"></templatestyles>
- Atkinson, James (1842). *The Expedition into Affghanistan*[349]. London: Wm. H. Allen & Company. Retrieved 2 May 2013.<templatestyles src="Module:Citation/CS1/styles.css"></templatestyles>
- Baillie, An Officer of Colonel Baillie's Detachment (1788). *Memoirs of the late war in Asia*[350]. **1**. London: Self-published. Retrieved 2 May 2013.<templatestyles src="Module:Citation/CS1/styles.css"></templatestyles>
- Bakshi, S.R. (1997). *Kashmir Through Ages*[351]. New Delhi: Sarup & Sons. ISBN 978-81-85431-71-0. Retrieved 2 May 2013.<templatestyles src="Module:Citation/CS1/styles.css"></templatestyles>
- Baldwin, R (1785). *The London Magazine Enlarged and Improved*[352]. **4**. London: R. Baldwin. Retrieved 2 May 2013.<templatestyles src="Module:Citation/CS1/styles.css"></templatestyles>
- Ball, Charles (1859). *The History of the Indian Mutiny*[353]. **3**. London: London Printing and Publishing Company. Retrieved 2 May 2013.<templatestyles src="Module:Citation/CS1/styles.css"></templatestyles>
- Blakiston, John (1829). *Twelve Years' Military Adventure in Three Quarters of the Globe*[354]. **1**. London: Henry Colburn. Retrieved 2 May 2013.<templatestyles src="Module:Citation/CS1/styles.css"></templatestyles>
- Boyar, Ebru; Fleet, Kate (2010). *A Social History of Ottoman Istanbul*[355]. Cambridge University Press. ISBN 978-1-139-48444-2. Retrieved 2 May 2013.<templatestyles src="Module:Citation/CS1/styles.css"></templatestyles>
- Broome, Arthur (1850). *History of the Rise and Progress of the Bengal Army*[356]. **1**. London, Calcutta: Smith, Elder and Company, W. Thacker

- and Company.<templatestyles src="Module:Citation/CS1/styles.css"></templatestyles>
- Butalia, Romesh C. (1998). *The Evolution of the Artillery in India*[357]. Mumbai etc: Allied Publishers. ISBN 978-81-7023-872-0. Retrieved 2 May 2013.<templatestyles src="Module:Citation/CS1/styles.css"></templatestyles>
- Calcutta Review (January–June 1851). *The Calcutta Review*[358]. **xv**. Calcutta. Retrieved 2 May 2013.<templatestyles src="Module:Citation/CS1/styles.css"></templatestyles>
- Campbell, William (1839). *British India in Its Relation to the Decline of Hindooism*[359]. London: John Snow. Retrieved 2 May 2013.<templatestyles src="Module:Citation/CS1/styles.css"></templatestyles>
- Cullather, Nick; Meyerowitz, Joanne J. (editor) (2003). "Damming Afghanistan". *History and September Eleventh*[360]. Philadelphia: Temple University Press. ISBN 978-1-59213-203-4. Retrieved 2 May 2013.<templatestyles src="Module:Citation/CS1/styles.css"></templatestyles>
- Deerrett, J. (1783). *The Remembrancer*[361]. London: J. Deerrett. Retrieved 2 May 2013.<templatestyles src="Module:Citation/CS1/styles.css"></templatestyles>
- Doveton, Cpt. (contributor) (November–April 1844). *The Asiatic journal and monthly miscellany*[362]. 2,Third Series. London: W.H. Allen. Retrieved 2 May 2013. Check date values in: | date= (help)<templatestyles src="Module:Citation/CS1/styles.css"></templatestyles>
- Duff, James G. (1826). *A history of the Mahrattas*[363]. **3**. London: Longmans, Rees, Orme, Brown, and Green. Retrieved 2 May 2013.<templatestyles src="Module:Citation/CS1/styles.css"></templatestyles>
- Edwards, David B. (1996). *Heroes of the Age:Moral Fault Lines on the Afghan Frontier*[364]. Berkeley and Los Angeles, California: University of California Press. ISBN 978-0-520-91631-9. Retrieved 2 May 2013.<templatestyles src="Module:Citation/CS1/styles.css"></templatestyles>
- Ferrier, Joseph P. (1858). *History of the Afghans*[365]. London: John Murray. Retrieved 2 May 2013.<templatestyles src="Module:Citation/CS1/styles.css"></templatestyles>
- Forbes, James (1815). *Oriental memoirs*[366]. London: White, Cochrane&co. Retrieved 2 May 2013.<templatestyles src="Module:Citation/CS1/styles.css"></templatestyles>
- Fremont-Barnes, Gregory (2007). *The Indian Mutiny 1857–58*[367]. Oxford: Osprey Publishing. ISBN 978-1-84603-209-7. Retrieved 2 May 2013.<templatestyles src="Module:Citation/CS1/styles.css"></templatestyles>
- Government Records (1911). *Government Records: Mutiny records.*

Correspondence and reports[368]. Punjab: Punjab Government Press. Retrieved 2 May 2013.<templatestyles src="Module:Citation/CS1/styles.css"></templatestyles>
- Grey, C.; Garrett, N.H.O (1996). *European Adventurers of Northern India, 1785 to 1849*[369]. New Delhi: Asian Educational Services. ISBN 978-81-206-0853-5. Retrieved 2 May 2013.<templatestyles src="Module:Citation/CS1/styles.css"></templatestyles>
- Havholm, Peter (2008). *Politics and Awe in Rudyard Kipling's Fiction*[370]. Aldershot, England and Burlington, VT, USA: Ashgate Publishing, Ltd. ISBN 978-0-7546-6164-1. Retrieved 2 May 2013.<templatestyles src="Module:Citation/CS1/styles.css"></templatestyles>
- Hazārah, Fayz Muhammad Kātib; McChesney, R.D; Khorrami, M.M. (2012). *The History of Afghanistan*[371]. **1**. Leyden: BRILL. ISBN 978-90-04-23491-8. Retrieved 2 May 2013.<templatestyles src="Module:Citation/CS1/styles.css"></templatestyles>
- Heathcote, T.A. (1995). *The Military in British India*[372]. Manchester: Manchester University Press. ISBN 978-0-7190-3570-8. Retrieved 2 May 2013.<templatestyles src="Module:Citation/CS1/styles.css"></templatestyles>
- Indian News, Abraham V.W. (1858). *The Indian News and Chronicle of Eastern Affaires*[373]. London. Retrieved 2 May 2013.<templatestyles src="Module:Citation/CS1/styles.css"></templatestyles>
- Irvine, William (1922). *Later Mughals*[374]. **1**. London: Luzac. Retrieved 2 May 2013.<templatestyles src="Module:Citation/CS1/styles.css"></templatestyles>
- Knight, Lionel (2012). *Britain in India, 1858–1947*[375]. London: Anthem Press. ISBN 978-0-85728-517-1. Retrieved 2 May 2013.<templatestyles src="Module:Citation/CS1/styles.css"></templatestyles>
- Lal, Basavan; Prinsep, Henry T. (1832). *Memoirs of the Puthan Soldier of Fortune*[376]. Calcutta: G. H. Huttmann, military orphan Press. Retrieved 2 May 2013.<templatestyles src="Module:Citation/CS1/styles.css"></templatestyles>
- Lee, Jonathan L. (1996). *The "Ancient Supremacy"*[377]. Leyden: Brill. ISBN 978-90-04-10399-3. Retrieved 2 May 2013.<templatestyles src="Module:Citation/CS1/styles.css"></templatestyles>
- Long, James (1869). *Selections from unpublished records of government for the years 1748–1767*[378]. Calcutta: Office of Superintendent of Government Printing. Retrieved 2 May 2013.<templatestyles src="Module:Citation/CS1/styles.css"></templatestyles>
- Macready, Major Edward (1853). "Extracts from the journals of the late Major Edward Macready". *Colburn's United Service Magazine*[379]. Londonissue=Part 1: Colburn&co. Retrieved 2 May 2013.<templatestyles

- Muir, William; Coldstream, William(editor) (1902). *Records of the Intelligence Department of the Government of the North-west Provinces of India during the mutiny of 1857*[380]. Edinburgh: T&T Clark. Retrieved 2 May 2013.
- Munro, Innes (1789). *A narrative of the military operations of the Coromandel Coast*[381]. London: T. Bensley. Retrieved 2 May 2013.
- Noel, Baptist Wriothesley (1859). *England and India*[382]. London: James Nisbet and Co. Retrieved 2 May 2013.
- Noelle, Christine (2012). *State and Tribe in Nineteenth-Century Afghanistan*[383]. New York: Routledge. ISBN 978-1-136-60317-4. Retrieved 2 May 2013.
- Parlby, Samuel (1822). *The British Indian Military Repository*[384]. **1**. Calcutta: Church mission Press. Retrieved 2 May 2013.
- Parliament of Great Britain, House of Commons (1859). *Accounts and papers of the House of Commons*[385]. 5 month=Session 3 February-19 April 1859. London: House of Commons, by order. Retrieved 2 May 2013.
- Philippart, John (1823). *The East India Military Calendar:Containing the Services of General and Field Officers of the Indian Army*[386]. **2**. London: Kingsbury, Parbury and Allen. Retrieved 5 May 2013.
- Pogson, Wredenhall R. (1833). *Memoir of the mutiny at Barrackpore*[387]. Serampore: Self published. Retrieved 5 May 2013.
- Ribeiro, João; Le Grand, Joachim; Lee, George (tr. from French edition) (1847). *History of Ceylon*[388]. Colombo: Government Press. Retrieved 5 May 2013.
- Roberts, Jeffrey J. (2003). *The Origins of Conflict in Afghanistan*[389]. Greenwood Publishing Group. ISBN 978-0-275-97878-5. Retrieved 5 May 2013.
- Rosselli, John (1974). *Lord William Bentinck*[390]. Berkeley, California: University of California Press. ISBN 978-0-520-02299-7. Retrieved 5 May 2013.

templatestyles>
- Russell, William H. (1860). *My Diary in India, in the Year 1858-9*[391]. **2**. London: Routledge, Warne, and Routledge. Retrieved 5 May 2013.<templatestyles src="Module:Citation/CS1/styles.css"></templatestyles>
- Sabahuddin, Abdul; Shukla, Rajshree (2003). *The Mughal Strategy of War*[392]. Delhi: Global Vision Publishing House. ISBN 978-81-87746-99-7. Retrieved 5 May 2013.<templatestyles src="Module:Citation/CS1/styles.css"></templatestyles>
- Salt, Henry (1814). *A Voyage to Abyssinia, and Travels into the Interior of that Country*[393]. London: J. Rivington. Retrieved 5 May 2013.<templatestyles src="Module:Citation/CS1/styles.css"></templatestyles>
- Seton-Karr, Walter S. (1865). *Selections from Calcutta Gazettes*[394]. **2**. Calcutta: Government of India.<templatestyles src="Module:Citation/CS1/styles.css"></templatestyles>
- Shrivastav, P.N. (1971). *Madhya Pradesh District Gazetteers*[395]. Madhya Pradesh, Bhopal: District Gazetteers Department.<templatestyles src="Module:Citation/CS1/styles.css"></templatestyles>
- Singh, Bhai Nahar; Singh, Bhai Kirpal (1995). *Rebels Against the British Rule*[396]. New Delhi: Atlantic Publishers & Dist. ISBN 978-81-7156-164-3.<templatestyles src="Module:Citation/CS1/styles.css"></templatestyles>
- Southey, Robert (1822). *History of Brazil*[397]. **1**. London: Longman, Hurst, Rees, Orme, and Brown. Retrieved 5 May 2013.<templatestyles src="Module:Citation/CS1/styles.css"></templatestyles>
- Tate, George P. (1911). *The kingdom of Afghanistan*[398]. Calcutta: Times of India. Retrieved 5 May 2013.<templatestyles src="Module:Citation/CS1/styles.css"></templatestyles>
- Thoman, Mauritz (1869). *Mauriz Thoman's, ehemaligen Jesuitens und Missionärs in Asien und Afrika, Reise- und Lebensbeschreibung*[399]. Lindau: Stettner. Retrieved 5 May 2013.<templatestyles src="Module:Citation/CS1/styles.css"></templatestyles>
- Wellington, Arthur Wellesley, Duke of; Wellington, Arthur R. wellesley, 2nd Duke of (ed.) (1868). *Despatches, Correspondence, and Memoranda of Field Marshal Arthur, Duke of Wellington, K. G.: 1825–1827*[400]. London: John Murray. Retrieved 5 May 2013.<templatestyles src="Module:Citation/CS1/styles.css"></templatestyles>
- Wilkes, John (editor) (1815). *Encyclopaedia Londinensis*[401]. **13**. London: John Wilkes. Retrieved 5 May 2013.<templatestyles src="Module:Citation/CS1/styles.css"></templatestyles>

Blood eagle

The **blood eagle** is a ritualized method of execution, detailed in late skaldic poetry. According to the two instances mentioned in the Sagas, the victims (in both cases members of royal families) were placed in a prone position, their ribs severed from the spine with a sharp tool, and their lungs pulled through the opening to create a pair of "wings". There is continuing debate about whether the ritual was a literary invention, a mistranslation of the original texts, or an authentic historical practice.

Accounts

The blood eagle ritual killing rite appears in just two instances in Norse literature, plus oblique references some have interpreted as referring to the same ritual. The primary versions share certain commonalities: the victims are both noblemen (Halfdan Haaleg or "Long-leg" was a prince; Ælla of Northumbria a king) and both of the executions were in retaliation for the murder of a father.

Einarr and Halfdan

 Wikisourcehas original text related to this article:
Heimskringla/Harald Harfager's Saga#Halfdan Haleg's Death.

Figure 77: *Detail from Stora Hammars I shows a man lying on his belly with another man using a weapon on his back, a Valknut, and two birds, one of which is held by a man to the right.*

In the *Orkneyinga saga*, the blood eagle is described as a sacrifice to Odin. Torf-Einarr has Harald Fairhair's son Halfdan Long-Leg ritually executed:

> Þar fundu þeir Hálfdan hálegg, ok lèt Einarr rísta örn á baki honum með sverði, ok skera rifin öll frá hrygginum ok draga þar út lúngun, ok gaf hann Óðni til sigrs sèr.
>
> Einarr made them carve an eagle on his back with a sword, and cut the ribs all from the backbone, and draw the lungs there out, and gave him to Odin for the victory he had won.

Snorri Sturluson's *Heimskringla* contains an account of the same event described in *Orkneyinga saga*, with Einarr actually performing the deed himself:

> Þá gékk Einarr jarl til Hálfdanar; hann reist örn á baki honum með þeima hætti, at hann lagði sverði á hol við hrygginn ok reist rifin öll ofan alt á lendar, dró þar út lungun; var þat bani Hálfdanar.
>
> Afterwards, Earl Einarr went up to Halfdan and cut the "blood eagle" on his back, in this fashion that he thrust his sword into his chest by the backbone and severed all the ribs down to the loins, and then pulled out the lungs; and that was Halfdan's death.

Ivar and King Ælla

In *Þáttr af Ragnars sonum* (the "Tale of Ragnar's sons"), Ivar the Boneless has captured king Ælla of Northumbria, who had killed Ivar's father Ragnar Loðbrók. The killing of Ælla, after a battle for control of York, is described thus:

> They caused the bloody eagle to be carved on the back of Ælla, and they cut away all of the ribs from the spine, and then they ripped out his lungs.

The blood eagle is referred to by the eleventh-century poet Sigvatr Þórðarson, who, some time between 1020 and 1038, wrote a skaldic verse named *Knútsdrápa* that recounts and establishes Ivar the Boneless as having killed Ælla and subsequently cutting his back.

Sighvatr's skaldic verse in Old Norse:

Original	Literal translation	Suggested reordering
Ok Ellu bak,	And Ella's back,	And Ívarr, the one
At lét hinn's sat,	at had the one who dwelt	who dwelt at York,
Ívarr, ara,	Ívarr, with eagle,	had Ella's back
Iorví, skorit.	York, cut.	cut with [an] eagle.

Skaldic verse, a common medium of Norse poets, was meant to be cryptic and allusive, and the idiomatic nature of Sighvatr's poem as a description of what has become known as the blood eagle is a matter of historical contention, particularly since in Norse imagery the eagle was strongly associated with blood and death.

Other accounts

Another possible oblique reference to the ritual appear in *Norna-Gests þáttr*. There are two stanzas of verse near the end of its section 6, "Sigurd Felled the Sons of Hunding", where a character describing previous events says:

Nú er blóðugr örn	Now the blood eagle
breiðum hjörvi	With a broad sword
bana Sigmundar	The killer of Sigmund
á baki ristinn.	Carved on the back.
Fár var fremri,	Fewer were more valiant
sá er fold rýðr,	As the troops dispersed
hilmis nefi,	A chief of people
ok hugin gladdi.	Who made the raven glad.

The word translated "raven" is not *hrafn* but *hugin*, one of Odin's ravens.

Authenticity

There is debate about whether the blood eagle was historically practiced, or whether it was a literary device invented by the authors who transcribed the sagas. No contemporary accounts of the ritual exist, and the scant references in the sagas are several hundred years after the Christianization of Scandinavia.

Alfred Smyth supported the historicity of the ritual, stating that it is clearly human sacrifice to the Norse god Odin. He characterized St. Dunstan's description of the Ælla's killing as an "accurate account of a body subjected to the ritual of the blood eagle".[402]

Roberta Frank reviewed the historical evidence for the ritual in her "Viking Atrocity and Skaldic Verse: The Rite of the Blood-Eagle", where she writes: "By the beginning of the nineteenth century, the various saga motifs—eagle sketch, rib division, lung surgery, and 'saline stimulant'—were combined in inventive sequences designed for maximum horror." She concludes that the authors of the sagas misunderstood alliterative kennings which described carnivorous birds scavenging after battles, i.e. killing a foe and allowing their backs to be torn by eagles as battlefield carrion. She compared the lurid details of the blood eagle to Christian martyrdom tracts, such as that relating the tortures of Saint Sebastian, shot so full of arrows that his ribs and internal organs were exposed. She suggests that these tales of martyrdom inspired further exaggeration of the misunderstood skaldic verses into a grandiose torture and death ritual with no actual historical basis. David Horspool in his book *King Alfred: Burnt Cakes and Other Legends*, while not committing to the historical veracity of the ritual, also saw parallels to martyrdom tracts. Frank's paper sparked a "lively debate".[403]

Ronald Hutton's *The Pagan Religions of the Ancient British Isles: Their Nature and Legacy* states that "the hitherto notorious rite of the 'Blood Eagle,' the killing of a defeated warrior by pulling up his ribs and lungs through his back, has been shown to be almost certainly a Christian myth resulting from the misunderstanding of some older verse."

References

<templatestyles src="Template:Refbegin/styles.css" />

Death by boiling

Death by boiling is a method of execution in which a person is killed by being immersed in a boiling liquid. While not as common as other methods of execution, boiling to death has been used in many parts of Europe and Asia.

Executions of this type were often carried out using a large vessel such as a cauldron or a sealed kettle that was filled with a liquid such as water, oil, tar, or tallow, and a hook and pulley system.[404]

Historical practice

Europe

In England, the 9th statute passed in 1531 (the 22nd year of the reign of King Henry VIII) made boiling alive the prescriptive form of capital punishment for murder committed by poisoning, which by the same Act was defined as High Treason.[405] This arose from an incident in which the Bishop of Rochester's cook, Richard Roose, gave several people poisoned porridge, resulting in two deaths in February 1531. A partial confession having been

Figure 78: *Execution cauldron at Deventer (Netherlands)*

extracted by torture, the sentence was thus imposed by attainder and without benefit of clergy. A contemporary chronicle reports the following:[406] <templatestyles src="Template:Quote/styles.css"/>

> *He roared mighty loud, and divers women who were big with child did feel sick at the sight of what they saw, and were carried away half dead; and other men and women did not seem frightened by the boiling alive, but would prefer to see the headsman at his work.*

Boiling to death was employed again in 1542 for a woman, Margaret Davy,[407] who had also used poison.[408] During the reign of Edward VI, in 1547, the 1531 act was repealed.

Scotland has several traditions of persons boiled to death. For example, in 1222, with the consent of Jon Haraldsson, the "Bloody Earl" of Orkney, the bishop of Caithness Adam of Melrose and a monk named Surlo, are said to have been boiled to death by angry husbandmen over the bishop's aggressive means of collecting tithes. Alexander II is said to have executed upwards to eighty persons as a punishment for the crime, and the earl fled his lands.[409] According to the Melrose Chronicle, Adam of Melrose was "burned alive", rather than boiled, and Alexander III executed up to 400.[410] William de Soules, a nobleman involved in a conspiracy against Robert the Bruce, was reputed to be a sorcerer consorting with evil spirits, and was boiled alive in 1321 at Ninestane Rig.[411] Around 1420, Melville, the sheriff of the Mearns and laird of Glenbervie, who was resented for his strictness, was apprehended by some other nobles and thrown into the kettle. The nobles are said each to have taken a spoonful of the brew afterwards.[412]

Figure 79: *Bandit Ishikawa Goemon was boiled to death for the attempted assassination of warlord Toyotomi Hideyoshi in 16th-century Japan.*

Boiling as an execution method was also used for counterfeiters, swindlers and coin forgers during the Middle Ages. In the Holy Roman Empire, for example, being boiled to death in oil is recorded for coin forgers and extremely grave murderers. In 1392, a man was boiled alive in Nuremberg for having raped and murdered his own mother.[413] Coin forgers were boiled to death in 1452 in Danzig[414] and in 1471 in Stralsund.[415] Even as late as in 1687, a man was boiled to death in oil in Bremen for having been of valuable help to some coin forgers who had escaped justice.[416]

In the Dutch town of Deventer, the kettle that was used for boiling criminals to death can still be seen.

Asia

In 16th-century Japan, the semi-legendary Japanese bandit Ishikawa Goemon was boiled alive in a large iron kettle-shaped bathtub.[417] His public execution, which might have included his entire family, was done after he failed to kill warlord Toyotomi Hideyoshi.

In 1675, a Sikh martyr, called Bhai Dayala, was boiled to death in Delhi after he refused to accept Islam. He was put into a cauldron full of cold water which was then heated to boiling point. Sikh scriptures record that Dayala recited the Japji of Guru Nanak and the Sukhmani of Guru Arjan as he died.

Modern times

The government of Uzbekistan under Islam Karimov has been alleged to have boiled suspected terrorists.

In a 2004 document from US Department of State, the following is written:<templatestyles src="Template:Quote/styles.css"/>

> During the year, there were no developments or investigations in the following 2002 deaths in custody: Mirzakomil Avazov and Khusnuddin Olimov, members of Hizb ut-Tahrir who were tortured to death in Jaslyk Prison in Karakalpakstan resulting in extensive bruises and burns, the latter reportedly caused by immersion in boiling water.

Former ISIS commander Abu Abboud al-Raqqawi referred to ISIS' brutal execution methods, among others, boiling prisoners alive in engine oil:

<templatestyles src="Template:Quote/styles.css"/>

> Some people were boiled alive in oil. Engine oil. They burned wood on a fire for an hour before throwing the victim into boiling oil. It's the Tunisians who were responsible for that.[418]

Depictions in Western culture

Early reports of cannibals from islands in the Pacific, such as Fiji or Papua New Guinea, killing western Christian missionaries were assumed to involve some form of boiling alive. This became a fertile ground for film makers and especially cartoonists, whose clichéd depiction of tourists or missionaries sitting restrained in a large cauldron above a wood fire and surrounded by bone-nosed tribesmen was a staple of popular magazines and film for decades. Examples include the dream sequence in the movie *Bagdad Café*.

External links

- Human Rights Watch: Torture Worldwide: Uzbekistan[419]

Brazen bull

The **brazen bull**, **bronze bull**, or **Sicilian bull**, was allegedly a torture and execution device designed in ancient Greece. According to Diodorus Siculus, recounting the story in *Bibliotheca historica*, Perillos of Athens invented and proposed it to Phalaris, the tyrant of Akragas, Sicily, as a new means of executing criminals.[420] The bull was said to be made entirely out of bronze, hollow, with a door in one side. According to legends the brazen bull was designed in the form and size of an actual bull and had an acoustic apparatus that converted screams into the sound of a bull. The condemned were locked inside the device, and a fire was set under it, heating the metal until the person inside was roasted to death. Some modern scholars question if the brazen bull ever really existed, attributing reports of the fearsome invention to early propaganda.

Creation of the brazen bull for Phalaris

The head of the bull was designed with a system of tubes and stops so that the prisoner's screams were converted into sounds like the bellowing of an infuriated bull. Phalaris is said to have commanded that the bull be designed in such a way that its smoke rose in spicy clouds of incense.Wikipedia:Citation needed According to legend, when the bull was reopened after a body was charred, the victim's scorched bones then "shone like jewels and were made into bracelets."

Stories allege after finishing construction on the execution device, Perillos said to Phalaris: "His screams will come to you through the pipes as the tenderest, most pathetic, most melodious of bellowings." Perillos believed he would receive a reward for his invention. Instead, Phalaris, who was disgusted by these words, ordered its horn sound system to be tested by Perillos himself, tricking him into getting in the bull. When Perillos entered, he was immediately locked in and the fire was set, so that Phalaris could hear the sound of his screams. Before Perillos could die, Phalaris opened the door and took him away. After freeing him from the bull, Phalaris is then said to have taken Perillos to the top of a hill and thrown him off, killing him. Phalaris himself is claimed to have been killed in the brazen bull when he was overthrown by Telemachus, the ancestor of Theron.Wikipedia:Citation needed

Pindar, who lived less than a century afterwards, expressly associates this instrument of torture with the name of the tyrant Phalaris.[421]

Figure 80: *Perillos being forced into the brazen bull that he built for Phalaris.*

Figure 81: *The brazen bull (left) depicted on an old engraving*

Figure 82: *Francesco Ferdinandi, The Martyrdom of St. Eustace. Behind the main altar at the Church of Sant'Eustachio, Rome, this painting follows the narrative in the Golden Legend: For refusing to sacrifice to the gods, Saint Eustace and his wife and sons are to be executed in a brazen bull.*

Roman persecution of Christians

The Romans were reputed to have used this torture device to kill some Christians, notably Saint Eustace, who, according to Christian tradition, was roasted in a brazen bull with his wife and children by Emperor Hadrian. The same happened to Saint Antipas, Bishop of Pergamon during the persecutions of Emperor Domitian and the first martyr in Asia Minor, who was roasted to death in a brazen bull in AD 92.[422] The device is claimed to have still been in use two centuries later, when another Christian, Pelagia of Tarsus, is said to have been burned in one in 287 by the Emperor Diocletian.Wikipedia:Citation needed

The Catholic Church discounts the story of Saint Eustace's martyrdom as "completely false".[423]

Visigothic kingdom of Toulouse

According to the *Chronica caesaraugustana*, Burdunellus, a Roman usurper, was roasted in a brazen bull by the king Alaric II in 497.

In media

The 2011 film *Immortals* shows three maidens of an oracle being tortured in a brazen bull.

The 2011 film *Red Riding Hood* features a nearly identical device, albeit in the form of an elephant.

The 2010 movie *Saw 3D* shows a woman dying in a device similar to a brazen bull.

The 2010 video game *Amnesia: The Dark Descent* features a brazen bull previously used as a torture device.

The third season of *1000 Ways To Die* features a segment (titled "My Big Fat Greek Death") on the story of Perillos of Athens demonstrating the device, and becoming the first victim of his invention.

The 2014 movie *A Pigeon Sat on a Branch Reflecting on Existence* features a torture device similar to a brazen bull used to kill many people at once.

References

Notes

Bibliography

<templatestyles src="Template:Refbegin/styles.css" />

- Diehl, Daniel; Donnelly, Mark P. (2008), *The Big Book of Pain: Punishment and Torture Through History*, The History Press, ISBN 978-0-7509-4583-7<templatestyles src="Module:Citation/CS1/styles.css"></templatestyles>
- Thompson, Irene (2008), *The A to Z of Punishment and Torture: From Amputations to Zero Tolerance*, Book Guild Publishing, ISBN 978-1-84624-203-8<templatestyles src="Module:Citation/CS1/styles.css"></templatestyles>

External links

- Media related to Bronze Bull at Wikimedia Commons

Breaking wheel

The **breaking wheel** or **execution wheel**, also known as the **Catherine wheel** or simply the **Wheel**, was a torture method used for public execution from antiquity through Middle Ages into the early modern period by breaking a criminal's bones and/or bludgeoning them to death. The practice was abolished in Bavaria in 1813 and in the Electorate of Hesse in 1836: the last known execution by the "Wheel" took place in Prussia in 1841. In the Holy Roman Empire, it was a "mirror punishment" for highwaymen and street thieves but was also set out in the *Sachsenspiegel* for murder and arson.

Punishment

Execution by wheel

Those convicted as murderers and/or robbers to be executed by "the Wheel", sometimes termed to be "Wheeled" or "broken by the Wheel", would be taken to a public stage scaffold site and tied to the floor. The execution Wheel was typically a large wooden spoked wheel same as used on wooden transport carts and carriages (often with iron rim), sometimes purposely modified with a rectangular iron thrust attached and extending blade-like from part of the rim. The primary goal of the first act was the agonizing mutilation of the body, not death. Therefore, the most common form would start with breaking the leg bones. To this end, the executioner dropped the execution Wheel on the shinbones of the convicted person and then worked his way up to the arms. Here, rhythm and number of beatings were prescribed in each case, sometimes also the number of spokes on the Wheel. To increase its effect, often sharp-edged timbers were placed under the convict's joints. Later, there were devices in which the convicted person could be "harnessed". Although not commonplace, the executioner could be instructed to execute the convicted person at the end of the first act, by aiming for the neck or heart in a "coup de grace". Even less often, this occurred immediately from the start (from the head down).

In the second act, the body was braided into another wooden spoked wheel, which was possible through the broken limbs, or tied to the wheel. The wheel was then erected on a mast or pole, like a crucifixion. After this, the executioner was permitted to decapitate or garrotte the convicted if need be. Alternatively, fire was kindled under the Wheel, or the "Wheeled" convict was simply thrown into a fire. Occasionally, a small gallows was set up on the Wheel, for example, if the guilty verdict in addition to murder was by theft.

Since the body remained on the Wheel after execution, left to scavenging animals, birds and decay, this form of punishment, like the ancient crucifixion,

Figure 83: *Execution wheel (German: Richtrad) with underlays, 18th century; on display at the Märkisches Museum, Berlin*

had a sacral function beyond death: According to the belief at that time, this would hinder transition from death to resurrection.:[180]

If the convict fell from the Wheel still alive or the execution failed in some other way, it was interpreted as God's intervention. There exist votive images of saved victims of the Wheel, and there is literature on how best to treat such sustained injuries.:[204]

The survival time after being "wheeled" or "broken" could be extensive. Accounts exist of a 14th-century murderer who remained conscious for three days after undergoing the punishment. In 1348, during the time of the Black Death, a Jewish man named Bona Dies underwent the punishment. The authorities stated he remained conscious for four days and nights afterwards. In 1581, the possibly fictitious German serial killer Christman Genipperteinga remained conscious for nine days on the breaking wheel before expiring, having been deliberately kept alive with "strong drink".

Alternatively, the condemned were spreadeagled and broken on a saltire, a cross consisting of two wooden beams nailed in an "X" shape, after which the victim's mangled body might be displayed on the wheel.

Breaking wheel

Figure 84: *Illustration of execution by wheel (Augsburg, Bavaria, 1586): Classic example of the "breaking wheel" punishment, with wheel crucifixions in the background*

Figure 85: *An execution wheel (German: Richtrad) exhibited in the Museum of Cultural History Franziskanerkloster in Zittau, Saxony, Germany, dated in the centre with year 1775. Bolted to the lower rim edge is an iron blade-like thrust attachment*

History

Possible Frankish origins

Pieter Spierenburg mentions a reference in sixth-century author Gregory of Tours as a possible origin for the punishment of breaking someone on the wheel. In Gregory's time, a criminal could be placed in a deep track, and then a heavily laden wagon was driven over him. Thus, the latter practice could be seen as a symbolic re-enactment of the previous penalty in which people were literally driven over by a wagon.

France

In France, the condemned were placed on a cartwheel with their limbs stretched out along the spokes over two sturdy wooden beams. The wheel was made to revolve slowly, and a large hammer or an iron bar was then applied to the limb over the gap between the beams, breaking the bones. This process was repeated several times per limb. Sometimes it was "mercifully" ordered that the executioner should strike the condemned on the chest and abdomen, blows known as *coups de grâce* (French: *"blows of mercy"*), which caused fatal injuries. Without those, the broken man could last hours and even days, during which birds could peck at the helpless victim. Eventually, shock and dehydration caused death. In France, a special grace, the *retentum*, could be granted, by which the condemned was strangled after the second or third blow, or in special cases, even before the breaking began.

Holy Roman Empire

In the Holy Roman Empire, the wheel was punishment reserved primarily for men convicted of aggravated murder (murder committed during another crime, or against a family member). Less severe offenders would be cudgelled "top down", with a lethal first blow to the neck. More heinous criminals were punished "bottom up", starting with the legs, and sometimes being beaten for hours. The number and sequence of blows was specified in the court's sentence (for example, in 1581, the arch-killer Peter Niers, found guilty of 544 murders was, after two days of extended torture, given 42 strikes with the wheel, and was, at last, quartered alive). Corpses were left for carrion-eaters, and the criminals' heads often placed on a spike.

The "Zürcher Blutgerichtsordnung" (Procedures for the Blood Court in Zurich) dates from the 15th century and contains a detailed description of how the breaking on the wheel shall occur: Firstly, the delinquent is placed belly down, bound hands and feet outstretched to a board, and thus dragged by a horse to the place of execution. The wheel is then slammed two times on each arm, one

Breaking wheel

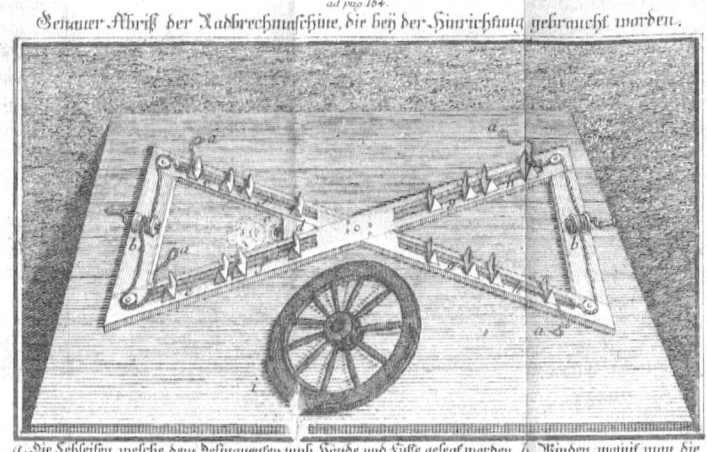

Figure 86: *Breaking-wheel machine used to execute Matthias Klostermayr, Bavaria, 1772.*

blow above the elbow, the other below. Then, each leg gets the same treatment, above and below the knees. The final ninth blow is given at the middle of the spine, so that it breaks. Then, the broken body is woven onto the wheel (i.e., between the spokes), and the wheel is then hammered onto a pole, which is then fastened upright in its other end in the ground. The criminal is then to be left dying "afloat" on the wheel, and be left to rot.

Dolle case; unclear case

On 1 October 1786 in the County of Tecklenburg, Heinrich Dolle was to be executed by being broken on the wheel, on account of the aggravated murder of a Jew. The court had decided that Dolle should be broken *von oben herab*: the first stroke of the wheel should crush his chest (traditionally thought to kill him instantly). The court instructed the executioner, Essmeyer, that Dolle should be clandestinely strangled (by garrotte) prior to the first stroke. The bystanders were shocked by what they thought was a severely botched execution by Essmeyer and his son, and thought Dolle had been alive during the entire proceeding, and also after Essmeyer had secured Dolle onto the wheel, and raised it on a pole. The town physician climbed up on a ladder (the Essmeyers had gone by then), and could ascertain that Dolle was indeed alive; he died six hours later.Wikipedia:Citation needed

The Essmeyers were taken to court for severe malpractice. It was established that the string around Dolle's neck had not been drawn tightly enough, and that Essmeyer had, contrary to his duties as an executioner, accepted the use of a wheel that was not heavy enough. That lacking weight meant that the chest had not been crushed. Furthermore, one arm and one leg of Dolle's had not broken according to proper penal procedure. And finally, the nail that was customarily hammered through the convict's brain in order to fasten him upon the wheel had been hammered in far too low.Wikipedia:Citation needed Many believed that Essmeyer's act of malpractice had been not so much a display of gross incompetence as it had been a deliberate act of cruelty because Dolle, just prior to his execution, had converted from Catholicism to that of the Reformed Church (the executioner Essmeyer was a devout Catholic). The court did not find sufficient evidence for deliberate malice on Essmeyer's part, but sentenced him to two years' hard labour and banned him from ever working again as an executioner. His young son was, on grounds of mercy, acquitted of any culpable wrongdoings.

Indian Subcontinent

A long struggle between the Sikh community and Islamic rulers resulted in execution of Sikhs. In 1746, Bhai Subeg Singh and Bhai Shahbaz Singh were executed on rotating wheels.

Scotland

In Scotland, a servant named Robert Weir was broken on the wheel at Edinburgh in 1603 or 1604 (sources disagree). This punishment had been used infrequently there. The crime had been the murder of John Kincaid, Lord of Warriston, on behalf of his wife, Jean Kincaid. Weir was secured to a cart wheel and was struck and broken with the coulter of a plough. Lady Warriston was later beheaded.[424]

British and French colonial empires

This method of execution was used in 18th-century North America following slave revolts. It was once used in New York after several British citizens were killed during a slave rebellion in 1712. Between 1730 and 1754, 11 slaves in French-controlled Louisiana, who had revolted against their masters, were killed on the wheel.

Figure 87: *The execution of Peter Stumpp, involving the breaking wheel in use in Cologne in the early modern period*

Habsburg Empire

At the end of the Revolt of Horea, Cloşca and Crişan, in 1785 (in the Austrian Principality of Transylvania (1711–1867)), two of the revolt leaders, Horea and Cloşca, were sentenced to be executed by the breaking wheel. Crişan hanged himself in prison before that sentence could be carried out. According to a book published the same year by Adam F. Geisler, the two leaders were broken "von unten auf", from bottom up, meaning the lower limbs were broken before the upper limbs, prolonging the torture.

Russia

The breaking wheel was frequently used in the Great Northern War in the early 1700s when the Tsardom of Russia challenged the supremacy of the Swedish Empire in northern Central Europe and Eastern Europe.

Sweden

Johann Patkul was a Livonian gentleman who was condemned on charges of treason by Swedish king Charles XII in 1707. The priest Lorentz Hagen was a friend of Patkul's and described the horrors his friend had to endure when Patkul was condemned to be broken on the wheel:

<templatestyles src="Template:Quote/styles.css"/>

Here the executioner gave him the first stroke. His cries were terrible. "O Jesus! Jesus, have mercy upon me!" This cruel scene was much lengthened out, and of the utmost horror; for as the headsman had no skill in his business, the wretch under his hands received upwards of fifteen blows, with each of which were intermixed the most piteous groans, and invocations of the name of God. At length, after two strokes given on the breast, his strength and voice failed him. In a faltering dying tone, he was just heard to say, "Cut off my head!" and the executioner still lingering, he himself placed his head on the scaffold: in a word, after four strokes with an hatchet, the head was separated from the body, and the body quartered. Such was the end of the renowned Patkul: and may God have mercy on his soul!

Later use

The breaking wheel was used as a form of execution in Germany as recently as the early 19th century. Its use as a method of execution was not fully abolished in Bavaria until 1813, and still in use until 1836 in Hesse-Kassel. In Prussia, the punishment of death was inflicted by decapitation with a large sword, by burning, and by breaking on the wheel. At the time, the Prussian penal code required a criminal to be broken upon the wheel when a particularly heinous crime had been committed. The king always issued an order to the executioner to strangle the criminal (which was done by a small cord not easily seen) before his limbs were broken. The last execution by this stronger form of capital punishment, of Rudolf Kühnapfel, was on 13 August 1841.[425]

Archaeology

Since victims' bodies of the breaking wheel were often left exposed to environmental influences over a long period of time, so hardly any archaeological features for the "breaking wheel" exist; as a deterrence, the bodies were often left on public display over many years, exposed to wind and weather, birds and other scavenging animals could also take away the remains and bones. In the German-speaking areas, only one archaeological discovery of a breaking wheel victim has been documented so far: In autumn 2013, the skeleton of a man was found in Groß Pankow, Germany, the sensational find was discovered during the laying of Federal Highway 189 (*Bundesstraße 189*) between Perleberg and Pritzwalk in Brandenburg, whose position and signs of injury indicate death by the "breaking wheel". Based on an iron belt buckle, the skeleton was dated to the 15th to 17th centuries, the identity of the man is unknown. A similar archaeological find has since also been discovered in 2014, in Pöls-Oberkurzheim, Styria, Austria.

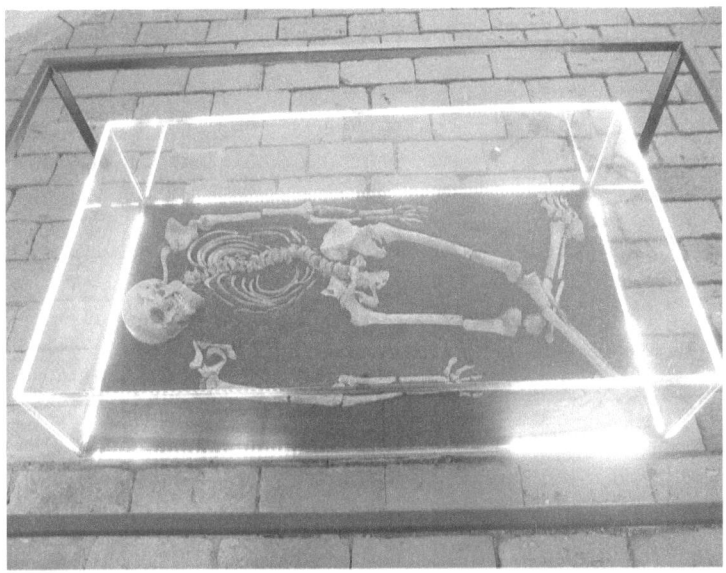

Figure 88: *Skeletal remains of a man executed by "breaking wheel", aged about 25 to 30 years, from the 16th to 18th century. Discovered in 2014, in the place of execution Pöls-Oberkurzheim (Styria), Austria. The skeleton is displayed at Riegersburg Castle in Austria*

Metaphorical uses

The breaking wheel was also known as a great dishonor, and appeared in several expressions as such. In Dutch, there is the expression *opgroeien voor galg en rad*, "to grow up for the gallows and wheel," meaning to be destined to come to no good. It is also mentioned in the Chilean expression *morir en la rueda*, "to die on the wheel," meaning to keep silent about something. The Dutch expression *ik ben geradbraakt*, literally "I have been broken on the wheel", is used to describe physical exhaustion and pain, like the German expression *sich gerädert fühlen*, "to feel wheeled," and the Danish expression "radbrækket" refer almost exclusively to physical exhaustion and great discomfort.

In Finnish *teilata*, "to execute by the wheel," refers to forceful and violent critique or rejection of performance, ideas or innovations. The German verb *radebrechen* ("to break on the wheel") can refer to speaking incorrectly, for example with a strong foreign accent or with a great deal of foreign vocabulary. Similarly, the Norwegian *radbrekke* can be applied to art and language, and refers to use which is seen as despoiling tradition and courtesy, with connotations of willful ignorance or malice. In Swedish, *rådbråka* can be used in the same sense as the English idiom "rack one's brain" or, as in German, to mangle language.[426]

The word *roué*, meaning a debauched or lecherous person, is French, and its original meaning was "broken on the wheel." As execution by breaking on the wheel in France and some other countries was reserved for crimes of particular atrocity, *roué* came by a natural process to be understood to mean a man morally worse than a "gallows-bird," a criminal who only deserved hanging for common crimes. He was also a leader in wickedness, since the chief of a gang of brigands (for instance) would be broken on the wheel, while his obscure followers were merely hanged. Philip, Duke of Orléans, who was regent of France from 1715 to 1723, gave the term the sense of impious and callous debauchee, which it has borne since his time, by habitually applying it to the very bad male company who amused his privacy and his leisure. The *locus classicus* for the origin of this use of the epithet is in the Memoirs of Saint-Simon.

Another french expression is "rouer de coups", which means giving a severe beating to someone.

In English, the quotation "Who breaks a butterfly upon a wheel?" from Alexander Pope's "Epistle to Dr Arbuthnot" is occasionally seen, referring to putting great effort into achieving something minor or unimportant.

Execution of St. Catherine

Medieval hagiographies, such as the *Legenda sanctorum*, record that St. Catherine of Alexandria was executed on one of these devices for refusing to renounce her Christian belief, which thereafter became known as the *Catherine wheel*, also used as her iconographic attribute. It is said the wheel miraculously broke when she touched it; she was then beheaded. As an attribute it is usually shown broken in a small version beside her, or sometimes as a miniature she holds in her hand; the sword then used is also often shown.

Coats of arms with Catherine wheels

Persons

- Thomas de Brantingham
- Katherine Swynford

Breaking wheel

Figure 89: *Catherine wheel symbol*

Figure 90: *Saint Catherine of Alexandria with a wheel as her attribute*

Figure 91: *The college shield of St Catherine's College, Oxford, depicting four breaking wheels*

Figure 92: *Coat of Arms of Kremnica displaying the broken Catherine wheel*

Organizations

- St Catharine's College, Cambridge
- St Catherine's College, Oxford

Places

- Altena, Germany
- Goa, India, when it was in Portuguese possession
- Hjørring, Denmark, where Saint Catherine is the patron-saint of the Town.
- Kaarina, Finland, until 2009 and Piikkiö's union with Kaarina
- Kremnica, Slovakia
- Kuldīga, Latvia
- Molsheim, France
- Niedererbach, Germany
- Prien am Chiemsee, Germany, where Saint Catherine is the patron saint of the town
- Sinaai, Belgium
- Wachtebeke, Belgium

Gallery

Figure 93: *Triumph des Todes (detail), by Pieter Brueghel the Elder, ca. 1562–1563*

Figure 94: *Detail from #11, Les Grandes Misères de la guerre, Jacques Callot, 1633*

Figure 95: *Executions of Cossacks in Lebedin. From early 18th-century engraving.*

Breaking wheel

Figure 96: *The execution of Louis Dominique Cartouche, 1721*

Figure 97: *The death of Jean Calas, Toulouse, 1762*

Figure 98: *The execution of Matthias Klostermayr, 1771*

External links

 Wikimedia Commons has media related to *Breaking wheels*.

- Probertenencyclopaedia – illustrated[427]
- Miriam Greenblatt: *Rulers and their Times: Peter the Great and Tsarist Russia*, Benchmark Books <templatestyles src="Module:Citation/CS1/styles.css" />ISBN 0-7614-0914-9
- Lyrics in Modern Songs: www.thrashmetalbands.com[428]Wikipedia:Link rot

Premature burial

Premature burial, also known as **live burial**, **burial alive**, or **vivisepulture**, means to be buried while still alive.

Animals or humans may be buried alive accidentally on the mistaken assumption that they are dead, or intentionally as a form of torture, murder, or execution. It may also occur with consent of the victim as a part of a stunt, with the intention to escape.

Fear of being buried alive is reported to be among the most common phobias.[429]

Biology

Premature burial can lead to death through the following: asphyxiation, dehydration, starvation, or (in cold climates) hypothermia. A person trapped with fresh air to breathe can last a considerable time and burial has been used as a very cruel method of execution (as in cases of Vestal Virgins who violated the oath of celibacy), lasting sufficiently long for the victim to comprehend and imagine every stage of what is happening (being trapped in total darkness with very limited or no movement) and to experience great psychological and physical torment including extreme panic. The medical term for the fear of being buried alive is taphophobia.

Unintentional live burial

At least one (almost certainly apocryphal) report of accidental burial dates back to the fourteenth century. Upon the reopening of his tomb, the philosopher John Duns Scotus (1266–1308) was reportedly found outside his coffin with his hands torn and bloody after attempting to escape.[430] Alice Blunden of Basingstoke was said in a contemporaneous account to have been buried alive, not once but twice, in 1674.

Revivals of supposed "corpses" have been triggered by dropped coffins, grave robbers, embalming, and attempted dissections.[431] Folklorist Paul Barber has argued that the incidence of unintentional live burial has been overestimated, and that the normal, physical effects of decomposition are sometimes misinterpreted as signs that the person whose remains are being exhumed had revived in his or her coffin.[432] Nevertheless, patients have been documented as late as the 1890s as accidentally being sent to the morgue or trapped in a steel box after erroneously being declared dead.[433]

Figure 99: *Antoine Wiertz's painting of a man buried alive*

Newspapers have reported cases of exhumed corpses which appear to have been accidentally buried alive. On February 21, 1885, *The New York Times* gave a disturbing account of such a case. The victim was a man from Buncombe County whose name was given as "Jenkins". His body was found turned over onto its front inside the coffin, with much of his hair pulled out. Scratch marks were also visible on all sides of the coffin's interior. His family were reportedly "distressed beyond measure at the criminal carelessness" associated with the case. Another similar story was reported in *The Times* on January 18, 1886, the victim of this case being described simply as a "girl" named "Collins" from Woodstock, Ontario, Canada. Her body was described as being found with the knees tucked up under the body, and her burial shroud "torn into shreds".

In 2005, a body bag was delivered to the Matarese Funeral home in Ashland, Massachusetts with a live occupant. Funeral director John Matarese discovered this, called paramedics, and avoided live embalming or premature burial.

In 2014 in Peraia, Thessaloniki, in Macedonia, Greece, the police discovered that a 45-year-old woman was buried alive and died of asphyxia after being declared clinically dead by a private hospital; she was discovered just shortly after being buried by children playing near the cemetery who heard screams from inside the earth and afterwards her family was reported as considering suing the private hospital. In 2015 it was reported that in 2014 again in Peraia,

Premature Burial Is Impossible When This Vault is Used. A Person could Live for Hours in One of the Compartments, or, at Any Rate, Long Enough to Open the Cover by Turning the Handwheel

Figure 100: *A burial vault built c. 1890 with internal escape hatches to allow the victim of accidental premature burial to escape.*

Thessaloniki, in Macedonia, Greece, police investigation concluded that a 49-year-old woman was buried alive after being declared dead due to cancer; her family reported that they could hear her scream from inside the earth at the cemetery shortly after burial and the investigation revealed that she died of heart failure inside the coffin and found out that it was the medicines given to her by her doctors for her cancer that caused her to be declared clinically dead and buried alive.

Attempts to prevent live burial

Robert Robinson died in Manchester in 1791. A movable glass pane was inserted in his coffin, and the mausoleum had a door for purposes of inspection by a watchman, who was to see if he breathed on the glass. He instructed his relatives to visit his grave periodically to check that he was actually dead.[434]

Safety coffins were devised to prevent premature burial, although there is no evidence that any have ever been successfully used to save an accidentally buried person. On 5 December 1882, J. G. Krichbaum received U.S. Patent 268,693[435] for his "Device For Life In Buried Persons". It consisted of a movable periscope-like pipe which provided air and, when rotated or pushed by the person interred, indicated to passersby that someone was buried alive. The

Figure 101: *Chinese civilians being buried alive by Japanese soldiers during the Nanking Massacre*

patent text refers to "that class of devices for indicating life in buried persons," suggesting that such inventions were common at the time.

In 1890, a family designed and built a burial vault at the Wildwood Cemetery in Williamsport, Pennsylvania, with an internal hatch to allow the victim of accidental premature burial to escape. The vault had an air supply and was lined in felt to protect a panic-stricken victim from self-inflicted injury before escape. Bodies were to be removed from the casket before interment.[436]

The London Association for the Prevention of Premature Burial was co-founded in 1896 by William Tebb and Walter Hadwen.

Execution by burial

Tacitus, in his work *Germania*, records that German tribes practiced two forms of capital punishment; the first where the victim was hanged from a tree, and another where the victim was tied to a wicker frame, pushed face down into mud and buried. The first was used to make an example of traitors; the second was used for punishment of dishonourable or shameful vices, such as cowardice. According to Tacitus, the Ancient Germans thought that crime should be exposed, whereas infamy should be buried out of sight.[437]

Figure 102: *Jan Luyken's drawing of the Anabaptist nl:Anna Utenhoven being buried alive at Vilvoorde in 1597. In the drawing, her head is still above the ground and the priest is exhorting her to recant her faith, while the executioner stands ready to completely cover her up upon her refusal*

In ancient Rome, a Vestal Virgin convicted of violating her vows of celibacy was "buried alive" by being sealed in a cave with a small amount of bread and water, ostensibly so that the goddess Vesta could save her were she truly innocent,[438] essentially making it into a trial by ordeal. This practice was, strictly speaking, immurement (i.e., being walled up and left to die) rather than premature burial. According to Christian tradition, a number of saints were martyred this way, including Saint Castulus[439] and Saint Vitalis of Milan.[440]

In Denmark, in the Ribe city statute, which was promulgated in 1269, a female thief was to be buried alive, and in the law by Queen Margaret I, adulterous women were to be punished with premature burial, men with beheading.[441]

Within the Holy Roman Empire a variety of offenses including rape, infanticide and theft could be punished with live burial. For example, the Schwabenspiegel, a law code from the 13th century, specified that the rape of a virgin should be punished by live burial (whereas the rapist of a non-virgin was to be beheaded).[442] Female murderers of their own employers also risked being buried alive. In Augsburg 1505, for example, a 12-year-old boy and a 13-year-old girl were found guilty of killing their master, in conspiracy with the cook.

The boy was beheaded, and the girl and the cook were buried alive beneath the gallows.[443] The jurist Eduard Henke observed that in the Middle Ages, live burial of women guilty of infanticide was a "very frequent" punishment in city statutes and *Landrechten*. For example, he notes those in Hesse, Bohemia, Tyrol.[444] The "Berlinisches Stadtbuch" records that between 1412 and 1447, 10 women were buried alive there,[445] and as late as in 1583, the archbishop of Bremen promulgated (alongside the somewhat milder 1532 Constitutio Criminalis Carolina punishment of drowning) live burial as an alternate execution method for punishing mothers found guilty of infanticide.[446]

As noted by Elias Pufendorf, a woman buried alive would afterwards be impaled through the heart. This combined punishment of live burial and impalement was practiced in Nuremberg until 1508 also for women found guilty of theft, but the city council decided in 1515 that the punishment was too cruel, and opted for drowning instead.[447] Impalement was, however, not always mentioned together with live burial. Eduard Osenbrüggen relates how the live burial of a woman convicted of infanticide could be pronounced in a court verdict. For example, in a 1570 case in Ensisheim: <templatestyles src="Template:Quote/styles.css"/>

> *The verdict commanded the executioner to place the perpetrator in the grave alive, "and place two layers of thorns, the one beneath, the other above her. Prior to that he should place a bowl over her face, in which he had made a hole, and to give her through that*[448] *a reed/tube into the mouth, then jump three times upon her, and lastly cover her with earth"*[449]

In this particular case, however, some noblewomen made an appeal for mercy, and the convicted woman was drowned instead.[450]

Dieter Furcht speculates that the impalement was not so much to be regarded as an execution method, but as a way to prevent the condemned from becoming an avenging, undead Wiedergänger.[451] In medieval Italy, unrepentant murderers were buried alive, head down, feet in the air, a practice referred to in passing in Canto XIX of Dante's *Inferno*.[452]

In the Faroe Islands, a powerful 14th-century woman landowner in the village of Húsavík was said to have buried two servants alive.

In the 16th-century Habsburg Netherlands, where the Catholic authorities made a prolonged effort to stamp out the Protestant churches, live burial was commonly used as the punishment of women found guilty of heresy. The last to be so executed was Anna Utenhoven, an Anabaptist buried alive at Vilvoorde in 1597. Reportedly, when her head was still above the ground she was given a last chance to recant her faith, and upon her refusal she was completely covered up and suffocated. The case aroused a great deal of protest in the rebellious north provinces, and foiled the peace feelers which King Philip III was at the time extending to the Dutch. Thereafter the Habsburg authorities avoided further such cases, punishing heresy with fines and deportations rather than death.Wikipedia:Citation needed

Into the seventeenth century in feudal Russia, live burial as execution method was known as "the pit" and used against women who were condemned for killing their husbands. In 1689, the punishment of live burial was changed to beheading.[453] Live burial of Jews in such countries as Ukraine is reported; for example some instances occurred during the Chmielnicki Massacre (1648–1649) in Ukraine.[454]

Among some contemporary indigenous people of Brazil with no or limited contact with the outside world, children with disabilities or other undesirable traits are still customarily buried alive[455]

Modern examples

There have been a number of cases of people pronounced incorrectly dead and thereafter buried alive.

Natural disasters

Natural disasters have also largely buried people alive, as well as collapsing mines.

Wars

It has been used during wars and by mafia organizations.

Serbian officials are documented to have buried alive Bulgarian civilians from Pehčevo (now in the Republic of Macedonia) during the Balkan Wars.[456] During World War II, Japanese soldiers were documented to have buried Chinese civilians alive, notably during the Nanking Massacre.[457] This method of execution was also used by German leaders against Jews in Ukraine and Belarus during World War II.[458,459,460,461,462]

During the Vietnam War, burials alive were documented at the Massacre at Huế in 1968.

During the Gulf War, Iraqi soldiers were knowingly buried alive by American tanks of the First Infantry Division shoveling earth into their trenches. Estimates for the number of soldiers killed this way vary: one source puts it at "between 80 and 250", while Col. Anthony Moreno suggested it may have been thousands.

In 2014, ISIS buried Yazidi women and children alive in an attempt to annihilate the Yazidi tribe.

Figure 103: *16th-century Portuguese illustration from the Códice Casanatense, depicting a Hindu ritual, in which a widow is buried alive with her dead husband*

Execution

There are also accounts of the Khmer Rouge using premature burials as a form of execution in the Killing Fields.[463]

During Mao Zedong's regime, there are some accounts that premature burials were used in executions.[464]

Voluntary burial

On rare occasions, people have willingly arranged to be buried alive, reportedly as a demonstration of their controversial ability to survive such an event. In one story taking place around 1840, Sadhu Haridas, an Indian fakir, is said to have been buried in the presence of a British military officer and under the supervision of the local maharajah, by being placed in a sealed bag in a wooden box in a vault. The vault was then interred, earth was flattened over the site and crops were sown over the place for a very long time. The whole location was guarded day and night to prevent fraud and the site was dug up twice in a ten-month period to verify the burial, before the fakir was finally dug out and slowly revived in the presence of another officer. The fakir said that his only fear during his "wonderful sleep" was to be eaten by underground worms.

However, according to current medical science, it is not possible for a human to survive for a period of ten months without food, water, and air.[465] According to other sources the entire burial was 40 days long. The Indian government has since made the act of voluntary premature burial illegal, because of the unintended deaths of individuals attempting to recreate this feat.

In 2010 a Russian man died after being buried alive to try to overcome his fear of death but he was crushed to death by the earth on top of him.[466] The following year, another Russian died after being buried overnight in a makeshift coffin "for good luck".

Buried Alive is a controversial art and lecture performance series by art-tech group monochrom. Participants have the opportunity to be buried alive in a coffin for fifteen to twenty minutes. As a framework program monochrom offers lectures about the history of the science of determining death and the medical cultural history of premature burial.

Myths and legends

St. Oran was a druid living on the Island of Iona in Scotland's Inner Hebrides. He became a follower of St. Columba, who brought Christianity to Iona from Ireland in 563 AD. When St. Columba had repeated problems building the original Iona Abbey, citing interference from the Devil, St. Oran offered himself as a human sacrifice and was buried alive. He was later dug up and found to be still alive, but he uttered such words describing what of the afterlife he had seen and how it involved no heaven or hell, that he was ordered to be covered up again. The building of the abbey went ahead, untroubled, and St. Oran's chapel marks the spot where the saint was buried.[467]

In the fourteenth through nineteenth centuries, a popular tale about premature burial in European folklore was the "Lady with the Ring". In the story, a woman who was prematurely buried awakens to frighten a grave robber who is attempting to cut a ring off her finger.[468]

The TV show *MythBusters* tested the myth to see if someone could survive being buried alive for two hours before being rescued. Host Jamie Hyneman attempted the feat, but when his steel coffin began to bend under the weight of the earth used to cover it, the experiment was aborted.[469]

Bibliography

Books

- Alighieri, Dante; O'Donnell, E. (1852). *Translation of the Divina Commedia*[470]. London: Thomas Richardson&Son.
- Barber, Paul (1988). *Vampires, Burial and Death: Folklore and Reality*. Yale University Press. ISBN 978-0-300-04859-9.
- Berner, Albert F. (1866). *Lehrbuch des deutschen Strafrechtes*[471]. Leipzig: Bernhard Tauchnitz.
- Bondeson, Jan (2001). *Buried Alive: The Terrifying History of Our Most Primal Fear*. W.W. Norton&Company. ISBN 0-393-04906-X.
- Bondeson, Jan (2002). *Buried Alive: The Terrifying History of Our Most Primal Fear*. W.W. Norton&Company. ISBN 978-0-393-32222-4.
- Chang, Iris (1997). *The Rape of Nanking: The Forgotten Holocaust of World War II*. New York: Basic Books. ISBN 0-465-06835-9.
- Encyclopædia Britannica (1823). *Encyclopædia Britannica: Or, A Dictionary of Arts, Sciences, and Miscellaneous Literature, Enlarged and Improved, Volume 5*[472]. London: Archibald Constable.
- Feucht, Dieter (1967). *Grube und Pfahl: Ein Beitrag zur Geschichte der deutschen Hinrichtungsbräuche*. Tübingen: J.C.B. Mohr. OCLC 462909742[473].
- Fidicin, E. (1837). *Berlinisches Stadtbuch*[474]. Berlin: A. W. Hayn.
- Henke, Hermann W. E. (1809). *Grundriss einer Geschichte des deutschen peinlichen Rechts und der peinlichen Rechtwissenschaft, Volume 2*[475]. Sulzbach: J.E. Seidel.

- Muravyeva, Marianna G.; Rosslyn, Wendy (ed.); Tosi, Alessandra (ed.) (2012). *"Between Law and Morality" in Women in Nineteenth-Century Russia: Lives and Culture*[476]. Cambridge: Open Book Publishers. pp. 209–238. ISBN 978-1-906924-65-2.<templatestyles src="Module:Citation/CS1/styles.css"></templatestyles>
- Osenbrüggen, Eduard (1868). *Studien zur deutschen und schweizerischen Rechtsgeschichte*[477]. Schaffhausen: F. Hurter.<templatestyles src="Module:Citation/CS1/styles.css"></templatestyles>
- von Pufendorf, Friedrich E. (1757). *Observationes iuris universi: Quibus Praecipue Res Judicatae Summi Tribunalis Regii Et Electoralis Continentur. Adjecta Est Appendix Variorum Statutorvm Et Jurium, Volume 1*[478]. Lüneburg: Gsellius.<templatestyles src="Module:Citation/CS1/styles.css"></templatestyles>
- Stemann, Christian L.E. (1871). *Den danske retshistorie indtil Chistian v.'s lov*[479]. Copenhagen: Gyldendal (F. Hegel).<templatestyles src="Module:Citation/CS1/styles.css"></templatestyles>
- Tacitus, Lucius Cornelius; Church, Alfred J. (tr.); Brodribb, William J. (tr.) (1868). *The Agricola and Germany of Tacitus*[480]. London: MacMillan&Co.<templatestyles src="Module:Citation/CS1/styles.css"></templatestyles>
- Siebenkees, Johann C.; Kiefhaber, Johann C. S. (1792). *Materialien zur Nürnbergischen Geschichte, Volume 2*[481]. Nuremberg: Schneider.<templatestyles src="Module:Citation/CS1/styles.css"></templatestyles>
- Weinryb, Bernard D. (1973). *The Jews of Poland: A Social and Economic History of the Jewish Community in Poland from 1100 to 1800*. Jewish Publication Society. ISBN 978-0-8276-0016-4.<templatestyles src="Module:Citation/CS1/styles.css"></templatestyles>
- Welser, Marcus; Werlich, Engelbertus; Gasser, Achilles P. (1595). *Chronica der Weitberuempten... Statt Augspurg*[482]. Frankfurt am Main: Hartmann, Wolffgangus.<templatestyles src="Module:Citation/CS1/styles.css"></templatestyles>

Journals, Newspapers, Periodicals etc.

- BBC News (2 June 2011). "Russian who buried himself alive dies by mistake"[483]. *BBC News*. BBC.<templatestyles src="Module:Citation/CS1/styles.css"></templatestyles>
- "Pakistani police arrest man accused of burying alive his newborn daughter"[484]. *Calgary Herald*. Associated Press. 14 July 2012. Retrieved 16 July 2012.<templatestyles src="Module:Citation/CS1/styles.css"></templatestyles>

- "Newborn girl 'buried alive by her father in Pakistan because she was deformed'"[485]. *Daily Mail*. 15 July 2012. Retrieved 16 July 2012.
- MacLeod Banks, M. (1931). "A Hebridean Version of Colum Cille and St. Oran". *Folklore*. **42** (1): 55–60. JSTOR 1256410[486].
- "A Man Buried Alive"[487] (PDF). *The New York Times*. The New York Times. 20 February 1885.
- "Buried Alive"[488] (PDF). *The New York Times*. The New York Times. 19 January 1886.
- Windsor, Henry H. (July 1921). ""Odd Family Vault Prevents Premature Burial" in Popular Mechanics"[489]. **36**. Popular Mechanics Co.
- Dibble, Christopher. "The Dead Ringer: Medicine, Poe, and the fear of premature burial"[490]. *Medicinae*.

Web resources

- Arem, Jacob; Bock, Fran (ed.) (August 2003). "My Family Trip to Belarus"[491]. jewishgen.org. Retrieved 2013-07-29.
- Администрация, опубликовано (2008). "ЙОРЦАЙТ"[492]. holocaust-museum.org. Retrieved 2013-07-29.
- Catholic Encyclopedia. "St. Vitalis"[493]. New Advent. Retrieved 2013-07-29.
- Cheong, Shahan (2011). "The Killing Fields – Pol Pot and the Khmer Rouge"[494]. scheong.wordpress.com. Retrieved 2013-07-29.
- Medicine Net.com. "Definition of Taphephobia"[495]. Retrieved 2013-07-29.
- Mikkelson, Barbara (2006). "Just Dying To Get Out"[496]. Snopes.com. Retrieved 2013-07-29.
- Mysterious People. "Mind Power – Strange Cases of Suspended Animation"[497]. mysteriouspeople.com. Retrieved 2013-07-29.

- Ökumenisches Heiligenlexicon. "Castulus"[498]. heiligenlexicon.de. Retrieved 2013-07-29.<templatestyles src="Module:Citation/CS1/styles.css"></templatestyles>
- Plutarch; Perrin, Bernadotte (1914). "The Parallel Lives by Plutarch"[499]. LacusCurtius (Loeb Classical Library). Retrieved 2013-07-29.<templatestyles src="Module:Citation/CS1/styles.css"></templatestyles>
- Rosen, Rachel (2005). "Virtual Jewish History Tour: Ukraine"[500]. jewishvirtuallibrary.org. Retrieved 2013-07-29.<templatestyles src="Module:Citation/CS1/styles.css"></templatestyles>
- Sciolino, Elaine (October 6, 2007). "A Priest Methodically Reveals Ukrainian Jews' Fate"[501]. The New York Times. Retrieved 2013-07-29.<templatestyles src="Module:Citation/CS1/styles.css"></templatestyles>
- World Holocaust Forum. "Uman. Memoirs of Manie Feinholtz"[502]. World Holocaust Forum. Retrieved 2013-07-29.<templatestyles src="Module:Citation/CS1/styles.css"></templatestyles>
- Yad Vashem. "Killing Sites: Stalino Region 1941–1942"[503]. yad-vashem.org. Retrieved 2013-07-29.<templatestyles src="Module:Citation/CS1/styles.css"></templatestyles>

External links

 Wikimedia Commons has media related to *Premature burial*.

- "Nightmares from the Mind of Poe"[504] full text, summary and film information.
- Gracey, James (August 2004). "Your Place And Mine – The Living Dead in Lurgan"[505]. *BBC Online*.<templatestyles src="Module:Citation/CS1/styles.css"></templatestyles>
- William Tebb. *Premature Burial and How it may be Prevented* at Project Gutenberg

Death by burning

Death by burning is a type of execution in which the condemned is bound to a large wooden stake (this is usually called **burning at the stake**, or in some cases, *auto-da-fé*). Deliberately causing death through the effects of combustion, or effects of exposure to extreme heat, has a long history as a form of capital punishment. Many societies have employed it as an execution method for activities considered criminal such as treason, rebellious actions by slaves, heresy, witchcraft, arson (in Japan) and sexual transgressions, such as incest or homosexuality.

For burnings at the stake, if the fire was large (for instance, when a number of prisoners were executed at the same time), death often came from carbon monoxide poisoning before flames actually caused lethal harm to the body. If the fire was small, however, the condemned would burn for some time until death from hypovolemia (the loss of blood and/or fluids, since extensive burns often require large amounts of intravenous fluid, because the subsequent inflammatory response causes significant capillary fluid leakage and oedema), heatstroke and/or simply the thermal decomposition of vital body parts.[506]

Other forms of death resulting from exposure to extreme heat are known. For example, pouring substances such as molten metal onto a person (or down their throat or into their ears), as well as enclosing persons within, or attaching them to, metal contraptions subsequently heated. Immersion in a heated liquid as a form of execution is considered distinct from death by burning, and classified as death by boiling.

Historical usage

Antiquity

Ancient Near East

Old Babylonia

The 18th century BC law code promulgated by Babylonian king Hammurabi specifies several crimes in which death by burning was thought appropriate. Looters of houses on fire could be cast into the flames, and priestesses who abandoned cloisters and began frequenting inns and taverns could also be punished by being burnt alive. Furthermore, a man who began committing incest with his mother after the death of his father could be ordered by courts to be burned alive.[507]

Figure 104: *The "baptism by fire" of Old Believer leader Avvakum in 1682*

Ancient Egypt

In Ancient Egypt, several incidents of burning alive perceived rebels are attested. For example, Senusret I (r. 1971–1926 BC) is said to have rounded up the rebels in campaign, and burnt them as human torches. Under the civil war flaring under Takelot II more than a thousand years later, the Crown Prince Osorkon showed no mercy, and burned several rebels alive.[508] On the statute books, at least, women committing adultery might be burned to death. Jon Manchip White, however, did not think capital judicial punishments were often carried out, pointing to the fact that the pharaoh had to personally ratify each verdict.[509] Furthermore, the Greek historian Diodorus Siculus (fl. 1st century BC) asserts that the Egyptians had a particularly terrible punishment for children who murdered their parents: With sharpened reeds, bits of flesh the size of a finger were cut from the criminal's body. Then he was placed on a bed of thorns and burnt alive.[510]

Assyria

In the Middle Assyrian period, paragraph 40 in a preserved law text concerns the obligatory unveiled face for the professional prostitute, and the concomitant punishment if she violated that by veiling herself (the way wives were to dress in public): <templatestyles src="Template:Quote/styles.css"/>

> *A prostitute shall not be veiled. Whoever sees a veiled prostitute shall seize her ... and bring her to the palace entrance. ... they shall pour hot pitch over her head.*[511]

For the Neo-Assyrians, mass executions seem to have been not only designed to instill terror and to enforce obedience, but also as proof of their might. For example, Neo-Assyrian King Asuhurnasirpal II (r. 883–859 BC) was evidently proud enough of his bloody work that he committed it to monument and eternal memory as follows:[512]

> *I cut off their hands, I burned them with fire, a pile of the living men and of heads over against the city gate I set up, men I impaled on stakes, the city I destroyed and devastated, I turned it into mounds and ruin heaps, the young men and the maidens in the fire I burned.*

Hebraic tradition

In Genesis 38, Judah orders Tamar—the widow of his son, living in her father's household—to be burned when she is believed to have become pregnant by an extramarital sexual relation. Tamar saves herself by proving that Judah is himself the father of her child. In the Book of Jubilees, the same story is basically told, with some intriguing differences, according to Caryn A. Reeder. In Genesis, Judah is exercising his patriarchal power at a distance, whereas he and the relatives seem more actively involved in Tamar's impending execution.[513]

In Hebraic law, death by burning was prescribed for ten forms of sexual crimes: The imputed crime of Tamar, namely that a married daughter of a priest commits adultery, and nine versions of relationships considered as incestuous, such as having sex with one's own daughter, or granddaughter, but also, for example, to have sex with one's mother-in-law or with one's wife's daughter.[514]

In the Mishnah, the following manner of burning the criminal is described:

> *The obligatory procedure for execution by burning: They immersed him in dung up to his knees, rolled a rough cloth into a soft one and wound it about his neck. One pulled it one way, one the other until he opened his mouth. Thereupon one ignites the (lead) wick and throws it in his mouth, and it descends to his bowels and sears his bowels.*

That is, the person dies from being fed molten lead.[515] The Mishnah is, however, a fairly late collections of laws, from about the 3rd century AD, and scholars believe it *replaced* the actual punishment of burning in the old biblical texts.[516]

Ancient Rome

In the 6th century AD collection of the sayings and rulings of the pre-eminent jurists from earlier ages, the Digest, a number of crimes are regarded as punishable by death by burning. The 3rd century jurist Ulpian, for example, says that enemies of the state, and deserters to the enemy are to be burned alive. His rough contemporary, the juristical writer Callistratus mentions that arsonists are typically burnt, as well as slaves who have conspired against the well-being of their masters (this last also, on occasion, being meted out to free persons of "low rank").[517] The punishment of burning alive arsonists (and traitors) seems to have been particularly ancient; it was included in the Twelve Tables, a mid-5th BC law code, that is, about 700 years prior to the times of Ulpian and Callistratus.[518] According to ancient reports, Roman authorities executed many of the early Christian martyrs by burning. An example of this is the earliest chronicle of a martyrdom, that of Polycarp.[519] Sometimes this was by means of the *tunica molesta*,[520] a flammable tunic:[521] <templatestyles src="Template:Quote/styles.css"/>

> ... the Christian, stripped naked, was forced to put on a garment called the tunica molesta, made of papyrus, smeared on both sides with wax, and was then fastened to a high pole, from the top of which they continued to pour down burning pitch and lard, a spike fastened under the chin preventing the excruciated victim from turning the head to either side, so as to escape the liquid fire, until the whole body, and every part of it, was literally clad and cased in flame.

In AD 326, Constantine the Great promulgated a law that increased the penalties for parentally non-sanctioned "abduction" of their girls, and concomitant sexual intercourse/rape. The man would be burnt alive without the possibility of appeal, and the girl would receive the same treatment if she had participated willingly. Nurses who had corrupted their female wards and led them to sexual encounters would have molten lead poured down their throats.[522] In the same year, Constantine also passed a law that said if a woman married her own slave, both would be subjected to capital punishment, the slave by burning.[523] In AD 390, Emperor Theodosius issued an edict against male prostitutes and brothels offering such services; those found guilty should be burned alive.[524]

Ritual child sacrifice in Carthage

Beginning in the early 3rd century BC, Greek and Roman writers have commented on the purported institutionalized child sacrifice the North African Carthaginians are said to have performed in honour of the gods Baal Hammon and Tanit. The earliest writer, Cleitarchus is among the most explicit. He says live infants were placed in the arms of a bronze statue, the statue's hands over a brazier, so that the infant slowly rolled into the fire. As it did

Figure 105: *Tanit with a lion's head*

so, the limbs of the infant contracted and the face was distorted into a sort of laughing grimace, hence called "the act of laughing". Other, later authors such as Diodorus Siculus and Plutarch says the throats of the infants were generally cut, before they were placed in the statue's embrace[525] In the vicinity of ancient Carthage, large scale grave yards containing the incinerated remains of infants, typically up to the age of 3, have been found; such graves are called "tophets". However, some scholars have argued that these findings are not evidence of *systematic* child sacrifice, and that estimated figures of ancient natural infant mortality (with cremation afterwards and reverent separate burial) might be the real historical basis behind the hostile reporting from non-Carthaginians. A late charge of the imputed sacrifice is found by the North African bishop Tertullian, who says that child sacrifices were still carried out, in secret, in the countryside at his time, 3rd century AD.[526]

Celtic traditions

According to Julius Caesar, the ancient Celts practiced the burning alive of humans in a number of settings. For example, in Book 6, chapter 16, he writes of the Druidic sacrifice of criminals within huge wicker frames shaped as men:
<templatestyles src="Template:Quote/styles.css"/>

> *Others have figures of vast size, the limbs of which formed of osiers they fill with living men, which being set on fire, the men perish enveloped in the*

flames. They consider that the oblation of such as have been taken in theft, or in robbery, or any other offence, is more acceptable to the immortal gods; but when a supply of that class is wanting, they have recourse to the oblation of even the innocent.

Slightly later, in Book 6, chapter 19, Caesar also says the Celts perform, on the occasion of death of great men, the funeral sacrifice on the pyre of living slaves and dependants ascertained to have been "beloved by them". Earlier on, in Book 1, chapter 4, he relates of the conspiracy of the nobleman Orgetorix, charged by the Celts for having planned a *coup d'état*, for which the customary penalty would be burning to death. It is said Orgetorix committed suicide to avoid that fate.[527]

Human sacrifice around the Eastern Baltic

Throughout the 12th–14th centuries, a number of non-Christian peoples living around the Eastern Baltic Sea, such as Old Prussians and Lithuanians were charged by Christian writers with performing human sacrifice. For example, Pope Gregory IX issued a papal bull denouncing an alleged practice among the Prussians, that girls were dressed in fresh flowers and wreaths and were then burned alive as offerings to evil spirits.[528]

Christian states

Eastern Roman Empire

Under 6th-century emperor Justinian I, the death penalty had been decreed for impenitent Manicheans, but a specific punishment was not made explicit. By the 7th century, however, those found guilty of "dualist heresy" could risk being burned at the stake.[529] Those found guilty of performing magical rites, and corrupting sacred objects in the process, might face death by burning, as evidenced in a 7th-century case.[530] In the 10th century AD, the Byzantines instituted death by burning for parricides, i.e. those who had killed their own relatives, replacing the older punishment of *poena cullei*, the stuffing of the convict in a leather sack along with a rooster, a viper, a dog and a monkey, and then throwing the sack into the sea.[531]

Medieval Inquisition and the burning of heretics

Civil authorities burned persons judged to be heretics under the medieval Inquisition. Burning heretics had become customary practice in the latter half of the twelfth century in continental Europe, and death by burning became *statutory* punishment from the early 13th century. Death by burning for heretics was made positive law by Pedro II of Aragon in 1197. In 1224, Frederick II, Holy Roman Emperor, made burning a legal alternative, and in 1238, it

Figure 106: *The burning of the Cathar heretics*

Figure 107: *Burning of the Knights Templar, 1314*

Figure 108: *Jews burned to death in the Strasbourg massacre*

became the principal punishment in the Empire. In Sicily, the punishment was made law in 1231, whereas in France, Louis IX made it binding law in 1270.[532]

As England in the 15th century grew weary of the teachings of John Wycliffe and the Lollards, kings, priests, and parliaments reacted with fire. In 1401, Parliament passed the De heretico comburendo act, which can be loosely translated as "Regarding the burning of heretics." Lollard persecution would continue for over a hundred years in England. The Fire and Faggot Parliament met in May 1414 at Grey Friars Priory in Leicester to lay out the notorious Suppression of Heresy Act 1414, enabling the burning of heretics by making the crime enforceable by the Justices of the peace. John Oldcastle, a prominent Lollard leader, was not saved from the gallows by his old friend King Henry V. Oldcastle was hanged and his gallows burned in 1417. Jan Hus was burned at the stake after being accused at the Roman Catholic Council of Constance (1414–18) of heresy. The ecumenical council also decreed that the remains of John Wycliffe, dead for 30 years, should be exhumed and burned. (This posthumous execution was carried out in 1428.)

Burnings of Jews

Several incidents are recorded of massacres on Jews from the 12th through 16th centuries in which they were burned alive, often on account of the blood libel. In 1171 in Blois, for example, 51 Jews were burned alive (the entire adult community). In 1191, King Philip Augustus ordered around 100 Jews burnt alive.[533] That Jews purportedly performed host desecration also led to mass burnings; In 1243 in Beelitz, the entire Jewish community was burnt alive, and in 1510 in Berlin, some 26 Jews were burnt alive for the same crime.[534] During the "Black Death" in the mid-14th century a spate of large-scale massacres occurred. One libel was that the Jews had poisoned the wells. In 1349, as panic grew along with the increasing death toll from the plague, general massacres, but also specifically mass burnings, began to occur. Six hundred (600) Jews were burnt alive in Basel alone. A large mass burning occurred in Strasbourg, where several hundred Jews were burnt alive in what became known as the Strasbourg massacre.[535]

A Jewish male, Johannes Pfefferkorn, met a particularly gruesome death in 1514 in Halle. He had been charged with a number of crimes, such as having impersonated a priest for twenty years, performed host desecration, stolen Christian children to be tortured and killed by other Jews, poisoning 13 people and poisoning wells. He was lashed to a pillar in such a way that he could run about it. Then, a ring of glowing coal was made around him, a fiery ring that was gradually pushed ever closer to him, until he was roasted to death.[536]

The Lepers' Plot of 1321

Not only Jews could be victims of mass hysteria on charges like that of poisoning wells. This particular charge, well-poisoning, was the basis for a large scale hunt of lepers in 1321 France. In the spring of 1321, in Périgueux, people became convinced that the local lepers had poisoned the wells, causing ill-health among the normal populace. The lepers were rounded up and burned alive. The action against the lepers didn't stay local, though, but had repercussions throughout France, not least because King Philip V issued an order to arrest all lepers, those found guilty to be burnt alive. Jews became tangentially included as well; at Chinon alone, 160 Jews were burnt alive.[537] All in all, around 5000 lepers and Jews are recorded in one tradition to have been killed during the Lepers' Plot hysteria.[538]

The charge of the lepers' plot was not wholly confined to France; existent records from England show that on Jersey the same year, at least one family of lepers were burnt alive for having poisoned others.[539]

Spanish Inquisition against Moriscos and Marranos

The Spanish Inquisition was established in 1478, with the aim of preserving Catholic orthodoxy; some of its principal targets were "Marranos", formally converted Jews thought to have relapsed into Judaism, or the Moriscos, formally converted Muslims thought to have relapsed into Islam. The public executions of the Spanish Inquisition were called autos-da-fé; convicts were "released" (handed over) to secular authorities in order to be burnt.

Death by burning 209

Figure 109: *The burning of a 16th-century Dutch Anabaptist, Anneken Hendriks, who was charged with heresy.*

Estimates of how many were executed on behest of the Spanish Inquisition have been offered from early on; historian Hernando del Pulgar (1436–c. 1492) estimated that 2000 people were burned at the stake between 1478 and 1490.[540] Estimates range from 30,000 to 50,000 burnt at the stake (alive or not) at the behest of the Spanish Inquisition during its 300 years of activity have previously been given and are still to be found in popular books.[541]

In February 1481, in what is said to be the first auto-da-fé, six Marranos were burnt alive in Seville. In November 1481, 298 Marranos were burnt publicly at the same place, their property confiscated by the Church.[542] Not all Maranos executed by being burnt at the stake seem to have been burnt alive. If the Jew "confessed his heresy", the Church would show mercy, and he would be strangled prior to the burning. Autos-da-fé against Maranos extended beyond the Spanish heartland. In Sicily, in 1511–15, 79 were burnt at the stake, while from 1511 to 1560, 441 Maranos were condemned to be burned alive.[543] In Spanish American colonies, autos-da-fé were held as well. For example, in 1664, a man and his wife were burned alive in Río de la Plata, and in 1699, a Jew was burnt alive in Mexico City.[544]

In 1535, five Moriscos were burned at the stake on Majorca, the images of a further four were also burnt in effigy, since the actual individuals had managed to flee. During the 1540s, some 232 Moriscos were paraded in autos-da-fé in Zaragoza; five of those were burnt at the stake.[545] The claim that out of 917 Moriscos appearing in autos of the Inquisition in Granada between 1550–95, just 20 were executed[546] seems at odds with the English government's state papers which claim that, while at war with Spain, they received a report from Seville of 17 June 1593 that over 70 of the richest men of Granada were burnt.[547] As late as 1728 as many as 45 Moriscos were recorded burned for heresy.[548] In the May 1691 "bonfire of the Jews", Rafael Valls, Rafael Benito Terongi and Catalina Terongi were burned alive.[549,550]

Portuguese Inquisition at Goa

In 1560, the Portuguese Inquisition opened offices in the Indian colony Goa, known as Goa Inquisition. Its aim was to protect Catholic orthodoxy among new converts to Christianity, and retain hold on the old, particularly against "Judaizing" deviancy. From the 17th century, Europeans were shocked at the tales of how brutal and extensive the activities of the Inquisition were.Wikipedia:Citation needed What modern scholars have established, is that some 4046 individuals in the time 1560–1773 received some sort of punishment from the Portuguese Inquisition, whereof 121 persons were condemned to be burned alive, of those 57 who actually suffered that fate, while the rest escaped it, and were burnt in effigy, instead.[551] For the Portuguese Inquisition in total, not just at Goa, modern estimates of persons actually executed on its behest is about 1200, whether burnt alive or not.[552]

Legislation concerning "crimes against nature"

From the 12th to the 18th centuries, various European authorities legislated (and held judicial proceedings) against sexual crimes such as sodomy or bestiality; often, the prescribed punishment was that of death by burning. Many scholars think that the first time death by burning appeared within explicit codes of law for the crime of sodomy was at the ecclesiastical 1120 Council of Nablus in the crusader Kingdom of Jerusalem. Here, if public repentance were done, the death penalty might be avoided.[553] In Spain, the earliest records for executions for the crime of sodomy are from the 13th–14th centuries, and it is noted there that the preferred mode of execution was death by burning. The Partidas of King Alfonso "El Sabio" condemned sodomites to be castrated and hung upside down to die from the bleeding, following the old testament phrase "their blood shall be upon them".[554] At Geneva, the first recorded burning of sodomites occurred in 1555, and up to 1678, some two dozen met the same fate. In Venice, the first burning took place in 1492, and a monk was burnt as late as 1771.[555] The last case in France where two men were condemned by court to be burned alive for engaging in consensual homosexual sex was in 1750 (although, it seems, they were actually strangled prior to being burned).

Death by burning

Figure 110: *Burning of two homosexuals at the stake outside Zürich, 1482 (Spiezer Schilling)*

The last case in France where a man was condemned to be burned for a murderous rape of a boy occurred in 1784.[556]

Crackdowns and the public burning of a couple of homosexuals might lead to local panic, and persons thus inclined fleeing from the place. The traveller William Lithgow witnessed such a dynamic when he visited Malta in 1616:

> *The fifth day of my staying here, I saw a Spanish soldier and a Maltezen boy burnt in ashes, for the public profession of sodomy; and long before night, there were above an hundred bardassoes, whorish boys, that fled away to Sicily in a galliot, for fear of fire; but never one bugeron stirred, being few or none there free of it.*[557]

The actual punishment meted out to, for example, pederasts could differ according to status. While both in 1532 and 1409 Augsburg two men were burned alive for their offenses, a rather different procedure was meted out to four *clerics* in the 1409 case guilty of the same offence: Instead of being burnt alive, they were locked into a wooden casket that was hung up in the Perlachturm and they starved to death in that manner.[558]

Figure 111: *Perlachturm with St. Peter by Perlach*

The 1532 penal code of Charles V

In 1532, Holy Roman Emperor Charles V promulgated his penal code Constitutio Criminalis Carolina. A number of crimes were punishable with death by burning, such as coin forgery, arson, and sexual acts "contrary to nature".[559] Also, those guilty of aggravated theft of sacred objects from a church could be condemned to be burnt alive.[560] Only those found guilty of *malevolent* witchcraft[561] could be punished by death by fire.[562]

The last burnings from 1804 and 1813

According to the jurist Eduard Osenbrüggen, the last case he knew of where a person had been judicially burned alive on account of arson in Germany happened in 1804, in Hötzelsroda, close by Eisenach.[563] The manner in which Johannes Thomas[564] was executed on 13 July that year is described as follows: Some feet above the actual pyre, attached to a stake, a wooden chamber had been constructed, into which the delinquent was placed. Pipes or chimneys, filled with sulphuric material led up to the chamber, and that was first lit, so that Thomas died from inhaling the sulphuric smoke, rather than being strictly burnt alive, before his body was consumed by the general fire. Some 20,000 people had gathered to watch Thomas' execution.[565]

Figure 112: *Burning of three witches in Baden (1585), painted by Johann Jakob Wick*

Although Thomas is regarded as the last to have been actually executed by means of fire (in this case, through suffocation), the couple Johann Christoph Peter Horst and his lover Friederike Louise Christiane Delitz, who had made a career of robberies in the confusion made by their acts of arson, were condemned to be burnt alive in Berlin 28 May 1813. They were, however, according to Gustav Radbruch, secretly strangled just prior to being burnt, namely when their arms and legs were tied fast to the stake.[566]

Although these two cases are the last where execution by burning might be said to have been *carried out* in some degree, Eduard Osenbrüggen mentions that *verdicts* to be burned alive were given in several cases in different German states afterwards, such as in cases from 1814, 1821, 1823, 1829 and finally in a case from 1835.[567]

Witch-hunts

Burning was used by Christians during the witch-hunts of Europe. The penal code known as the Constitutio Criminalis Carolina (1532) decreed that sorcery throughout the Holy Roman Empire should be treated as a criminal offence, and if it purported to inflict injury upon any person the witch was to be burnt at the stake. In 1572, Augustus, Elector of Saxony imposed the penalty of burning for witchcraft of every kind, including simple fortunetelling.[568] From the

Figure 113: *Jan Hus burnt at the stake*

latter half of the 18th century, the number of "nine million witches burned in Europe" has been bandied about in popular accounts and media, but has never had a following among specialist researchers.[569] Today, based on meticulous study of trial records, ecclesiastical and inquisitorial registers and so on, as well as on the utilization of modern statistical methods, the specialist research community on witchcraft has reached an agreement for roughly 40,000–50,000 people executed for witchcraft in Europe in total,[570] and by no means all of them executed by being burned alive. Furthermore, it is solidly established that the peak period of witch-hunts was the century 1550–1650, with a slow increase preceding it, from the 15th century onward, as well as a sharp drop following it, with "witch-hunts" having basically fizzled out by the first half of the 18th century.[571]

Famous cases

Notable individuals executed by burning include Jacques de Molay (1314),[572] Jan Hus (1415),[573] Joan of Arc (1431),[574] Girolamo Savonarola (1498),[575] Patrick Hamilton (1528),[576] John Frith (1533),[577] William Tyndale (1536), Michael Servetus (1553),[578] Giordano Bruno (1600),[579] Urbain Grandier (1634),[580] and Avvakum (1682).[581] Anglican martyrs John Rogers,[582] Hugh Latimer and Nicholas Ridley were burned at the stake in 1555.[583] Thomas Cranmer followed the next year (1556).[584]

Figure 114: *Joan of Arc's Death at the Stake, by Hermann Stilkede:Hermann Stilke (1843)*

Denmark

In Denmark, after the 1536 reformation, Christian IV of Denmark (r. 1588–1648) encouraged the practice of burning witches, in particular by the law against witchcraft in 1617. In Jutland, the mainland part of Denmark, more than half the recorded cases of witchcraft in the 16th and 17th centuries occurred after 1617. Rough estimates says about a thousand persons were executed due to convictions for witchcraft in the 1500–1600s, but it is not wholly clear if all of the transgressors were burned to death.[585]

England

Mary I ordered hundreds of Protestants burnt at the stake during her reign (1553–58) in what would be known as the "Marian Persecutions" earning her the epithet of 'Bloody' Mary.[586] Many of those martyred by Mary and the Roman Catholic Church are listed in *Actes and Monuments*, written by Foxe in 1563 and 1570. Edward Wightman, a Baptist from Burton on Trent, was the last person burned at the stake for heresy in England in Lichfield, Staffordshire on 11 April 1612.[587] Although cases can be found of burning heretics in the 16th and 17th centuries England, that penalty for heretics was historically relatively new. For example, it did not exist in 14th century England, and when the bishops in England petitioned King Richard II to institute death by burning for heretics in 1397, he flatly refused, and no one was burnt for heresy during his reign.[588] Just one year after his death, however, in 1401, William Sawtrey was burnt alive for heresy.[589] Death by burning for heresy was formally abolished by King Charles II in 1676.[590]

The traditional punishment for women found guilty of treason was to be burned at the stake, where they did not need to be publicly displayed naked, whereas men were hanged, drawn and quartered. The jurist William Blackstone argued as follows for the differential punishment of females vs. males: <templatestyles src="Template:Quote/styles.css"/>

> *For as the decency due to sex forbids the exposing and public mangling of their bodies, their sentence (which is to the full as terrible to sensation as the other) is to be drawn to the gallows and there be burned alive*[591]

However, as described in Camille Naish's "Death Comes to the Maiden", in practice, the woman's shift would burn away at the beginning, and she would be left naked anyway.Wikipedia:Citation needed There were two types of treason, high treason for crimes against the sovereign, and petty treason for the murder of one's lawful superior, including that of a husband by his wife. Commenting on the 18th century execution practice, Frank McLynn says that most convicts condemned to burning were not burnt alive, and that the executioners made sure the women were dead before consigning them to the flames.[592]

The last to have been condemned to death for "petty treason" was Mary Bailey, whose body was burned in 1784. The last woman to be convicted for "high treason", and have her body burnt, in this case for the crime of coin forgery, was Catherine Murphy in 1789.[593] The last case where a woman was actually burnt alive in England is that of Catherine Hayes in 1726, for the murder of her husband. In this case, one account says this happened because the executioner accidentally set fire to the pyre before he had hanged Hayes properly.[594] The historian Rictor Norton has assembled a number of contemporary newspaper reports on the actual death of Mrs. Hayes, internally somewhat divergent. The following excerpt is one example: <templatestyles src="Template:Quote/styles.css"/>

> *The fuel being placed round her, and lighted with a torch, she begg'd for the sake of Jesus, to be strangled first: whereupon the Executioner drew tight the halter, but the flame coming to his hand in the space of a second, he let it go, when she gave three dreadful shrieks; but the flames taking her on all sides, she was heard no more; and the Executioner throwing a piece of timber into the Fire, it broke her skull, when her brains came plentifully out; and in about an hour more she was entirely reduced to ashes.*[595]

Scotland

James VI of Scotland (later James I of England) shared the Danish king's interest in witch trials. This special interest of the king resulted in the North Berwick witch trials, which led more than seventy people to be accused of witchcraft in Scotland due to inclement weather. James sailed in 1590 to Denmark to meet his betrothed, Anne of Denmark, who, ironically, is believed by some to have secretly converted to Roman Catholicism herself from Lutheranism around 1598, although historians are divided on whether she ever was received into the Roman Catholic faith.[596]

The last to be executed as a witch in Scotland was Janet Horne in 1727, condemned to death for using her own daughter as a flying horse in order to travel. Janet Horne was burnt alive in a tar barrel.[597]

Ireland

Petronilla de Meath (c. 1300–1324) was the maidservant of Dame Alice Kyteler, a 14th-century Hiberno-Norman noblewoman. After the death of Kyteler's fourth husband, the widow was accused of practicing witchcraft and Petronilla of being her accomplice. Petronilla was tortured and forced to proclaim that she and Kyteler were guilty of witchcraft. Petronilla was then flogged and eventually burnt at the stake on 3 November 1324, in Kilkenny, Ireland.[598,599] Hers was the first known case in the history of the British Isles of death by fire for the crime of heresy. Kyteler was charged by the Bishop of Ossory, Richard de Ledrede, with a wide slate of crimes, from sorcery and demonism to the murders of several husbands. She was accused of having illegally acquired her wealth through witchcraft, which accusations came principally from her stepchildren, the children of her late husbands by their previous marriages. The trial predated any formal witchcraft statute in Ireland, thus relying on ecclesiastical law (which treated witchcraft as heresy) rather than English common law (which treated it as a felony). Under torture, Petronilla claimed she and her mistress applied a magical ointment to a wooden beam, which enabled both women to fly. She was then forced to proclaim publicly that Lady Alice and her followers were guilty of witchcraft. Some were convicted and whipped, but others, Petronilla included, were burnt at the stake. With the help of relatives, Alice Kyteler fled, taking with her Petronilla's daughter, Basilia.[600]

In 1895, Bridget Cleary (née Boland), a County Tipperary woman, was burnt by her husband and others, the stated motive for the crime being the belief that the real Bridget had been abducted by fairies with a changeling left in her place. Her husband claimed to have slain only the changeling. The gruesome nature of the case prompted extensive press coverage. The trial was closely followed by newspapers in both Ireland and Britain.[601] As one reviewer commented,

Figure 115: *Execution of Mariana de Carabajal (converted Jew), Mexico City, 1601*

nobody, with the possible exception of the presiding judge, thought it was an ordinary murder case.

Slavery and colonialism in the Americas

North America

Indigenous North Americans often used burning as a form of execution, against members of other tribes or white settlers during the 18th and 19th centuries. Roasting over a slow fire was a customary method.[602] {See Captives in American Indian Wars}

In Massachusetts, there are two known cases of burning at the stake. First, in 1681, a slave named Maria tried to kill her owner by setting his house on fire. She was convicted of arson and burned at the stake in Roxbury.[603] Concurrently, a slave named Jack, convicted in a separate arson case, was hanged at a nearby gallows, and after death his body was thrown into the fire with that of Maria. Second, in 1755, a group of slaves had conspired and killed their owner, with servants Mark and Phillis executed for his murder. Mark was hanged and his body gibbeted, and Phillis burned at the stake, at Cambridge.[604]

In Montreal, then part of New France, Marie-Joseph Angélique, a black slave, was sentenced to being burned alive for an arson which destroyed 45 homes

Figure 116: *Native Americans scalping and roasting their prisoners, published in 1873*

and a hospital in 1734. The sentence was commuted on appeal to burning after death by stangulation.[605] WP:NOTRS

In New York, several burnings at the stake are recorded, particularly following suspected slave revolt plots. In 1708, one woman was burnt and one man hanged. In the aftermath of the New York Slave Revolt of 1712, 20 people were burnt (one of the leaders slowly roasted, before he died after 10 hours of torture[606]) and during the alleged slave conspiracy of 1741, at least 13 slaves were burnt at the stake.[607]

Bartolomé de las Casas, a 16th-century eyewitness to the brutal subjugation of the Native Americans by the Spanish conquistadores, has left a particularly harrowing description of how roasting alive was a favoured technique of repression:[608] <templatestyles src="Template:Quote/styles.css"/>

They usually dealt with the chieftains and nobles in the following way: they made a grid of rods which they placed on forked sticks, then lashed the victims to the grid and lighted a smoldering fire underneath, so that little by little, as those captives screamed in despair and torment, their souls would leave them. I once saw this, when there were four or five nobles lashed on grids and burning; I seem even to recall that there were two or three pairs where others were burning, and because they uttered such loud screams that they disturbed the captain's sleep, he ordered them to be strangled. And the constable, who was worse than an executioner, did not want to obey that order (and I know the name of that constable and know his relatives in Seville), but instead put a stick over the victims' tongues, so they could not make a sound, and he stirred up the fire, but not too much, so that they roasted slowly, as he liked.

The last known burning by the Spanish Colonial government in Latin America was of Mariana de Castro, in Lima, Peru Wikipedia:Please clarify in February 1732.[609]

British West Indies

In 1760, the slave rebellion known as Tacky's War broke out in Jamaica. Apparently, some of the defeated rebels were burned alive, while others were gibbeted alive, left to die of thirst and starvation.[610]

In 1774, nine African slaves at Tobago were found complicit of murdering a white man. Eight of them had first their right arms chopped off, and were then burned alive bound to stakes, according to the report of an eyewitness.[611]

Dutch Suriname

In 1855 the Dutch abolitionist and historian Julien Wolbers spoke to the Anti Slavery Society in Amsterdam. Painting a dark picture of the condition of slaves in Suriname, he mentions in particular that as late as in 1853, just two years previously, "three Negroes were burnt alive".[612]

Greek War of Independence

The Greek War of Independence in the 1820s contained several instances of death by burning. When the Greeks in April 1821 captured a corvette near Hydra, the Greeks chose to roast to death the 57 Ottoman crew members. After the fall of Tripolitsa in September 1821, European officers were horrified to note that not only were Muslims suspected of hiding money being slowly roasted after having had their arms and legs cut off but, in one instance, three Muslim children were roasted over a fire while their parents were forced to watch. On their part, the Ottomans committed many similar acts; for example, in retaliation they gathered up Greeks in Constantinople, throwing several of them into huge ovens, baking them to death.[613]

Islamic countries

Followers of a false claimant of prophethood

The Arab chieftain Tulayha ibn Khuwaylid ibn Nawfal al-Asad set himself up as a prophet in AD 630. Tulayha had a strong following which was, however, soon quashed in the so-called Ridda Wars. He himself escaped, though, and later was reconverted to Islam, but many of his rebel followers were burnt to death; his mother chose to embrace the same fate.[614]Wikipedia:Citation needed

Catholic monks in 13th-century Tunis and Morocco

A number of monks are said to have been burnt alive in Tunis and Morocco in the 13th century. In 1243, two English monks, Brothers Rodulph and Berengarius, after having secured the release of some 60 captives, were charged with being English spies, and were burnt alive on 9 September. In 1262, Brothers Patrick and William, again having freed captives, but also sought to proselytize among Muslims, were burnt alive in Morocco. In 1271, 11 Catholic monks were burnt alive in Tunis. Several other cases are reported.[615]

Converts to Christianity

Apostasy, i.e. the act of converting to another religion, was (and remains so in a few countries) punishable with death.

The French traveller Jean de Thevenot, traveling the East in the 1650s, says: *'Those that turn Christians, they burn alive, hanging a bag of Powder about their neck, and putting a pitched Cap upon their Head.'*[616] Travelling the same regions some 60 years earlier, Fynes Moryson writes: <templatestyles src="Template:Quote/styles.css"/>

> *A Turke forsaking his Fayth and a Christian speaking or doing anything against the law of Mahomett are burnt with fyer.*[617]

(*NOTE:* De Thevenot says Christians committing blasphemy against Islam were impaled, rather than burnt, if they do not convert to Islam.)

Muslim heretics

Certain accursed ones of no significance is the term used by Taş Köprü Zade in the *Şakaiki Numaniye* to describe some members of the Hurufiyya who became intimate with the Sultan Mehmed II to the extent of initiating him as a follower. This alarmed members of the Ulema, particularly Mahmut Paşa, who then consulted Mevlana Fahreddin. Fahreddin hid in the Sultan's palace and heard the Hurufis propound their doctrines. Considering these heretical, he reviled them with curses. The Hurufis fled to the Sultan, but Fahreddin's denunciation of them was so virulent that Mehmed II was unable to defend them. Farhreddin then took them in front of the Üç Şerefeli Mosque, Edirne, where he publicly condemned them to death. While preparing the fire for their execution, Fahreddin accidentally set fire to his beard. However the Hurufis were burnt to death.

Barbary States, 18th century

John Braithwaite, staying in Morocco in the late 1720s, says that apostates from Islam would be burnt alive:

> THOSE that can be proved after Circumcision to have revolted, are stripped quite naked, then anointed with Tallow, and with a Chain about the Body, brought to the Place of Execution, where they are burnt.

Similarly, he notes that non-Muslims entering mosques or being blasphemous against Islam will be burnt, unless they convert to Islam.[618] The chaplain for the English in Algiers at the same time, Thomas Shaw, wrote that whenever capital crimes were committed either by Christian slaves or Jews, the Christian or Jew was to be burnt alive.[619] Several generations later, in Morocco in 1772, a Jewish interpreter to the British, and a merchant in his own right, sought from the Emperor of Morocco restitution for some goods confiscated, and was burnt alive for his impertinence. His widow made her woes clear in a letter to the British.[620]

In 1792 in Ifrane, Morocco, 50 Jews preferred to be burned alive, rather than convert to Islam.[621] In 1794 in Algiers, the Jewish Rabbi Mordecai Narboni was accused of having maligned Islam in a quarrel with his neighbour. He was ordered to be burnt alive unless he converted to Islam, but he refused and was therefore executed on 14 July 1794.[622]

In 1793, Ali Benghul made a short-lived *coup d'état* in Tripoli, deposing the ruling Karamanli dynasty. During his short, violent reign he seized for example, the two interpreters for the Dutch and English consuls, both of them Jews, and roasted them over a slow fire, on charges of conspiracy and espionage.[623]

Persia

During a famine in Persia in 1668, the government took severe measures against those trying to profiteer from the misfortune of the populace. Restaurant owners found guilty of profiteering were slowly roasted on spits, and greedy bakers were baked in their own ovens.[624]

A physician, Dr C.J. Wills, traveling through Persia in 1866–81 noted that shortly before his (Wills') arrival, a "priest" had been burned alive. Wills wrote:[625] <templatestyles src="Template:Quote/styles.css"/>

> *Just prior to my first arrival in Persia, the "Hissam-u-Sultaneh", another uncle of the king, had burned a priest to death for a horrible crime and murder; the priest was chained to a stake, and the matting from the mosques piled on him to a great height, the pile of mats was lighted and burnt freely, but when the mats were consumed the priest was found groaning, but still alive. The executioner went to Hissam-u-Sultaneh who ordered him to obtain more mats, pour naphtha on them, and apply a light, which 'after some hours' he did.*

Roasting by means of heated metal

The previous cases concern primarily death by burning through contact with open fire or burning material; a slightly different principle is to enclose an individual within, or attach him to, a metal contraption which is subsequently heated. In the following, some reports of such incidents, or anecdotes about such are included.

The brazen bull

Perhaps the most infamous example of a brazen bull, which is a hollow metal structure shaped like a bull within which the condemned is put, and then roasted alive as the metal bull is gradually heated up, is the one allegedly constructed by Perillos of Athens for the 6th-century BC tyrant Phalaris at Agrigentum, Sicily. As the story goes, the first victim of the bull was its constructor Perillos himself. The historian George Grote was among those regarding this story as having sufficient evidence behind it to be true, and points particularly to that the Greek poet Pindar, working just one or two generations after the times of Phalaris refers to the brazen bull. A bronze bull was, in fact, one of the spoils of victory when the Carthaginians conquered Agrigentum.[626] The story of a brazen bull as an execution device is not wholly unique. About 1000 years later, for example, in AD 497, it can be read in an old chronicle about the Visigoths on the Iberian Peninsula and the south of France: <templatestyles src="Template:Quote/styles.css"/>

Figure 117: *Perillos being forced into the brazen bull that he built for Phalaris*

Burdunellus became a tyrant in Spain and a year later was ... handed over by his own men and having been sent to Toulouse, he was placed inside a bronze bull and burnt to death.[627]

Fate of a Scottish regicide

Walter Stewart, Earl of Atholl was a Scottish nobleman complicit in the murder of King James I of Scotland. On 26 March 1437 Stewart had a red hot iron crown placed upon his head, was cut in pieces alive, his heart was taken out, and then thrown in a fire. A papal nuncio, the later Pope Pius II witnessed the execution of Stewart and his associate Sir Robert Graham, and, reportedly, said he was at a loss to determine whether the *crime* committed by the regicides, or the *punishment* of them was the greater.[628]

György Dózsa on the iron throne

György Dózsa led a peasants' revolt in Hungary, and was captured in 1514. He was bound to a glowing iron throne and a likewise hot iron crown was placed on his head, and he was roasted to death.[629]

Georgius Zekel
Figure 118: *Dózsa's execution (contemporary woodcut)*

The tale of the murderous midwife

In a few English 18th- and 19th-century newspapers and magazines, a tale was circulated about the particularly brutal manner in which a French midwife was put to death on 28 May 1673 in Paris. No fewer than 62 infant skeletons were found buried on her premises, and she was condemned on multiple accounts of abortion/infanticide. One detailed account of her supposed execution runs as follows: <templatestyles src="Template:Quote/styles.css"/>

> *A gibbet was erected, under which a fire was made, and the prisoner being brought to the place of execution, was hung up in a large iron cage, in which were also placed sixteen wild cats, which had been catched in the woods for the purpose.—When the heat of the fire became too great to be endured with patience, the cats flew upon the woman, as the cause of the intense pain they felt.—In about fifteen minutes they had pulled out her intrails, though she continued yet alive, and sensible, imploring, as the greatest favour, an immediate death from the hands of some charitable spectator. No one however dared to afford her the least assistance; and she continued in this wretched situation for the space of thirty-five minutes, and then expired in unspeakable torture. At the time of her death, twelve of the cats were expired, and the other four were all dead in less than two minutes afterwards.*

The English commentator adds his own view on the matter:<templatestyles src="Template:Quote/styles.css"/>

> *However cruel this execution may appear with regard to the poor animals, it certainly cannot be thought too severe a punishment for such a monster of iniquity, as could calmly proceed in acquiring a fortune by the deliberate murder of such numbers of unoffending, harmless innocents. And if a method of executing murderers, in a manner somewhat similar to this was adapted in England, perhaps the horrid crime of murder might not so frequently disgrace the annals of the present times.*[630]

The English story is derived from a pamphlet published in 1673.[631]

Pouring molten metal down the throat or ears

Molten gold poured down the throat

A number of stories concern individuals who are said to have been executed by having molten gold (melting point 1064 °C/1947 °F) poured down their throats. For example, in 88 BC, Mithridates VI of Pontus captured the Roman general Manius Aquillius, and executed him by pouring molten gold down his throat.[632] A popular but unsubstantiated rumor also had the Parthians executing the famously greedy Roman general Marcus Licinius Crassus in this manner in 53 BC.[633]

Genghis Khan is said to have poured molten gold down the throat of a perfidious governor in 1220,[634] and an early 14th-century chronicle mentions that his grandson Hulagu Khan did likewise to the sultan Al-Musta'sim after the fall of Baghdad in 1258 to the Mongol army.[635]

The Spanish in 16th-century Americas gave horrified reports that the Spanish who had been captured by the natives (who had learnt of the Spanish thirst for gold) had their feet and hands bound, and then molten gold poured down their throats as the victims were mocked: "Eat, eat gold, Christians".[636]

From the 19th century reports from the Kingdom of Siam (present day Thailand) stated that those who have defrauded the public treasury could have either molten gold or silver poured down their throat.[637]

A punishment for inebriation and tobacco smoking

The 16th-/early 17th-century prime minister Malik Ambar in the Deccan Ahmadnagar Sultanate would not tolerate inebriation among his subjects, and would pour molten lead (melting point 327 °C/621.43 °F) down the mouths of those caught in that condition.[638] Similarly, in the 17th century Sultanate of Aceh Sultan Iskandar Muda (r. 1607–36) is said to have poured molten lead into the mouths of at least two drunken subjects.[639] Military discipline in 19th-century Burma was reportedly harsh, with strict prohibition of smoking opium or drinking arrack. Some monarchs, it appears, had ordained pouring molten lead down the throats of those who drank anyway, "but it has been found necessary to relax this severity, in order to conciliate the army"[640]

Shah Safi I of Persia is said to have abhorred tobacco, and apparently in 1634, he prescribed the punishment of pouring molten lead into the throats of smokers.[641]

A Mongol punishment for horse thieves

According to historian Pushpa Sharma, stealing a horse was considered the most heinous offence within the Mongol army, and the culprit would either have molten lead poured into his ears, or alternatively, his punishment would be the breaking of the spinal cord or beheading.[642]

Chinese tradition of Buddhist self-immolation

Apparently, for many centuries, a tradition of devotional self-immolation existed among Buddhist monks in China. One monk who immolated himself in AD 527, explained his intent a year before, in the following manner: <templatestyles src="Template:Quote/styles.css"/>

> The body is like a poisonous plant; it would really be right to burn it and extinguish its life. I have been weary of this physical frame for many a long day. I vow to worship the buddhas, just like Xijian.[643]

A severe critic in the 16th century wrote the following comment on this practice: <templatestyles src="Template:Quote/styles.css"/>

> There are demonic people ... who pour on oil, stack up firewood, and burn their bodies while still alive. Those who look on are overawed and consider it the attainment of enlightenment. This is erroneous.[644]

Japanese persecution of Christians

In the first half of the 17th century, Japanese authorities sporadically persecuted Christians, with some executions seeing persons being burnt alive. At Nagasaki in 1622, for example, some 25 monks were burnt alive,[645] and in Edo in 1624, 50 Christians were burnt alive.[646]

Stories of cannibalism

Americas

Even fateful encounters with cannibals are recorded: in 1514, in the Americas, Francis of Córdoba and five companions were, reportedly, caught, impaled on spits, roasted and eaten by the natives. In 1543, such was also the end of a previous bishop, Vincent de Valle Viridi.[647]

Fiji

In 1844, the missionary John Watsford wrote a letter about the internecine wars on Fiji, and how captives could be eaten, after being roasted alive: <templatestyles src="Template:Quote/styles.css"/>

> At Mbau, perhaps, more human beings are eaten than anywhere else. A few weeks ago they ate twenty-eight in one day. They had seized their wretched victims while fishing, and brought them alive to Mbau, and there half-killed them, and then put them into their ovens. Some of them made several vain attempts to escape from the scorching flame.[648]

The actual manner of the roasting process was described by the missionary pioneer David Cargill, in 1838: <templatestyles src="Template:Quote/styles.css"/>

> When about to be immolated, he is made to sit on the ground with his feet under his thighs and his hands placed before him. He is then bound so that he cannot move a limb or a joint. In this posture he is placed on stones heated for the occasion (and some of them are red-hot), and then covered with leaves and earth, to be roasted alive. When cooked, he is taken out of the oven and, his face and other parts being painted black, that he may resemble a living man ornamented for a feast or for war, he is carried to the temple of the gods and, being still retained in a sitting posture, is offered as a propitiatory sacrifice.[649]

Death by burning 229

Figure 119: *A Hindu widow burning herself with the corpse of her husband, 1820s*

Immolation of widows

Indian subcontinent

Sati refers to a funeral practice among some communities of Indian subcontinent in which a recently widowed woman immolates herself on her husband's funeral pyre. The first reliable evidence for the practice of *sati* appears from the time of the Gupta Empire (AD 400), when instances of sati began to be marked by inscribed memorial stones.[650]

According to one model of history thinking, the practice of *sati* only became really widespread with the Muslim invasions of India, and the practice of *sati* now acquired a new meaning as a means to preserve the honour of women whose men had been slain. As S.S.Sashi lays out the argument, "The argument is that the practice came into effect during the Islamic invasion of India, to protect their honor from Muslims who were known to commit mass rape on the women of cities that they could capture successfully."[651] It is also said that according to the memorial stone evidence, the practice was carried out in appreciable numbers in western and southern parts of India, and even in some areas, before pre-Islamic times.[652] Some of the rulers and activist of the time sought actively to suppress the practice of *sati*.[653]

The British began to compile statistics of the incidences of *sati* for all their domains from 1815 and onwards. The official statistics for Bengal represents that the practice was much more common here than elsewhere, recorded numbers typically in the range 500-600 per year, up to the year 1829, when the British

Figure 120: *Ceremony of Burning a Hindu Widow with the Body of her Late Husband, from Pictorial History of China and India, 1851*

authorities banned the practice.[654] Since 19th - 20th Century, the practice remains outlawed in Indian subcontinent.

Jauhar was a practice among royal Hindu women to prevent capture by Muslim conquerors.

Bali and Nepal

The practice of burning widows has not been restricted to the Indian subcontinent; at Bali, the practice was called *masatia* and, apparently, restricted to the burning of royal widows. Although the Dutch colonial authorities had banned the practice, one such occasion is attested as late as in 1903, probably for the last time.[655] In Nepal, the practice was not banned until 1920.[656]

Traditions in sub-Saharan African cultures

C.H.L. Hahn[657] wrote that within the O-ndnonga tribe among the Ovambo people in modern-day Namibia, abortion was not used at all (in contrast to among the other tribes), and that furthermore, if two young unwed individuals had sex resulting in pregnancy, then both the girl and the boy were "taken out to the bush, bound up in bundles of grass and ... burnt alive."[658]

Legislation against the practice

In 1790, Sir Benjamin Hammett introduced a bill into Parliament to end the practice of judicial burning. He explained that the year before, as Sheriff of London, he had been responsible for the burning of Catherine Murphy, found guilty of counterfeiting, but that he had allowed her to be hanged first. He pointed out that as the law stood, he himself could have been found guilty of a crime in not carrying out the lawful punishment and, as no woman had been burnt alive in the kingdom for more than half a century, so could all those still alive who had held an official position at all of the previous burnings. The Treason Act 1790 was duly passed by Parliament and given royal assent by King George III (30 George III. C. 48).[659]

Modern burnings

Retaliation against Nazis

Benjamin B. Ferencz, one of the prosecutors in the Nuremberg trials who, in May 1945, investigated occurrences at the Ebensee concentration camp, and narrated them to Tom Hofmann, a family member and biographer. He was completely outraged at what the Nazis had done there. When people discovered an SS guard who attempted to flee, they tied him to one of the metal trays used to transport bodies into the crematorium. They then proceeded to light the oven, and slowly roast the SS guard to death, taking him in and out of the oven several times. Ferencz said to Hofmann that at the time, he was in no position to stop the proceedings of the mob, and frankly admitted that he had not been inclined to try. Hofmann adds, "There seemed to be no limit to human brutality in wartime."[660]

Lynching of Germans in Czechoslovakia

During the expulsion of Germans from Czechoslovakia after the end of World War II, a number of massacres against the German minority occurred. In one case in Prague in May 1945, a Czech mob hanged several Germans upside down on lampposts, doused them in fuel and set them on fire, burning them alive.[661,662] WP:NOTRS

Necklacing

Necklacing is the practice of summary execution and torture carried out by forcing a rubber tire, filled with petrol, around a victim's chest and arms, and setting it on fire. The victim may take up to 20 minutes to die, suffering severe burns in the process. The method was widely used in Haiti and South Africa.

Extrajudicial burnings in Latin America

In Rio de Janeiro, Brazil, burning people standing inside a pile of tires is a common form of murder used by drug dealers to punish those who have supposedly collaborated with the police. This form of burning is called *micro-ondas* (microwave oven).[663] The film *Tropa de Elite* (*Elite Squad*) and the video game *Max Payne 3* contain scenes depicting this practice.[664]

During the Guatemalan Civil War the Guatemalan Army and security forces carried out an unknown number of extrajudicial killings by burning. In one instance in March 1967, Guatemalan guerrilla and poet Otto René Castillo was captured by Guatemalan government forces and taken to Zacapa army barracks alongside one of his comrades, Nora Paíz Cárcamo. The two were interrogated, tortured for four days, and burned alive.[665] Other reported instances of immolation by Guatemalan government forces occurred in the Guatemalan government's rural counterinsurgency operations in the Guatemalan Altiplano in the 1980s. In April 1982, 13 members of a Quanjobal Pentecostal congregation in Xalbal, Ixcan, were burnt alive in their church by the Guatemalan Army.[666]

On 31 August 1996, a Mexican man, Rodolfo Soler Hernandez, was burned to death in Playa Vicente, Mexico, after he was accused of raping and strangling a local woman to death. Local residents tied Hernandez to a tree, doused him in a flammable liquid and then set him ablaze. His death was also filmed by residents of the village. Shots taken before the killing showed that he had been badly beaten. On 5 September 1996, Mexican television stations broadcast footage of the murder. Locals carried out the killing because they were fed up with crime and believed that the police and courts were both incompetent. Footage was also shown in the 1998 shockumentary film, *Banned from Television*.

A young Guatemalan woman, Alejandra María Torres, was attacked by a mob in Guatemala City on 15 December 2009. The mob alleged that Torres had attempted to rob passengers on a bus. Torres was beaten, doused with gasoline, and set on fire, but was able to put the fire out before sustaining life-threatening burns. Police intervened and arrested Torres. Torres was forced to go topless throughout the ordeal and subsequent arrest, and many photographs were taken and published. Approximately 219 people were lynched in Guatemala in 2009, of whom 45 died.

In May 2015, a sixteen-year-old girl was allegedly burned to death in Rio Bravo by a vigilante mob after being accused by some of involvement in the killing of a taxi driver earlier in the month.[667]

In Chile during public mass protests held against the military regime of General Augusto Pinochet on 2 July 1986, engineering student Carmen Gloria Quintana, 18, and Chilean-American photographer Rodrigo Rojas DeNegri, 19, were arrested by a Chilean Army patrol in the Los Nogales neighborhood of Santiago. The two were searched and beaten before being doused in gasoline and burned alive by Chilean troops. Rojas was killed, while Quintana survived but with severe burns.[668]

Lynchings and mass killings by burning in the US

During the 1980 New Mexico State Penitentiary riot, a number of inmates were burnt to death by fellow inmates, who used blow torches. Modern burnings continued as a method of lynching in the United States in the late 19th and early 20th centuries, particularly in the South. One of the most notorious extrajudicial burnings in modern history occurred in Waco, Texas on 15 May 1916. Jesse Washington, an African-American farmhand, after having been convicted of the rape and subsequent murder of a white woman, was taken by a mob to a bonfire, castrated, doused in coal oil, and hanged by the neck from a chain over the bonfire, slowly burning to death. A postcard from the event still exists, showing a crowd standing next to Washington's charred corpse with the words on the back "This is the barbecue we had last night. My picture is to the left with a cross over it. Your son, Joe". This attracted international condemnation and is remembered as the "Waco Horror".[669,670]

Unconfirmed act of execution in the Soviet Union

A former Soviet Main Intelligence Directorate (GRU) officer writing under the alias Victor Suvorov described, in his book *Aquarium*, a Soviet "traitor" being burned alive in a crematorium.[671] There has been some speculation that this officer was Oleg Penkovsky. However, during a radio interview with the Echo of Moscow, Suvorov denied this, saying "I never mentioned it was Penkovsky".[672] No executed GRU traitors other than Penkovsky are known to match Suvorov's description of the spy in *Aquarium*.[673]

Executions in North Korea

In connection to the purge of Jang Song-taek, O Sang-hon, a deputy minister at the Ministry of Public Security (North Korea) associated with Jang, was 'executed by flamethrower' in 2014, according to unconfirmed reports.[674]

African cases

In South Africa, extrajudicial executions by burning were carried out via "necklacing", wherein rubber tires filled with kerosene (or gasoline) are placed around the neck of a live individual. The fuel is then ignited, the rubber melts, and the victim is burnt to death.[675,676]

It was reported that in Kenya, on 21 May 2008, a mob had burned to death at least 11 accused witches.[677]

Cases from the Middle East and Indian subcontinent

Dr Graham Stuart Staines, an Australian Christian missionary, and his two sons Philip (aged ten) and Timothy (aged six), were burnt to death by a gang while the three slept in the family car (a station wagon), at Manoharpur village in Keonjhar District, Odisha, India on 22 January 1999. Four years later, in 2003, a Bajrang Dal activist, Dara Singh, was convicted of leading the gang that murdered Staines and his sons, and was sentenced to life in prison. Staines had worked in Odisha with the tribal poor and lepers since 1965. Some Hindu groups made allegations that Staines had forcibly converted or lured many Hindus into Christianity.[678,679]

On 19 June 2008, the Taliban, at Sadda, Lower Kurram, Pakistan, burned three truck drivers of the Turi tribe alive after attacking a convoy of trucks en route from Kohat to Parachinar, possibly for supplying the Pakistan Armed Forces.[680]

In January 2015, Jordanian pilot Moaz al-Kasasbeh was burned in a cage by the Islamic State of Iraq and the Levant (ISIS). The pilot was captured when his plane crashed near Raqqa, Syria, during a mission against IS in December 2014.[681]

In August 2015, ISIS burned to death four Iraqi Shia prisoners.

In December 2016, ISIS burned to death two Turkish soldiers, publishing high quality video of the atrocity.[682]

Bride-burning

On 20 January 2011, a 28-year-old woman, Ranjeeta Sharma, was found burning to death on a road in rural New Zealand. The police confirmed the woman was alive before being covered in an accelerant and set on fire.[683] Sharma's husband, Davesh Sharma, was charged with her murder.

Bibliography

<templatestyles src="Template:Refbegin/styles.css" />

- de Almeida, Fortunato (1923). "Appendix IX". *História da Igreja em Portugal*. **4, 3**. Oporto: Imprensa académica.<templatestyles src="Module:Citation/CS1/styles.css"></templatestyles>
- Anderson, James M. (2002). *Daily Life During the Spanish Inquisition*[684]. Westport, Connecticut: Greenwood Publishing Group. ISBN 9780313316678.<templatestyles src="Module:Citation/CS1/styles.css"></templatestyles>
- Anouchi, Avram (2009). *The Hidden Scroll*[685]. Xlibris Corporation. ISBN 9781450002035.<templatestyles src="Module:Citation/CS1/styles.css"></templatestyles>Wikipedia:Verifiability#Self-published sources
- Barber, Malcolm (1993). *The Trial of the Templars*[686]. Cambridge: Cambridge University Press. ISBN 9780521457279.<templatestyles src="Module:Citation/CS1/styles.css"></templatestyles>
- "Missionary widow continues leprosy work"[687]. *BBC News*. 27 January 1999.<templatestyles src="Module:Citation/CS1/styles.css"></templatestyles>
- Begbie, Peter J. (1834). *The Malayan Peninsula: Embracing Its History, Manners and Customs of the Inhabitants, Politics, Natural History, Etc. from Its Earliest Records*[688]. Madras: Author.<templatestyles src="Module:Citation/CS1/styles.css"></templatestyles>
- Behringer, Wolfgang (2006). "Neun Millionen Hexen. Entstehung, Tradition und Kritik eines populären Mythos"[689]. *historicum.net*.<templatestyles src="Module:Citation/CS1/styles.css"></templatestyles>
- Ben-Menahem, Hanina (author, ed.); Edrei, Arye (ed.); Hecht, Neil S. (ed.) (2012). "3, Exigency Authority". *Windows Onto Jewish Legal Culture: Fourteen Exploratory Essays*[690]. London: Routledge. ISBN 9780415500494.<templatestyles src="Module:Citation/CS1/styles.css"></templatestyles>
- Benn, James A. (2007). *Burning for the Buddha: Self-Immolation in Chinese Buddhism*[691]. University of Hawaii Press. ISBN 9780824829926.<templatestyles src="Module:Citation/CS1/styles.css"></templatestyles>
- Berger, Stefan (ed.); Sicker, Dieter (2009). *Classics in Spectroscopy*[692]. John Wiley & Sons. ISBN 9783527325160.<templatestyles src="Module:Citation/CS1/styles.css"></templatestyles>
- Bischoff; Hitzig, Julius (ed.) (1832). Julius Hitzig, ed. "Wer ist im Sinne der Carolina als ein "boshafter überwundener Brenner" zu bestrafen?"[693].

Annalen der deutschen und ausländischen Criminal-Rechtspflege. Berlin: Ferdinand Dümmler. 2 (Neue Folge), 14 (In total) (27): 109–178.

- Blake, William O. (1857). *The History of Slavery and the Slave Trade, Ancient and Modern*[694]. Columnus, Ohio: J. and H. Miller. pp. 154–155. ISBN 9780312272883.
- Buckingham, J.S. (28 March 1835). James S. Buckingham, ed. "The Athenæum"[695]. **387**. London: J. Francis.
- Bülau, Friedrich (1860). *Geheime Geschichten und räthselhafte Menschen, Sammlung verborgener oder vergessener Merkwürdigkeiten*[696]. **12**. Leipzig: Brockhaus.
- Burns, William E. (2003). *Witch Hunts in Europe and America: An Encyclopedia*[697]. Westport, Connecticut: Greenwood Publishing Group. ISBN 9780313321429.
- Calvert, James; Rowe, George S. (ed.) (1858). *Fiji and the Fijians: Mission history*[698]. **2**. London: A. Heylin.
- Cameron, Scott (ed.); Sela, Ron (ed.) (2010). *Islamic Central Asia: An Anthology of Historical Sources*[699]. Bloomington, Indiana: Indiana University Press. ISBN 9780253353856.
- Carey, William (April 1814). J. Hooper, ed. "Burning a leper to death"[700]. *Evangelical Magazine and Missionary Chronicle*. London: Williams&Son. **22**.
- Carr, Matthew (2009). *Blood and Faith: The Purging of Muslim Spain*[701]. New York: The New Press. ISBN 9781595583611.
- Carvacho, René M. (2004). *La Inquisición de Lima: signos de su decadencia, 1726–1750*[702]. LOM Ediciones. ISBN 9789562827089.
- De las Casas, Bartolomé (1974). *The Devastation of the Indies: A Brief Account*[703]. JHU Press. ISBN 9780801844300.
- Braithwaite, John (1729). *The history of the revolutions in the empire of Morocco*[704]. London, UK: Knapton and Betterworth.

- Cipolla, Gaetano (2005). *Siciliana: Studies on the Sicilian Ethos*[705]. Mineola, New York: Legas. ISBN 9781881901457.
- Collins, Roger (2004). *Visigothic Spain 409-711*. Oxford: Blackwell Publishing. ISBN 0631181857.
- Coward, D.A; Dynes, Wayne R. (ed.); Donaldson, Stephen (ed.) (1992). "Attitudes to Homosexuality in Eighteenth Century France". *History of Homosexuality in Europe and America*[706]. Taylor & Francis. ISBN 9780815305507.
- Croft, J.Pauline (2003). *King James*. Basingstoke and New York: Palgrave Macmillan. ISBN 0-333-61395-3.
- Crawford, Paul (ed.) (2003). *The 'Templar of Tyre': Part III of the 'Deeds of the Cypriots'*[707]. Aldershot, England: Ashgate Publishing, Ltd. p. 149. ISBN 9781840146189.
- Crompton, Louis (2006). *Homosexuality and Civilization*[708]. Boston: Harvard University Press. ISBN 9780674030060.
- Cummins, Thomas; Cole, Martin W. (ed.); Zorach (ed.), Rebecca (2009). "The Golden Calf in America". *The Idol in the Age of Art: Objects, Devotions and the Early Modern World*[709]. Burlington, Vermont: Ashgate Publishing, Ltd. p. 99. ISBN 9780754652908.
- Das, Sukla (1977). *Crime and Punishment in Ancient India: (C. A.D. 300 to A.D. 1100)*[710]. Abhinav Publications. ISBN 978-81-7017-054-9.
- Decker, Roy (2001). "Religion of Carthage"[711]. *About.com*.
- Dietze, Karl H. (July 1995). "1804, der letzte Scheiterhaufen lohte im Kreis Eisenach". *StadtZeit.Stadtjournal mit Informationen aus dem Wartburgkreis*. Eisenach: MFB-Verlagsgesellschaft, Frisch: 24.
- Digby, Kenelm H. (1853). *Compitum, Or The Meeting of the Ways at the Catholic Church*[712]. **3**. London: C. Dolman.

- DuBois, W.E.B. (July 1916). "The Waco Horror"[713] (PDF). *The Crisis*. Archived by the Modernist Journals Project. **12** (Supplement to no. 3): 1–8.
- Dumas, Alexandre (1843). *Celebrated crimes*[714]. London: Chapman and Hall.
- Durso, Keith E. (2007). *No Armor for the Back: Baptist Prison Writings, 1600s-1700s*[715]. Macon, Georgia: Mercer University Press. ISBN 9780881460919.
- Perthensis, Encyclopaedia (1816). *Encyclopaedia Perthensis; or, Universal dictionary of Knowledge*[716]. **20**. Edinburgh.
- Eaton, Richard M. (2005). *A Social History of the Deccan, 1300-1761: Eight Indian Lives*[717]. **1**. Cambridge: Cambridge University Press. ISBN 9780521254847.
- Eraly, Abraham (2011). *The First Spring: The Golden Age of India*[718]. New Delhi: Penguin Books India. ISBN 9780670084784.
- Feek, Belinda (24 January 2011). "Burnt body victim named as search goes offshore"[719]. *Waikato Times*. Retrieved 27 September 2011.
- Ferrier, Ronald W. (1996). *A Journey To Persia*[720]. London: I.B.Tauris. ISBN 9781850435648.
- Foxe, John; Townsend, George (commentary); Cattley, Stephen R. (ed.) (1838). *The Acts and Monuments of John Foxe: A New and Complete Edition*[721]. **5**. London: R. B. Seeley and W. Burnside.
- Foxe, John; Milner, John; Cobbin, Ingram (1856). *Foxe's book of martyrs: a complete and authentic account of the lives, sufferings, and triumphant deaths of the primitive and Protestant martyrs in all parts of the world, with notes, comments and illustrations*[722]. London: Knight and Son. pp. 608–09.
- França, Ronaldo. "Como na Chicago de Capone"[723]. *Veja on-line (30 January 2002)*. Retrieved 8 October 2007.
- Fraser, Antonia (1997). *Faith and Treason: The Story of the Gunpowder Plot*. Anchor Books. ISBN 9780385471909.

src="Module:Citation/CS1/styles.css"></templatestyles>
- Garrard-Burnett, Virginia (2010). *Terror in the Land of the Holy Spirit: Guatemala Under General Efrain Rios Montt 1982-1983*[724]. Oxford: Oxford University Press. ISBN 9780195379648.<templatestyles src="Module:Citation/CS1/styles.css"></templatestyles>
- Gilbert, John T. (ed.) (2012). *Chartularies of St Mary's Abbey, Dublin: With the Register of Its House at Dunbrody, and Annals of Ireland*[725]. **2**. Cambridge: Cambridge University Press. ISBN 9781108052245.<templatestyles src="Module:Citation/CS1/styles.css"></templatestyles>
- Gräff, Heinrich (1834). *Sammlung sämmtlicher Verordnungen, welche bis Ende 1833 in den von Kamptz'schen Jahrbüchern für Preußische Gesetzgebung enthalten sind*[726]. **7**. Breslau: Georg Philipp Aderholz.<templatestyles src="Module:Citation/CS1/styles.css"></templatestyles>
- Grellet, Fábio (24 May 2010). "Autorizado a visitar família, condenado por morte de Tim Lopes foge da prisão"[727] (in Portuguese). Rio de Janeiro: Folha de S.Paulo. Retrieved 6 July 2013.<templatestyles src="Module:Citation/CS1/styles.css"></templatestyles>
- Grote, George (2013). *History of Greece*[728]. London: Routledge. ISBN 9781134593781.<templatestyles src="Module:Citation/CS1/styles.css"></templatestyles>
- Haldon, John (1997). *Byzantium in the Seventh Century: The Transformation of a Culture*[729]. Cambridge: Cambridge University Press. ISBN 9780521319171.<templatestyles src="Module:Citation/CS1/styles.css"></templatestyles>
- Hamilton, Janet; Hamilton, Bernard; Stoyanov, Yuri (1998). *Christian Dualist Heresies in the Byzantine World, C. 650-c. 1450: Selected Sources*[730]. Manchester: Manchester University Press. ISBN 9780719047657.<templatestyles src="Module:Citation/CS1/styles.css"></templatestyles>
- Hahn, C-G.L. (1966). "The Ovambo". *The Native Tribes of South West Africa*[731]. Abingdon: Frank Cass and Company Limited. pp. 1–37. ISBN 0-7146-1670-2.<templatestyles src="Module:Citation/CS1/styles.css"></templatestyles>
- Heng, Geraldine (2013). *Empire of Magic: Medieval Romance and the Politics of Cultural Fantasy*[732]. New York: Columbia University Press. ISBN 9780231500678.<templatestyles src="Module:Citation/CS1/styles.css"></templatestyles>
- Herden, Ralph B. (2005). *Roter Hahn und Rotes Kreuz: Chronik der Geschichte des Feuerlösch- und Rettungswesens ; von den syphonari der römischen Kaiser über die dienenden Brüder der Hospitaliter-Ritterorden*

bis zu Feuerwehren und Katastrophenschutz, Sanitäts- und Samariterdiensten in der ersten Hälfte des 20. Jahrhunderts[733]. Norderstedt: BoD Books on Demand. ISBN 9783833426209.
- Hermann, Heinrich L. (1818). *Kurze Geschichte des Criminal-Prozesses wider den Brandstifter Johann Christoph Peter Horst, und dessen Geliebte, die unverehelichte Friederike Louise Christiane Delitz.* Berlin.
- Hirschberg, H.Z. (1981). *A history of the Jews in North Africa: From the Ottoman conquests to the present time*[734]. **2**. Leyden: BRILL. ISBN 9789004062955.
- Hoey, Edwin (June 1974). "Terror in New York-1741". *www.americanheritage.com*. **25** (4). ISSN 0002-8738[735].
- Hofmann, Tom (2013). *Benjamin Ferencz, Nuremberg Prosecutor and Peace Advocate*[736]. Jefferson, North Carolina: McFarland. ISBN 9780786474936.
- Hogg, Gary (1980). *Cannibalism & Human Sacrifice*. Coles. ISBN 9780774029254.
- Hogge, Alice (2005). *God's Secret Agents: Queen Elizabeth's Forbidden Priests and the Hatching of the Gunpowder Plot*. London: Harper Collins. ISBN 0-00-715637-5.
- Hübner, Lorenz (7 August 1804). "Eisenach, den 15ten July"[737]. *Kurpfalzbaierische gnädigst priviligierte Münchner Staats-Zeitung*. Munich: Kurpfb. Münchner Zeitungs-Comptoir. **5** (185): 760.
- Hunter, W.W (2013). *The Indian Empire: Its People, History and Products*[738]. London: Routledge. ISBN 9781136383014.
- Ikram, S.M.; Embree, Ainslie T. (1964). "Economic and Social Developments under the Mughals". *Muslim Civilization in India*. New York: Columbia University Press. ISBN 978-0231025805.
- John, Barbara; Pope, Robert (ed.) (2003). "An Examination of the Origins and Development of the Legend of the Jewish Mass Poisoner". *Honouring the Past and Shaping the Future: Religious and Biblical Studies in Wales : Essays in Honour of Gareth Lloyd Jones*[739]. Leomin-

ster: Gracewing Publishing. ISBN 9780852444016.<templatestyles src="Module:Citation/CS1/styles.css"></templatestyles>
- Julius Caesar, Gaius; McDevitt (tr.); Bohn (tr.) (1851). *Cæsar's commentaries on the Gallic and civil wars*[740]. London: Henry G. Bohn.<templatestyles src="Module:Citation/CS1/styles.css"></templatestyles>
- Kamen, Henry (1999). *The Spanish Inquisition: A Historical Revision*. Boston: Yale University Press. ISBN 9780300078800.<templatestyles src="Module:Citation/CS1/styles.css"></templatestyles>
- Kanina, Wangui (21 May 2008). "Mob burns to death 11 Kenyan 'witches'"[741]. *reuters.com*.<templatestyles src="Module:Citation/CS1/styles.css"></templatestyles>
- Kantor, Mattis (1993). *The Jewish Time Line Encyclopedia: A Year-by-Year History From Creation to the Present*[742]. Lanham, Maryland: Jason Aronson, Incorporated. ISBN 9781461631491.<templatestyles src="Module:Citation/CS1/styles.css"></templatestyles>
- Kantor, Máttis (2005). *Codex Judaica: Chronological Index of Jewish History, Covering 5,764 Years of Biblical, Talmudic & Post-Talmudic History*[743]. Zichron Press. ISBN 9780967037837.<templatestyles src="Module:Citation/CS1/styles.css"></templatestyles>
- Klein, Samuel (1833). *Handbuch der Geschichte von Ungarn und seiner Verfaßung*[744]. Leipzig: Wigand.<templatestyles src="Module:Citation/CS1/styles.css"></templatestyles>
- Koch, Johann C. (1824). *Hals-oder peinliche Gerichtsordnung Kaiser Carls V*[745]. Marburg: Krieger.<templatestyles src="Module:Citation/CS1/styles.css"></templatestyles>
- Kurth, Peter (12 November 2002). ""Out of the Flames" by Lawrence and Nancy Goldstone"[746]. *Salon.com*. salon.com. Retrieved 11 February 2014.<templatestyles src="Module:Citation/CS1/styles.css"></templatestyles>
- Kyle, Donald G. (2002). *Spectacles of Death in Ancient Rome*[747]. London: Routledge. ISBN 9780203006351.<templatestyles src="Module:Citation/CS1/styles.css"></templatestyles>
- Landucci, Luca; Jarvis, Alice de Rosen (tr.) (1927). *A Florentine diary from 1450 to 1516*[748]. London: J.M. Dent&Sons, Ltd.<templatestyles src="Module:Citation/CS1/styles.css"></templatestyles>
- Lattimer, Mark (13 December 2007). "Freedom Lost"[749]. *The Guardian*.<templatestyles src="Module:Citation/CS1/styles.css"></templatestyles>
- de La Vega, Garcilaso; Rycaut, Paul (tr.) (1688). *The Royal Commentaries of Peru*[750]. London: Christopher Wilkinson. pp. 216–217.<templatestyles src="Module:Citation/CS1/styles.css"></

templatestyles>
- de Ledrede, Richard; Wright, Thomas (ed.) (1843). *A Contemporary Narrative of the Proceedings Against Dame Alice Kyteler, Prosecuted for Sorcery in 1324, by Richard de Ledrede, Bishop of Ossory*[751]. London: The Camden Society.<templatestyles src="Module:Citation/CS1/styles.css"></templatestyles>
- de Ledrede, Richard; Davidson, Sharon (ed.); Ward, John (2004). *The Sorcery Trial of Alice Kyteler: A Contemporary Account (1324)*. Asheville, North Carolina: Pegasus Press. ISBN 978-1889818429.<templatestyles src="Module:Citation/CS1/styles.css"></templatestyles>
- Lee, Samuel (2010). *Rediscovering Japan, Reintroducing Christendom: Two Thousand Years of Christian History in Japan*[752]. Lanham, Maryland: Hamilton Books. ISBN 9780761849506.<templatestyles src="Module:Citation/CS1/styles.css"></templatestyles>
- Lithgow, William (1814). *Travels & Voyages Through Europe, Asia, and Africa, for Nineteen Years*[753]. London: Longman, Hurst, Rees, Orme&Brown.<templatestyles src="Module:Citation/CS1/styles.css"></templatestyles>
- McCullough, David W. (8 October 2000). "The Fairy Defense"[754]. *New York Times*. Retrieved 23 March 2007.<templatestyles src="Module:Citation/CS1/styles.css"></templatestyles>
- McLynn, Frank (2013). *Crime and Punishment in Eighteenth Century England*[755]. London: Routledge. ISBN 9781136093081.<templatestyles src="Module:Citation/CS1/styles.css"></templatestyles>
- McManus, Edgar J. (1973). *Black Bondage in the North*[756]. Syracuse, New York: Syracuse University Press. ISBN 9780815628934.<templatestyles src="Module:Citation/CS1/styles.css"></templatestyles>
- Manu; Haughton, Graves C., editor and translator (1825). *The Institutes of Menu*[757]. **2**. London: Cox and Baylis.<templatestyles src="Module:Citation/CS1/styles.css"></templatestyles>
- Markoe, Glenn (2000). *Phoenicians*[758]. Berkeley, Los Angeles: University of California Press. ISBN 9780520226142.<templatestyles src="Module:Citation/CS1/styles.css"></templatestyles>
- Matar, Nabil I. (2013). *Europe Through Arab Eyes, 1578-1727*[759]. New York: Columbia University Press. ISBN 9780231512084.<templatestyles src="Module:Citation/CS1/styles.css"></templatestyles>
- Matsumoto, Dianna (2009). *The Soul of a Nation: Japan's Destiny*[760]. Garden City, New York: Morgan James Publishing. ISBN 9781600375538.<templatestyles src="Module:Citation/CS1/styles.css"></templatestyles>

- Miley, John (1843). *Rome, as it was Under Paganism, and as it Became Under the Popes, Volume 1*[761]. London: J. Madden. pp. 223–224.<templatestyles src="Module:Citation/CS1/styles.css"></templatestyles>
- Miller, John (1972). *Popery and Politics in England 1660–1688*[762]. Cambridge: Cambridge University Press. ISBN 9780521202367.<templatestyles src="Module:Citation/CS1/styles.css"></templatestyles>
- Mittra, Sangh; Kumar, Bachchan (2004). *Encyclopaedia of Women in South Asia: Nepal*[763]. **6**. Gyan Publishing House. ISBN 9788178351933.<templatestyles src="Module:Citation/CS1/styles.css"></templatestyles>
- Mooney, John A. (1919). *Joan of Arc*. New York: Encyclopedia Press, Incorporated.<templatestyles src="Module:Citation/CS1/styles.css"></templatestyles>
- Mooney, John A.; Patterson, Gail (ed.) (2002). "From Domremy to Chinon". *Joan of Arc: Historical Overview and Bibliography*[764]. Hauppauge, New York: Nova Publishers. ISBN 9781590335031.<templatestyles src="Module:Citation/CS1/styles.css"></templatestyles>
- Moryson, Fynes; Hadfield, Andrew (2001). "Fynes Moryson, *An Itinerary* (1617)". *Amazons, Savages, and Machiavels*[765]. Oxford: Oxford University Press. pp. 166–179. ISBN 9780198711865.<templatestyles src="Module:Citation/CS1/styles.css"></templatestyles>
- Murphy, Cullen (2012). *God's Jury: The Inquisition and the making of the Modern World*[766]. New York: Houghton Mifflin Harcourt. ISBN 978-0-618-09156-0.<templatestyles src="Module:Citation/CS1/styles.css"></templatestyles>
- Nassau, George R. S. (1824). *Catalogue of the ... library of ... George Nassau, which will be sold by auction, by mr. Evans, Feb. 16*[767]. p. 17.<templatestyles src="Module:Citation/CS1/styles.css"></templatestyles>
- Oehlschlaeger, Emil (1866). *Posen. Kurz gefasste Geschichte und Beschreibung der Stadt Posen*[768]. Posen: Louis Merzbach.<templatestyles src="Module:Citation/CS1/styles.css"></templatestyles>
- Olmstead, Albert Ten Eyck (February 1918). "Assyrian Government of Dependencies". *The American Political Science Review*. American Political Science Association. **12, 1**: 63–77. ISSN 0003-0554[769]. JSTOR 1946342[770].<templatestyles src="Module:Citation/CS1/styles.css"></templatestyles>
- Osenbrüggen, Eduard (1854). *Die brandstiftung in den strafgesetzbüchern Deutschlands und der deutschen Schweiz*[771]. Leipzig: J.G.

Hinrich.<templatestyles src="Module:Citation/CS1/styles.css"></templatestyles>
- Osenbrüggen, Eduard (1860). *Das alamannische Strafrecht im deutschen Mittelalter*[772]. Schaffhausen: Hurter.<templatestyles src="Module:Citation/CS1/styles.css"></templatestyles>
- O'Shea, Kathleen A. (1999). *Women and the Death Penalty in the United States, 1900-1998*[773]. Westport, Connecticut: Greenwood Publishing Group. ISBN 9780275959524.<templatestyles src="Module:Citation/CS1/styles.css"></templatestyles>
- Pagán, Victoria (2012). *Conspiracy Theory in Latin Literature*[774]. Austin, Texas: University of Texas Press. ISBN 9780292749795.<templatestyles src="Module:Citation/CS1/styles.css"></templatestyles>
- Paige, Jeffery M (November 1983). "Social Theory and Peasant Revolution in Vietnam and Guatemala"[775] (PDF). *Theory and Society*. **12** (6): 699–737. doi: 10.1007/bf00912078[776]. ISSN 0304-2421[777].<templatestyles src="Module:Citation/CS1/styles.css"></templatestyles>
- Pasachoff, Naomi E.; Littman, Robert J. (2005). *A Concise History of the Jewish People*[778]. Lanham, Maryland: Rowman & Littlefield. ISBN 9780742543669.<templatestyles src="Module:Citation/CS1/styles.css"></templatestyles>
- Pavlac, Brian A. (2009). *Witch Hunts in the Western World: Persecution and Punishment from the Inquisition Through the Salem Trials*[779]. Westport, Connecticut: ABC-CLIO. ISBN 9780313348730.<templatestyles src="Module:Citation/CS1/styles.css"></templatestyles>
- Peletz, Michael G. (2002). *Islamic Modern: Religious Courts and Cultural Politics in Malaysia*[780]. Princeton, New Jersey: Princeton University Press. ISBN 9780691095080.<templatestyles src="Module:Citation/CS1/styles.css"></templatestyles>
- Perckmayr, Reginbald (1738). *Geschichte und Predig-Buch*[781]. **2**. Augsburg: Martin Veith.<templatestyles src="Module:Citation/CS1/styles.css"></templatestyles>
- Peter from Mladanovic (2003). "How was executed Jan Hus"[782]. *Newyorske listy*. ISSN 1093-2887[783]. Retrieved 11 February 2014.<templatestyles src="Module:Citation/CS1/styles.css"></templatestyles>
- Pharr, Clyde (tr.) (2001). *The Theodosian Code*[784]. Union, New Jersey: The Lawbook Exchange, Ltd. ISBN 978-1-58477-146-3.<templatestyles src="Module:Citation/CS1/styles.css"></templatestyles>
- Pickett, Brent L. (2009). *The A to Z of Homosexuality*[785]. Lanham, Maryland: Scarecrow Press. ISBN 9780810870727.<templatestyles src="Module:Citation/CS1/styles.css"></templatestyles>

- Pluskowski, Aleksander (2013). *The Archaeology of the Prussian Crusade: Holy War and Colonisation*[786]. London: Routledge. ISBN 9781136162817.<templatestyles src="Module:Citation/CS1/styles.css"></templatestyles>
- Prager, Dennis; Telushkin, Joseph (2007). *Why the Jews?: The Reason for Antisemitism*[787]. New York: Touchstone. ISBN 9781416591238.<templatestyles src="Module:Citation/CS1/styles.css"></templatestyles>
- Puff, Helmut; Bennett, Judith M.(ed.); Karras, Ruth M. (ed.) (2013). "Same Sex Possibilities". *The Oxford Handbook of Women and Gender in Medieval Europe*[788]. Oxford: Oxford University Press. ISBN 9780199582174.<templatestyles src="Module:Citation/CS1/styles.css"></templatestyles>
- Quint, Emmanuel B. (2005). *A Restatement of Rabbinic Civil Law*[789]. **10**. Jerusalem: Gefen Publishing House Ltd. ISBN 9789652293237.<templatestyles src="Module:Citation/CS1/styles.css"></templatestyles>
- Radbruch, Gustav (1992). "Abbau des Strafrechts. Bemerkungen über den Entwurf 1925 mit Anmerkungen über den Entwurf 1927 (published 1927)". *Gesamtausgabe, Band 9: Strafrechtsreform*[790]. Heidelberg: C.F. Müller. pp. 246–252. ISBN 9783811450912.<templatestyles src="Module:Citation/CS1/styles.css"></templatestyles>
- Rapley, Robert (2001). *A Case of Witchcraft: The Trial of Urbain Grandier*[791]. McGill-Queen's Press – MQUP. ISBN 9780773523128.<templatestyles src="Module:Citation/CS1/styles.css"></templatestyles>
- Reeder, Caryn A. (2012). *The Enemy in the Household: Family Violence in Deuteronomy and Beyond*[792]. Grand Rapids, Michigan: Baker Books. ISBN 9781441236197.<templatestyles src="Module:Citation/CS1/styles.css"></templatestyles>
- Richards, Jeffrey (2013). *Sex, Dissidence and Damnation: Minority Groups in the Middle Ages*[793]. London: Routledge. ISBN 9781136127007.<templatestyles src="Module:Citation/CS1/styles.css"></templatestyles>
- Richards, William (1812). *The History of Lynn: Civil, Ecclesiastical, Political, Commercial, Biographical, Municipal, and Military, from the Earliest Accounts to the Present Time*[794]. **2**. Lynn: W. G. Whittingham.<templatestyles src="Module:Citation/CS1/styles.css"></templatestyles>
- Roth, Mitchel (2010). *Crime and Punishment: A History of the Criminal Justice System*[795]. Belmont, California: Cengage Learning. ISBN 9780495809883.<templatestyles src="Module:Citation/CS1/

styles.css"></templatestyles>
- Rowland, Ingrid D. (2009). *Giordano Bruno: Philosopher/Heretic*[796]. Chicago: University of Chicago Press. p. 10. ISBN 9780226730240.<templatestyles src="Module:Citation/CS1/styles.css"></templatestyles>
- Salomon, H.P.; Sassoon, I. S.D.; Saraiva, Antonio Jose (2001). "Appendix Four: The Portuguese Inquisition in Goa (India), 1561–1812". *The Marrano Factory. The Portuguese Inquisition and Its New Christians, 1536–1765*. Leyden: Brill. ISBN 9789004120808.<templatestyles src="Module:Citation/CS1/styles.css"></templatestyles>
- Sangvi, Vir (8 February 1999). "A Kill Before Dying"[797]. *Rediff on the Net*. Rediff.com.<templatestyles src="Module:Citation/CS1/styles.css"></templatestyles>
- Sashi, S.S. (1996). *Encyclopaedia Indica: India, Pakistan, Bangladesh*. **100**. Anmol Publications. ISBN 9788170418597.<templatestyles src="Module:Citation/CS1/styles.css"></templatestyles>
- Saunders, John J. (2001). *The History of the Mongol Conquests*[798]. Philadelphia: University of Pennsylvania Press. ISBN 9780812217667.<templatestyles src="Module:Citation/CS1/styles.css"></templatestyles>
- Sayles, George O. (17 February 1971). "King Richard II of England, A Fresh Look"[799]. *Proceedings of the American Philosophical Society*. Philadelphia: The American Philosophical Society. 115,1: 28–32. ISSN 0003-049X[800].<templatestyles src="Module:Citation/CS1/styles.css"></templatestyles>
- Schneider, Tammi J. (2008). *Mothers of Promise: Women in the Book of Genesis*[801]. Grand Rapids, Michigan: Baker Academic. ISBN 9781441206015.<templatestyles src="Module:Citation/CS1/styles.css"></templatestyles>
- Schulte Nordholt, H.G.C. (2010). *The Spell of Power: A History of Balinese Politics, 1650-1940*[802]. Leyden: BRILL. ISBN 9789004253759.<templatestyles src="Module:Citation/CS1/styles.css"></templatestyles>
- Schwartz, Jeffrey; Houghton, Frank; Macchiarelli, Roberto; Bondioli, Luca (17 February 2010). "Skeletal Remains from Punic Carthage Do Not Support Systematic Sacrifice of Infants"[803]. *PLoS ONE*. **5** (2): e9177. Bibcode: 2010PLoSO...5.9177S[804]. doi: 10.1371/journal.pone.0009177[805]. PMC 2822869[806]. PMID 20174667[807] – via PLoS ONE.<templatestyles src="Module:Citation/CS1/styles.css"></templatestyles>
- Scott, George R. (2003) [1940]. *History of Torture throughout the Ages*. Kila, Montana/US: Kessinger Publishing Co.

ISBN 9780766140639.<templatestyles src="Module:Citation/CS1/styles.css"></templatestyles>
- Sharma, Pushpa; Srivastava, Vijay Shankar (1981). "The Military System of the Mongols". *Cultural Contours of India: Dr. Satya Prakash Felicitation Volume*[808]. Abhinav Publications. p. 361. ISBN 9780391023581.<templatestyles src="Module:Citation/CS1/styles.css"></templatestyles>
- Shaw, Thomas (1757). *Travels, or Observations relating to several parts of Barbary and the Levant*[809]. London, UK: Millar and Sandby. p. 253.<templatestyles src="Module:Citation/CS1/styles.css"></templatestyles>
- Smirke, Edward (1865). "Extracts from original Records relating to the Burning of Lepers in the reign of Edward II"[810]. *The Archaeological Journal*. London: Central Committee of the Archaeological Institute. **22**: 326–331. doi: 10.1080/00665983.1865.10851326[811].<templatestyles src="Module:Citation/CS1/styles.css"></templatestyles>
- Soukhorukov, Sergey (13 June 2004). "Train blast was 'a plot to kill North Korea's leader"[812]. *The Daily Telegraph*.<templatestyles src="Module:Citation/CS1/styles.css"></templatestyles>
- Springer, Alex (24 September 2008). "Der Letzte Feuer"[813]. *Die Welt*.<templatestyles src="Module:Citation/CS1/styles.css"></templatestyles>
- St. Clair, William (2008) [1972]. *That Greece Might Still Be Free*[814] (revised ed.). Cambridge: Open Book Publishers. ISBN 978-1-906924-00-3.<templatestyles src="Module:Citation/CS1/styles.css"></templatestyles>
- Steel, Catherine (2013). *The End of the Roman Republic 146 to 44 BC: Conquest and Crisis*[815]. Edinburgh: Edinburgh University Press. p. 98. ISBN 9780748619443.<templatestyles src="Module:Citation/CS1/styles.css"></templatestyles>
- Stevens, George A. (1764). *The Beauties of All Magazines Selected for the Year 1764 (including several Comic Pieces)*[816]. **3**. London: T. Waller.<templatestyles src="Module:Citation/CS1/styles.css"></templatestyles>
- Stewart, Alan (2003). *The Cradle King: A Life of James VI & 1*. London: Chatto and Windus. ISBN 0-7011-6984-2.<templatestyles src="Module:Citation/CS1/styles.css"></templatestyles>
- Stillman, Norman A. (1979). *The Jews of Arab Lands: A History and Source Book*[817]. Jewish Publication Society. ISBN 9780827611559.<templatestyles src="Module:Citation/CS1/styles.css"></templatestyles>

- Stillman, Yedida K. (ed.); Zucker, George K.(ed.) (1993). *New Horizons in Sephardic Studies*[818]. Albany, New York: SUNY Press. ISBN 9780791414026.<templatestyles src="Module:Citation/CS1/styles.css"></templatestyles>
- Sumner, William G. (2007). *Folkways: A Study of Mores, Manners, Customs and Morals*[819]. New York: Cosimo, Inc. ISBN 9781602067585.<templatestyles src="Module:Citation/CS1/styles.css"></templatestyles>
- Suwurow, Victor (1995). *GRU – Die Speerspitze: Was der KGB für die Polit-Führung, ist die GRU für die Rote Armee* (3rd ed.). Solingen: Barett. ISBN 3-924753-18-0.<templatestyles src="Module:Citation/CS1/styles.css"></templatestyles>
- Telchin, Stan (2004). *Messianic Judaism is Not Christianity: A Loving Call to Unity*[820]. Chosen Books. ISBN 9780800793722.<templatestyles src="Module:Citation/CS1/styles.css"></templatestyles>
- De Thévenot, Jean; Lovell, Archibald (1687). *The Travels Of Monsieur De Thevenot Into The Levant*[821]. 1. London: Faithorne.<templatestyles src="Module:Citation/CS1/styles.css"></templatestyles>
- Thurston, H. (1912). "Witchcraft"[822]. *The Catholic Encyclopedia*. New York: Robert Appleton Company. Retrieved 12 December 2010.<templatestyles src="Module:Citation/CS1/styles.css"></templatestyles>
- Tjernagel, N.S. (1974). "Patrick Hamilton: Precursor of the Reformation in Scotland"[823]. *Wisconsin Lutheran Quarterly*. 74. ISSN 0362-5648[824]. Archived from the original[825] on 7 July 2010.<templatestyles src="Module:Citation/CS1/styles.css"></templatestyles>
- Trenchard-Smith, Margaret; Turner, Wendy (ed.) (2010). "Insanity, Exculpation and Disempowerment in Byzantine Law". *Madness in Medieval Law and Custom*[826]. Leiden: BRILL. ISBN 978-90-04-18749-8.<templatestyles src="Module:Citation/CS1/styles.css"></templatestyles>
- Tully, Miss (1817). *Narrative of a ten years' residence at Tripoli in Africa*[827]. London: Henry Colburn.<templatestyles src="Module:Citation/CS1/styles.css"></templatestyles>
- Universal House of Justice (2001). *Applicability of the Laws and Ordinances of the Kitab-i-Aqdas*[828].<templatestyles src="Module:Citation/CS1/styles.css"></templatestyles>
- Waddell, Hope M. (1863). *Twenty-nine years in the West Indies and Central Africa: a review of missionary work and adventure. 1829-1858*[829]. London: T. Nelson and sons. p. 19.<templatestyles src="Module:Citation/CS1/styles.css"></templatestyles>
- Watson, Alan (ed.) (1998). *The Digest of Justinian*. 4. Philadelphia: University of Pennsylvania Press. ISBN 9780812220360.<templatestyles

- Weinberger-Thomas, Catherine (1999). *Ashes of Immortality: Widow-Burning in India*[830]. Chicago: University of Chicago Press,. ISBN 9780226885681.
- Weiss, Moshe (2004). *A Brief History of the Jewish People*[831]. Lanham, Maryland: Rowman & Littlefield. ISBN 9780742544024.
- White, Jon M. (2011). *Everyday Life in Ancient Egypt*[832]. Minneola, New York: Courier Dover Publications. ISBN 9780486425108.
- Wiener, Margaret J. (1995). *Visible and Invisible Realms: Power, Magic, and Colonial Conquest in Bali*[833]. Chicago: University of Chicago Press. ISBN 9780226885827.
- Wilkinson, Toby (2011). *The Rise and Fall of Ancient Egypt*[834]. London: Bloomsbury Publishing. ISBN 9781408810026.
- Willis-Bund, J.W. (1982). *A Selection of Cases from the State Trials. Vol. II Part I. Trials for Treason (1660–1678)*[835]. Cambridge: CUP Archive. ASIN B0029U3KWY[836].
- Wills, C.J. (1891). *In the land of the lion and sun*[837]. p. 204.
- Wilson, David H. (1963) [original edition 1956]. *King James VI & 1*. London, UK: Jonathan Cape Ltd. ISBN 0-224-60572-0.
- Wilson, James Holbert. (1853). *Temple bar, the city Golgotha, by a member of the Inner Temple*[838]. London: David Bogue. p. 4.
- Winroth, Anders; Müller, Wolfgang P. (ed.); Sommar, Mary E.(ed.). "Neither Slave Nor Free:Theology and Law in Gratian's Thoughts on the Definition of Marriage and Unfree Persons". *Medieval Church Law and the Origins of the Western Legal Tradition: A Tribute to Kenneth Pennington*[839]. CUA Press. ISBN 9780813214627.
- Woblers, Julien (1 September 1855). "Speech for the Amsterdam Anti Slavery Society, 19th July 1855"[840]. *The Anti Slavery Reporter*. London: Peter Jones Bolton. **3**.

styles.css"></templatestyles>
- Wood, Alan (2011). *Russia's Frozen Frontier: A History of Siberia and the Russian Far East 1581 - 1991*[841]. London: Bloomsbury Academic. p. 44. ISBN 9780340971246.<templatestyles src="Module:Citation/CS1/styles.css"></templatestyles>
- Zurkhana, Taif (ed.); Houtsma, M. (1987). *E.J. Brill's First Encyclopaedia of Islam 1913-1936*[842]. **8**. Leyden: BRILL. ISBN 9789004082656.<templatestyles src="Module:Citation/CS1/styles.css"></templatestyles>
- Yang, Anand A.; Sarkar, Sumit (ed.); Sarkar, Tanika (ed.) (2008). "Whose Sati?Widow-Burning in early Nineteenth Century India". *Women and Social Reform in Modern India: A Reader*[843]. Bloomington, Indiana: Indiana University Press. ISBN 9780253352699.<templatestyles src="Module:Citation/CS1/styles.css"></templatestyles>
- Zvi Gilat, Israel; Lifshitz, Berachyahu (ed.) (2013). "Exegetical creativity in Interpreting Biblical Laws". *Jewish Law Annual*[844]. **20**. London: Routledge. p. 62, footnote 73. ISBN 9781136013768.<templatestyles src="Module:Citation/CS1/styles.css"></templatestyles>

External links

 Wikisourcehas the text of the 1911 *Encyclopædia Britannica*article ***Burning to Death***.

- CapitalPunishmentUK.org[845]
- List of deaths by fire throughout history[846]

Crucifixion

Crucifixion is a method of capital punishment in which the victim is tied or nailed to a large wooden beam and left to hang for several days until eventual death from exhaustion and asphyxiation.

The crucifixion of Jesus is a central narrative in Christianity, and the cross (sometimes depicting Jesus nailed onto it) is the main religious symbol for many Christian churches.

Figure 121: *Christ at the Cross by Carl Bloch, painting c. 1870*

Terminology

Ancient Greek has two verbs for crucify: *ana-stauro* (ἀνασταυρόω), from *stauros*, "stake", and *apo-tumpanizo* (ἀποτυμπανίζω) "crucify on a plank",[847] together with *anaskolopizo* (ἀνασκολοπίζω "impale"). In earlier pre-Roman Greek texts *anastauro* usually means "impale".[848,849,850]

New Testament Greek uses four verbs, three of them based upon *stauros* (σταυρός), usually translated "cross". The most common term is *stauroo* (σταυρόω), "to crucify", occurring 43 times; *sustauroo* (συσταυρόω), "to crucify with" or "alongside" occurs five times, while *anastauroo* (ἀνασταυρόω), "to crucify again" occurs only once at the Epistle to the Hebrews 6:6. *prospegnumi* (προσπήγνυμι), "to fix or fasten to, impale, crucify" occurs only once at the Acts of the Apostles 2:23.

The English term *cross* derives from the Latin word *crux*. The Latin term *crux* classically referred to a tree or any construction of wood used to hang criminals as a form of execution. The term later came to refer specifically to a cross.[851]

The English term *crucifix* derives from the Latin *crucifixus* or *cruci fixus*, past participle passive of *crucifigere* or *cruci figere*, meaning "to crucify" or "to fasten to a cross".

Figure 122: *This crucifix is attributed to Michelangelo, notable for showing naked crucifixion.*

Details

Crucifixion was most often performed to dissuade its witnesses from perpetrating similar (usually particularly heinous) crimes. Victims were sometimes left on display after death as a warning to any other potential criminals. Crucifixion was usually intended to provide a death that was particularly slow, painful (hence the term *excruciating*, literally "out of crucifying"), gruesome, humiliating, and public, using whatever means were most expedient for that goal. Crucifixion methods varied considerably with location and time period.

The Greek and Latin words corresponding to "crucifixion" applied to many different forms of painful execution, including being impaled on a stake, or affixed to a tree, upright pole (a crux simplex), or (most famous now) to a combination of an upright (in Latin, *stipes*) and a crossbeam (in Latin, *patibulum*). Seneca the Younger wrote: "I see crosses there, not just of one kind but made in many different ways: some have their victims with head down to the ground; some impale their private parts; others stretch out their arms on the gibbet".[852]

In some cases, the condemned was forced to carry the crossbeam to the place of execution. A whole cross would weigh well over 135 kg (300 lb), but the crossbeam would not be quite as burdensome, weighing around 45 kg (100 lb)

The Roman historian Tacitus records that the city of Rome had a specific place for carrying out executions, situated outside the Esquiline Gate, and had a specific area reserved for the execution of slaves by crucifixion. Upright posts would presumably be fixed permanently in that place, and the crossbeam, with the condemned person perhaps already nailed to it, would then be attached to the post.

The person executed may have been attached to the cross by rope, though nails and other sharp materials are mentioned in a passage by the Judean historian Josephus, where he states that at the Siege of Jerusalem (70), "the soldiers out of rage and hatred, *nailed* those they caught, one after one way, and another after another, to the crosses, by way of jest". Objects used in the crucifixion of criminals, such as nails, were sought as amulets with perceived medicinal qualities.[853]

While a crucifixion was an execution, it was also a humiliation, by making the condemned as vulnerable as possible. Although artists have traditionally depicted the figure on a cross with a loin cloth or a covering of the genitals, the person being crucified was usually stripped naked. Writings by Seneca the Younger state some victims suffered a stick forced upwards through their groin.[854] Despite its frequent use by the Romans, the horrors of crucifixion did not escape criticism by some eminent Roman orators. Cicero, for example, described crucifixion as "a most cruel and disgusting punishment", and suggested that "the very mention of the cross should be far removed not only from a Roman citizen's body, but from his mind, his eyes, his ears".[855] Elsewhere he says, "It is a crime to bind a Roman citizen; to scourge him is a wickedness; to put him to death is almost parricide. What shall I say of crucifying him? So guilty an action cannot by any possibility be adequately expressed by any name bad enough for it."

Frequently, the legs of the person executed were broken or shattered with an iron club, an act called *crurifragium*, which was also frequently applied without crucifixion to slaves. This act hastened the death of the person but was also meant to deter those who observed the crucifixion from committing offenses.

Cross shape

<templatestyles src="Multiple_image/styles.css" />

Crux simplex, a simple wooden stake. Image by Justus Lipsius.

The crucifixion of Jesus. Image by Justus Lipsius[856]

The gibbet on which crucifixion was carried out could be of many shapes. Josephus describes several tortures and positions of crucifixion during the Siege of Jerusalem as Titus crucified the rebels; and Seneca the Younger recounts: "I see crosses there, not just of one kind but made in many different ways: some have their victims with head down to the ground; some impale their private parts; others stretch out their arms on the gibbet."

At times the gibbet was only one vertical stake, called in Latin *crux simplex*. This was the simplest available construction for torturing and killing the condemned. Frequently, however, there was a cross-piece attached either at the top to give the shape of a T (*crux commissa*) or just below the top, as in the form most familiar in Christian symbolism (*crux immissa*).[857] The most ancient image of a Roman crucifixion depicts an individual on a T-shaped cross. It is a graffito found in a taberna (hostel for wayfarers) in Puteoli, dating to the time of Trajan or Hadrian (late 1st century to early 2nd century AD).

Some 2nd-century writers took it for granted that a crucified person's arms would be stretched out, not connected to a single stake: Lucian speaks of Prometheus as crucified "above the ravine with his hands outstretched" and explains that the letter T (the Greek letter tau) was looked upon as an unlucky letter or sign (similar to the way the number thirteen is looked upon today as

Figure 123: *Crucifixion window by Henry E. Sharp, 1872, in St. Matthew's German Evangelical Lutheran Church, Charleston, South Carolina*

an unlucky number), saying that the letter got its "evil significance" because of the "evil instrument" which had that shape, an instrument on which tyrants crucified people. Jehovah's Witnesses argue that Jesus was crucified on a *crux simplex*, and that the *crux immissa* was first used as a Christian symbol near the time of the supposed conversion of Emperor Constantine. Other forms were in the shape of the letters X and Y.

The New Testament writings about the crucifixion of Jesus do not speak specifically about the shape of that cross, but the early writings that do speak of its shape, from about the year AD 100 on, describe it as shaped like the letter T (the Greek letter tau)[858] or as composed of an upright and a transverse beam, sometimes with a small projection in the upright.[859,860]

Nail placement

In popular depictions of the crucifixion of Jesus (possibly because in translations of John 20:25[861] the wounds are described as being "in his hands"), Jesus is shown with nails in his hands. But in Greek the word "χείρ", usually translated as "hand", could refer to the entire portion of the arm below the elbow,[862] and to denote the *hand* as distinct from the *arm* some other word could be added, as "ἄκρην οὔτασε χεῖρα" (he wounded the end of the χείρ, i.e., "he wounded her in the hand".

A possibility that does not require tying is that the nails were inserted just above the wrist, between the two bones of the forearm (the radius and the ulna).

An experiment that was the subject of a documentary on the National Geographic Channel's *Quest For Truth: The Crucifixion*, showed that nailed feet provided enough support for the body, and that the hands could have been merely tied. Nailing the feet to the side of the cross relieves strain on the wrists by placing most of the weight on the lower body.

Another possibility, suggested by Frederick Zugibe, is that the nails may have been driven in at an angle, entering in the palm in the crease that delineates the bulky region at the base of the thumb, and exiting in the wrist, passing through the carpal tunnel.

A foot-rest (*suppedaneum*) attached to the cross, perhaps for the purpose of taking the person's weight off the wrists, is sometimes included in representations of the crucifixion of Jesus, but is not discussed in ancient sources. Some scholars interpret the Alexamenos graffito, the earliest surviving depiction of the Crucifixion, as including such a foot-rest. Ancient sources also mention the *sedile*, a small seat attached to the front of the cross, about halfway down, which could have served a similar purpose.

In 1968, archaeologists discovered at Giv'at ha-Mivtar in northeast Jerusalem the remains of one Jehohanan, who had been crucified in the 1st century. The remains included a heel bone with a nail driven through it from the side. The tip of the nail was bent, perhaps because of striking a knot in the upright beam, which prevented it being extracted from the foot. A first inaccurate account of the length of the nail led some to believe that it had been driven through both heels, suggesting that the man had been placed in a sort of sidesaddle position, but the true length of the nail, 11.5 cm (4.53 inches), suggests instead that in this case of crucifixion the heels were nailed to opposite sides of the upright.[863] The skeleton from Giv'at ha-Mivtar is currently the only recovered example of ancient crucifixion in the archaeological record.

Cause of death

The length of time required to reach death could range from hours to days depending on method, the victim's health, and the environment. A literature review by Maslen and Mitchell identified scholarly support for several possible causes of death: cardiac rupture, heart failure, hypovolemic shock, acidosis, asphyxia, arrhythmia, and pulmonary embolism. Death could result from any combination of those factors or from other causes, including sepsis following

Figure 124: *"Burmese Dacoits Readied for Execution"*, photography by Willough Wallace Hooper (c. 1880). "Dacoit" is the Anglicized form of the Hindustani word for "bandit".

infection due to the wounds caused by the nails or by the scourging that often preceded crucifixion, eventual dehydration, or animal predation.

A theory attributed to Pierre Barbet holds that, when the whole body weight was supported by the stretched arms, the typical cause of death was asphyxiation. He wrote that the condemned would have severe difficulty inhaling, due to hyper-expansion of the chest muscles and lungs. The condemned would therefore have to draw himself up by the arms, leading to exhaustion, or have his feet supported by tying or by a wood block. When no longer able to lift himself, the condemned would die within a few minutes. Some scholars, including Frederick Zugibe, posit other causes of death. Zugibe suspended test subjects with their arms at 60° to 70° from the vertical. The test subjects had no difficulty breathing during experiments, but did suffer rapidly increasing pain, which is consistent with the Roman use of crucifixion to achieve a prolonged, agonizing death. However, Zugibe's positioning of the test subjects' feet is not supported by any archaeological or historical evidence.

Survival

Since death does not follow immediately on crucifixion, survival after a short period of crucifixion is possible, as in the case of those who choose each year as a devotional practice to be non-lethally crucified.

There is an ancient record of one person who survived a crucifixion that was intended to be lethal, but that was interrupted. Josephus recounts: "I saw many captives crucified, and remembered three of them as my former acquaintance. I was very sorry at this in my mind, and went with tears in my eyes to Titus, and told him of them; so he immediately commanded them to be taken down, and to have the greatest care taken of them, in order to their recovery; yet two of them died under the physician's hands, while the third recovered."[864] Josephus gives no details of the method or duration of the crucifixion of his three friends before their reprieve.

Archaeological evidence

Although the ancient Jewish historian Josephus, as well as other sources,Wikipedia:Avoid weasel words refers to the crucifixion of thousands of people by the Romans, there is only a single archaeological discovery of a crucified body dating back to the Roman Empire around the time of Jesus. This was discovered at Givat HaMivtar, Jerusalem in 1968.[865] It is not necessarily surprising that there is only one such discovery, because a crucified body was usually left to decay on the cross and therefore would not be preserved. The only reason these archaeological remains were preserved was because family members gave this particular individual a customary burial.

The remains were found accidentally in an ossuary with the crucified man's name on it, 'Jehohanan, the son of Hagakol'.[866] Nicu Haas, an anthropologist at the Hebrew University Medical School in Jerusalem, examined the ossuary and discovered that it contained a heel bone with a nail driven through its side, indicating that the man had been crucified. The position of the nail relative to the bone indicates that the feet had been nailed to the cross from their side, not from their front; various opinions have been proposed as to whether they were both nailed together to the front of the cross or one on the left side, one on the right side. The point of the nail had olive wood fragments on it indicating that he was crucified on a cross made of olive wood or on an olive tree. Since olive trees are not very tall, this would suggest that the condemned was crucified at eye level.

Additionally, a piece of acacia wood was located between the bones and the head of the nail, presumably to keep the condemned from freeing his foot by sliding it over the nail. His legs were found broken, possibly to hasten his death. It is thought that because in Roman times iron was rare, the nails were removed from the dead body to conserve costs. According to Haas, this could help to explain why only one nail has been found, as the tip of the nail in question was bent in such a way that it could not be removed.

Haas had also identified a scratch on the inner surface of the right radius bone of the forearm, close to the wrist. He deduced from the form of the scratch, as well as from the intact wrist bones, that a nail had been driven into the forearm at that position. However, many of Haas' findings have been challenged. For instance, it was subsequently determined that the scratches in the wrist area were non-traumatic – and, therefore, not evidence of crucifixion – while reexamination of the heel bone revealed that the two heels were not nailed together, but rather separately to either side of the upright post of the cross.

History and religious texts

Pre-Roman states

Crucifixion (or impalement), in one form or another, was used by Persians, Carthaginians, and Macedonians.

The Greeks were generally opposed to performing crucifixions.[867] However, in his *Histories*, ix.120–122, the Greek writer Herodotus describes the execution of a Persian general at the hands of Athenians in about 479 BC: "They nailed him to a plank and hung him up ... this Artayctes who suffered death by crucifixion."[868] The *Commentary on Herodotus* by How and Wells remarks: "They crucified him with hands and feet stretched out and nailed to crosspieces; cf. vii.33. This barbarity, unusual on the part of Greeks, may be explained by the enormity of the outrage or by Athenian deference to local feeling."[869]

Some Christian theologians, beginning with Paul of Tarsus writing in Galatians 3:13[870], have interpreted an allusion to crucifixion in Deuteronomy 21:22-23[871]. This reference is to being hanged from a tree, and may be associated with lynching or traditional hanging. However, Rabbinic law limited capital punishment to just 4 methods of execution: stoning, burning, strangulation, and decapitation, while the passage in Deuteronomy was interpreted as an obligation to hang the corpse on a tree as a form of deterrence.[872] The fragmentary Aramaic Testament of Levi (DSS 4Q541) interprets in column 6: "God ... (partially legible)-*will set* ... right errors. ... (partially legible)-*He will judge* ... revealed sins. Investigate and seek and know how Jonah wept. Thus, you shall not destroy the weak by wasting away or by ... (partially legible)-*crucifixion* ... Let not the nail touch him."[873]

The Jewish king Alexander Jannaeus, king of Judea from 103 BC to 76 BC, crucified 800 rebels, said to be Pharisees, in the middle of Jerusalem.

Alexander the Great is reputed to have crucified 2,000 survivors from his siege of the Phoenician city of Tyre,[874] as well as the doctor who unsuccessfully treated Alexander's friend Hephaestion. Some historians have also conjectured that Alexander crucified Callisthenes, his official historian and biographer, for objecting to Alexander's adoption of the Persian ceremony of royal adoration.

In Carthage, crucifixion was an established mode of execution, which could even be imposed on generals for suffering a major defeat.

The oldest crucifixion may be a post-mortem one mentioned by Herodotus. Polycrates, the tyrant of Samos, was put to death in 522 B.C. by Persians, and his dead body was then crucified.[875]

Ancient Rome

History

The hypothesis that the Ancient Roman custom of crucifixion may have developed out of a primitive custom of *arbori suspendere*—hanging on an *arbor infelix* ("inauspicious tree") dedicated to the gods of the nether world—is rejected by William A. Oldfather, who shows that this form of execution (the *supplicium more maiorum*, punishment in accordance with the custom of our ancestors) consisted of suspending someone from a tree, not dedicated to any particular gods, and flogging him to death. Tertullian mentions a 1st-century AD case in which trees were used for crucifixion, but Seneca the Younger earlier used the phrase *infelix lignum* (unfortunate wood) for the transom ("patibulum") or the whole cross.[876] Plautus and Plutarch are the two main sources for accounts of criminals carrying their own patibula to the upright *stipes*.[877]

Notorious mass crucifixions followed the Third Servile War in 73–71 BC (the slave rebellion under Spartacus), other Roman civil wars in the 2nd and 1st centuries BC, and the destruction of Jerusalem in AD 70. Crassus crucified 6,000 of Spartacus' followers hunted down and captured after his defeat in battle. Josephus tells a story of the Romans crucifying people along the walls of Jerusalem. He also says that the Roman soldiers would amuse themselves by crucifying criminals in different positions.

Constantine the Great, the first Christian emperor, abolished crucifixion in the Roman Empire in 337 out of veneration for Jesus Christ, its most famous victim.[878]

Society and law

<templatestyles src="Multiple_image/styles.css" />

The Alexamenos graffito, a satirical representation of the Christian worship, depicting a man worshiping a crucified donkey (Rome, c AD 85 to 3rd century). It is inscribed ΑΛΕΞΑΜΕΝΟΣ (ΑΛΕΞΑΜΕΝΟC) ΣΕΒΕΤΕ (CEBETE) ΘΕΟΝ, which translates as "Alexamenos respects god". Visible at the museum on the Palatine Hill, Rome, Italy (*left*). A modern-day tracing (*right*).

Crucifixion was intended to be a gruesome spectacle: the most painful and humiliating death imaginable. It was used to punish slaves, pirates, and enemies of the state. It was originally reserved for slaves (hence still called "supplicium servile" by Seneca), and later extended to citizens of the lower classes (*humiliores*). The victims of crucifixion were stripped naked[879] and put on public display while they were slowly tortured to death so that they would serve as a spectacle and an example.

According to Roman law, if a slave killed his or her master, all of the master's slaves would be crucified as punishment. Both men and women were crucified. Tacitus writes in his *Annals* that when Lucius Pedanius Secondus was murdered by a slave, some in the Senate tried to prevent the mass crucifixion of four hundred of his slaves because there were so many women and children, but in the end tradition prevailed and they were all executed.[880] Although not conclusive evidence for female crucifixion by itself, the most ancient image of a Roman crucifixion may depict a crucified woman, whether real or imaginary.[881] Crucifixion was such a gruesome and humiliating way to die that the subject was somewhat of a taboo in Roman culture, and few crucifixions were specifically documented. One of the only specific female crucifixions we have documented is that of Ida, a freedwoman (former slave) who was crucified by order of Tiberius.

Process

Crucifixion was typically carried out by specialized teams, consisting of a commanding centurion and his soldiers. First, the condemned would be stripped naked and scourged. This would cause the person to lose a large amount of blood, and approach a state of shock. The convict then usually had to carry the horizontal beam (*patibulum* in Latin) to the place of execution, but not necessarily the whole cross.

During the death march, the prisoner, probably[882] still nude after the scourging, would be led through the most crowded streets bearing a *titulus* — a sign board proclaiming the prisoner's name and crime. Upon arrival at the place of execution, selected to be especially public, the convict would be stripped of any remaining clothing, then nailed to the cross naked. If the crucifixion took place in an established place of execution, the vertical beam (*stipes*) might be permanently embedded in the ground. In this case, the condemned person's wrists would first be nailed to the *patibulum*, and then he or she would be hoisted off the ground with ropes to hang from the elevated *patibulum* while it was fastened to the *stipes*. Next the feet or ankles would be nailed to the upright stake. The 'nails' were tapered iron spikes approximately 5 to 7 inches (13 to 18 cm) long, with a square shaft $3/8$ inch (10 mm) across. The *titulus* would also be fastened to the cross to notify onlookers of the person's name and crime as they hung on the cross, further maximizing the public impact.

There may have been considerable variation in the position in which prisoners were nailed to their crosses and how their bodies were supported while they died. Seneca the Younger recounts: "I see crosses there, not just of one kind but made in many different ways: some have their victims with head down to the ground; some impale their private parts; others stretch out their arms on the gibbet." One source claims that for Jews (apparently not for others), a man would be crucified with his back to the cross as is traditionally depicted, while a woman would be nailed facing her cross, probably with her back to onlookers, or at least with the *stipes* providing some semblance of modesty if viewed from the front. Such concessions were "unique" and not made outside a Jewish context. Several sources mention some sort of seat fastened to the *stipes* to help support the person's body,[883,884,885] thereby prolonging the person's suffering and humiliation by preventing the asphyxiation caused by hanging without support. Justin Martyr calls the seat a *cornu*, or "horn," leading some scholars to believe it may have had a pointed shape designed to torment the crucified person.[886] This would be consistent with Seneca's observation of victims with their private parts impaled.

In Roman-style crucifixion, the condemned could take up to a few days to die, but death was sometimes hastened by human action. "The attending Roman guards could leave the site only after the victim had died, and were known to precipitate death by means of deliberate fracturing of the tibia and/or fibula, spear stab wounds into the heart, sharp blows to the front of the chest, or a smoking fire built at the foot of the cross to asphyxiate the victim." The Romans sometimes broke the prisoner's legs to hasten death and usually forbade burial. On the other hand, the person was often deliberately kept alive as long as possible to prolong their suffering and humiliation, so as to provide the maximum deterrent effect. Corpses of the crucified were typically left on the crosses to decompose and be eaten by animals.

In Islam

Islam spread in a region where many societies, including the Persian and Roman empires, had used crucifixion to punish traitors, rebels, robbers and criminal slaves. The Qur'an refers to crucifixion in six passages, of which the most significant for later legal developments is verse 5:33:

<templatestyles src="Template:Quote/styles.css"/>

> *The punishment of those who wage war against Allah and His Apostle, and strive with might and main for mischief through the land is: execution, or crucifixion, or the cutting off of hands and feet from opposite sides, or exile from the land: that is their disgrace in this world, and a heavy punishment is theirs in the Hereafter.*

The corpus of hadith provides contradictory statements about the first use of crucifixion under Islamic rule, attributing it variously to Muhammad himself (for murder and robbery of a shepherd) or to the second caliph Umar (applied to two slaves who murdered their mistress). Classical Islamic jurisprudence applies the verse 5:33 chiefly to highway robbers, as a *hadd* (scripturally prescribed) punishment. The preference for crucifixion over the other punishments mentioned in the verse or for their combination (which Sadakat Kadri has called "Islam's equivalent of the hanging, drawing and quartering that medieval Europeans inflicted on traitors") is subject to "complex and contested rules" in classical jurisprudence. Most scholars required crucifixion for highway robbery combined with murder, while others allowed execution by other methods for this scenario. The main methods of crucifixion are:

- Exposure of the culprit's body after execution by another method, ascribed to "most scholars" and in particular to Ibn Hanbal and Al-Shafi'i; or Hanbalis and Shafi'is.
- Crucifying the culprit alive, then executing him with a lance thrust or another method, ascribed to Malikis, most Hanafis and most Twelver Shi'is; the majority of the Malikis; Malik, Abu Hanifa, and al-Awza'i; or Malikis, Hanafis, and Shafi'is.

Figure 125: *Early Meiji period crucifixion (c. 1865–1868), Yokohama, Japan. A 25-year-old servant, Sokichi, was executed by crucifixion for murdering his employer's son during the course of a robbery. He was affixed by tying, rather than nailing, to a stake with two cross-pieces.*

- Crucifying the culprit alive and sparing his life if he survives for three days, ascribed to Shiites.

Most classical jurists limit the period of crucifixion to three days. Crucifixion involves affixing or impaling the body to a beam or a tree trunk. Various minority opinions also prescribed crucifixion as punishment for a number of other crimes. Cases of crucifixion under most of the legally prescribed categories have been recorded in the history of Islam, and prolonged exposure of crucified bodies was especially common for political and religious opponents.

Japan

Crucifixion was introduced into Japan during the Sengoku period (1467–1573), after a 350-year period with no capital punishment. It is believed to have been suggested to the Japanese by the introduction of Christianity into the region, although similar types of punishment had been used as early as the Kamakura period. Known in Japanese as *haritsuke* (磔), crucifixion was used in Japan before and during the Tokugawa Shogunate. Several related crucifixion techniques were used. Petra Schmidt, in

Figure 126: *The Twenty Six Martyrs of Japan*

"Capital Punishment in Japan", writes:<templatestyles src="Template:Quote/styles.css"/>

> Execution by crucifixion included, first of all, hikimawashi (i.e, being paraded about town on horseback); then the unfortunate was tied to a cross made from one vertical and two horizontal poles. The cross was raised, the convict speared several times from two sides, and eventually killed with a final thrust through the throat. The corpse was left on the cross for three days. If one condemned to crucifixion died in prison, his body was pickled and the punishment executed on the dead body. Under Toyotomi Hideyoshi, one of the great 16th-century unifiers, crucifixion upside down (i.e, sakasaharitsuke) was frequently used. Water crucifixion (mizuharitsuke) awaited mostly Christians: a cross was raised at low tide; when the high tide came, the convict was submerged under water up to the head, prolonging death for many days

In 1597 twenty-six Christian Martyrs were nailed to crosses at Nagasaki, Japan. Among those executed were Saints Paulo Miki, Philip of Jesus and Pedro Bautista, a Spanish Franciscan who had worked about ten years in the Philippines. The executions marked the beginning of a long history of persecution of Christianity in Japan, which continued until its decriminalization in 1871.

Crucifixion was used as a punishment for prisoners of war during World War II. Ringer Edwards, an Australian prisoner of war, was crucified for killing cattle, along with two others. He survived 63 hours before being let down.

Burma

In Burma, crucifixion was a central element in several execution rituals. Felix Carey, a missionary in Burma from 1806 to 1812, wrote the following:
<templatestyles src="Template:Quote/styles.css"/>

> Four or five persons, after being nailed through their hands and feet to a scaffold, had first their tongues cut out, then their mouths slit open from ear to ear, then their ears cut off, and finally their bellies ripped open.
>
> Six people were crucified in the following manner: their hands and feet nailed to a scaffold; then their eyes were extracted with a blunt hook; and in this condition they were left to expire; two died in the course of four days; the rest were liberated, but died of mortification on the sixth or seventh day.
>
> Four persons were crucified, viz. not nailed but tied with their hands and feet stretched out at full length, in an erect posture. In this posture they were to remain till death; every thing they wished to eat was ordered them with a view to prolong their lives and misery. In cases like this, the legs and feet of the criminals begin to swell and mortify at the expiration of three or four days; some are said to live in this state for a fortnight, and expire at last from fatigue and mortification. Those which I saw, were liberated at the end of three or four days.

Europe

During World War I, there were persistent rumors that German soldiers had crucified a Canadian soldier on a tree or barn door with bayonets or combat knives. The event was initially reported in 1915 by Private George Barrie of the 1st Canadian Division. Two investigations, one a post-war official investigation, and the other an independent investigation by the Canadian Broadcasting Corporation, concluded that there was no evidence to support the story. However, British documentary maker Iain Overton in 2001 published an article claiming that the story was true, identifying the soldier as Harry Band. Overton's article was the basis for a 2002 episode of the Channel 4 documentary show *Secret History*.

It has been reported that crucifixion was used in several cases against the German civil population of East Prussia when it was occupied by Soviet forces at the end of the Second World War.[887]

Figure 127: *Poster showing a German soldier nailing a man to a tree, as American soldiers come to his rescue. Published in Manila by Bureau of Printing (1917).*

Modern use

Crucifixion is still used as a rare method of execution in some countries. The punishment of crucifixion (*ṣalb*) imposed in Islamic law is variously interpreted as exposure of the body after execution, crucifixion followed by stabbing in the chest, or crucifixion for three days, survivors of which are allowed to live.

Legal execution

Several people have been executed by crucifixion in Saudi Arabia in the 2000s, although on occasion they were first beheaded and then crucified. Most recently, in March 2013, a robber was set to be executed by being crucified for three days. However, the method was changed.

Ali Mohammed Baqir al-Nimr was arrested in 2012 when he was 17 years old for taking part in an anti-government protests in Saudi Arabia during the Arab Spring.[888] In May 2014, Ali al-Nimr was sentenced to be publicly beheaded and crucified.[889]

Theoretically, crucifixion is still one of the Hadd punishments in Iran.[890] If a crucified person were to survive three days of crucifixion, that person would be allowed to live. Execution by hanging is described as follows: "In execution

Figure 128: *Prisoner kneeling on chains, thumbs supporting arms, photographic print on stereo card, Mukden, China (c. 1906)*

by hanging, the prisoner will be hung on a hanging truss which should look like a cross, while his (her) back is toward the cross, and (s)he faces the direction of Mecca [in Saudi Arabia], and his (her) legs are vertical and distant from the ground."

Sudan's penal code, based upon the government's interpretation of shari'a,[891] includes execution followed by crucifixion as a penalty. When, in 2002, 88 people were sentenced to death for crimes relating to murder, armed robbery, and participating in ethnic clashes, Amnesty International wrote that they could be executed by either hanging or crucifixion.

Crucifixion is a legal punishment in the United Arab Emirates.

Jihadism

On 5 February 2015 the United Nations Committee on the Rights of the Child (CRC) reported that the Islamic State of Iraq and the Levant (ISIL) had committed "several cases of mass executions of boys, as well as reports of beheadings, crucifixions of children and burying children alive".

On 30 April 2014 Islamic extremists carried out a total of seven public executions in Raqqa, northern Syria. The pictures, originally posted to Twitter by a student at Oxford University, were retweeted by a Twitter account owned by a known member of the Islamic State of Iraq and the Levant (ISIL) causing major media outlets to incorrectly attribute the crucifixions to the militant group. In most of these cases of "crucifixion" the victims are shot first then their bodies are displayed but there have also been reports of "crucifixion" preceding shootings or decapitations as well as a case where a man was said to have been "crucified alive for eight hours" with no indication of whether he died.

Other terrorist incidents

The human rights group Karen Women Organization documented a case of Tatmadaw forces crucifying several Karen villagers in 2000 in the Dooplaya District in Burma's Kayin State.

On 22 January 2014, an anti-government activist and member of AutoMaidan was kidnapped by unknown parties and tortured for a week. His captors kept him in the dark, beat him, cut off a piece of his ear, and nailed him to a cross. His captors ultimately left him in a forest outside Kiev after forcing him to confess to being an American spy and accepting money from the US Embassy in Ukraine to organize protests against then-President Viktor Yanukovych.

In 2015, a video surfaced depicting members of the Azov Battalion, an official regiment of the Ukrainian Armed Forces, allegedly crucifying a separatist rebel of Novorossiya and burning him alive. Therein they declare, "all the separatists, traitors of Ukraine and militia fighters [sic] will be treated the same". The Azov Battalion is associated with neo-Nazism and flaunts symbols associated with the SS such as the wolfsangel and black sun. They allegedly sent the video to the pro-Russian hacktivist organization CyberBerkut, which responded by threatening to take no Ukrainian Army soldiers or militia fighters as prisoners from then on. The authenticity of this video is unconfirmed.

In culture and arts

Figure 129: *Sculpture construction: Crucifixion, homage to Mondrian, by Barbara Hepworth, United Kingdom (2007)*

Figure 130: *Allegory of Poland (1914–1918), postcard by Sergey Solomko*

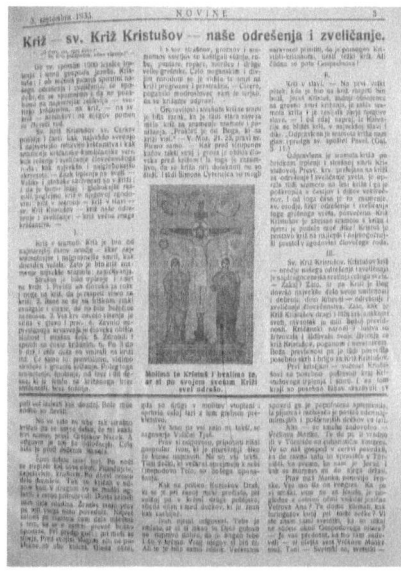

Figure 131: *The Holy Cross, article of the Novine (September 3, 1933)*

Figure 132: *Car-float at the feast of the Virgin of San Juan de los Lagos, Colonia Doctores, Mexico City (2011)*

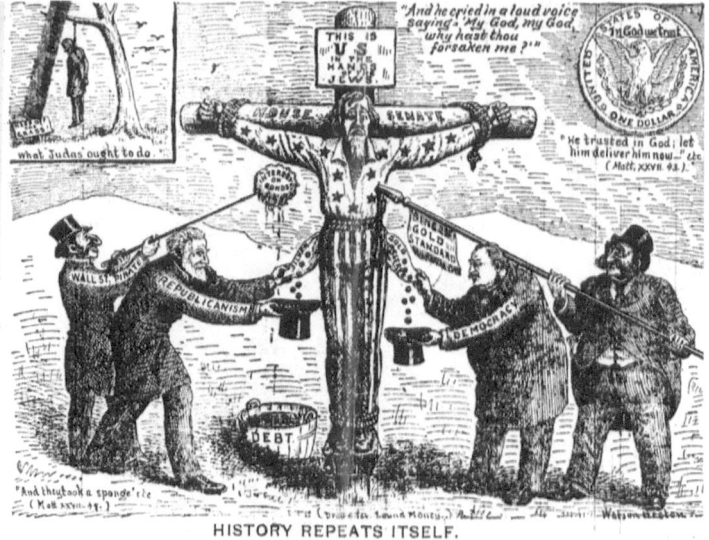

Figure 133: *Antisemitic American political cartoon, Sound Money magazine, April 15, 1896 issue*

Figure 134: *Protester tied to a cross in Washington D.C. (1970)*

Figure 135: *Devotional crucifixion in San Fernando, Pampanga, Philippines, Easter 2006*

As a devotional practice

The Catholic Church frowns upon self-crucifixion as a form of devotion: "Penitential practices leading to self-crucifixion with nails are not to be encouraged."[892] Nevertheless, the practice is not unknown.

In the Philippines, some Catholics are voluntarily, non-lethally crucified for a limited time on Good Friday to imitate the sufferings of Christ. Pre-sterilised nails are driven through the palm of the hand between the bones, while there is a footrest to which the feet are nailed. Rolando del Campo, a carpenter in Pampanga, vowed to be crucified every Good Friday for 15 years if God would carry his wife through a difficult childbirth, while in San Pedro Cutud, Ruben Enaje has been crucified 27 times. The Church in the Philippines has repeatedly voiced disapproval of crucifixions and self-flagellation, while the government has noted that it cannot deter devotees. The Department of Health insists that participants in the rites should have tetanus shots and that the nails used should be sterilized.

In other cases, a crucifixion is only simulated within a passion play, as in the ceremonial re-enactment that has been performed yearly in the town of Iztapalapa, on the outskirts of Mexico City, since 1833, and in the more famous Oberammergau Passion Play. Also, since at least the mid-19th century, a group of flagellants in New Mexico, called *Hermanos de Luz* ("Brothers of Light"), have annually conducted reenactments of Christ's crucifixion during Holy Week, in which a penitent is tied—but not nailed—to a cross.

Famous crucifixions

- The rebel slaves of the Third Servile War: Between 73 BC and 71 BC a band of slaves, eventually numbering about 120,000, under the (at least partial) leadership of Spartacus were in open revolt against the Roman republic. The rebellion was eventually crushed and, while Spartacus himself most likely died in the final battle of the revolt, approximately 6,000 of his followers were crucified along the 200 km Appian Way between Capua and Rome as a warning to any other would-be rebels.
- Jehohanan: Jewish man who was crucified around the same time as Jesus of Nazareth and it is widely accepted that his ankles were nailed to the side of the *stipes* of the cross
- Jesus of Nazareth: his death by crucifixion under Pontius Pilate (c. AD 30 or 33), recounted in the four 1st-century canonical Gospels, is referred to repeatedly as something well known in the earlier letters of Saint Paul, for instance, five times in his First Letter to the Corinthians, written in 57 AD (1:13, 1:18, 1:23, 2:2, 2:8). Pilate was the Roman governor of Iudaea province at the time, and he is explicitly linked with the condemnation of Jesus not only by the Gospels but also by Tacitus,[893] (see Responsibility for the death of Jesus for details). The civil charge was a claim to be King of the Jews.
- Saint Peter: Christian apostle, who according to tradition was crucified upside-down at his own request (hence the Cross of St. Peter), because he did not feel worthy enough to die the same way as Jesus.
- Saint Andrew: Christian apostle and Saint Peter's brother, who is traditionally said to have been crucified on an X-shaped cross (hence the St. Andrew's Cross).
- Simeon of Jerusalem: second Bishop of Jerusalem, crucified in either 106 or 107.
- Mani: the founder of Manicheanism, he was depicted by followers as having died by crucifixion in 274 AD.
- Eulalia of Barcelona was venerated as a saint. According to her hagiography, she was stripped naked, tortured, and ultimately crucified on an X-shaped cross.
- Wilgefortis was venerated as a saint and represented as a crucified woman, however her legend comes from a misinterpretation of a full-clothed crucifix known as the Volto Santo of Lucca.

External links

 Wikimedia Commons has media related to *Crucifixion*.

- "Forensic and Clinical Knowledge of the Practice of Crucifixion" by Frederick Zugibe[894]
- Jesus's death on the cross, from a medical perspective[895]
- "Crucifixion in antiquity - The Anthropological evidence" by Joe Zias[896] at the Wayback Machine (archived February 12, 2012)
- "Dishonour, Degradation and Display: Crucifixion in the Roman World" by Philip Hughes[897]
- Jewish Encyclopedia: Crucifixion[898]
- Crucifixion of Joachim of Nizhny-Novgorod[899]

Crushing (execution)

Death by **crushing** or **pressing** is a method of execution that has a history during which the techniques used varied greatly from place to place, generally involving the placement of intense weight upon a person with the intent to kill. This form of execution is no longer sanctioned by any governing body.

Crushing by elephant

A common method of death throughout South and South-East Asia for over 4,000 years was crushing by elephants. The Romans and Carthaginians used this method on occasion.Wikipedia:Citation needed

Roman mythology

In Roman mythology, Tarpeia was a Roman maiden who betrayed the city of Rome to the Sabines in exchange for what she thought would be a reward of jewelry. She was instead crushed to death and her body cast from the Tarpeian Rock which now bears her name.

Crushing in pre-Columbian America

Crushing is also reported from pre-Columbian America, notably in the Aztec Empire.[900,901]

Figure 136: *Louis Rousselet described this Central Indian execution in "Le Tour du Monde" in 1868.*

Crushing under common law

Peine forte et dure (Law French for "forceful and hard punishment") was a method of torture formerly used in the common law legal system, in which a defendant who refused to plead ("stood mute") would be subjected to having heavier and heavier stones placed upon his or her chest until a plea was entered, or as the weight of the stones on the chest became too great for the condemned to breathe, fatal suffocation would occur.

The common law courts originally took a very limited view of their own jurisdiction. They considered themselves to lack jurisdiction over a defendant until he had voluntarily submitted to it by entering a plea seeking judgment from the court.[902] Obviously, a criminal justice system that punished only those who volunteered for punishment was unworkable; this was the means chosen to coerce them.[903]

Many defendants charged with capital offences nonetheless refused to plead, since thereby they would escape forfeiture of property, and their heirs would still inherit their estate; but if the defendant pleaded guilty and was executed, their heirs would inherit nothing, their property escheating to the Crown. *Peine forte et dure* was abolished in Great Britain in 1772, and the last known use of the practice was in 1741.[904] In 1772, refusing to plead was deemed to be equivalent to pleading guilty. This was changed in 1827 to being deemed a plea of not guilty. Today, in all common law jurisdictions, standing mute is treated by the courts as equivalent to a plea of not guilty.

The elaborate procedure was recorded by a 15th-century witness in an oft-quoted description: "he will lie upon his back, with his head covered and his feet, and one arm will be drawn to one quarter of the house with a cord, and the other arm to another quarter, and in the same manner it will be done with his legs; and let there be laid upon his body iron and stone, as much as he can bear, or more ..."[905]

"Pressing to death" might take several days, and not necessarily with a continued increase in the load. The Frenchman Guy Miege, who from 1668 taught languages in London[906] says the following about the English practice:[907] <templatestyles src="Template:Quote/styles.css"/>

> *For such as stand Mute at their Trial, and refuse to answer Guilty, or Not Guilty, Pressing to Death is the proper Punishment. In such a Case the Prisoner is laid in a low dark Room in the Prison, all naked but his Privy Members, his Back upon the bare Ground his Arms and Legs stretched with Cords, and fastned to the several Quarters of the Room. This done, he has a great Weight of Iron and Stone laid upon him. His Diet, till he dies, is of three Morsels of Barley bread without Drink the next Day; and if he lives beyond it, he has nothing daily, but as much foul Water as he can drink three several Time , and that without any Bread: Which grievous Death some resolute Offenders have chosen, to save their Estates to their Children. But, in case of High Treason, the Criminal's Estate is forfeited to the Sovereign, as in all capital Crimes, notwithstanding his being pressed to Death.*

The most famous case in the United Kingdom was that of Roman Catholic martyr St Margaret Clitherow, who (in order to avoid a trial in which her own children would be obliged to give evidence) was pressed to death on March 25, 1586, after refusing to plead to the charge of having harboured Catholic (then outlawed) priests in her house. She died within fifteen minutes under a weight of at least 700 pounds (320 kg). Several hardened criminals, including William Spigott (1721) and Edward Burnworth, lasted a half hour under 400 pounds (180 kg) before pleading to the indictment. Others, such as Major Strangways (1658) and John Weekes (1731), refused to plead, even under 400 pounds (180 kg), and were killed when bystanders, out of mercy, sat on them.

The only death by *peine forte et dure* in American history was Giles Corey, who was pressed to death on September 19, 1692, during the Salem witch trials, after he refused to enter a plea in the judicial proceeding. According to legend, his last words as he was being crushed were "More weight", and he

Figure 137: *Giles Corey was pressed to death during the Salem Witch Trials in the 1690s.*

was thought to be dead as the weight was applied. This is referred to in Arthur Miller's political drama *The Crucible* (1953), where Giles Corey is pressed to death after refusing to plead "aye or nay" to the charge of witchcraft. In the 1996 film version of this play, the screenplay also written by Arthur Miller, Corey is crushed to death for refusing to reveal the name of a source of information.

In medieval Europe, the slow crushing of body parts in screw-operated "bone vises" of iron was a common method of torture, and a tremendous variety of cruel instruments were used to savagely crush the head, the knee, the hand, and, most commonly, either the thumb or the naked foot. Such instruments were finely threaded and variously provided with spiked inner surfaces or heated red-hot before their application to the limb to be tortured.

Further reading

- McKenzie, Andrea. "'This Death Some Strong and Stout Hearted Man Doth Choose': The Practice of Peine Forte et Dure in Seventeenth- and Eighteenth-Century England". *Law and History Review*, Summer 2005, Vol. 23, No. 2, pp. 279–313.[908]

External links

- Forfeiture in England and Colonial America[909]
- *The Proceedings of the Old Bailey,* Reference Number: t16760823-6 (23 August 1676)[910]

Disembowelment

Disembowelment or **evisceration** is the removal of some or all of the organs of the gastrointestinal tract (the bowels, or viscera), usually through a horizontal incision made across the abdominal area. Disembowelment may result from an accident but has also been used as a method of torture and execution. In such practices, disembowelment may be accompanied by other forms of torture, or the removal of other vital organs.

Disembowelment as torture

If a living creature is disemboweled, it is invariably fatal without major medical intervention. Historically, disembowelment has been used as a severe form of capital punishment. If the intestinal tract alone is removed, death follows after several hours of gruesome pain. However, in some forms of intentional disembowelment, decapitation or the removal of the heart and lungs would hasten the victim's death.

Asia

Japan

In Japan, disembowelment played a central part as a method of execution or the ritualized suicide of a samurai. In killing themselves by this method, they were deemed to be free from the dishonor resulting from their crimes. The most common form of disembowelment was referred to in Japanese as *seppuku* (or, colloquially, *hara-kiri*), literally "stomach cutting," involving two cuts across the abdomen, sometimes followed by pulling out one's own viscera. The act of decapitation by a second (*kaishaku-nin*) was added to this ritual suicide in later times in order to shorten the suffering of the samurai or leader, an attempt at rendering the ritual more humane. Even later the knife was just a simple formality and the swordsman would decapitate before the subject could reach for it. The commission of a crime or dishonorable act was only one of many reasons for the performance of seppuku; others included the atonement of cowardice, as a means of apology, or following the loss of a battle or the surrender of a castle.

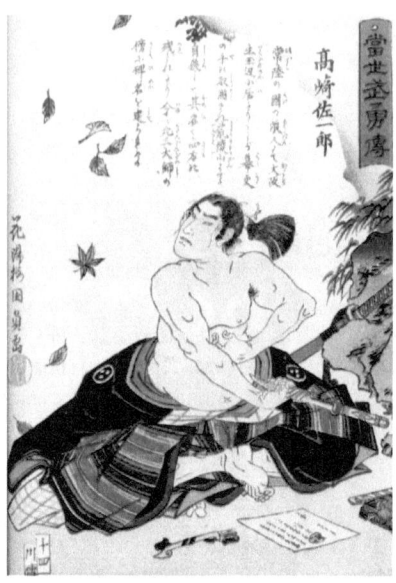

Figure 138: *Ukiyo-e woodblock print of warrior about to perform seppuku, from the Edo period.*

Vietnam

Various accounts have asserted that during the Vietnam War, members of the Viet Cong sometimes made calculated use of disembowelment as a means of psychological warfare, to coerce and intimidate rural peasants. Peer De Silva, former head of the Saigon department of the Central Intelligence Agency (CIA), wrote that from as early as 1963, Viet Cong units were using disembowelment and other methods of mutilation as psychological warfare. The extent, however, to which this punishment was perpetrated may be impossible to gauge and while detailed accounts survive regarding how civilians were disemboweled by Viet Cong, the use of this torture appears to have been quite arbitrary and there is no record that such actions were sanctioned by the North Vietnamese government in Hanoi. Disembowelment and other methods of intimidation and torture were intended to frighten civilian peasants at a local level into cooperating with the Viet Cong or discourage them from cooperating with the South Vietnamese Army or its allies.

Europe

Romania

In early 1941, during the Bucharest pogrom in which 125 Jewish civilians were killed, multiple cases of torture including disembowelment were recorded.[911]

Netherlands

On 10 July 1584, Balthasar Gérard shot and killed William of Orange, who had advocated for Dutch independence from the King of Spain. The assassin was interrogated and condemned to death almost immediately. On 14 July, after suffering various tortures during each of the five days since the assassination, Gérard was disemboweled and dismembered while still alive, after which his heart was torn out and then he was beheaded by his Dutch executioners.

Roman Empire

Christian tradition states that Erasmus of Formiae, also known as Saint Elmo, was finally executed by disembowelment in about A.D. 303, after he had suffered extreme forms of torture during the persecutions of Emperor Diocletian and Maximian.

England

In England, the punishment of being "hanged, drawn and quartered" was typically used for men convicted of high treason. This referred to the practice of dragging a man by a hurdle (similar to a fence) through the streets, removing him from the hurdle and (1) hanging him from the neck (but removing him before death), (2) drawing (i.e. disembowelling) him slowly on a wooden block by slitting open his abdomen, removing his entrails and his other organs (which were frequently thrown on a fire), and then decapitating him and (3) quartering, i.e. dividing the body into four pieces. The man's head and quarters would often be parboiled and displayed as a warning to others. As part of the disembowelment, the man was also typically emasculated and his genitals and entrails would be burned.

William Harrington is an example of someone tortured on the rack, hanged until not quite dead, then subjected to disembowelment.

Figure 139: *The execution of Hugh Despenser the Younger, who was hanged, drawn and quartered for high treason in 1326*

Germany

From the 15th century, ordinances are retained that threaten with a terrible punishment for those who stripped off the bark of a standing tree in the common woods. A typical wording is found in the 1401 ordinance from Oberursel:[912] <templatestyles src="Template:Quote/styles.css"/>

> "and whoever is caught stripping off a standing tree, mercy would have been more beneficial to him than the law is; for when law is to be fulfilled, then one is to cut up his stomach at the navel, and pull out a length of the gut. The gut is to be nailed to the tree, and one is keep going around that tree with the person, so long as he still has any part of the gut left in his body"

Jacob Grimm observes that no case of the punishment being carried out has been found in records from that period (15th century), but 300 to 500 years earlier, the Western Slavic tribes like the Wends are said to have revenged themselves upon Christians by binding the guts to an erect pole and driving them around until the person was fully eviscerated.[913] In the 13th century, members of the now extinct Baltic ethnic group of Old Prussians in one of the battles against the Teutonic Knights, are said to have captured one such knight in 1248, and made to undergo this punishment.

Figure 140: *Nezahualcoyotl as shown in the Codex Ixtlilxochitl, folio 106R, painted roughly a century after Nezahualcoyotl's death.*

Americas

Texcoco

Nezahualcoyotl, a 15th-century Acolhuan ruler of Texcoco, a member of the Aztec Triple Alliance (now Mexico), promulgated a law code that was partially preserved. Those who had engaged in the passive role of homosexual anal intercourse had their intestines pulled out, then their bodies were filled with ash, and finally, were burnt. The active or penetrating partner was simply suffocated in a heap of ash.

Suicide

The Japanese tradition of *seppuku* is a well known example of highly ritualized suicide, within a wider cultural world of norms and symbolism. However, reported examples of suicides exist, in which a person performed disembowelment on himself or herself, without any ambient culture of approved, or expected, suicide.

The Spartan king Cleomenes I is reported, in a fit of madness, to have slit his stomach open, and ripped his own bowels out.

Roman statesman Cato the Younger committed suicide in Utica, after his side lost to Caesar, by plunging a knife in his own gut, in the dead of night. According to Plutarch, Cato's son heard the commotion from a nearby room, and called a doctor who stitched the wound close; after his son and the doctor left, Cato tore the stitching open with his hand and died. On account of his tragic, highly symbolic suicide, Cato is often termed *Uticensis* ("of Utica"), in order to differentiate him from his homonymous ancestor, Cato "the Elder" or "the Censor".

In 1593, a suicide occurred in Wimpfen. A young, pregnant woman, who had become a widow a few weeks before, was lying in her bed. She took a large knife, opened her belly in a cross, and threw out the fetus, her own intestines, and dug out her spleen and flung that out as well. She lived for 10 hours after the act, and when the priests sought to bring her a final consolation and blessing, she said it would all be in vain, because she was a daughter of the devil, and was beyond any sort of redemption. Then, she died, was put in a sack and thrown in the river. She was affluent, so it was clear that poverty had not driven her to this act.[914]

In 1617, a merchant in the municipality Grossglockau[915] slit up his abdomen so that the intestines fell out; he then pulled out his stomach and threw it on the bed. The chronicler notes he lived long enough to regret his action.

Transanal evisceration

When a portion of the intestinal tract is forcefully pulled from or expelled from the body through the anus, it is referred to as *transanal evisceration*. Following the first report of transanal small intestine evisceration by Brodie in 1827, more than 70 cases have been reported to date, the majority occurring spontaneously in elderly individuals. Straining, chronic constipation, and rectal ulcerations predispose to spontaneous perforation in elderly individuals. Cases of transanal evisceration of children whilst sitting over uncovered swimming pool drains have been reported; notable cases include Valerie Lakey (1993) and Abigail Taylor (2007). In Taylor's case, the suction dislodged and damaged her liver and pancreas; several meters of her small intestine were forcefully pulled through her anus. In both these cases, the victims were left with short bowel syndrome and required feeding by total parenteral nutrition. After multiple operations, Taylor later died from transplant-related cancer.

A person, usually a child, can suffer a similar injury if a heavy weight is applied directly over the abdomen. Large intestine (Rectosigmoid) rupture with transanal evisceration has been reported from blunt abdominal trauma and suction injuries. A direct blow or impingement of intestine between the vertebrae and anterior abdominal wall results in sudden increase in the intra-abdominal or intraluminal pressure of the intestine and rupture. The downward pressure forces a portion of the intestine to burst from the anus.

Cultural references

The short story "Guts" from the book *Haunted* by Chuck Palahniuk is based on the concept of transanal evisceration.

In Japanese folklore, it was believed that malicious *Kappa* – water-goblins that inhabited ponds and rivers – might thrust a hand into the anus of a human swimmer, seeking a mythical sphere called a *shirikodama*.

In American Horror Story: Roanoke (2016), Cricket is disemboweled by The Butcher (Thomyson White)

In the video game Fallout: New Vegas, if the character Arcade Gannon is sold into slavery, during the ending slideshow he narrates how, during an unguarded moment, he used a medical scalpel to disembowel himself.

Embalming

The process of embalming sometimes includes removing the internal organs. Mummification, especially as practised by the ancient Egyptians, entailed the removal of the internal organs prior to the preservation of the remainder of the body. The organs removed were embalmed, stored in canopic jars and then placed in the tomb with the body.

James Cook, on his second voyage, noted an embalming custom on some of the Pacific islands his crew visited, a custom utilizing transanal evisceration:<templatestyles src="Template:Quote/styles.css"/>

> We found the body not only entire in every part; but, what surprised us much more, was, that putrefaction had scarcely begun (...); though the climate is one of the hottest, and Tee had been dead above five months.(...) Such were Mr. Anderson's remarks to me, who also told me, on his enquiring inte the method of effecting this preservation of their dead bodies, he had been informed, that, soon after their death, they are disemboweled, by drawing their intestines, and other viscera, out at the anus; and the whole cavity is then filled or stuffed with cloth; introduced through the same part(...)

Dismemberment

Dismemberment is the act of cutting, tearing, pulling, wrenching or otherwise removing the limbs of a living thing. It has been practised upon human beings as a form of capital punishment, can occur as a result of a traumatic accident, or in connection with murder, suicide, or cannibalism. As opposed to surgical amputation of the limbs, dismemberment is often fatal to all but the simplest of creatures. In criminology, a distinction is made between offensive and defensive dismemberment. Intentional, criminal dismemberment is known as *mayhem*.

History

Cut apart

Sliced to pieces by elephant

Particularly in South-Eastern Asia, execution by trained elephants was a form of capital punishment practiced for several centuries. The techniques by which the convicted person was actually executed varied widely but did, on occasion, include the elephant dismembering the victim by means of sharp blades attached to its feet. The Muslim traveller Ibn Battuta, visiting Delhi in the 1330s, has left the following eyewitness account of this particular type of execution by elephants:[916] <templatestyles src="Template:Quote/styles.css"/>

> *"Upon a certain day, when I myself was present, some men were brought out who had been accused of having attempted the life of the Vizier. They were ordered, accordingly, to be thrown to the elephants, which had been taught to cut their victims to pieces. Their hoofs were cased with sharp iron instruments, and the extremities of these were like knives. On such occasions the elephant-driver rode upon them: and, when a man was thrown to them, they would wrap the trunk about him and toss him up, then take him with the teeth and throw him between their fore feet upon the breast, and do just as the driver should bid them, and according to the orders of the Emperor. If the order was to cut him to pieces, the elephant would do so with his irons, and then throw the pieces among the assembled multitude: but if the order was to leave him, he would be left lying before the Emperor, until the skin should be taken off, and stuffed with hay, and the flesh given to the dogs"*

Figure 141: *The Martyrdom of St. Hippolytus by Dieric Bouts*

Figure 142: *Aztec stone disk depicting a dismembered Coyolxauhqui which was found during construction in 1978 in Mexico City. Its discovery led to the excavation of the Templo Mayor.*

Figure 143: *The execution of Sir Thomas Armstrong, who was hanged, drawn and quartered in England for high treason in 1684*

Figure 144: *Tiradentes Quartered, Pedro Américo (1893)*

Quartering procedure in the Holy Roman Empire

In the Holy Roman Empire emperor Charles V's 1532 Constitutio Criminalis Carolina specifies how *every* dismemberment (quartering) should ideally occur:[917]

> "Concerning quartering: To cut and hack apart his entire body into four pieces, and thus be punished unto death, and such four parts are to be hanged on stakes publicly on four common thorough-fares"

Thus, the imperially approved way to dismember the convict within the Holy Roman Empire was by means of *cutting*, rather than dismemberment through *ripping* the individual apart. In paragraph 124 of the same code, beheading prior to quartering is mentioned as allowable when extenuating circumstances are present, whereas aggravating circumstances may allow pinching/ripping the criminal with glowing pincers, prior to quartering.

The fate of Wilhelm von Grumbach in 1567, a maverick knight in the Holy Roman Empire who was fond of making his own private wars and was thus condemned for treason, is also worthy of note. Gout-ridden, he was carried to the execution site in a chair and bound fast to a table. The executioner then ripped out his heart, and stuck it in von Grumbach's face with the words: "von Grumbach! Behold your false heart!" Afterwards, the executioner quartered von Grumbach's body. His principal associate was given the same treatment, and an eyewitness avers that *after* his heart had been ripped out, Chancellor Brück screamed horribly for "quite some time".

One example of a highly aggravated execution is illustrated by the fate of Bastian Karnhars on 16 July 1600. Karnhars was found guilty of 52 separate acts of murder, including the rape and murder of 8 women, and the murder of a child, whose heart he had allegedly eaten for rituals of black magic. To begin, Karnhars had three strips of flesh torn from his back, before being pinched 18 times with glowing pincers, having his fingers clipped off one by one, his arms and legs broken on the wheel, and finally, while still alive, quartered.[918]

A fabled Turkish execution method

In the seventeenth century, a number of travel reports speak of an exotic "Turkish" execution method, where first, the waist of a man was constricted by ropes and cords, and then a swift bisection of the trunk was performed. William Lithgow presents a comparatively prosaic description of the method:

> If a Turke should happen to kill another Turke (...) he is brought forth to the market place, and a blocke being brought hither of foure foote high; the malefactor is stripd naked; and then layd thereupon with his belly downeward, they drawe in his middle together so small with running cords,

that they strike his body a two with one blow: his hinder parts they cast to be eaten by hungry dogges kept for the same purpose; and the forequarters and head they throw into a grievous fire, made there for the same end .- and this is the punishment for man-slaughter

George Sandys, however, during the same period, tells of a method as no longer in use, in a rather more mythologized way:

...they twitch the offender about the waist with a towell, enforcing him to draw up his breath by often pricking him in the body, until they have drawn him within the compasse of a span; then tying it hard, they cut him off in the middle, and setting the body on a hot plate of copper, which seareth the veines, they so up-propping him during their cruell pleasure: who not only retaineth his sense, but the faculties of discourse, until he be taken downe; and then he departeth in an instant

Shekkeh in Persia

In 1850s Persia, a particular dismemberment technique called *shekkeh* is reported to have been used. Travelling as an official for the East India Company Robert Binning[919] describes it as follows:

"the criminal is hung up by the heels, head downwards, from a ladder or between two posts, and the executioner hacks away with a sword, until the body is bisected lengthways, terminating at the head. The two several halves are then suspended on a camel, and paraded through the streets, for the edification of all beholders. When the shekkeh is to be inflicted in a merciful manner, the culprit's head is struck off, previous to bisecting the trunk"

Korea

Dismemberment was a form of capital punishment for convicts of high treason in the Korean kingdom of the Joseon Dynasty. This punishment was, for example, meted out to Hwang Sa-Yong in 1801.

China

The Five Pains is a Chinese variation invented during the Qin dynasty. During the Tang dynasty (618-907 CE), truncation of the body at the waist by means of a fodder knife was a death penalty reserved for those who were seen to have done something particularly treacherous or repugnant. That practice of cutting in two did not originate in the Tang dynasty; in sources concerning the Han dynasty (206 BCE-220 CE), no less than 33 cases of execution by cutting at the waist are mentioned, but occurs very rarely in earlier material.

Current use

Dismemberment is no longer used by most modern governments as a form of execution or torture, though amputation is still carried out in countries that practice Sharia law.[920]

Torn apart

Dismemberment was carried out in the Medieval and Early Modern era and could be effected, for example, by tying a person's limbs to chains or other restraints, then attaching the restraints to separate movable entities (e.g. vehicles) and moving them in opposite directions.

Torn apart by four horses

Also referred to as "disruption" or being "drawn and quartered", dismemberment could be brought about by chaining four horses to the condemned's arms and legs, thus making them pull him apart, as was the case with the executions of François Ravaillac in 1610 and Robert-François Damiens in 1757. Ravaillac's extended torture and execution has been described like this:<templatestyles src="Template:Quote/styles.css"/>

> "He was condemned to be tortured with red-hot pincers on four limbs and on each breast. His wounds were to be sprinkled with molten lead and boiling oil and his body was then to be torn in pieces by four horses, the remains being subsequently burnt."

In the case of Damiens, he was condemned to essentially the same fate as Ravaillac, but the execution did not quite work according to plan, as the eyewitness Giacomo Casanova could relate:[921]<templatestyles src="Template:Quote/styles.css"/>

> Damiens' agony went on for hours as each torture was applied. When the horses failed to disconnect the sinews between his body and his limbs, his body, still alive, was quartered with a knife. His friend, the infamous Casanova, reports that he "watched the dreadful sight for four hours." "I was obliged to turn away my face and to stop my ears as I heard his piercing shrieks, half his body having been torn from him"

As late as in 1781, this gruesome punishment was meted out to the Peruvian rebel leader Túpac Amaru II by the Spanish colonial authorities. The following is an extract from the official judicial death sentence issued by the Spanish authorities which condemns Túpac Amaru II to torture and death. It was ordered in the sentence that Túpac Amaru II be condemned to have his tongue cut out, after watching the executions of his family, and to have his hands and feet tied... <templatestyles src="Template:Quote/styles.css"/>

Figure 145: *The execution of Túpac Amaru II, who was dismembered by four horses 18 May 1781.*

...to four horses who will then be driven at once toward the four corners of the plaza, pulling the arms and legs from his body. The torso will then be taken to the hill overlooking the city... where it will be burned in a bonfire... Tupac Amaru's head will be sent to Tinta to be displayed for three days in the place of public execution and then placed upon a pike at the principal entrance to the city. One of his arms will be sent to Tungasuca, where he was the cacique, and the other arm to the capital province of Carabaya, to be similarly displayed in those locations. His legs will be sent to Livitica and Santa Rosas in the provinces of Chumbivilcas and Lampa, respectively.

The fate of Queen Brunhilda

Queen Brunhilda of Austrasia, executed in 613, is generally regarded to have suffered the same death, though one account has it that she was tied to the tail of a single horse and thus suffered more of a dragging death. The Liber Historiae Francorum, an eighth century chronicle, describes her death by dismemberment as follows:[922]<templatestyles src="Template:Quote/styles.css"/>

> Then King Chlothar ordered that she be lifted onto a camel and led through the entire army. Then she was tied to the feet of wild horses and torn apart limb from limb. Finally, she died.

The story of Brunhilda being tied to the tail of a *single* horse (and then to die in some gruesome manner) is promoted, for example, by Ted Byfield (2003), in which he writes: "Then they tied her to the tail of a wild horse; whipped into frenzy, it kicked her to death" The cited source for this claim, however, the seventh century "Life of St. Columban" by the monk Jonas, does not support

Dismemberment

Figure 146: *Execution of Brunhilda, engraving by Paul Girardet after Henri Félix Emmanuel Philippoteaux*

this claim. In paragraph 58 in his work, Jonas just writes: "..but Brunhilda he had placed first on a camel in mockery and so exhibited to all her enemies round about then she was bound to the tails of wild horses and thus perished wretchedly"[923]

The storyline of Brunhilde being tied to the tail of a single horse and being subsequently *dragged* to death has become a classical motif in artistic representations, as can be seen by the included image.

Torn apart by four ships

According to Olfert Dapper, a 17th-century Dutchman who meticulously collected reports from faraway countries from seamen and other travelers, a fairly frequent maritime death penalty among the corsairs on the Barbary coast was to affix the hands and feet to chains on four different ships. When the ships then sailed off in different directions, the chains grew taut, and the man in between was torn apart after a while.

Torn apart by two trees

Roman military discipline could be extremely severe, and the emperor Aurelian (r. 270–275 CE), who had a reputation for extreme strictness, instituted the rule that soldiers who seduced the wives of their hosts should have their legs fastened to two bent-down trees, which were then released, ripping the man in two. Similarly, in an unsuccessful rebellion against the emperor Valens in 366 CE, the usurper Procopius met the same fate.

After the defeat of Darius III by Alexander the Great, the Persian monarchy was thrown into turmoil, and Darius was killed. One man, Bessus, claimed the throne as Artaxerxes V, but in 329 BCE, Alexander had him executed. The manner of Bessus' death is rather disputed, and Waldemar Heckel writes:<templatestyles src="Template:Quote/styles.css"/>

> The exact details of Bessus' death are disputed. He may have been crucified, or torn apart by recoiling trees, or (what is most likely) mutilated before being sent to Ecbatana for execution.

The method of tying people to bent down trees, which are then allowed to recoil, ripping the individual to pieces in the process is, however, mentioned by several travelers to nineteenth century Persia. The British diplomat James Justinian Morier travelled as a special envoy to the Shah in 1808, and Morier writes the following concerning then prevailing criminal justice:<templatestyles src="Template:Quote/styles.css"/>

> ..for the King never pardons theft, and orders a convicted thief to be executed instantly. The mode is as follows: two young trees are by main strength brought together at their summits, and there fastened with cords together. The culprit is then brought out, and his legs are tied with ropes, which are again carried up and: fixed to the top of the trees. The cords that force the trees together are then cut; and, in the elasticity and power of this spring, the body of the thief is torn asunder, and left thus to hang divided on each separate tree. The inflexibility of the King in this point has given to the roads a security, which, in former times, was little known.

Torn apart by stones

An obscure Christian martyr, Severianus[924] was, about the year 300 AD, martyred in the following way, according to one tale: One stone was fastened to his head, another bound to his feet. His middle was then fastened by a rope to the top of a wall, and the stones released from the height. His body was ripped apart.

A Christian martyr withstands being torn apart

During the reign of the Roman Emperor Diocletian a Christian named Shamuna was, allegedly, torn apart in the following manner:<templatestyles src="Template:Quote/styles.css"/>

> The governor immediately ordered that Shamuna should be made to kneel down on one side and that an iron chain should be fastened on his knee. This having been done, he hung him up head downwards by the foot with which he had made him kneel; the other he pulled downwards with a heavy piece of iron, which cannot be described in words: thus endeavouring to rend the champion in two. By this means the socket of the hip-bone was wrenched out of its place and Shamuna became lame.

Some time thereafter, Shamuna was taken down from his hanging position, and was beheaded instead.[925]

Homicide cases

There are many instances of dismemberment in murder cases. Examples of victims include Bernard Oliver, Bill Nelson, Jana Claudia Gómez Menéndez, Jessica Ridgeway, Becky Watts, Ingrid Lyne and Kim Wall. Serial killer Jeffrey Dahmer is also known to have dismembered and cannibalized his victims.[926]

Examples in fiction

Anime

- *Baccano!*, premiered in 2007
- *Dansai Bunri no Crime Edge*, premiered on 4 April 2013

Film

Dismemberment has been portrayed in many films; although a few are depictions of historical or actual events, a significant number are within the horror genre. Filmmakers can be quite innovative in the methods depicted, and thus reflect the public's fear and fascination with this method of torture, homicide, and/or body disposal. The following movies portray or imply dismemberment in some form; exceptional methods or motives are described. Bahubali The Beginning (2015)https://en.wikipedia.org/wiki/Baahubali:_The_Beginning - dismemberment of Bhadra by Mahendra Bahubali Bahubali The Conclusion (2017)https://en.wikipedia.org/wiki/Baahubali_2:_The_Conclusion - dismemberment of Sethupati by Amarendra Bahubali

- *127 Hours* (2010) – self-dismemberment of hand

- *2001 Maniacs* (2005) – dismemberment by horses
- *Black Death* (2010) – dismemberment by horses
- *Bone Tomahawk* (2015) – dismembered
- *Braindead* (1992)
- *Braveheart* (1995) – Sir William Wallace is hanged, drawn, and quartered, then beheaded.
- *Bride of Chucky* (1998) – victims dismembered by falling shards of glass
- *Cabin Fever 2: Spring Fever* (2009) – self-dismemberment
- *Donnie Brasco* (1997) – mob hit victims are dismembered in a basement
- *Earth* (1998) – victim pulled apart between two cars
- *Friday the 13th Part III* (1982) - Jason Voorhees hacks off a victim's hand before killing him
- *Green Inferno* (2013) – victim gouged and cut apart with axe while alive
- *Kill Bill* (2003)
- *Kraken: Tentacles of the Deep* (2006) female scuba diver's leg gets ripped off by a giant squid
- *Law Abiding Citizen* (2009) – victim paralyzed with toxin and provided with mirror before live dismemberment
- *Monty Python and the Holy Grail* (1975) – during a sword fight, the victim has each of his limbs severed one by one, all the while taunting his opponent and refusing to back down.
- *Pathfinder* (2007)
- *Saw* (2004) – self-dismemberment of foot
- *Saw IV* (2007) – dismemberment by automated machine
- *Scarface* (1983) – dismemberment of arms by chainsaw
- *Shaun of the Dead* (2004) – disembowelment followed by dismemberment by zombies
- *Sin City* (2005)
- *The Hitcher* (1986) and *The Hitcher* (2007) – victim chained between a truck and trailer and pulled apart
- *The Lost World: Jurassic Park* (1997) – Eddie Carr (Richard Schiff) is dismembered from the waist by two tyrannosaurus rexes before being devoured
- *The Paleface* (1948) – attempted execution by tying the victim's feet to two bent-down trees, then using the trees to rip him apart
- *The Texas Chain Saw Massacre* (1974)
- *The Thaw* (2009) – self-dismemberment
- *Twilight* (2008) – decapitation followed by dismemberment
- *Wagons East!* (1994) – dismembered by horses

Folklore

- In Aztec mythology, the god Huitzilopochtli dismembers his sister Coyolxauhqui for trying to kill their mother, Coatlicue; he tossed his sister's head into the sky, where it became the moon
- In Egyptian mythology, the demon Set dismembers his brother Osiris so he could not be resurrected
- In Greek mythology, the god Dionysus is dismembered by the Titans, and Orpheus, according to Ovid, is dismembered by Ciconian women.
- In Japanese mythology, Izanagi dismembers Kagutsuchi in revenge for the death of his lover Izanami

Literature

- In *The Divine Comedy*, falsifiers are dismembered, only to be healed and have the process start over again
- In *The Lovely Bones*, a 14-year-old girl is murdered and dismembered.
- In the "Tell-Tale Heart" the unnamed victim is murdered, dismembered and hid under the floorboards of his own house.

Television

- Multiple episodes of *The Sopranos* discussed or showed mafiosi dismembering bodies; for example, in "Whoever Did This", Tony Soprano and Christopher Moltisanti dismember and decapitate the body of Ralph Cifaretto.
- The television series *24* showed many dismemberments by both protagonists and antagonists alike. For example, in the first two episodes of the second season, Jack Bauer decapitates a federal witness to get back undercover with a terrorist group that can lead authorities to a stolen nuclear weapon.
- On Spartacus: War of the Damned, a man captured in battle is dismembered by a group of soldiers.
- On Moon Embracing the Sun, a Shaman is dismembered because of being accused of a crime.
- In the Joseon-era Korean drama *Maids*, Guk In-yeob is made to watch her father be dismembered after he is accused of treason.
- In the Netflix original show *Narcos*, Pacho publicly draws and quarters Salazar via motorcycle
- Happens in nearly every episode of *Superjail!*

Video games

- *Call of Duty: Black Ops*
- *Call of Duty: World at War*
- *Dead Island*
- *Dead Space*
- *Doom*
- *Dwarf Fortress*
- *Quake 4*
- *Gears of War 3*
- *Gun*
- *Metal Gear Rising*
- *Naruto Shippuden: Ultimate Ninja Storm 3*
- *Left 4 Dead*
- *Conker's Bad Fur Day*
- *God of War*
- *Mortal Kombat*
- *Carmageddon*
- *Fallout*

External links

 Wikimedia Commons has media related to *Dismemberment*.

Hanged, drawn and quartered

To be **hanged, drawn and quartered** was from 1352 a statutory penalty in England for men convicted of high treason, although the ritual was first recorded during the reign of King Henry III (1216–1272). A convicted traitor was fastened to a hurdle, or wooden panel, and drawn by horse to the place of execution, where he was then hanged (almost to the point of death), emasculated, disembowelled, beheaded, and quartered (chopped into four pieces). The traitor's remains were often displayed in prominent places across the country, such as London Bridge. For reasons of public decency, women convicted of high treason were instead burned at the stake.

The severity of the sentence was measured against the seriousness of the crime. As an attack on the monarch's authority, high treason was considered a deplorable act demanding the most extreme form of punishment. Although some convicts had their sentences modified and suffered a less ignominious end,

Figure 147: *The execution of Hugh Despenser the Younger, as depicted in the Froissart of Louis of Gruuthuse*

over a period of several hundred years many men found guilty of high treason were subjected to the law's ultimate sanction. They included many English Catholic priests executed during the Elizabethan era, and several of the regicides involved in the 1649 execution of Charles I.

Although the Act of Parliament defining high treason remains on the United Kingdom's statute books, during a long period of 19th-century legal reform the sentence of hanging, drawing, and quartering was changed to drawing, hanging until dead, and posthumous beheading and quartering, before being abolished in England in 1870. The death penalty for treason was abolished in 1998.

Treason in England

During the High Middle Ages those in England guilty of treason were punished in a variety of ways, including drawing and hanging. In the 13th century other, more brutal penalties were introduced, such as disembowelling, burning, beheading and quartering. The 13th-century English chronicler Matthew Paris described how in 1238 "a certain man at arms, a man of some education (*armiger literatus*)" attempted to kill King Henry III. His account records in gruesome detail how the would-be assassin was executed: "dragged asunder, then beheaded, and his body divided into three parts; each part was

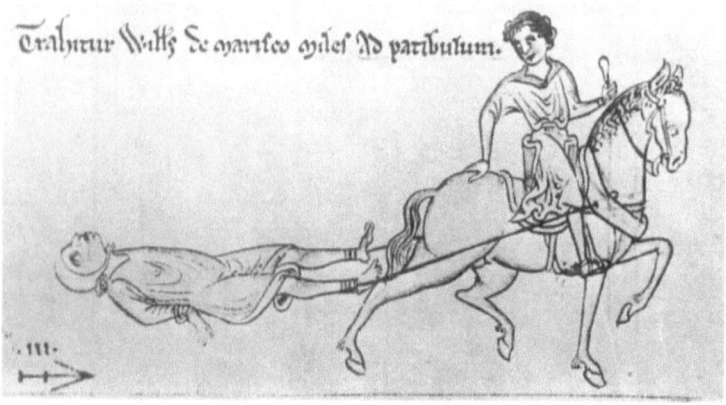

Figure 148: *As illustrated in Matthew Paris's Chronica Majora, William de Marisco is drawn to his execution behind a horse.*

then dragged through one of the principal cities of England, and was afterwards hung on a gibbet used for robbers."[927]</ref> He was apparently sent by William de Marisco, an outlaw who some years earlier had killed a man under royal protection before fleeing to Lundy Island. De Marisco was captured in 1242 and on Henry's order dragged from Westminster to the Tower of London to be executed. There he was hanged from a gibbet until dead. His corpse was disembowelled, his entrails burned, his body quartered and the parts distributed to cities across the country. The punishment is more frequently recorded during Edward I's reign. Welshman Dafydd ap Gruffydd became the first nobleman in England to be hanged, drawn, and quartered after he turned against the king and proclaimed himself Prince of Wales and Lord of Snowdon. Dafydd's rebellion infuriated Edward so much that he demanded a novel punishment. Therefore, following his capture and trial in 1283, for his betrayal he was drawn by horse to his place of execution. For killing English nobles he was hanged alive. For killing those nobles at Easter he was eviscerated and his entrails burned. For conspiring to kill the king in various parts of the realm, his body was quartered and the parts sent across the country; his head was placed on top of the Tower of London. A similar fate was suffered by the Scottish leader Sir William Wallace. Captured and tried in 1305, he was forced to wear a crown of laurel leaves and was drawn to Smithfield, where he was hanged and beheaded. His entrails were then burned and his corpse quartered. His head was set on London Bridge and the quarters sent to Newcastle, Berwick, Stirling, and Perth.

These and other executions, such as those of Andrew Harclay, 1st Earl of Carlisle, and Hugh Despenser the Younger, which each occurred during King

Figure 149: *Edward III, under whose rule the Treason Act 1351 was enacted. It defined in law what constituted high treason.*

Edward II's reign, happened when acts of treason in England, and their punishments, were not clearly defined in common law.[928]</ref> Treason was based on an allegiance to the sovereign from all subjects aged 14 or over and it remained for the king and his judges to determine whether that allegiance had been broken. Edward III's justices had offered somewhat over-zealous interpretations of what activities constituted treason, "calling felonies treasons and afforcing indictments by talk of accroachment of the royal power", prompting parliamentary demands to clarify the law. Edward therefore introduced the Treason Act 1351. It was enacted at a time in English history when a monarch's right to rule was indisputable and was therefore written principally to protect the throne and sovereign. The new law offered a narrower definition of treason than had existed before and split the old feudal offence into two classes. Petty treason referred to the killing of a master (or lord) by his servant, a husband by his wife, or a prelate by his clergyman. Men guilty of petty treason were drawn and hanged, whereas women were burned.[929] and so a woman convicted of killing her husband was guilty not of murder, but petty treason. For disrupting the social order a degree of retribution was therefore required; hanging was considered insufficient for such a heinous crime.</ref>

High treason was the most egregious offence an individual could commit. Attempts to undermine the king's authority were viewed with as much seriousness as if the accused had attacked him personally, which itself would be an assault on his status as sovereign and a direct threat to his right to govern. As this might undermine the state, retribution was considered an absolute necessity and the crime deserving of the ultimate punishment. The practical difference between the two offences therefore was in the consequence of being convicted; rather than being drawn and hanged, men were to be hanged, drawn, and quartered, while for reasons of public decency (their anatomy being considered inappropriate for the sentence), women were instead drawn and burned. The Act declared that a person had committed high treason if they were: compassing or imagining the death of the king, his wife or his eldest son and heir; violating the king's wife, his eldest daughter if she were unmarried, or the wife of his eldest son and heir; levying war against the king in his realm; adhering to the king's enemies in his realm, giving them aid and comfort in his realm or elsewhere; counterfeiting the Great Seal or the Privy Seal, or the king's coinage; knowingly importing counterfeit money; killing the Chancellor, Treasurer or one of the king's Justices while performing their offices. The Act did not limit the king's authority in defining the scope of treason. It contained a proviso giving English judges discretion to extend that scope whenever required, a process more commonly known as constructive treason.[930]</ref> It also applied to subjects overseas in British colonies in the Americas, but the only documented incident of an individual there being hanged, drawn, and quartered was that of Joshua Tefft, an English colonist accused of having fought on the side of the Narragansett during the Great Swamp Fight. He was executed in January 1676. Later sentences resulted either in a pardon or a hanging.

Only one witness was required to convict a person of treason, although in 1547 this was increased to two. Suspects were first questioned in private by the Privy Council before they were publicly tried. They were allowed no witnesses or defence counsel, and were generally presumed guilty from the outset. This meant that for centuries anyone accused of treason was severely legally disadvantaged, a situation which lasted until the late 17th century, when several years of politically motivated treason charges made against Whig politicians prompted the introduction of the Treason Act 1695. This allowed a defendant counsel, witnesses, a copy of the indictment, and a jury, and when not charged with an attempt on the monarch's life, to be prosecuted within three years of the alleged offence.

Edward Stafford, 3rd Duke of Buckingham was executed on 17 May 1521 for the crime of treason. The wording of his sentence has survived and indicates the precision with which the method of execution was described; he was to be "laid on a hurdle and so drawn to the place of execution, and there to be hanged, cut down alive, your members to be cut off and cast in the fire, your bowels burnt before you, your head smitten off, and your body quartered and divided at the King's will, and God have mercy on your soul."[931]

Execution of the sentence

Once sentenced, malefactors were usually held in prison for a few days before being taken to the place of execution. During the early Middle Ages this journey may have been made tied directly to the back of a horse, but it subsequently became customary for the victim to be fastened instead to a wicker hurdle, or wooden panel, itself tied to the horse. Historian Frederic William Maitland thought that this was probably to "[secure] for the hangman a yet living body". The use of the word drawn, as in "to draw", has caused a degree of confusion. One of the *Oxford English Dictionary's* definitions of draw is "to draw out the viscera or intestines of; to disembowel (a fowl, etc. before cooking, a traitor or other criminal after hanging)", but this is followed by "in many cases of executions it is uncertain whether this, or [to drag (a criminal) at a horse's tail, or on a hurdle or the like, to the place of execution; formerly a legal punishment of high treason], is meant. The presumption is that where *drawn* is mentioned after *hanged*, the sense is as here." Historian Ram Sharan Sharma arrived at the same conclusion: "Where, as in the popular *hung, drawn and quartered* [use] (meaning facetiously, of a person, completely disposed of), *drawn* follows *hanged* or *hung*, it is to be referred to as the disembowelling of the traitor." The historian and author Ian Mortimer disagrees. In an essay published on his website, he writes that the separate mention of evisceration is a relatively modern device, and that while it certainly took place on many occasions, the presumption that *drawing* means to disembowel is spurious. Instead, drawing (as a method of transportation) may be mentioned after hanging because it was a supplementary part of the execution.

Some reports indicate that during Queen Mary I's reign bystanders were vocal in their support: while in transit convicts sometimes suffered directly at the hands of the crowd. William Wallace was whipped, attacked and had rotten food and waste thrown at him, and the priest Thomas Pilchard was reportedly barely alive by the time he reached the gallows in 1587. Others found themselves admonished by "zealous and godly men"; it became customary for a preacher to follow the condemned, asking them to repent. According to Samuel Clarke, the Puritan clergyman William Perkins (1558–1602) once managed to convince a young man at the gallows that he had been forgiven, enabling the youth to go to his death "with tears of joy in his eyes ... as if he actually saw himself delivered from the hell which he feared before, and heaven opened for receiving his soul."

After the king's commission had been read aloud, the crowd was normally asked to move back from the scaffold before being addressed by the convict.

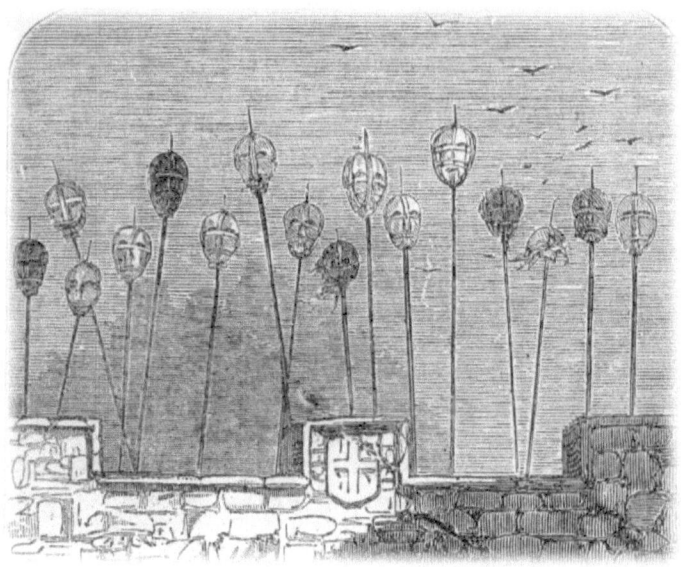

Figure 150: *The spiked heads of executed criminals once adorned the gatehouse of the medieval London Bridge.*

While these speeches were mostly an admission of guilt (although few admitted treason), still they were carefully monitored by the sheriff and chaplain, who were occasionally forced to act; in 1588, Catholic priest William Dean's address to the crowd was considered so inappropriate that he was gagged almost to the point of suffocation. Questions on matters of allegiance and politics were sometimes put to the prisoner, as happened to Edmund Gennings in 1591. He was asked by priest hunter Richard Topcliffe to "confess his treason", but when Gennings responded "if to say Mass be treason, I confess to have done it and glory in it", Topcliffe ordered him to be quiet and instructed the hangman to push him off the ladder. Sometimes the witness responsible for the condemned man's execution was also present. A government spy, John Munday, was in 1582 present for the execution of Thomas Ford. Munday supported the sheriff, who had reminded the priest of his confession when he protested his innocence. The sentiments expressed in such speeches may be related to the conditions encountered during imprisonment. Many Jesuit priests suffered badly at the hands of their captors but were frequently the most defiant; conversely, those of a higher station were often the most apologetic. Such contrition may have arisen from the sheer terror felt by those who thought they might be disembowelled rather than simply beheaded as they would normally expect, and any apparent acceptance of their fate may have stemmed from the

Figure 151: *A liuely Representation of the manner how his late Majesty was beheaded uppon the Scaffold Ian 30: 1648; A representation of the execution of the King's Judges. In the top pane, Charles I is shown awaiting his execution. In the bottom pane, one regicide is hanged and another quartered, while the latter's head is shown to the crowd.*

belief that a serious, but not treasonable act, had been committed. Good behaviour at the gallows may also have been due to a convict's desire for his heirs not to be disinherited.

The condemned were occasionally forced to watch as other traitors, sometimes their confederates, were executed before them. The priest James Bell was in 1584 made to watch as his companion, John Finch, was "a-quarter-inge". Edward James and Francis Edwardes were made to witness Ralph Crockett's execution in 1588, in an effort to elicit their co-operation and acceptance of Elizabeth I's religious supremacy before they were themselves executed. Normally stripped to the shirt with their arms bound in front of them, prisoners were then hanged for a short period, either from a ladder or cart. On the sheriff's orders the cart would be taken away (or if a ladder, turned), leaving the man suspended in mid-air. The aim was usually to cause strangulation and near-death, although some victims were killed prematurely, the priest John Payne's death in 1582 being hastened by a group of men pulling on his legs. Conversely, some, such as the deeply unpopular William Hacket (d. 1591), were cut down instantly and taken to be disembowelled and normally emasculated—the latter, according to Sir Edward Coke, to "show his issue was disinherited with corruption of blood."[932].

A victim still conscious at that point might have seen his entrails burned, before his heart was removed and the body decapitated and quartered (chopped into four pieces). The regicide Major-General Thomas Harrison, after being hanged for several minutes and then cut open in October 1660, was reported to have leaned across and hit his executioner—resulting in the swift removal of his head. His entrails were thrown onto a nearby fire.[933] His head adorned the sledge that drew fellow regicide John Cooke to his execution, before being displayed in Westminster Hall; his quarters were fastened to the city gates.</ref> John Houghton was reported to have prayed while being disembowelled in 1535, and in his final moments to have cried "Good Jesu, what will you do with my heart?" Executioners were often inexperienced and proceedings did not always run smoothly. In 1584 Richard White's executioner removed his bowels piece by piece, through a small hole in his belly, "the which device taking no good success, he mangled his breast with a butcher's axe to the very chine most pitifully."[934] In Professor Robert Kastenbaum's opinion the disfigurement of Despenser's corpse (presuming that his disembowelment was post-mortem) may have served as a reminder to the crowd that the authorities did not tolerate dissent. He speculates that the reasoning behind such bloody displays may have been to assuage the crowd's anger, to remove any human characteristics from the corpse, to rob the criminal's family of any opportunity to hold a meaningful funeral, or even to release any evil spirits contained within. The practice of disembowelling the body may have originated in the medieval belief that treasonable thoughts were housed there, requiring that the convict's entrails be "purged by fire". Andrew Harclay's "treasonous thoughts had originated in his 'heart, bowels, and entrails'", and so were to be "extracted and burnt to ashes, which would then be dispersed", as had happened with William Wallace and Gilbert de Middleton.</ref> At his execution in January 1606 for his involvement in the Gunpowder Plot, Guy Fawkes managed to break his neck by jumping from the gallows, cheating the executioner.

No records exist to demonstrate exactly how the corpse was quartered, although an engraving of the quartering of Sir Thomas Armstrong in 1684 shows the executioner making vertical cuts through the spine and removing the legs at the hip.[935] The distribution of Dafydd ap Gruffydd's remains was described by Herbert Maxwell: "the right arm with a ring on the finger in York; the left arm in Bristol; the right leg and hip at Northampton; the left [leg] at Hereford. But the villain's head was bound with iron, lest it should fall to pieces from putrefaction, and set conspicuously upon a long spear-shaft for the mockery of London." After the execution in 1660 of several of the regicides involved

Figure 152: *Engraving depicting the execution of Sir Thomas Armstrong in 1684*

in the death of King Charles I eleven years earlier, the diarist John Evelyn remarked: "I saw not their execution, but met their quarters, mangled, and cut, and reeking, as they were brought from the gallows in baskets on the hurdle." Such remains were typically parboiled and displayed as a gruesome reminder of the penalty for high treason, usually wherever the traitor had conspired or found support. Salt and cumin seed would be added during the boiling process: the salt to prevent putrefaction, and the cumin seed to prevent birds pecking at the flesh.[936]

The head was often displayed on London Bridge, for centuries the route by which many travellers from the south entered the city. Several eminent commentators remarked on the displays. In 1566 Joseph Justus Scaliger wrote that "in London there were many heads on the bridge ... I have seen there, as if they were masts of ships, and at the top of them, quarters of men's corpses." In 1602 the Duke of Pommerania-Stettin emphasised the ominous nature of their presence when he wrote "near the end of the bridge, on the suburb side, were stuck up the heads of thirty gentlemen of high standing who had been beheaded on account of treason and secret practices against the Queen."[937]</ref> The practice of using London Bridge in this manner ended following the hanging, drawing, and quartering in 1678 of William Staley, a victim of the fictitious Popish Plot. His quarters were given to his relatives, who promptly arranged a "grand" funeral; this incensed the coroner so much that he ordered the body to be dug up and set upon the city gates. Staley's was the last head to be placed on London Bridge.

Later history

Another victim of the Popish Plot, Oliver Plunkett the Archbishop of Armagh, was hanged, drawn, and quartered at Tyburn in July 1681. His executioner was bribed so that Plunket's body parts were saved from the fire; the head is now displayed at St Peter's Church in Drogheda. Francis Towneley and several other captured Jacobite officers involved in the Jacobite Rising of 1745 were executed, but by then the executioner possessed some discretion as to how much they should suffer and thus they were killed before their bodies were eviscerated. The French spy François Henri de la Motte was hanged in 1781 for almost an hour before his heart was cut out and burned, and the following year David Tyrie was hanged, decapitated, and then quartered at Portsmouth. Pieces of his corpse were fought over by members of the 20,000-strong crowd there, some making trophies of his limbs and fingers. In 1803 Edward Despard and six co-conspirators in the Despard Plot were sentenced to be hanged, drawn, and quartered. Before they were hanged and beheaded at Horsemonger Lane Gaol, they were first placed on sledges attached to horses, and ritually pulled in circuits around the gaol yards. Their execution was attended by an audience of about 20,000. A contemporary report describes the scene after Despard had made his speech:

<templatestyles src="Template:Quote/styles.css"/>

> *This energetic, but inflammatory appeal, was followed by such enthusiastic plaudits, that the Sheriff hinted to the Clergyman to withdraw, and forbade Colonel Despard to proceed. The cap was then drawn over their eyes, during which the Colonel was observed again to fix the knot under his left ear, and, at seven minutes before nine o'clock the signal being given, the platform dropped, and they were all launched into eternity. From the precaution taken by the Colonel, he appeared to suffer very little, neither did the others struggle much, except Broughton, who had been the most indecently profane of the whole. Wood, the soldier, died very hard. The Executioners went under, and kept pulling them by the feet. Several drops of blood fell from the fingers of Macnamara and Wood, during the time they were suspended. After hanging thirty-seven minutes, the Colonel's body was cut down, at half an hour past nine o'clock, and being stripped of his coat and waistcoat, it was laid upon saw-dust, with the head reclined upon a block. A surgeon then in attempting to sever the head from the body by a common dissecting knife, missed the particular joint aimed at, when he kept haggling it, till the executioner was obliged to take the head*

Figure 153: *The severed head of Jeremiah Brandreth, one of the last men in England sentenced to be hanged, drawn, and quartered*

between his hands, and to twist it several times round, when it was with difficulty severed from the body. It was then held up by the executioner, who exclaimed—"Behold the head of EDWARD MARCUS DESPARD, a Traitor!" The same ceremony followed with the others respectively; and the whole concluded by ten o'clock.

At the burnings of Isabella Condon in 1779 and Phoebe Harris in 1786, the sheriffs present inflated their expenses; in the opinion of Simon Devereaux they were probably dismayed at being forced to attend such spectacles. Harris's fate prompted William Wilberforce to sponsor a bill which if passed would have abolished the practice, but as one of its proposals would have allowed the anatomical dissection of criminals other than murderers, the House of Lords rejected it. The burning in 1789 of Catherine Murphy, a counterfeiter,[938] was impugned in Parliament by Sir Benjamin Hammett. He called it one of "the savage remains of Norman policy". Amidst a growing tide of public disgust at the burning of women, Parliament passed the Treason Act 1790, which for women guilty of treason substituted hanging for burning. It was followed by the Treason Act 1814, introduced by Samuel Romilly, a legal reformer. Influenced by his friend, Jeremy Bentham, Romilly had long argued that punitive laws should serve to reform criminal behaviour and that far from acting as a deterrent, the severity of England's laws was responsible for an increase in crime. When appointed the MP for Queensborough in 1806 he resolved to improve what he described as "Our sanguinary and barbarous penal code, written in blood". He managed to repeal the death penalty for certain thefts and vagrancy, and in 1814 proposed to change the sentence for men guilty of treason to being hanged until dead and the body left at the king's disposal. However, when it was pointed out that this would be a less severe punishment than that given for murder, he agreed that the corpse should also be decapitated, "as a fit punishment and appropriate stigma." This is what happened to Jeremiah Brandreth, leader of a 100-strong contingent of men in the Pentrich rising and one of three men executed in 1817 at Derby Gaol. As with Edward Despard and his confederates the three were drawn to the scaffold on sledges before being hanged for about an hour, and then on the insistence of the Prince Regent were beheaded with an axe. The local miner appointed to the task of beheading them was inexperienced though, and having failed with the first two blows, completed his job with a knife. As he held the first head up and made the customary announcement, the crowd reacted with horror and fled. A different reaction was seen in 1820, when amidst more social unrest five men involved in the Cato Street Conspiracy were hanged and beheaded at Newgate Prison. Although the beheading was performed by a surgeon, following the usual proclamation the crowd was angry enough to force the executioners to find safety behind the prison walls. The plot was the last crime for which the sentence was applied.

Reformation of England's capital punishment laws continued throughout the 19th century, as politicians such as John Russell, 1st Earl Russell, sought to remove from the statute books many of the capital offences that remained. Robert Peel's drive to ameliorate law enforcement saw petty treason abolished by the Offences against the Person Act 1828, which removed the distinction between crimes formerly considered as petty treason, and murder. The Royal Commission on Capital Punishment 1864-1866 recommended that there be no change to treason law, quoting the "more merciful" Treason Felony Act 1848, which limited the punishment for most treasonous acts to penal servitude. Its report recommended that for "rebellion, assassination or other violence ...we are of opinion that the extreme penalty must remain", although the most recent occasion (and ultimately, the last) on which anyone had been sentenced to be hanged, drawn, and quartered was in November 1839, following the Chartist Newport Rising—and those men sentenced to death were instead transported. The report highlighted the changing public mood toward public executions (brought about in part by the growing prosperity created by the Industrial Revolution). Home Secretary Spencer Horatio Walpole told the commission that executions had "become so demoralizing that, instead of its having a good effect, it has a tendency rather to brutalize the public mind than to deter the criminal class from committing crime". The commission recommended that executions should be performed privately, behind prison walls and away from the public's view, "under such regulations as may be considered necessary to prevent abuse, and to satisfy the public that the law has been complied with." The practice of executing murderers in public was ended two years later by the Capital Punishment Amendment Act 1868, introduced by Home Secretary Gathorne Hardy, but this did not apply to traitors.[939] An amendment to abolish capital punishment completely, suggested before the bill's third reading, failed by 127 votes to 23.

Hanging, drawing, and quartering was abolished in England by the Forfeiture Act 1870, Liberal politician Charles Forster's second attempt since 1864[940]</ref> to end the forfeiture of a felon's lands and goods (thereby not making paupers of his family). The Act limited the penalty for treason to hanging alone, although it did not remove the monarch's right under the 1814 Act to replace hanging with beheading. Beheading was abolished in 1973,[941] although it had long been obsolete. The death penalty for treason was abolished by the Crime and Disorder Act 1998, enabling the UK to ratify protocol six of the European Convention on Human Rights in 1999.

In the United States

In some of the places where the American War of Independence developed into a fierce civil war among American factions, there are recorded cases of both sides resorting to hanging, drawing, and quartering - both Loyalists and Patriots finding reasons to construe their opponents as being "traitors" deserving of such a fate.[942,943,944,945]

The Eighth Amendment to the United States Constitution's prohibition of "Cruel and Unusual Punishments" clearly (and successfully) aimed at preventing any further such usage on American soil.

References

Footnotes

Notes

Bibliography <templatestyles src="Template:Refbegin/styles.css" />

- Anon (1870), *The Law Times*[946], **49**, London: Office of the Law Times<templatestyles src="Module:Citation/CS1/styles.css"></templatestyles>
- Anon 2 (1870), *The Solicitors' journal & reporter*[947], London: Law Newspaper<templatestyles src="Module:Citation/CS1/styles.css"></templatestyles>

- Anon 3 (1870), *Public Bills*[948], **2**, Great Britain Parliament
- Abbott, Geoffrey (2005) [1994], *Execution, a Guide to the Ultimate Penalty*, Chichester, West Sussex: Summersdale Publishers, ISBN 1-84024-433-X
- Beadle, Jeremy; Harrison, Ian (2008), *Firsts, Lasts & Onlys: Crime*[949], London: Anova Books, ISBN 1-905798-04-0
- Bellamy, John (1979), *The Tudor Law of Treason*, London: Routledge & Kegan Paul, ISBN 0-7100-8729-2
- Bellamy, John (2004), *The Law of Treason in England in the Later Middle Ages*[950] (Reprinted ed.), Cambridge: Cambridge University Press, ISBN 0-521-52638-8
- Blackstone, William; Christian, Edward; Chitty, Joseph; Hovenden, John Eykyn; Ryland, Archer (1832), *Commentaries on the Laws of England*[951], **2** (18th London ed.), New York: Collins and Hannay
- Block, Brian P.; Hostettler, John (1997), *Hanging in the balance: a history of the abolition of capital punishment in Britain*[952], Winchester: Waterside Press, ISBN 1-872870-47-3
- Briggs, John (1996), *Crime and Punishment in England: an introductory history*[953], London: Palgrave Macmillan, ISBN 0-312-16331-2
- Caine, Barbara; Sluga, Glenda (2002), *Gendering European History: 1780–1920*[954], London: Continuum, ISBN 0-8264-6775-X
- Chase, Malcolm (2007), *Chartism: A New History*, Manchester: Manchester University Press, ISBN 0-7190-6087-7
- Clarke, Samuel (1654), *The marrow of ecclesiastical history*[955], Unicorn in Pauls-Church-yard: William Roybould
- Coke, Edward; Littleton, Thomas; Hargrave, Francis (1817), *The ... part of the institutes of the laws of England; or, a commentary upon Littleton*[956], London: Clarke

- Devereaux, Simon (2006), "The Abolition of the Burning of Women", *Crime, Histoire et Sociétés, 2005/2*[957], **9**, International Association for the History of Crime and Criminal Justice, ISBN 2-600-01054-8
- Diehl, Daniel; Donnelly, Mark P. (2009), *The Big Book of Pain: Torture & Punishment Through History*[958], Stroud: Sutton Publishing, ISBN 978-0-7509-4583-7
- Dubber, Markus Dirk (2005), *The police power: patriarchy and the foundations of American government*[959], New York: Columbia University Press, ISBN 0-231-13207-7
- Evelyn, John (1850), William Bray, ed., *Diary and correspondence of John Evelyn*[960], London: Henry Colburn
- Feilden, Henry St. Clair (2009) [1910], *A Short Constitutional History of England*[961], Read Books, ISBN 978-1-4446-9107-8
- Fraser, Antonia (2005) [1996], *The Gunpowder Plot*, Phoenix, ISBN 0-7538-1401-3
- Foucault, Michel (1995), *Discipline & Punish: The Birth of the Prison* (Second ed.), New York: Vintage, ISBN 0-679-75255-2
- Gatrell, V. A. C. (1996), *The Hanging Tree: Execution and the English People 1770–1868*[962], Oxford: Oxford University Press, ISBN 0-19-285332-5
- Giles, J. A. (1852), *Matthew Paris's English history: From the year 1235 to 1273*[963], London: H. G. Bohn
- Granger, William; Caulfield, James (1804), *The new wonderful museum, and extraordinary magazine*[964], Paternoster-Row, London: Alex Hogg & Co
- Joyce, James Avery (1955) [1952], *Justice at Work: The Human Side of the Law*[965], London: Pan Books
- Kastenbaum, Robert (2004), "On our way: the final passage through life and death"[966], *Life Passages*, Berkeley and Los Angeles: University of California Press, **3**, ISBN 0-520-21880-9

- Lewis, Mary E (2008) [2006], "A Traitor's Death? The identity of a drawn, hanged and quartered man from Hulton Abbey, Staffordshire"[967] (PDF), *Antiquity*, reading.academia.edu, pp. 113–124
- Lewis, Suzanne; Paris, Matthew (1987), *The art of Matthew Paris in the Chronica majora*[968], California: University of California Press, ISBN 0-520-04981-0
- Levi, Leone (1866), *Annals of British Legislation*[969], London: Smith, Elder & Co
- Maxwell, Sir Herbert (1913), *The Chronicle of Lanercost, 1272–1346*[970], Glasgow: J Maclehose
- McConville, Seán (1995), *English local prisons, 1860–1900: next only to death*[971], London: Routledge, ISBN 0-415-03295-4
- Murison, Alexander Falconer (2003), *William Wallace: Guardian of Scotland*[972], New York: Courier Dover Publications, ISBN 0-486-43182-7
- Naish, Camille (1991), *Death comes to the maiden: sex and execution, 1431–1933*[973], London: Taylor & Francis, ISBN 0-415-05585-7
- Northcote Parkinson, C. (1976), *Gunpowder Treason and Plot*, Weidenfeld and Nicolson, ISBN 0-297-77224-4
- Phillips, Seymour (2010), *Edward II*, New Haven and London: Yale University Press, ISBN 978-0-300-15657-7
- Poole, Steve (2000), *The politics of regicide in England, 1760–1850: Troublesome subjects*[974], Manchester: Manchester University Press, ISBN 0-7190-5035-9
- Pollen, John Hungerford (1908), *Unpublished documents relating to the English martyrs*[975], London: J. Whitehead
- Pollock, Frederick; Maitland, F. W. (2007), *The History of English Law Before the Time of Edward I*[976] (Second ed.), New Jersey: The Lawbook Exchange, ISBN 1-58477-718-4
- Powicke, F. M. (1949), *Ways of Medieval Life and Thought*[977], New York: Biblo & Tannen Publishers, ISBN 0-8196-0137-3

- Roberts, John Leonard (2002), *The Jacobite wars: Scotland and the military campaigns of 1715 and 1745*[978], Edinburgh: Edinburgh University Press, ISBN 1-902930-29-0
- Romilly, Samuel (1820), *The Speeches of Sir Samuel Romilly in the House of Commons: in two volumes*[979], London: Ridgway
- Sharma, Ram Sharan (2003), *Encyclopaedia of Jurisprudence*[980], New Delhi: Anmol Publications PVT., ISBN 81-261-1474-6
- Shelton, Don (2009), *The Real Mr Frankenstein*[981] (e-book), Portmin Press
- Smith, Greg T. (1996), "The Decline of Public Physical Punishment in London", in Carolyn Strange, *Qualities of mercy: Justice, Punishment, and Discretion*[982], Vancouver: UBC Press, ISBN 978-0-7748-0585-8
- Tanner, Joseph Robson (1940), *Tudor constitutional documents, A.D. 1485–1603: with an historical commentary*[983] (second ed.), Cambridge: Cambridge University Press Archive
- Tomkovicz, James J. (2002), *The right to the assistance of counsel: a reference guide to the United States Constitution*[984], Westport, CT: Greenwood Publishing Group, ISBN 0-313-31448-9
- Ward, Harry M. (2009), *Going down hill: legacies of the American Revolutionary War*[985], Palo Alto, CA: Academica Press, ISBN 978-1-933146-57-7
- Westerhof, Danielle (2008), *Death and the noble body in medieval England*[986], Woodbridge: Boydell & Brewer, ISBN 978-1-84383-416-8
- Wiener, Martin J. (2004), *Men of blood: violence, manliness and criminal justice in Victorian England*[987], Cambridge: Cambridge University Press, ISBN 0-521-83198-9Wikipedia:Link rot
- Windlesham, Baron David James George Hennessy (2001), "Dispensing justice"[988], *Responses to Crime*, Oxford: Oxford University Press, **4**, ISBN 0-19-829844-7

- Wormald, Patrick (2001) [1999], *The Making of English Law: King Alfred to the Twelfth Century, Legislation and Its Limits*[989], Oxford: Wiley-Blackwell, ISBN 0-631-22740-7<templatestyles src="Module:Citation/CS1/styles.css"></templatestyles>

Further reading

<templatestyles src="Template:Refbegin/styles.css" />

- Andrews, William (1890), *Old-Time Punishments*[990], Hull: William Andrews & Co.<templatestyles src="Module:Citation/CS1/styles.css"></templatestyles>
- Hamburger, Philip (2008), *Law and judicial duty*[991], Harvard University Press, ISBN 0-674-03131-8<templatestyles src="Module:Citation/CS1/styles.css"></templatestyles>

<indicator name="featured-star"> ⭐ </indicator>

Falling (execution)

Throwing or dropping people from great heights has been used as a form of execution since ancient times. People executed in this way die from injuries caused by hitting the ground at high velocity.

In ancient Delphi the sacrilegious were hurled from the top of the Hyampeia, the high crag of the Phaedriades to the east of the Castalian Spring.[992]

In pre-Roman Sardinia, elderly people who were unable to support themselves were ritually killed. They were intoxicated with a neurotoxic plant known as the "sardonic herb" (which some scientists think is hemlock water dropwort) and then dropped from a high rock or beaten to death.[993]

During the Roman Republic, the Tarpeian Rock, a steep cliff at the southern summit of the Capitoline Hill, was used for public executions. Murderers and traitors, if convicted by the quaestores parricidii, were flung from the cliff to their deaths. Those who had a mental or significant physical disability also suffered the same fate as they were thought to have been cursed by the gods.[994]

Later, during the Roman Empire, the Gemonian stairs were used for this purpose. Their use as a place of execution is most closely associated with the later part of the reign of the emperor Tiberius.[995,996] The condemned were usually strangled before their bodies were bound and thrown down the stairs. Occasionally the corpses of the executed were transferred here for display from other places of execution in Rome. Corpses were usually left to rot on the staircase for extended periods of time in full view of the Forum, scavenged by dogs or other carrion animals, until eventually being thrown into the Tiber. Death on the stairs was considered extremely dishonourable and dreadful, yet several senators and even an emperor met their demise here.

Suetonius records the rumours of lurid tales of sexual perversity and cruelty of Tiberius during the later part of his reign while he was living at Capri, Tiberius would execute people by having them thrown from a cliff into the sea while he watched. These people were tortured before being executed and if they survived the fall, men waiting below in boats would break their bones with oars and boathooks.

In pre-colonial South Africa, several tribes including the Xhosa and the Zulu had named Execution Hills, from which miscreants were hurled to their deaths. These societies had no form of imprisonment so punishment was corporal, capital or expulsion. It is believed that during the Namibian war of independence numerous SWAPO rebels were dropped from South African helicopters over the sea.

During the Spanish Civil War, both the right-wing Nationalist and left-wing Republican sides of the conflict made use of this execution method on their prisoners, though the practice was far more widespread on the part of the Nationalists.

During Argentina's Dirty War of the late 1970s, those secretly abducted were often thrown from aircraft, in what were known as death flights.

Iran may have used this form of execution for the crime of sodomy. According to Amnesty International in 2008, two men were convicted of raping two university students and sentenced to death.[997] They were to be thrown off a cliff or from a great height. Other men involved in this incident were sentenced to lashes, presumably because they did not engage in penetrative sex with the victims.[998]

In 2015, members of the Islamic State of Iraq and the Levant executed men who were accused of being gay by pushing them off towers.[999]

References

<templatestyles src="Template:Refbegin/styles.css" />

Flaying

Flaying, also known colloquially as skinning, is a method of slow and painful execution in which skin is removed from the body. Generally, an attempt is made to keep the removed portion of skin intact.Wikipedia:Citation needed

Scope

A dead animal may be flayed when preparing it to be used as human food, or for its hide or fur. This is more commonly called skinning.Wikipedia:Citation needed

Flaying of humans is used as a method of torture or execution, depending on how much of the skin is removed. This is often referred to as "flaying alive". There are also records of people flayed after death, generally as a means of debasing the corpse of a prominent enemy or criminal, sometimes related to religious beliefs (e.g. to deny an afterlife); sometimes the skin is used, again for deterrence, esoteric/ritualistic purposes, etc. (e.g. scalping).Wikipedia:Citation needed

Causes of death

Dermatologist Ernst G. Jung notes that the typical causes of death due to flaying are shock, critical loss of blood or other body fluids, hypothermia, or infections, and that the actual death is estimated to occur from a few hours up to a few days after the flaying.[1000] Hypothermia is possible, as skin is essential for maintaining a person's body temperature, as it provides a person's natural insulation.

History

The Assyrian tradition

Ernst G. Jung, in his *"Kleine Kulturgeschichte der Haut"* ("A small cultural history of the skin"), provides an essay in which he outlines the Neo-Assyrian tradition of flaying human beings.[1001] Already from the times of Ashurnasirpal II (r. 883-859 BC), the practice is displayed and commemorated in both carvings and official royal edicts. The carvings show that the actual flaying process might begin at various places on the body, such as at the crus (lower leg), the thighs, or the buttocks.

In their royal edicts, the Neo-Assyrian kings seem to gloat over the terrible fate they imposed upon their captives, and that flaying seems, in particular,

Figure 154: *Michelangelo's The Last Judgment - St Bartholomew holding the knife of his martyrdom and his flayed skin; it is conjectured that Michelangelo included a self-portrait depicting himself as St Bartholomew after he had been flayed alive.*

Figure 155: *Assyrians flaying their prisoners alive*

to be the fate meted out to rebel leaders. Jung provides some examples of this triumphant rhetoric. Here are some from Ashurnasirpal II:<templatestyles src="Template:Quote/styles.css"/>

> *I have made a pillar facing the city gate, and have flayed all the rebel leaders; I have clad the pillar in the flayed skins. I let the leaders of the conquered cities be flayed, and clad the city walls with their skins. The captives I have killed by the sword and flung on the dung heap, the little boys and girls were burnt.Wikipedia:Citation needed*

The Rassam Cylinder, in the British Museum demonstrates this.<templatestyles src="Template:Quote/styles.css"/>

> *Their corpses they hung on stakes, they stripped off their skins and covered the city wall with them.*[1002]

Other examples

Searing or cutting the flesh from the body was sometimes used as part of the public execution of traitors in medieval Europe. A similar mode of execution was used as late as the early 18th century in France; one such episode is graphically recounted in the opening chapter of Michel Foucault's *Discipline and Punish* (1979).

In 1303, the Treasury of Westminster Abbey was robbed while holding a large sum of money belonging to King Edward I. After arrest and interrogation of 48 monks, three of them, including the subprior and sacrist, were found guilty of the robbery and flayed. Their skin was attached to three doors as a warning against robbers of Church and State. The Copford church in Essex, England, has been found to have human skin attached to a door.[1003]

In Chinese history, Sun Hao, Fu Sheng and Gao Heng were known for removing skin from people's faces.[1004] The Hongwu Emperor flayed many servants, officials and rebels.[1005] In 1396 he ordered the flaying of 5000 women.[1006] Hai Rui suggested that his emperor flay corrupt officials. The Zhengde Emperor flayed six rebels,[1007] and Zhang Xianzhong also flayed many people. Lu Xun said the Ming Dynasty was begun and ended by flaying.[1008]

Figure 156: *Apollo flaying Marsyas by Antonio Corradini (1658-1752), Victoria and Albert Museum, London*

Examples and depictions of flayings

Artistic

- One of the plastinated exhibits in Body Worlds includes an entire posthumously flayed skin, and many of the other exhibits have had their skin removed.

Mythological

- In Greek mythology, Marsyas, a satyr, was flayed alive for daring to challenge Apollo to a musical contest, which he lost.
- Also according to Greek mythology, Aloeus is said to have had his wife flayed.
- In Aztec mythology, Xipe Totec is the flayed god of death and rebirth. Slaves were flayed annually as sacrifices to him.

Figure 157: *The Flaying of Marsyas after challenging Apollo. Painting by Titian.*

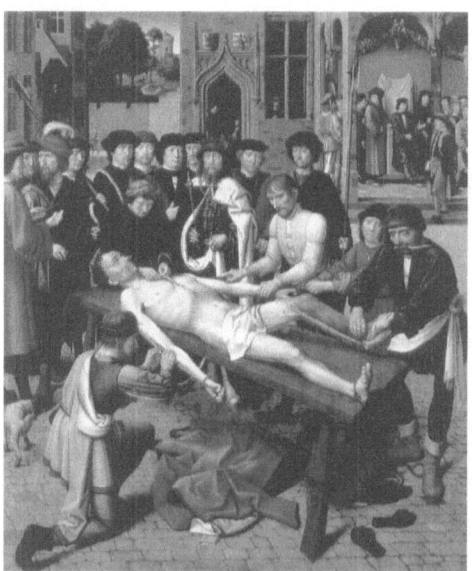

Figure 158: *The Judgement of Cambyses, part 2, half of a diptych painted by Gerard David in 1498.*

Historical

- Yahu-Bihdi, ruler of Hamath, was flayed alive by the Assyrians under Sargon II.
- According to Herodotus, Sisamnes, a corrupt judge under Cambyses II of Persia, was flayed for accepting a bribe.
- The Talmud discusses how Rabbi Akiva was flayed alive by the Romans for publicly teaching Torah.
- Catholic and Orthodox tradition holds that Saint Bartholomew was flayed before being crucified.
- Mani, founding prophet of Manichaeism, was said to have been flayed or beheaded (c. 275).
- In March 415, Hypatia of Alexandria, a Neoplatonist philosopher, was murdered by a Christian mob of Nitrian monks who accused her of paganism. They stripped her naked, skinned her with *ostraca* (pot shards), and then burned her remains.
- Totila is said to have ordered the bishop of Perugia, Herculanus, to be flayed when he captured that city in 549.
- In 991 AD, during a Viking raid in England, a Danish Viking is said to have been flayed by London locals for ransacking a church. Alleged human skin found on a local church door has, for many years, been considered as proof for this legend, but a deeper analysis made during the production of the 2001 BBC documentary, *Blood of the Vikings*, came to the conclusion that the preserved skin came from a cow hide and was part of a 19th-century hoax.
- Pierre Basile was flayed alive and all defenders of the chateau hanged on 6 April 1199, by order of the mercenary leader Mercadier, for shooting and killing King Richard I of England with a crossbow at the siege of Châlus, in March 1199.
- In 1314, the brothers d'Aulnoy, who were lovers of the daughters-in-law of king Philip IV of France, were flayed alive, then castrated and beheaded, and their bodies were exposed on a gibbet (*Tour de Nesle Affair*). The extreme severity of their punishment was due to the *lèse majesté* nature of the crime.
- In 1404 or 1417, the Hurufi Imad ud-Din Nesîmî, an Islamic poet of Turkic extraction, was flayed alive, apparently on orders of a Timurid governor, and for heresy.
- In August 1571, Marcantonio Bragadin, a defeated Venetian commander, was flayed to death by the Ottomans, causing enormous outrage in Venice and perhaps inspiring Titian's *Flaying of Marsyas*.
- In 1657, the Polish Jesuit martyr, Andrew Bobola, was burned, half strangled, partly flayed alive, and killed by a sabre stroke by Eastern Orthodox Cossacks.

- In 1771, Daskalogiannis, a Cretan rebel against the Ottoman Empire, was flayed alive, and it is said that he suffered in dignified silence.
- In the United States, Nat Turner, leader of an unsuccessful slave rebellion, was hanged on November 11, 1831. His body was then flayed, beheaded, and quartered.
- In the year 1689, Aurangzeb captured Sambhaji, the second ruler of the Maratha kingdom. He was ordered to bow before Aurangzeb and convert to Islam. It was his refusal to do so, Aurangzeb brutally tortured Sambhaji for more than 40 days where his skin was flayed along with other tortures before he was finally killed.
- The Rawhide Valley in Wyoming is said to have acquired its name from a white settler who was flayed alive there for murdering a Native American woman.Wikipedia:Citation needed
- In Marcel Ophüls' documentary, *Hôtel Terminus: The Life and Times of Klaus Barbie*, the daughter of a French Resistance leader claims her father was tortured, including being flayed, by Klaus Barbie during his time at Lyon, 1942-44.
- In 1957, a victim of Ed Gein was found "dressed out like a deer". His story fueled the inspiration of movie characters of Norman Bates (Psycho), Jame Gumb "Buffalo Bill" (The Silence of the Lambs) and Leatherface (The Texas Chainsaw Massacre).

Fictional

- In Thomas Harris' novel, *The Silence of the Lambs*, the character Buffalo Bill is a serial killer whose *modus operandi* includes flaying his victims.
- In the fantasy series, *A Song of Ice and Fire*, the Boltons of the Dreadfort flay their prisoners. The sigil of House Bolton is a flayed man. The Boltons allegedly gave up this practice 1,000 years before the series begins; however, the sadistic bastard of the family, Ramsay Snow/Bolton, delights in flaying people and wants to restore its use.
- The titular monster of *Predator* flays its victims.
- In Haruki Murakami's novel, *The Wind-Up Bird Chronicle* (1994-1995), the character Mamiya is traumatised by having witnessed a colleague being flayed to death in Manchukuo, in the late 1930s.
- The opening case of the French crime thriller TV series, *The Frozen Dead* (2017), concerns a valuable horse which has been flayed and beheaded.
- In the sixth season of the television series *Buffy the Vampire Slayer,* the witch Willow Rosenberg notoriously used dark magic to flay Warren Mears alive in retaliation for the murder of her girlfriend, Tara Maclay. The fallout from this incident plays a significant role in Rosenberg's arc during both the show's seventh and final season, and in the canonical

comic continuation, where Mears is revealed to have survived the incident thanks to the timely magical intervention of Amy Madison.

Bibliography

- Jung, Ernst G. (2007). *"Von Ursprung des Schindens in Assyrien"*, in *"Kleine Kulturgeschichte Der Haut"*. Springer Verlag. ISBN 9783798517578.<templatestyles src="Module:Citation/CS1/styles.css"></templatestyles>

External links

 Wikimedia Commons has media related to *Flaying*.

- 1575 Painting: The Flaying of Marsyas, by Titian[1009].

Garrote

A **garrote** or **garrote vil** (a Spanish word; alternative spellings include **garotte** and similar variants[1010]) is a weapon, most often a handheld ligature of chain, rope, scarf, wire or fishing line used to strangle a person.[1011]

Assassination weapon

A garrote can be made out of many different materials, including ropes, cable ties, fishing lines, nylon, guitar strings, telephone cord or piano wire.[1012,1013]

A stick may be used to tighten the garrote; the Spanish word actually refers to the stick itself, so it is a *pars pro toto* where the eponymous component may actually be absent. In Spanish, the term may also refer to a rope and stick used to constrict a limb as a torture device.[1014]

Since World War II, the garrote has been regularly employed as a weapon by soldiers as a silent means of killing sentries and other enemy personnel. Instruction in the use of purpose-built and improvised garrottes is included in the training of many elite military units and special forces. A typical military garrote consists of two wooden handles attached to a length of flexible wire; the wire is looped over a sentry's head and pulled taut in one motion. Soldiers of the French Foreign Legion have used a particular type of double-loop garrote (referred to as *la loupe*), where a double coil of rope or cord is dropped around

Figure 159: *A 1901 execution at the old Bilibid Prison, Manila, Philippines*

Figure 160: *From the torture museum of Freiburg im Breisgau*

Figure 161: *In this 15th-century depiction of the burning of Albigensians after an auto da fe, the condemned had been garroted previously. It is one of the first depictions of a garrote. Pedro Berruguete, Saint Dominic Presiding over an Auto-da-fe.*

a victim's neck and then pulled taut. Even if the victim pulls on one of the coils, he only succeeds in tightening the other.

The garrote was widely employed in 17th- and 18th-century India as an assassination device, particularly by the Thuggee cult. Practitioners used a yellow silk or cloth scarf called a rumāl. The Indian version of the garrote frequently incorporates a knot at the center intended to aid in crushing the larynx while someone applies pressure to the victim's back, usually with a foot or knee.

Execution device

The garrote (Latin: *laqueus*) is known to have been used in the first century BC in Rome. It is referred to in accounts of the Second Catilinian Conspiracy, where conspirators including Publius Cornelius Lentulus Sura were strangled with a *laqueus* in the Tullianum, and the implement is shown in some early reliefs, e.g., *Répertoire de Reliefs grecs et romains*, tome I, p. 341 (1919). It was also used in the Middle Ages in Spain and Portugal. It was employed during the *conquista* of the Americas, notably in the execution of the Inca emperor Atahualpa.

In the Ottoman Empire, execution by strangulation was reserved for very high officials and members of the ruling family. Unlike the Spanish version, a bowstring was used instead of a tightening collar.

During the Peninsular War of 1808–1814, French forces regularly used the garrote to execute Spanish *guerrilleros*, priests, and other opponents of Napoleonic rule. Around 1810 the earliest known metallic garrote appeared in Spain, and on 28 April 1828, the garrote was declared the sole method of executing civilians in that country. In May 1897, the last public garroting in Spain was performed in Barcelona. After that, all executions were performed inside prisons.

Abolition

The last civilian executions in Spain, both by garroting, were those of Pilar Prades in May 1959 and José María Jarabo in July 1959. Recent legislation had caused many crimes (such as robbery-murder) to fall under the jurisdiction of military law; thus, prosecutors rarely requested civilian executions. Military executions were still performed in Spain until the 1970s. The garrotings of Heinz Chez (real name Georg Michael Welzel) and Salvador Puig Antich in March 1974, both convicted in the Francoist State of killing police officers, were the last state-sanctioned garrotings in Spain and in the world.Wikipedia:Citation needed

With the 1973 Penal Code, prosecutors once again started requesting execution in civilian cases. If the death penalty had not been abolished in 1978 after caudillo Francisco Franco's death, it is most likely that civilian executions would have resumed.Wikipedia:Citation needed The last man to be sentenced to death by garroting was José Luis Cerveto "el asesino de Pedralbes" in October 1977, for a double robbery–murder in May 1974.Wikipedia:Citation needed Cerveto requested execution, but his sentence was commuted. Another prisoner whose civilian death sentence was commuted was businessman Juan Ballot, for the contract killing of his wife in Navarre in November 1973.

In Spain, the death penalty was abolished after a new constitution was adopted in 1978. The writer Camilo José Cela obtained a garrote (which had probably been used for the execution of Puig Antich) from the *Consejo General del Poder Judicial* to display at his foundation. The device was kept in storage in Barcelona. It was displayed in the room that the Cela Foundation devoted to his novel *La familia de Pascual Duarte* until Puig Antich's family asked for its removal.[1015]

In 1990, Andorra became the last country to officially abolish the death penalty by garrotting, though this method had not been employed there since the late 12th century.

List of executed

Sortable and collapsible table

Name	Year
Atahualpa	1533
Benigno Andrade	1952
Michele Angiolillo	1897
Leonardo Bravo	1812
Heinz Chez	
Juan Díaz de Garayo	1881
Francisco Javier de Elío	1822
Baldomero Fernández Ladreda	1947
Francisco Castro Bueno	
Agapito García Atadell	
Juan García Suárez	
Mariano Gómez	1872
José María Jarabo	1959
José Apolonio Burgos	1872
Juan Vázquez Pérez	
Julio López Guixot	1958
Narciso López	1851
Luis Candelas	
Martín Merino y Gómez	
Francisco Otero González	
Mariana de Pineda Muñoz	1831
Salvador Puig Antich	1974
Pilar Prades Santamaría	1959
António José da Silva	1739
Şehzade Bayezid	1561
Jacinto Zamora	1872
Kara Mustafa Pasha	1683

References

 Wikimedia Commons has media related to *Garrote*.

Gibbeting

See also Halifax gibbet, a kind of guillotine.

A **gibbet** /ˈdʒɪbɪt/ is any instrument of public execution (including guillotine, executioner's block, impalement stake, hanging gallows, or related scaffold), but **gibbeting** refers to the use of a gallows-type structure from which the dead or dying bodies of criminals were hung on public display to deter other existing or potential criminals. Occasionally the gibbet was also used as a method of execution, with the criminal being left to die of exposure, thirst and/or starvation. The term *gibbet* may also be used to refer to the practice of placing a criminal on display within a gibbet.[1016] This practice is also called "hanging in chains".

Display

Gibbeting was a common law punishment, which a judge could impose in addition to execution. This practice was regularised in England by the Murder Act 1751, which empowered judges to impose this for murder. It was most often used for traitors, murderers, highwaymen, pirates, and sheep stealers and was intended to discourage others from committing similar offences. The structures were therefore often placed next to public highways (frequently at crossroads) and waterways.

Exhibiting a body could backfire against a monarch, especially if the monarch was unpopular. The rebels Henry of Montfort and Henry of Wylynton, enemies of Edward II, were drawn and hanged before being exhibited on a gibbet near Bristol. However, the people made relics of these bloody and mutilated remains out of respect and later used the relics in violent protest. Miracles were even reported at the spot where the bodies were hanging.

Although the intention was deterrence, the public response was complex. Samuel Pepys expressed disgust at the practice. There was Christian objection that prosecution of criminals should end with their death. The sight and smell of decaying corpses was offensive and regarded as "pestilential", so it was seen as a threat to public health.

Figure 162: *The reconstructed gallows-style gibbet at Caxton Gibbet, in Cambridgeshire, England*

Figure 163: *Captain Kidd, who was tried and executed for piracy, hanging in chains*

Figure 164: *A gibbet with a dummy inside*

Pirates were sometimes executed by hanging on a gibbet erected close to the low-water mark by the sea or a tidal section of a river. Their bodies would be left dangling until they had been submerged by the tide three times. In London, Execution Dock is located on the north bank of the River Thames in Wapping; after tidal immersion, particularly notorious criminals' bodies could be hung in cages a little farther downstream at either Cuckold's Point or Blackwall Point, as a warning to other waterborne criminals of the possible consequences of their actions (such a fate befell Captain William Kidd in May 1701). There were objections that these displays offended foreign visitors and did not uphold the reputation of the law, though the scenes even became gruesome tourist attractions.[1017]

Variants

In some cases, the bodies would be left until their clothes rotted or even until the bodies were almost completely decomposed, after which the bones would be scattered.

In cases of drawing and quartering, the body of the criminal was cut into four or five portions, with the several parts often gibbeted in different places.

So that the public display might be prolonged, bodies were sometimes coated in tar or bound in chains. Sometimes, body-shaped iron cages were used to

Figure 165: *Hanging cage at the main gate to Corciano, Province of Perugia, Italy*

contain the decomposing corpses. For example, in March 1743 in the town of Rye, East Sussex, Allen Grebell was murdered by John Breads. Breads was imprisoned in the Ypres Tower and then hanged, after which his body was left to rot for more than 20 years in an iron cage on Gibbet Marsh. The cage and Breads' skull are still kept in the town hall.

Another example of the cage variation is the gibbet iron, on display at the Atwater Kent Museum in Philadelphia, Pennsylvania. The cage, created in 1781, was intended to be used to display the body of convicted pirate Thomas Wilkinson, so that sailors on passing ships might be warned of the consequences of piracy; Wilkinson's planned execution never took place, so the gibbet was never used.

An example of an iron cage used to string up bodies on a gibbet can still be seen in the Westgate Museum at Winchester.

Historical examples

Antiquity

The Old Testament (Torah) law forbids gibbeting beyond sundown of the day that the body is hanged on the tree.[1018] Public crucifixion with prolonged display of the body after death can be seen as a form of gibbeting.[1019] Gibbeting was one of the methods said by Tacitus and Cassius Dio to have been used by Boudica's army in the massacre of Roman settlers in the destruction of Camulodunum (Colchester), Londinium (London) and Verulamium (St. Albans) in AD 60–61.

Bermuda

Being a seafaring nation in the 17th and 18th centuries, Bermuda inherited many of the same customs as England, including the gibbet. Located in Smith's Parish at the entrance to Flatt's Inlet is Gibbet Island, which was used to hang the bodies of escaped slaves as a deterrent to others. The small island was used for this purpose because it was not on the mainland and therefore satisfied the superstitious beliefs of locals who did not want gibbets near their homes.

Canada

Marie-Josephte Corriveau (1733–1763), better known as "La Corriveau", is one of the most popular figures in Québécois folklore. She lived in New France, was sentenced to death by a British court martial for the murder of her second husband, and was hanged for it, and her body was hung in chains. Her story has become legendary in Quebec, and she is the subject of numerous books and plays.

During the Napoleonic Wars, the Royal Navy used Hangman's Beach on McNab's Island in Halifax Harbour to display the hanged bodies of deserters, in order to deter the crews of passing warships.

England

The body of Oliver Cromwell was gibbeted after his death, after monarchists disinterred it during the restoration of the monarchy. Robert Aske, who led the rebellion against Henry VIII known as Pilgrimage of Grace, was hanged in chains in 1537.

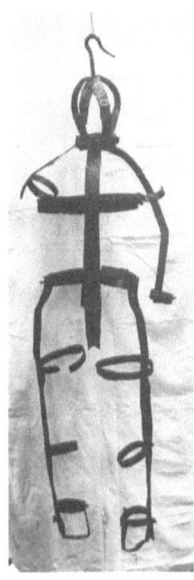

Figure 166: *The gibbet in which Corriveau was exhibited after her execution, the "cage" of La Corriveau*

Figure 167: *Hanging of Cromwell, Bradshaw and Ireton.*

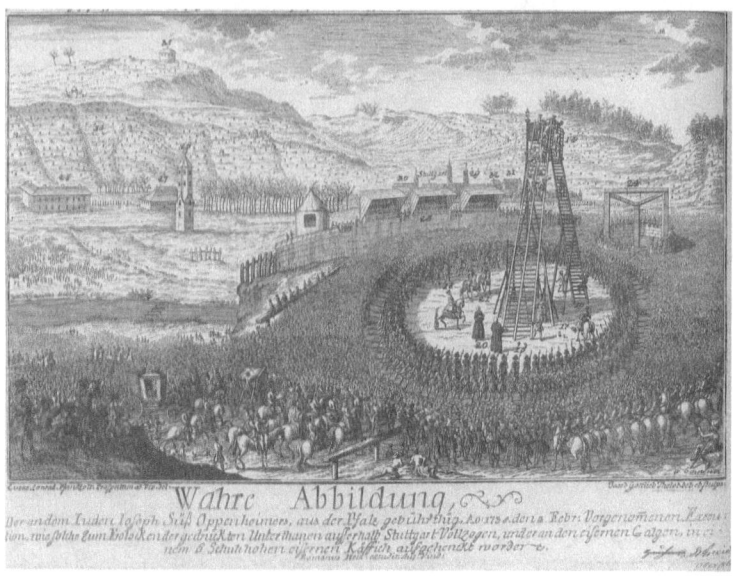

Figure 168: *Execution of Joseph Süss*

Germany

The leaders of the Anabaptist movement in Münster were executed in 1536, and their dead bodies were gibbeted in iron cages hanging from the steeple of St. Lambert's Church, and the cages are still on display there today. Similarly, following his execution by hanging in 1738, the corpse of Jewish financier Joseph Süß Oppenheimer was gibbeted in a human-sized bird cage that hung outside of Stuttgart on the so-called Pragsattel (the public execution place at the time) for six years, until the inauguration of Karl Eugen, Duke of Württemberg, who permitted the hasty burial of his corpse at an unknown location.

Iran

In 838, Babak Khorramdin had his hands and feet cut off and was then gibbeted alive while sewn into a cow's skin with the horns at ear level to crush his head gradually as the skin dried out.[1020]

United States

While still under British rule Bird Island and Nix's Mate island in Boston Harbor were used for gibbeting pirates and sailors executed for crimes in Massachusetts. Their bodies were left hanging as a warning to sailors coming into the harbor and approaching Boston.[1021] About 1755 a slave named Mark was hanged and gibbeted in Charlestown, Massachusetts; twenty years later Paul Revere passed the remains of Mark on his famous ride.

After independence, a gang of Cuban pirates was gibbeted in New York ca. 1815.[1022]

Last recorded gibbetings

Afghanistan

The January 1921 issue of *National Geographic Magazine* contains two photographs of gibbet cages, referenced as "man-cages," in use in Afghanistan. Commentary included with the photograph indicates that the gibbet was a practice still in active use. Persons sentenced to death were placed alive in the cage and remained there until some undefined time weeks or months after their deaths.

Australia

In 1837, five years after the practice had ceased in England, the body of John McKay was gibbeted near the spot where he had murdered Joseph Wilson near Perth, Tasmania.[1023] There was great outcry, but the body was not removed until an acquaintance of Wilson passed the spot and, horrified by the spectacle of McKay's rotting corpse, pleaded with the authorities to remove it. The place where this occurred was just to the right (when travelling towards Launceston, not to be confused with the private road with the same name) on the Midlands Highway on the northern side of Perth. It is the last case of gibbetting in a British colony.

United Kingdom

The Murder Act 1751 stipulated that "in no case whatsoever shall the body of any murderer be suffered to be buried";[1024] the cadaver was either to be publicly dissected or left "hanging in chains". The use of gibbeting had been in decline for some years before it was formally repealed by statute in 1834. In Scotland, the final case of gibbeting was that of Alexander Gillan in 1810.[1025] The last two men gibbeted in England were William Jobling and James Cook,

Figure 169: *Combe Gibbet, a replica gibbet in Berkshire*

both in 1832. Their cases are good examples of the changing attitudes toward the practice.

William Jobling was a miner hanged and gibbeted for the murder of Nicholas Fairles, a colliery owner and local magistrate, near Jarrow, Durham. After being hanged, the body was taken off the rope and loaded into a cart and taken on a tour of the area before arriving at Jarrow Slake, where the crime had been committed. Here, the body was placed into an iron gibbet cage. The cage and the scene were described thus:

<templatestyles src="Template:Quote/styles.css"/>

> *The body was encased in flat bars of iron of two and a half inches in breadth, the feet were placed in stirrups, from which a bar of iron went up each side of the head, and ended in a ring by which he was suspended; a bar from the collar went down the breast, and another down the back, there were also bars in the inside of the legs which communicated with the above; and crossbars at the ankles, the knees, the thighs, the bowels the breast and the shoulders; the hands were hung by the side and covered with pitch, the face was pitched and covered with a piece of white cloth.*

Wikipedia:Citation needed

The gibbet was a foot in diameter with strong bars of iron up each side. The post was fixed into a one-and-a-half-ton stone base sunk into the Slake. The body was soon removed by fellow miners and given a decent burial.

James Cook was a bookbinder convicted of the murder of his creditor Paas, a manufacturer of brass instruments, in Leicester. He was executed on Friday, 10 August 1832, in front of Leicester prison. Afterwards: <templatestyles src="Template:Quote/styles.css"/>

> The head was shaved and tarred, to preserve it from the action of the weather; and the cap in which he had suffered was drawn over his face. On Saturday afternoon his body, attired as at the time of his execution, having been firmly fixed in the irons necessary to keep the limbs together, was carried to the place of its intended suspension.

His body was to be displayed on a purpose-built gallows 33 ft high in Saffron Lane near the Aylestone Tollgate. According to *The Newgate Calendar*: <templatestyles src="Template:Quote/styles.css"/>

> Thousands of persons were attracted to the spot, to view this novel but most barbarous exhibition; and considerable annoyance was felt by persons resident in the neighbourhood of the dreadful scene. Representations were in consequence made to the authorities, and on the following Tuesday morning instructions were received from the Home Office directing the removal of the gibbet.

Although the practice of gibbeting had been abandoned by 1834 in Britain, during the British Raj of India in 1843, Charles James Napier threatened to have such structures built in parallel to any attempt to practice Sati, the ritualized burning of widows, to execute the perpetrators.[1026]

References

- Gatrell, V. A. C. (1996). *The hanging tree: execution and the English people, 1770–1868*. Oxford: Oxford University Press. pp.   266–269. ISBN 978-0-19-820413-8.<templatestyles src="Module:Citation/CS1/styles.css"></templatestyles>

Immurement

Immurement (from Latin *im-* "in" and *murus* "wall"; literally "walling in") is a form of imprisonment, usually for life, in which a person is placed within an enclosed space with no exits.[1027] This includes instances where people have been enclosed in extremely tight confinement, such as within a coffin. When used as a means of execution, the prisoner is simply left to die from starvation or dehydration. This form of execution is distinct from being buried alive, in which the victim typically dies of asphyxiation.

Some examples of immurement as an established executional practice (with death from thirst or starvation as the intended aim) are attested. Roman Vestal Virgins could face immurement as punishment if they broke their vows of chastity and immurement has been well-established as a punishment of robbers in Persia, even into the early 20th century. Some ambiguous evidence exists of immurement as a practice of coffin-type confinement in Mongolia.

However, isolated incidents of immurement, rather than elements of continuous traditions, are attested or alleged from numerous parts of the world as well, and some of these notable incidents are included. Instances of immurement as an element of massacre within the context of war or revolution are also noted. Immuring living persons as a type of human sacrifice is also reported, for example as part of grand burial ceremonies in some cultures.

As a motif in legends and folklore, many tales of immurement exist. In the folklore, immurement is prominent as a form of capital punishment, but its use as a type of human sacrifice to make buildings sturdy has many tales attached to it as well. Skeletal remains have been, from time to time, found behind walls and in hidden rooms and on several occasions have been asserted to be evidence of such sacrificial practices or of such a form of punishment.

History

Method of execution

There is a difference between a form of execution established as a tradition (for example, one crystallized into formal law), and isolated incidents of immurement. This section illustrates that distinction. Furthermore, incidents at war time are explored separately.Wikipedia:Citation needed

Established practice

Vestal Virgins in ancient Rome

The Vestal Virgins in ancient Rome constituted a class of priestesses whose principal duty was to maintain the sacred fire dedicated to Vesta (goddess of the home and the family), and they lived under a strict vow of chastity and celibacy. If that vow of chastity was broken, the offending priestess was immured alive as follows:[1028] <templatestyles src="Template:Quote/styles.css"/>

> When condemned by the college of pontifices, she was stripped of her vittae and other badges of office, was scourged, was attired like a corpse, placed in a close litter, and borne through the forum attended by her weeping kindred, with all the ceremonies of a real funeral, to a rising ground called the Campus Sceleratus, just within the city walls, close to the Colline gate. There a small vault underground had been previously prepared, containing a couch, a lamp, and a table with a little food. The pontifex maximus, having lifted up his hands to heaven and uttered a secret prayer, opened the litter, led forth the culprit, and placing her on the steps of the ladder which gave access to the subterranean cell, delivered her over to the common executioner and his assistants, who conducted her down, drew up the ladder, and having filled the pit with earth until the surface was level with the surrounding ground, left her to perish deprived of all the tributes of respect usually paid to the spirits of the departed

The order of the Vestal Virgins existed for about 1,000 years, but only about 10 effected immurements are attested in extant sources.[1029]

In Persia

A tradition existed in Persia of walling up criminals and leaving them to die of hunger or thirst. The traveller M. A. Hume-Griffith stayed in Persia from 1900 to 1903, and she wrote the following:[1030] <templatestyles src="Template:Quote/styles.css"/>

> Another sad sight to be seen in the desert sometimes, are brick pillars in which some unfortunate victim is walled up alive...The victim is put into the pillar, which is half built up in readiness; then if the executioner is merciful he will cement quickly up to the face, and death comes speedily. But sometimes a small amount of air is allowed to permeate through the bricks, and in this case the torture is cruel and the agony prolonged. Men bricked up in this way have been heard groaning and calling for water at the end of three days

Travelling back and forth to Persia from 1630 to 1668 as a gem merchant, Jean Baptiste Tavernier observed much the same custom that Hume-Griffith noted some 250 years later. Tavernier notes that immuring was principally a punishment for thieves, and that immurement left the convict's head out in the open. According to him, many of these individuals would implore passersby to cut off their heads, an amelioration of the punishment forbidden by law.[1031] John Fryer,[1032] travelling Persia in the 1670s writes the following:[1033]

> From this Plain to Lhor, both in the Highways, and on the high Mountains, were frequent Monuments of Thieves immured in Terror of others who might commit the like Offence; they having literally a Stone-Doublet, whereas we say metaphorically, when any is in Prison, He has it Stone Doublet on; for these are plastered up, all but their Heads, in a round Stone Tomb, which are left out, not out of kindness, but to expose them to the Injury of the Weather, and Assaults of the Birds of Prey, who wreak their Rapin with as little Remorse, as they did devour their Fellow-Subjects.

Staying as a diplomat in Persia from 1860–63, E. B. Eastwick met at one time, the Sardar i Kull, or military high commander, Aziz Khan. Eastwick notes that he "did not strike me as one who would greatly err on the side of leniency". Eastwick was told that just recently, Aziz Khan had ordered 14 robbers walled up alive, two of them head-downwards.[1034] Staying for the year 1887–1888 primarily in Shiraz, Edward Granville Browne noted the gloomy reminders of a particularly bloodthirsty governor there, Firza Ahmed, who in his four years of office (ending *circa* 1880), had caused, for example, more than 700 hands cut off for various offences. Browne continues:[1035]

> Besides these minor punishments, many robbers and others suffered death; not a few were walled up alive in pillars of mortar, there to perish miserably. The remains of these living tombs may still be seen outside Derwaze-i-kassah-khane ("Slaughter-house Gate") at Shiraz, while another series lines the road as it enters the little town of Abade...

Mongolia

Immurement was practiced in Mongolia as recently as the early 20th century. It is not clear that all thus immured were meant to die of starvation. In a newspaper report from 1914, it is written:[1036]

> ..the prisons and dungeons of the Far Eastern country contain a number of refined Chinese shut up for life in heavy iron-bound coffins, which do not permit them to sit upright or lie down. These prisoners see daylight for only a few minutes daily when the food is thrown into their coffins through a small hole

Immurement

Figure 170: *A Mongolian woman condemned to die Wikipedia:Citation needed of immurement, c. 1913*

Neo-Assyrian vengeance

The Neo-Assyrian Empire is infamous for its brutal repression techniques, not the least of those reasons being because several of its rulers congratulated themselves upon the vengeance they wrought by going into detail of how they dealt with their enemies. Here is a commemoration Ashurnasirpal II (r. 883–859 BC) made that includes immurement:[1037] <templatestyles src="Template:Quote/styles.css"/>

> *I erected a wall in front of the great gate of the city. I flayed the chiefs and covered this wall with their skins. Some of them were walled in alive in the masonry; others were impaled along the wall. I flayed a great number of them in my presence, and I clothed the wall with their skins. I collected their heads in the form of crowns, and their corpses I pierced in the shape of garlands... My figure blooms on the ruins; in the glutting of my rage I find my content*

Revolution at Corfu

In book 3 of his *History of the Peloponnesian War*, Thucydides goes into great detail on the revolution that broke out at Corfu in 427 BC. Book three, chapter 81, passage five reads as follows:[1038] <templatestyles src="Template:Quote/styles.css"/>

> Death thus raged in every shape; and, as usually happens at such times, there was no length to which violence did not go; sons were killed by their fathers, and suppliants dragged from the altar or slain upon it; while some were even walled up in the temple of Dionysus and died there.

Notable incidents

Execution of Livilla

Livilla, a member of the imperial dynasty under Emperor Tiberius, was condemned in AD 31 for being complicit in the plot Sejanus staged to overthrow the Emperor. According to Cassius Dio, Tiberius handed Livilla over to her mother, Antonia Minor, who locked her own daughter in the bedroom, ensuring that she starved to death.[1039]

Death of an emperor

Flavius Basiliscus, emperor in the Eastern Roman Empire from AD 475-476, was deposed. In winter he was sent to Cappadocia with his family, where they were imprisoned in either a dry cistern,[1040] or a tower,[1041] and perished. The historian Procopius said they died exposed to cold and hunger,[1042] while other sources, such as Priscus, merely speaks of death by starvation.[1043]

Patriarch and the doge

The patriarch of Aquileia, Poppo of Treffen (r. 1019–1045) was a mighty secular potentate, and in 1044 he sacked Grado. The newly elected Doge of Venice, Domenico I Contarini, captured him and allegedly let him be buried up to his neck, and left guards to watch over him until he died.[1044]

England

Maud de Braose and her son, William, were imprisoned and starved to death under John, King of England, after de Braose accused John of murdering his nephew.[1045]

Figure 171: *Perlachturm with St. Peter by Perlach*

Moravia

In 1149 Duke Otto III of Olomouc of the Moravian Přemyslid dynasty immured the abbot Deocar and 20 monks in the refectory in the monastery of Rhadisch, where they starved to death. Ostensibly this was because one of the monks had fondled his wife Duranna when she had spent the night there. However, Otto III confiscated the monastery's wealth, and some said this was the motive for the immurement.[1046]

Paederasts in the Perlachturm

The actual punishment meted out to men found guilty of paederasty (homosexual intercourse with boys) might vary between different status groups. In 1409 and 1532 in Augsburg, two men were burned alive for their offences, but a rather different procedure was meted out to four clerics in the 1409 case, guilty of the same offence. Instead of being burned alive, they were locked into a wooden casket that was hung up in the Perlachturm, and they starved to death.[1047]

Guillaume Agassa

After confessing in an Inquisition Court to an alleged conspiracy involving lepers, the Jewry, the King of Granada and the Sultan of Babylon, Guillaume Agassa, head of the leper asylum at Lestang, was condemned in 1322 to be immured in shackles for life.[1048]

Elizabeth Báthory*Talk:Immurement#*

Hungarian countess Elizabeth Báthory de Ecsed (*Báthory Erzsébet* in Hungarian; 7 August 1560 – 21 August 1614) was immured in a set of rooms in 1610 for the death of several girls, with figures being as high as several hundred, though the actual number of victims is uncertain. Being labeled the most prolific female serial killer in history has earned her the nickname of the "Blood Countess", and she is often compared with Vlad III the Impaler of Wallachia in folklore. She was allowed to live in immurement until she died, four years after being sealed, ultimately dying of causes other than starvation; evidently her rooms were well supplied with food.

Fugitive royal family from the Mughal Empire

In the late 1650s, various sons of the Mughal emperor Shah Jahan became embroiled in wars of succession, in which Aurangzeb was victorious. One of his half-brothers, Shah Shujah proved particularly troublesome, but in 1661 Aurangzeb defeated him, and Shah Shuja and his family sought the protection of the King of Arakan. According to Francois Bernier, the King reneged on his promise of asylum, and Shuja's sons were decapitated, while his daughters were immured, and died of starvation.[1049]

Jezzar Pasha, the tyrant at Beirut

Jezzar Pasha, the Ottoman governor of provinces in modern Lebanon, and Palestine from 1775 to 1804, was infamous for his cruelties. When building the new walls of Beirut, he was charged, inter alia, with the following:[1050]
<templatestyles src="Template:Quote/styles.css"/>

> *..and this monster had taken the name of Dgezar (Butcher) as an illustrious addition to his title. It was, no doubt, well deserved; for he had immured alive a great number of Greek Christians when he rebuilt the Walls of Barut..The heads of these miserable victims, which the butcher had left out, in order to enjoy their tortures, are still to be seen*

Moroccan serial killer

In a newspaper clipping from 1906, the fate of a cobbler from Marrakesh who was found guilty of murdering 36 women (the bodies were found buried underneath his shop and in his garden) is recounted. In order to deter others from similar heinous crimes, he was sentenced to be walled up alive. For two days after his immurement his screams were heard incessantly, but from the third day, all was silent from him.

Sons of Sikh Guru Gobind Singh

During the battle against Wazir Khan, Guru Gobind Singh's two elder sons died and the two younger ones, aged nine and seven, were bricked up alive in Wazir Khan's palace.

Human sacrifice

Entombed with the deceased

In several cultures, it is attested that living persons were entombed along with a deceased person, as part of the funerary ritual. Some such borderline cases between buried alive and immurement are included here.

Excavations at Ur

In the ancient Sumerian city of Ur some graves (as early as 2500 BC.) clearly show the burial of attendants, along with that of the principal dead person. In one such grave, Gerda Lerner writes: <templatestyles src="Template:Quote/styles.css"/>

> *The human sacrifices were probably first drugged or poisoned, as evidenced by a drinking cup near each body, then the pit was immured, and covered with earth*[1051]

China

In 102 BC, the Qin Shi Huang died, and all the imperial concubines and the artisans who had worked on the mausoleum were immured alive along with him.[1052]

Burial of a Mongol Khan

The 14th century traveller Ibn Batuta observed once the burial of a great khan, and writes the following, pertinent to immurement:[1053]

> The Khan who had been killed, with about a hundred of his relatives, was then brought, and a large sepulchre was dug for him under the earth, in which a most beautiful couch was spread, and the Khan was with his weapons laid upon it. With him they placed all the gold and silver vessels he had in his house,' together with four female slaves, and six of his favourite Mamluks, with a few vessels of drink. They were then all closed up, and the earth heaped upon them to the height of a large hill.

The Bonny Widows in Africa

Harold Edward Bindloss, in his 1898 non-fiction "In the Niger country" writes the following transpiring when a great chief died:

> Only a few years ago, when a powerful headman died not very far from Bonny, several of his wives had their legs broken, and were buried alive with him[1054]

Other types of human sacrifice

Sun festival among Incas

Within Inca culture, it is reported that as one element in the great Sun festival was the sacrifice of young maidens (between ten and twelve years old), who after their ceremonial duties done were lowered down in a waterless cistern and were immured alive.[1055]

Asceticism/Religious practice

Anchorites

A particularly severe form of asceticism within Christianity is that of anchorites, who typically allowed themselves to be immured, and subsisting on minimal food. For example, in the 4th century AD, one nun named "Alexandra immured herself in a tomb for ten years with a tiny aperture enabling her to receive meager provisions...Saint Jerome (ca.340-420) spoke of one follower who spent his entire life in a cistern, consuming no more than five figs a day".[1056]

Figure 172: *Immurement of a nun (fictitious depiction in a painting from 1868)*

Vade in pace

In Catholic monastic tradition, there existed a type of enforced, lifelong confinement against nuns or monks who had broken their vows of chastity, or espoused heretical ideas, and some have believed that this type of imprisonment was, indeed, a form of immurement. The judgment was preceded by the phrase *"vade in pacem"*, that is, "go *into* peace", rather than "go *in* peace". (Latin "in" can be translated to English as either "in" or "into", depending on the case of its object—ablative for "in" or accusative for "into".) As Henry Charles Lea puts it, the tradition seems to have been that of complete, utter isolation from other human beings, but that food was, indeed, provided:[1057] <templatestyles src="Template:Quote/styles.css"/>

> *In the case of Jeanne, widow of B. de la Tour, a nun of Lespenasse, in 1246, who had committed acts of both Catharan and Waldensian heresy, and had prevaricated in her confession, the sentence was confinement in a separate cell in her own convent, where no one was to enter or see her, her food being pushed in through an opening left for the purpose—in fact, the living tomb known as the "in pace."*

In the footnote appended to this passage, Lea writes:[1058] <templatestyles src="Template:Quote/styles.css"/>

> *The cruelty of the monastic system of imprisonment known as in pace, or vade in pacem, was such that those subjected to it speedily died in all the agonies of despair. In 1350 the Archbishop of Toulouse appealed to King John to interfere for its mitigation, and he issued an Ordonnance that the superior of the convent should twice a month visit and console the prisoner, who, moreover, should have the right twice a month to ask for the company of one of the monks. Even this slender innovation provoked the bitterest resistance of the Dominicans and Franciscans, who appealed to Pope Clement VI., but in vain*

Although the "Vade in Pace" tradition therefore seems to one of perpetual, aggravated confinement, but not immurement where the individual was meant to starve to death, several have thought "vade in pace" was just that, a death sentence. For example, Sir Walter Scott, himself an antiquarian, notes in a remark to his poem *Marmion* (1808):[1059]

> *It is well known, that the religious, who broke their vows of chastity, were subjected to the same penalty as the Roman Vestals in a similar case. A small niche, sufficient to enclose their bodies, was made in the massive wall of the convent; a slender pittance of food and water was deposited in it and the awful words Vade in pace, were the signal for immuring the criminal. It is not likely that, in latter times, this punishment was often resorted to; but, among the ruins of the abbey of Coldingham were some years ago discovered the remains of a female skeleton which, from the shape of the niche, and the position of the figure seemed to be that of an immured nun*

The practice of immuring nuns or monks on breaches of chastity has a long history, and Francesca Medioli writes the following in her essay "Dimensions of the Cloister":[1060]

> *At Lodi in 1662 Sister Antonia Margherita Limera stood trial for having introduced a man into her cell and entertained him for a few days; she was sentenced to be walled in alive on a diet of bread and water. In the same year, the trial for breach of enclosure and sexual intercourse against the cleric Domenico Cagianella and Sister Vinzenza Intanti of the convent of San Salvatore in Ariano had an identical outcome*

Japanese suicide tradition

Emile Durkheim in his work *Suicide* writes the following about certain followers of Amida Buddha:[1061]

> *The sectarians of Amida have themselves immured in caverns where there is barely space to be seated and where they can breathe only through an air shaft. There they quietly allow themselves to die of hunger.*

Figure 173: *Recreation of a sixteenth-century knight, who was believed to be immured in a wall of Kuressaare Castle, Estonia.*

Legend and folklore

Punishments in folklore

Sweden, Finland and Estonia

According to Finnish legends, a young maiden was wrongfully immured into the castle wall of Olavinlinna as a punishment for treason. The subsequent growth of a rowan tree at the location of her execution, whose flowers were as white as her innocence and berries as red as her blood, inspired a ballad.[1062] Similar legends stem from Haapsalu,[1063] Kuressaare,[1064] Põlva[1065] and Visby.[1066]

Latvia

According to a Latvian legend as many as three people might have been immured in tunnels under the Grobiņa Castle. A daughter of a knight living in the castle did not approve of her father's choice of a young nobleman as her future husband. Said knight also pillaged surrounding areas and took prisoners to live in the tunnels, among these a handsome young man whom the daughter took a liking to, helping him escape. Her fate wasn't so lucky as the knight and his future son-in-law punished her by immuring her in one of the tunnels. Another nobleman's daughter and a Swedish soldier are also said to be immured in one of the tunnels after she had fallen in love with the Swedish soldier and requested her father to allow her to marry him. According to another legend a maiden and a servant have been immured after a failed attempt at spying on Germans wanting to know what their plans were for what is now Latvia.

Mughal Empire

By popular legend, Anarkali was immured between two walls in Lahore, Pakistan by order of Mughal Emperor Akbar for having a relationship with crown prince Salim (later Emperor Jehangir) in the 16th century. A bazaar developed around the site, and was named Anarkali Bazaar in her honour.[1067]

Human sacrifice when constructing buildings

A number of cultures have tales and ballads containing as a motif the sacrifice of a human being to ensure the strength of a building.

South-Eastern Europe

The folklore of many Southeastern European peoples refers to immurement as the mode of death for the victim sacrificed during the completion of a construction project, such as a bridge or fortress (mostly real buildings). The Castle of Shkodra is the subject of such stories in both the Albanian oral tradition and in the Slavic one: in the Albanian version, three brothers uselessly toiled at building walls that disappeared at night: when told that they had to bury one of their wives in the wall, they pledge to choose the one that will bring them lunch the next day, and not to warn their respective spouse. Two brothers do, however (the topos of two fellows betraying one is common in Balkan poetry, cfr. Miorița or the Song of Çelo Mezani), leave Rozafa, the wife of the honest brother, to die. She accepts her fate, but asks to leave exposed her foot (to rock the infant son's cradle), the breast (to feed him) and the hand (to stroke his hair). The Serbian version is The Building of Skadar, and differs on a few details (the name "Rozafa" and the topic of betrayal are absent). A very similar Romanian legend, that of Meșterul Manole, tells of the building of the Curtea de Argeș Monastery: ten expert masons, among whom Master Manole himself, are ordered by Neagu Voda to build a beautiful monastery, but incur the same fate, and decide to immure the wife who will bring them lunch. Manole, working on the roof, sees her approach, and pleads with God to unleash the elements, in order to stop her, but in vain: when she arrives, he proceeds to wall her in, pretending to be doing so in jest, with his wife increasingly crying out in pain and distress. When the building is finished, Neagu Voda takes away the masons' ladders, fearing they will build a more beautiful building, and they try to escape but all fall to their death. Only from Manole's fall a stream is created.[1068]

Many other Bulgarian and Romanian folk poems and songs describe a bride offered for such purposes, and her subsequent pleas to the builders to leave her hands and breasts free, that she might still nurse her child. Later versions of the songs revise the bride's death; her fate to languish, entombed in the stones of the construction, is transmuted to her nonphysical shadow, and its loss yet leads to her pining away and eventual death.[1069]

Other variations include the Hungarian folk ballad "Kőmíves Kelemen" (Kelemen the Stonemason). This is the story of twelve unfortunate stonemasons tasked with building the fort of Déva (a real building). To remedy its recurring collapses, it is agreed that one of the builders must sacrifice his bride, and the bride to be sacrificed will be she who first comes to visit.[1070] In some versions of the ballad the victim is shown some mercy; rather than being trapped alive she is burned and only her ashes are immured.[1071].

Greece and Malta

A Greek story "The Bridge of Arta" (Greek: Γεφύρι της Άρτας) describes numerous failed attempts to build a bridge in that city. A cycle whereby a team of skilled builders toils all day only to return the next morning to find their work demolished is eventually ended when the master mason's wife is immured.[1072]

Like many other European folktales, legend has it that a maiden was immured in the walls of Madliena church as a sacrifice or offering after continuous failed attempts at building it. The pastor achieved this by inviting all of the most beautiful maidens to a feast and the most beautiful one, Madaļa, falling into a deep sleep after he'd offered her wine from a "certain goblet".[1073]

Animal sacrifice

Acknowledging the traditions of **human** sacrifice in the context of the building of structures within German and Slavic folklore, Jacob Grimm proffers some examples of the sacrifice of *animals* as well. According to him, within Danish traditions, a lamb was immured under an erected altar in order to preserve it, while a churchyard was to be ensured protection by immuring a living horse as part of the ceremony. In the ceremonies of erection of other types of constructions, Grimm notices that other animals were sacrificed as well, such as pigs, hens and dogs.[1074]

Figure 174: *Ruins of Thornton Abbey*

Quarantine

Scotland

There exist legends that the residents of Mary King's Close in Edinburgh had been immured, and left to perish during an outbreak of the plague; however, this is considered to be untrue.

Immured skeletons

In several places, immured skeletons have been found in buildings and ruins. Many of these finds have been asserted, at one time or another, to be evidence of a historical practice in consonance with the tales and legends of sacrificing human beings when constructing a building, or as being the remains of persons punished by immurement, or possibly, victims of murder.

Thornton Abbey

In the ruins of Thornton Abbey, Lincolnshire, an immured skeleton was found behind a wall; along with a table, book and a candlestick. By some, he is believed to be the fourteenth abbot, immured for some crime he committed.[1075]

Figure 175: *Cesvaine Palace*

Castle in Dublin

In 1755, it is reported that in a castle belonging to the Duke of Dorset, the skeleton of a man was found behind the wall of a servant's room. No clothes were found, but a seal with a religious inscription was found, and the skeleton had a pair of wooden clogs on the feet. The author discusses the possibility of the person having been some sort of state prisoner immured, but opts for him being the victim of murder instead.[1076]

Cesvaine Palace, Latvia

In 1778, when some reconstruction was done at Cesvaine Palace, a skeleton in a woman's dress was found behind a wall. Old people assured the visitor August Hupel that she had been immured alive at the building of the castle, but Hupel regarded the whole story as rather fanciful, and remained skeptical.[1077]

The immured knight in Tiefburg, Handschuhsheim

In 1770, human remains were found at the medieval castle Tiefburg in what is now a quarter of Heidelberg, then the village of Handschuhsheim.[1078] Going down a winding stair, the castle owner noticed one wall sounded hollow, and called for a mason to break it open. Inside was a niche that contained a skeleton in full armour; at the opening, it fell together. The helmet still carried traces of gilding, along with several sword strokes. It was assumed that the individual had been defeated in a feud, and had been immured alive at some remote time.[1079]

The monk in Malmö

In the 1770s, Sir Nathaniel Wraxall, 1st Baronet toured countries like Sweden and Denmark, and wrote a memoir on his journeys. He was wholly displeased with his visit to Malmö, and said the only thing of interest was that of the skeleton of a monk who had been immured in the church wall. According to tradition, the monk had been found guilty of fornication, and had lived nine days immured, having been fed eggs though a small hole.[1080]

Immured coffins of infants

In 1686 Bremen, when a 132-year-old city gate was rebuilt, a tiny coffin containing the skeletal remains of a child was found. A century earlier, in 1589, the city walls had been reconstructed. More than 200 years later, in 1812, there was discovered embedded in the walls some 50 tiny oak coffins. These were, however, empty.[1081] At Plesse castle, close by Göttingen, a small child coffin with remains was found in the early 19th century. In 1819, when the city walls of Harburg were renewed, a whole series of child coffins were found, just as in the walls of Bremen. The coffins in Harburg, however, did contain skeletal remains. Several other such finds are attested.[1082]

Cultural references

Antiquity to Middle Ages

Sophocles

Antigone, the heroine of the eponymous play by Sophocles, is sentenced to execution by being placed in a cave and having the exits covered with stones. Both she and her lover Haemon kill themselves, though, after interment.[1083]

Seven Sleepers

One version of the legend of the Seven Sleepers alleges that during the persecutions by the Roman emperor Decius, around 250 AD, seven young men were accused of following Christianity. They were given some time to recant their faith, but chose instead to give their worldly goods to the poor and retire to a mountain cave to pray, where they fell asleep. The emperor, seeing that their attitude towards paganism had not improved, ordered the mouth of the cave to be sealed. Others amongst many involve various tales in Christianity and Islam utilizing various cave sites.

Figure 176: *Decius orders the walling in of the Seven Sleepers. From a 14th-century manuscript.*

Dante

For alleged treachery, Ugolino della Gherardesca and his sons and grandsons were immured in the Torre dei Gualandi in the thirteenth century. Dante mentions the Ghibelline Pisan leader in the ninth circle of hell in his *Divine Comedy*.[1084]

19th century

Walter Scott

In his 1808 poem Marmion, Walter Scott has as one of his motifs the immurement of the fictional nun, Clara de Clare, on grounds of unchastity. The stanza XXV reads: <templatestyles src="Template:Quote/styles.css"/>

> And now the blind old abbot rose, To speak the chapter's doom. On those the wall was to enclose, Alive, within the tomb

Scott, himself an antiquarian, believed that the Catholic Church in earlier times immured monks and nuns found guilty of breaking their vows of chastity, explains his belief in a note appended to the poem.[1085]

Edgar Allan Poe

This form of death appears in several of Edgar Allan Poe's works, including "The Cask of Amontillado". Montresor, the narrator, immures his enemy, Fortunato, within the catacombs beyond the wine cellar under his palazzo. In "The Black Cat", the narrator's pet cat accidentally suffers immurement, but is discovered and rescued. The cat's rescue leads to the discovery of the body of the narrator's wife, since the cat was walled in with it after the murder.[1086]

William Harrison Ainsworth

In the opening of William Harrison Ainsworth's, *The Lancashire Witches*, John Paslew, the abbot of Whalley, reveals to his confessor that he conspired to have his rival for the position of abbot accused of witchcraft and immured in the walls of the abbey. The confessor then reveals himself to be the former rival, escapes from the immurement by consorting with dark powers, and returns to exact his vengeance on the abbot.

Oscar Wilde

In "The Canterville Ghost" by Oscar Wilde it is implied that Sir Simon was immured by his wife's brothers after having killed his wife. When speaking to little Virginia Otis, the ghost remarks, "I don't think it was very nice of her brothers to starve me to death." His skeleton is found chained to the wall in a secret room of Canterville Chase.[1087]

Mark Twain

In Mark Twain's *The Adventures of Tom Sawyer*, Injun Joe died after being accidentally sealed in a cave. His corpse is discovered later when the cave is reopened.[1088]

Giuseppe Verdi

In Giuseppe Verdi's *Aida*, Radames is sealed in a vault at the Temple of Vulcan as punishment for treason. His lover Aida, without his knowledge, has hidden herself in the vault so they can die together. Aida dies as the tomb is being sealed, with Radames awaiting his own death after the final curtain.[1089]

20th century

Elmore Leonard

In Elmore Leonard's 1980 novel *City Primeval*, a criminal is threatened with immurement in a concealed basement safe room.

Bibliography

<templatestyles src="Template:Refbegin/styles.css" />

- Altekar, Anant S. (1959). *The Position of Women in Hindu Civilization: From Prehistoric Times to the Present Day*[1090]. Madras: Motilal Banarsidass Publ. ISBN 9788120803244.<templatestyles src="Module:Citation/CS1/styles.css"></templatestyles>
- Baltikumresan. "The immured knight"[1091]. *http://www.aulik.se''*. Baltikumresan. Archived from the original[1092] on 2013-12-03. External link in |website= (help)<templatestyles src="Module:Citation/CS1/styles.css''></templatestyles>
- ibn Batuta; Lee (1829). *THE TRAVELS OF IBN BATUTA*[1093]. London: Oriental Translation Committee.<templatestyles src="Module:Citation/CS1/styles.css"></templatestyles>
- Bechstein, Ludwig (1858). *Thüringer sagenbuch*[1094]. Coburg: C. A. Hartleben.<templatestyles src="Module:Citation/CS1/styles.css"></templatestyles>
- Bernier, Francois (1916). *Travels in the Mogul Empire, A.D. 1656-1668*[1095]. London: Milford, Oxford University Press.<templatestyles src="Module:Citation/CS1/styles.css"></templatestyles>
- Bindloss, Harold (1898). *In the Niger country*[1096]. Edinburgh and London: W. Blachwood and Sons.<templatestyles src="Module:Citation/CS1/styles.css"></templatestyles>
- Blumenbach; Spangenberg, Ernst (1828). "Ueber eingemauerte Kinderleichen"[1097]. *Neues vaterländisches Archiv oder Beiträge zur allseitigen Kenntniß d. Königreichs Hannover u. d. Herzogthums Braunschweig*. Lüneburg: Herold & Wahlstab. **14**: 268–282.<templatestyles src="Module:Citation/CS1/styles.css"></templatestyles>
- Brown, Harry J. (2004). *Injun Joe's Ghost: The Indian Mixed-blood in American Writing*[1098]. Columbia, Missouri: University of Missouri Press. ISBN 9780826262448.<templatestyles src="Module:Citation/CS1/styles.css"></templatestyles>
- Browne, Edward G. (2013). *A Year Amongst The Persians*[1099]. London: Routledge. ISBN 9781136183966.<templatestyles src="Module:Citation/CS1/styles.css"></templatestyles>
- Burian, Peter; Shapiro, Alan (2010). *The Complete Sophocles: Volume I: The Theban Plays*[1100]. Oxford: Oxford University Press. ISBN 9780199830930.<templatestyles src="Module:Citation/CS1/styles.css"></templatestyles>
- Chmel, Joseph (1841). *Der österreichische Geschichtsforscher, Volume 2*[1101]. Vienna: Carl Gerold.<templatestyles src="Module:Citation/CS1/styles.css"></templatestyles>

- Dodsley, R (1744). *The Geography of England: Done in the Manner of Gordon's Geographical Grammar*[1102]. London: R. Dodsley.<templatestyles src="Module:Citation/CS1/styles.css"></templatestyles>
- Dowling, Melissa (2001). "Vestal Virgins-Chaste keepers of the flame"[1103]. *BAS Library*. Biblical Archaeological Society.<templatestyles src="Module:Citation/CS1/styles.css"></templatestyles>
- Durkheim, Emile (2010). *Suicide*[1104]. Simon and Schuster. ISBN 9781439118269.<templatestyles src="Module:Citation/CS1/styles.css"></templatestyles>
- Elliade, Mircea; Dundes, Alan (ed.) (1996). *The Walled-up Wife: A Casebook*[1105]. Madison, Wisconsin: Univ of Wisconsin Press. ISBN 9780299150730.<templatestyles src="Module:Citation/CS1/styles.css"></templatestyles>
- Eastwick, Edward B. (1864). *Journal of a Diplomate's Three Years' Residence in Persia, Volume 1*[1106]. London: Smith, Elder and Company.<templatestyles src="Module:Citation/CS1/styles.css"></templatestyles>
- Evagrius (2000). *The Ecclesiastical History of Evagrius Scholasticus*[1107]. Liverpool: Liverpool University Press. ISBN 9780853236054.<templatestyles src="Module:Citation/CS1/styles.css"></templatestyles>
- ExecutedToday.com. "1762: Crown Prince Sado, locked in a rice chest"[1108]. *ExecutedToday.com*.<templatestyles src="Module:Citation/CS1/styles.css"></templatestyles>
- French, Marilyn (2008). *From Eve to Dawn: A History of Women, Volume 1*[1109]. New York, NY: Feminist Press at CUNY. ISBN 9781558616196.<templatestyles src="Module:Citation/CS1/styles.css"></templatestyles>
- Fryer, John (1698). *A New Account of East-India and Persia, in Eight Letters: Being Nine Years Travels Begun 1672 and Finished 1681*[1110]. London: Chiswell.<templatestyles src="Module:Citation/CS1/styles.css"></templatestyles>
- Fumagalli, Maria C. (2001). *The Flight of the Vernacular: Seamus Heaney, Derek Walcott and the Impress of Dante*[1111]. Amsterdam: Rodopi. ISBN 9789042014763.<templatestyles src="Module:Citation/CS1/styles.css"></templatestyles>
- Grimm, Jacob (1854). *Deutsche Mythologie. [With] Anhang*[1112]. Göttingen: Dieterische Buchh.<templatestyles src="Module:Citation/CS1/styles.css"></templatestyles>
- Haapsalu. "The Immured Lady"[1113]. *http://www.haapsalu.ee"*. Haapsalu township. Archived from the original[1114] on 2009-08-19. External

link in | website= (help)<templatestyles src="Module:Citation/CS1/styles.css"></templatestyles>
- Hayes, Kevin (ed.) (2012). *Edgar Allan Poe in Context*[1115]. Cambridge: Cambridge University Press. ISBN 9781107009974.<templatestyles src="Module:Citation/CS1/styles.css"></templatestyles>
- Hübner, Johann (1700). *Kurze Fragen aus der politischen Historia biß auf gegenwärtige Zeit, Volume 3*[1116]. Gleditsch.<templatestyles src="Module:Citation/CS1/styles.css"></templatestyles>
- Hume-Griffith, M.E. (1909). *Behind the veil in Persia and Turkish Arabia; an account of an Englishwoman's eight years' residence amongst the women of the East. With narratives of experiences in both countries*[1117]. Philadelphia: J.P. Lippincott Company.<templatestyles src="Module:Citation/CS1/styles.css"></templatestyles>
- Hupel, August W. (1782). *Topographische Nachrichten von Lief- und Ehstland: Nebst vollständigen Register über alle drey Bände, Volume 3*[1118]. Riga: Hartknoch.<templatestyles src="Module:Citation/CS1/styles.css"></templatestyles>
- Jansone, Una. "Grobiņas pils"[1119]. *www.pasakas.net*. Retrieved November 9, 2013.<templatestyles src="Module:Citation/CS1/styles.css"></templatestyles>
- Krehbiel, Henry (2006). *Book of Operas EasyRead Edition*[1120]. ReadHowYouWant.com. ISBN 9781442938106.<templatestyles src="Module:Citation/CS1/styles.css"></templatestyles>
- Kurkijan, Vahan M. (2008). *A History of Armenia*[1121]. New York, NY: Indo-European Publishing. ISBN 9781604440126.<templatestyles src="Module:Citation/CS1/styles.css"></templatestyles>
- Lea, Henry C (2012). *A History of The Inquisition of The Middle Ages; volume 1*[1122]. Project Gutenberg.<templatestyles src="Module:Citation/CS1/styles.css"></templatestyles>
- Lerner, Gerda (1986). *The Creation of Patriarchy, Volume 1*[1123]. Oxford: Oxford University Press. ISBN 9780195051858.<templatestyles src="Module:Citation/CS1/styles.css"></templatestyles>
- Levy, Reuben (1957). *The Social Structure of Islam: Being the Second Edition of The Sociology of Islam*[1124]. Cambridge: CUP Archive. ISBN 978-0521091824.<templatestyles src="Module:Citation/CS1/styles.css"></templatestyles>
- Mallows, Lucy (2013). *Transylvania*[1125]. Bradt Travel Guides. ISBN 9781841624198.<templatestyles src="Module:Citation/CS1/styles.css"></templatestyles>
- Medioli, Francesca; Schutte, Anna Jacobson (ed); Kuehn, Thomas (ed); Menchi, Silvana Seidel (ed) (2001). *Time, Space, and Women's Lives in Early Modern Europe*[1126]. Kirksville, Missouri: Truman State Univ

Press. ISBN 9780943549903.<templatestyles src="Module:Citation/CS1/styles.css"></templatestyles>
- Miesegaes, Carsten (1829). *Chronik der freyen Hansestadt Bremen, Volume 2*[1127]. Bremen: Miesegaes.<templatestyles src="Module:Citation/CS1/styles.css"></templatestyles>
- Моллов, Тодор (14 August 2002). "Троица братя града градяха"[1128] (in Bulgarian). LiterNet. Retrieved 2007-05-19.<templatestyles src="Module:Citation/CS1/styles.css"></templatestyles>
- Muhammad Ali, Maulana (2011). *Holy Quran, English Translation and Commentary*[1129]. eBookIt.com. ISBN 9781934271148.<templatestyles src="Module:Citation/CS1/styles.css"></templatestyles>
- New Zealand Herald (17 February 1914). "Immured in Coffins"[1130]. *New Zealand Herald*. **LI**.<templatestyles src="Module:Citation/CS1/styles.css"></templatestyles>
- Noor, Raza. "Anarkali's Tomb"[1131]. *Staff Page for Raza Noor*. University of Alberta.<templatestyles src="Module:Citation/CS1/styles.css"></templatestyles>
- O'Reilly, Sean; O'Reilly, James (2000). *Pilgrimage: Adventures of the Spirit*[1132]. Travelers' Tales. ISBN 9781885211569.<templatestyles src="Module:Citation/CS1/styles.css"></templatestyles>
- Osenbrüggen, Eduard (1860). *Das alamannische Strafrecht im deutschen Mittelalter*[1133]. Schaffhausen: Hurter.<templatestyles src="Module:Citation/CS1/styles.css"></templatestyles>
- Planetware. "Visby Tourist Attractions"[1134]. *Planetware*.<templatestyles src="Module:Citation/CS1/styles.css"></templatestyles>
- "Põlva linn"[1135]. *http://www.polva.ee/tourism"*. Polva Tourism. *External link in |website= (help)*<templatestyles src="Module:Citation/CS1/styles.css"></templatestyles>
- Pozemovskis, Ēriks. "Kā cēlies Madlienas nosaukums"[1136]. Retrieved November 9, 2013.<templatestyles src="Module:Citation/CS1/styles.css"></templatestyles>
- Procopius (2007). *History of the Wars: Books 3-4 (Vandalic War)*[1137]. Cosimo, Inc. ISBN 9781602064461.<templatestyles src="Module:Citation/CS1/styles.css"></templatestyles>
- Riepl, Ludwig. "Aus der Geschichte von Weitersfelden"[1138]. *http://www.weitersfelden.ooe.gv.at"*. Weitersfelden Government. *External link in |website= (help)*<templatestyles src="Module:Citation/CS1/styles.css"></templatestyles>
- Rohrbacher, David (2013). *The Historians of Late Antiquity*[1139]. London: Routledge. ISBN 9781134628858.<templatestyles src="Module:Citation/CS1/styles.css"></templatestyles>
- Sarris, Peter (2011). *Empires of Faith: The Fall of Rome to the*

Rise of Islam, 500-700[1140]. Oxford: Oxford University Press. ISBN 9780191620027.<templatestyles src="Module:Citation/CS1/styles.css"></templatestyles>
- Sbornici. "Three Brothers Were Building a Fortress"[1141]. liternet.bg.<templatestyles src="Module:Citation/CS1/styles.css"></templatestyles>
- Sbornici. "Immured Bride"[1142]. liternet.bg.<templatestyles src="Module:Citation/CS1/styles.css"></templatestyles>
- Schreiber, Alois W. (1811). *Heidelberg und seine Umgebungen historisch und topographisch beschrieben*[1143]. Heidelberg: Engelmann.<templatestyles src="Module:Citation/CS1/styles.css"></templatestyles>
- Scott, Walter (1833). *The Complete Works of Sir Walter Scott: With a Biography, and His Last Additions and Illustrations, Volume 1*[1144]. New York: Conner & Cooke.<templatestyles src="Module:Citation/CS1/styles.css"></templatestyles>
- Smith, Anthon (1846). *A school dictionary of Greek and Roman antiquities*[1145]. London: Harper.<templatestyles src="Module:Citation/CS1/styles.css"></templatestyles>
- Tappe, Eric (1984). "A Rumanian Ballad and its English Adaptation"[1146]. *Folklore*. Folklore Enterprises Ltd. **95** (1): 113–119. doi: 10.1080/0015587x.1984.9716302[1147]. ISSN 0015-587X[1148].<templatestyles src="Module:Citation/CS1/styles.css"></templatestyles>
- Tavernier, Jean-Baptiste; Phillips, John (1678). *The six voyages of John Baptista Tavernier*[1149]. London: R.L and M.P.<templatestyles src="Module:Citation/CS1/styles.css"></templatestyles>
- Taylor, Lou (2009) [1983]. *Mourning Dress (Routledge Revivals): A Costume and Social History*[1150]. London: Routledge. ISBN 9780203871324.<templatestyles src="Module:Citation/CS1/styles.css"></templatestyles>
- The St.John Sun (8 September 1906). "Walled in Alive"[1151]. *The St.John Sun*. Ruby Douglas. **30**: 13.<templatestyles src="Module:Citation/CS1/styles.css"></templatestyles>
- Thucydides. "The Pelopennesian War 3.69-3.85:Civil War at Corcyra"[1152]. *The Perseus Digital Library*. Tufts University.<templatestyles src="Module:Citation/CS1/styles.css"></templatestyles>
- de Tott, Francois, baron (1786). *Memoirs of Baron de Tott: Containing the State of the Turkish Empire & the Crimea, During the Late War with Russia. With Numerous Anecdotes, Facts, & Observations, on the Manners & Customs of the Turks & Tartars, Volume 2*[1153]. London: G.G.J. & J. Robinson.<templatestyles src="Module:Citation/CS1/styles.css"></templatestyles>

templatestyles>
- Urban, Sylvanus (1755). *The Gentleman's Magazine, and Historical Chronicle, Volume 25*[1154]. London: E.Cave.<templatestyles src="Module:Citation/CS1/styles.css"></templatestyles>
- Varner, Eric R. (2004). *Monumenta Graeca et Romana: Mutilation and transformation : damnatio memoriae and Roman imperial portraiture*[1155]. Leiden: BRILL. ISBN 9789004135772.<templatestyles src="Module:Citation/CS1/styles.css"></templatestyles>
- Wekebrod, Franz Xaver (1814). *Mährens Kirchengeschichte, Volume 1*[1156]. Brünn (Brno): Traßler.<templatestyles src="Module:Citation/CS1/styles.css"></templatestyles>
- Wilde, Oscar; Murray (ed.), Isobel (1998). *Complete Shorter Fiction*[1157]. Oxford: Oxford University Press. ISBN 9780192833761.<templatestyles src="Module:Citation/CS1/styles.css"></templatestyles>
- Wraxall, Nathaniel W. (1797). *A tour through some of the northern parts of Europe, Particularly Copenhagen, Stockholm, and Petersburgh: In a series of letters*[1158]. Vienna: R. Sammer.<templatestyles src="Module:Citation/CS1/styles.css"></templatestyles>

Impalement

<indicator name="good-star"> ⊕ </indicator>

Impalement, as a method of execution and also torture, is the penetration of a human by an object such as a stake, pole, spear, or hook, often by complete or partial perforation of the torso. It was used particularly in response to "crimes against the state" and regarded across a number of cultures as a very harsh form of capital punishment and recorded in myth and art. Impalement was also used during wartime to suppress rebellion, punish traitors or collaborators, and as a punishment for breaches of military discipline.

Offenses where impalement was occasionally employed include: contempt for the state's responsibility for safe roads and trade routes by committing highway robbery or grave robbery, violating state policies or monopolies, or subverting standards for trade. Offenders have also been impaled for a variety of cultural, sexual and religious reasons.

References to impalement in Babylonia and the Neo-Assyrian Empire are found as early as the 18th century BC.

Impalement

Figure 177: *Vertical impalement*

Methods

Longitudinal impalement

Impaling an individual along the body length has been documented in several cases, and the merchant Jean de Thevenot provides an eyewitness account of this, from 17th century Egypt, in the case of a Jewish man condemned to death for the use of false weights:[1159]

> They lay the Malefactor upon his Belly, with his Hands tied behind his Back, then they slit up his Fundament with a Razor, and throw into it a handful of Paste that they have in readiness, which immediately stops the Blood. After that they thrust up into his Body a very long Stake as big as a Mans Arm, sharp at the point and tapered, which they grease a little before; when they have driven it in with a Mallet, till it come out at his Breast, or at his Head or Shoulders, they lift him up, and plant this Stake very streight in the Ground, upon which they leave him so exposed for a day. One day I saw a Man upon the Pale, who was Sentenced to continue so for three Hours alive and that he might not die too soon, the Stake was not thrust up far enough to come out at any part of his Body, and they also put a stay or rest upon the Pale, to hinder the weight of his body

Figure 178: *Mural on the ceiling of Avudaiyarkoil at Pudukottai District, Tamil Nadu, India showing the impalement scene.*

from making him sink down upon it, or the point of it from piercing him through, which would have presently killed him: In this manner he was left for some Hours, (during which time he spoke) and turning from one side to another, prayed those that passed by to kill him, making a thousand wry Mouths and Faces, because of the pain he suffered when he stirred himself, but after Dinner the Basha sent one to dispatch him; which was easily done, by making the point of the Stake come out at his Breast, and then he was left till next Morning, when he was taken down, because he stunk horridly.

Survival time

The *survival time* on the stake is reported as quite varied, from a few seconds or minutes[1160] to a few hours[1161] or 1 to 3 days.[1162] The Dutch overlords at Batavia, present day Jakarta, seem to have been particularly proficient in prolonging the lifetime of the impaled, one witnessing a man surviving 6 days on the stake,[1163] another hearing from local surgeons that some could survive 8 or more days.[1164] A critical determinant for survival length seems to be precisely *how* the stake was inserted: If it went into the "interior" parts, vital organs could easily be damaged, leading to a swift death. However, by letting the stake follow the spine, the impalement procedure would not damage the vital organs, and the person could survive for several days.[1165]

Transversal impalement

Alternatively, the impalement could be transversely performed, for example in the frontal-to-dorsal direction, that is, from front (through abdomen,[1166] chest[1167] or directly through the heart[1168]) to back or *vice versa*.[1169]

In the Holy Roman Empire (and elsewhere in Central/Eastern Europe), women who killed their newborn especially keeping in mind any implications of witchcraft could be liable to be placed in an open grave, and have a stake hammered into their heart. A detailed description of an execution in this manner comes from 17th century Košice (then in Hungary, now in eastern Slovakia). A woman to be executed for infanticide involved an executioner and two assistants to help him. First, a grave some one-and-a-half ell deep was dug. The woman was placed within it, her hands and feet secured by driving nails through them. The executioner placed a small thorn bush upon her face. He then placed, and held vertically, a wooden stave at her heart to mark its location, while his assistants piled earth on the woman, keeping her head free of earth at the behest of the clerics, however, as to do otherwise would have quickened the death process. Once the earth had been piled upon her, the executioner grabbed with a pair of tongs a rod made of iron, which had been made red hot. He positioned the glowing iron rod beside the wooden stave, and as one of his assistants hammered the rod in, the other assistant emptied a trough of earth upon the woman's head. It is said that a scream was heard, and that the earth actually moved upwards for a moment, before all was over.[1170]

Variations

Gaunching

Joseph Pitton de Tournefort, travelling on botanical research in the Levant 1700–1702, observed both ordinary longitudinal impalement, but also a method called "gaunching", in which the condemned is hoisted up by means of a rope over a bed of sharp metal hooks. He is then released, and depending on how the hooks enter his body, he may survive in impaled condition for a few days.[1171] Forty years earlier than de Tournefort, de Thévenot described much the same process, adding that it was seldom used because it was regarded as too cruel.[1172] Some 80 years prior to de Thevenot, in 1579, Hans Jacob Breuning von Buchenbach[1173] witnessed a variant of the gaunching ritual. A large iron hook was fixed on the horizontal cross-bar of the gallows and the individual was forced upon this hook, piercing him from the abdomen through his back, so that he hung from it, hands, feet and head downward. On top of the cross bar, the executioner situated himself and performed various torture on the impaled man below him.[1174]

Figure 179: *Original in-image text from 1741 edition of Tournefort: "The Gaunche, a sort of punishment in use among the Turks."*

Hooks in the city wall

While gaunching as de Tournefort describes involves the erection of a scaffold, it seems that in the city of Algiers, hooks were embedded in the city walls, and on occasion, people were thrown upon them from the battlements.

Thomas Shaw,[1175] who was chaplain for the Levant Company stationed at Algiers during the 1720s, describes the various forms of executions practiced as follows:[1176]

<templatestyles src="Template:Quote/styles.css"/>

> ... but the Moors and Arabs are either impaled for the same crime, or else they are hung up by the neck, over the battlements of the city walls, or else they are thrown upon the chingan or hooks that are fixed all over the walls below, where sometimes they break from one hook to another, and hang in the most exquisite torments, thirty or forty hours.

According to one source, these hooks in the wall as an execution method were introduced with the construction of the new city gate in 1573. Before that time, gaunching as described by de Tournefort was in use.[1177] As for the actual *frequency* of throwing persons on hooks in Algiers, Capt. Henry Boyde notes[1178] that in his own 20 years of captivity there, he knew of only one

Impalement 369

Figure 180: *"A Negro Hung Alive by the Ribs to a Gallows," by William Blake. Originally published in Stedman's Narrative.*

case where a Christian slave who had murdered his master had met that fate, and "not above" two or three Moors besides.[1179] Taken captive in 1596, the barber-surgeon William Davies relates something of the heights involved when thrown upon hooks (although it is somewhat unclear if this relates specifically to the city of Algiers, or elsewhere in the Barbary States): "Their ganshing is after this manner: he sitteth upon a wall, being five fathoms high, within two fathoms of the top of the wall; right under the place where he sits, is a strong iron hook fastened, being very sharp; then he is thrust off the wall upon this hook, with some part of his body, and there he hangeth, sometimes two or three days, before he dieth." Davies adds that "these deaths are very seldom", but that he had personally witnessed it.[1180]

Hanged by the ribs

A slightly variant way of executing people by means of impalement was to force an iron meat hook beneath a person's ribs and hang him up to die slowly. This technique was in 18th century Ottoman-controlled Bosnia called the *cengela*,[1181] but the practice is also attested, for example, in 1770s Dutch Suriname as a punishment meted out to rebellious slaves.[1182]

Bamboo torture

A recurring horror story on many websites and popular media outlets is that Japanese soldiers during World War II inflicted bamboo torture upon prisoners of war.[1183] The victim was supposedly tied securely in place above a young bamboo shoot. Over several days, the sharp, fast growing shoot would first puncture, then completely penetrate the victim's body, eventually emerging through the other side. The plausibility of this method was tested on an episode of *MythBusters*, and confirmed.

History

Antiquity

Mesopotamia and the ancient Near East

The earliest known use of impalement as a form of execution occurred in civilizations of the ancient Near East. For example, the Code of Hammurabi, promulgated about 1772 BC[1184] by the Babylonian king Hammurabi specifies impaling for a woman who killed her husband for the sake of another man.[1185] In the late Isin/Larsa period, from about the same time, it seems that, in some city states, mere adultery on the wife's part (without murder of her husband mentioned) could be punished by impalement.[1186] From the royal archives of the city of Mari (at the Syrian-Iraqi border by the western bank of Euphrates), most of it also roughly contemporary to Hammurabi, it is known that soldiers taken captive in war were on occasion impaled.[1187] Roughly contemporary with Babylonia under Hammurabi, king Siwe-Palar-huhpak of Elam, a country lying directly east of Babylonia in present-day Iran, made official edicts in which he threatened the allies of his enemies with impalement, among other terrible fates.[1188] For acts of perceived great sacrilege, some individuals, in diverse cultures, have been impaled for their effrontery. For example, roughly 1200 BC, merchants of Ugarit express deep concern to each other that a fellow citizen is to be impaled in the Phoenician town Sidon, due to some "great sin" committed against the patron deity of Sidon.[1189]

Pharaonic Egypt

During Dynasty 19, Merneptah had Libu prisoners of war impaled ("caused to be set upon a stake") to the south of Memphis, following an attempted invasion of Egypt during his Regnal Year 5. The relevant determinative for $ḫt$ ("stake") depicts an individual transfixed through the abdomen.[1190] Other Egyptian kings employing impalements include Sobekhotep II, Akhenaten, Seti, and Ramesses IX.

Impalement 371

Figure 181: *Impalement of Judeans in a Neo-Assyrian relief*

Neo-Assyrian Empire

Evidence by carvings and statues is found as well, for example from Neo-Assyrian empire (c. 934–609 BCE). The image of the impaled Judeans is a detail from the public commemoration of the Assyrian victory in 701 BC after the Siege of Lachish,[1191] under King Sennacherib (r. 705–681 BC), who proceeded similarly against the inhabitants of Ekron during the same campaign.[1192] From Sennacherib's father Sargon II's time (r. 722–705 BCE), a relief from his palace at Khorsabad shows the impalement of 14 enemies during an attack on the city of Pazashi.[1193] A peculiarity[1194] about the "Neo-Assyrian" way of impaling was that the stake was "driven into the body immediately under the ribs",[1195] rather than along the full body length. For the Neo-Assyrians, mass executions seem to have been not only designed to instill terror and to enforce obedience, but also, it can seem, as proofs of their *might* that they took pride in. For example, Neo-Assyrian King Ashurnasirpal II (r. 883–859 BC) was evidently proud enough of his bloody work that he committed it to monument and eternal memory as follows:[1196]<templatestyles src="Template:Quote/styles.css"/>

> *I cut off their hands, I burned them with fire, a pile of the living men and of heads over against the city gate I set up, men I impaled on stakes, the city I destroyed and devastated, I turned it into mounds and ruin heaps, the young men and the maidens in the fire I burned*

Paul Kern,[1197] in his (1999) "Ancient Siege Warfare", provides some statistics on how different Neo-Assyrian kings from the times of Ashurnasirpal II commemorated their punishments of rebels.[1198]

Although impalement of rebels and enemies is particularly well-attested from Neo-Assyrian times, the 14th century BCE Mitanni king Shattiwaza charges his predecessor, the usurper Shuttarna III for having delivered unto the (Middle) Assyrians[1199] several nobles, who had them promptly impaled.[1200] Some scholars have said, though, that it is only with king Ashur-bel-kala (r. 1074–1056) that we have solid evidence that punishments like flaying and impaling came into use.[1201] From the Middle Assyrian period, we have evidence about impalement as a form of punishment relative to other types of perceived crimes as well. The law code discovered and deciphered by Dr. Otto Schroeder[1202] contains in its paragraph 51 the following injunction against abortion:[1203]

<templatestyles src="Template:Quote/styles.css"/>

> *If a woman with her consent brings on a miscarriage, they seize her, and determine her guilt. On a stake they impale her, and do not bury her; and if through the miscarriage she dies, they likewise impale her and do not bury her.*

Achaemenid Persia

The Greek historian Herodotus recounts that, when Darius I, king of Persia, conquered Babylon, he impaled 3000 Babylonians.[1204] In the Behistun Inscription, Darius himself boasts of having impaled his enemies.[1205]

Ambiguous Biblical evidence

Some controversy exist between different Bible translations concerning the actual fate of the 5th century BC Persian minister Haman and his ten sons, whether they were impaled or hanged[1206] For example, the English Standard Version, Esther 5:14 opts for *hanging*,[1207] whereas The New International Reader's version opts for *impalement*.[1208] The Assyriologist Paul Haupt opts for impalement in his 1908 essay "Critical notes on Esther",[1209] while Benjamin Shaw has an extended discussion of the topic on the website ligonier.org from 2012.[1210]

Other passages in the Bible allude to the practice of impalement, such as II Samuel 21:9, concerning the fate of the sons of Saul.

<templatestyles src="Template:Quote/styles.css"/>

> *And they handed them over to the Gibeonites, and they impaled them* ויקיעם *(VeYiQY'aM) on the mountain before YHVH, and all seven of*

them fell together. And they were killed in the first days of the harvest, at the beginning of the barley harvest.[1211]

Although conclusive evidence might be wanting either way for whether Hebrew Law allowed for impalement, or just hanging, the Neo-Assyrian method of impalement as seen in the carvings could, perhaps, equally easily be seen as a form of *hanging* upon a pole, rather than focusing upon the stake's actual *penetration* of the body.

Rome

From John Granger Cook, 2014: "*Stipes* is Seneca's term of the object used for impalement. This narrative and his *Ep*. 14.5 are the only two textually explicit references of impalement in Latin texts:"

<templatestyles src="Template:Quote/styles.css"/>

> *I see crosses there, not just of one kind but made differently by different [fabricators]; some individuals suspended their victims with heads inverted toward the ground; some drove a stake (stipes) through their excretory organs/genitals; others stretched out their [victims'] arms on a patibulum [cross bar]; I see racks, I see lashes ...*
>
> *Video istic cruces ne unius quidem generis sed aliter ab aliis fabricatas; capite quidam conuersos in terram suspendere, alii per obscena stipitem egerunt, alii brachia patibulo explicuerunt; video fidiculas, video uerbera ...*[1212]

Europe

Transversal impalement

Within the Holy Roman Empire, in article 131 of the 1532 Constitutio Criminalis Carolina, the following punishment was stated for women found guilty of infanticide. Generally, they should be drowned, but the law code allowed for, in particularly severe cases, that the old punishment could be implemented. That is, the woman would be buried alive, and then a stake would be driven through her heart.[1213] Similarly, burial alive, combined with transversal impalement is attested as an early execution method for people found guilty of adultery. For example, from the 1348 statutes of Zwickau, it seems that an adulterous couple could be punished in the following way: They were to be placed on top of each other in a grave, with a layer of thorns between them. Then, a single stake was to be hammered through them.[1214] A similar punishment by impalement for a proven male adulterer is mentioned in a 13th-century ordinance for Bohemian mining town Jihlava (then and German Iglau),[1215] whereas in a 1340 Vienna statute, the husband of a woman caught *in flagrante* in adultery could, if he wished to, demand that his wife and her lover be impaled, or alternatively demand a monetary restitution.[1216] Occasionally, women found guilty of witchcraft have been condemned to be impaled. In 1587 Kiel, 101-year-old Sunde Bohlen was, on being condemned as a witch, buried alive, and afterwards had a stake driven through her heart.[1217]

Rapists of virgins and children are also attested to have been buried alive, with a stake driven through them. In one such judicial tradition, the rapist was to be placed in an open grave, and the rape victim was ordered to make the three first strokes on the stake herself; the executioners then finishing the impalement procedure.[1218] Serving as an example of the fate of a child molester, in August 1465 in Zurich, Switzerland, Ulrich Moser was condemned to be impaled, for having sexually violated six girls between the ages four and nine. His clothes were taken off, and he was placed on his back. His arms and legs were stretched out, each secured to a pole. Then a stake was driven through his navel down into the ground. Thereafter, people left him to die.[1219]

Longitudinal impalement

Cases of *longitudinal* impalement can be found typically in the context of war or as a punishment of robbers, the latter being attested as practice in Central and Eastern Europe.

Individuals perceived of collaborating with the enemy have, on occasion, been impaled. For example, in 1632 during the Thirty Years' War, the German officer Fuchs was impaled on suspicion of defecting to the Swedes,[1220] a Swedish corporal was likewise impaled for trying to defect to the Germans.[1221] In 1654, under the Ottoman siege of the Venetian garrison at Crete, several peasants were impaled for supplying provisions to the besieged.[1222] Likewise in 1685, some Christians were impaled by the Hungarians for having provided supplies to the Turks.[1223]

In 1677, a particularly brutal German General Kops leading the forces of Holy Roman Emperor Leopold I designed to keep Hungary dominated by the Germans, rather than to become dominated by the Turks, began impaling and quartering his Hungarian subjects/opponents. An opposing general for the Hungarians, Wesselényi, responded in kind, by flaying alive Imperial troops, and fixing sharp iron hooks in fortress walls, upon which he threw captured Germans to be impaled. Finally, Emperor Leopold I had had enough of the mutual bloodshed, and banished Kops in order to establish a needed cessation of hostilities.[1224] After the Treaty of The Hague (1720), Sicily fell under Habsburg rule, but the locals deeply resented the German overlords. One parish priest (who exhorted his parishioners to kill the Germans) is said to have broken into joy when a German soldier arrived at his village, exclaiming that a whole eight days had gone by since he had last killed a German, and shot the soldier off his horse. The priest was later impaled.[1225] In the short-lived 1784 Horea Revolt against the Austrians and Hungarians, the rebels gained hold of two officers, whom they promptly impaled. On their side, the imperial troops got hold of Horea's 13-year-old son, and impaled him. That seems to have merely inflamed the rebel leader's determination, although the revolt was quashed shortly afterwards.[1226] After the revolt was crushed by early 1785, some 150 rebels are said to have been impaled.[1227]

From 1748 and onwards, German regiments organized manhunts on "robbers" in Hungary/Croatia, impaling those caught.[1228]

Heinous murderers

Occasionally, individual murderers were perceived to have been so heinous that standard punishments like beheading or to be broken on the wheel were regarded as incommensurate with their crimes, and extended rituals of execution that might include impalement were devised. An example is that of Pavel Vašanský (Paul Wasansky in German transcript), who was executed on 1 March 1570 in Ivančice in present-day Czech Republic, on account of 124 confessed murders (he was a roaming highwayman). He underwent a particularly gruelling execution procedure: first, his limbs were cut off and his nipples were ripped off with glowing pincers; he was then flayed, impaled and finally roasted alive. A pamphlet that purports to give Wasansky's verbatim confession, does not record how he was apprehended, nor what means of torture was used to extract his confessions.[1229]

Other such accounts of "heinous murderers" in which impalement is a prominent element include cases in 1504 and 1519,[1230] the murderer nicknamed Puschpeter executed in 1575 for killing thirty people, including six pregnant women whose unborn children he ate in the hope of thereby acquiring invisibility,[1231] the head of the Pappenheimer family in 1600,[1232] and an unnamed murderer executed in Breslau in 1615, who under torture had confessed to 96 acts of murder by arson.[1233]

Dracula

During the 15th century, Vlad III ("Dracula"), Prince of Wallachia, is credited as the first notable figure to prefer this method of execution during the late medieval period,[1234] and became so notorious for its liberal employment that among his several nicknames he was known as Vlad the Impaler.[1235] After being orphaned, betrayed, forced into exile and pursued by his enemies, he retook control of Wallachia in 1456. He dealt harshly with his enemies, especially those who had betrayed his family in the past, or had profited from the misfortunes of Wallachia. Though a variety of methods were employed, he

Figure 182: *Woodblock print of Vlad III "Dracula" attending a mass impalement*

has been most associated with his use of impalement. The liberal use of capital punishment was eventually extended to Saxon settlers, members of a rival clan, and criminals in his domain, whether they were members of the boyar nobility or peasants, and eventually to any among his subjects that displeased him. Following the multiple campaigns against the invading Ottoman Turks, Vlad would never show mercy to his prisoners of war. After The Night Attack of Vlad Țepeș in mid-June 1462 failed to assassinate the Ottoman sultan, the road to Târgoviște, the capital of Vlad's principality of Wallachia, eventually became inundated in a "forest" of 20,000 impaled and decaying corpses, and it is reported that Mehmet II's invading army of Turks turned back to Constantinople in 1462 after encountering thousands of impaled corpses along the Danube River. Woodblock prints from the era portray his victims impaled from either the frontal or the dorsal aspect, but not vertically.

As an example of how Vlad Țepeș soon became iconic for all horrors unimaginable, the following pamphlet from 1521 pours out putative incidents like this one: <templatestyles src="Template:Quote/styles.css"/>

> He let children be roasted; those, their mothers were forced to eat. And (he) cut off the breasts of women; those, their husbands were forced to eat. After that, he had them all impaled
>
> ___.[1236]

Ottoman Empire

Longitudinal impalement is an execution method often attested within the Ottoman Empire, for a variety of offenses.

Siege of Constantinople

The Ottoman Empire used impalement during, and before, the last siege of Constantinople in 1453. For example, during the buildup phase to the great siege the year before, in 1452, the sultan declared that all ships sailing up or down through the Bosphorus had to anchor at his fortress there, for inspection. One Venetian captain, Antonio Rizzo, sought to defy the ban, but his ship was hit by a cannonball. He and his crew were picked up from the waters, the crew members to be beheaded (or sawn asunder according to Niccolò Barbaro[1237]), whereas Rizzo was impaled.[1238] In the early days of the siege in May 1453, contingents of the Ottoman army made mop-up operations at minor fortifications like Therapia and Studium. The surrendered soldiers, some 40 individuals from each place, were impaled.[1239]

Civil crimes

Within the Ottoman Empire, some civil crimes (rather than rebel activity/ treasonous behavior), such as highway robbery, might be punished by impalement. For some periods at least, executions for civil crimes were claimed to have been rather rare in the Ottoman Empire. For example, Aubry de La Motraye, lived in the realm for 14 years from 1699 to 1713 and claimed that he hadn't heard of twenty thieves in Constantinople during that time. As for highway robbers, who sure enough had been impaled, Aubry heard of only 6 such cases during his residence there.[1240] Staying at Aleppo from 1740–54, Alexander Russell notes that in the 20 years gone by, there were no more than "half a dozen" public executions there.[1241] Jean de Thévenot, traveling in the Ottoman Empire and its territories like Egypt in the late 1650s, emphasizes the *regional* variations in impalement frequency. Of Constantinople and Turkey, de Thévenot writes that impalement was "not much practised" and "very rarely put in practice." An exception he highlighted was the situation of Christians in Constantinople. If a Christian spoke or acted out against the "Law of Mahomet", or consorted with a Turkish woman, or broke into a mosque, then he might face impalement unless he converted to Islam. In contrast, de Thévenot says that in Egypt impalement was a "very ordinary punishment" against the Arabs there, whereas Turks in Egypt were strangled in prison instead of being publicly executed like the natives.[1242] Thus, the actual frequency of impalement within the Ottoman Empire varied greatly, not only from time to time, but also from place to place, and between different population groups in the empire.

Highway robbers were still impaled into the 1830s, but one source says the practice was rare by then.[1243] Travelling to Smyrna and Constantinople in 1843, Stephen Massett[1244] was told by a man who witnessed the event that "just a few years ago", a dozen or so robbers were impaled at Adrianople. All of them, however, had been strangled prior to impalement.[1245] Writing around 1850, the archaeologist Austen Henry Layard mentions that the latest case he was acquainted with happened "about ten years ago" in Baghdad, on four rebel Arab sheikhs.[1246]

Impalement of *pirates*, rather than highway robbers, is also occasionally recorded. In October 1767, for example, Hassan Bey, who had preyed on Turkish ships in the Euxine Sea for a number of years, was captured and impaled, even though he had offered 500,000 ducats for his pardon.[1247]

Klephts and rebels in Greece

During the Ottoman rule of Greece, impalement became an important tool of psychological warfare, intended to put terror into the peasant population. By the 18th century, Greek bandits turned guerrilla insurgents (known as *klephts*) became an increasing annoyance to the Ottoman government. Captured klephts were often impaled, as were peasants that harbored or aided them. Victims were publicly impaled and placed at highly visible points, and had the intended effect on many villages who not only refused to help the klephts, but would even turn them in to the authorities.[1248] The Ottomans engaged in active campaigns to capture these insurgents in 1805 and 1806, and were able to enlist Greek villagers, eager to avoid the stake, in the hunt for their outlaw countrymen.[1249]

Impalement was, on occasion, aggravated with being set over a fire, the impaling stake acting as a spit, so that the impaled victim might be roasted alive.[1250] Among other severities, Ali Pasha, an Albanian-born Ottoman noble who ruled Ioannina, had rebels, criminals, and even the descendants of those who had wronged him or his family in the past, impaled and roasted alive. For example, Thomas Smart Hughes, visiting Greece and Albania in 1812–13, says the following about his stay in Ioannina:[1251]

<templatestyles src="Template:Quote/styles.css"/>

> *Here criminals have been roasted alive over a slow fire, impaled, and skinned alive; others have had their extremities chopped off, and some have been left to perish with the skin of the face stripped over their necks. At first I doubted the truth of these assertions, but they were abundantly confirmed to me by persons of undoubted veracity. Some of the most respectable inhabitants of Ioannina assured me that they had sometimes conversed with these wretched victims on the very stake, being prevented*

from yielding to their torturing requests for water by fear of a similar fate themselves. Our own resident, as he was once going into the serai of Litaritza, saw a Greek priest, the leader of a gang of robbers, nailed alive to the outer wall of the palace, in sight of the whole city.

During the Greek War of Independence (1821–1832), Greek revolutionaries or civilians were tortured and executed by impalement. A German witness of the Constantinople massacre (April 1821) narrates the impalement of about 65 Greeks by Turkish mob.[1252] In April 1821, thirty Greeks from the Ionian island of Zante (Zakynthos) had been impalled in Patras, in front of the British consulate. This was recorded in the diary of the French consul Hughes Pouqueville and published by his brother François Pouqueville.[1253] Athanasios Diakos, a klepht and later a rebel military commander, was captured after the Battle of Alamana (1821), near Thermopylae, and after refusing to convert to Islam and join the Ottoman army, he was impaled.[1254] Diakos became a martyr for a Greek independence and was later honored as a national hero.[1255,1256] Non-combatant Greeks (elders, monks, women etc.) were impaled around Athens during the first year of the revolution (1821).[1257]

Rebels elsewhere in the Ottoman Empire

Impaling perceived rebels was an attested practice in other parts of the empire as well, such as the 1809 quelling of a Bosnian revolt,[1258] and during the Serbian Revolution (1804–1835) against the Ottoman Empire, about 200 Serbs were impaled in Belgrade in 1814.[1259] Historian James J. Reid,[1260] in his *Crisis of the Ottoman Empire: Prelude to Collapse 1839–1878*, notes several instances of later use, in particular in times of crises, ordered by military commanders (if not, that is, directly ordered by the supreme authority possessed by the sultan). He notes late instances of impalement during rebellions (rather than cases of robbery) like the Bosnian revolt of 1852, during the Cretan insurrection of 1866–69, and during the insurrections in Bosnia and Herzegovina in 1876–77.[1261] In the Nobel Prize-winning novel *The Bridge on the Drina*, by Ivo Andrić, in the third chapter is described impalement of a Bosnian Serb, who was trying to sabotage the bridge's construction.

Occurrences in genocides

Impalement during the Assyrian and Armenian genocides has also been purported.

Aurora Mardiganian, a survivor of the Armenian genocide of 1915–1923, claimed sixteen young Armenian girls were "crucified" by Ottomans. The film *Auction of Souls* (1919), which was based on her book *Ravished Armenia*, showed the victims nailed to crosses. However, almost 70 years

Figure 183: *Purported image of a Polish prisoner of war being tortured by Bolshevik soldiers, Polish–Soviet War, 1918 image by Frenchman telling his story to The New York Times, 1920*[1262]

later Mardiganian claimed that the scene was inaccurate:[1263] <templatestyles src="Template:Quote/styles.css"/>

> *'The Turks didn't make their crosses like that. The Turks made little pointed crosses. They took the clothes off the girls. They made them bend down, and after raping them, they made them sit on the pointed wood, through the vagina. That's the way they killed - the Turks. Americans have made it a more civilized way. They can't show such terrible things."*

A Russian clergyman visiting ravaged Christian villages in northwestern Persia claimed to find the remains of several impaled people. He wrote: "The bodies were so firmly fixed, in some instances, that the stakes could not be withdrawn; it was necessary to saw them off and bury the victims as they were."[1264]

References and notes

 Wikimedia Commons has media related to ***Impalement***.

Bibliography

Books

<templatestyles src="Template:Refbegin/styles.css" />

- Alison, Archibald (1856). *History of Europe from the fall of Napoleon in MDCCCXV to the accession of Louis Napoleon in MDCCCLII, volume 3*[1265]. Edinburgh and London: W.Blackwood and Sons.<templatestyles src="Module:Citation/CS1/styles.css"></templatestyles>
- Andric, Ivo (1977). *The Bridge on the Drina*[1266]. University Of Chicago Press. ISBN 0-226-02045-2.<templatestyles src="Module:Citation/CS1/styles.css"></templatestyles>
- d'Arvieux, Laurent; Labat, Jean B. (1755). *Des Herrn von Arvieux ... hinterlassene merkwürdige Nachrichten*[1267]. **5–6**. Copenhagen and Leipzig: J.B. Ackermann.<templatestyles src="Module:Citation/CS1/styles.css"></templatestyles>
- Bastian, Adolf (1860). *Der Mensch in der Geschichte*[1268]. **3**. Leipzig: Otto Wigand.<templatestyles src="Module:Citation/CS1/styles.css"></templatestyles>
- Beer, Johann C. (1713). *Der durchleuchtigsten Erzherzogen zu Oesterreich Leben, Regierung und Großthaten*[1269]. Nuremberg: Martin Endter.<templatestyles src="Module:Citation/CS1/styles.css"></templatestyles>
- Blount, Henry (1636). *A Voyage into the Levant*[1270]. London: Andrew Crooke.<templatestyles src="Module:Citation/CS1/styles.css"></templatestyles>
- Bond, Edward A. (editor); Horsey, Jerome; Fletcher, Giles (1856). *Russia at the close of the sixteenth century*[1271]. New York: Hakluyt Society (Burt Franklin reprint).<templatestyles src="Module:Citation/CS1/styles.css"></templatestyles>
- Boyde, Henry (1736). *Several voyages to Barbary*[1272]. London: O. Payne.<templatestyles src="Module:Citation/CS1/styles.css"></templatestyles>
- Braithwaite, John (1729). *The history of the revolutions in the empire of Morocco*[1273]. London: Knapton and Betterworth.<templatestyles src="Module:Citation/CS1/styles.css"></templatestyles>
- Bryce, Trevor (2012). *The World of The Neo-Hittite Kingdoms*[1274]. Oxford: Oxford University Press. ISBN 978-0-19-921872-1.<templatestyles src="Module:Citation/CS1/styles.css"></templatestyles>
- von Buchenbach, Hans J. B. (1612). *Orientalische Reyß deß edlen unnd vesten, Hanß Jacob Breüning, von und zu Buochenbach*[1275]. Strassburg: Johann Carolo.<templatestyles src="Module:Citation/CS1/styles.css"></templatestyles>

- Burgess, Richard (1835). *Greece and the Levant*[1276]. **2**. London: Longman, Rees, Orme, Brown, Green & Longman.
- Callaway, Joseph A. (1995). *Faces of the Old Testament*[1277]. Macon, Georgia: Smyth & Helwys Publishing, Inc. ISBN 978-1-880837-56-6.
- Clarke, Adam (1831). *The Holy Bible.. with a Commentary and Critical Notes*. J. Emory and B. Waugh.
- Crouch, C.L. (2009). *War and Ethics in the Ancient Near East*[1278]. Berlin: Walter de Gruyter. ISBN 978-3-11-022352-1.
- Dampier, William (1729). *A Collection Of Voyages*[1279]. **2**. London: Knapton.
- Daschitsky, Georg (1570). *Erschreckliche Zeytunge von zweyen Mördern, mit namen Merten Farkaß, und Paul Wasansky*[1280]. Prague: Georg Daschitsky.
- Döpler, Jacob (1697). *Theatrum Poenarum*[1281]. **2**. Leipzig: Friedrich Lanckishen Erben.
- Dumas, Alexandre (2008). *Celebrated Crimes Ali Pacha*. Arc Manor.
- Ehrlich, Anna (2005). *Auf den Spuren der Josefine Mutzenbacher*. Amalthea. ISBN 9783850025263.
- Ehrlich, Paul R.; Ehrlich, Anne H. (2004). *One With Nineveh*[1282]. Washington DC: Island Press. ISBN 978-1-55963-879-1.
- Elias, Ney (editor); Ross, Edward D. (translator) (2009 (1898)). *The Tarikh-i-rashidi*[1283]. Srinagar Kashmir: Karakorum Books. Check date values in: |year= (help)
- Engel, Evamaria; Jacob, Frank-Dietrich (2006). *Städtisches Leben im Mittelalter*[1284]. Köln, Weimar: Böhlau Verlag. ISBN 978-3-412-20205-7.
- Eph'al, Israel (2009). *Ke-'ir Netsurah*[1285]. Leiden: Brill. ISBN 978-90-04-17410-8.

- Erish, Andrew A. (2012). *Col. William N. Selig, the Man Who Invented Hollywood*[1286]. University of Texas Press. ISBN 9780292742697.
- Fick, Conrad F. (1867). *Kleine Mittheilungen aus Kiel's Vergangenheit*[1287]. Kiel: Carl Schröder&Comp.
- Florescu, Radu R. (1999). *Essays on Romanian History*. The Center for Romanian Studies. ISBN 973-9432-03-4.
- Gadd, C.J. (1965). *The Cambridge Ancient History: Assyria and Babylon, c. 1370–1300 B.C.*[1288] Cambridge University Press. ISBN 978-1-00-134579-6.
- Goodrich, C.A. (1836). *The universal traveller*[1289]. Hartford: Canfield & Robins.
- Gottfried, Johann L. (1633). *Grundliche und warhaffte Beschreibung de Konigreichs Schweden und dessen incorporirten Provintzen*[1290]. Frankfurt am Main: Friedrich van Hulsius.
- Green, Philip J.; Green, R.L. (1827). *Sketches of the war in Greece*[1291]. London: Thomas Hurst and Co.
- Guer, Jean-Antoine (1747). *Moeurs et usages des Turcs*[1292]. **2**. Paris: Coustelier.
- Gutknecht, Jobst (1521). *Von dem Dracole Wayda, dem großen Tyrannen*[1293]. Nuremberg: Jobst Gutknecht.
- Hamblin, William J. (2006). *Warfare in the Ancient Near East to 1600 BC*[1294]. New York: Routledge. ISBN 978-0-203-96556-6.
- Han, Paul C.B. (1669). *Venediger Löwen-Muth Und Türckischer Ubermuth*[1295]. Hoffmann.
- Hartmann, Johann M.; Büsching, Anton F. (1799). *Erdbeschreibung und Geschichte von Afrika*[1296]. **1, 12**. Hamburg: Bohn.
- Herrenschmidt, Clarisse; Bottéro, Jean (2000). *Ancestor of the West*[1297]. Chicago: University of Chicago Press.

ISBN 9780226067162.
- His, Rudoulf (1967) [1928]. *Geschichte des deutschen Strafrechts bis zur Karolina* (Reprint ed.). Oldenbourg. ASIN B0000BRMK3[1298].
- Holland, Henry (1815). *Travels in the Ionian Isles, Albania, Thessaly, Macedonia*[1299]. **1**. London: Longman, Hurst, Rees, Orme, and Brown.
- Hueber, Fortunatus (1693). *Stammenbuch...*[1300] Munich: Joh. Jäcklin.
- Hughes, Thomas S. (1820). *Travels in Sicily, Greece & Albania*[1301]. **1**. London: J. Mawman.
- von Imhoff, Andrea L. (1736). *Neu-Eroffneter Historien-Saal*[1302]. **4**. Basel: Johann Brandmüller.
- Kern, Paul B. (1999). *Ancient siege warfare*[1303]. Bloomington, Indiana: Indiana University Press. ISBN 978-0-253-33546-3.
- Koch, Johann C. (1824). *Hals- oder peinliche Gerichtsordnung Kaiser Carls V*[1304]. Marburg: Krieger.
- Koller, Markus (2004). *Bosnien an der Schwelle zur Neuzeit*[1305]. Munich: Oldenbourg Verlag. ISBN 978-3-486-57639-9.
- Korabinsky, Johann M. (1786). *Geographisch-historisches und Produkten-Lexikon von Ungarn*[1306]. Pressburg: Weber u. Korabinsky.
- Kuhrt, Amelie (1995). *The Ancient Near East*[1307]. London: Routledge. ISBN 978-0-415-16763-5.
- de La Motraye, Aubry (1723). *A. de La Motraye's Travels*[1308]. **1**. London: Printed for the Author.
- Layard, Austen H (1850). *Nineveh and its remains*[1309]. **1**. London: Murray.
- Layard, Austen H (1871). *Discoveries among the ruins of Nineveh*

- *and Babylon*[1310]. New York: Harper & brothers.
- von Loen, Johann M. (1751). *Des Herrn von Loen Entwurf einer Staats-Kunst*[1311]. Frankfurt, Leipzig: Johann Friedrich Fleischer.
- Massett, Stephen (1863). *Drifting about*[1312]. New York: Carleton.
- Mentzel, O.F.; Allemann, R.F.; Greenlees, Margaret (tr.) (1919). *Life at the Cape in Mid-eighteenth Century: Being the Biography of Rudolf Siegfried Allemann*[1313]. Van Riebeeck Society. ISBN 9780958452250.
- Merry, Bruce (2004). *Encyclopedia of modern Greek literature*[1314]. Westport, CT: Greenwood Publishing Group. ISBN 978-0-313-30813-0.
- Morgan, Joseph (1729). *A Complete History of Algiers*[1315]. **2**. London: Bettenham.
- Moryson, Fynes; Hadfield, Andrew (2001). "Fynes Moryson, *An Itinerary* (1617)"[1316]. *Amazons, Savages, and Machiavels*. Oxford: Oxford University Press: 166–179. ISBN 9780198711865.
- Muir, Edward (1997). *Ritual in early modern Europe*[1317]. Cambridge: Cambridge University Press. ISBN 978-0-521-40967-4.
- Mundy, Peter; Temple, Richard (editor) (1907). *The travels of Peter Mundy in Europe and Asia, 1608–1667*[1318]. **1**. Cambridge: Hakluyt Society.
- Osborne, Thomas (1745). *A Collection of Voyages and Travels*[1319]. London: Thomas Osborne.
- Osenbrüggen, Eduard (1868). *Studien zur deutschen und schweizerischen Rechtsgeschichte*[1320]. Schaffhausen: F. Hurter.
- de Pages, P.M.F (1791). *Travels Round the World*[1321]. London: J. Murray.
- Paroulakis, Peter H. (1984). *The Greeks: Their Struggle for Independence*. Hellenic International Press. ISBN 0-9590894-0-3.

- Pears, Edwin (2004). *The Destruction of the Greek Empire And the Story of the Capture of Constantinople by the Turks*[1322]. Kessinger Publishing. ISBN 978-1-4179-4776-8.
- Philippides, Marios; Hanak, Walter K. (2011). *The Siege and the Fall of Constantinople in 1453*[1323]. Farnham, Surrey: Ashgate Publishing, Ltd. ISBN 978-1-4094-1064-5.
- Raymond, André (2000). *Cairo*[1324]. Boston: Harvard University Press. ISBN 978-0-674-00316-3.
- Reid, James R. (2000). *Crisis of the Ottoman Empire*[1325]. Stuttgart: Steiner. ISBN 3-515-07687-5.
- Richardson, Seth; Laneri, Nicola (2007). "Death and dismemberment in Mesopotamia". *Performing Death*. Chicago: Oriental Institute of the University of Chicago. ISBN 9781885923509.
- Roch, Heinrich (1687). *Neue Lausitz'sche Böhm-und Schlesische Chronica*[1326]. Torgau: Johann Herbordt Klossen.
- Runciman, Steven (1965). *The Fall of Constantinople 1453*[1327]. Cambridge: Cambridge University Press. ISBN 978-0-521-39832-9.
- Russell, Alexander (1794). *The Natural History of Aleppo*[1328]. 1. London: Robinson.
- St. Clair, William (2008 (revised edition, original from 1972)). *That Greece Might Still Be Free*[1329]. Cambridge: Open Book Publishers. ISBN 978-1-906924-00-3. Check date values in: |year= (help)
- Schroeder, Otto (1920). *Keilschrifttexte aus Assur verschiedenen Inhalts*[1330]. Leipzig: Hinrich.
- Schwab, Gustav (1827). *Der Bodensee nebst dem Rheinthale von St Luziensteig bis Rheinegg*[1331]. Stuttgart, Tübingen: Cotta.
- Schweigger, Salomon (1613). *Ein newe Reißbeschreibung auß Teutschland.*[1332] Nuremberg: Katharina Lantzenbergerin.

- Shahbaz, Yonan (1918). *The rage of Islam*[1333]. Philadelphia, Boston: Roger Williams Press.
- Shaw, Thomas (1757). *Travels, or Observations relating to several parts of Barbary and the Levant*[1334]. London: Millar and Sandby.
- Shepherd, William (1814). *Paris, in eighteen hundred and two, and eighteen hundred and fourteen*[1335]. London: Longman, Hurst, Rees, Orme, and Brown.
- Slade, Adolphus (1837). *Turkey, Greece and Malta*[1336]. **2**. London: Saunders and Otley.
- Stavorinus, J.S.; Wilcocke, Samuel H. (tr.) (1798). *Voyages to the East-Indies*[1337]. **1**. London: G.G. and J. Robinson.
- Stedman, John Gabriel (1813). *Narrative, of a Five Years' Expedition, Against the Revolted Negroes of Surinam*[1338]. **1**. London: Johnson and Payne.
- Stevens, J. (1711). *A new collection of voyages and travels*[1339]. **2**. London: Knapton and Bell.
- von Taube, Friedrich W. (1777). *Historische und geographische Beschreibung des Königreiches Slavonien und des Herzogthums Syrmien*[1340]. **2**. Leipzig.
- Tetlow, Elisabeth M. (2004). *Women, Crime and Punishment in Ancient Law and Society*[1341]. **1**. New York: Continuum International Publishing Group. ISBN 978-0-8264-1628-5.
- de Thévenot, Jean; Lovell, Archibald (1687). *The Travels Of Monsieur De Thevenot Into The Levant*[1342]. **1**. London: Faithorne.
- de Tournefort, Joseph Pitton; Ozell, John (tr.) (1741). *A Voyage Into the Levant*[1343]. **1**. London: D. Midwinter.
- von Troilo, Franz Ferdinand (1676). *Orientalische Reise-Beschreibung*[1344]. Dresden: Bergen.

- Ussishkin, David; Amit, Yairah (2006). "Sennacherib's Campaign to Philistia and Judah: Ekron, Lachish, and Jerusalem". *Essays on Ancient Israel in Its Near Eastern Context: A Tribute to Nadav Na'aman*[1345]. Eisenbrauns. ISBN 978-1-57506-128-3.<templatestyles src="Module:Citation/CS1/styles.css"></templatestyles>
- Vaporis, Nomikos M. (2000). *Witnesses for Christ*[1346]. Crestwood, NY: St Vladimir's Seminary Press. ISBN 9780881411966.<templatestyles src="Module:Citation/CS1/styles.css"></templatestyles>
- di Varthema, Ludovica; Jones, John W. (tr.) (1863). *The Travels of Ludovico Di Varthema*[1347]. London: Hakluyt Society.<templatestyles src="Module:Citation/CS1/styles.css"></templatestyles>
- Vehse, Karl E.; Demmler, Franz (tr.) (1856). *Memoirs of the Court, Aristocracy, and Diplomacy of Austria*[1348]. **2**. London: Longman, Brown, Green, and Longmans.<templatestyles src="Module:Citation/CS1/styles.css"></templatestyles>
- Waddington, George (1825). *A Visit to Greece, in 1823 and 1824*[1349]. London: Murray.<templatestyles src="Module:Citation/CS1/styles.css"></templatestyles>
- Wiltenburg, Joy (2012). *Crime and Culture in Early Modern Germany*[1350]. University of Virginia Press. ISBN 9780813933023.<templatestyles src="Module:Citation/CS1/styles.css"></templatestyles>
- Wagner, Johann C. (1687). *Christlich- und Türckischer Staedt- und Geschicht-Spiegel*[1351]. Augsburg: Jacob Kopppmayer.<templatestyles src="Module:Citation/CS1/styles.css"></templatestyles>
- Woltersdorf (1812). *Die illyrischen provinzen und ihre einwohner*[1352]. Vienna: Camesinaschen buchh.<templatestyles src="Module:Citation/CS1/styles.css"></templatestyles>

Newspapers, magazines and periodicals

<templatestyles src="Template:Refbegin/styles.css" />

- Colburn and co (February 1822). "Political Events-Foreign"[1353]. *The New Monthly Magazine*. London: Colburn and co. **6**: 55–56.<templatestyles src="Module:Citation/CS1/styles.css"></templatestyles>
- Constable (September 1821). *Foreign Intelligence.Turkey*[1354]. *The Edinburgh Magazine and Literary Miscellany*. **88**. Edinburgh: Archibald Constable. pp. 274–275.<templatestyles src="Module:Citation/CS1/styles.css"></templatestyles>
- Engelmann (1834). Leopold von Ledebur, ed. *Geschichte und Verfassung des Cröverreiches (part 2)*[1355]. *Allgemeines Archiv für die Geschichtskunde des Preußischen Staates*. **14**. Berlin: E.S. Mittler.

pp. 140–165.<templatestyles src="Module:Citation/CS1/styles.css"></templatestyles>
- Fick, D.H (26 June 1821). *Triumph, das Kreuz siegt!*[1356]. *Erlanger Real-Zeitung*. **52**. Erlangen: G.L.A.Gross. pp. 233–235.<templatestyles src="Module:Citation/CS1/styles.css"></templatestyles>
- Grund (26 February 1822). *Türkisch-Griechische Angelegenheiten*[1357]. *Staats und gelehrte zeitung des hamburgischen unpartheyischen correspondenten*. **33**. Hamburg: Grundschen Erben. p. 4.<templatestyles src="Module:Citation/CS1/styles.css"></templatestyles>
- Haupt, Paul (January 1908). "Critical Notes on Esther". *The American Journal of Semitic Languages and Literatures*. Chicago: The University of Chicago Press. **24, 2**: 97–186. ISSN 1062-0516[1358]. JSTOR 527925[1359].<templatestyles src="Module:Citation/CS1/styles.css"></templatestyles>
- Hughes, Thomas S. (1822). *An Address to the people of England in the CAUSE OF THE GREEKS.*[1360] *The Pamphleteer*. **21**. London: A.J. Valpy. pp. 167–188.<templatestyles src="Module:Citation/CS1/styles.css"></templatestyles>
- Jastrow Jr., Morris (1921). "An Assyrian Law Code". *Journal of the American Oriental Society*. Baltimore: American Oriental Society. **41**: 1–59. doi: 10.2307/593702[1361]. ISSN 0003-0279[1362]. JSTOR 593702[1363].<templatestyles src="Module:Citation/CS1/styles.css"></templatestyles>
- M***r, G. (November 1833). "An Incursion into Turkey"[1364]. *The Metropolitan Magazine*. New Haven: Peck and Newton: 439–442.<templatestyles src="Module:Citation/CS1/styles.css"></templatestyles>
- Mannheimer Zeitung (27 December 1784). "Wien, den 15. Christm"[1365]. *Mannheimer Zeitung*. Mannheim. **156**: 637–638.<templatestyles src="Module:Citation/CS1/styles.css"></templatestyles>
- Mayer, Werner (ed.) (2005). *Orientalia, Vol.74, Fasc. 1*[1366]. Rome, Italy: The Pontifical Biblical Institute.<templatestyles src="Module:Citation/CS1/styles.css"></templatestyles>
- von Meyer von Knonau, Gerold (July 1855). *Unzuchtstrafen im Mittelalter*[1367]. *Anzeiger für Kunde der deutschen Vorzeit, Neue Folge*. **2, 7**. Nuremberg: Germanisches Museum. p. 175.<templatestyles src="Module:Citation/CS1/styles.css"></templatestyles>
- Olmstead, Albert Ten Eyck (February 1918). "Assyrian Government of Dependencies". *The American Political Science Review*. American Political Science Association. **12, 1**: 63–77. ISSN 0003-0554[1368]. JSTOR 1946342[1369].<templatestyles src="Module:Citation/CS1/styles.css"></templatestyles>

- Olmstead, Albert Ten Eyck (1921). "Shalmaneser III and the Establishment of the Assyrian Power". *Journal of the American Oriental Society*. Baltimore: American Oriental Society. **41**: 345–82. doi: 10.2307/593746[1370]. ISSN 0003-0279[1362]. JSTOR 593702[1363].<templatestyles src="Module:Citation/CS1/styles.css"></templatestyles>
- Presbyterian Magazine (January 1847). *Massacre of the Nestorian Christians*[1371]. *The United Presbyterian magazine*. **1**. Edinburgh: Oliphant and sons. pp. 33–34.<templatestyles src="Module:Citation/CS1/styles.css"></templatestyles>
- Purser (1 December 1827). "A Turkish Execution"[1372]. *The Casket*. London: Cowie and Strange and co. **1, 47**: 337–339.<templatestyles src="Module:Citation/CS1/styles.css"></templatestyles>
- Ranft, Michael (1769). *Von den Türkischen und andern Orientalischen Begebenheiten 1767*[1373]. *Fortgesetzte neue genealogisch-historische Nachrichten von den vornehmsten Begebenheiten, welche sich an den europäischen Höfen zugetragen*. **89**. Leipzig: Heinsius. pp. 342–352.<templatestyles src="Module:Citation/CS1/styles.css"></templatestyles>
- Schwetschke, J.C. (1789). *Allgemeine Literatur-Zeitung, Volumes 1-3*[1374]. Jena: C.A. Schwetschke.<templatestyles src="Module:Citation/CS1/styles.css"></templatestyles>
- Siegman, E.J. (ed) (4 September 1821). "Türkei"[1375]. *Allgemeine Zeitung, mit allerhöchste Privilegien*. Cotta'shen Buch. **247**: 987–988.<templatestyles src="Module:Citation/CS1/styles.css"></templatestyles>
- Urban, Sylvanus (pseud) (January 1810). Sylvanus Urban (pseud.), ed. *Abstract of foreign Occurnces.Turkey*[1376]. *Gentleman's Magazine, and Historical Chronicle*. **80.1**. London: Nichols and Son. pp. 74–75.<templatestyles src="Module:Citation/CS1/styles.css"></templatestyles>

Web resources

<templatestyles src="Template:Refbegin/styles.css" />

- Aiolos (2004). "Turkish Culture: The Art of Impalement"[1377]. Archived from the original on 2015-01-13. Retrieved 2015-01-13.<templatestyles src="Module:Citation/CS1/styles.css"></templatestyles>
- Axinte, Adrian. "Dracula: Between myth and reality"[1378]. Stanford University. Retrieved 2013-03-01.<templatestyles src="Module:Citation/CS1/styles.css"></templatestyles>

- Bible, ESV (2012). "Book of Esther 5, English Standard Version"[1379]. BibleGateway.com. Retrieved 2013-03-01.<templatestyles src="Module:Citation/CS1/styles.css"></templatestyles>
- Bible, NIRV (2012). "Book of Esther 5, New International Readers' Version"[1380]. Biblica.com. Retrieved 2013-03-01.<templatestyles src="Module:Citation/CS1/styles.css"></templatestyles>
- Harper, Robert Francis, translator (1904). "The Code of Hammurabi"[1381]. Retrieved 2013-03-01.<templatestyles src="Module:Citation/CS1/styles.css"></templatestyles>
- Shaw, Benjamin (2012). "Was Haman Hanged or Impaled?"[1382]. ligonier.org. Retrieved 2013-03-01.<templatestyles src="Module:Citation/CS1/styles.css"></templatestyles>
- Sowards, Steven W. (2009). "The Serbian Revolution and the Serbian State"[1383]. *Twenty-Five Lectures on Modern Balkan History (The Balkans in the Age of Nationalism)*. Michigan State University Libraries. Retrieved 2013-03-01.<templatestyles src="Module:Citation/CS1/styles.css"></templatestyles>
- WW2, People's War (2005). "Japanese torture techniques"[1384]. BBC. Retrieved 2013-03-01.<templatestyles src="Module:Citation/CS1/styles.css"></templatestyles>

Keelhauling

Keelhauling (Dutch *kielhalen*; "to drag along the keel") is a form of punishment and potential execution once meted out to sailors at sea. The sailor was tied to a line that is looped beneath the vessel, thrown overboard on one side of the ship, and dragged under the ship's keel, either from one side of the ship to the other, or the length of the ship (from bow to stern).

The common supposition is that keelhauling amounted to a sentence of either death by extreme torture, or minimally a physical trauma likely to permanently maim. The hull of the ship was usually covered in barnacles and other marine growth, and thus, keelhauling would typically result in serious lacerations, of which the victim could later suffer infection and scarring. If the victim was dragged slowly, his weight might lower him sufficiently to miss the barnacles, but this method would frequently result in his drowning. There was also a risk of head trauma, especially if the ship was in motion.

There is limited evidence that keelhauling in this form was used by pirate ships, especially in the ancient world. The earliest known mention of keelhauling is from the Greeks in the Rhodian Maritime Code (Lex Rhodia), of c. 700 AD, which outlines punishment for piracy. There is an image on a Greek vase, for example, from the same era.[1385]

Figure 184: *Keelhauling in the Tudor period (1485–1603)*

Figure 185: *The keelhauling of the ship's surgeon of admiral Jan van Nes, Lieve Pietersz. Verschuier, 1660 to 1686*

Several 17th-century English writers such as Monson and Boteler[1386] recorded the use of keel-hauling on English naval sailing ships. However, their references are vague and provide no date. There seems to be no record of it in English ships' logs of the era, and naval historian Nicholas Rodger has stated he knows of no firm evidence that it ever happened.[1387]Wikipedia:No original research In 1880, Mr. Shaw Lefevre (MP), confronted in Parliament with a recent report from Italy of a keelhauling on HMS *Alexandra*, denied that such an incident had taken place.[1388]

It was an official, though rare, punishment in the Dutch navy,[1389] as shown in the painting at right, "The keel-hauling of the ship's surgeon of Admiral Jan van Nes." This shows a large crowd gathered to watch the event, as though it was a "show" punishment intended to frighten other potential offenders, as was flogging round the fleet. A contemporary description suggests it was not intended to be fatal:

> *Keel-Hauling, a punishment inflicted for various offences in the Dutch Navy. It is performed by plunging the delinquent repeatedly under the ship's bottom on one side, and hoisting him up on the other, after having passed under the keel. The blocks, or pullies, by which he is suspended, are fastened to the opposite extremities of the main-yard, and a weight of lead or iron is hung upon his legs to sink him to a competent depth. By this apparatus he is drawn close up to the yard-arm, and thence let fall suddenly into the sea, where, passing under the ship's bottom, he is hoisted up on the opposite side of the vessel. As this extraordinary sentence is executed with a serenity of temper peculiar to the Dutch, the culprit is allowed sufficient intervals to recover the sense of pain, of which indeed he is frequently deprived during the operation. In truth, a temporary insensibility to his sufferings ought by no means to be construed into a disrespect of his judges, when we consider that this punishment is supposed to have peculiar propriety in the depth of winter, whilst the flakes of ice are floating on the stream; and that it is continued till the culprit is almost suffocated for want of air, benumbed with the cold of water, or stunned with the blows his head received by striking the ship's bottom.*[1390]

A footnote in one source suggests that it may have evolved from the medieval punishment of ducking.[1391]

The term still survives today, although usually in the sense of being overpunished or receiving extreme discipline for lightly violating the rules.

References

- *kielholen* entry[1392] in: Johann Hinrich Röding: *Allgemeines Wörterbuch der Marine in allen Europäischen Seesprachen nebst vollständigen Erklärungen*. Nemnich, Hamburg & J.J. Gebauer, Halle, 1793-1798.

External links

- An explanation of the terms "drawn and quartered" and "keelhauling"[1393] on The Straight Dope

Poena cullei

<indicator name="good-star"> ⊕ </indicator>

Poena cullei (from Latin 'penalty of the sack')[1394] under Roman law was a type of death penalty imposed on a subject who had been found guilty of parricide. The punishment consisted of being sewn up in a leather sack, with an assortment of live animal including a dog, snake, monkey, and a chicken or rooster, and then being thrown into water.

The punishment may have varied widely in its frequency and precise form during the Roman period. For example, the earliest fully documented case is from ca. 100 BCE, although scholars think the punishment may have developed about a century earlier. Inclusion of live animals in the sack is only documented from Early Imperial times, and at the beginning, only snakes were mentioned. At the time of Emperor Hadrian (2nd century CE), the most well known form of the punishment was documented, where a cock, a dog, a monkey and a viper were inserted in the sack. At the time of Hadrian *poena cullei* was made into an optional form of punishment for parricides (the alternative was being thrown to the beasts in the arena).

During the 3rd century CE up to the accession of Emperor Constantine, *poena cullei* fell out of use; Constantine revived it, now with only serpents to be added in the sack. Well over 200 years later, Emperor Justinian reinstituted the punishment with the four animals, and *poena cullei* remained the statutory penalty for parricides within Byzantine law for the next 400 years, when it was replaced with being burned alive. *Poena cullei* gained a revival of sorts in late medieval and early modern Germany, with late cases of being drowned in a sack along with live animals being documented from Saxony in the first half of the 18th century.

Execution ritual

The 19th-century historian Theodor Mommsen compiled and described in detail the various elements that at one time or another have been asserted as elements within the ritualistic execution of a parricide during the Roman Era. The following paragraph is based on that description, it is *not* to be regarded as a static ritual that always was observed, but as a descriptive enumeration of elements gleaned from several sources written over a period of several centuries. Mommsen, for example, notes that the monkey hardly can have been an ancient element in the execution ritual.[1395]

The person was first whipped, or beaten, with *virgis sanguinis* ("blood-colored rods", probably[1396]), and his head was clad/covered in a bag made of a wolf's hide. On his feet were placed clogs, or wooden shoes, and he was then put into the *poena cullei*, a sack made of ox-leather. Placed along with him into the sack was also an assortment of live animals, arguably the most famous combination being that of a serpent, a cock, a monkey and a dog. The sack was put on a cart, and the cart driven by black oxen to a running stream or to the sea. Then, the sack with its inhabitants was thrown into the water.

Other variations occur, and some of the Latin phrases have been interpreted differently. For example, in his early work *De Inventione*, Cicero says the criminal's mouth was covered by a leather bag, rather than a wolf's hide. He also says the person was held in prison until the large sack was made ready, whereas at least one modern author believes the sack, *culleus*, involved, would have been one of the large, very common sacks Romans transported wine in, so that such a sack would have been readily available. According to the same author, such a wine sack had a volume of 144.5 US gallons (547 l).[1397]

Another point of contention concerns precisely how, and by what means, the individual was beaten. In his 1920 essay "*The Lex Pompeia and the Poena Cullei*", Max Radin observes that, as expiation, convicts were typically flogged until they bled (some commentators translate the phrase as "beaten with rods till he bleeds"), but that it might very well be the case that the rods themselves were painted red. Radin also points to a third option, namely that the "rods" actually were some type of shrub, since it documented from other sources that whipping with some kinds of shrub was thought to be purifying in nature.[1398]

Publicius Malleolus

The picture gained of the ritual above is compiled from sources ranging in their generally agreed upon dates of composition from the 1st century BCE, to the 6th century CE, that is, over a period of six to seven hundred years. Different elements are mentioned in the various sources, so that the *actual* execution ritual at any one particular time may have been substantially distinct from that ritual performed at other times. For example, the *Rhetoricia ad Herennium*, a treatise by an unknown author from about 90 BCE details the execution of a Publicius Malleolus, found guilty of murdering his own mother, along with citing the relevant law as follows: <templatestyles src="Template:Quote/styles.css"/>

> *Another law says: "He who has been convicted of murdering his parent shall be completely wrapped and bound in a leather sack and thrown in a running stream"... Malleolus was convicted of matricide. Immediately after he had received sentence, his head was wrapped in a bag of wolf's hide, the "wooden shoes" were put upon his feet and he was led away to prison. His defenders bring tablets into the jail, write his will in his presence, witnesses duly attending. The penalty is exacted of him*[1399]

As can be seen from the above, in this early reference, *no* mention is made of live animals as co-inhabitants within the sack, nor is the mention of any initial whipping contained, nor that Malleolus, contained within the sack, was transported to the river in a cart driven by black oxen.

The Roman historian Livy places the execution of Malleolus to just about 10 years earlier than the composition of *Rhetoricia ad Herennium* (i.e., roughly 100 BCE) and claims, furthermore, that Malleolus was the first in Roman history who was convicted to be sewn into a sack and thrown into the water, on account of parricide.[1400]

Possible antecedents

The historians Dionysius of Halicarnassus and Valerius Maximus,[1401] connect the practice of *poena cullei* with an alleged incident under king Tarquinius Superbus (legendary reign being 535–509 BCE). During his reign, the Roman state apparently acquired the so-called Sibylline Oracles, books of prophecy and sacred rituals. The king appointed a couple of priests, the so-called Duumviri sacrorum, to guard the books, but one of them, Marcus Atilius, was bribed, and in consequence, divulged some of the book's secrets (to a certain Sabine foreigner Petronius, according to Valerius). For that breach of religion, Tarquinius had him sewn up in a sack and thrown into the sea. According to Valerius Maximus, it was very long after this event that this punishment was instituted for the crime of parricide as well, whereas Dionysius says that in addition to be suspected of divulging the secret texts, Atilius was, indeed, accused of having killed his own father.[1402]

The Greek historian Plutarch, however, in his "Life of Romulus" claims that the first case in Roman history of a son killing his own father happened more than five centuries after the foundation of Rome (traditional foundation date 753 BCE), when a man called Lucius Hostius murdered his own father after the wars with Hannibal, that is, after the Second Punic War (which ended in 201 BCE). Plutarch, however, does not specify *how* Lucius Hostius was executed, or even if he was executed by the Roman state at all. Additionally, he notes that at the time of Romulus and for the first centuries onwards, "parricide" was regarded as roughly synonymous with what is now called homicide, and that prior to the times of Luicus Hostius, the murder of one's own *father*, (i.e., patricide), was simply morally "unthinkable".[1403]

According to Cloud and other modern scholars of Roman classical antiquity, a fundamental shift in the punishment of murderers may have occurred towards the end of the 3rd century BCE, possibly spurred on by *specific* incidents like that of Lucius Hostius' murder of his father, and, more *generally*, occasioned by the concomitant brutalization of society in the wake of the protracted wars with Hannibal. Previously, murderers would have been handed over to the family of the victim to exact their vengeance, whereas from the 2nd century BCE and onwards, the punishment of murderers became the affair of the Roman *state*, rather than giving the offended family full licence to mete out what *they* deemed appropriate punishment to the murderer of a family member.[1404] Within that particular context, Cloud points out that certain jokes contained in the plays of the early 2nd century dramatist Plautus may be read as referring to the recent introduction of the punishment by the sack for parricides specifically (without the animals being involved).[1405]

Yet another incident prior to the execution of Malleolus is relevant. Some 30 years before the times of Malleolus, in the upheavals and riotings caused by the reform program urged on by Tiberius Gracchus, a man called Caius Villius, an ally of Gracchus, was condemned on some charge, and was shut up in a vessel or jar, to which serpents were added, and he was killed in that manner.[1406]

First century BCE legislation

Two laws documented from the first century BCE are principally relevant to Roman murder legislation in general, and legislation on parricide in particular. These are the *Lex Cornelia De Sicariis*, promulgated in the 80s BCE, and the *Lex Pompeia de Parricidiis* promulgated about 55 BCE. According to a 19th-century commentator, the relation between these two old laws might have been that it was the *Lex Pompeia* that specified the *poena cullei* (i.e., sewing the convict up in a sack and throwing him in the water) as the particular punishment for a *parricide*, because a direct reference to the *Lex Cornelia* shows that the typical punishment for a poisoner or assassin in general (rather than for the specific crime of parricide) was that of banishment, i.e., *Lex Pompeia* makes explicit distinctions for the crime of parricide not present in *Lex Cornelia*.[1407]

Support for a possible distinction in the inferred contents of *Lex Cornelia* and *Lex Pompeia* from the remaining primary source material may be found in comments by the 3rd century CE jurist Aelius Marcianus, as preserved in the 6th century collection of juristical sayings, the *Digest*:

> By the lex Pompeia on parricides it is laid down that if anyone kills his father, his mother, his grandfather, his grandmother, his brother, his sister, first cousin on his father's side, first cousin on his mother's side, paternal or maternal uncle, paternal (or maternal) aunt, first cousin (male or female) by mother's sister, wife, husband, father-in-law, son-in-law, mother-in-law, (daughter-in-law), stepfather, stepson, stepdaughter, patron, or patroness, or with malicious intent brings this about, shall be liable to the same penalty as that of the lex Cornelia on murderers. And a mother who kills her son or daughter suffers the penalty of the same statute, as does a grandfather who kills a grandson; and in addition, a person who buys poison to give to his father, even though he is unable to administer it.[1408]

Modern experts continue to have some disagreements as to the actual meaning of the offence called "parricide", on the *precise* relation between the *Lex Cornelia* and the *Lex Pompeia* generally, and on the practice and form of the *poena cullei* specifically. For example, Kyle (2012) summarizes, in a footnote, one of the contemporary relevant controversies in the following manner:

> Cloud (1971), 42–66, suggests that Pompey's law on parricide, the Lex Pompeia de Parricidiis (Dig. 48.9.1), probably of 55 or 52 BC defined parricide in terms of the murder of parents or close relatives, assimilated it with other forms of homicide, and suspended the sack and replaced it with the interdictio;[1409] but see Bauman's cautions, (1996) 30–2, about whether Pompey changed the nature of the penalty[1410]

Writings of Marcus Tullius Cicero

Marcus Tullius Cicero, the renowned lawyer, orator and politician from the 1st century BCE, provides in his copious writings several references to the punishment of *poena cullei*, but none of the live animals documented within the writings by others from later periods. In his defence speech of 80 BCE for Sextus Roscius (accused of having murdered his own father), he expounds on the *symbolic* importance of the punishment as follows, for example, as Cicero believed it was devised and designed by the previous Roman generations:

> *They therefore stipulated that parricides should be sewn up in a sack while still alive and thrown into a river. What remarkable wisdom they showed, gentlemen! Do they not seem to have cut the parricide off and separated him from the whole realm of nature, depriving him at a stroke of sky, sun, water and earth – and thus ensuring that he who had killed the man who gave him life should himself be denied the elements from which, it is said, all life derives? They did not want his body to be exposed to wild animals, in case the animals should turn more savage after coming into contact with such a monstrosity. Nor did they want to throw him naked into a river, for fear that his body, carried down to the sea, might pollute that very element by which all other defilements are thought to be purified. In short, there is nothing so cheap, or so commonly available that they allowed parricides to share in it. For what is so free as air to the living, earth to the dead, the sea to those tossed by the waves, or the land to those cast to the shores? Yet these men live, while they can, without being able to draw breath from the open air; they die without earth touching their bones; they are tossed by the waves without ever being cleansed; and in the end they are cast ashore without being granted, even on the rocks, a resting-place in death*[1411]

That the practice of sewing murderers of their parents in sacks and throwing them in the water was still an active type of punishment at Cicero's time, at least on the *provincial* level, is made clear within a preserved letter Marcus wrote to his own brother Quintus, who as governor in Asia Minor in the 50s BCE had, in fact, meted out that precise punishment to two locals in Smyrna, as Marcus observes.[1412]

Julio-Claudian Dynasty, the two Senecas and Juvenal

In whatever form or frequency the punishment of the sack was actually practiced in late Republican Rome or early Imperial Rome, the historian Suetonius, in his biography of Octavian, that is Emperor Augustus (r.27 BCE–14 CE), notes the following reluctance on the emperor's part to actively authorize, and effect, that dread penalty: <templatestyles src="Template:Quote/styles.css"/>

> *Furthermore, he administered justice not only with the utmost care but also with compassion as is illustrated in the case of a defendant clearly guilty of parricide; to keep him from being sewn into the sack (only those who confessed suffered this punishment) Augustus reportedly asked, "Surely you did not kill your father?"*[1413]

Quite the opposite mentality seems to have been the case with Emperor Claudius (r.41 – 54 CE) For example, Emperor Nero's mentor, Seneca the Younger sighed about the times of Claudius as follows:

> The Emperor Claudius sewed more men into the *culleus* in five years than history says were sewn up in all previous centuries. We saw more *cullei* than crucifixions[1414]

It is also with a writer like Seneca that serpents are mentioned in context with the punishment;.[1415] Even before Seneca the Younger, his father, Seneca the Elder, who lived in the reigns of Augustus, Tiberius and Caligula, indicates in a comment that snakes would be put in the *culleus*:

> The postponement of my punishment was unpleasant: waiting for it seem worse than suffering it. I kept imagining the culleus, the snake, the deep[1414]

The rather later satirist Juvenal (born, probably, in the 50s CE) also provides evidence for the *monkey*, he even pities the monkey, at one point, as an innocent sufferer.[1416] Not so with how Emperor Nero was reviled. In one play, Juvenal suggests that for Nero, being put in merely one sack is not good enough.[1417] This might, for example, be a reference both to the death of Nero's mother Agrippina Minor, widely believed to have been murdered on Nero's orders, and also to how Nero murdered his fatherland.[1418] Not only Juvenal thought the sack was the standard by which the appropriate punishment for Nero should be measured; the statues of Nero were despoiled and vandalized, and according to the Roman historian Suetonius, one statue was draped in a sack given a placard that said "I have done what I could. But you deserve the sack!".[1419]

Emperor Hadrian and later jurists

It is within the law collection Digest 48.9.9 that perhaps the most famous formulation of the *poena cullei* is retained, from the sayings of the mid-3rd century CE jurist Modestinus. In Olivia Robinsons translation, it reads:

> According to the custom of our ancestors, the punishment instituted for parricide was as follows; A parricide is flogged with blood-colored rods, then sewn up in a sack with a dog, a dunghill cock, a viper, and a monkey; then the sack is thrown into the depths of the sea. This is the procedure if the sea is close at hand; otherwise, he is thrown to the beasts, according to the constitution of the deified Hadrian[1420]

Thus, it is seen in the time of Emperor Hadrian (r.117–138 CE), the punishment for parricide was basically made *optional*, in that the convict might be thrown into the arena instead. Furthermore, a rescript from Hadrian is preserved in the 4th century CE grammarian Dositheus Magister that contains the information that the cart with the sack and its live contents was driven by black oxen.

In the time of the late 3rd century CE jurist Paulus, he said that the *poena cullei* had fallen out of use, and that parricides were either burnt alive or thrown to the beasts instead.[1421]

However, although Paulus regards the punishment of *poena cullei* as obsolete in his day, the church father Eusebius, in his "Martyrs of Palestine" notes a case of a Christian man Ulpianus in Tyre who was "cruelly scourged" and then placed in a raw ox-hide, together with a dog and a venomous serpent and cast in the sea.[1422] The incident is said to have taken place in 304 CE.[1423]

Revival by Constantine the Great

On account of Paulus' comment, several scholars think[1424] the punishment of *poena cuelli* fell out of use in the 3rd century CE, but the punishment was revived, and made broader (by including fathers who killed their children as liable to the punishment) by Emperor Constantine in a rescript from 318 CE. This rescript was retained in the 6th century Codex Justinianus and reads as follows: <templatestyles src="Template:Quote/styles.css"/>

> *Emperor Constantine to Verinus, Vicar of Africa.*
>
> *Whoever, secretly or openly, shall hasten the death of a parent, or son or other near relative, whose murder is accounted as parricide, will suffer the penalty of parricide. He will not be punished by the sword, by fire or by some other ordinary form of execution, but he will be sewn up in a sack and, in this dismal prison, have serpents as his companions. Depending on the nature of the locality, he shall be thrown into the neighboring sea or into the river, so that even while living he may be deprived of the enjoyment of the elements, the air being denied him while living and interment in the earth when dead.*
>
> *Given November 16 (318).*[1425]

Legislation of Justinian

The Corpus Juris Civilis, the name for the massive body of law promulgated by Emperor Justinian from the 530s CE and onwards, consists of two historical collections of laws and their interpretation (the *Digest*, opinions of the pre-eminent lawyers from the past, and the *Codex Justinianus*, a collection of edicts and rescripts by earlier emperors), along with Jusinian's prefatory introduction text for students of Law, Institutes, plus the Novels, Justinian's own, later edicts. That the earlier collections were meant to be sources for the *actual, current practice of law*, rather than just being of historical interest, can be seen, for example, from the inclusion, and modification of Modestinus' famous description of *poena cullei* (Digest 48.9.9), in Justinian's own law text in Institutes 4.18.6. <templatestyles src="Template:Quote/styles.css"/>

> *A novel penalty has been devised for a most odious crime by another statute, called the lex Pompeia on parricide, which provides that any person who by secret machination or open act shall hasten the death of his parent, or child, or other relation whose murder amounts in law to parricide, or who shall be an instigator or accomplice of such crime, although a stranger, shall suffer the penalty of parricide. This is not execution by the sword or by fire, or any ordinary form of punishment, but the criminal is sewn up in a sack with a dog, a cock, a viper, and an ape, and in this dismal prison is thrown into the sea or a river, according to the nature of the locality, in order that even before death he may begin to be deprived of the enjoyment of the elements, the air being denied him while alive, and interment in the earth when dead. Those who kill persons related to them by kinship or affinity, but whose murder is not parricide, will suffer the penalties of the lex Cornelia on assassination.*[1426]

It is seen that Justinian regards this as a *novel* enactment of an old law, and that he includes not only the symbolic interpretations of the punishment as found in for example Cicero, but also Constantine's extension of the penalty to fathers who murder their own children. In Justinian, relative to Constantine, we see the inclusion in the sack of the dog, cock and monkey, not just the serpent(s) in Constantine. Some modern historians, such as O.F. Robinson, suspects that the precise wording of the text in the *Institutes* 4.18.6 suggests that the claimed reference in *Digest* 48.9.9 from Modestinus is actually a sixth CE *interpolation* into the 3rd century CE law text, rather than being a faithful citation of Modestinus.[1427]

Abolition

The *poena cullei* was eliminated as the punishment for parricides within the Byzantine Empire in the law code Basilika, promulgated more than 300 years after the times of Justinian, around 892 CE. As Margaret Trenchard-Smith notes, however, in her essay "Insanity, Exculpation and Disempowerment", that "this does not necessarily denote a softening of attitude. According to the *Synopsis Basilicorum* (an abridged edition of *Basilika*), parricides are to be cast into the flames."[1428]

German revival in the Middle Ages and beyond

The penalty of the sack, with the animals included, experienced a revival in parts of late medieval, and early modern Germany (particularly in Saxony). The 14th century commentator on the 13th century compilation of laws/customs Sachsenspiegel, Johann von Buch,[1429] for example, states that the *poena cullei* is the appropriate punishment for parricides. Some differences evolved within the German ritual, relative to the original Roman ritual, though. Apparently, the rooster was not included, and the serpent might be replaced with a painting of a serpent on a piece of paper and the monkey could be replaced with a cat. Furthermore, the cat and the dog were sometimes physically separated from the person, and the sack itself (with its two partitions) was made of linen, rather than of leather.[1430]

The difference between using *linen*, rather than *leather* is that linen soaks easily, and the inhabitants will drown, whereas a *watertight* leather sack will effect death by suffocation due to lack of air (or death by a drawn-out drowning process, relative to a comparatively quick one), rather than death by drowning. In a 1548 case from Dresden, the intention was to suffocate the culprit (who had killed his mother), rather than drown him. With him into the leather sack was a cat and a dog, and the sack was made airtight by coating it with pitch. However, the sack chosen was too small, and had been overstretched, so as the sack hit the waters after being thrown from the bridge, it ripped open. The cat and the dog managed to swim away and survive, while the criminal (presumably bound) "got his punishment rather earlier than had been the intention", that is, death by drowning instead.[1431]

The last case where this punishment is, by some, alleged to have been meted out in 1734, somewhere in Saxony.[1432] Another tradition, however, is evidenced from the Saxonian city Zittau, where the last case is alleged to have happened in 1749. In at least one case in Zittau 1712, a non-venomous colubrid snake was used. The Zittau ritual was to put the victims in a black sack, and keep it under water for no less than six hours. In the mean time, the choir boys in town had the duty to sing the Psalm composed by Martin Luther, "Aus tiefer Not schrei ich zu dir" (From deep affliction I cry out to you).[1433] The punishment of the sack was expressly abolished in Saxony in a rescript dated 17 June 1761[1434]

From Chinese accounts

The *Wenxian Tongkao*, written by Chinese historian Ma Duanlin (1245-1322), and the *History of Song* describe how the Byzantine emperor Michael VII Parapinakēs Caesar (*Mie li sha ling kai sa* 滅力沙靈改撒) of *Fu lin* (拂菻, i.e. Byzantium) sent an embassy to China's Song dynasty, arriving in November 1081, during the reign of Emperor Shenzong of Song (r. 1067-1085). The *History of Song* described the tributary gifts given by the Byzantine embassy as well as the products made in Byzantium. It also described forms of punishment in Byzantine law, such as caning, as well as the capital punishment of being stuffed into a "feather bag" and thrown into the sea. This description seems to correspond with the Romano-Byzantine punishment of *poena cullei*.

Modern fiction

In his (1991) novel *Roman Blood*, Steven Saylor renders a fictionalized, yet informed, rendition of how the Roman punishment *poena cullei* might occur. The reference to the punishment is in connection with Cicero's (historically correct, and successful) endeavours to acquit Sextus Roscius of the charge of having murdered his own father.

China Miéville's short story "Säcken", collected in *Three Moments of an Explosion: Stories*, is a modern horror story which incorporates the punishment.

Bibliography

Books and journals

<templatestyles src="Template:Refbegin/styles.css" />

- Auler, Jost (2012). *Richtstättenarchäologie 3*[1435]. Dormagen: *archeotopos* Buchverlag. ISBN 978-3-938473-17-7.<templatestyles src="Module:Citation/CS1/styles.css"></templatestyles>
- Bradley, Mark (2012). *Rome, Pollution and Propriety: Dirt, Disease and Hygiene in the Eternal City from Antiquity to Modernity*[1436]. Cambridge: Cambridge University Press. ISBN 978-1-107-01443-5.<templatestyles src="Module:Citation/CS1/styles.css"></templatestyles>

- Böhmer, Dr. Ge. Wilh. (1820). "Ueber die Wahl der Todesstrafen, Zweiter Abschnitt"[1437]. *Archiv des Criminalrechts*. Halle: Hemmerde und Schwetschke. 11.<templatestyles src="Module:Citation/CS1/styles.css"></templatestyles>
- Caplan, Harry (tr.) (1954). *Ad C. Herennium de ratione dicendi (Rhetorica ad Herennium)*[1438]. London, Cambridge;Mass.: Heinemann, Harvard University Press.<templatestyles src="Module:Citation/CS1/styles.css"></templatestyles>
- Cicero, Marcus Tullius; Watson, J.S. (tr.) (1871). *Cicero on Oratory and Orators: With His Letters to Quintus and Brutus*[1439]. London: Bell&Daldy.<templatestyles src="Module:Citation/CS1/styles.css"></templatestyles>
- Cicero, Marcus Tullius; Yonge, C.D. (tr.) (1852). *The orations of Marcus Tullius Cicero*[1440]. London: Henry G. Bohn.<templatestyles src="Module:Citation/CS1/styles.css"></templatestyles>
- Dionysius of Halicarnassus; Spelman, Edward (tr.) (1758). *The Roman antiquities of Dionysius Halicarnassensis, Volume 2*[1441]. London.<templatestyles src="Module:Citation/CS1/styles.css"></templatestyles>
- Elliott, Neil; Reasoner, Mark (2011). *Documents and Images for the Study of Paul*[1442]. Minneapolis, MN: Fortress Press. ISBN 978-1-4514-1514-8.<templatestyles src="Module:Citation/CS1/styles.css"></templatestyles>
- Eusebius of Caesarea; Cureton, William (1861). *History of the Martyrs in Palestine: Discovered in a Very Antient Syriac Manuscript*[1443]. London, Paris: Williams and Norgate, C.Borrani.<templatestyles src="Module:Citation/CS1/styles.css"></templatestyles>
- Francese, Christopher (2007). *Ancient Rome in So Many Words*[1444]. New York, NY: Hippocrene Books. ISBN 978-0-7818-1153-8.<templatestyles src="Module:Citation/CS1/styles.css"></templatestyles>
- Gaughan, Judy E. (2010). *Murder Was Not a Crime: Homicide and Power in the Roman Republic*[1445]. Austin, TX: University of Texas Press. ISBN 978-0-292-77992-1.<templatestyles src="Module:Citation/CS1/styles.css"></templatestyles>
- Grimm, Jacob (1828). *Deutsche Rechtsalterthuemer*[1446]. Göttingen: Dieterichsche Buchhandlung.<templatestyles src="Module:Citation/CS1/styles.css"></templatestyles>
- Juvenal, Decimus Junius; Gifford, William (tr.); Nuttall, P. Austin (1836). *The Satires of Decimus Junius Juvenalis*[1447]. London: Nuttall, self-published.<templatestyles src="Module:Citation/CS1/styles.css"></templatestyles>
- Kahn, Arthur D. (2005). *Byron's Single Difference with Homer and*

- Virgil: And Other Essays on the Poet's Interplay with the Literatures of Greece and Rome[1448]. Bloomington, Indiana: AuthorHouse. ISBN 978-1-4634-8046-2.
- Kyle, Donald C. (2012). *Spectacles of Death in Ancient Rome*[1449]. Oxford: Routledge. ISBN 978-1-134-86271-9.
- Lintott, Andrew W. (1999). *Violence in Republican Rome*[1450]. Oxford: Oxford University Press. ISBN 978-0-19-815282-8.
- Livy; Baker, George (tr.) (1797). *The History of Rome, volume 6*[1451]. London: A. Strahan and T. Cadell jun. and W. Davies.
- Long, George (1855). *M. Tullii Ciceronis Orationes, Volume 2*[1452]. London: Whittaker and Company, G. Bell.
- Mommsen, Theodor (1899). *Römisches Strafrecht*[1453]. Leipzig: Duncker&Humblot. Retrieved 13 March 2014.
- Pescheck, Christian A. (1837). *Handbuch der Geschichte von Zittau, Volume 2*[1454]. Zittau: in Commission der J. D. Schöpfischen Buch- und Kunsthandlung.
- Plutarch; Dryden, John (tr.) (2008). *Plutarch's Lives of Illustrious Men, Volume 1*[1455]. Wildside Press LLC. ISBN 978-1-4344-7533-6.
- Plutarch; Stadter, Philip A.(tr.) (1999). *Roman Lives: A Selection of Eight Lives*[1456]. Oxford: Oxford University Press. ISBN 978-0-19-160508-6.
- Radin, Max (1920). "The Lex Pompeia and the Poena Cullei". *The Journal of Roman Studies*. Society for the Promotion of Roman Studies. **10**: 119–130. doi: 10.2307/295798[1457]. ISSN 0075-4358[1458]. JSTOR 295798[1459].
- Robinson, O.F. (2007). *Penal Practice and Penal Policy in Ancient Rome*[1460]. Oxford: Taylor & Francis. ISBN 978-0-203-96554-2.
- Saylor, Steven (2011). *Roman Blood*[1461]. Constable & Robinson Ltd. ISBN 978-1-84901-985-9.

styles.css"></templatestyles>
- Scarborough, Connie; Classen, Albrecht (ed.); Scarborough, Connie (ed.) (2012). "Women as Victims and Criminals in the Siete Partidas". *Crime and Punishment in the Middle Ages and Early Modern Age: Mental-Historical Investigations of Basic Human Problems and Social Responses*[1462]. Berlin,Boston: Walter de Gruyter. pp. 225–246. ISBN 9783110294583.<templatestyles src="Module:Citation/CS1/styles.css"></templatestyles>
- Suetonius; Hurley, Donna W.(tr.) (2011). *The Caesars*[1463]. Indianapolis, IN: Hackett Publishing,. ISBN 978-1-60384-613-4.<templatestyles src="Module:Citation/CS1/styles.css"></templatestyles>
- Trenchard-Smith, Margaret; Turner, Wendy (ed.) (2010). *Madness in Medieval Law and Custom*[1464]. Leiden: BRILL. ISBN 978-90-04-18749-8.<templatestyles src="Module:Citation/CS1/styles.css"></templatestyles>
- Valerius Maximus; Walker, Henry J. (tr.) (2004). *Memorable Deeds and Sayings: One Thousand Tales from Ancient Rome*[1465]. Indianapolis,IN: Hackett Publishing. ISBN 978-0-87220-674-8.<templatestyles src="Module:Citation/CS1/styles.css"></templatestyles>
- Varner, Eric R. (2004). *Monumenta Graeca et Romana: Mutilation and transformation : damnatio memoriae and Roman imperial portraiture*[1466]. Leiden: BRILL. ISBN 978-90-04-13577-2.<templatestyles src="Module:Citation/CS1/styles.css"></templatestyles>
- Watson, Alan (ed.); Robinson, Olivia (tr.) (1998). *The Digest of Justinian, Volume 4, Book 48*. Philadelphia: University of Pennsylvania Press. ISBN 978-0-8122-2036-0.<templatestyles src="Module:Citation/CS1/styles.css"></templatestyles>
- Weck, Antonius (1680). *"Der" Chur-Fürstlichen Sächsischen weitberuffenen Residentz- und Haupt-Vestung Dresden Beschreib- und Vorstellung*[1467]. Dresden: Hoffmann.<templatestyles src="Module:Citation/CS1/styles.css"></templatestyles>
- Weiske, Julius (1833). *Handbuch der Strafgesetze des Königreiches Sachsen von 1572 bis auf die neueste Zeit*[1468]. Leipzig: Gustav Schaarschmidt.<templatestyles src="Module:Citation/CS1/styles.css"></templatestyles>

Web resources

- Blume, Fred H. "Annotated Justinian Code"[1469]. *George W. Hopper Law Library*. Kearley, Timothy at College of Law George William Hopper Law Library. Retrieved 11 December 2013.<templatestyles src="Module:Citation/CS1/styles.css"></templatestyles>
- Mertens, A. "WHO WAS A CHRISTIAN IN THE HOLY LAND?"[1470]. *www.christusrex.org*. Christus Rex, Inc. Retrieved 11 December

2013.<templatestyles src="Module:Citation/CS1/styles.css"></templatestyles>
- Moyle, J.B. "JUSTINIAN, INSTITUTES"[1471] (PDF). *amesfoundation.law.harvard.edu*. The Ames Foundation, Harvard University. Retrieved 11 December 2013.<templatestyles src="Module:Citation/CS1/styles.css"></templatestyles>
- Scott, S.P. "THE ENACTMENTS OF JUSTINIAN. THE DIGEST OR PANDECTS"[1472]. *The Roman Law Library*. Y. Lassard&A.Koptev. Retrieved 11 December 2013.<templatestyles src="Module:Citation/CS1/styles.css"></templatestyles>

Further reading

- Bauman, Richard A. (2012). *Crime and Punishment in Ancient Rome*. Oxford: Taylor & Francis Group. pp. 30–32. ISBN 978-0-415-69254-0.<templatestyles src="Module:Citation/CS1/styles.css"></templatestyles>
- Beness, Lea (1998). "When the Punishment Rivals the Crime: The Sack Treatment and the Execution of C. Villius". *Ancient History: Resources for Teachers*. **28.2**: 95–112.<templatestyles src="Module:Citation/CS1/styles.css"></templatestyles>
- Beness, Lea (2000). "The Punishment of the Gracchani and the Execution of C. Villius in 133/132". *Antichthon*. **34**: 1–17.<templatestyles src="Module:Citation/CS1/styles.css"></templatestyles>
- Cantarella, Eva (1991). *I supplizi capitali in Grecia e a Roma*. Milan: Rizzoli. ISBN 978-88-17-33173-9.<templatestyles src="Module:Citation/CS1/styles.css"></templatestyles>
- Cloud J.D. (1971). "Parricidium from the lex Numae to the Lex Pompeia de parricidiis". *Zeitschrift der Savigny-Stiftung für Rechtsgeschichte, romanistische Abteilung*. Weimar: Böhlau. **88**: 1–66. doi:10.7767/zrgra.1971.88.1.1[1473]. ISSN 0323-4096[1474].<templatestyles src="Module:Citation/CS1/styles.css"></templatestyles>
- Düll, R. (1935). "Zur Bedeutung der poena cullei im Römischen Strafrecht". *Atti del Congresso Int. di diritto romano (R 1933)*. Pavia: 363–408.<templatestyles src="Module:Citation/CS1/styles.css"></templatestyles>
- Egmond, Florike (1995). "The Cock, the Dog, the Serpent, and the Monkey. Reception and Transmission of a Roman Punishment, or Historiography as History". *International Journal of the Classical Tradition*. Springer. **2, 2**: 159–192. ISSN 1874-6292[1475]. JSTOR 30222199[1476].<templatestyles src="Module:Citation/CS1/styles.css"></templatestyles>

- Gorgoni, Christina Bukowska (1979). "Die Strafe des Säckens-Wahrheit und Legende". *Forschungen zur Rechtsarchäologie und rechtlichen Volkskunde*. Zürich: Schulthess Polygraphischer Verlag. **2**: 149–162. OCLC 492555150[1477].<templatestyles src="Module:Citation/CS1/styles.css"></templatestyles>
- Radin, Max (1920). "The Lex Pompeia and the Poena Cullei". *The Journal of Roman Studies*. Society for the Promotion of Roman Studies. **10**: 119–130. doi: 10.2307/295798[1457]. ISSN 0075-4358[1458]. JSTOR 295798[1459].<templatestyles src="Module:Citation/CS1/styles.css"></templatestyles>
- Watson, Alan (editor) (1998). *The Digest of Justinian, Volumes 1–4*. Philadelphia: University of Pennsylvania Press. ISBN 978-0-8122-2036-0.<templatestyles src="Module:Citation/CS1/styles.css"></templatestyles>

Poisoning

Poisoning	
Synonym	Envenomation

The symbol of a toxic substance

Classification and external resources	
ICD-10	Xxx.x[1478]
ICD-9-CM	xxx[1479]

Poisoning is a condition or a process in which an organism becomes chemically harmed severely (**poisoned**) by a toxic substance or venom of an animal.

Acute poisoning is exposure to a poison on one occasion or during a short period of time. Symptoms develop in close relation to the degree of exposure. Absorption of a poison is necessary for systemic poisoning (that is, in the blood throughout the body). In contrast, substances that destroy tissue but do not absorb, such as lye, are classified as corrosives rather than poisons. Furthermore, many common household medications are not labeled with skull and crossbones, although they can cause severe illness or even death. In the medical sense, toxicity and poisoning can be caused by less dangerous substances than those legally classified as a poison. Toxicology is the study and practice of the symptoms, mechanisms, diagnosis, and treatment of poisoning.

Chronic poisoning is long-term repeated or continuous exposure to a poison where symptoms do not occur immediately or after each exposure. The patient gradually becomes ill, or becomes ill after a long latent period. Chronic poisoning most commonly occurs following exposure to poisons that bioaccumulate, or are biomagnified, such as mercury, gadolinium, and lead.

Contact or absorption of poisons can cause rapid death or impairment. Agents that act on the nervous system can paralyze in seconds or less, and include both biologically derived neurotoxins and so-called nerve gases, which may be synthesized for warfare or industry.

Inhaled or ingested cyanide, used as a method of execution in gas chambers, almost instantly starves the body of energy by inhibiting the enzymes in mitochondria that make ATP. Intravenous injection of an unnaturally high concentration of potassium chloride, such as in the execution of prisoners in parts of the United States, quickly stops the heart by eliminating the cell potential necessary for muscle contraction.

Most biocides, including pesticides, are created to act as poisons to target organisms, although acute or less observable chronic poisoning can also occur in non-target organisms (secondary poisoning), including the humans who apply the biocides and other beneficial organisms. For example, the herbicide 2,4-D imitates the action of a plant hormone, which makes its lethal toxicity specific to plants. Indeed, 2,4-D is not a poison, but classified as "harmful" (EU).

Many substances regarded as poisons are toxic only indirectly, by toxication. An example is "wood alcohol" or methanol, which is not poisonous itself, but is chemically converted to toxic formaldehyde and formic acid in the liver. Many drug molecules are made toxic in the liver, and the genetic variability of certain liver enzymes makes the toxicity of many compounds differ between individuals.

Exposure to radioactive substances can produce radiation poisoning, an unrelated phenomenon.

Pendulum

<indicator name="pp-default"> </indicator>

A **pendulum** is a weight suspended from a pivot so that it can swing freely. When a pendulum is displaced sideways from its resting, equilibrium position, it is subject to a restoring force due to gravity that will accelerate it back toward the equilibrium position. When released, the restoring force acting on the pendulum's mass causes it to oscillate about the equilibrium position, swinging back and forth. The time for one complete cycle, a left swing and a right swing, is called the period. The period depends on the length of the pendulum and also to a slight degree on the amplitude, the width of the pendulum's swing.

From the first scientific investigations of the pendulum around 1602 by Galileo Galilei, the regular motion of pendulums was used for timekeeping, and was the world's most accurate timekeeping technology until the 1930s. The pendulum clock invented by Christian Huygens in 1658 became the world's standard timekeeper, used in homes and offices for 270 years, and achieved accuracy

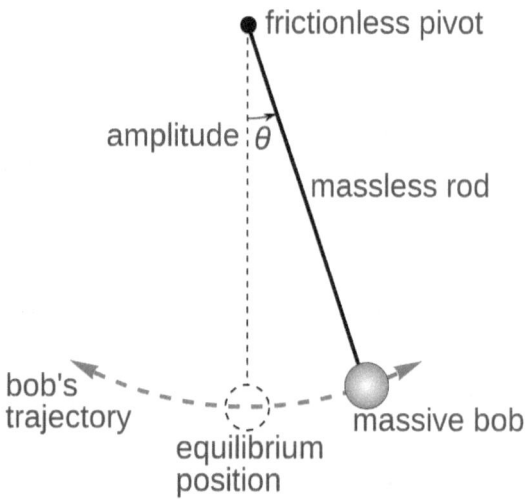

Figure 186: *"Simple gravity pendulum" model assumes no friction or air resistance.*

of about one second per year before it was superseded as a time standard by the quartz clock in the 1930s. Pendulums are also used in scientific instruments such as accelerometers and seismometers. Historically they were used as gravimeters to measure the acceleration of gravity in geophysical surveys, and even as a standard of length. The word "pendulum" is new Latin, from the Latin *pendulus*, meaning 'hanging'.

Simple gravity pendulum

The *simple gravity pendulum*[1480] is an idealized mathematical model of a pendulum. This is a weight (or bob) on the end of a massless cord suspended from a pivot, without friction. When given an initial push, it will swing back and forth at a constant amplitude. Real pendulums are subject to friction and air drag, so the amplitude of their swings declines.

<templatestyles src="Multiple_image/styles.css" />

Pendulum

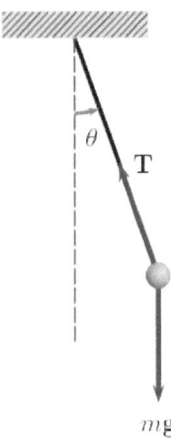

Animation of a pendulum showing forces acting on the bob: the tension T in the rod and the gravitational force mg.

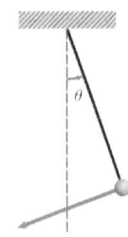

Animation of a pendulum showing the velocity and acceleration vectors.

Period of oscillation

<templatestyles src="Multiple_image/styles.css" />

The period of a pendulum gets longer as the amplitude θ_0 (width of swing) increases.

The period of swing of a simple gravity pendulum depends on its length, the local strength of gravity, and to a small extent on the maximum angle that the pendulum swings away from vertical, θ_0, called the amplitude.[1481] It is independent of the mass of the bob. If the amplitude is limited to small swings,[1482] the period T of a simple pendulum, the time taken for a complete cycle, is:

$$T \approx 2\pi \sqrt{\frac{L}{g}} \qquad \theta_0 \ll 1 \text{ radian} \qquad (1)$$

where L is the length of the pendulum and g is the local acceleration of gravity.

For small swings the period of swing is approximately the same for different size swings: that is, *the period is independent of amplitude*. This property, called isochronism, is the reason pendulums are so useful for timekeeping. Successive swings of the pendulum, even if changing in amplitude, take the same amount of time.

For larger amplitudes, the period increases gradually with amplitude so it is longer than given by equation (1). For example, at an amplitude of $\theta_0 = 23°$ it is 1% larger than given by (1). The period increases asymptotically (to infinity) as θ_0 approaches 180°, because the value $\theta_0 = 180°$ is an unstable equilibrium point for the pendulum. The true period of an ideal simple gravity pendulum can be written in several different forms (see Pendulum (mathematics)), one example being the infinite series:[1483]

$$T = 2\pi \sqrt{\frac{L}{g}} \left(1 + \frac{1}{16}\theta_0^2 + \frac{11}{3072}\theta_0^4 + \cdots \right)$$

where θ_0 is in radians.

The difference between this true period and the period for small swings (1) above is called the *circular error*. In the case of a typical grandfather clock whose pendulum has a swing of 6° and thus an amplitude of 3° (0.05 radians), the difference between the true period and the small angle approximation (1) amounts to about 15 seconds per day.

For small swings the pendulum approximates a harmonic oscillator, and its motion as a function of time, t, is approximately simple harmonic motion:

$$\theta(t) = \theta_0 \cos\left(\frac{2\pi}{T} t + \varphi\right)$$

where φ is a constant value, dependent on initial conditions.

For real pendulums, the period varies slightly with factors such as the buoyancy and viscous resistance of the air, the mass of the string or rod, the size and shape of the bob and how it is attached to the string, and flexibility and stretching of the string. In precision applications, corrections for these factors may need to be applied to eq. (1) to give the period accurately.

Compound pendulum

Any swinging rigid body free to rotate about a fixed horizontal axis is called a **compound pendulum** or **physical pendulum**. The appropriate equivalent length L for calculating the period of any such pendulum is the distance from the pivot to the *center of oscillation*.[1484] This point is located under the center of mass at a distance from the pivot traditionally called the radius of oscillation, which depends on the mass distribution of the pendulum. If most of the mass is concentrated in a relatively small bob compared to the pendulum length, the center of oscillation is close to the center of mass.

The radius of oscillation or equivalent length L of any physical pendulum can be shown to be

$$L = \frac{I}{mR}$$

where I is the moment of inertia of the pendulum about the pivot point, m is the mass of the pendulum, and R is the distance between the pivot point and the center of mass. Substituting this expression in (1) above, the period T of a compound pendulum is given by

$$T = 2\pi \sqrt{\frac{I}{mgR}}$$

for sufficiently small oscillations.

For example, a rigid uniform rod of length L pivoted about one end has moment of inertia $I = mL^2/3$. The center of mass is located at the center of the rod, so $R = L/2$ Substituting these values into the above equation gives

Figure 187: *Replica of Zhang Heng's seismometer. The pendulum is contained inside.*

$T = 2\pi\sqrt{2L/3g}$. This shows that a rigid rod pendulum has the same period as a simple pendulum of 2/3 its length.

Christiaan Huygens proved in 1673 that the pivot point and the center of oscillation are interchangeable.[1485] This means if any pendulum is turned upside down and swung from a pivot located at its previous center of oscillation, it will have the same period as before and the new center of oscillation will be at the old pivot point. In 1817 Henry Kater used this idea to produce a type of reversible pendulum, now known as a Kater pendulum, for improved measurements of the acceleration due to gravity.

History

One of the earliest known uses of a pendulum was a 1st-century seismometer device of Han Dynasty Chinese scientist Zhang Heng.[1486] Its function was to sway and activate one of a series of levers after being disturbed by the tremor of an earthquake far away.[1487] Released by a lever, a small ball would fall out of the urn-shaped device into one of eight metal toad's mouths below, at the eight points of the compass, signifying the direction the earthquake was located.

Many sources claim that the 10th-century Egyptian astronomer Ibn Yunus used a pendulum for time measurement, but this was an error that originated in 1684 with the British historian Edward Bernard.

During the Renaissance, large hand-pumped pendulums were used as sources of power for manual reciprocating machines such as saws, bellows, and pumps. Leonardo da Vinci made many drawings of the motion of pendulums, though without realizing its value for timekeeping.

1602: Galileo's research

Italian scientist Galileo Galilei was the first to study the properties of pendulums, beginning around 1602. The earliest extant report of his research is contained in a letter to Guido Ubaldo dal Monte, from Padua, dated November 29, 1602. His biographer and student, Vincenzo Viviani, claimed his interest had been sparked around 1582 by the swinging motion of a chandelier in Pisa Cathedral.[1488] Galileo discovered the crucial property that makes pendulums useful as timekeepers, called isochronism; the period of the pendulum is approximately independent of the amplitude or width of the swing. He also found that the period is independent of the mass of the bob, and proportional to the square root of the length of the pendulum. He first employed freeswinging pendulums in simple timing applications. His physician friend, Santorio Santorii, invented a device which measured a patient's pulse by the length of a pendulum; the *pulsilogium*. In 1641 Galileo conceived and dictated to his son Vincenzo a design for a pendulum clock; Vincenzo began construction, but had not completed it when he died in 1649.[1489] The pendulum was the first harmonic oscillator used by man.

1656: The pendulum clock

<templatestyles src="Multiple_image/styles.css" />

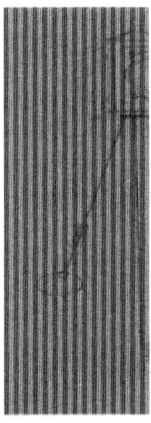

The first pendulum clock

In 1656 the Dutch scientist Christiaan Huygens built the first pendulum clock.[1490] This was a great improvement over existing mechanical clocks; their best accuracy was improved from around 15 minutes deviation a day to around 15 seconds a day. Pendulums spread over Europe as existing clocks were retrofitted with them.[1491]

The English scientist Robert Hooke studied the conical pendulum around 1666, consisting of a pendulum that is free to swing in two dimensions, with the bob rotating in a circle or ellipse. He used the motions of this device as a model to analyze the orbital motions of the planets. Hooke suggested to Isaac Newton in 1679 that the components of orbital motion consisted of inertial motion along a tangent direction plus an attractive motion in the radial direction. This played a part in Newton's formulation of the law of universal gravitation. Robert Hooke was also responsible for suggesting as early as 1666 that the pendulum could be used to measure the force of gravity.

During his expedition to Cayenne, French Guiana in 1671, Jean Richer found that a pendulum clock was $2\,^1/_2$ minutes per day slower at Cayenne than at Paris. From this he deduced that the force of gravity was lower at Cayenne.[1492] In 1687, Isaac Newton in *Principia Mathematica* showed that this was because the Earth was not a true sphere but slightly oblate (flattened at the poles) from the effect of centrifugal force due to its rotation, causing gravity to increase with latitude.[1493] Portable pendulums began to be taken on voyages to distant lands, as precision gravimeters to measure the acceleration of gravity at different points on Earth, eventually resulting in accurate models of the shape of the Earth.

1673: Huygens' *Horologium Oscillatorium*

In 1673, 17 years after he invented the pendulum clock, Christiaan Huygens published his theory of the pendulum, *Horologium Oscillatorium sive de motu pendulorum*.[1494] Marin Mersenne and René Descartes had discovered around 1636 that the pendulum was not quite isochronous; its period increased somewhat with its amplitude. Huygens analyzed this problem by determining what curve an object must follow to descend by gravity to the same point in the same time interval, regardless of starting point; the so-called *tautochrone curve*. By a complicated method that was an early use of calculus, he showed this curve was a cycloid, rather than the circular arc of a pendulum,[1495] confirming that the pendulum was not isochronous and Galileo's observation of isochronism was accurate only for small swings. Huygens also solved the problem of how to calculate the period of an arbitrarily shaped pendulum (called a *compound pendulum*), discovering the *center of oscillation*, and its interchangeability with the pivot point.[1496]

The existing clock movement, the verge escapement, made pendulums swing in very wide arcs of about 100°. Huygens showed this was a source of inaccuracy, causing the period to vary with amplitude changes caused by small unavoidable variations in the clock's drive force.[1497] To make its period isochronous, Huygens mounted cycloidal-shaped metal 'chops' next to the pivots in his clocks, that constrained the suspension cord and forced the pendulum to follow a cycloid arc.[1498] This solution didn't prove as practical as simply limiting the pendulum's swing to small angles of a few degrees. The realization that only small swings were isochronous motivated the development of the anchor escapement around 1670, which reduced the pendulum swing in clocks to 4°–6°.[1499]

1721: Temperature compensated pendulums

During the 18th and 19th century, the pendulum clock's role as the most accurate timekeeper motivated much practical research into improving pendulums. It was found that a major source of error was that the pendulum rod expanded and contracted with changes in ambient temperature, changing the period of swing. This was solved with the invention of temperature compensated pendulums, the mercury pendulum in 1721[1500] and the gridiron pendulum in 1726, reducing errors in precision pendulum clocks to a few seconds per week.

The accuracy of gravity measurements made with pendulums was limited by the difficulty of finding the location of their center of oscillation. Huygens had discovered in 1673 that a pendulum has the same period when hung from its center of oscillation as when hung from its pivot, and the distance between the two points was equal to the length of a simple gravity pendulum of the

Figure 188: *The Foucault pendulum in 1851 was the first demonstration of the Earth's rotation that did not involve celestial observations, and it created a "pendulum mania". In this animation the rate of precession is greatly exaggerated.*

same period. In 1818 British Captain Henry Kater invented the reversible Kater's pendulum which used this principle, making possible very accurate measurements of gravity. For the next century the reversible pendulum was the standard method of measuring absolute gravitational acceleration.

1851: Foucault pendulum

In 1851, Jean Bernard Léon Foucault showed that the plane of oscillation of a pendulum, like a gyroscope, tends to stay constant regardless of the motion of the pivot, and that this could be used to demonstrate the rotation of the Earth. He suspended a pendulum free to swing in two dimensions (later named the Foucault pendulum) from the dome of the Panthéon in Paris. The length of the cord was 67 m (220 ft). Once the pendulum was set in motion, the plane of swing was observed to precess or rotate 360° clockwise in about 32 hours. This was the first demonstration of the Earth's rotation that didn't depend on celestial observations,[1501] and a "pendulum mania" broke out, as Foucault pendulums were displayed in many cities and attracted large crowds.

1930: Decline in use

Around 1900 low-thermal-expansion materials began to be used for pendulum rods in the highest precision clocks and other instruments, first invar, a nickel steel alloy, and later fused quartz, which made temperature compensation trivial. Precision pendulums were housed in low pressure tanks, which kept the air pressure constant to prevent changes in the period due to changes in buoyancy of the pendulum due to changing atmospheric pressure. The best pendulum clocks achieved accuracy of around a second per year.

The timekeeping accuracy of the pendulum was exceeded by the quartz crystal oscillator, invented in 1921, and quartz clocks, invented in 1927, replaced pendulum clocks as the world's best timekeepers. Pendulum clocks were used as time standards until World War 2, although the French Time Service continued using them in their official time standard ensemble until 1954. Pendulum gravimeters were superseded by "free fall" gravimeters in the 1950s, but pendulum instruments continued to be used into the 1970s.

<templatestyles src="Multiple_image/styles.css" />

Clock pendulums

Longcase clock (Grandfather clock) pendulum

Ornamented pendulum in a French Comtoise clock

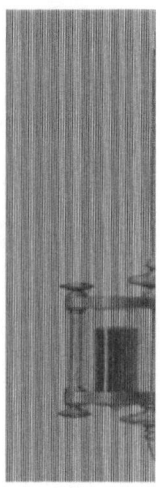

Mercury pendulum

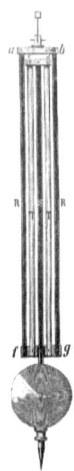

Gridiron pendulum

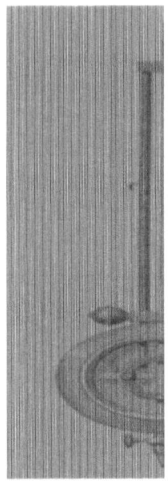

Ellicott pendulum, another temperature compensated type

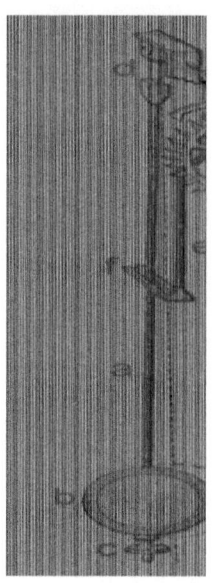

Figure 189: *Pendulum and anchor escapement from a grandfather clock*

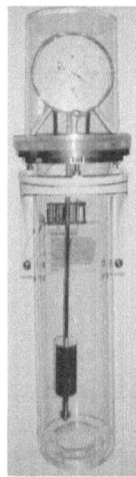

Invar pendulum in low pressure tank in Riefler regulator clock, used as the US time standard from 1909 to 1929

Figure 190: *Animation of anchor escapement, one of the most widely used escapements in pendulum clock.*

Use for time measurement

For 300 years, from its discovery around 1582 until development of the quartz clock in the 1930s, the pendulum was the world's standard for accurate timekeeping.[1502] In addition to clock pendulums, freeswinging seconds pendulums were widely used as precision timers in scientific experiments in the 17th and 18th centuries. Pendulums require great mechanical stability: a length change of only 0.02%, 0.2 mm in a grandfather clock pendulum, will cause an error of a minute per week.[1503]

Clock pendulums

Pendulums in clocks (see example at right) are usually made of a weight or bob *(b)* suspended by a rod of wood or metal *(a)*. To reduce air resistance (which accounts for most of the energy loss in precision clocks) the bob is traditionally a smooth disk with a lens-shaped cross section, although in antique clocks it often had carvings or decorations specific to the type of clock. In quality clocks the bob is made as heavy as the suspension can support and the movement can drive, since this improves the regulation of the clock (see Accuracy below). A common weight for seconds pendulum bobs is 15 pounds (6.8 kg).[1504] Instead of hanging from a pivot, clock pendulums are usually supported by a short straight spring *(d)* of flexible metal ribbon. This avoids the friction and 'play' caused by a pivot, and the slight bending force of the spring merely adds to the pendulum's restoring force. A few precision clocks have pivots of 'knife' blades resting on agate plates. The impulses to keep the pendulum swinging are provided by an arm hanging behind the pendulum called the *crutch, (e)*, which ends in a *fork, (f)* whose prongs embrace the pendulum rod. The crutch is pushed back and forth by the clock's escapement, *(g,h)*.

Each time the pendulum swings through its centre position, it releases one tooth of the *escape wheel (g)*. The force of the clock's mainspring or a driving weight hanging from a pulley, transmitted through the clock's gear train, causes the wheel to turn, and a tooth presses against one of the pallets *(h)*, giving the pendulum a short push. The clock's wheels, geared to the escape wheel, move forward a fixed amount with each pendulum swing, advancing the clock's hands at a steady rate.

The pendulum always has a means of adjusting the period, usually by an adjustment nut *(c)* under the bob which moves it up or down on the rod.[1505] Moving the bob up decreases the pendulum's length, causing the pendulum to swing faster and the clock to gain time. Some precision clocks have a small auxiliary adjustment weight on a threaded shaft on the bob, to allow finer adjustment. Some tower clocks and precision clocks use a tray attached near to the midpoint of the pendulum rod, to which small weights can be added or removed. This effectively shifts the centre of oscillation and allows the rate to be adjusted without stopping the clock.[1506]

The pendulum must be suspended from a rigid support.[1507] During operation, any elasticity will allow tiny imperceptible swaying motions of the support, which disturbs the clock's period, resulting in error. Pendulum clocks should be attached firmly to a sturdy wall.

The most common pendulum length in quality clocks, which is always used in grandfather clocks, is the seconds pendulum, about 1 metre (39 inches) long. In mantel clocks, half-second pendulums, 25 cm (9.8 in) long, or shorter, are used. Only a few large tower clocks use longer pendulums, the 1.5 second pendulum, 2.25 m (7.4 ft) long, or occasionally the two-second pendulum, 4 m (13 ft)[1508] which is used in Big Ben.

Temperature compensation

The largest source of error in early pendulums was slight changes in length due to thermal expansion and contraction of the pendulum rod with changes in ambient temperature.[1509] This was discovered when people noticed that pendulum clocks ran slower in summer, by as much as a minute per week (one of the first was Godefroy Wendelin, as reported by Huygens in 1658).[1510] Thermal

Pendulum

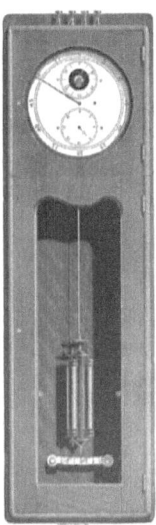

Figure 191: *Mercury pendulum in Howard astronomical regulator clock, 1887*

expansion of pendulum rods was first studied by Jean Picard in 1669.[1511] A pendulum with a steel rod will expand by about 11.3 parts per million (ppm) with each degree Celsius increase, causing it to lose about 0.27 seconds per day for every degree Celsius increase in temperature, or 9 seconds per day for a 33 °C (59 °F) change. Wood rods expand less, losing only about 6 seconds per day for a 33 °C (59 °F) change, which is why quality clocks often had wooden pendulum rods. The wood had to be varnished to prevent water vapor from getting in, because changes in humidity also affected the length.

Mercury pendulum

The first device to compensate for this error was the mercury pendulum, invented by George Graham in 1721. The liquid metal mercury expands in volume with temperature. In a mercury pendulum, the pendulum's weight (bob) is a container of mercury. With a temperature rise, the pendulum rod gets longer, but the mercury also expands and its surface level rises slightly in the container, moving its centre of mass closer to the pendulum pivot. By using the correct height of mercury in the container these two effects will cancel, leaving the pendulum's centre of mass, and its period, unchanged with temperature. Its main disadvantage was that when the temperature changed, the rod would come to the new temperature quickly but the mass of mercury might

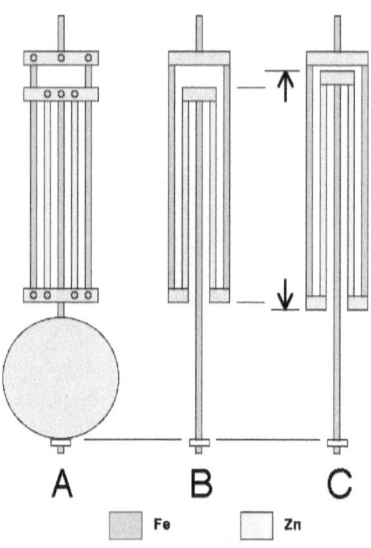

Figure 192: *Diagram of a gridiron pendulum*
A: exterior schematic
B: normal temperature
C: higher temperature

take a day or two to reach the new temperature, causing the rate to deviate during that time.[1512] To improve thermal accommodation several thin containers were often used, made of metal. Mercury pendulums were the standard used in precision regulator clocks into the 20th century.[1513]

Gridiron pendulum

The most widely used compensated pendulum was the gridiron pendulum, invented in 1726 by John Harrison. This consists of alternating rods of two different metals, one with lower thermal expansion (CTE), steel, and one with higher thermal expansion, zinc or brass. The rods are connected by a frame, as shown in the drawing at the right, so that an increase in length of the zinc rods pushes the bob up, shortening the pendulum. With a temperature increase, the low expansion steel rods make the pendulum longer, while the high expansion zinc rods make it shorter. By making the rods of the correct lengths, the greater expansion of the zinc cancels out the expansion of the steel rods which have a greater combined length, and the pendulum stays the same length with temperature.

Zinc-steel gridiron pendulums are made with 5 rods, but the thermal expansion of brass is closer to steel, so brass-steel gridirons usually require 9 rods. Gridiron pendulums adjust to temperature changes faster than mercury pendulums, but scientists found that friction of the rods sliding in their holes in the frame caused gridiron pendulums to adjust in a series of tiny jumps. In high precision clocks this caused the clock's rate to change suddenly with each jump. Later it was found that zinc is subject to creep. For these reasons mercury pendulums were used in the highest precision clocks, but gridirons were used in quality regulator clocks.

Gridiron pendulums became so associated with good quality that, to this day, many ordinary clock pendulums have decorative 'fake' gridirons that don't actually have any temperature compensation function.

Invar and fused quartz

Around 1900, low thermal expansion materials were developed which could be used as pendulum rods in order to make elaborate temperature compensation unnecessary. These were only used in a few of the highest precision clocks before the pendulum became obsolete as a time standard. In 1896 Charles Édouard Guillaume invented the nickel steel alloy Invar. This has a CTE of around 0.5 μin/(in·°F), resulting in pendulum temperature errors over 71 °F of only 1.3 seconds per day, and this residual error could be compensated to zero with a few centimeters of aluminium under the pendulum bob (this can be seen in the Riefler clock image above). Invar pendulums were first used in 1898 in the Riefler regulator clock[1514] which achieved accuracy of 15 milliseconds per day. Suspension springs of Elinvar were used to eliminate temperature variation of the spring's restoring force on the pendulum. Later fused quartz was used which had even lower CTE. These materials are the choice for modern high accuracy pendulums.[1515]

Atmospheric pressure

The effect of the surrounding air on a moving pendulum is complex and requires fluid mechanics to calculate precisely, but for most purposes its influence on the period can be accounted for by three effects:[1516]

- By Archimedes' principle the effective weight of the bob is reduced by the buoyancy of the air it displaces, while the mass (inertia) remains the same, reducing the pendulum's acceleration during its swing and increasing the period. This depends on the air pressure and the density of the pendulum, but not its shape.

- The pendulum carries an amount of air with it as it swings, and the mass of this air increases the inertia of the pendulum, again reducing the acceleration and increasing the period. This depends on both its density and shape.
- Viscous air resistance slows the pendulum's velocity. This has a negligible effect on the period, but dissipates energy, reducing the amplitude. This reduces the pendulum's Q factor, requiring a stronger drive force from the clock's mechanism to keep it moving, which causes increased disturbance to the period.

Increases in barometric pressure increase a pendulum's period slightly due to the first two effects, by about 0.11 seconds per day per kilopascal (0.37 seconds per day per inch of mercury or 0.015 seconds per day per torr). Researchers using pendulums to measure the acceleration of gravity had to correct the period for the air pressure at the altitude of measurement, computing the equivalent period of a pendulum swinging in vacuum. A pendulum clock was first operated in a constant-pressure tank by Friedrich Tiede in 1865 at the Berlin Observatory, and by 1900 the highest precision clocks were mounted in tanks that were kept at a constant pressure to eliminate changes in atmospheric pressure. Alternatively, in some a small aneroid barometer mechanism attached to the pendulum compensated for this effect.

Gravity

Pendulums are affected by changes in gravitational acceleration, which varies by as much as 0.5% at different locations on Earth, so precision pendulum clocks have to be recalibrated after a move. Even moving a pendulum clock to the top of a tall building can cause it to lose measurable time from the reduction in gravity.

Accuracy of pendulums as timekeepers

The timekeeping elements in all clocks, which include pendulums, balance wheels, the quartz crystals used in quartz watches, and even the vibrating atoms in atomic clocks, are in physics called harmonic oscillators. The reason harmonic oscillators are used in clocks is that they vibrate or oscillate at a specific resonant frequency or period and resist oscillating at other rates. However, the resonant frequency is not infinitely 'sharp'. Around the resonant frequency there is a narrow natural band of frequencies (or periods), called the resonance width or bandwidth, where the harmonic oscillator will oscillate.[1517] In a clock, the actual frequency of the pendulum may vary randomly within this resonance width in response to disturbances, but at frequencies outside this band, the clock will not function at all.

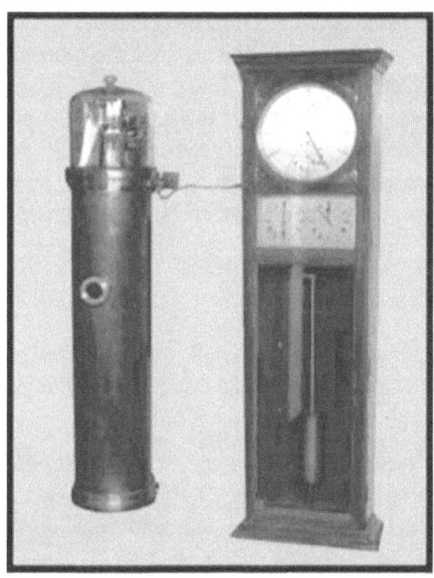

Figure 193: *A Shortt-Synchronome free pendulum clock, the most accurate pendulum clock ever made, at the NIST museum, Gaithersburg, MD, USA. It kept time with two synchronized pendulums. The master pendulum in the vacuum tank (left) swung free of virtually any disturbance, and controlled the slave pendulum in the clock case (right) which performed the impulsing and timekeeping tasks. Its accuracy was about a second per year.*

Q factor

The measure of a harmonic oscillator's resistance to disturbances to its oscillation period is a dimensionless parameter called the Q factor equal to the resonant frequency divided by the resonance width.[1518] The higher the Q, the smaller the resonance width, and the more constant the frequency or period of the oscillator for a given disturbance. The reciprocal of the Q is roughly proportional to the limiting accuracy achievable by a harmonic oscillator as a time standard.[1519]

The Q is related to how long it takes for the oscillations of an oscillator to die out. The Q of a pendulum can be measured by counting the number of oscillations it takes for the amplitude of the pendulum's swing to decay to $1/e$ = 36.8% of its initial swing, and multiplying by 2π.

In a clock, the pendulum must receive pushes from the clock's movement to keep it swinging, to replace the energy the pendulum loses to friction. These pushes, applied by a mechanism called the escapement, are the main source of disturbance to the pendulum's motion. The Q is equal to 2π times the energy stored in the pendulum, divided by the energy lost to friction during each oscillation period, which is the same as the energy added by the escapement each period. It can be seen that the smaller the fraction of the pendulum's energy that is lost to friction, the less energy needs to be added, the less the disturbance from the escapement, the more 'independent' the pendulum is of the clock's mechanism, and the more constant its period is. The Q of a pendulum is given by:

$$Q = \frac{M\omega}{\Gamma}$$

where M is the mass of the bob, $\omega = 2\pi/T$ is the pendulum's radian frequency of oscillation, and Γ is the frictional damping force on the pendulum per unit velocity.

ω is fixed by the pendulum's period, and M is limited by the load capacity and rigidity of the suspension. So the Q of clock pendulums is increased by minimizing frictional losses (Γ). Precision pendulums are suspended on low friction pivots consisting of triangular shaped 'knife' edges resting on agate plates. Around 99% of the energy loss in a freeswinging pendulum is due to air friction, so mounting a pendulum in a vacuum tank can increase the Q, and thus the accuracy, by a factor of 100.[1520]

The Q of pendulums ranges from several thousand in an ordinary clock to several hundred thousand for precision regulator pendulums swinging in vacuum. A quality home pendulum clock might have a Q of 10,000 and an accuracy of 10 seconds per month. The most accurate commercially produced pendulum clock was the Shortt-Synchronome free pendulum clock, invented in 1921.[1521] Its Invar master pendulum swinging in a vacuum tank had a Q of 110,000 and an error rate of around a second per year.

Their Q of 10^3–10^5 is one reason why pendulums are more accurate timekeepers than the balance wheels in watches, with Q around 100–300, but less accurate than the quartz crystals in quartz clocks, with Q of 10^5–10^6.

Escapement

Pendulums (unlike, for example, quartz crystals) have a low enough Q that the disturbance caused by the impulses to keep them moving is generally the limiting factor on their timekeeping accuracy. Therefore, the design of the escapement, the mechanism that provides these impulses, has a large effect on the accuracy of a clock pendulum. If the impulses given to the pendulum by the escapement each swing could be exactly identical, the response of the pendulum would be identical, and its period would be constant. However, this is not achievable; unavoidable random fluctuations in the force due to friction of the clock's pallets, lubrication variations, and changes in the torque provided by the clock's power source as it runs down, mean that the force of the impulse applied by the escapement varies.

If these variations in the escapement's force cause changes in the pendulum's width of swing (amplitude), this will cause corresponding slight changes in the period, since (as discussed at top) a pendulum with a finite swing is not quite isochronous. Therefore, the goal of traditional escapement design is to apply the force with the proper profile, and at the correct point in the pendulum's cycle, so force variations have no effect on the pendulum's amplitude. This is called an *isochronous escapement*.

The Airy condition

In 1826 British astronomer George Airy proved what clockmakers had known for centuries; that the disturbing effect of a drive force on the period of a pendulum is smallest if given as a short impulse as the pendulum passes through its bottom equilibrium position. Specifically, he proved that if a pendulum is driven by an impulse that is symmetrical about its bottom equilibrium position, the pendulum's period will be unaffected by changes in the drive force. The most accurate escapements, such as the deadbeat, approximately satisfy this condition.[1522]

Gravity measurement

The presence of the acceleration of gravity g in the periodicity equation (1) for a pendulum means that the local gravitational acceleration of the Earth can be calculated from the period of a pendulum. A pendulum can therefore be used as a gravimeter to measure the local gravity, which varies by over 0.5% across the surface of the Earth.[1523] The pendulum in a clock is disturbed by the pushes it receives from the clock movement, so freeswinging pendulums were used, and were the standard instruments of gravimetry up to the 1930s.

The difference between clock pendulums and gravimeter pendulums is that to measure gravity, the pendulum's length as well as its period has to be measured. The period of freeswinging pendulums could be found to great precision by comparing their swing with a precision clock that had been adjusted to keep correct time by the passage of stars overhead. In the early measurements, a weight on a cord was suspended in front of the clock pendulum, and its length adjusted until the two pendulums swung in exact synchronism. Then the length of the cord was measured. From the length and the period, g could be calculated from equation (1).

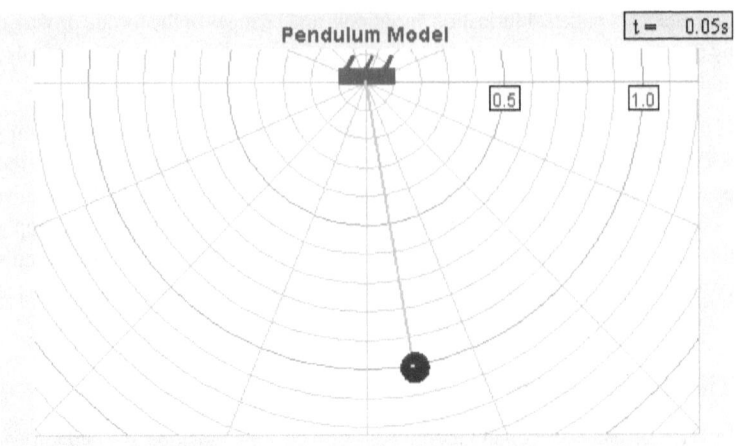

Figure 194: *The seconds pendulum, a pendulum with a period of two seconds so each swing takes one second*

The seconds pendulum

The seconds pendulum, a pendulum with a period of two seconds so each swing takes one second, was widely used to measure gravity, because its period could be easily measured by comparing it to precision regulator clocks, which all had seconds pendulums. By the late 17th century, the length of the seconds pendulum became the standard measure of the strength of gravitational acceleration at a location. By 1700 its length had been measured with submillimeter accuracy at several cities in Europe. For a seconds pendulum, g is proportional to its length:

$$g \propto L.$$

Early observations

- **1620**: British scientist Francis Bacon was one of the first to propose using a pendulum to measure gravity, suggesting taking one up a mountain to see if gravity varies with altitude.
- **1644**: Even before the pendulum clock, French priest Marin Mersenne first determined the length of the seconds pendulum was 39.1 inches (990 mm), by comparing the swing of a pendulum to the time it took a weight to fall a measured distance.
- **1669**: Jean Picard determined the length of the seconds pendulum at Paris, using a 1-inch (25 mm) copper ball suspended by an aloe fiber, obtaining 39.09 inches (993 mm).[1524]

Figure 195: *Borda & Cassini's 1792 measurement of the length of the seconds pendulum*

- **1672**: The first observation that gravity varied at different points on Earth was made in 1672 by Jean Richer, who took a pendulum clock to Cayenne, French Guiana and found that it lost 2 $1/2$ minutes per day; its seconds pendulum had to be shortened by 1 $1/4$ *lignes* (2.6 mm) shorter than at Paris, to keep correct time. In 1687 Isaac Newton in *Principia Mathematica* showed this was because the Earth had a slightly oblate shape (flattened at the poles) caused by the centrifugal force of its rotation. At higher latitudes the surface was closer to the center of the Earth, so gravity increased with latitude. From this time on, pendulums began to be taken to distant lands to measure gravity, and tables were compiled of the length of the seconds pendulum at different locations on Earth. In 1743 Alexis Claude Clairaut created the first hydrostatic model of the Earth, Clairaut's theorem, which allowed the ellipticity of the Earth to be calculated from gravity measurements. Progressively more accurate models of the shape of the Earth followed.
- **1687**: Newton experimented with pendulums (described in *Principia*) and found that equal length pendulums with bobs made of different materials had the same period, proving that the gravitational force on different substances was exactly proportional to their mass (inertia).
- **1737**: French mathematician Pierre Bouguer made a sophisticated series

of pendulum observations in the Andes mountains, Peru.[1525] He used a copper pendulum bob in the shape of a double pointed cone suspended by a thread; the bob could be reversed to eliminate the effects of nonuniform density. He calculated the length to the center of oscillation of thread and bob combined, instead of using the center of the bob. He corrected for thermal expansion of the measuring rod and barometric pressure, giving his results for a pendulum swinging in vacuum. Bouguer swung the same pendulum at three different elevations, from sea level to the top of the high Peruvian *altiplano*. Gravity should fall with the inverse square of the distance from the center of the Earth. Bouguer found that it fell off slower, and correctly attributed the 'extra' gravity to the gravitational field of the huge Peruvian plateau. From the density of rock samples he calculated an estimate of the effect of the *altiplano* on the pendulum, and comparing this with the gravity of the Earth was able to make the first rough estimate of the density of the Earth.

- **1747**: Daniel Bernoulli showed how to correct for the lengthening of the period due to a finite angle of swing θ_0 by using the first order correction $\theta_0^2/16$, giving the period of a pendulum with an extremely small swing.
- **1792**: To define a pendulum standard of length for use with the new metric system, in 1792 Jean-Charles de Borda and Jean-Dominique Cassini made a precise measurement of the seconds pendulum at Paris. They used a 1 1/2-inch (14 mm) platinum ball suspended by a 12-foot (3.7 m) iron wire. Their main innovation was a technique called the "*method of coincidences*" which allowed the period of pendulums to be compared with great precision. (Bouguer had also used this method). The time interval ΔT between the recurring instants when the two pendulums swung in synchronism was timed. From this the difference between the periods of the pendulums, T_1 and T_2, could be calculated:

$$\frac{1}{\Delta T} = \frac{1}{T_1} - \frac{1}{T_2}$$

- **1821**: Francesco Carlini made pendulum observations on top of Mount Cenis, Italy, from which, using methods similar to Bouguer's, he calculated the density of the Earth. He compared his measurements to an estimate of the gravity at his location assuming the mountain wasn't there, calculated from previous nearby pendulum measurements at sea level. His measurements showed 'excess' gravity, which he allocated to the effect of the mountain. Modeling the mountain as a segment of a sphere 11 miles (18 km) in diameter and 1 mile (1.6 km) high, from rock samples he calculated its gravitational field, and estimated the density of the Earth at 4.39 times that of water. Later recalculations by others gave values of 4.77 and 4.95, illustrating the uncertainties in these geographical methods.

Kater's pendulum

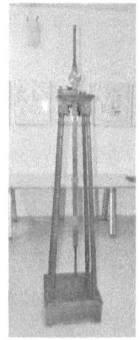 

Figure 196: *Kater's pendulum and stand*

Figure 197: *Measuring gravity with Kater's reversible pendulum, from Kater's 1818 paper*

The precision of the early gravity measurements above was limited by the difficulty of measuring the length of the pendulum, L. L was the length of an idealized simple gravity pendulum (described at top), which has all its mass concentrated in a point at the end of the cord. In 1673 Huygens had shown that the period of a rigid bar pendulum (called a *compound pendulum*) was equal to the period of a simple pendulum with a length equal to the distance between the pivot point and a point called the center of oscillation, located under the center of gravity, that depends on the mass distribution along the pendulum. But there was no accurate way of determining the center of oscillation in a real pendulum.

To get around this problem, the early researchers above approximated an ideal simple pendulum as closely as possible by using a metal sphere suspended by a light wire or cord. If the wire was light enough, the center of oscillation was close to the center of gravity of the ball, at its geometric center. This "ball and wire" type of pendulum wasn't very accurate, because it didn't swing as a rigid body, and the elasticity of the wire caused its length to change slightly as the pendulum swung.

However Huygens had also proved that in any pendulum, the pivot point and the center of oscillation were interchangeable. That is, if a pendulum were turned upside down and hung from its center of oscillation, it would have the same period as it did in the previous position, and the old pivot point would be the new center of oscillation.

Figure 198: *A Kater's pendulum*

British physicist and army captain Henry Kater in 1817 realized that Huygens' principle could be used to find the length of a simple pendulum with the same period as a real pendulum. If a pendulum was built with a second adjustable pivot point near the bottom so it could be hung upside down, and the second pivot was adjusted until the periods when hung from both pivots were the same, the second pivot would be at the center of oscillation, and the distance between the two pivots would be the length L of a simple pendulum with the same period.

Kater built a reversible pendulum (shown at right) consisting of a brass bar with two opposing pivots made of short triangular "knife" blades *(a)* near either end. It could be swung from either pivot, with the knife blades supported on agate plates. Rather than make one pivot adjustable, he attached the pivots a meter apart and instead adjusted the periods with a moveable weight on the pendulum rod *(b,c)*. In operation, the pendulum is hung in front of a precision clock, and the period timed, then turned upside down and the period timed again. The weight is adjusted with the adjustment screw until the periods are equal. Then putting this period and the distance between the pivots into equation (1) gives the gravitational acceleration g very accurately.

Kater timed the swing of his pendulum using the *"method of coincidences"* and measured the distance between the two pivots with a micrometer. After

Figure 199: *Measuring gravity with an invariable pendulum, Madras, India, 1821*

applying corrections for the finite amplitude of swing, the buoyancy of the bob, the barometric pressure and altitude, and temperature, he obtained a value of 39.13929 inches for the seconds pendulum at London, in vacuum, at sea level, at 62 °F. The largest variation from the mean of his 12 observations was 0.00028 in. representing a precision of gravity measurement of 7×10^{-6} (7 mGal or 70 µm/s^2). Kater's measurement was used as Britain's official standard of length (see below) from 1824 to 1855.

Reversible pendulums (known technically as "convertible" pendulums) employing Kater's principle were used for absolute gravity measurements into the 1930s.

Later pendulum gravimeters

The increased accuracy made possible by Kater's pendulum helped make gravimetry a standard part of geodesy. Since the exact location (latitude and longitude) of the 'station' where the gravity measurement was made was necessary, gravity measurements became part of surveying, and pendulums were taken on the great geodetic surveys of the 18th century, particularly the Great Trigonometric Survey of India.

- **Invariable pendulums:** Kater introduced the idea of *relative* gravity measurements, to supplement the *absolute* measurements made by a Kater's pendulum.[1526] Comparing the gravity at two different points was an easier process than measuring it absolutely by the Kater method. All that was necessary was to time the period of an ordinary (single pivot) pendulum at the first point, then transport the pendulum to the other point and time its period there. Since the pendulum's length was constant, from (1) the ratio of the gravitational accelerations was equal to the inverse of the ratio of the periods squared, and no precision length measurements were necessary. So once the gravity had been measured absolutely at some central station, by the Kater or other accurate method, the gravity at other points could be found by swinging pendulums at the central station and then taking them to the other location and timing their swing there. Kater made up a set of "invariable" pendulums, with only one knife edge pivot, which were taken to many countries after first being swung at a central station at Kew Observatory, UK.

- **Airy's coal pit experiments**: Starting in 1826, using methods similar to Bouguer, British astronomer George Airy attempted to determine the density of the Earth by pendulum gravity measurements at the top and bottom of a coal mine. The gravitational force below the surface of the Earth decreases rather than increasing with depth, because by Gauss's law the mass of the spherical shell of crust above the subsurface point does not contribute to the gravity. The 1826 experiment was aborted by the flooding of the mine, but in 1854 he conducted an improved experiment at the Harton coal mine, using seconds pendulums swinging on agate plates, timed by precision chronometers synchronized by an electrical circuit. He found the lower pendulum was slower by 2.24 seconds per day. This meant that the gravitational acceleration at the bottom of the mine, 1250 ft below the surface, was 1/14,000 less than it should have been from the inverse square law; that is the attraction of the spherical shell was 1/14,000 of the attraction of the Earth. From samples of surface rock he estimated the mass of the spherical shell of crust, and from this estimated that the density of the Earth was 6.565 times that of water. Von Sterneck attempted to repeat the experiment in 1882 but found inconsistent results.

- **Repsold-Bessel pendulum:** It was time-consuming and error-prone to repeatedly swing the Kater's pendulum and adjust the weights until the periods were equal. Friedrich Bessel showed in 1835 that this was unnecessary.[1527] As long as the periods were close together, the gravity could be calculated from the two periods and the center of gravity of the pendulum.[1528] So the reversible pendulum didn't need to be adjustable, it could just be a bar with two pivots. Bessel also showed that if the pendulum was made symmetrical in form about its center, but was weighted internally at one end, the errors due to air drag would cancel out. Further, another

Figure 200: *Repsold pendulum, 1864*

error due to the finite diameter of the knife edges could be made to cancel out if they were interchanged between measurements. Bessel didn't construct such a pendulum, but in 1864 Adolf Repsold, under contract by the Swiss Geodetic Commission made a pendulum along these lines. The Repsold pendulum was about 56 cm long and had a period of about $3/4$ second. It was used extensively by European geodetic agencies, and with the Kater pendulum in the Survey of India. Similar pendulums of this type were designed by Charles Pierce and C. Defforges.

- **Von Sterneck and Mendenhall gravimeters:** In 1887 Austro-Hungarian scientist Robert von Sterneck developed a small gravimeter pendulum mounted in a temperature-controlled vacuum tank to eliminate the effects of temperature and air pressure. It used a "half-second pendulum," having a period close to one second, about 25 cm long. The pendulum was nonreversible, so the instrument was used for relative gravity measurements, but their small size made them small and portable. The period of the pendulum was picked off by reflecting the image of an electric spark created by a precision chronometer off a mirror mounted at the top of the pendulum rod. The Von Sterneck instrument, and a similar instrument developed by Thomas C. Mendenhall of the US Coast and Geodetic Survey in 1890, were used extensively for surveys into the 1920s.

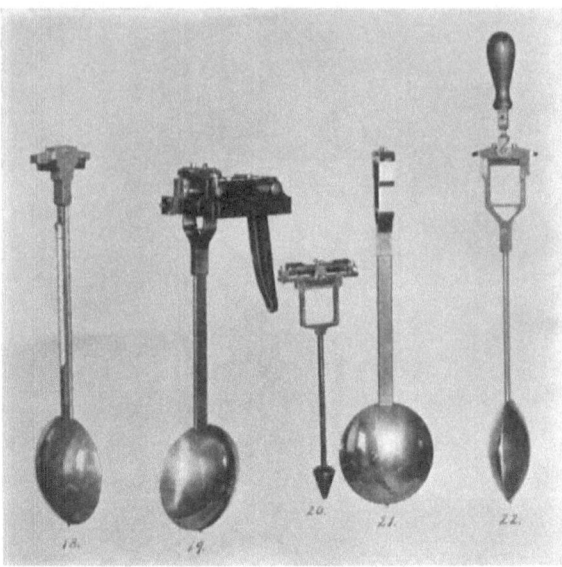

Figure 201: *Pendulums used in Mendenhall gravimeter, 1890*

The Mendenhall pendulum was actually a more accurate timekeeper than the highest precision clocks of the time, and as the 'world's best clock' it was used by Albert A. Michelson in his 1924 measurements of the speed of light on Mt. Wilson, California.

- **Double pendulum gravimeters:** Starting in 1875, the increasing accuracy of pendulum measurements revealed another source of error in existing instruments: the swing of the pendulum caused a slight swaying of the tripod stand used to support portable pendulums, introducing error. In 1875 Charles S Peirce calculated that measurements of the length of the seconds pendulum made with the Repsold instrument required a correction of 0.2 mm due to this error.[1529] In 1880 C. Defforges used a Michelson interferometer to measure the sway of the stand dynamically, and interferometers were added to the standard Mendenhall apparatus to calculate sway corrections.[1530] A method of preventing this error was first suggested in 1877 by Hervé Faye and advocated by Peirce, Cellérier and Furtwangler: mount two identical pendulums on the same support, swinging with the same amplitude, 180° out of phase. The opposite motion of the pendulums would cancel out any sideways forces on the support. The idea was opposed due to its complexity, but by the start of the 20th century the Von Sterneck device and other instruments were modified to swing multiple pendulums simultaneously.

Figure 202: *Quartz pendulums used in Gulf gravimeter, 1929*

- **Gulf gravimeter**: One of the last and most accurate pendulum gravimeters was the apparatus developed in 1929 by the Gulf Research and Development Co.[1531] It used two pendulums made of fused quartz, each 10.7 inches (270 mm) in length with a period of 0.89 second, swinging on pyrex knife edge pivots, 180° out of phase. They were mounted in a permanently sealed temperature and humidity controlled vacuum chamber. Stray electrostatic charges on the quartz pendulums had to be discharged by exposing them to a radioactive salt before use. The period was detected by reflecting a light beam from a mirror at the top of the pendulum, recorded by a chart recorder and compared to a precision crystal oscillator calibrated against the WWV radio time signal. This instrument was accurate to within $(0.3-0.5) \times 10^{-7}$ (30–50 microgals or 3–5 nm/s^2). It was used into the 1960s.

Relative pendulum gravimeters were superseded by the simpler LaCoste zero-length spring gravimeter, invented in 1934 by Lucien LaCoste. Absolute (reversible) pendulum gravimeters were replaced in the 1950s by free fall gravimeters, in which a weight is allowed to fall in a vacuum tank and its acceleration is measured by an optical interferometer.

Standard of length

Because the acceleration of gravity is constant at a given point on Earth, the period of a simple pendulum at a given location depends only on its length. Additionally, gravity varies only slightly at different locations. Almost from the pendulum's discovery until the early 19th century, this property led scientists to suggest using a pendulum of a given period as a standard of length.

Until the 19th century, countries based their systems of length measurement on prototypes, metal bar primary standards, such as the standard yard in Britain kept at the Houses of Parliament, and the standard *toise* in France, kept at Paris. These were vulnerable to damage or destruction over the years, and because of the difficulty of comparing prototypes, the same unit often had different lengths in distant towns, creating opportunities for fraud. During the Enlightenment scientists argued for a length standard that was based on some property of nature that could be determined by measurement, creating an indestructible, universal standard. The period of pendulums could be measured very precisely by timing them with clocks that were set by the stars. A pendulum standard amounted to defining the unit of length by the gravitational force of the Earth, for all intents constant, and the second, which was defined by the rotation rate of the Earth, also constant. The idea was that anyone, anywhere on Earth, could recreate the standard by constructing a pendulum that swung with the defined period and measuring its length.

Virtually all proposals were based on the seconds pendulum, in which each swing (a half period) takes one second, which is about a meter (39 inches) long, because by the late 17th century it had become a standard for measuring gravity (see previous section). By the 18th century its length had been measured with sub-millimeter accuracy at a number of cities in Europe and around the world.

The initial attraction of the pendulum length standard was that it was believed (by early scientists such as Huygens and Wren) that gravity was constant over the Earth's surface, so a given pendulum had the same period at any point on Earth. So the length of the standard pendulum could be measured at any location, and would not be tied to any given nation or region; it would be a truly democratic, worldwide standard. Although Richer found in 1672 that gravity varies at different points on the globe, the idea of a pendulum length standard remained popular, because it was found that gravity only varies with latitude. Gravitational acceleration increases smoothly from the equator to the poles, due to the oblate shape of the Earth, so at any given latitude (east-west line), gravity was constant enough that the length of a seconds pendulum was the same within the measurement capability of the 18th century. Thus the unit of length could be defined at a given latitude and measured at any point along that latitude. For example, a pendulum standard defined at 45° north latitude, a popular choice, could be measured in parts of France, Italy, Croatia, Serbia, Romania, Russia, Kazakhstan, China, Mongolia, the United States and Canada. In addition, it could be recreated at any location at which the gravitational acceleration had been accurately measured.

By the mid 19th century, increasingly accurate pendulum measurements by Edward Sabine and Thomas Young revealed that gravity, and thus the length of any pendulum standard, varied measurably with local geologic features such as mountains and dense subsurface rocks. So a pendulum length standard had to be defined at a single point on Earth and could only be measured there. This took much of the appeal from the concept, and efforts to adopt pendulum standards were abandoned.

Early proposals

One of the first to suggest defining length with a pendulum was Flemish scientist Isaac Beeckman who in 1631 recommended making the seconds pendulum "the invariable measure for all people at all times in all places".[1532] Marin Mersenne, who first measured the seconds pendulum in 1644, also suggested it. The first official proposal for a pendulum standard was made by the British Royal Society in 1660, advocated by Christiaan Huygens and Ole Rømer, basing it on Mersenne's work, and Huygens in *Horologium Oscillatorium* proposed a "horary foot" defined as 1/3 of the seconds pendulum. Christopher Wren was another early supporter. The idea of a pendulum standard of length must have been familiar to people as early as 1663, because Samuel Butler satirizes it in *Hudibras*:[1533]

> Upon the bench I will so handle 'em
>
> That the vibration of this pendulum
>
> Shall make all taylors' yards of one
>
> Unanimous opinion

In 1671 Jean Picard proposed a pendulum-defined 'universal foot' in his influential *Mesure de la Terre*.[1534] Gabriel Mouton around 1670 suggested defining the *toise* either by a seconds pendulum or a minute of terrestrial degree. A plan for a complete system of units based on the pendulum was advanced in 1675 by Italian polymath Tito Livio Burratini. In France in 1747, geographer Charles Marie de la Condamine proposed defining length by a seconds pendulum at the equator; since at this location a pendulum's swing wouldn't be distorted by the Earth's rotation. James Steuart (1780) and George Skene Keith were also supporters.

By the end of the 18th century, when many nations were reforming their weight and measure systems, the seconds pendulum was the leading choice for a new definition of length, advocated by prominent scientists in several major nations. In 1790, then US Secretary of State Thomas Jefferson proposed to Congress a comprehensive decimalized US 'metric system' based on the seconds pendulum at 38° North latitude, the mean latitude of the United States.[1535] No action was taken on this proposal. In Britain the leading advocate of the pendulum was politician John Riggs Miller.[1536] When his efforts to promote a joint British–French–American metric system fell through in 1790, he proposed a British system based on the length of the seconds pendulum at London. This standard was adopted in 1824 (below).

The metre

In the discussions leading up to the French adoption of the metric system in 1791, the leading candidate for the definition of the new unit of length, the metre, was the seconds pendulum at 45° North latitude. It was advocated by a group led by French politician Talleyrand and mathematician Antoine Nicolas Caritat de Condorcet. This was one of the three final options considered by the French Academy of Sciences committee. However, on March 19, 1791 the committee instead chose to base the metre on the length of the meridian through Paris. A pendulum definition was rejected because of its variability at different locations, and because it defined length by a unit of time. (However, since 1983 the metre has been officially defined in terms of the length of the second and the speed of light.) A possible additional reason is that the radical French Academy didn't want to base their new system on the second, a traditional and nondecimal unit from the *ancien regime*.

Although not defined by the pendulum, the final length chosen for the metre, 10^{-7} of the pole-to-equator meridian arc, was very close to the length of the seconds pendulum (0.9937 m), within 0.63%. Although no reason for this particular choice was given at the time, it was probably to facilitate the use of the seconds pendulum as a secondary standard, as was proposed in the official document. So the modern world's standard unit of length is certainly closely linked historically with the seconds pendulum.

Britain and Denmark

Britain and Denmark appear to be the only nations that (for a short time) based their units of length on the pendulum. In 1821 the Danish inch was defined as 1/38 of the length of the mean solar seconds pendulum at 45° latitude at the meridian of Skagen, at sea level, in vacuum. The British parliament passed the *Imperial Weights and Measures Act* in 1824, a reform of the British standard system which declared that if the prototype standard yard was destroyed, it would be recovered by defining the inch so that the length of the solar seconds pendulum at London, at sea level, in a vacuum, at 62 °F was 39.1393 inches.

This also became the US standard, since at the time the US used British measures. However, when the prototype yard was lost in the 1834 Houses of Parliament fire, it proved impossible to recreate it accurately from the pendulum definition, and in 1855 Britain repealed the pendulum standard and returned to prototype standards.

Other uses

Seismometers

A pendulum in which the rod is not vertical but almost horizontal was used in early seismometers for measuring earth tremors. The bob of the pendulum does not move when its mounting does, and the difference in the movements is recorded on a drum chart.

Schuler tuning

As first explained by Maximilian Schuler in a 1923 paper, a pendulum whose period exactly equals the orbital period of a hypothetical satellite orbiting just above the surface of the earth (about 84 minutes) will tend to remain pointing at the center of the earth when its support is suddenly displaced. This principle, called Schuler tuning, is used in inertial guidance systems in ships and aircraft that operate on the surface of the Earth. No physical pendulum is used, but the control system that keeps the inertial platform containing the gyroscopes stable is modified so the device acts as though it is attached to such a pendulum, keeping the platform always facing down as the vehicle moves on the curved surface of the Earth.

Coupled pendulums

In 1665 Huygens made a curious observation about pendulum clocks. Two clocks had been placed on his mantlepiece, and he noted that they had acquired an opposing motion. That is, their pendulums were beating in unison but in the opposite direction; 180° out of phase. Regardless of how the two clocks were started, he found that they would eventually return to this state, thus making the first recorded observation of a coupled oscillator.

The cause of this behavior was that the two pendulums were affecting each other through slight motions of the supporting mantlepiece. This process is called entrainment or mode locking in physics and is observed in other coupled oscillators. Synchronized pendulums have been used in clocks and were widely used in gravimeters in the early 20th century. Although Huygens only observed out-of-phase synchronization, recent investigations have shown the existence of in-phase synchronization, as well as "death" states wherein one or both clocks stops.[1537,1538]

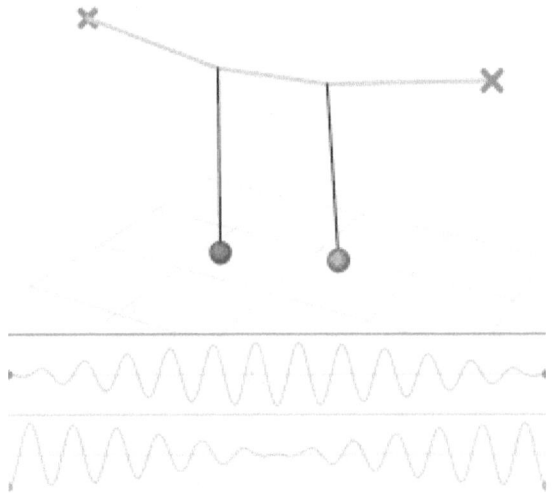

Figure 203: *Two pendulums with the same period coupled by suspending them from a common support string. The oscillation alternates between the two.*

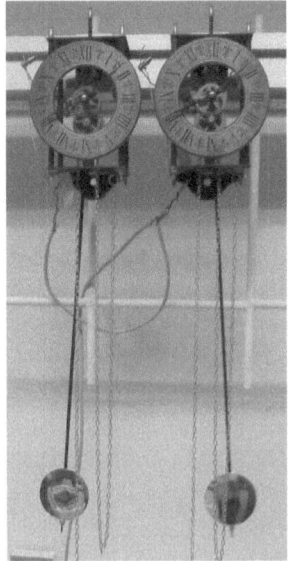

Figure 204: *Repetition of Huygens experiment showing synchronization of two clocks*

Figure 205: *Pendulum in the Metropolitan Cathedral, Mexico City.*

Religious practice

Pendulum motion appears in religious ceremonies as well. The swinging incense burner called a censer, also known as a thurible, is an example of a pendulum.[1539] Pendulums are also seen at many gatherings in eastern Mexico where they mark the turning of the tides on the day which the tides are at their highest point. See also pendulums for divination and dowsing.

Education

Pendulums are widely used in science education as an example of a harmonic oscillator, to teach dynamics and oscillatory motion. One use is to demonstrate the law of conservation of energy. A heavy object such as a bowling ball or wrecking ball is attached to a string. The weight is then moved to within a few inches of a volunteer's face, then released and allowed to swing and come back. In most instances, the weight reverses direction and then returns to (almost) the same position as the original release location — *i.e.* a small distance from the volunteer's face — thus leaving the volunteer unharmed. On occasion the volunteer is injured if either the volunteer does not stand still or the pendulum is initially released with a push (so that when it returns it surpasses the release position).

Torture device

It is claimed that the pendulum was used as an instrument of torture and execution by the Spanish Inquisition in the 18th century. The allegation is contained in the 1826 book *The history of the Inquisition of Spain* by the Spanish priest, historian and liberal activist Juan Antonio Llorente. A swinging pendulum whose edge is a knife blade slowly descends toward a bound prisoner until it cuts into his body. This method of torture came to popular consciousness through the 1842 short story "The Pit and the Pendulum" by American author Edgar Allan Poe but there is considerable skepticism that it actually was used.

Most knowledgeable sources are skeptical that this torture was ever actually used. The only evidence of its use is one paragraph in the preface to Llorente's 1826 *History*, relating a second-hand account by a single prisoner released from the Inquisition's Madrid dungeon in 1820, who purportedly described the pendulum torture method. Modern sources point out that due to Jesus' admonition against bloodshed, Inquisitors were only allowed to use torture methods which did not spill blood, and the pendulum method would have violated this stricture. One theory is that Llorente misunderstood the account he heard; the prisoner was actually referring to another common Inquisition torture, the *strappado* (garrucha), in which the prisoner has his hands tied behind his back and is hoisted off the floor by a rope tied to his hands. This method was also known as the "pendulum". Poe's popular horror tale, and public awareness of the Inquisition's other brutal methods, has kept the myth of this elaborate torture method alive.

Notes

The value of g reflected by the period of a pendulum varies from place to place. The gravitational force varies with distance from the center of the Earth, i.e. with altitude - or because the Earth's shape is oblate, g varies with latitude. A more important cause of this reduction in g at the equator is because the equator is spinning at one revolution per day, reducing the gravitational force there.

References

Note: most of the sources below, including books, can be viewed online through the links given.

Further reading

<templatestyles src="Template:Refbegin/styles.css" />

- G. L. Baker and J. A. Blackburn (2009). *The Pendulum: A Case Study in Physics* (Oxford University Press).
- M. Gitterman (2010). *The Chaotic Pendulum* (World Scientific).
- Michael R. Matthews, Arthur Stinner, Colin F. Gauld (2005)*The Pendulum: Scientific, Historical, Philosophical and Educational Perspectives*, Springer
- Matthews, Michael R.; Gauld, Colin; Stinner, Arthur (2005). "The Pendulum: Its Place in Science, Culture and Pedagogy". *Science & Education*. **13** (4/5): 261–277. Bibcode: 2004Sc&Ed..13..261M[1540]. doi: 10.1023/b:sced.0000041867.60452.18[1541].<templatestyles src="Module:Citation/CS1/styles.css"></templatestyles>
- Schlomo Silbermann,(2014) "Pendulum Fundamental; The Path Of Nowhere" (Book)

Matthys, Robert J. (2004). *Accurate Pendulum Clocks*. UK: Oxford Univ. Press. ISBN 978-0-19-852971-2.<templatestyles src="Module:Citation/CS1/styles.css"></templatestyles>

- Nelson, Robert; M. G. Olsson (February 1986). "The pendulum – Rich physics from a simple system". *American Journal of Physics*. **54** (2): 112–121. Bibcode: 1986AmJPh..54..112N[1542]. doi: 10.1119/1.14703[1543].<templatestyles src="Module:Citation/CS1/styles.css"></templatestyles>
- L. P. Pook (2011). *Understanding Pendulums: A Brief Introduction* (Springer).

 Wikimedia Commons has media related to *Pendulums*.

Death by sawing

The term "**death by sawing**" indicates the act of sawing a living person in half, either sagitally (usually midsagitally), or transversely. Thus, decapitation by sawing or dismemberment by sawing are tangential sub-themes, though some ambiguous cases might be included. Death by sawing was a method of execution reportedly used in different parts of the world. Some of the reviewed examples are legendary. At least one source states that the method was probably never used.[1544]

Methods

Different methods of death by sawing have been recorded. In cases related to the Roman Emperor Caligula, the sawing is said to be through the middle (transversely).[1545] In the cases of Morocco, it is stated that the sawing was lengthwise, both from the groin and upwards and from the skull and downwards (midsagittally).[1546]

In only one case, in the story about Simon the Zealot, the person is explicitly described as being hung upside-down and sawn apart vertically through the middle, starting at the groin, with no mention of fastening or support boards around the person, in the manner depicted in illustrations.[1547] In other cases where details about the method beyond the mere sawing act are explicitly supplied, the condemned person was apparently fastened to either one or two boards prior to sawing.

Archaic Age and antiquity

Ancient Persia

The legend of Jamshid

Jamshid was a legendary shah of Persia, whose story is told in the *Shahnameh* by Ferdowsi. After 300 years of blessed reign, Jamshid forgot the blessings came from God, and began demanding that he be revered as a god himself. The people rebelled, and Zahhak had him sawn asunder.[1548]

Figure 206: *Sawing of three men, from a 15th-century print*

Parysatis

Parysatis, wife and half-sister of Darius II (r. 423–405 BC) was the real power behind the throne of the Achaemenid Empire; she instigated and became involved in a number of court intrigues, made several enemies, yet had an uncanny knack for dispatching them at an opportune time. At one point, she decided to have the siblings of her daughter-in-law Stateira killed, and only relented from killing Stateira as well due to the desperate pleas of her son, Artaxerxes II. Stateira's sister Roxana was the first of her siblings to be killed, by being sawn in half. When Dareius II died, Parysatis moved quickly, and was able to have the new queen Stateira poisoned; Parysatis still remained a power to be reckoned with for years after.[1549]

Hormizd IV

Hormizd IV (Persian: هرمز چهارم), son of Khosrow I, reigned as the twenty-first King of Persia from AD 579 to 590.[1550] As the years went by, he was, due to his "cruelties", deeply resented by the nobility. In 590, a palace coup was staged in which his son, Khosrow II, was declared king. Hormizd IV was forced to watch his wife and one of his sons sawn in two, and the deposed king was then blinded. After a few days, the new king is said to have killed his old, blind father in a fit of rage.[1551]

Thracians

Thracians were regarded as warlike, ferocious, and bloodthirsty by Romans and Greeks.[1552] One of the most notorious was the king Diegylis, possibly only topped by his son Ziselmius. According to Diodorus Siculus, Ziselmius sawed several persons to death and commanded their families to eat the flesh of their murdered relatives. The Thracians eventually rebelled, captured him and sought to inflict every conceivable torture upon him prior to his death.[1553]

Ancient Rome

The Twelve Tables

Promulgated about 451 BC, the Twelve Tables is the oldest extant law code for the Romans. Aulus Gellius, whose work "Attic Nights" is partially preserved, states that death by the saw was mentioned for some offenses in the tables, but that the use of which was so infrequent that no one could remember ever having seen it done.[1554] Of the retained laws in the Twelve Tables, the following concerning how creditors should proceed with debtors is found in Table 3, article 6: "On the third market-day they [the creditors] shall cut pieces. If they shall have cut more or less [than their shares], it shall be with impunity (_s[in]e fraude_)." The translator notes the ambiguity of the original text, but says that later Roman writers understood this to mean that creditors were allowed to cut their shares from the body of the debtor. If true, that would constitute dismemberment, rather than sawing.[1555]

Caligula

This method of execution was uncommon throughout the time of the Roman Empire. However, it was used extensively during the reign of Caligula[1556] when the condemned, including members of his own family, were sawn across the torso rather than lengthways down the body. It is said that Caligula would watch such executions while he ate, stating that witnessing the suffering acted as an appetiser.

The Kitos War

The Kitos War occurred 115–117 AD, and was a rebellion by the Jews within the Roman Empire. Major revolts happened several places, and the main source by Cassius Dio claims that in Cyrene, 220,000 Greeks were massacred by the Jews; in Cyprus, 240,000. Dio adds that many of the victims were sawn asunder, and that the Jews licked up the blood of the slain, and "twisted the entrails like a girdle about their bodies"[1557]

Figure 207: *Illustration by Lucas Cranach the Elder of St. Simon sawn in two*

Valens

In 365 AD, Procopius declared himself emperor, and moved against Valens. He was defeated in battle, and due to the treachery of his two generals Agilonius and Gomoarius (they had been promised they would be "shown favour" by Valens), he was captured. In 366, he was fastened to two trees bent down with force; when the trees were released, Procopius was ripped apart. The "favour" Valens showed to Agilonius and Gomoarius was to have them both sawn asunder.[1558]

Jewish tradition

Death of Isaiah

The prophet Isaiah was, according to some traditional rabbinic texts, sawn apart on orders of King Manasseh of Juda.[1559] One tradition states that he was put within a tree, and then sawn apart; another says he was sawn apart by means of a wooden saw.[1560]

Christian Martyrs

Simon the Zealot

Several early Christians are credited with being martyred by means of a saw. The earliest, and most famous, is the obscure apostle of Jesus, Simon the Zealot. He is said to have been martyred in Persia, and that the express mode by which he was executed was to be hanged up by the feet, as in the woodcut illustration.

Conus and his son

Living in the age of Domitian, Conus went, after his wife's death, with his 7-year-old son into a desert. However, he then had the idea of attacking paganism, and destroyed several idols in Cogni, Asia Minor (Anatolia). Caught, he and his son were tortured by starvation and fire, but they were finally put to the saw, dying while they prayed.[1561]

Symphorosa and her seven sons

Symphorosa was, allegedly, a widow with seven sons living in the age of emperor Trajan (98-117). They were commanded to pray at a heathen temple, but refusing, Symphorosa was scourged, and then with a large stone fastened to her, thrown in the river Aniene. The six eldest sons were all killed by stab wounds, but the youngest, Eugenius, was sawn apart.[1562] However, she may have been killed ca. 138, near the end of the reign of Hadrian (117–138).[1563]

The 38 monks and martyrs on Mount Sinai

Supposedly during the reign of Diocletian, a community of monks lived at Mount Sinai. One day, the "wild barbarians" (said to be inveterate robbers and even cannibalizing their own sons occasionally) decided to rob the community. But, there was nothing of material wealth there, and in their rage, the Arabs slaughtered them all, several by flaying, others by sawing them with dull saws.[1564]

St. Tarbula

Accused of practicing witchcraft and of causing sickness to befall the wife of the ardently anti-Christian Persian king Shapur II, she was condemned and executed by being sawed in half in the year 345.[1565]

Africa

Egypt

The monk from Montepulciano

In the 1630s, there are several reports from the Levant and Egypt that monks were killed. One of them, Brother Conrad d'Elis Barthelemy, a native of Montepulciano is said to have been sawn in two, from the head and downwards.[1566]

The renegade Coptic governor

Writing in 1843, William Holt Yates speaks of a governor under Muhammad Ali (r.1801–49), Abd-ur-Rahman Bey, who was said to be particularly cruel and avaricious. He was a renegade Copt, and abused his position to gain hold of wealth. He is even credited with having sawed people in two. Yates further supplies the detail: "This fellow has since been assassinated-report says, with sanction and approval of the Government"[1567]

Morocco

1705 The sawing of Alcaide Melec

One of the most notorious cases of sawing as execution is that of the Alcaide (castellan/governor) Melec under emperor Moulay Ishmael (r. 1672–1727). The fullest description of this execution is found in Dominique Busnot's[1568] 1714 work *Histoire du règne de Mouley Ismael*, although a brief notice of the event can be found in the January 1706 edition of *Present state of Europe*.[1569] In the following, the tale as told by Busnot will be given.

Melec was judged as the chief rebel to be punished in a rebellion instigated by one of the emperor's sons, Mulay Muhammad. In particular, according to Busnot, the empress was incensed that Melec had personally beheaded one of her cousins, Ali Bouchasra.[1570] In September/October 1705, Mulay Ismail sent for his chief carpenter and asked if his saws were capable of sawing a man in two. The carpenter answered "Sure enough". He was then given the grisly task, and before he left, he asked him whether Melec should be sawn across or along the length. The emperor said the sawing should proceed lengthwise, from the head downwards. He told, however, Boachasra's sons, they should follow the carpenter and decide for themselves how best to take revenge upon the murderer (i.e., Melec) of their father. Taking with him 8 of the public executioner's assistants, the master carpenter went to the prison where Melec was held, two of his brand new saws packed in cloth, in order to keep from Melec information of the intended manner of execution. Melec was now placed on a mule, bound with an iron chain, and led to the public square, where some 4000 of his relatives and members of his tribe were assembled. These made a "terrifying" spectacle through screaming, and clawing their faces in a public display of grief. Melec, on the other hand, seemed unperturbed, calmly smoking from his tobacco pipe. When taken down from the mule, Melec's clothes were removed, damning letters "proving" his treason was cast in the fire.

Then, he was strapped onto a board, and placed upon a sawbench, his arms and legs fastened. The executioner's team then sought to start by sawing him from the head downwards, but Boucasra's sons intervened, and demanded that one began between Melec's legs instead, because otherwise, he would die too quickly. Under the terrible screams of Melec and his relatives, thus began his execution. Once they had sawed him up to the navel, they pulled out the saw in order to commence from the other side. Melec is said to have been still conscious, asking for some water. His friends, though, thought it best to hasten his demise and shorten his sufferings, and the executioners went on, sawing him from skull to navel so he fell apart. In the process, chunks of flesh were ripped out by the saw's teeth, causing blood to splatter everywhere, thus making the execution quite unbearable to watch.

Around 300 other conspirators were impaled alive, and another report states that in addition to these, some other 20 chief conspirators had their arms and legs sawed off, and left to expire in the marketplace.

1721 The sawing of Larbe Shott

19 July 1721, a noble descended from the Andalusian Moors, Larbe Shott was put to the saw. He had spent considerable time at Gibraltar, and one of the crimes imputed to him was to have spent time in Christian kingdoms without his emperor's leave. Furthermore, he had been found guilty of defiling himself with Christian women, and often drunk alcohol. In short, he was charged as an apostate and unbeliever, in addition to being charged with having invited the "Spaniards" to invade Barbary (i.e., treason). They brought him to one of the gates in the city, fastened him between two boards, and sawed him in two, from skull and downwards. After his death, Mulay Ishmael pardoned him, so that his body could be picked up and given a decent burial at least, instead of being eaten by the dogs.[1571]

Americas

Swiss sawing

In 1757, a French officer was executed by his men in a mutiny on Cat Island in current-day Mississippi. Three of the mutineers were eventually captured and brought to New Orleans for trial. After conviction, two of the mutineers died on the French wheel. The last mutineer, a Swiss from the Karrer regiment, was allegedly, nailed into a coffin-shaped wooden box, and it was sawed into with a cross-cut saw. This claim of a Swiss being sawed in two was first made by the French captain and traveller Jean Bernard Bossu in his 1768 *Nouveaux Voyages aux Indes Occidentales*, translated into English by Johann Reinhold Forster in 1771.[1572]

Commenting on Bossu's general reliability in a footnote to his essay *A Map within an Indian Painting?*, jurist Morris S. Arnold says the following: "Bossu's books contain a lot of tall tales, so one needs to be cautious about relying on him".[1573] Bossu claims that being "sawed asunder" was a traditional Swiss military punishment, and alleges that one Swiss mutineer actually committed suicide to avoid that punishment.[1574] Therefore, the one who was allegedly sawed in half had his punishment as governed by Swiss military law, rather than French. An incident from 1741 (in Louisbourg, Canada) shows that at that time, when two Frenchmen and a Swiss were executed, Swiss mercenary troops had been placed under French military law, rather than under Swiss.[1575] Furthermore, detailing the recorded executions in the Swiss Canton of Zürich through the 15th-18th century, Gerold Meyer von Knonau records 1445 executions in total, none of them being through death by sawing.[1576]

Haitian revolution

In August 1791, a great slave revolt broke out at Saint-Domingue, eventually leading to Haitian independence. In the process, some 4,000 white planters and their family members were massacred.[1577] One of the victims was a carpenter by trade, Robert. The rebels decided he "should die in the way of his occupation" and accordingly fastened him between two boards and sawed him apart.[1578]

Asia

Levant

An episode from the Crusades

In 1123, Joscelin de Courtenay and Baldwin II were separately ambushed and surprised by a Turkish emir, Balac, and made prisoners at the castle at Quartapiert. Some 50 Armenians, bound by oath to Joscelin as Count of Edessa, decided to free their liege lord as well as Baldwin II. Dressed as monks and pedlars, they gained entry in the town where the two nobles were held captive, and managed, through massacre, to take control of the castle. Joscelin slipped out in order to raise a force, while Baldwin II and his nephew Galeran remained behind to hold the castle. Apprised of the capture of the castle, Balac sent quickly a force to recapture it, and Baldwin II saw no possibility of holding it. Graciously, Balac took Baldwin and his nephew merely prisoners. Not so merciful was he towards the Armenians: Several of them were flayed, others buried up to the neck and used as target practice, the rest were sawn apart.[1579]

The Assassins

The Assassins, a misnomer for the Nizari, an Ismaili sect, had an independent kingdom in the Levant during the age of the Crusades, and were feared and loathed by Muslims and Christians alike. The Jewish traveller Benjamin of Tudela, travelling the region around 1157 notes that the Assassins were reputed to saw in two the kings of other peoples, if they managed to capture them.[1580]

Ottoman Empire

A number of accounts exist where the Ottomans are said to have sawn persons in two, most of them said to occur in Mehmed the Conqueror's reign (1451–81).

1453 conquest of Constantinople

A number of cruel excesses against the populace of Constantinople is said to have happened in the wake of the taking of the city. according to one rendering of the tale:[1581] <templatestyles src="Template:Quote/styles.css"/>

> They no sooner found themselves masters of it, than they began to exercise On the inhabitants the most unremitting barbarities, destroying them by every method of ingenious cruelty. Some they roasted alive on spits, others they starved, some they flayed alive, and left them in that horrid manner to perish; many were sawn asunder, and others torn to pieces by horses. Three days and nights was the city given to spoil, in which time the soldiers were licensed to commit every enormity

1460 Capture of Mystras

After the last Despot of Morea, Demetrios Palaiologos in 1460 switched allegiance to the Turks and gave them entry to Mystras, a tale grew up that the actual castellan at the castle of Mystras was ordered sawn in two. This tale was "well known" in later centuries, whatever actual veracity.[1582]

1460 Michael Szilágyi

In 1460, the Hungarian general Michael Szilágyi was seized by the Turks, and since he was regarded as a traitor and spy, he was sawed in half at Constantinople.[1583]

1460-64 campaigns and slaughter in the Morea

In the following years, inhabitants in Greece under the Venetians fought several battles in the Morea. In 1464, for example, a small city is said to have been subdued, and 500 prisoners sent to Constantinople. There, they were put to the saw, according to one account.[1584]

1463 conquest of Mytilene, Lesbos

The Knights Hospitallers, then stationed at Rhodes, sent several knights to aid in the defence of Mytilene from the Turks. They eventually surrendered, under promise of having their lives spared. Instead, according to some reports, they were sawed asunder.[1585] According to Kenneth Meyer Setton, the sultan had actually promised to spare the heads of some 400 knights, and sawed them in half to keep his oath of not harming the heads.[1586]

1469/1470 conquest of Negroponte

The Triarchy of Negroponte, a Crusader state or *Stato da Màr* under control of the Republic of Venice, was extinguished by the capture of the city in 1469/1470, and the governor Paolo Erizzo, is said to treacherously to have been ordered sawn in two, after have being promised his life would be spared. The sultan, Mehmed the Conqueror, is said to have cut off the head of Erizzo's daughter by his own hands, because she would not yield to his desires.[1587]

1473 the arsonist at Gallipoli

In 1473, a Sicilian called Anthony, is said to have managed set fire to the sultan's ships at the Sanjak of Gelibolu, Gallipoli. After being captured at Negroponte, he was brought before the sultan who asked him what harm had been done to him that he performed such an evil deed? The young man answered that he simply wanted to harm the enemy of Christianity in some glorious way. The sultan is said to have ordered that Anthony should be sawn in two.[1588]

1480 invasion of Otranto

In 1480, the Ottomans, led by Gedik Ahmed Pasha, invaded mainland Italy, occupying Otranto. A general massacre, of disputed magnitude,[1589] occurred. Archbishop Stefano Pendinelli was, by some reports, ordered to be sawn in half.[1590]

1611 revolt of Dionysius the Philosopher

Dionysius the Philosopher led an eventually unsuccessful revolt against the Ottomans, seeking to establish a power base at Ioannina. Dionysius was flayed alive, and his skin, stuffed with straw, was sent as a present to the sultan, Ahmed I, at Constantinople. The other principal conspirators were said to be punished in various ways, some were burnt alive, others impaled, and yet others sawn asunder.[1591]

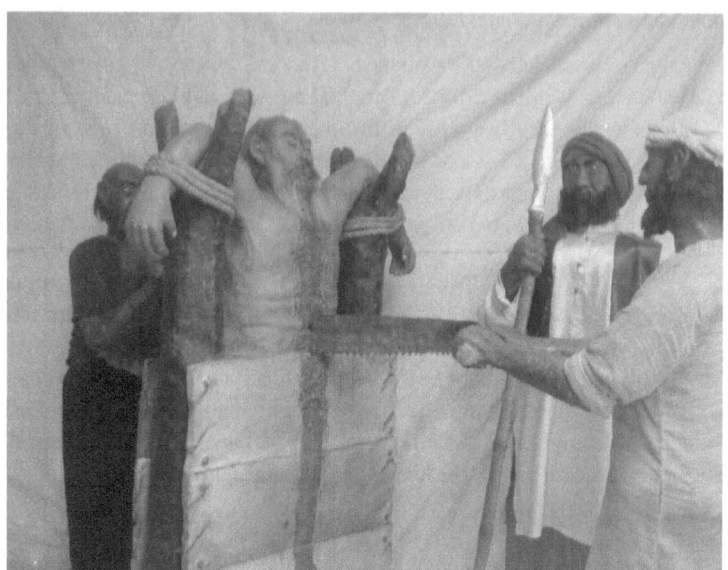

Figure 208: *Martyrdom of Bhai Mati Das*

The mythologized death of Rhigas, the protomartyr of Greek independence

Rigas Feraios (1760–98), was an early Greek patriot, whose struggle for independence of Greece preceded with about 30 years the general uprising known as the Greek War of Independence. His actual manner of death has garnered many tales; Encyclopædia Britannica 1911, for example, states that he was shot in the back.[1592] Yet others state that he was strangled. Some 19th century stories report that he was sawn in two.[1593] Finally, one source asserts he was beheaded.[1594]

Mughal Empire

The Sikh Bhai Mati Das, a follower of the 9th guru, Guru Tegh Bahadur was in 1675 AD ordered executed by emperor Aurangzeb, along with several other prominent Sikhs, including their Guru, because of their refusal to convert to Islam. Bhai Mati Das was sawed in half, the others in different manners.[1595]

Burma

Several reports state that even in the 1820s, sawing criminals in two was an occasional punishment in Burma for "certain offenses". The criminals were fastened between two planks prior to the sawing.[1596] However, this might possibly have been conflated by reports of *disembowelment*, for which eyewitness reports exist.[1597]

The Burmese general Maha Bandula is said to have had one of his high-ranking officers sawn in two, due to some act of disobedience, the person being fastened between two planks for that purpose.[1598]

Vietnam

Martyrdom of Augustin Huy

On occasion, a confusion of reports may exist where, for example, performed post-mortem indignities are misinterpreted as the actual manner of execution:

In 1839, the governor of Vietnam's Nam Định Province summoned five hundred soldiers to a banquet to pressure them into trampling upon a cross in renunciation of Christianity. Most of the guests complied, but three Catholic soldiers refused.[1599] One of the Vietnamese Martyrs, Augustin Huy, is reported by some sources to have been sawed in two.[1600] Others report that he was hacked to death,[1601] or cut in two.[1602] But, a letter from 1839, just three weeks after the execution 12 June, states that he was beheaded.:[1603]<templatestyles src="Template:Quote/styles.css"/>

> *'I have to announce to you the death of two Tonquinese, who here shed their blood for the faith on the 12th of June, 1839. They were beheaded near the port of Cua-thuan-an, the principal port of Hue. Their bodies were first cut into five pieces and then cast into the sea.*

Imperial China

Technique

The movement of a saw may cause a body to sway back and forth making the process difficult for the executioners. The Chinese overcame this problem by securing the victim in an upright position between two boards firmly fixed between stakes driven deep into the ground. Two executioners, one at each end of the saw, would saw downwards through the stabilized boards and enclosed victim.[1604] Whether sawing as an execution method actually existed, or that cases referred to are garbled accounts of the "slow slicing" method of execution will remain an open question.

Tang dynasty

The emperor Zhaozong of Tang (r. 888–904) is said to have commanded one of his prisoners sawn asunder.[1605]

Qing dynasty

When the last emperor of the Ming dynasty committed suicide in 1644, the new emperor had one of the previous regime's strongest supporters, Chen, said to be viceroy of Canton, sawed in two. However, growing in popularity in his martyrdom, the new regime condemned the execution of Chen, declared him to have been a holy man, and erected a pagoda in Canton for his memory.[1606]

Europe

Spain

Morisco revolt

In the aftermath of the destruction of the last Islamic kingdom in Spain, Granada in 1492, the Moriscoes, the descendants of Muslims and those who still were, in secret, adherents of Islam, felt increasingly persecuted. In 1568, the Morisco revolt broke out, under leadership of Aben Humeya. The crushing of the revolt was extremely bloody, and at Almería 1569, the historian Luis del Marmol Carvajal states that one Morisco was sawn apart alive.[1607]

La Mancha rebellion

In the Spanish rebellion of 1808 against the occupying French forces, reports exist that some French officers were sawed in two. In one of those reports, it is colonel Rene (or Frene[1608]) who met this fate.[1609] In another report, Rene was merely thrown into a kettle of boiling water, whereas the officers Caynier and Vaugien were the ones sawed in two.[1610]

Russia

1812 the *Grande Armée*

After the Fire of Moscow in September 1812, the French Grande Armée had not exactly endeared itself to the local population. The peasant population is said to have become embittered, fanaticized, and even developed an effective guerrilla. In addition, the "wild Cossacks" lurked about, and both groups of Russians could be a deadly enemy to solitary French soldiers. Some of those unfortunates are said to have been sawed apart.[1611]

Hungary

1848 Revolution

The Hungarian Revolution of 1848 was a bitter struggle where different ethnicities and people of different religious persuasions committed atrocities against others. A decidedly partisan pamphlet from 1850, *Ungarns gutes recht (The well-founded right of Hungary)* from 1850, states that in the struggles around Banat, some 4,000 Serbians, spurred on by the preaching of the Metropolitan of Karlovci, Josif Rajačić, committed heinous deeds against the Hungarians. Women, children and old men were mutilated, roasted over slow fires, some sawn apart.[1612]

Cultural references

Tortures in Hell

Hindu mythology

In Hindu lore, Yama is the god of death. He determines the punishments to those who were wicked in life. Those guilty of robbing a Brahmin, are to be sawn apart while being in *Naraka* (Hell).[1613]

Chinese mythology

Sawing people asunder is one of the punishments said to occur in Buddhist Hell, and the priests knew how to make a visible spectacle of sufferings in the beyond, by commissioning artists to make paintings the populace were meant to see and reflect upon:[1614]<templatestyles src="Template:Quote/styles.css"/>

> At a Buddhist temple in Canton, at certain seasons of the year, the court is set round with pictures, which pourtray in a fearful manner the sufferings of the dead. Some are sawn asunder; some are gored with pitchforks; some are thrown into a cauldron of boiling water; others are burnt. The artists, under the gifted instruction of the priests, succeeded in representing every sight that is terrible to the eye or revolting to the senses. In the recess at Mongha beforementioned, a few of these choice subjects were displayed with an edifying effect. The presumed existence of a place of torment brings a revenue into the coffers of the priest, who is assumed to have the power of appeasing the wrath of the judges..

Segare la vecchia

In Italy and Spain, a curious tradition of "segare la vecchia" ("sawing the old woman") was upheld on Laetare Sunday (Mid-Lent Sunday) in hamlets and towns, well into the 19th century. The custom consisted of the boys running about to find the "oldest woman in the village", and then make a wooden effigy in her likeness. Then, the wooden figure was sawn across the middle. The folklorist Jacob Grimm regards this as an odd spring ritual, in which the "old year"/winter is symbolically defeated. He also notes that a rather similar custom existed in his day among Southern Slavs.[1615]

Bibliography

 Wikimedia Commons has media related to *Sawing (torture)*.

- Abbott, G. (2004). *Execution: A Guide To The Ultimate Penalty*. Summersdale Publishers Ltd. ISBN 1-84024-433-X.<templatestyles src="Module:Citation/CS1/styles.css"></templatestyles>
- Anonymous (1850). *Ungarns gutes recht:eine historische denkschrift von einem diplomaten*[1616]. London: W.M. Watts. Retrieved 2013-02-28.<templatestyles src="Module:Citation/CS1/styles.css"></templatestyles>
- Asiatic Journal (1840). *Asiatic Journal, volume 32 New series*[1617]. London: Allen&co. Retrieved 2013-02-28.<templatestyles src="Module:Citation/CS1/styles.css"></templatestyles>
- von der Aurachl, Ph. S. (1859). *Das Heil kommt nicht aus Oesterreich: Eine Stimme aus Bayern*[1618]. Berlin: Ferdinand Riegel. Retrieved 2013-02-28.<templatestyles src="Module:Citation/CS1/styles.css"></templatestyles>
- Benjamin of Tudela; Martinet, Adam (tr) (1858). *Reisetagbuch:Ein Beitr. zur Kenntniß d. Juden in d. Diaspora während d. XII. Jhs*[1619]. Bamberg. Retrieved 2013-02-28.<templatestyles src="Module:Citation/CS1/styles.css"></templatestyles>
- Bridgman, Elijah C.; Williams, Samuel W. (1841). *The Chinese Repository, Volume 10*[1620]. Canton: Bridgman and Williams. Retrieved 2013-02-28.<templatestyles src="Module:Citation/CS1/styles.css"></templatestyles>
- Busnot, Dominique (1716). *Das Leben des Blutdürstigen Tyrannen Muley-Ismael, jetztregierenden Kaysers von Marocco*[1621]. Hamburg: von Wiering. Retrieved 2013-02-28.<templatestyles src="Module:Citation/CS1/styles.css"></templatestyles>

- Censer, Jack; Hunt, Lynn (2001). *Liberty, Equality, Fraternity: Exploring the French Revolution*. University Park, Pennsylvania: Pennsylvania State University Press. ISBN 0-271-02088-1.<templatestyles src="Module:Citation/CS1/styles.css"></templatestyles>
- Chateaubriand, François-Réné (1812). *Travels in Greece, Palestine, Egypt, and Barbary during the years 1806 and 1807, Volume 2*[1622]. London: h. Colburn. Retrieved 2013-02-28.<templatestyles src="Module:Citation/CS1/styles.css"></templatestyles>
- Coleman-Norton, P.R. (1948). *The Twelve Tables*[1623]. Princeton Univ. Dept. of Classics. ASIN B0007HKWAO[1624]. Retrieved 2013-02-28.<templatestyles src="Module:Citation/CS1/styles.css"></templatestyles>
- Collins, Arthur; Brydges, Sir Egerton (1812). *Collins's Peerage of England; Genealogical, Biographical, and Historical, Volum 6*[1625]. London: F. C. and J. Rivington, Otridge and son. Retrieved 2013-02-28.<templatestyles src="Module:Citation/CS1/styles.css"></templatestyles>
- Deinl, Franz (1830). *Römisches Martyrologium, wie es von dem Papste Gregor dem Dreyzehnten eingerichtet, und von Benedikt dem Vierzehnten verbessert wurde*[1626]. Munich: Daisenberger. Retrieved 2013-02-28.<templatestyles src="Module:Citation/CS1/styles.css"></templatestyles>
- Dignas, Beate; Winter, Engelbert (2007). *Rome and Persia in late antiquity: neighbours and rivals*. Cambridge University Press.<templatestyles src="Module:Citation/CS1/styles.css"></templatestyles>
- Diodorus Seculus; Wurm, Julius F. (tr.) (1840). *Historische Bibliothek, Volum 19*[1627]. Stuttgart: J.B. Metzler. Retrieved 2013-02-28.<templatestyles src="Module:Citation/CS1/styles.css"></templatestyles>
- Du Pin, Louis E. (1699). *A compleat history of the canon and writers of the books of the Old and New Testament: by way of dissertation with useful remarks on that subject, Volume 1*[1628]. London: H. Rhodes. Retrieved 2013-02-28.<templatestyles src="Module:Citation/CS1/styles.css"></templatestyles>
- Edwards, Bryan (1819). *The History, Civil and Commercial, of the British West Indies, Volum 3*[1629]. London: G. and W.B. Whittaker. Retrieved 2013-02-28.<templatestyles src="Module:Citation/CS1/styles.css"></templatestyles>
- Fallmerayer, Jakob P. (1836). *Geschichte der Halbinsel Morea während des Mittelalters: Bd. Morea, durch innere Kriege zwischen Franken und Byzantin verwüstet und von albanesischen Colonisten überschwemmt, wird endlich von den Türken erobert. Von 1250-1500*

- *nach Christus*[1630]. Stuttgart: J.G. Cotta'schen Buchhandlung. Retrieved 2013-02-28.<templatestyles src="Module:Citation/CS1/styles.css"></templatestyles>
- de Ferreras, Juan; Semler, Johann S. (1760). *Algemeine Historie von Spanien: Mit den Zusätzen der französischen Uebersetzung nebst der Fortsetzung bis auf gegenwärtige Zeit, Volume 10*[1631]. Halle: Gebauer. Retrieved 2013-02-28.<templatestyles src="Module:Citation/CS1/styles.css"></templatestyles>
- Forster, Johann R.; Bossu, Jean-Bernard (1771). *Travels Through that Part of North America Formerly Called Louisiana, Volum 1*[1632]. London: T. Davies. Retrieved 2013-02-28.<templatestyles src="Module:Citation/CS1/styles.css"></templatestyles>
- Foxe, John (1840). *Book of Martyrs: A Universal History of Christian Martyrdom from the Birth of Our Blessed Saviour to the Latest Periods of Persecution, Volumes 1-2*[1633]. Philadelphia: E.C. Biddle. Retrieved 2013-02-28.<templatestyles src="Module:Citation/CS1/styles.css"></templatestyles>
- Foy, Maximilien S. (1827). *Geschichte des Krieges auf der pyrenäischen Halbinsel unter Napoleon, 3*[1634]. Stuttgart: Francky. Retrieved 2013-02-28.<templatestyles src="Module:Citation/CS1/styles.css"></templatestyles>
- Geyer, J.K. (1738). *Christ-Catholische Hauß-Postill Oder Auslegung Deren Sonn- und Feyertäglichen Evangelien, Volume 2*[1635]. Passau: Lang. Retrieved 2013-02-28.<templatestyles src="Module:Citation/CS1/styles.css"></templatestyles>
- Gibbon, Edward (1776). *The History of the Decline and Fall of the Roman Empire, Volum 1*[1636]. London: W. Strahan and T. Cadell. Retrieved 2013-02-28.<templatestyles src="Module:Citation/CS1/styles.css"></templatestyles>
- Gliddon, George R. (1841). *A Memoir on the Cotton of Egypt*[1637]. London: J. Madden. Retrieved 2013-02-28.<templatestyles src="Module:Citation/CS1/styles.css"></templatestyles>
- Grimm, Jacob (1835). *Deutsche Mythologie*[1638]. Göttingen: Dieterichsche Buchhandlung. Retrieved 2013-02-28.<templatestyles src="Module:Citation/CS1/styles.css"></templatestyles>
- Grumeza, Ion (2010). *The Roots of Balkanization: Eastern Europe C.E. 500-1500*[1639]. Lanham, Maryland: University Press of America. ISBN 9780761851356. Retrieved 2013-02-28.<templatestyles src="Module:Citation/CS1/styles.css"></templatestyles>
- Günther, Johannes; Schulz, Otto A. (1856). *Handbuch für Autographensammler*[1640]. Leipzig: O.A. Schulz. Retrieved 2013-02-28.<templatestyles src="Module:Citation/CS1/styles.css"></

templatestyles>
- Hahn, Heinrich (1860). *Geschichte der katholischen Missionen seit Jesus Christus bis auf die neueste Zeit: Für die Mitglieder der katholischen Missions-Vereine und alle Freunde der Missionen, Volum 3*[1641]. Cologne: DuMont-Schauberg. Retrieved 2013-02-28.<templatestyles src="Module:Citation/CS1/styles.css"></templatestyles>
- Head, Duncan; Heath, Ian (1982). *Armies of the Macedonian and Punic Wars 359 BC to 146 BC: Organisation, Tactics, Dress and Weapons*. Wargames Research Group.<templatestyles src="Module:Citation/CS1/styles.css"></templatestyles>
- Heyne, Carl T. (1840). *Geschichte Napoleons von der Wiege bis zum Grabe: Für alle Völker deutschen Sinnes und deutscher Zunge in Wort und Bild, Volum 2*[1642]. Chemnitz: Goedsche. Retrieved 2013-02-28.<templatestyles src="Module:Citation/CS1/styles.css"></templatestyles>
- Hughes, Thomas S. (1820). *Travels in Sicily, Greece & Albania, Volum 2*[1643]. London: J. Mawman. Retrieved 2013-02-28.<templatestyles src="Module:Citation/CS1/styles.css"></templatestyles>
- Inderbitzi, Thomas (1840). *Annalen der Verbreitung des Glaubens: Monatsschr. D. Vereins der Glaubensverbreitung, Volum 8*[1644]. Mainz: Kirchheim, Schott&Thielmann. Retrieved 2013-02-28.<templatestyles src="Module:Citation/CS1/styles.css"></templatestyles>
- Institution for the Progation of the Faith (1840). *Annals of the propagation of the faith: a periodical collection of letters from the bishops and missionaries employed in the missions of the old and new word, volume 1*[1645]. London: Andrews. Retrieved 2013-02-28.<templatestyles src="Module:Citation/CS1/styles.css"></templatestyles>
- Judson, Ann H. (1823). *An account of the American Baptist mission to the Burman empire: in a series of letters, addressed to a gentleman in London*[1646]. London: J. Butterworth & Son and T. Clark. Retrieved 2013-02-28.<templatestyles src="Module:Citation/CS1/styles.css"></templatestyles>
- Knonau, Gerold M. von (1846). *1901 Reprint: Der canton Zürich, historisch-geographisch-statistisch geschildert von den ältesten zeiten bis auf die gegenwart Volume 2*[1647]. Zürich: Huber und compagnie.<templatestyles src="Module:Citation/CS1/styles.css"></templatestyles>
- Knowles, James D. (1830). *Life of Mrs. Ann H. Judson: late missionary to Burmah*[1648]. Philadelphia: American Sunday school union. Retrieved 2013-02-28.<templatestyles src="Module:Citation/CS1/styles.css"></templatestyles>
- von Kreckwitz, Abraham (1654). *Sylvula Politico-Historica Lustwäldlin*

Allerhand Politischer Gnomen und Historien: Auß vielen Glaubwürdigen Scribenten meistes Auß dem Latein- vnnd Frantzösischen Inns Deütsche transferiret, Vnd Summarisch ohn allen ornat also verfasset Daß es in Täglicher Conversation Discoursen vnd Gesprächen Fug- vnd Nutzlich kan gebraucht werden, Volume 1[1649]. Leipzig: Riese. Retrieved 2013-02-28.<templatestyles src="Module:Citation/CS1/styles.css"></templatestyles>

- Lay, George T. (1841). *The Chinese as they are: their moral, social, and literary character. A new analysis of the language; with succinct views of their principal arts and sciences*[1650]. London: W. Ball and Co. Retrieved 2013-02-28.<templatestyles src="Module:Citation/CS1/styles.css"></templatestyles>
- Lempriere, John; Lord, Eleazar (1825). *Lempriere's universal biography:containing a critical and historical account of the lives, characters, and labours of eminent persons, in all ages and countries. Together with selections of foreign biography from Watkin's dictionary, recently published, and about eight hundred original articles of American biography, Volume 1*[1651]. New York: R. Lockwood. Retrieved 2013-02-28.<templatestyles src="Module:Citation/CS1/styles.css"></templatestyles>
- Lewis, G.Malcolm; Arnold, Morris S. (1998). *"A Map within an Indian Painting?" in Cartographic Encounters: Perspectives on Native American Mapmaking and Map Use*[1652]. Chicago: University of Chicago Press. ISBN 9780226476940. Retrieved 2013-02-28.<templatestyles src="Module:Citation/CS1/styles.css"></templatestyles>
- Majer, Friedrich; Gruber, Johann G. (1804). *Allgemeines Mythologisches Lexicon: Aus Original-Quellen bearbeitet. Welche die nicht altklassischen Mythologien, nämlich die heiligen Mythen und Fabeln, so wie die religiösen Ideen und Gebräuche der Sinesen, Japaner ... enthält, volume 2*[1653]. Weimar: Verlag des Landes-Industrie-Comptoirs. Retrieved 2013-02-28.<templatestyles src="Module:Citation/CS1/styles.css"></templatestyles>
- Mignot, Vincent; Hawkins, A. (tr) (1787). *The history of the Turkish, or Ottoman Empire: from its foundation in 1300, to the peace of Belgrade in 1740. To which is prefixed An historical discourse on Mahomet and his successors, Volum 1*[1654]. Exeter: R. Thorn. Retrieved 2013-02-28.<templatestyles src="Module:Citation/CS1/styles.css"></templatestyles>
- Murray, J (1829). *The Quarterly Review, volume 41*[1655]. London: J. Murray. Retrieved 2013-02-28.<templatestyles src="Module:Citation/CS1/styles.css"></templatestyles>
- Napier, William F. P. (1862). *History of the war in the Peninsula and

in the south of France: from the year 1807 to the year 1814, Volum 1[1656]. New York: W.J. Widdleton. Retrieved 2013-02-28.<templatestyles src="Module:Citation/CS1/styles.css"></templatestyles>
- Napier, William F. P. (1839). *History of the war in the Peninsula and in the south of France: from the year 1807 to the year 1814, Volum 1*[1657]. Paris: Charles Hingray. Retrieved 2013-02-28.<templatestyles src="Module:Citation/CS1/styles.css"></templatestyles>
- Osborne, T. (1742). *An Universal History, from the Earliest Account of Time to the Present; Compiled from Original Authors and Illustrated with Maps, Cuts, Notes, Chronological and Other Tables, Volum 6*[1658]. London: T. Osborne et. al. Retrieved 2013-02-28.<templatestyles src="Module:Citation/CS1/styles.css"></templatestyles>
- Osborne, T. (1744). *An Universal History, from the Earliest Account of Time to the Present; Compiled from Original Authors and Illustrated with Maps, Cuts, Notes, Chronological and Other Tables, Volum 2*[1659]. London: T. Osborne et. al. Retrieved 2013-02-28.<templatestyles src="Module:Citation/CS1/styles.css"></templatestyles>
- Osborne, T. (1747). *An Universal History, from the Earliest Account of Time to the Present; Compiled from Original Authors and Illustrated with Maps, Cuts, Notes, Chronological and Other Tables, Volum 5*[1660]. London: T. Osborne et. al. Retrieved 2013-02-28.<templatestyles src="Module:Citation/CS1/styles.css"></templatestyles>
- Pachtler, Georg M. (1861). *Das Christenthum in Tonkin und Cochinchina, dem heutigen Annamreiche: von seiner Einführung bis auf die Gegenwart*[1661]. Paderborn: F. Schöningh. Retrieved 2013-02-28.<templatestyles src="Module:Citation/CS1/styles.css"></templatestyles>
- Pouqueville, Francois C.H.L. (1813). *Travels in the Morea, Albania, and Other Parts of the Ottoman Empire*[1662]. London: Henry Colburn. Retrieved 2013-02-28.<templatestyles src="Module:Citation/CS1/styles.css"></templatestyles>
- Reider, William D, (1841). *The new tablet of memory; or, Recorder of remarkable events, alphabetically arranged, from the earliest period*[1663]. London: John Clements. Retrieved 2013-02-28.<templatestyles src="Module:Citation/CS1/styles.css"></templatestyles>
- Rhodes, Henry (1706). *The Present State of Europe, Or, The Historical and Political Mercury, Volum 17*[1664]. London: Henry Rhodes. Retrieved 2013-02-28.<templatestyles src="Module:Citation/CS1/styles.css"></templatestyles>
- Rosenmüller, E.F.K. (1820). *Das alte und neue Morgenland oder Erläuterungen der heiligen Schrift aus der natürlichen Beschaffenheit, den Sagen, Sitten und Gebräuchen des Morgenlandes, Volum*

- 5^{1665}. Leipzig: Baumgärtner. Retrieved 2013-02-28.<templatestyles src="Module:Citation/CS1/styles.css"></templatestyles>
- Sadler, Johann E.; Heim, Franz J. (1858). *Vollständiges Heiligen-Lexikon, oder Lebensgeschichten aller Heiligen, Seligen aller Orte und aller Jahrhunderte, deren Andenken in der katholischen Kirche gefeiert oder sonst geehrt Wird*[1666]. Augsburg: F.C. Retrieved 2013-02-28.<templatestyles src="Module:Citation/CS1/styles.css"></templatestyles>
- Salisbury, A. (1830). *A History of the most distinguished martyrs: in various ages and countries of the world*[1667]. Philadelphia: A. Salisbury. Retrieved 2013-02-28.<templatestyles src="Module:Citation/CS1/styles.css"></templatestyles>
- Scott, G.R. (1995). *A History Of Torture*. Merchant Book Company Limited. ISBN 1-85958-174-9.<templatestyles src="Module:Citation/CS1/styles.css"></templatestyles>
- Schild, Wolfgang (1997). *Die Geschichte der Gerichtsbarkeit*. Munich: Callwey Verlag 1980. Lizenz für Nikol Verlagsgesellschaft mbH, Hamburg.<templatestyles src="Module:Citation/CS1/styles.css"></templatestyles>
- Schmauss, Johann J. (1719). *Ausführliches Heiligen-Lexicon: Darinn Das gottseelige Leben und der Tugend-Wandel, das standhaffte Leyden und Sterben, und die grossen Wunderwercke aller Heiligen Gottes... Beschrieben werden*[1668]. Cologne and Frankfurt. Retrieved 2013-02-28.<templatestyles src="Module:Citation/CS1/styles.css"></templatestyles>
- Setton, Kenneth M (1978). *The Papacy and the Levant, 1204-1571: The Fifteenth Century, volume 2*[1669]. Philadelphia: American Philosophical Society. ISBN 9780871691279. Retrieved 2013-02-28.<templatestyles src="Module:Citation/CS1/styles.css"></templatestyles>
- Singha, H.S (2000). *The Encyclopedia of Sikhism*[1670]. New Delhi: Hemkunt Press. ISBN 9788170103011. Retrieved 2013-02-28.<templatestyles src="Module:Citation/CS1/styles.css"></templatestyles>
- Smedley, Edward (1832). *Sketches from Venetian history, volume 2*[1671]. New York: J, J. Harper. Retrieved 2013-02-28.<templatestyles src="Module:Citation/CS1/styles.css"></templatestyles>
- Sozomen (1846). *A History of the Church in nine books, from A.D. 324 to A.D.440*[1672]. London: S. Bagster and Sons. Retrieved 2013-02-28.<templatestyles src="Module:Citation/CS1/styles.css"></templatestyles>
- Warnekros, Heinrich E. (1832). *Entwurf der Hebräischen Alterthümer*[1673]. Weimar: Hoffmann. Retrieved 2013-02-28.<templatestyles

- src="Module:Citation/CS1/styles.css"></templatestyles>
- Watkins, John (1806). *A biographical, historical and chronological dictionary*[1674]. London: Richard Phillips. Retrieved 2013-02-28.<templatestyles src="Module:Citation/CS1/styles.css"></templatestyles>
- Webber, Christopher; McBride, Angus (2001). *The Thracians 700 BC-AD 46 (Men-at-Arms)*. Osprey Publishing.<templatestyles src="Module:Citation/CS1/styles.css"></templatestyles>
- Wigand, Otto (1844). *Wigands Vierteljahrsschrift volume 1*[1675]. Leipzig: Otto Wigand. Retrieved 2013-02-28.<templatestyles src="Module:Citation/CS1/styles.css"></templatestyles>
- Windus, John (1725). *A journey to Mequinez, the residence of the present emperor of Fez and Morocco: On the occasion of Commodore Stewart's embassy thither for the redemption of the british captives in the year 1721*[1676]. London: J. Tonson. Retrieved 2013-02-28.<templatestyles src="Module:Citation/CS1/styles.css"></templatestyles>
- Yates, William H. (1843). *The Modern History and Condition of Egypt, Its Climate, Diseases, and Capabilities, Volum 2*[1677]. London: Smith, Elder and Company. Retrieved 2013-02-28.<templatestyles src="Module:Citation/CS1/styles.css"></templatestyles>

Web resources

- Suetonius; Rolfe, J.C. (tr.) (1914). "The Lives of the Twelve Caesars"[1678]. Loeb Classical Library. Retrieved 2013-02-28.<templatestyles src="Module:Citation/CS1/styles.css"></templatestyles>
- catholic.org. "St. Tarbula"[1679]. catholic.org. Retrieved 2013-02-28.<templatestyles src="Module:Citation/CS1/styles.css"></templatestyles>
- Encyclopædia Britannica 1911. "Constantine Rhigas"[1680]. theodora.com. Retrieved 2013-02-28.<templatestyles src="Module:Citation/CS1/styles.css"></templatestyles>
- catholic Online. "St. Domingo Nicolas Dat Dinh"[1681]. catholic.org. Retrieved 2013-02-28.<templatestyles src="Module:Citation/CS1/styles.css"></templatestyles>

Scaphism

Scaphism, also known as **the boats**, is an alleged ancient Persian method of execution. The word comes from the Greek σκάφη, *skáphe*, meaning "anything scooped (or hollowed) out". It entailed trapping the victim between two boats, feeding and covering him[1682] with milk and honey, and allowing him to fester and be devoured by vermin. The primary source is Plutarch's 'Life of Artaxerxes II', where he attributes the story to Ctesias; a notoriously suspect source.[1683,1684,1685]

Historical descriptions

The first mention of scaphism is Plutarch's description of the execution of Mithridates:

<templatestyles src="Template:Quote/styles.css"/>

> [*The king*] *decreed that Mithridates should be put to death in boats; which execution is after the following manner: Taking two boats framed exactly to fit and answer each other, they lay down in one of them the malefactor that suffers, upon his back; then, covering it with the other, and so setting them together that the head, hands, and feet of him are left outside, and the rest of his body lies shut up within, they offer him food, and if he refuse to eat it, they force him to do it by pricking his eyes; then, after he has eaten, they drench him with a mixture of milk and honey, pouring it not only into his mouth, but all over his face. They then keep his face continually turned towards the sun; and it becomes completely covered up and hidden by the multitude of flies that settle on it. And as within the boats he does what those that eat and drink must needs do, creeping things and vermin spring out of the corruption and rottenness of the excrement, and these entering into the bowels of him, his body is consumed. When the man is manifestly dead, the uppermost boat being taken off, they find his flesh devoured, and swarms of such noisome creatures preying upon and, as it were, growing to his inwards. In this way Mithridates, after suffering for seventeen days, at last expired.*
>
> —Plutarch, Life of Artaxerxes

The 12th century Byzantine chronicler Joannes Zonaras later described the punishment, based on Plutarch:

<templatestyles src="Template:Quote/styles.css"/>

> *The Persians outvie all other barbarians in the horrid cruelty of their punishments, employing tortures that are peculiarly terrible and long-drawn,*

namely the 'boats' and sewing men up in raw hides. But what is meant by the 'boats,' I must now explain for the benefit of less well informed readers. Two boats are joined together one on top of the other, with holes cut in them in such a way that the victim's head, hands, and feet only are left outside. Within these boats the man to be punished is placed lying on his back, and the boats then nailed together with bolts. Next they pour a mixture of milk and honey into the wretched man's mouth, till he is filled to the point of nausea, smearing his face, feet, and arms with the same mixture, and so leave him exposed to the sun. This is repeated every day, the effect being that flies, wasps, and bees, attracted by the sweetness, settle on his face and all such parts of him as project outside the boats, and miserably torment and sting the wretched man. Moreover his belly, distended as it is with milk and honey, throws off liquid excrements, and these putrefying breed swarms of worms, intestinal and of all sorts. Thus the victim lying in the boats, his flesh rotting away in his own filth and devoured by worms, dies a lingering and horrible death.

—Zonaras, Annals

In fiction

- In Shakespeare's *The Winter's Tale*, the rogue Autolycus tells the shepherd and his son that because Perdita has fallen in love with the prince, her adoptive father will be stoned, while her adoptive brother will be subjected to the following punishment: "He has a son,—who shall be flayed alive; then 'nointed over with honey, set on the head of a wasp's nest; then stand till he be three quarters and a dram dead; then recovered again with aqua-vitae or some other hot infusion; then, raw as he is, and in the hottest day prognostication proclaims, shall he be set against a brick wall, the sun looking with a southward eye upon him,—where he is to behold him with flies blown to death."
- In H. Rider Haggard's *The Ancient Allan* the protagonist Allan Quatermain experiences a vision of one of his past lives, in which he was a great Egyptian hunter named Shabaka. At one time he is condemned to "death by the boat" by the "King of kings" because of a hunting bet they had made. When Shabaka asks what is to happen to him, he is told by a eunuch "This, O Egyptian slayer of lions. You will be laid upon a bed in a little boat upon the river and another boat will be placed over you, for these boats are called the Twins, Egyptian, in such a fashion that your head and your hands will project at one end and your feet at the other. There you will be left, comfortable as a baby in its cradle, and twice every day the best of food and drink will be brought to you. Should your appetite fail, moreover, it will be my duty to revive it by pricking your

eyes with the point of a knife until it returns. Also after each meal I shall wash your face, your hands and your feet with milk and honey, lest the flies that buzz about them should suffer hunger, and to preserve your skin from burning by the sun. Thus slowly you will grow weaker and at length fall asleep. The last one who went into the boat—he, unlucky man, had by accident wandered into the court of the House of Women and seen some of the ladies there unveiled—only lived for twelve days, but you, being so strong, may hope to last for eighteen."

External links

- Traité des instruments de martyre et des divers modes de supplice employés par les paiens contre les chrétiens[1686] (French)
- BREWER: Dictionary of Phrase and Fable, Scaphism[1687]
- Artaxerxes by Plutarch[1688]
- Lexicon Universale, Historiam Sacram Et Profanam Omnis aevi, omniumque Gentium[1689] (Late Latin/some Greek)
- Tortures and Torments of the Christian Martyrs[1690]

Lingchi

Lingchi	
"*Lingchi* in Traditional (top) and Simplified (bottom) Chinese characters"	
Traditional Chinese	凌遲
Simplified Chinese	凌迟

Lingchi

Transcriptions	
Standard Mandarin	
Hanyu Pinyin	língchí
Wade–Giles	ling^2-ch'ih^2
IPA	[lɪŋ.tsʰɻ̩]
Yue: Cantonese	
Yale Romanization	lìhng-chìh
IPA	[lɐ̏ŋ.tsʰȉː]
Jyutping	ling^4-ci^4
Southern Min	
Tâi-lô	lêng-tî

Lingchi (Chinese: 凌遲), translated variously as the **slow process**, the **lingering death**, or **slow slicing**, and also known as **death by a thousand cuts**, was a form of torture and execution used in China from roughly 900 CE until it was banned in 1905. It was also used in Vietnam. In this form of execution, a knife was used to methodically remove portions of the body over an extended period of time, eventually resulting in death.

Lingchi was reserved for crimes viewed as especially severe, such as treason. Some Westerners were executed in this manner. Even after the practice was outlawed, the concept itself has still appeared across many types of media.

Etymology

The term *lingchi* first appeared in a line in Chapter 28 of the classical philosophical text *Xunzi*. The line originally described the difficulty in travelling in a horse-drawn carriage on mountainous terrain. Later on, it was used to describe the prolonging of a person's agony when the person is being killed.

Description

The process involved tying the condemned prisoner to a wooden frame, usually in a public place. The flesh was then cut from the body in multiple slices in a process that was not specified in detail in Chinese law, and therefore most likely varied. The punishment worked on three levels: as a form of public humiliation, as a slow and lingering death, and as a punishment after death.

According to the Confucian principle of filial piety, to alter one's body or to cut the body are considered unfilial practices. *Lingchi* therefore contravenes the demands of filial piety. In addition, to be cut to pieces meant that the body of the victim would not be "whole" in spiritual life after death. This method of execution became a fixture in the image of China among some Westerners.

Figure 209: *An 1858 illustration from the French newspaper Le Monde illustré, of the lingchi execution of a French missionary, Auguste Chapdelaine, in China. In actuality, Chapdelaine died from physical abuse in prison, and was beheaded after death.*

Lingchi could be used for the torture and execution of a living person, or applied as an act of humiliation after death. It was meted out for major offences such as high treason, mass murder, patricide/matricide or the murder of one's master or employer. Emperors used it to threaten people and sometimes ordered it for minor offences.[1691,1692] There were forced convictions and wrongful executions.[1693,1694] Some emperors meted out this punishment to the family members of their enemies.

While it is difficult to obtain accurate details of how the executions took place, they generally consisted of cuts to the arms, legs, and chest leading to amputation of limbs, followed by decapitation or a stab to the heart. If the crime was less serious or the executioner merciful, the first cut would be to the throat causing death; subsequent cuts served solely to dismember the corpse.

Art historian James Elkins argues that extant photos of the execution clearly show that the "death by division" (as it was termed by German criminologist Robert Heindl) involved some degree of dismemberment while the subject was living.[1695] Elkins also argues that, contrary to the apocryphal version of "death by a thousand cuts", the actual process could not have lasted long. The condemned individual is not likely to have remained conscious and aware (if even alive) after one or two severe wounds, so the entire process could not have included more than a "few dozen" wounds.

In the Yuan dynasty, 100 cuts were inflicted[1696] but by the Ming dynasty there were records of 3,000 incisions.[1697,1698] It is described as a fast process lasting no longer than 15 to 20 minutes. Available photographic records seem to prove the speed of the event as the crowd remains consistent across the series of photographs. Moreover, these photographs show a striking contrast between the stream of blood that soaks the left flank of the victim and the lack of blood on the right side, possibly showing that the first or the second cut has reached the heart. The *coup de grâce* was all the more certain when the family could afford a bribe to have a stab to the heart inflicted first. Some emperors ordered three days of cutting[1699,1700] while others may have ordered specific tortures before the execution,[1701] or a longer execution.[1702,1703,1704] For example, records showed that during Yuan Chonghuan's execution, Yuan was heard shouting for half a day before his death.[1705]

The flesh of the victims may also have been sold as medicine.[1706] As an official punishment, death by slicing may also have involved slicing the bones, cremation, and scattering of the deceased's ashes.

Western perceptions

The Western perception of *lingchi* has often differed considerably from the actual practice, and some misconceptions persist to the present. The distinction between the sensationalised Western myth and the Chinese reality was noted by Westerners as early as 1895. That year, Australian traveller George Ernest Morrison, who claimed to have witnessed an execution by slicing, wrote that "*lingchi* [was] commonly, and quite wrongly, translated as 'death by slicing into 10,000 pieces' — a truly awful description of a punishment whose cruelty has been extraordinarily misrepresented... The mutilation is ghastly and excites our horror as an example of barbarian cruelty; but it is not cruel, and need not excite our horror, since the mutilation is done, not before death, but after."

According to apocryphal lore, *lingchi* began when the torturer, wielding an extremely sharp knife, began by putting out the eyes, rendering the condemned incapable of seeing the remainder of the torture and, presumably, adding considerably to the psychological terror of the procedure. Successive rather minor cuts chopped off ears, nose, tongue, fingers, toes and genitals before proceeding to cuts that removed large portions of flesh from more sizable parts, e.g., thighs and shoulders.

The entire process was said to last three days, and to total 3,600 cuts. The heavily carved bodies of the deceased were then put on a parade for a show in the public. Some victims were reportedly given doses of opium to alleviate suffering.Wikipedia:Citation needed

John Morris Roberts, in *Twentieth Century: The History of the World, 1901 to 2000* (2000), writes "the traditional punishment of death by slicing... became part of the western image of Chinese backwardness as the 'death of a thousand cuts.'" Roberts then notes that slicing "was ordered, in fact, for K'ang Yu-Wei, a man termed the 'Rousseau of China', and a major advocate of intellectual and government reform in the 1890s."[1707]

Although officially outlawed by the government of the Qing dynasty in 1905, *lingchi* became a widespread Western symbol of the Chinese penal system from the 1910s on, and in Zhao Erfeng's administration. Three sets of photographs shot by French soldiers in 1904–05 were the basis for later mythification. The abolition was immediately enforced, and definite: no official sentences of *lingchi* were performed in China after April 1905.

Regarding the use of opium, as related in the introduction to Morrison's book, Meyrick Hewlett insisted that "most Chinese people sentenced to death were given large quantities of opium before execution, and Morrison avers that a charitable person would be permitted to push opium into the mouth of someone dying in agony, thus hastening the moment of decease." At the very least, such tales were deemed credible to British officials in China and other Western observers.

History

Lingchi existed under the earliest emperors,Wikipedia:Citation needed although similar but less cruel tortures were often prescribed instead. Under the reign of Qin Er Shi, the second emperor of the Qin dynasty, multiple tortures were used to punish officials.Wikipedia:Please clarify The arbitrary, cruel, and short-lived Liu Ziye was apt to kill innocent officials by *lingchi*. Gao Yang killed only six people by this method, and An Lushan killed only one man. *Lingchi* was known in the Five Dynasties period (907–960 CE); but, in one of the earliest such acts, Shi Jingtang abolished it. Other rulers continued to use it.

The method was prescribed in the Liao dynasty law codes, and was sometimes used. Emperor Tianzuo often executed people in this way during his rule. It became more widely used in the Song dynasty under Emperor Renzong and Emperor Shenzong.

Another early proposal for abolishing *lingchi* was submitted by Lu You (1125–1210) in a memorandum to the imperial court of the Southern Song dynasty. Lu You's elaborate argument against *lingchi* was piously copied and

Figure 210: *Execution of Joseph Marchand in Vietnam, 1835.*

transmitted by generations of scholars, among them influential jurists of all dynasties, until the late Qing dynasty reformist Shen Jiaben (1840–1913) included it in his 1905 memorandum that obtained the abolition. This anti-*lingchi* trend coincided with a more general attitude opposed to "cruel and unusual" punishments (such as the exposure of the head) that the Tang dynasty had not included in the canonic table of the Five Punishments, which defined the legal ways of punishing crime. Hence the abolitionist trend is deeply ingrained in the Chinese legal tradition, rather than being purely derived from Western influences.

Under later emperors, *lingchi* was reserved for only the most heinous acts, such as treason,[1708] a charge often dubious or false, as exemplified by the deaths of Liu Jin, a Ming dynasty eunuch, and Yuan Chonghuan, a Ming dynasty general. In 1542, *lingchi* was inflicted on a group of palace women who had attempted to assassinate the Jiajing Emperor, along with his favourite concubine, Consort Duan. The bodies of the women were then displayed in public. Reports from Qing dynasty jurists such as Shen Jiaben show that executioners' customs varied, as the regular way to perform this penalty was not specified in detail in the penal code.Wikipedia:Citation needed

Lingchi was also known in Vietnam, notably being used as the method of execution of the French missionary Joseph Marchand, in 1835, as part of the repression following the unsuccessful Lê Văn Khôi revolt.

An 1858 account by *Harper's Weekly* claimed the martyr Auguste Chapdelaine was killed by *lingchi*; in reality he was beaten to death.

As Western countries moved to abolish similar punishments, some Westerners began to focus attention on the methods of execution used in China. As early as 1866, the time when Britain itself moved to abolish its own cruel method of hanging, drawing, and quartering, Thomas Francis Wade, then serving with the British diplomatic mission in China, unsuccessfully urged the abolition of *lingchi*.

Lingchi remained in the Qing dynasty's code of laws for persons convicted of high treason and other serious crimes, but the punishment was abolished as a result of the 1905 revision of the Chinese penal code by Shen Jiaben.[1709]

Published accounts

- Sir Henry Norman, *The People and Politics of the Far East* (1895). Norman was a widely travelled writer and photographer whose collection is now owned by the University of Cambridge. Norman gives an eyewitness account of various physical punishments and tortures inflicted in a magistrate's court (*yamen*) and of the execution by beheading of 15 men. He gives the following graphic account of a *lingchi* execution but does not claim to have witnessed such an execution himself. "[The executioner] grasping handfuls from the fleshy parts of the body such as the thighs and breasts slices them away... the limbs are cut off piecemeal at the wrists and ankles, the elbows and knees, shoulders and hips. Finally the condemned is stabbed to the heart and the head is cut off."[1710]
- George Ernest Morrison, *An Australian in China* (1895) differs from some other reports in stating that most *lingchi* mutilations are in fact made post-mortem. Morrison wrote his description based on an account related by a claimed eyewitness: "The prisoner is tied to a rude cross: he is invariably deeply under the influence of opium. The executioner, standing before him, with a sharp sword makes two quick incisions above the eyebrows, and draws down the portion of skin over each eye, then he makes two more quick incisions across the breast, and in the next moment he pierces the heart, and death is instantaneous. Then he cuts the body in pieces; and the degradation consists in the fragmentary shape in which the prisoner has to appear in heaven."
- Tienstin (Tianjin), *The China Year Book* (1927), p. 1401, contains contemporary reports from fighting in Guangzhou (Canton) between the Nanjing government and Communist forces. Stories of various atrocities are related, including accounts of *lingchi*. There is no mention of opium, and these cases appear to be government propaganda.

- *The Times*, (9 December 1927), a journalist reported from the city of Guangzhou (Canton) that the Communists were targeting Christian priests and that "It was announced that Father Wong was to be publicly executed by the slicing process."
- George Roerich, "Trails to Inmost Asia" (1931), p . 119, relates the story of the assassination of Yang Tseng-hsin, Governor of Sinkiang in July 1928, by the bodyguard of his foreign minister Fan Yao-han. Fan was seized, and he and his daughter were both executed by *lingchi*, the minister made to watch his daughter's execution first. Roerich was not an eyewitness to this event, having already returned to India by the date of the execution.
- George Ryley Scott, *History of Torture* (1940) claims that many were executed this way by the Chinese Communist insurgents; he cites claims made by the Nanking government in 1927. It is perhaps uncertain whether these claims were anti-communist propaganda. Scott also uses the term "the slicing process" and differentiates between the different types of execution in different parts of the country. There is no mention of opium. Riley's book contains a picture of a sliced corpse (with no mark to the heart) that was killed in Guangzhou (Canton) in 1927. It gives no indication of whether the slicing was done post-mortem. Scott claims it was common for the relatives of the condemned to bribe the executioner to kill the condemned before the slicing procedure began.

Photographs

The first Western photographs of *lingchi* were taken in 1890 by William Arthur Curtis of Kentucky in Guangzhou (Canton).

French soldiers stationed in Beijing had the opportunity to photograph three different *lingchi* executions in 1905:

- Wang Weiqin (王維勤), a former official who killed two families, executed on 31 October 1904.
- Unknown, reason unknown, possibly a young deranged boy who killed his mother, and was executed in January 1905. Photographs were published in various volumes of Georges Dumas' *Nouveau traité de psychologie*, 8 vols., Paris, 1930–43, and again nominally by Bataille (in fact by Lo Duca), who mistakenly appended abstracts of Fou-tchou-li's executions as related by Carpeaux (see below).
- Fou-tchou-li or Fuzhuli (符珠哩),[1711] a Mongol guard who killed his master, the Prince of the Aohan Banner of Inner Mongolia, and who was executed on 10 April 1905; as *lingchi* was to be abolished two weeks later, this was presumably the last attested case of *lingchi* in Chinese history, or said Kang Xiaoba (康小八)[1712] Photographs appeared in books

by Matignon (1910), and Carpeaux (1913), the latter claiming (falsely) that he was present.Wikipedia:Citation needed Carpeaux's narrative was mistakenly, but persistently, associated with photographs published by Dumas and Bataille. Even related to the correct set of photos, Carpeaux's narrative is highly dubious; for instance, an examination of the Chinese judicial archives show that Carpeaux bluntly invented the execution decree. The proclamation is reported to state: "The Mongolian princes demand that the aforesaid Fou-Tchou-Le, guilty of the murder of Prince Ao-Han-Ouan, be burned alive, but the Emperor finds this torture too cruel and condemns Fou-Tchou-Li to slow death by *leng-tch-e* (different spelling of *lingchi*, cutting into pieces)."

Photographic material and other sources are available online at the Chinese Torture Database (Iconographic, Historical and Literary Approaches of an Exotic Representation) hosted by the Institut d'Asie Orientale (CNRS, France).

In popular culture

Accounts of *lingchi* or the extant photographs have inspired or referenced in numerous artistic, literary, and cinematic media. Some works have attempted to put the process in a historical context; others, possibly due to the scarcity of detailed historical information, have attempted to extrapolate the details or present innovations of method that may be products of an author's creative license. Some of these descriptions may have influenced modern public perceptions of the historic practice.

Non-fiction

Susan Sontag mentions the 1905 case in *Regarding the Pain of Others* (2003). One reviewer wrote that though Sontag includes no photographs in her book – a volume about photography – "she does tantalisingly describe a photograph that obsessed the philosopher Georges Bataille, in which a Chinese criminal, while being chopped up and slowly flayed by executioners, rolls his eyes heavenwards in transcendent bliss."

The philosopher Georges Bataille wrote about *lingchi* in *L'expérience intérieure* (1943) and in *Le coupable* (1944). He included five pictures in his *The Tears of Eros* (1961; translated into English and published by City Lights in 1989). Historians Timothy Brook, Jérome Bourgon and Gregory Blue, criticised Bataille for his language, mistakes and dubious content.

Literature

The "death by a thousand cuts" with reference to China is also mentioned in Malcolm Bosse's novel *The Examination*, Amy Tan's novel *The Joy Luck Club*, and Robert van Gulik's *Judge Dee* novels. The 1905 photos are mentioned in Thomas Harris' novel *Hannibal* and in Julio Cortázar's novel *Hopscotch*.

Film

Inspired by the 1905 photos, Chinese artist Chen Chien-jen created a 25-minute film called *Lingchi*, which has generated some controversy.

A scene of Lingchi also appeared on the film The Sand Pebbles (film).

References

 Wikimedia Commons has media related to *Lingchi*.

- Brook, Timothy; Bourgon, Jérôme; Blue, Gregory (2008). *Death by a Thousand Cuts*. Cambridge, MA: Harvard University Press. ISBN 978-0-674-02773-2.<templatestyles src="Module:Citation/CS1/styles.css"></templatestyles>
- Bourgon, Jérôme (2003). "Abolishing 'Cruel Punishments': A Reappraisal of the Chinese Roots and Long-Term Efficiency of the in Legal Reforms". *Modern Asian Studies*. **37** (4): 851–62. doi: 10.1017/S0026749X03004050[1713].<templatestyles src="Module:Citation/CS1/styles.css"></templatestyles>

Suffocation in ash

Suffocation in ash was a method of capital punishment in which the individual is suffocated by being in some way immersed into ash to cause asphyxiation. As an execution practice, it is attested from ancient Persia and within a certain Meso-American culture.

Ancient Persia

In ancient Persia, there existed an execution method where a tower/room was filled with ash, into which the condemned person was plunged. Wheels were constantly turned while he was alive, making the ash whirl about, and the person died by gradual suffocation as he inhaled the ash.[1714] The description can be found in Valerius Maximus and 2 Maccabees 13:5-8.[1715]

Reputedly, the first to suffer this punishment was Sogdianus. He killed his half-brother Xerxes II around 423 BC. Another half-brother, Ochus (later called Darius II) rebelled against him, and killed Sogdianus in this manner because he had promised Sogdianus he would not die by the sword, by poison or by hunger.[1716] At the instigation of his wife Parysatis, Darius II had his brother, Arsites, executed in the same manner for rebellion, along with Arsites' general Artyphius. Some time later, a rebelling general Pisuthnes met the same fate.

In about 162 BC, Menelaus, Jewish high priest at Jerusalem was apparently put to death in this manner by Lysias, regent for Antiochus V, on charges of rebellion.

Texcoco

Nezahualcoyotl, a 15th-century, pre-Columbian, non-Aztec Acolhuan ruler of Texcoco in modern Mexico, designed a law code that is partially preserved. Those who had engaged in the active role of homosexual anal intercourse were suffocated in a heap of ash. Their passive partners had their intestines pulled out, then their bodies were filled with ash, and finally, were burnt.

Stoning

Stoning, or **lapidation**, is a method of capital punishment whereby a group throws stones at a person until the subject dies. No individual among the group can be identified as the one who kills the subject. This is in contrast to the case of a judicial executioner. Often slower than other forms of execution, stoning within the context of contemporary Western culture is considered a form of execution by torture.

Stoning is called *rajm* (Arabic: رجم) in Islamic literature, and is a legal or customary punishment found in the United Arab Emirates, Iran, Iraq, Qatar, Mauritania, Saudi Arabia, Somalia, Sudan, Yemen, northern Nigeria, Aceh Province of Indonesia, Afghanistan, and tribal parts of Pakistan, including northwest Kurram Valley and the northwest Khwezai-Baezai region.[1717] In some countries, such as Afghanistan and Iraq, stoning has been declared illegal by the state, but is practiced extrajudicially. In several others, people have been sentenced to death by stoning, but the sentence has not been carried out. In modern times, allegations of stoning are politically sensitive; the government of Iran, for example, describes allegations of stoning as political propaganda.

Ancient history

Judaism

Torah

The Jewish Torah (the first five books of the Hebrew Bible: Genesis, Exodus, Leviticus, Numbers, and Deuteronomy) serves as a common religious reference for Judaism. Stoning is the method of execution mentioned most frequently in the Torah. (Murder is not mentioned as an offense punishable by stoning, but it seems that a member of the victim's family was allowed to kill the murderer; see avenger of blood.) The crimes punishable by stoning were the following:

- Touching Mount Sinai while God was giving Moses the Ten Commandments, Exodus 19:13[1718]
- An ox that gores someone to death should be stoned, Exodus 21:28[1719]
- Breaking Sabbath, Numbers 15:32[1720]–36
- Giving one's "seed" (presumably child sacrifice of one's offspring) "to Molech" Leviticus 20:2[1721]-5
- Having a "familiar spirit" (or being a necromancer) or being a "wizard", Leviticus 20:27[1722]
- Enticing others to polytheism, Deuteronomy 13:7[1723]–11

Figure 211: *Saint Stephen, first martyr of Christianity, painted in 1506 by Marx Reichlich (1460–1520) (Pinakothek of Munich)*

- Cursing God, Leviticus 24:10[1724]–16
- Engaging in idolatry, Deuteronomy 17:2-7; or seducing others to do so, Deuteronomy 13:7[1723]–12
- "Rebellion" against parents, after repeated warnings, Deuteronomy 21:18[1725]–21
- Getting married as though a virgin, when not a virgin, Deuteronomy 22:13[1726]–21
- Sexual intercourse between a man and a woman engaged to another man in a town, since she did not cry out, Deuteronomy 22:23[1727]–24; both parties should be stoned to death
- Forced sexual intercourse between a man and a woman engaged to another man in a field, where no one could hear her cries and save her, Deuteronomy 22:25[1728]–27; the man should be stoned

Describing the stoning of those who entice others to apostates from Judaism, the Torah states: <templatestyles src="Template:Quote/styles.css"/>

If thy brother, the son of thy mother, or thy son, or thy daughter, or the wife of thy bosom, or thy friend, which [is] as thine own soul, entice thee secretly, saying, Let us go and serve other gods, which thou hast not known,

Stoning

Figure 212: *Virasundara is stoned to death on the order of Rajasinha II of Kandy (Sri Lanka, c. 1672)*

thou, nor thy fathers; [Namely], of the gods of the people which [are] round about you, nigh unto thee, or far off from thee, from the [one] end of the earth even unto the [other] end of the earth; Thou shalt not consent unto him, nor hearken unto him; neither shall thine eye pity him, neither shalt thou spare, neither shalt thou conceal him: But thou shalt surely kill him; thine hand shall be first upon him to put him to death, and afterwards the hand of all the people. And thou shalt stone him with stones, that he die; because he hath sought to thrust thee away from the LORD thy God, which brought thee out of the land of Egypt, from the house of bondage.

—*Deuteronomy 13:6–10*[1729]

A case noted in the Bible, not falling into any of the above categories, was that of Achan, stoned to death together with his sheep, other livestock and his children for having pillaged valuables from Jericho during Joshua's Conquest of Canaan.

Mishna

The Talmud describes four methods of execution: stoning, pouring molten lead down the throat of the condemned person, beheading, and strangulation (see Capital and corporal punishment in Judaism). The Mishna gives the following list of persons who should be stoned.[1730]

"To the following sinners stoning applies – הנסקלין הן אלו

- one who has had relations with his mother – האם על הבא
- with his father's wife – האב אשת ועל
- with his daughter-in-law – הכלה ועל
- a human male with a human male – הזכור ועל
- or with cattle – הבהמה ועל
- and the same is the case with a woman who uncovers herself before cattle – הבהמה את המביאה והאשה
- with a blasphemer – והמגדף
- an idolater – כוכבים עבודת והעובד
- he who sacrifices one of his children to Molech – למולך מזרעו והנותן
- one that occupies himself with familiar spirits – אוב ובעל
- a wizard – וידעוני
- one who violates Sabbath – השבת את והמחלל
- one who curses his father or mother – ואמו אביו ומקלל
- one who has assaulted a betrothed damsel – המאורסה נערה על והבא
- a seducer who has seduced men to worship idols – והמסית
- and the one who misleads a whole town – והמדיח
- a witch (male or female) – והמכשף
- a stubborn and rebellious son – ומורה" סורר ובן

As God alone was deemed to be the only arbiter in the use of capital punishment, not fallible people, the Sanhedrin made stoning a hypothetical upper limit on the severity of punishment.[1731]

Prior to early Christianity, particularly in the Mishnah, doubts were growing in Jewish society about the effectiveness of capital punishment in general (and stoning in particular) in acting as a useful deterrent. Subsequently, its use was dissuaded by the central legislators. The Mishnah states:

> *A Sanhedrin that puts a man to death once in seven years is called destructive. Rabbi Eliezer ben Azariah says that this extends to a Sanhedrin that puts a man to death even once in seventy years. Rabbi Akiba and Rabbi Tarfon say: Had we been in the Sanhedrin none would ever have been put to death. Rabban Simeon ben Gamaliel says: they would have multiplied shedders of blood in Israel.*[1732]

In the following centuries the leading Jewish sages imposed so many restrictions on the implementation of capital punishment as to make it *de facto* illegal.

Figure 213: *The Punishment of Korah and the Stoning of Moses and Aaron (1480–1482), by Sandro Botticelli, Sistine Chapel, Rome.*

The restrictions were to prevent execution of the innocent, and included many conditions for a testimony to be admissible that were difficult to fulfill.

Philosopher Moses Maimonides wrote, "It is better and more satisfactory to acquit a thousand guilty persons than to put a single innocent one to death."[1733] He was concerned that the law guard its public perception, to preserve its majesty and retain the people's respect. He saw errors of commission as much more threatening to the integrity of law than errors of omission.[1734]

Mode of Judgment

In rabbinic law, capital punishment may only be inflicted by the verdict of a regularly constituted court of twenty-three qualified members. There must be the most trustworthy and convincing testimony of at least two qualified eyewitnesses to the crime, who must also depose that the culprit had been forewarned of the criminality and the consequences of his project. The culprit must be a person of legal age and of sound mind, and the crime must be proved to have been committed of the culprit's free will and without the aid of others.

On the day the verdict is pronounced, the convict is led forth to execution. The Torah law (Leviticus 19:18) prescribes, "Thou shalt love thy neighbor as thyself"; and the Rabbis maintain that this love must be extended beyond the limits of social intercourse in life, and applied even to the convicted criminal who, "though a sinner, is still thy brother" (Mak. 3:15; Sanh. 44a): "The spirit of love must be manifested by according him a decent death" (Sanh. 45a, 52a).

Torah law provides (Deut. 24:16), "The parents shall not be put to death for the children, neither shall the children be put to death for the parents; every man shall be put to death for his own sins", and rabbinic jurisprudence follows this principle both to the letter and in spirit. A sentence is not attended by confiscation of the convict's goods; the person's possessions descend to their legal heirs.

The Talmud limits the use of the death penalty to Jewish criminals who:

- (A) while about to do the crime were warned not to commit the crime while in the presence of two witnesses (and only individuals who meet a strict list of standards are considered acceptable witnesses); and
- (B) having been warned, committed the crime in front of the same two witnesses.

In theory, the Talmudic method of how stoning is to be carried out differs from mob stoning. According to the Jewish oral law, after the Jewish criminal has been determined as guilty before the Great Sanhedrin, the two valid witnesses and the sentenced criminal go to the edge of a two-story building. From there the two witnesses are to push the criminal off the roof of a two-story building. The two-story height is chosen as this height is estimated by the Talmud to effect a quick and painless demise but is not so high that the body will become dismembered. After the criminal has fallen, the two witnesses are to drop a large boulder onto the criminal – requiring both of the witnesses to lift the boulder together. If the criminal did not die from the fall or from the crushing of the large boulder, then any people in the surrounding area are to quickly cause him to die by stoning with whatever rocks they can find.

Islam

Islamic sharia law is based on the Quran and the hadith as primary sources.

Quran

The Qur'an does not mention the act of stoning (Rajm) for any crime.

Contrary to popular belief, the punishment for Adultery (Zina) in the Quran is not stoning to death but flogging with a 100 lashes (if the accuser can provide 4 witnesses to the act). If the accuser cannot produce 4 witnesses, he himself will be punished by flogging with 80 lashes. <templatestyles src="Template:Quote/styles.css"/>

> "The woman and the man guilty of fornication/adultery,- flog each of them with a hundred stripes: Let not compassion move you in their case, in a matter prescribed by Allah, if ye believe in Allah and the Last Day: and let a party of the Believers witness their punishment."

Figure 214: *Stoning of the Devil, 2006 Hajj*

—*Qur'an, Sura 24 (An-Nur), ayat 2*

> "And those who accuse chaste women then do not bring four witnesses, flog them, (giving) eighty stripes, and do not admit any evidence from them ever; and these it is that are the transgressors. Except those who repent after this and act aright, for surely Allah is Forgiving, Merciful."

—*Qur'an, Sura 24 (An-Nur), ayat 4-5*

Hadith

Hadith refers to orally transmitted reports of statements or actions attributed to Muhammad. It was forbidden to record any Hadith on paper by Muhammad himself, the first 4 righteous Caliphs after the death of Muhammed and the later Caliphs. They believed the Quran was clear, fully detailed, complete, perfect and sufficient. There were fears that people would confuse hadith with the Qur'an, influence would seep in from other creeds, fear for fabrications by heretics,for personal or political gain. The first Hadith (that have survived) were recorded 200 years after the prophets death. There were tens of thousands Muhaddiths who had each memorised at least 400,000 narrations along with the chain of narrators for each narration. Out of the hundreds of thousands of Hadith only a very, very small percentage were declared authentic (Sahih) by Hadith Scholars. Hadith Scholars used a number of methods of evaluation to determine the veracity of the recorded oral reports. This is achieved by analyzing the text of the report, the scale of the report's transmission, the routes through which the report was transmitted, the individual narrators involved in its transmission and cross-referincing the reports.

Muslims vary in degrees of acceptance of the Hadith. To many Sunnite and Shiite Muslims (different collections of) the hadith are almost on par with the Quran itself. To others the Quran is the word of Allah but the Hadith are the words and deeds of a human (the prophet Muhammed) transmitted down by the 200 years old fallible memory of men. Useful but not completely reliable. Some Muslims give little to no credence to the Hadith. Then there are also the different sets of Hadith accepted by different branches of Islam (Temporary Marriage or Female Genital Mutilation) who consider each other's Hadith fake.

Stoning in the Sunnah mainly follows on the Jewish stoning rules of the Torah. A few hadiths refer to Muhammad ordering the stoning of a marriedWikipedia:Verifiability Jewish man and a marriedWikipedia:Verifiability woman committing an illegal sexual act after consulting the Torah.

<templatestyles src="Template:Quote/styles.css"/>

> *Narrated Ibn 'Umar: A Jew and Jewess were brought to the Prophet on a charge of committing an illegal sexual intercourse. The Prophet asked the Jews, "What do you (usually) do with them?" They said, "We blacken their faces and disgrace them." He said, "Bring here the Torah and recite it, if you are truthful." They (fetched it and) came and asked a one-eyed man to recite. He went on reciting till he reached a portion on which he put his hand. The Prophet said, "Lift up your hand!" He lifted his hand up and behold, there appeared the verse of Ar-Rajm (stoning of the adulterers to death). Then he said, "O Muhammad! They should be stoned to death but we conceal this Divine Law among ourselves." Then the Prophet ordered that the two sinners be stoned to death and, and they were stoned to death, and I saw the man protecting the woman from the stones.*
>
> *— Volume 9, Book 93, Number 633: (See Hadith No. 809, Vol. 8)*

<templatestyles src="Template:Quote/styles.css"/>

> *Narrated by 'Abdullah bin 'Umar:The Jews came to Allah's Apostle and told him that a man and a woman from amongst them had committed illegal sexual intercourse. Allah's Apostle said to them, "What do you find in the Torah (old Testament) about the legal punishment of Ar-Rajm (stoning)?" They replied, (But) we announce their crime and lash them." Abdullah bin Salam said, "You are telling a lie; Torah contains the order*

of Rajm. " They brought and opened the Torah and one of them solaced his hand on the Verse of Rajm and read the verses preceding and following it. Abdullah bin Salam said to him, "Lift your hand. " When he lifted his hand, the Verse of Rajm was written there. They said, "Muhammad has told the truth; the Torah has the Verse of Rajm. The Prophet then gave the order that both of them should be stoned to death. ('Abdullah bin 'Umar said, "I saw the man leaning over the woman to shelter her from the stones. "

— Volume 4, Book 56, Number 829:

In a few others, a Bedouin man is lashed, while a Jewish woman is stoned to death, for having sex outside marriage.[1735]

Stoning is described as punishment in multiple hadiths.[1736] Shia and Sunni hadith collections differ because scholars from the two traditions differ as to the reliability of the narrators and transmitters and the Imamah. Shi'a sayings related to stoning can be found in Kitab al-Kafi,[1737] and Sunni sayings related to stoning can be found in the Sahih Bukhari and Sahih Muslim.[1738] Based on these hadiths, in some Muslim countries, married adulterers are sentenced to death, while consensual sex between unmarried people results in 100 lashes.

Hadiths describe stoning as punishment under sharia.[1739,1740,1741] In others stoning is prescribed as punishment for illegal sex between man and woman, illegal sex by a slave girl, as well as anyone involved in any homosexual relations. In some sunnah, the method of stoning, by first digging a pit and partly burying the person's lower half in it, is described.[1742]

<templatestyles src="Template:Quote/styles.css"/>

Narrated by Abu Huraira and Zaid bin Khalid Al-Juhani: A bedouin came to Allah's Apostle and said, "O Allah's apostle! I ask you by Allah to judge My case according to Allah's Laws." His opponent, who was more learned than he, said, "Yes, judge between us according to Allah's Laws, and allow me to speak." Allah's Apostle said, "Speak." He (i .e. the bedouin or the other man) said, "My son was working as a laborer for this (man) and he committed illegal sexual intercourse with his wife. The people told me that it was obligatory that my son should be stoned to death, so in lieu of that I ransomed my son by paying one hundred sheep and a slave girl. Then I asked the religious scholars about it, and they informed me that my son must be lashed one hundred lashes, and be exiled for one year, and the wife of this (man) must be stoned to death." Allah's Apostle said, "By Him in Whose Hands my soul is, I will judge between you according to Allah's Laws. The slave-girl and the sheep are to be returned to you, your son is to receive a hundred lashes and be exiled for one year. You, Unais, go to the wife of this (man) and if she confesses her guilt, stone

> her to death." Unais went to that woman next morning and she confessed. Allah's Apostle ordered that she be stoned to death.
> —*Sahih al-Bukhari, 3:50:885*[1743] see also *Sahih al-Bukhari, 3:49:860*[1744], *8:82:842*[1745], *9:89:303*[1746]

<templatestyles src="Template:Quote/styles.css"/>

> Narrated by Ash-Shaibani: I asked 'Abdullah bin Abi 'Aufa about the Rajam (stoning somebody to death for committing illegal sexual intercourse). He replied, "The Prophet carried out the penalty of Rajam," I asked, "Was that before or after the revelation of Surat-an-Nur?" He replied, "I do not know."
> —*Sahih al-Bukhari, 8:82:824*[1747] see also *Sahih al-Bukhari, 8:82:809*[1748] *9:92:432*[1749]

<templatestyles src="Template:Quote/styles.css"/>

> Aisha reported: Abd b. Zam'a said Messenger of Allah, he is my brother as he was born on the bed of my father from his slave-girl. Allah's Messenger looked at his resemblance and found a clear resemblance with 'Utba. (But) he said: He is yours 'Abd (b. Zam'a), for the child is to be attributed to one on whose bed it is born, and stoning for a fornicator.
> —*Sahih Muslim, 8:3435*[1750] see also *Sahih Muslim, 17:4216*[1751], *17:4191*[1752], *17:4212*[1753]

Islamic jurisprudence (fiqh)

Stoning (Arabic: رجم, *Rajm*, sometimes spelled as *Rajam*) has been extensively discussed in the texts of early, medieval and modern era Islamic jurisprudence (fiqh).[1754]

According to traditional jurisprudence, zina can include adultery (of married parties), fornication (of unmarried parties), prostitution, bestiality, and rape. Classification of homosexual intercourse as zina differs according to legal school. Although stoning for zina is not mentioned in the Quran, all schools of traditional jurisprudence agreed on the basis of hadith that it is to be punished by stoning if the offender is *muhsan* (adult, free, Muslim, and having been married), with some extending this punishment to certain other cases and milder punishment prescribed in other scenarios. The offenders must have acted of their own free will. According to traditional jurisprudence, zina must be proved by testimony of four eyewitnesses to the actual act of penetration, or a confession repeated four times and not retracted later. The Maliki legal school also allows an unmarried woman's pregnancy to be used as evidence, but the punishment can be averted by a number of legal "semblances" (*shubuhat*), such as existence of an invalid marriage contract. These requirements made zina virtually impossible to prove in practice. Rape was traditionally prosecuted under different legal categories which used normal evidentiary rules.[1755] Making an accusation of zina without presenting the required eyewitnesses is called *qadhf* (القذف), which is itself a *hadd* crime[1756,1757] liable to a punishment of 80 lashes and to be unacceptable as witnesses unless they repent and reform.

According to the Islamic concept of *Li'an*, the testimony of a man who accuses his own wife without any other witnesses may be accepted if he swears by God four times that he is telling the truth with a fifth oath to incur God's condemnation if they be lying. In this case, if his wife counter swears, no punishment will be enforced.[1758]

One of the widely followed Islamic legal commentaries, *Al-Muwatta* by Malik ibn Anas, state that contested pregnancy is sufficient proof of adultery and the woman must be stoned to death.[1759]

Hanafi

Hanafi jurists have held that the accused must be a *muhsan* at the time of religiously disallowed sex, to be punished by *Rajm* (stoning). A *Muhsan* is an adult, free, Muslim who has previously enjoyed legitimate sexual relations in matrimony, regardless of whether the marriage still exists.[1760] In other words, stoning does not apply to someone who was never married in his or her life (only lashing in public is the mandatory punishment in such cases).[1761]

For evidence, Hanafi fiqh accepts the following: self-confession, or testimony of four male witnesses (female witness is not acceptable). Hanafi Islamic law literature specifies two types of stoning. One, when the punishment is based on *bayyina*, or concrete evidence (four male witnesses). In this case the person is bound, a pit dug, the bound person placed and partially buried inside the pit so that he or she may not escape, thereafter the public stoning punishment is executed. A woman sentenced to stoning must be partially buried up to her chest. The first stones are thrown by the witnesses and the accuser, thereafter the Muslim community present, stated Abū Ḥanīfa and other Hanafi scholars. In second type of stoning, when the punishment is based on self-confession, the stoning is to be performed without digging a pit or partially burying the person. In this case, the qadi (judge) should throw the first stone before other Muslims join in. Further, if the person flees, the person is allowed to leave.

Hanafi scholars specify the stone size to be used for *Rajm*, to be the size of one's hand. It should not be too large to cause death too quickly, nor too small to extend only pain.

Hanafis have traditionally held that the witnesses should throw the first stones in case the conviction was brought about by witnesses, and the *qadi* must throw the first stones in case the conviction was brought about by a confession.[1762]

Shafi'i

The Shafii school literature has the same Islamic law analysis as the Hanafi. However, it recommends, that the first stone be thrown by the Imam or his deputy in all cases, followed by the Muslim community witnessing the stoning punishment.[1763]

Hanbali

Hanbali jurist Ibn Qudamah states, "Muslim jurists are unanimous on the fact that stoning to death is a specified punishment for the married adulterer and adulteress. The punishment is recorded in number of traditions and the practice of Muhammad stands as an authentic source supporting it. This is the view held by all Companions, Successors and other Muslim scholars with the exception of Kharijites."

Hanbali Islamic law sentences all forms of consensual but religiously illegal sex as punishable with *Rajm*.[1764]

Maliki

Maliki school of jurisprudence (fiqh) holds that stoning is the required punishment for illegal sex by a married or widowed person, as well as for any form of homosexual relations among men. Malik ibn Anas, founded of Maliki fiqh, considered pregnancy in an unmarried woman as a conclusive proof of zina. He also stated that contested pregnancy is also sufficient proof of adultery and any Muslim woman who is pregnant by a man who she is not married to, at the time of getting pregnant, must be stoned to death. Later Maliki Muslim scholars admitted the concept of "sleeping embryo", where a divorced woman could escape the stoning punishment, if she remained unmarried and became pregnant anytime within five years of her divorce, and it was assumed that she was impregnated by her previous husband but the embryo remained dormant for five years.

Aztec

Stoning appears to have been practiced by the Aztecs.Wikipedia:Citation needed

Modern history

As of September 2010, stoning is a punishment that is included in the laws in some countries including Saudi Arabia, Sudan, Iran, Somalia, Yemen and some predominantly Muslim states in northern Nigeria as punishment for Zina ("adultery by married persons").

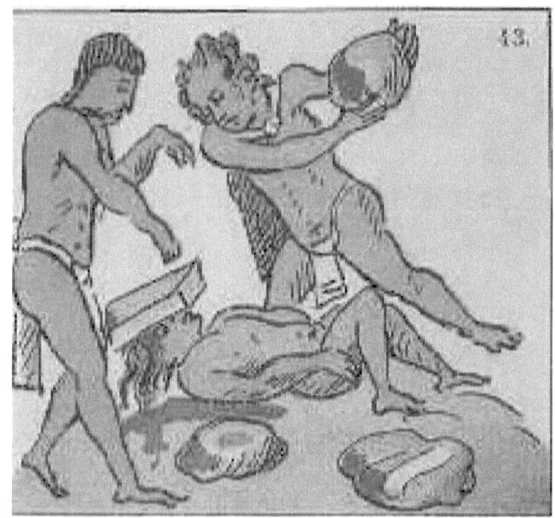

Figure 215: *An Aztec adulterer being stoned to death; Florentine Codex*

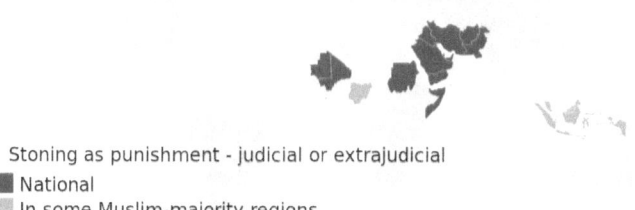

Stoning as punishment - judicial or extrajudicial
■ National
In some Muslim-majority regions

Figure 216: *A map showing countries where public stoning is a judicial or extrajudicial form of punishment, as of 2013.*

Afghanistan

Stoning is illegal in Afghanistan, but is sometimes carried out by tribal leaders and Taliban insurgents extrajudicially in certain parts of the country. Before the Taliban government, most areas of Afghanistan, aside from the capital, Kabul, were controlled by warlords or tribal leaders. The Afghan legal system depended highly on an individual community's local culture and the political or religious ideology of its leaders. Stoning also occurred in lawless areas, where vigilantes committed the act for political purposes. Once the Taliban took over, it became a form of punishment for certain serious crimes or adultery. After the fall of the Taliban government, the Karzai administration reenforced the 1976 penal code which made no provision for the use of stoning as a punishment. In 2013, the Ministry of Justice proposed public stoning as punishment for adultery. However, the government had to back down from the proposal after it was leaked and triggered international outcry. While stoning is officially banned in Afghanistan, it has continued to be reported occasionally as a crime.[1765]

Brunei

In October 2013, Sultan Hassanal Bolkiah announced that stoning, along with flogging and amputations, would be added to the country's laws in accordance with sharia law.

Indonesia

On 14 September 2009, the outgoing Aceh Legislative Council passed a bylaw that called for the stoning of married adulterers.[1766] However, then governor Irwandi Yusuf refused to sign the bylaw, thereby keeping it a law without legal force and, in some views, therefore still a law *draft*, rather than **actual** law.[1767] In March 2013, the Aceh government removed the stoning provision from its own draft of a new criminal code.[1768]

Iran

The Iranian judiciary officially placed a moratorium on stoning in 2002; however, in 2007, the Iranian judiciary confirmed that a man who had been convicted of adultery 10 years earlier, was stoned to death in Qazvin province. In 2008, the judiciary tried to eliminate the punishment from the books in legislation submitted to parliament for approval. In 2009, two people were stoned to death in Mashhad, Razavi Khorasan Province as punishment for the crime of adultery.[1769] In early 2013, a spokesman for judicial committee of Iran's parliament stated that stoning is no longer mentioned in Iran's legislation, but that punishment will remain the same as it is in Islamic law. He questioned

Western enmity against Iran, and termed the campaign to remove *rajm* as noise against the implementation of Islamic law in Iran.[1770] Legal scholars concur that while certain stoning-related passages have been removed from Iran's new penal code, other passages in the new code refer to stoning, and stoning remains a possible form of punishment under the new Iranian penal code. The most known case in Iran was the stoning of Soraya Manutchehri in 1986.

Methods

In the 2008 version of the Islamic Penal Code of Iran detailed how stoning punishments are to be carried out for adultery, and even hints in some contexts that the punishment may allow for its victims to avoid death:[1771]

Article 102 – An adulterous man shall be buried in a ditch up to near his waist and an adulterous woman up to near her chest and then stoned to death.

Article 103 – In case the person sentenced to stoning escapes the ditch in which they are buried, then if the adultery is proven by testimony then they will be returned for the punishment but if it is proven by their own confession then they will not be returned.

Article 104 – The size of the stone used in stoning shall not be too large to kill the convict by one or two throws and at the same time shall not be too small to be called a stone.

Depending upon the details of the case, the stoning may be initiated by the judge overseeing the matter or by one of the original witnesses to the adultery. Certain religious procedures may also need to be followed both before and after the implementation of a stoning execution, such as wrapping the person being stoned in traditional burial dress before the procedure.

The method of stoning set out in the 2008 code was similar to that in a 1999 version of Iran's penal code.[1772] Iran revised its penal code in 2013. The new code does not include the above passages, but does include stoning as a hadd punishment.[1773] For example, Book I, Part III, Chapter 5, Article 132 of the new Islamic Penal Code (IPC) of 2013 in the Islamic Republic of Iran states, "If a man and a woman commit zina together more than one time, if the death penalty and flogging or stoning and flogging are imposed, only the death penalty or stoning, whichever is applicable, shall be executed". Book 2, Part II, Chapter 1, Article 225 of the Iran's IPC released in 2013 states, "the hadd punishment for zina of a man and a woman who meet the conditions of ihsan shall be stoning to death".[1774,1775]

Iraq

In 2007, Du'a Khalil Aswad, a Yazidi girl, was stoned by her fellow tribesmen in northern Iraq for dating a Muslim boy.

In 2012 at least 14 youths were stoned to death in Baghdad, apparently as part of a Shi'ite militant campaign against Western-style "emo" fashion.

An Iraqi man was stoned to death, in August 2014, in the northern city of Mosul after one Sunni Islamic court sentenced him to die for the crime of adultery.[1776]

Nigeria

Since the sharia legal system was introduced in the predominantly Muslim north of Nigeria in 2000, more than a dozen Nigerian Muslims have been sentenced to death by stoning for sexual offences ranging from adultery to homosexuality. However, none of these sentences has actually been carried out. They have either been thrown out on appeal or commuted to prison terms as a result of pressure from human rights groups.

Pakistan

As part of Zia-ul-Haq's Islamization measures, stoning to death (*rajm*) at a public place was introduced into law via the 1979 Hudood Ordinances as punishment for adultery (*zina*) and rape (*zina-bil-jabr*) when committed by a married person. However, stoning has never been officially utilized since the law came into effect and all judicial executions occur by hanging. The first conviction and sentence of stoning (of Fehmida and Allah-Bakhsh) in September 1981 was overturned under national and international pressure. A conviction for adultery of Safia Bibi, a 13-year-old blind girl who alleged that she was raped by her employer and his son, was reversed and the conviction was set aside on appeal after bitter public criticism. Another conviction for adultery and sentence of stoning (of Shahida Parveen and Muhammad Sarwar) in early 1988 sparked outrage and led to a retrial and acquittal by the Federal Sharia Court. In this case the trial court took the view that notice of divorce by Shahida's former husband, Khushi Muhammad, should have been given to the Chairman of the local council, as stipulated under Section-7(3) of the *Muslim Family Laws Ordinance*, 1961. This section states that any man who divorces his wife must register it with the Union Council. Otherwise, the court concluded that the divorce stood invalidated and the couple became liable to conviction under the Adultery ordinance. In 2006, the ordinances providing for stoning in the case of adultery or rape were legislatively demoted from overriding status.

Extrajudicial stonings in Pakistan have been known to happen in recent times. In March 2013, Pakistani soldier Anwar Din, stationed in Parachinar, was publicly stoned to death for allegedly having a love affair with a girl from a village in the country's north western Kurram Agency. On 11 July 2013, Arifa Bibi, a young mother of two, was sentenced by a tribal court in Dera Ghazi Khan District, in Punjab, to be stoned to death for possessing a cell phone. Members of her family were ordered to execute her sentence and her body was buried in the desert far away from her village.

In February 2014, a couple in a remote area of Baluchistan province was stoned to death after being accused of an adulterous relationship. On 27 May 2014, Farzana Parveen, a 25-year-old married woman who was three months pregnant, was killed by being attacked with batons and bricks by nearly 20 members of her family outside the high court of Lahore in front of "a crowd of onlookers" according to a statement by a police investigator. The assailants, who allegedly included her father and brothers, attacked Farzana and her husband Mohammad Iqbal with batons and bricks. Her father Mohammad Azeem, who was arrested for murder, reportedly called the murder an "honor killing" and said "I killed my daughter as she had insulted all of our family by marrying a man without our consent." The man whose second wife Farzana had become, Iqbal, told a news agency that he had strangled his previous wife in order to marry Farzana, and police said that he had been released for killing his first wife because a "compromise" had been reached with his family.

Saudi Arabia

Legal stoning sentences have been reported in Saudi Arabia.

Sudan

In May 2012, a Sudanese court convicted Intisar Sharif Abdallah of adultery and sentenced her to death; the charges were appealed and dropped two months later. In July 2012, a criminal court in Khartoum, Sudan, sentenced 23-year-old Layla Ibrahim Issa Jumul to death by stoning for adultery. Amnesty International reported that she was denied legal counsel during the trial and was convicted only on the basis of her confession. The organization designated her a prisoner of conscience, "held in detention solely for consensual sexual relations", and lobbied for her release. In September, Article 126 of the 1991 Sudan Criminal Law, which provided for death by stoning for apostasy, was amended to provide for death by hanging.[1777]

Somalia

In October 2008, a girl, Aisha Ibrahim Duhulow, was buried up to her neck at a Somalian football stadium, then stoned to death in front of more than 1,000 people. The stoning occurred after she had allegedly pleaded guilty to adultery in a sharia court in Kismayo, a city that was controlled by Islamist insurgents. According to the insurgents she had stated that she wanted sharia law to apply. However, other sources state that the victim had been crying, had begged for mercy and had to be forced into the hole before being buried up to her neck in the ground. Amnesty International later learned that the girl was in fact 13 years old and had been arrested by al-Shabab militia after she had reported being gang-raped by three men.

In December 2009, another instance of stoning was publicised after Mohamed Abukar Ibrahim was accused of adultery by the Hizbul Islam militant group.

In September 2014, Somali al Shabaab militants stoned a woman to death, after she was declared guilty of adultery by an informal court.

United Arab Emirates

Stoning is a legal form of judicial punishment in UAE. In 2006, an expatriate was sentenced to death by stoning for committing adultery. Between 2009 and 2013, several people were sentenced to death by stoning. In May 2014, an Asian housemaid was sentenced to death by stoning in Abu Dhabi.

ISIL

Several adultery executions by stoning committed by IS have been reported in the autumn of 2014. The Islamic State's magazine, Dabiq, documented the stoning of a woman in Raqqa as a punishment for adultery.

In October 2014, IS released a video appearing to show a Syrian man stone his daughter to death for alleged adultery.[1778]

Views

Support

Among Christians

The late American Calvinist and Christian Reconstructionist cleric Rousas John (R. J.) Rushdoony, his son Mark and his son-in-law Gary North, supported the reinstatement of the Mosaic law's penal sanctions. Under such a system, the list of civil crimes which carried a death sentence by stoning would include homosexuality, adultery, incest, lying about one's virginity, bestiality, witchcraft, idolatry or apostasy, public blasphemy, false prophesying, kidnapping, rape, and bearing false witness in a capital case.[1779,1780]

Among Muslims

A survey conducted by the Pew Research Center in 2013 found varying support in the global Muslim population for stoning as a punishment for adultery (sex between people where at least one person is married; when both participants are unmarried they get 100 lashes). Highest support for stoning is found in Muslims of the Middle East-North Africa region and South-Asian countries while generally less support is found in Muslims living in the Mediterranean and Central Asian countries. Support is consistently higher in Muslims who want Sharia to be the law of the land than in Muslims who do not want Sharia. Support for stoning in various countries is as follows:

South Asia:

Pakistan (86% in all Muslims, 89% in Muslims who say Sharia should be the law of the land), **Afghanistan** (84% in all Muslims, 85% in Muslims who say Sharia should be the law of the land), **Bangladesh** (54% in all Muslims, 55% in Muslims who say Sharia should be the law of the land) **Middle East-North Africa:**

Palestinian territories (81% in all Muslims, 84% in Muslims who say Sharia should be the law of the land), **Egypt** (80% in all Muslims, 81% in Muslims who say Sharia should be the law of the land), **Jordan** (65% in all Muslims, 67% in Muslims who say Sharia should be the law of the land), **Iraq** (57% in all Muslims, 58% in Muslims who say Sharia should be the law of the land)

Southeast Asia:

Malaysia (54% in all Muslims, 60% in Muslims who say Sharia should be the law of the land), **Indonesia** (42% in all Muslims, 48% in Muslims who say Sharia should be the law of the land), **Thailand** (44% in all Muslims, 51% in Muslims who say Sharia should be the law of the land) **Sub-Saharan Africa:**

Niger (70% in all Muslims), **Djibouti** (67%), **Mali** (58%), **Senegal** (58%), **Guinea Bissau** (54%), **Tanzania** (45%), **Ghana** (42%), **DR Congo** (39%), **Cameroon** (36%), **Nigeria** (33%)

Central Asia:

Kyrgyzstan (26% in all Muslims, 39% in Muslims who say Sharia should be the law of the land), **Tajikistan** (25% in all Muslims, 51% in Muslims who say Sharia should be the law of the land), **Azerbaijan** (16%), **Turkey** (9% in all Muslims, 29% in Muslims who say Sharia should be the law of the land) **Southern and Eastern Europe:**

Russia (13% in all Muslims, 26% in Muslims who say sharia should be the law of the land), **Kosovo** (9% in all Muslims, 25% in Muslims who say Sharia should be the law of the land), **Albania** (6% in all Muslims, 25% in Muslims who say Sharia should be the law of the land), **Bosnia** (6% in all Muslims, 21% in Muslims who say Sharia should be the law of the land)

Places where substantial numbers of Muslims did not answer the survey's question or are undecided about whether they support stoning for adultery include Malaysia (19% of all Muslims), Kosovo (18%), Iraq (14%), Democratic Republic of the Congo (12%) and Tajikistan (10%).

Opposition

Stoning has been condemned by several human rights organizations. Some groups, such as Amnesty International and Human Rights Watch, oppose all capital punishment, including stoning. Other groups, such as RAWA (Revolutionary Association of the Women of Afghanistan), or the International Committee against Stoning (ICAS), oppose stoning *per se* as an especially cruel practice.

Specific sentences of stoning, such as the Amina Lawal case, have often generated international protest. Groups such as Human Rights Watch, while in sympathy with these protests, have raised a concern that the Western focus on stoning as an especially "exotic" or "barbaric" act distracts from what they view as the larger problems of capital punishment. They argue that the "more fundamental human rights issue in Nigeria is the dysfunctional justice system."

In Iran, the Stop Stoning Forever Campaign was formed by various women's rights activists after a man and a woman were stoned to death in Mashhad in May 2006. The campaign's main goal is to legally abolish stoning as a form of punishment for adultery in Iran.

Human rights

Stoning is condemned by human rights groups as a form of cruel and unusual punishment and torture, and a serious violation of human rights.

Women's rights

Stoning has been condemned as a violation of women's rights and a form of discrimination against women. Although stoning is also applied to men, the vast majority of the victims are reported to be women.[1781] According to the international group Women Living Under Muslim Laws stoning "is one of the most brutal forms of violence perpetrated against women in order to control and punish their sexuality and basic freedoms".

Amnesty International has argued that the reasons for which women suffer disproportionately from stoning include the fact that women are not treated

Figure 217: *The stoning of Saint Stephen (1863) by Gabriel-Jules Thomas*

equally and fairly by the courts; the fact that, being more likely to be illiterate than men, women are more likely to sign confessions to crimes which they did not commit; and the fact that general discrimination against women in other life aspects leaves them at higher risk of convictions for adultery.

LGBT rights

Stoning also targets homosexuals and others who have same-sex relations in certain jurisdictions. In Mauritania, northern Nigeria, Somalia and Yemen, the legal punishment for sodomy is death by stoning.

Right to private life

Human rights organizations argue that many acts targeted by stoning should not be illegal in the first place, as outlawing them interferes with people's right to a private life. Amnesty International said that stoning deals with "acts which should never be criminalized in the first place, including consensual sexual relations between adults, and choosing one's religion".

Examples

Ancient

- Palamedes, stoned to death as a traitor.

- Lucius Appuleius Saturninus, d. 100 BC, grandfather of later triumvir Marcus Aemilius Lepidus
- Pancras of Taormina, about AD 40
- James the Just, in AD 62, after being condemned by the Sanhedrin
- Possibly Saint Timothy (by Hellenistic pagans), after AD 67
- Constantine-Silvanus, founder of the Paulicians, stoned in 684 in Armenia
- Chase (son of Ioube), Muslim Byzantine official of Arab origin, stoned in 915 at Athens
- Saint Eskil, Anglo-Saxon monk stoned to death by Swedish Vikings, about 1080
- Moctezuma II, 1520, last Aztec Emperor (according to Western accounts; whereas, according to Aztec accounts, the Spanish killed him)

Modern

- Soraya Manutchehri, 1986, stoned to death in Iran after unconfirmed accusations of adultery
- Mahboubeh M. and Abbas H., at Behest-e Zahra cemetery, southern Teheran, Iran, 2006. The public was not invited to the stoning, and the incident was not reported to the media. However it was spread by word of mouth to a journalist and women's rights activist. The activist gathered information and further exposed the happening to the world. In response to this, several women's rights activists, lawyers and members of the Networks of Volunteers went on to form the Stop Stoning Forever campaign to stop stoning in Iran.
- Du'a Khalil Aswad, 2007, a 17-year-old stoned to death in Iraq
- Jafar Kiani, in Agche – kand, a small village near Takestan, Iran, 2007.
- Sara Jaffar Nimat, aged 11, in the town of Khanaqin, Iraqi Kurdistan, 2007. She had been hit by bricks and stones, and burnt.
- Aisha Ibrahim Duhulow, aged 13 in Kismayo, Somalia, 2008.
- Kurdistan Aziz, aged 16, Iraqi Kurdistan, 2008. She had been stoned in an act of "Honour" – killing.
- Shano and Daulat Khan Malikdeenkhe, in Khwezai – Baezai area, Pakistan, 2008
- Solange Medina, 2009, a 20-year-old stoned to death in Ciudad Juárez, Chihuahua, Mexico
- Vali Azad, 30, in Gilan province, Iran, 2009.
- Gustavo Santoro, 2010, a small town mayor in Mexico believed to have been murdered by stoning
- Murray Seidman, 2011, a 70-year-old senior in Lansdowne, Pennsylvania, near Philadelphia, stoned to death by 28-year-old John Thomas after

allegedly making sexual advances towards the younger man. Thomas' defence is that he did it because the Old Testament says to kill homosexuals in certain situations.

Averted

- Amina Lawal was sentenced to death by stoning in Nigeria in 2002 but freed on appeal.
- Sakineh Mohammadi Ashtiani was sentenced to death by stoning in Iran in 2007, but the sentence is under review.
- Safiya Husseini was sentenced to death by stoning in Nigeria but freed on appeal.[1782]
- Shaheen Abdel Rahman and an unnamed woman in Fujeirah, United Arab Emirates in 2006
- Zoleykhah Kadkhoda in Iran

Biblical

In the Tanakh (Old Testament):

- The son of an Israelite woman and an Egyptian man, for cursing God (Leviticus 24:10–23[1783])
- A man who gathered wood on Sabbath (Numbers 15:32–36[1784])
- Achan (Joshua 7[1785])
- Adoniram, King Rehoboam's tax man (1 Kings 12:18[1786])
- Naboth, (1 Kings 21[1787])
- Zechariah ben Jehoiada, who denounced the people's disobedience to the commandments (2 Chronicles 24:20–21[1788], perhaps also Matthew 23:35[1789])

In the New Testament:

- Saint Stephen, accused of blasphemy c. AD 31 (Acts 6:8–14[1790], 7:58–60[1791]).
- Paul the Apostle, stoned at Lystra at the instigation of Jews. He was left for dead, but then revived. (Acts 14:19[1792])

In the Talmud

- Yeshu the Nazarene "will be led out to be stoned" (Sanhedrin 43a)[1793]

Averted

In the Tanakh and Old Testament:

- Moses (Exodus 17:4[1794])
- Moses and Aaron (Numbers 14:6–10[1795])
- David (1 Samuel 30:6[1796])

In the New Testament:

- The Gospel of John chapter 8 gives the story of Jesus and the woman taken in adultery, in which people wanted to stone the woman.
- Jesus (John 8:59[1797], John 10:31[1798])
- The captain of the Temple and his officers feared that they might be stoned by the people of Jerusalem for preventing the Apostles from preaching about Jesus (Acts 5:26[1799])
- Paul and Barnabas, after provoking a division between believers and non-believers in Iconium (Acts 14:4[1800])

In literature

- Shirley Jackson's "The Lottery" depicts an annual lottery in which one member of a small, isolated American community is ritually stoned to death as a sacrifice. It explores themes of scapegoating, man's inherent evil and the destructive nature of observing ancient, outdated rituals. The music video for "Man That You Fear" by Marilyn Manson is based on the story.
- Robert A. Heinlein's *Stranger in a Strange Land* reaches its climax with a stoning execution.
- Freidoune Sahebjam's 1990 book *La Femme Lapidée* is based on the story of a woman who was stoned to death in Iran in 1986. The book was the basis of the 2008 film, *The Stoning of Soraya M.*.
- Simon Perry's *All Who Came Before* climaxes with a stoning as Barabbas enters Jerusalem.
- *Princess: A true story of life behind the veil in Saudi Arabia* by Jean Sasson describes a girl sentenced to death by stoning.
- In the 2003 novel *The Kite Runner* by Khaled Hosseini, a couple are stoned to death at a soccer stadium in Afghanistan.
- In the 2008 novel "The Dark Forest" by Liu Cixin, Wallfacer Rey Diaz was stoned to death by his own people for putting the entire world in danger.

In film and television

- *Seven Sleepers*, 2005 – A series running on Iranian TV, in which medieval (300–400 AD) Jews stone Christians.
- *A Stoning in Fulham County*, 1988 – A made-for-TV movie surrounding the vigilante stoning in an American Amish community.
- *Monty Python's Life of Brian* presents a Jesus of Nazareth-era stoning in a humorous context, ending with a massive boulder being dropped on the Jewish official, not the victim. The film mentions that women are not allowed at stonings, yet almost all of the stone-throwers turn out to be women disguised as men.
- Shirley Jackson's "The Lottery" was made into a short (20 minute) film by Larry Yust in 1969 as part of an educational release for Encyclopædia Britannica's "Short Story Showcase".
- The film *The Kite Runner* depicts the stoning of an adulteress by the Taliban in a public stadium during a football match.
- The film *Mission Istanbul* depicts the stoning of an adulteress in Kabul, by the fictional terrorist group Abu Nazir until it is interrupted by the protagonist Vikas Sagar.
- *The Stoning of Soraya M.*, a 2008 film
- *Zorba The Greek*, a 1946 novel by Nikos Kazantzakis and 1964 movie with Anthony Quinn, has a grim stoning scene where the woman is rescued only to be stabbed at the scene.
- *Osama* (2003) by director Siddiq Barmak depicts a woman being buried in preparation for stoning.
- In one CSI: Miami 2011 episode a female college bully is murdered by lapidation.
- In Lady Gaga's music video for her song Judas, a scene depicts Gaga being stoned to death.
- Although Islamic law prescribes stoning for married adulterers, the television series Sleeper Cell, about an underground radical Islamist group, depicts a scene where a member is stoned for treason.
- In Spartacus: War of the Damned (2010–13), Season 3, Episode 2, a slave is stoned by the Roman public.
- In *Timbuktu* (2014), a film about Islamist insurgents in Timbuktu, Mali, a man and woman are depicted buried up to the neck and stoned to death.

External links

Wikiquote has quotations related to: *Stoning*

Wikimedia Commons has media related to *Stonings*.

- Frequently Asked Questions About Stoning[1801]
- Stoning and Human Rights[1802]
- Stoning and Islam[1803]
- Extract of the Kitab Al-Hudud[1804] (The book pertaining to punishments prescribed by Islam)
- Khaleej Times[1805] (United Arab Emirates: Fujairah Shariah court orders man to be stoned to death for adultery – 11 June 2006)
- Muslims against stoning[1806]
- QuranicPath – Qur'an against stoning[1807]
- 1991 Video of Stoning of Death in Iran: WMV format[1808] | RealPlayer[1809]
- Graphic: Anatomy of a stoning (National Post, November 20, 2010)[1810]
- Amnesty International 2008, "Campaigning to end stoning in Iran"[1811]

Strangling

Strangling is compression of the neck that may lead to unconsciousness or death by causing an increasingly hypoxic state in the brain.[1812] Fatal strangling typically occurs in cases of violence, accidents, and is one of two main ways that hanging causes death (alongside breaking the victim's neck).

Strangling does not have to be fatal; limited or interrupted strangling is practised in erotic asphyxia, in the choking game, and is an important technique in many combat sports and self-defence systems. Strangling can be divided into three general types according to the mechanism used:[1813]

- **Hanging**—Suspension from a cord wound around the neck
- **Ligature strangulation**—Strangulation without suspension using some form of cord-like object called a garrote
- **Manual strangulation**—Strangulation using the fingers or other extremity

Figure 218: *A cheetah strangling an impala, Timbavati Game Reserve, South Africa*

General

Strangling involves one or several mechanisms that interfere with the normal flow of oxygen into the brain:[1814]

- Compression of the carotid arteries or jugular veins—causing cerebral ischemia.
- Compression of the laryngopharynx, larynx, or trachea—causing asphyxia.
- Stimulation of the carotid sinus reflex—causing bradycardia, hypotension, or both.

Depending on the particular method of strangulation, one or several of these typically occur in combination; vascular obstruction is usually the main mechanism. Complete obstruction of blood flow to the brain is associated with irreversible neurological damage and death,[1815] but during strangulation there is still unimpeded blood flow in the vertebral arteries.[1816] Estimates have been made that significant occlusion of the carotid arteries and jugular veins occurs with a pressure of around 3.4 N/cm^2 (4.9 psi), while the trachea demands six times more at approximately 22 N/cm^2 (32 psi).[1817]

As in all cases of strangulation, the rapidity of death can be affected by the susceptibility to carotid sinus stimulation. Carotid sinus reflex death is sometimes considered a mechanism of death in cases of strangulation, but it remains

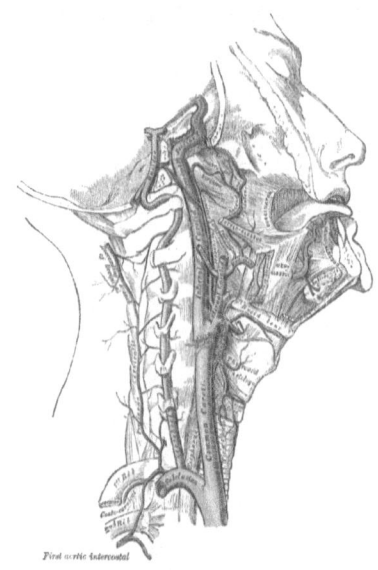

Figure 219: *The neck contains several vulnerable targets for compression including the carotid arteries.*

highly disputed.[1818] The reported time from application to unconsciousness varies from 7–14 seconds if effectively applied[1819] to one minute in other cases, with death occurring minutes after unconsciousness.

Manual strangulation

Manual strangulation (also known as "throttling") is strangling with the hands, fingers, or other extremities and sometimes also with blunt objects, such as batons. Depending on how the strangling is performed, it may compress the airway, interfere with the flow of blood in the neck, or work as a combination of the two. Consequently, manual strangulation may damage the larynx, and fracture the hyoid or other bones in the neck. In cases of airway compression, manual strangling leads to the frightening sensation of air hunger and may induce violent struggling.

More technical variants of manual strangulation are referred to as chokeholds, and are extensively practised and used in various martial arts, combat sports, self-defense systems, and in military hand-to-hand combat application. In some martial arts like judo and jujutsu, strangles or chokes that constrict blood flow are regarded as a safeWikipedia:Citation needed way to render the opponent unconscious as opposed to other attacks, e.g., strikes to the head. During the 18th century, a sentence of "Death by Throttling" would be passed upon the verdict of a Court Martial for the crime of desertion from the British Army.[1820]

Ligature strangulation

Ligature strangulation (also known as "garroting") is strangling with some form of cord such as rope, wire, or shoe laces, either partially or fully circumferencing the neck.[1821] Even though the mechanism of strangulation is similar, it is usually distinguished from hanging by the strangling force being something other than the person's own bodyweight. Incomplete occlusion of the carotid arteries is expected and, in cases of homicide, the victim may struggle for a period of time, with unconsciousness typically occurring in 10 to 15 seconds. Cases of ligature strangulation generally involve homicides of women, children, and the elderly, but accidents and suicides occur as well.[1822]

Compared to hanging, the ligature mark will most likely be located lower on the neck of the victim.

During the Spanish Inquisition, victims who admitted their alleged sins and recanted were killed via ligature strangulation (i.e. the garrote) before their bodies were burnt during the *auto-da-fé*.[1823] Throughout much of the 20th and 21st centuries, the American Mafia used ligature strangulation as a means of murdering their victims. Confessed American serial killer Altemio Sanchez used ligature strangulation in the rapes and/or murders of his victims, as did Gary Ridgway, the Green River Killer.

Notes

Look up *strangling* in Wiktionary, the free dictionary.

References

<templatestyles src="Template:Refbegin/styles.css" />
- Ohlenkamp, Neil (2006). *Judo Unleashed*[1824]. <templatestyles src="Module:Citation/CS1/styles.css" />ISBN 0-07-147534-6. Basic reference on judo choking techniques.

Appendix

References

[1] //en.wikipedia.org/w/index.php?title=Template:Criminal_procedure_(trial)&action=edit

[2] So common was the practice of compensation that the word *murder* is derived from the French word *mordre* (bite) a reference to the heavy compensation one must pay for causing an unjust death. The "bite" one had to pay was used as a term for the crime itself: "Mordre wol out; that se we day by day." – Geoffrey Chaucer (1340–1400), The Canterbury Tales, *The Nun's Priest's Tale*, l. 4242 (1387–1400), repr. In *The Works of Geoffrey Chaucer*, ed. Alfred W. Pollard, et al. (1898).

[3] Translated from Waldmann, *op.cit.*, p. 147.

[4] Lindow, *op.cit.* (primarily discusses Icelandic *things*).

[5] Benn, p. 8.

[6] Benn, pp. 209–210

[7] Benn, p. 210

[8] Moses Maimonides, *The Commandments, Neg. Comm. 290*, at 269–71 (Charles B. Chavel trans., 1967).

[9] *The Caliphate: Its Rise, Decline, and Fall.*, William Muir

[10] Durant, Will and Ariel, *The Story of Civilization, Volume IX: The Age of Voltaire* New York, 1965, p. 71

[11] Durant, Will and Ariel, *The Story of Civilization, Volume IX: The Age of Voltaire* New York, 1965, p. 72,

[12] Conquest, Robert, *The Great Terror: A Reassessment*, New York, pp. 485–86

[13] //en.wikipedia.org/w/index.php?title=Capital_punishment&action=edit

[14] Borg and Radelet, pp. 144–47

[15] Van Norman p. 287

[16] Paternoster, R. (2012-09-18). Capital Punishment. Oxford Handbooks Online. Retrieved 15 June 2016, from .

[17] Roger G. Hood. *The death penalty: a worldwide perspective*, Oxford University Press, 2002. p10

[18] See Caitlin pp. 420–22 http//quod.lib.umich.edu

[19] Rob Gallagher,

[20] https://iran-hrm.com/index.php/2018/10/08/cruel-and-inhuman-executions-in-iran/

[21] https://irannewswire.org/iran-executes-female-juvenile-offender-despite-grossly-unfair-legal-process/

[22] UNICEF, Convention of the Rights of the Child – FAQ http://www.unicef.org/crc/index_30229.html : "The Convention on the Rights of the Child is the most widely and rapidly ratified human rights treaty in history. Only two countries, Somalia and the United States, have not ratified this celebrated agreement. Somalia is currently unable to proceed to ratification as it has no recognised government. By signing the Convention, the United States has signaled its intention to ratify but has yet to do so."

[23] Iranian activists fight child executions http://usatoday30.usatoday.com/news/world/2008-09-17-child-executions_N.htm, Ali Akbar Dareini, Associated Press, 17 September 2008. Retrieved 2008-09-22.

[24] Iranian hanged after verdict stay http://news.bbc.co.uk/2/hi/middle_east/7130380.stm ; BBC-news.co.uk; 2007-12-06; Retrieved 2007-12-06

[25] "Somalia to Ratify UN Child Rights Treaty" http://allafrica.com/stories/201311210066.html , allAfrica.com, 20 November 2013.

[26] Brian Evans, "The Death Penalty In 2011: Three Things You Should Know" http://blog.amnestyusa.org/us/the-death-penalty-in-2011-three-things-you-should-know/ , Amnesty International, 26 March 2012, in particular the map, "Executions and Death Sentences in 2011" http://betablog.amnestyusa.org/wp-content/uploads/2012/03/death_penalty_world_map.jpg

[27] Film *Robert Blecker want me dead*, about retributive justice and capital punishment

[28] Joel Feinberg: Voluntary Euthanasia and the Inalienable Right to Life http://www.tannerlectures.utah.edu/lectures/documents/feinberg80.pdf The Tanner Lecture on Human Values, 1 April 1977.
[29] Capital Defense Weekly http://capitaldefenseweekly.com/innocent.html
[30] Van Norman p. 288
[31] Amnesty International, "Singapore – The death penalty: A hidden toll of executions" http://web.amnesty.org/library/index/engasa360012004 (January 2004)
[32] http://conventions.coe.int/Treaty/Commun/ChercheSig.asp?NT=187&CM=&DF=&CL=ENG
[33] http://conventions.coe.int/Treaty/Commun/ChercheSig.asp?NT=114&CM=&DF=&CL=ENG
[34] http://www.oas.org/juridico/english/treaties/a-53.html
[35] https://doi.org/10.1017%2FCBO9780511489273.006
[36] https://doi.org/10.1017%2FCBO9780511841361.051
[37] http://www.wcl.american.edu/hrbrief/13/3curry.pdf
[38] https://www.webcitation.org/6FVicGebt?url=http://www.wcl.american.edu/hrbrief/13/3curry.pdf
[39] https://books.google.com/books?id=FaUNdNuVjJYC&lpg=PP1&pg=PP1
[40] https://books.google.com/books/about/The_next_frontier.html?id=nZY8E6n-JAAC
[41] https://books.google.com/books?id=SOiuzOv061EC&lpg=PP1&pg=PP1
[42] https://books.google.com/books?id=n8P0BYf62wAC&lpg=PP1&pg=PP1
[43] https://books.google.com/books?id=KPIf6dPJ_jQC&lpg=PP1&pg=PP1
[44] https://books.google.com/books?id=nlOU4fUaiV8C&lpg=PP1&pg=PP1
[45] https://books.google.com/books?id=U3McAciWdWYC&lpg=PA1&pg=PA1
[46] https://books.google.com/books?id=tpmQDVdv3UgC&lpg=PP1&pg=PP1
[47] http://usliberals.about.com/od/deathpenalty/i/DeathPenalty.htm
[48] http://www.iep.utm.edu/cap-puni/
[49] http://www.clarkprosecutor.org/html/links/dplinks.htm
[50] http://www.capitaldefenseweekly.com/
[51] https://web.archive.org/web/20061108150222/http://www.tdcj.state.tx.us/stat/executedoffenders.htm
[52] http://www.deathpenaltyworldwide.org/index.cfm
[53] http://www.answers.com/topic/capital-punishment
[54] http://www.bbc.co.uk/sn/tvradio/programmes/horizon/broadband/tx/executions/
[55] https://web.archive.org/web/20060614135521/http://www.megalaw.com/top/deathpenalty.php
[56] https://web.archive.org/web/20070102134352/http://www.soundportraits.org/on-air/witness_to_an_execution/
[57] https://web.archive.org/web/20070118082741/http://www.soundportraits.org/on-air/execution_tapes/
[58] https://jurisoffice.com/blog/wrongfully-convicted-citizens/
[59] http://www.cjlf.org/deathpenalty/dpdeterrencefull.htm
[60] https://web.archive.org/web/20170504000359/http://www.cjlf.org/deathpenalty/deathpenalty.htm
[61] http://www.recordnet.com/apps/pbcs.dll/article?AID=/20090805/A_OPINION0619/908050306/-1/NEWSMAP
[62] http://www.explorernews.com/articles/2009/08/26/opinion/doc4a9478dabc9be260176264.txt
[63] https://web.archive.org/web/20050404011836/http://www.prodeathpenalty.com/
[64] http://www.wesleylowe.com/cp.html
[65] http://www.geometry.net/basic_c/capital_punishment_pro_death_penalty.php
[66] http://constitution.now77.com/
[67] https://www.washingtonpost.com/wp-dyn/content/article/2005/06/03/AR2005060301450.html
[68] http://www.clarkprosecutor.org/html/death/death.htm
[69] https://web.archive.org/web/20150407063507/http://www.capital-punishment.us/search/label/Pro
[70] http://www.msnbc.msn.com/id/19160965
[71] http://www.worldcoalition.org/

[72] http://www.deathwatchinternational.org/
[73] http://www.nodeathpenalty.org/
[74] http://www.antideathpenalty.org/
[75] http://www.deathpenaltyinfo.org/
[76] https://www.amnesty.org/en/death-penalty
[77] http://eeas.europa.eu/human_rights/adp/index_en.htm
[78] https://web.archive.org/web/20061024192722/http://www.ipsnews.net/new_focus/deathpenalty/index.asp
[79] http://www.deathpenalty.org/
[80] http://www.reprieve.org/
[81] https://www.aclu.org/DeathPenalty/DeathPenaltyMain.cfm
[82] http://www.ncadp.org/
[83] http://www.nswccl.org.au/nswccl_policy_on_the_death_penalty
[84] https://web.archive.org/web/20100506030411/http://www.thesomnambulist.org/2008/01/winning-a-war-on-terror-eliminating-the-death-penalty/
[85] http://pennreview.com/2011/12/electric-chair-at-sing-sing
[86] http//www.shreveporttimes.com
[87] https://web.archive.org/web/20020122104520/http://www.deathpenaltyreligious.org/education/perspectives/dalailama.html
[88] http://www.engaged-zen.org/articles/Damien_P_Horigan-Buddhism_Capital_Punishment.html
[89] https://web.archive.org/web/20060105042354/http://www.ou.org/torah/savannah/5760/behaalotcha60.htm
[90] http://www.priestsforlife.org/deathpenalty
[91] https://web.archive.org/web/20010614045347/http://americancatholic.org/Newsletters/CU/ac0195.asp
[92] http://www.americancatholic.org/
[93] https://web.archive.org/web/20030812072150/http://www.americancatholic.org/Newsletters/YU/ay0696.asp
[94] http://www.cacp.org/
[95] https://web.archive.org/web/20101202000306/http://kashifshahzada.com/2010/11/20/why-the-death-penalty-is-un-islamic/
[96] Oxford English Dictionary, 2nd ed. Hanging as method of execution is unknown, as method of suicide from 1325.
[97] Oxford English Dictionary (2015 update), OUP, Oxford, UK
[98] Report by Kingsbury Smith, International News Service, 16 October 1946.
[99] MacDonogh G., "After the Reich" John Murray, London (2008) p. 450.
[100] Life Magazine, 28 October 1946: The Gallows Chamber https://books.google.com/books?id=iU0EAAAAMBAJ&pg=PA42
[101] "Gruesome death in gas chamber pushes Arizona towards injections" https://query.nytimes.com/gst/fullpage.html?res=9E0CE5D7113BF936A15757C0A964958260, New York Times, 25 April 1992 (retrieved 7 January 2008).
[102] James R, Nasmyth-Jones R., *The occurrence of cervical fractures in victims of judicial hanging*, Forensic Science International, 1992 Apr;54(1):81–91.
[103] Executedtoday.com http://www.executedtoday.com/images/South_Africa_Pretoria_prison_gallows.jpg, South Africa Pretoria prison gallows.
[104] Wallace SK, Cohen WA, Stern EJ, Reay DT, *Judicial hanging: postmortem radiographic, CT, and MR imaging features with autopsy confirmation*, Radiology, 1994 Oct;193(1):263–7.
[105] Countries that have abandoned the use of the death penalty http://www.religioustolerance.org/executh.htm, Ontario Consultants on Religious Tolerance, 8 November 2005
[106] Death penalty in Australia http://www.nswccl.org.au/issues/death_penalty/australia.php , New South Wales Council for Civil Liberties
[107] Capital Punishment Worldwide http://encarta.msn.com/media_461543496/Capital_Punishment_Worldwide.html , MSN Encarta. Archived https://www.webcitation.org/5kwQafqG1?url=http://encarta.msn.com/media_461543496/capital_punishment_worldwide.html 31 October 2009.

[108] Susan Munroe, History of Capital Punishment in Canada http://canadaonline.about.com/cs/crime/a/cappuntimeline.htm, About: Canada Online,
[109] Richard Solash, Hungary: U.S. President To Honor 1956 Uprising http://www.rferl.org/featuresarticle/2006/06/3c9b40e0-f493-49d4-a33d-6d93c1580bb1.html (20 June 2006), radio Free Europe; RadioLiberty.
[110] IRAN: Halted execution highlights inherent cruelty of death penalty http://www.amnestyusa.org/document.php?id=ENGMDE131742008&lang=e . Amnesty International USA (9 December 2008). Retrieved on 2008-12-11.
[111] Iraq's "Chemical Ali" sentenced to death http://www.msnbc.msn.com/id/19394865/, *MSNBC.com*, 24 June 2007. Retrieved on 24 June 2007.
[112] Second death sentence for Iraq's 'Chemical Ali http://www.msnbc.msn.com/id/28011270/, *MSNBC.com*, 2 December 2008. Retrieved on 2 December 2008.
[113] Iraq's 'Chemical Ali' gets 3rd death sentence http://hosted.ap.org/dynamic/stories/M/ML_IRAQ?SITE=CAGRA&SECTION=HOME&TEMPLATE=DEFAULT, *Associated Press*, 2 March 2009. Retrieved on 17 January 2010.
[114] 'Chemical Ali' gets a new death sentence http://www.msnbc.msn.com/id/34904200/ns/world_news-mideastn_africa, *MSNBC.com*, 17 January 2010. Retrieved on 17 January 2010.
[115] The Maryland Ritual Murders. The Final Verdict: Death By Hanging http://www.liberiapastandpresent.org/MarylandRitualMurders08.htm. Liberiapastandpresent.org. Retrieved 11 December 2017.
[116] Ritualistic Killings Spark Mob Action in Maryland http://www.theperspective.org/2005/jan/ritualistickillings.html. Theperspective.org Jan 2005. Retrieved 11 December 2017.
[117] Burckhardt, J.L.:" Travels in Syria and the Holy Land https//books.google.com", London 1822, p.156
[118] Lords Hansard text for 12 February 1998 http://www.parliament.the-stationery-office.co.uk/pa/ld199798/ldhansrd/vo980212/text/80212-26.htm , Hansard, Col. 1350.
[119] Tengler, U: " Layenspiegel https//books.google.com" p.119
[120] Original German text: *Den Juden zwischen zweyen wütenden oder beissenden hunde zu der gewonlichen gerichtstatt zu ziehen. vel schlieffen, mit dem strang oder ketten bey seinen füssen an eynen besondern galgen zwischen die hund nach verkerter mass hencken damit er also von leben zom tod gericht wird*
[121] Cohen, Esther (1993): " The Crossroads of Justice: Law and Culture in Late Medieval France https://books.google.com/books?id=5lclnUXYB4sC&pg=PA92&lpg=PA92" Brill, p.92-93
[122] Kriegk, G.L._ " Deutsches bürgerthum im mittelalter https://books.google.com/books?id=QtQMAAAAIAAJ&pg=PA243" Frankfurt am Main 1868, p.243
[123] Limmer, K.A: " Bibliothek der Sächsischen Geschichte, Volum 2 https://books.google.com/books?id=N3UAAAAAcAAJ&pg=PA721", Ronneburg 1831 p.721
[124] " Monatsschrift für Geschichte und Wissenschaft des Judentums, Volum 9 https://books.google.com/books?id=soAoAAAAYAAJ&pg=PA90", Leipzig 1860, p.90
[125] Henne am Rhyn, O.:" Kulturgeschichte der neuern Zeit: Vom Wiederaufleben d. Wiss. Bis ..., Volum 1 https://books.google.com/books?id=ph1BAAAAcAAJ&pg=PA566" Leipzig 1870, p.566
[126] Battenberg, F.:" Von Enoch bis Kafka: Festschrift für Karl E. Grözinger zum 60. Geburtstag https://books.google.com/books?id=EuhCKcHBYJwC&pg=PA86" Wiesbaden 2002, p.86
[127] Haym, R: " Preussische Jahrbücher, Volum 8 https://books.google.com/books?id=lME21-6A8kgC&pg=PA123", Berlin 1861 p.122-23
[128] The author regards this as probably the last case in which a Jew (although in this case dead) was hanged up by the feet in Germany.
[129] On Kisch's assessment, see for example:, on locus in Adam of Bremen's text, see
[130] *Ryccardi di Sancto Germano Notarii Chronicon* http://www.leeds.ac.uk/history/weblearning/MedievalHistoryTextCentre/ricsgermano.doc trans. G. A. Loud
[131] " Modern-day 'outlaws' gather to honour Jánošík http://spectator.sme.sk/articles/view/46928/8/modern_day_outlaws_gather_to_honour janosik.html". *The Slovak Spectator*. 9 July 2012.
[132] Stedman, J.G.: " Narrative, of a five years' expedition https//books.google.com", Vol.1, London 1813, p.116

[133] Honour, Hugh (1975). The European Vision of America Cleveland, Ohio; The Cleveland Museum of Art, p.343
[134] Online
[135] Online
[136] https://web.archive.org/web/20070713073312/http://www.geradts.com/anil/ij/vol_002_no_002/papers/paper005.html
[137] https://web.archive.org/web/20070713073439/http://www.geradts.com/anil/ij/vol_007_no_001/papers/paper005.html
[138] http://www.deathpenaltyworldwide.org/index.cfm
[139] M. Watt Espy and John Ortiz Smylka's database, "Executions in the U.S. 1608-2002: The Espy File." (Inter-University Consortium for Political and Social Research) http://www.deathpenaltyinfo.org/executions-us-1608-2002-espy-file
[140] https://www.reuters.com/article/us-bahrain-security-execution-idUSKBN14Z08A
[141] http://3g.163.com/news/article_cambrian/DSMUD3R000001899O.html?clickfrom=baidu_daka
[142] # ^ Sahib: The British Soldier in India 1750-1914 Richard Holmes HarperCollins 2005
[143] "Le président mongol veut abolir la peine de mort" http://www.lemonde.fr/asie-pacifique/article/2010/01/14/le-president-mongol-veut-abolir-la-peine-de-mort_1291441_3216.html, *Le Monde*, January 14, 2009
[144] http://www.capitalpunishmentuk.org/mar16.html
[145] Amnesty Intl., Death Penalty, MDE 20/002/2001, May 8, 2001.
[146] Thailand Department of Corrections: Death Penalty http://www.correct.go.th/eng/deathpenalty.htm
[147] http://www.thaiprisonlife.com/books/the-last-executioner/
[148] https://www.voicetv.co.th/read/Bk8HUEHWm
[149] http://gulfnews.com/news/uae/courts/man-who-raped-killed-eight-year-old-boy-obaida-executed-1.2129225
[150] http://www.capitalpunishmentuk.org/world.html
[151] https://query.nytimes.com/gst/fullpage.html?res=950DE4D71039F931A15755C0A96F948260
[152] R. McGowen. The Lethal Injection: The Origins of Lethal Injection.
[153] State v. Adams, 194 Ariz. 408 (1999).
[154] Duty v. Sirmons, No. CIV-05-23-FHS-SPS, 2007 WL 2358648 (E.D. Okla. August 17, 2007).
[155] https://web.archive.org/web/20010625104340/http://www.courttv.com/news/mcveigh_special/botched_ctv.html
[156] http://www.courttv.com/news/mcveigh_special/botched_ctv.html
[157] http://people.howstuffworks.com/lethal-injection.htm
[158] http://www.scientificamerican.com/article/capital-punishment-by-lethal-injection/
[159] //doi.org/10.1007%2F978-0-387-71695-4_7
[160] //doi.org/10.1016%2FS0140-6736%2805%2966377-5
[161] //www.ncbi.nlm.nih.gov/pubmed/15836890
[162] https://www.nytimes.com/2003/10/07/us/critics-say-execution-drug-may-hide-suffering.html
[163] https://www.webcitation.org/6g9tpaDzd?url=https://www.law.berkeley.edu/clinics/dpclinic/LethalInjection/LI/documents/articles/journal/vassallo.pdf
[164] https://www.law.berkeley.edu/clinics/dpclinic/LethalInjection/LI/documents/articles/journal/vassallo.pdf
[165] http://www.ama-assn.org/ama/pub/physician-resources/medical-ethics/code-medical-ethics/principles-medical-ethics.page
[166] http://news.bbc.co.uk/2/hi/health/4444473.stm
[167] http://www.deathpenaltyworldwide.org
[168] http://www.lethalinjection.org
[169] Philippines: The Death Penalty: Criminality, Justice and Human Rights
[170] The Effects of Electric Shock on the Body http://www.healthguidance.org/entry/12834/1/The-Effects-of-Electric-Shock-on-the-Body.html
[171] Order Upholding Constitutionality of the Electric Chair http://www.dc.state.fl.us/oth/deathrow/drorder.html

[172] http://www.capitalpunishmentuk.org/chair.html
[173] Tennessee electric chair use could spur legal challenges http://www.tennessean.com/story/news/politics/2014/05/23/haslam-approves-electric-chair/9485545/
[174] Randall E. Stross, The Wizard of Menlo Park: How Thomas Alva Edison Invented the Modern World, Crown/Archetype - 2007, page 171-173
[175] Craig Brandon The Electric Chair: An Unnatural American History page 12
[176] Craig Brandon, The Electric Chair: An Unnatural American History page 14
[177] Craig Brandon The Electric Chair: An Unnatural American History page 21
[178] Craig Brandon The Electric Chair: An Unnatural American History page 24
[179] David Marc. "Southwick, Alfred Porter", American National Biography Online - 2000 http://www.anb.org/articles/20/20-01919.html
[180] Craig Brandon, The Electric Chair: An Unnatural American History, page 54
[181] Anthony Galvin, Old Sparky: The Electric Chair and the History of the Death Penalty, Skyhorse Publishing - 2015, pages 30-45
[182] Craig Brandon, The Electric Chair: An Unnatural American History, pages 57-58
[183] Jill Jonnes, Empires Of Light: Edison, Tesla, Westinghouse, And The Race To Electrify The World, Random House - 2004, page 420
[184] Richard Moran, Executioner's Current: Thomas Edison, George Westinghouse, and the Invention of the Electric Chair, Knopf Doubleday Publishing Group - 2007, page 4
[185] Richard Moran, Executioner's Current: Thomas Edison, George Westinghouse, and the Invention of the Electric Chair, Knopf Doubleday Publishing Group - 2007, page 102
[186] Craig Brandon, The Electric Chair: An Unnatural American History, McFarland - 1999, pages 70 and 261
[187] Jill Jonnes, Empires Of Light: Edison, Tesla, Westinghouse, And The Race To Electrify The World, Random House - 2004, page 166
[188] W. Bernard Carlson, Innovation as a Social Process: Elihu Thomson and the Rise of General Electric, Cambridge University Press - 2003, page 285
[189] Mark Essig, Edison and the Electric Chair: A Story of Light and Death, Bloomsbury Publishing USA - 2009, pages 152-155
[190] Craig Brandon The Electric Chair: An Unnatural American History page 82
[191] Terry S. Reynolds, Theodore Bernstein, Edison and "The Chair", Technology and Society Magazine, Institute of Electrical and Electronics Engineers (Volume 8, Issue 1) March 1989, pages 19 - 28
[192] Mark Essig, Edison and the Electric Chair: A Story of Light and Death, Bloomsbury Publishing USA - 2009, pages 225
[193] Sarah Davis., A "Bungled" Execution and a Doctor's Guilt: The Horrifying Debut of the Electric Chair, December 4, 2014 https://johnbalebooks.wordpress.com/2014/12/04/a-bungled-execution-and-a-doctors-guilt-the-horrifying-debut-of-the-electric-chair/
[194] Mark Essig, Edison and the Electric Chair: A Story of Light and Death, Bloomsbury Publishing - 2005, pages 190-195 https//books.google.com
[195] Stuart Banner, The Death Penalty: an American history, Harvard University Press - 2009, pages 194-195
[196] Carl Sifakis, The Encyclopedia of American Prisons, Infobase Publishing - 2014, page 39
[197] "Electric Executions: The New York Court of Appeals Passes on the Question: The Famous Kemmler Case Decided" https://news.google.com/newspapers?nid=ix4AEQmNN7wC&dat=18900101&printsec=frontpage&hl=en, Lawrence Daily Record, Jan. 1, 1890, pg. 1.
[198] Justice Dwight, quoted in "Electric Executions", Lawrence Daily Record, Jan. 1, 1890; pg. 1.
[199] AC/DC: The Savage Tale of the First Standards War; By Tom McNichol
[200] James D. Livingston, Arsenic and Clam Chowder: Murder in Gilded Age New York, SUNY Press - 2012, pge 64
[201] James D. Livingston, Arsenic and Clam Chowder: Murder in Gilded Age New York, SUNY Press - 2012, pages 64-65
[202] Time-Life Books, 1969, p. 185
[203] Gilbert King, The Two Executions Of Willie Francis, Wednesday, July 19, 2006, washingtonpost.com https://www.washingtonpost.com/wp-dyn/content/article/2006/07/18/AR2006071801376.html

[204] U.S. Supreme Court case, Francis v. Resweber:
[205] //en.wikipedia.org/w/index.php?title=Electric_chair&action=edit
[206] http://www.dc.state.fl.us/oth/deathrow/drorder.html
[207] Tightening the Nuts and Bolts of Death by Electric Chair, Tom Kuntz, New York Times, Aug 3 1997
[208] https://web.archive.org/web/20140515081413/http://www.mindfully.org/Reform/Kemmler-Torture-Death7aug1890.htm
[209] http://www.deathpenaltyworldwide.org/index.cfm
[210] Video testimonials by former guards and prisoners at Camp 22 http://freekorea.us/2007/02/18/holocaust-now-looking-down-into-hell-at-camp-22/ , where the experiments are said to have occurred, with Google Earth images Camp 22 and other camps
[211] Truth behind False Report about "Experiment of Chem. Weapons on Human Bodies" in DPRK Disclosed http://www.kcna.co.jp/item/2004/200403/news03/31.htm#10 (North Korean Central News Agency)
[212] Killer Of 3-Year-Old Mississippi Girl Executed After Justices Reject Plea https://select.nytimes.com/gst/abstract.html?res=F30B17FE395C0C718CDDA00894DB484D81. *The New York Times* (1983-09-02). Retrieved on 2007-11-12.
[213] *Handbook of Death and Dying* by Clifton D. Bryant - Page 499
[214] fourth paragraph
[215] "The History Channel" - *Modern Marvels* (gas chamber) http://www.history.com/shows/modern-marvels/videos/gas-chamber
[216] second paragraph
[217] Mississippi State Penitentiary, Leuchter report http://www.zundelsite.org/archive/leuchter/report3/ch7000.html section 7.002
[218] *Encyclopedia of Capital Punishment in the United States*, 2d ed. by Louis J. Palmer, Jr. (page 319)
[219] *The Death Penalty As Cruel Treatment And Torture* by William Schabas (page 194)
[220] Mississippi State Penitentiary, Leuchter report http://www.zundelsite.org/archive/leuchter/report3/ch7000.html section 7.007
[221] See Isadora Duncan § Death.
[222] Francis Larson. *Severed: a history of heads lost and heads found* Liveright, 2014.
[223] Webster's Revised Unabridged Dictionary, edited by Noah Porter, published by G & C. Merriam Co., 1913
[224] For Devereux's execution: Smollett, T.:" A Complete History of England, from the Descent of Julius Caesar ..., Volum 4 https//books.google.com" London 1758, p.488
[225] For Mary, Queen of Scots:Cheetham, J.K.:" On the Trail of Mary Queen of Scots https//books.google.com" Glasgow 2000, p.161
[226] *The Complete Peerage*, v. XII p. II, p. 393
[227] Hume, D.:" The history of the reign of Henry the eighth https://books.google.com/books?id=nl0TAAAAQAAJ&pg=PT7&dq=execution+countess+of+salisbury&hl=no&sa=X&ei=rtMgUcq-H9KK4gS_8YDADQ&ved=0CDgQ6AEwAg" London 1792, p.151
[228] Gabriel Beaurieux, writing in 1905, quoted in , cited by
[229] Cited in
[230] Dash, Mike. 'Some experiments with severed heads.' http://allkindsofhistory.wordpress.com/2011/01/25/some-experiments-with-severed-heads/ A Blast From The Past, January 2011. Retrieved 30 July 2011.
[231] Mignet, François, *History of the French Revolution from 1789 to 1814*, (1824).
[232] Meurtre de deux experts de l'ONU: la RDC présente une vidéo http://www.lalibre.be/dernieres-depeches/afp/meurtre-de-deux-experts-de-l-onu-la-rdc-presente-une-video-58fe3008cd70812a659fffed, Retrieved 5 August 2017|(In French)
[233] "无头人"挑战传统医学 人类还有个"腹脑"? http://□□□.cn/GB/kejiao/42/154/20030410/968308.html
[234] http://kotobank.jp/word/%E5%96%84%E4%BD%8F%E5%9D%8A Asahi Dictionary of Japanese Historical Figures
[235] UN – TRIBUNAL CONVICTS ENVER HADZIHASANOVIC AND AMIR KUBURA Press Release, March 2006 https://www.un.org/icty/pressreal/2006/p1054-e.htm

[236] Cunliffe, Barry (2010), *Druids: A Very Short Introduction*, Oxford University Press, pp 71–72.
[237] Cunliffe, *Op. cit.*, pg 72.
[238] Paul Jacobsthal *Early Celtic Art*
[239] ()
[240] http://grandcolombier.com/wp-content/uploads/2014/12/zuzaregui.jpg
[241] Execution of the Marquess of Ayamonte on the 11th. of December 1645 Described in "Varios relatos diversos de Cartas de Jesuitas" (1634–1648) Coll. Austral Buones Aires 1953 en Dr. J. Geers "Van het Barokke leven", Baarn 1957 Bl. 183–188.
[242] https://www.usnews.com/news/best-states/louisiana/articles/2017-07-28/old-south-grandeur-leavened-with-a-cold-look-at-slavery
[243] https://www.theguardian.com/world/2016/jul/20/syrian-opposition-group-which-killed-child-was-in-us-vetted-alliance
[244] http://apps.who.int/classifications/icd10/browse/2016/en#/S18
[245] http://www.crimelibrary.com/serial_killers/history/landru/guillotine_7.html
[246] http://www.capitalpunishmentuk.org/behead.html
[247] Allsen, p. 156.
[248] Schimmel, p. 96.
[249] Chevers, p. 261.
[250] Schafer, Edward H. "The Golden Peaches of Samarkand: A Study of T'ang Exotics". University of California Press, 1985. p. 80. ASIN: B0000CLTET
[251] Crawfurd, John. "Journal of an Embassy from the Governor-general of India to the Courts of Siam and Cochin China". H. Colburn and R. Bentley, 1830. p. 419 https//books.google.com.
[252] Olivelle, p. 125.
[253] Jack Weatherford-Genghis Khan, p.116
[254] Natesan, G.A. *The Indian Review*, p. 160
[255] Hamilton, p. 170.
[256] Eraly, p. 45.
[257] Battuta, " The travels of Ibn Battuta https//books.google.com", transl. Lee, S, London 1829, pp. 146-47
[258] Eraly, p. 479.
[259] Eraly, p. 498
[260] Kerr, p. 395.
[261] Buffon, Georges Louis Leclerc. "Natural history of man, the globe, and of quadrupeds". vol. 1. Leavitt & Allen, 1857. p. 113.
[262] Ryley Scott, George. "The Percy Anecdotes vol. VIII". *The History of Torture Throughout the Ages*. Torchstream Books, 1940. pp. 116-7.
[263] *Harper's Weekly*, February 3, 1872
[264] Maddock, Eleanor. "What the Crystal Revealed". *American Theosophist Magazine*, April to September 1914. p. 859.
[265] Knox, Robert. " An Historical Relation of the Island Ceylon http://www.gutenberg.org/etext/14346". London, 1681.
[266] Tennent, p. 281.
[267] Sirr, Sir Charles Henry, quoted in Barrow, George. "Ceylon: Past and Present". John Murray, 1857. pp. 135–6.
[268] Benisch, A. (trans). "Travels of Petachia of Ratisbon". London, 1856.
[269] Fox, Robin Lane. "Alexander the Great". Penguin, 2004. p. 474.
[270] Curt. 10.6-10 http://luna.cas.usf.edu/~murray/classes/aa/source22.htm (registration required)
[271] Futrell, Alison (Quoted by) (ed.). "A Sourcebook on the Roman Games". Blackwell Publishing, 2006. p. 8.
[272] 3 Maccabees 5
[273] 3 Maccabees 6
[274] Collins, p. 122.
[275] *Havholm* (2008), p. 77 https://books.google.com/books?id=vxuSORJ-Tv8C&pg=PA77
[276] *Calcutta Review* (1851), p. 395 https://books.google.com/books?id=mYdHAAAAYAAJ&pg=PA395
[277] *Alden* (1996), p. 55 https://books.google.com/books?id=7nVIBhrRb9AC&pg=PA55

[278] *Southey* (1822), p.469 https://books.google.com/books?id=h4AiAQAAMAAJ&pg=PA469
[279] 17th century case, *Afsos, Court* (1871), p. 64 https://books.google.com/books?id=a-BRAAAAcAAJ&pg=PA64, 18th century case *Hazārah, McChesney, Khorrami* (2012), p. 54 https://books.google.com/books?id=8tLE4hjSyjEC&pg=PA54
[280] *Long* (1869), p. 397–398 https://books.google.com/books?id=QXwoAAAAYAAJ&pg=PR397#v=onepage&q=blown&f=false
[281] **February 1781** *Parlby* (1822), p. 188 https://books.google.com/books?id=-d0KAQAAIAAJ&pg=PA188, **May 1783** *Baillie* (1788), p. 490 https://books.google.com/books?id=3SIUAAAAQAAJ&pg=PA490, **July 1783** *Forbes* (1815), p. 123 https://books.google.com/books?id=82AOAAAAQAAJ&pg=PA123, **October 1783** *Forbes* (1815), p. 133 https://books.google.com/books?id=82AOAAAAQAAJ&pg=PA133 **November 1783** *Baillie* (1788), p. 468 https://books.google.com/books?id=3SIUAAAAQAAJ&pg=PA468
[282] Long (1869), p. 51 https://books.google.com/books?id=QXwoAAAAYAAJ&pg=PR51 page 224 https://books.google.com/books?id=QXwoAAAAYAAJ&pg=PR224
[283] Past Present, Volume 233, Issue 1, November 2016, Pages 185-225, Calculated to Strike Terror: The Amritsar Massacre and the Spectacle of Colonial Violence by Kim A. Wagner, https://academic.oup.com/past/article/233/1/185/2915150/Calculated-to-Strike-Terror-The-Amritsar-Massacre
[284] *Cullather, Meyerowitz* (2003), p. 50 https://books.google.com/books?id=V5NdS-k7FUMC&pg=PA50
[285] *Atkinson* (1842), p. 189–190 https://books.google.com/books?id=lcwNAAAAIAAJ&pg=PA189
[286] *Boyar, Fleet* (2010), p. 112 https://books.google.com/books?id=hHd2OizxNCcC&pg=PA112
[287] *Campbell* (1839), p. 421 https://books.google.com/books?id=PHgOAAAAQAAJ&pg=PA421
[288] *Duff* (1826, 3), p. 190 https://books.google.com/books?id=_7A5AQAAIAAJ&pg=PA190, and *Lal, Prinsep* (1831), p. 127 https://books.google.com/books?id=OH5CAAAAIAAJ&pg=PA127
[289] Ball, (1859, 3), p. 411 https://books.google.com/books?id=v-ZCAAAAcAAJ&pg=PA411
[290] *American Peace Society* (1858) p. 23 https://books.google.com/books?id=EMYBAAAAYAAJ&pg=PA23
[291] "It is a curious fact, and well attested by many persons present, that a number of kites (a bird of prey very common in India) actually accompanied the melancholy party in their progress to the place of execution, as if they knew what was going on, and then kept hovering over the guns from which the culprits were to be blown away, flapping their wings, and shrieking, as if in anticipation of their bloody feast, till the fatal flash, which scattered the fragments of bodies in the air; when, pouncing on their prey, they positively caught in their talons many pieces of the quivering flesh before they could reach the ground! At sight of this the native troops employed on this duty, together with the crowd which had assembled to witness the execution, set up a yell of horror".. The description is from the execution of those found guilty in the Vellore Mutiny in 1806, *Blakiston* (1829), p. 309 https://books.google.com/books?id=wboRAAAAYAAJ&pg=PA309.
[292] In an 1845 Herat case: "It was a scene that I shall never forget—a horrid spectacle, and touched me to the very heart. The broken limbs of the unfortunate man were scattered in all directions, while his bowels, which had not been thrown to so great a distance, were in an instant devoured by the dogs that were loitering about the spot." *Ferrier* (1856), p. 189 https://books.google.com/books?id=eT4cLqALvtMC&pg=PA189.
[293] See, for example, *Heathcote* (1995), p. 105 https://books.google.com/books?id=YSK8AAAAIAAJ&pg=PA105, and *Fremont-Barnes* (2007), p. 79 https://books.google.com/books?id=DVoNNeKsKmgC&pg=PA79 .
[294] *Sabahuddin, Shukla* (2003), p. 122 https://books.google.com/books?id=FW4WqqLVzLEC&pg=PA122
[295] *Afsos* (1871), p. 64 https://books.google.com/books?id=a-BRAAAAcAAJ&pg=PA64
[296] *Asiatic Soicety of Bengal* (1847), p. 658 https://books.google.com/books?id=iAfgAAAAMAAJ&pg=PA658
[297] *Hazārah, McChesney, Khorrami* (2012), p. 54 https://books.google.com/books?id=8tLE4hjSyjEC&pg=PA54

[298] *Bakshi* (1997), p. 103–104 https://books.google.com/books?id=7O3dD1N93hUC&pg=PA103
[299] *Irvine* (1922), thieves, p. 287 https://archive.org/stream/latermughals01irviuoft#page/286/mode/2up, and deserters, p. 415 https://archive.org/stream/latermughals01irviuoft#page/414/mode/2up.
[300] *Ribeiro, Le Grand* (1847), p. 138 https://books.google.com/books?id=D6M2AAAAMAAJ&pg=PA138
[301] According to the same source, this punishment was only inflicted in cases of rebellion, otherwise, deportation was the most severe punishment *Thoman* (1869), p. 111 https://books.google.com/books?id=86xGAAAAcAAJ&pg=PA111
[302] *Salt* (1814), p. 39–40 https://books.google.com/books?id=QzGKBkUTLrkC&pg=PA39
[303] *Southey* (1822), p. 469 https://books.google.com/books?id=h4AiAQAAMAAJ&pg=PA469
[304] *Long* (1869), p. 51 https://books.google.com/books?id=QXwoAAAAYAAJ&pg=PR51 page 224 https://books.google.com/books?id=QXwoAAAAYAAJ&pg=PR224 for 17 November 1760 decision, footnote remarking that thief was a carpenter named Nayn
[305] *Anderson* (1859), p. 39 https://books.google.com/books?id=H2kJAAAAQAAJ&pg=PA39
[306] At that time, Shuja-ud-Daula, who was defeated by the British in the Battle of Buxar some months later
[307] *Broome* (1850), p. 435 https://books.google.com/books?id=JcQDM10JmcgC&pg=PA435
[308] For 1764 and 1775 events, *Butalia* (1998), p. 273 https://books.google.com/books?id=eV262iNGUb4C&pg=PA273. Hector Munro's report on 24 executed to the House of Commons may be read here: *Adolphus* (1840), p. 268 https://books.google.com/books?id=FhEOAQAAMAAJ&pg=PA268. In his letter dated 18 September to the East India Company, however, Monro says 25, detailing where they were sent for execution, *Long* (1869), p. 397–398 https://books.google.com/books?id=QXwoAAAAYAAJ&pg=PR397#v=onepage&q=blown&f=false.
[309] *Deerrett* (1783), p. 83–85 https://books.google.com/books?id=o5YrAQAAIAAJ&pg=PA83
[310] *Almon* (1791), p. 637 https://books.google.com/books?id=0zTgAAAAMAAJ&pg=PA637
[311] **February 1781** *Parlby* (1822), p. 188 https://books.google.com/books?id=-d0KAQAAIAAJ&pg=PA188, **May 1783** *Baillie* (1788), p. 490 https://books.google.com/books?id=3SIUAAAAQAAJ&pg=PA490, **July 1783** *Forbes* (1815), p. 123 https://books.google.com/books?id=82AOAAAAQAAJ&pg=PA123, **October 1783** *Forbes* (1815), p. 133 https://books.google.com/books?id=82AOAAAAQAAJ&pg=PA133, **November 1783** *Baillie* (1788), p. 468 https://books.google.com/books?id=3SIUAAAAQAAJ&pg=PA468
[312] *Butalia* (1998), p. 273–274 https://books.google.com/books?id=eV262iNGUb4C&pg=PA273
[313] *Grey, Garrett* (1996), p. 216 https://books.google.com/books?id=S8AN0-cO-RYC&pg=PA216. However, a case from 1784 in the cantonment at Arcot says that a mutiny over reduced pay broke out in October among European troops, and that one active serjeant was condemned to be blown from a gun. *Baldwin* (1785), p. 390 https://books.google.com/books?id=ixcAAAAAYAAJ&pg=PA390.
[314] *Philippart* (1823), p. 497 https://books.google.com/books?id=e_I8zCCqhV4C&pg=PA497
[315] *Rosselli* (1974), p. 52 https://books.google.com/books?id=px6WdehjC-MC&pg=PA52
[316] *Wilkes* (1815), p. 310 https://books.google.com/books?id=mJw1IV-EAAoC&pg=PA310
[317] *Macready* (1853), p. 236 https://books.google.com/books?id=rPobAQAAIAAJ&pg=PA236
[318] Detailed report by captain Doveton from 1844, *Doveton* (1844), p. 620–624 https://books.google.com/books?id=CihGAAAAcAAJ&pg=PA620
[319] On achieved rank under Madras governor George Macartney *Munro* (1789), p. 344 https://books.google.com/books?id=Eg8NAAAAYAAJ&pg=PA344
[320] *Munro* (1789), p. 358 https://books.google.com/books?id=Eg8NAAAAYAAJ&pg=PA358
[321] *Seton-Karr* (1865), p. 181–185 https://books.google.com/books?id=LdUMAAAAIAAJ&pg=PA181
[322] *Wellington, Wellington* (1868), p. 332 https://books.google.com/books?id=mx8yAQAAIAAJ&pg=PA332, and *Pogson* (1833), p. 30–31 https://books.google.com/books?id=ikAIAAAAQAAJ&pg=PA30
[323] *Asiatic Journal* (1837), p. 58 https://books.google.com/books?id=eSoLAQAAMAAJ&pg=RA1-PA58
[324] Number executed specified in "Government Records" (1911), p. 132 https//books.google.com

[325] *Allen's Indian Mail* https://books.google.com/books?id=JrgOAAAAQAAJ (1857), pp. 465, 466, 502, 549, 601, 731, 771, 911

[326] *Parliament of Great Britain* (1859), p. 80 https://books.google.com/books?id=Tq5bAAAAQAAJ&pg=RA1-PA80

[327] *Indian News* (1858), p. 125 https://books.google.com/books?id=43lNAAAAcAAJ&pg=PA125

[328] *Shrivastav* (1971), p. 108 https://books.google.com/books?id=hqE8AAAAIAAJ&pg=PA108

[329] See, for example, remark by colonel Mylne, *Russell* (1859), p. 45 https://books.google.com/books?id=Mk0QAAAAYAAJ&pg=PA45

[330] In a letter dated 30 August 1857, received by William Muir working as an intelligence officer, the persons were Mr. Bridges (an indigo planter), his wife, his mother-in-law and their daughter Mrs. Eckford. *Muir, Coldstream* (1902), p. 501 https://archive.org/stream/recordsintellig00indigoog#page/n510/mode/2up.

[331] The Inquirer & Commercial News, Wednesday 7 April 1858 http://nla.gov.au/nla.news-article66008933, "Phoenix", 10 September 1857 http://paperspast.natlib.govt.nz/cgi-bin/paperspast?a=d&d=LT18571212.2.15&l=mi&e=-------10--1----0--, *Noel* (1859), p. 461 https://books.google.com/books?id=O3gOAAAAQAAJ&pg=PA461

[332] What a skull in an English pub says about India's 1857 mutiny, BBC News, Thursday 5 April 2018 https://www.bbc.com/news/world-asia-india-43616597

[333] In this case, however, the viceroy of India, Richard Bourke, earl of Mayo, disowned the action of Mr. Cowan, who presided over the first 49 executions and dismissed that officer responsible for the mass execution. *Knight* (2012), p. 13 https://books.google.com/books?id=NVfTufIqlD8C&pg=PA13. However, this was on basis of a procedural point concerning how the trial under Cowan had been held; Mr. Forsyth, Mr. Cowan's hierarchical superior, also blew the last 16 from guns, some time thereafter, but according to requirements of "fair trial". *Singh* (1995), p. 503–507 https://books.google.com/books?id=2lu7HatPQCoC&pg=PA503.

[334] *Noelle* (2012), p. 290 https://books.google.com/books?id=ylTi-e2C_0IC&pg=PP290

[335] *Tate* (1911), on treachery, p. 115 https://archive.org/stream/kingdomofafghani00taterich#page/114/mode/2up, on blowing from a gun, p. 121 https://archive.org/stream/kingdomofafghani00taterich#page/120/mode/2up.

[336] Apart from blowing from guns, the source mention as well that people could be bayoneted to death, hanged, crucified, disemboweled, sawn in two, hanged or dragged to death behind horses. *Akbarzadeh, Macqueen* (2008), p. 93 https://books.google.com/books?id=hEGj-55dCvkC&pg=PA93. Lord Curzon, visiting Kabul in 1894, narrates the following chilling story about a rapist: "One official who had outraged a woman was stripped naked and placed in a hole dug for the purpose on the top of a high hill outside Kabul. It was in mid-winter; and water was then poured upon him until he was converted into an icicle and frozen alive. As the Amir sardonically remarked, 'He would never be too hot again.'" *Edwards* (1996), p. 111 https://books.google.com/books?id=IncGaivUHu8C&pg=PA111.

[337] *Lee* (1996), p. 551 https://books.google.com/books?id=nYaamE_3kD4C&pg=PA551. In 1891 Herat, a rebel leader was also blown from a gun, p. 580 https://books.google.com/books?id=nYaamE_3kD4C&pg=PA580.

[338] Letter from Humphreys to the foreign secretary from 20 January 1929, cited in *Roberts* (2003), p. 51 https://books.google.com/books?id=Pj8DIT_bva0C&pg=PA51 and p. 61 https://books.google.com/books?id=Pj8DIT_bva0C&pg=PA61. For the case of Ali Ahmad Khan blown by guns in July 1929, see *Lee* (1996), p. 378 https://books.google.com/books?id=nYaamE_3kD4C&pg=PA378.

[339] https://books.google.com/books?id=FhEOAQAAMAAJ
[340] https://books.google.com/books?id=a-BRAAAAcAAJ
[341] https://books.google.com/books?id=hEGj-55dCvkC
[342] https://books.google.com/books?id=7nVIBhrRb9AC
[343] https://books.google.com/books?id=JrgOAAAAQAAJ
[344] https://books.google.com/books?id=0zTgAAAAMAAJ
[345] https://books.google.com/books?id=EMYBAAAAYAAJ
[346] https://books.google.com/books?id=H2kJAAAAQAAJ
[347] https://books.google.com/books?id=eSoLAQAAMAAJ

[348] https://books.google.com/books?id=iAfgAAAAMAAJ
[349] https://books.google.com/books?id=lcwNAAAAIAAJ
[350] https://books.google.com/books?id=3SIUAAAAQAAJ
[351] https://books.google.com/books?id=7O3dD1N93hUC
[352] https://books.google.com/books?id=ixcAAAAAYAAJ
[353] https://books.google.com/books?id=v-ZCAAAAcAAJ
[354] https://books.google.com/books?id=wboRAAAAYAAJ
[355] https://books.google.com/books?id=hHd2OizxNCcC
[356] https://books.google.com/books?id=JcQDM10JmcgC
[357] https://books.google.com/books?id=eV262iNGUb4C
[358] https://books.google.com/books?id=mYdHAAAAYAAJ
[359] https://books.google.com/books?id=PHgOAAAAQAAJ
[360] https://books.google.com/books?id=V5NdS-k7FUMC
[361] https://books.google.com/books?id=o5YrAQAAIAAJ
[362] https://books.google.com/books?id=CihGAAAAcAAJ
[363] https://books.google.com/books?id=_7A5AQAAIAAJ
[364] https://books.google.com/books?id=IncGaivUHu8C
[365] https://books.google.com/books?id=Sr0IAAAAQAAJ
[366] https://books.google.com/books?id=82AOAAAAQAAJ
[367] https://books.google.com/books?id=DVoNNeKsKmgC
[368] https://books.google.com/books?hl=no&id=WiMeAQAAIAAJ
[369] https://books.google.com/books?id=S8AN0-cO-RYC
[370] https://books.google.com/books?id=vxuSORJ-Tv8C
[371] https://books.google.com/books?id=8tLE4hjSyjEC
[372] https://books.google.com/books?id=YSK8AAAAIAAJ
[373] https://books.google.com/books?id=43lNAAAAcAAJ
[374] https://archive.org/details/latermughals01irviuoft
[375] https://books.google.com/books?id=NVfTufIqlD8C
[376] https://books.google.com/books?id=OH5CAAAAIAAJ
[377] https://books.google.com/books?id=nYaamE_3kD4C
[378] https://books.google.com/books?id=QXwoAAAAYAAJ
[379] https://books.google.com/books?id=rPobAQAAIAAJ
[380] https://archive.org/stream/recordsintellig00indigoog#page/n6/mode/2up
[381] https://books.google.com/books?id=Eg8NAAAAYAAJ
[382] https://books.google.com/books?id=O3gOAAAAQAAJ
[383] https://books.google.com/books?hl=no&id=ylTi-e2C_0IC
[384] https://books.google.com/books?id=-d0KAQAAIAAJ
[385] https://books.google.com/books?id=Tq5bAAAAQAAJ
[386] https://books.google.com/books?id=e_I8zCCqhV4C
[387] https://books.google.com/books?id=ikAIAAAAQAAJ
[388] https://books.google.com/books?id=D6M2AAAAMAAJ
[389] https://books.google.com/books?id=Pj8DIT_bva0C
[390] https://books.google.com/books?id=px6WdehjC-MC
[391] https://books.google.com/books?id=Mk0QAAAAYAAJ
[392] https://books.google.com/books?id=FW4WqqLVzLEC
[393] https://books.google.com/books?id=QzGKBkUTLrkC
[394] https://books.google.com/books?id=LdUMAAAAIAAJ
[395] https://books.google.com/books?id=hqE8AAAAIAAJ
[396] https://books.google.com/books?id=2Iu7HatPQCoC
[397] https://books.google.com/books?id=h4AiAQAAMAAJ
[398] https://archive.org/details/kingdomofafghani00taterich
[399] https://books.google.com/books?id=86xGAAAAcAAJ
[400] https://books.google.com/books?id=mx8yAQAAIAAJ
[401] https://books.google.com/books?id=mJw1IV-EAAoC
[402] Alfred P. Smyth, *Scandinavian Kings in the British Isles, 850–880* (1977), Oxford, pp. 212–213

[403] , citing: Bjarni Einarsson, *"De Normanorum Atrocitate*, or on the Execution of Royalty by the Aqueline Method", *The Saga Book*, 22 (1988): 79–82; Roberta Frank, "The Blood-Eagle Again", *The Saga Book*, 22 (1988): 287–289; Bjarni Einarsson and Roberta Frank, "The Blood-Eagle Once More: Two Notes", *The Saga Book*, 23 (1990): 80–83.

[404] Geoffrey Abbott, *Execution blunders*, pages 21–22.

[405] 'Anno 22 Henry VIII (1530-31), Chapter 9', in *The Statutes of the Realm* Vol. 3: The Statutes of King Henry VIII, (By Command 1817), Reprint (Dawsons of Pall Mall, London 1963), p. 326 https://babel.hathitrust.org/cgi/pt?id=pst.000017915533;view=1up;seq=382 (Hathi Trust).

[406] (S.H. Burke), *The Men and Women of the English Reformation* (R. Washbourne, London 1870), p. 240 https://books.google.co.uk/books?id=b58HAAAAQAAJ&pg=RA1-PA240#v=onepage (Google).

[407] Chisholm 1911.

[408] Leslie, Frank, Frank Leslie, and Ellery Sedgwick. 1876. Frank Leslie's popular monthly. [New York]: Frank Leslie Pub. House. p 343

[409] Pinkerton: " A General Collection of the Best and Most Interesting Voyages https://books.google.com/books?id=mFJBAAAAcAAJ&pg=PA158, Volume 3", London 1809, p.158 The same tradition is transmitted in

[410] *Soc. Diff. Use. Knowl.* (1842), p.310 https://books.google.com/books?id=f5VUAAAAYAAJ&pg=PA310#v=onepage in

[411] " The Complete Works of Sir Walter Scott https://books.google.com/books?id=yRMeAAAAMAAJ&pg=PA216, New York 1833 p.216

[412] " The new statistical account of Scotland, Volum 18 https://books.google.com/books?id=6NE9AAAAcAAJ&pg=PA34", Edinburgh 1838, pp.34-35

[413] Mayer, M.M: " Kleine Chronik der Reichsstadt Nürnberg: Mit einem Grundrisse https://books.google.com/books?id=HS1BAAAAcAAJ&pg=PA102, Nuremberg 1847 p.102,

[414] Krüger, J.G: " Die beglückte und geschmückte Stadt Lübeck https://books.google.com/books?id=RnMAAAAcAAJ&pg=PA20", 1697, p.20

[415] Klemptzen, N.von:" Nicolaus Klemzen vom Pommer-lande und dessen fürsten geschlechtbeschreibung https://books.google.com/books?id=OldFAAAAYAAJ&pg=PA37", Stralsund 1771, p.39

[416] " Blätter für literarische Unterhaltung, Volum 1 https://books.google.com/books?id=BnIDAAAAYAAJ&pg=PA116, p.116, review of "Taschenbuch für vaterländische Geschichte", Berlin 1843

[417] Goemonburo - Goemon-style bath http://www.pixelmap.ca/gallery2/rumi/japan_2010/IMG_2189.jpg.html

[418] https://www.expressen.se/nyheter/qs/avhoppade-ledaren-talar-ut-om-livet-med-is/

[419] http://hrw.org/english/docs/2005/04/27/china10549.htm#UZBEKISTAN

[420] *Biblioteca Historica*, IX, 18-19

[421] Pindar, *Pythian 1*

[422] The Seat of Satan: Ancient Pergamum http://www.cbn.com/700club/features/churchhistory/pergamon/ez28_seat_of_satan_part_1.aspx

[423] "Martyrologium Romanum" (Libreria Editrice Vaticana, 2001)

[424] Chambers, Robert (1885). *Domestic Annals of Scotland*. Edinburgh: W & R Chambers.

[425] Blazek, Matthias: „Letzte Hinrichtung durch Rädern im Königreich Preußen am 13. August 1841" (In the Kingdom of Prussia a criminal was broken upon the wheel for the last time on 13 August 1841), in: Fachprosaforschung – Grenzüberschreitungen. Deutscher Wissenschafts-Verlag (DWV), Baden-Baden, ed. 7, 2011, p. 339–343. Rudolf Kühnapfel, assassin of Andreas Stanislaus von Hatten, the Bishop of Warmia, was sentenced to be executed in this manner, though he was killed by strangulation before his corpse was broken on the wheel.

[426] Svenska Akademiens Ordbok: Rådbråka http://g3.spraakdata.gu.se/saob/show.phtml?filenr=1/223/158.html (Swedish only) Retrieved 12 December 2011.

[427] https://web.archive.org/web/20071028170512/http://www.probertencyclopaedia.com/cgi-bin/res.pl?keyword=Breaking+on+the+Wheel&offset=0

[428] http://www.thrashmetalbands.com/lyrics1.html

[429] *Bondeson* (2002)

[430] For a variant, see *Encycl. Brit.* (1823) p.24 https://encrypted.google.com/books?id= r8YnAAAAMAAJ&pg=PA24#v=onepage&q&f=false
[431] *E.g.*, *Mikkelson* (2006), Just Dying To Get Out http://www.snopes.com/horrors/gruesome/buried.asp
[432] *Barber* (1988)
[433] *Mikkelson* (2006), Just Dying To Get Out http://www.snopes.com/horrors/gruesome/buried.asp
[434] James Cocks; *Memorials of Hatherlow and of the old Chadkick Chapel*; Stockport, 1895.
[435] //www.google.com/patents/US268693
[436] *Windsor* (1921), p.47-48
[437] Tacitus, Church, Brodribb (1868), p. 9 https://books.google.com/books?id= P9pUAAAAcAAJ&pg=PA50#v=onepage&q=buried&f=false
[438] Plutarch, Perrin (1914), Life of Numa Pompilius http://penelope.uchicago.edu/Thayer/E/Roman/Texts/Plutarch/Lives/Numa*.html#10
[439] Ökumen. HeilgenLex. Castulus http://www.heiligenlexikon.de/BiographienC/Castulus_Kastulus.htm
[440] *Catholic Encyclopedia* St. Vitalis http://www.newadvent.org/cathen/15486a.htm
[441] Stemann (1871), pp. 633–634 https://books.google.com/books?id=gF4DAAAAQAAJ&pg=PA633
[442] *Berner* (1866), p. 417 https://books.google.com/books?id=6PFCAAAAcAAJ&pg=PA417
[443] Welser, Werlich, Gasser (1595), pp. 264–265 https://books.google.com/books?hl=no&id= TodPAAAAcAAJ&q=k%C3%B6chin+m%C3%A4gdlin#v=snippet&q=k%C3%B6chin%20m%C3%A4gdlin
[444] Henke (1809), p. 96, footnote r https://books.google.com/books?id= G0MUAAAAQAAJ&pg=PA96
[445] Fidicin (1837), pp. 275–276 https://books.google.com/books?id=x6BSAAAAcAAJ&pg=PA275
[446] Pufendorf (1757) p. 649, p. 57 in "Appendix Variorum Statutorum et Jurium", article 16 https://books.google.com/books?hl=no&id=MQpBAAAAcAAJ&q=gliedmassen+empfangen#v=snippet&q=gliedmassen%20empfangen
[447] *Siebenkees, Kiefhaber* (1792), p.599-600 https://books.google.com/books?id= 2X8AAAAcAAJ&pg=PA599
[448] (in order that she would live for a longer time and expiate the evil act she was condemned for), parenthesis included in original
[449] German original: Das Urtheil befahl dem Nachrichter, die Thäterin lebendig in das Grab zu legen, "und zwo Wellen Dornen, die eine under, die ander uff sie,-, doch das es Irn zuvor ein Schüssel uff das Angesicht legen, in welche er ein Loch machen und ihr durch dasselb (damit sie desto lenger leben und bemelte böse Misshandlung abbiesen möge) ein Ror in Mund geben, volgens uff sie drey spring thun und sie darnach mit Erden bedecken solle
[450] Osenbrüggen (1868), p. 357 https://books.google.com/books?id=YWE7AAAAcAAJ&pg=PA357
[451] Feucht (1967)
[452] Alighieri, O'Donnell (1852), p. 120 https://books.google.com/books?id= 1qFWAAAAcAAJ&pg=PA120
[453] *Muravyeva, Rosslyn, Tosi* (2012), p. 227 https://books.google.com/books?id= rUqU5305GxEC&pg=PA227 Source in Russian:http://allpravo.ru/library/doc101p/instrum2363/
[454] Rosen (2005) Virtual Jewish History Tour: Ukraine https://www.jewishvirtuallibrary.org/jsource/vjw/ukraine.html, for example: Chmielnicki Massacre (1648–1649): "In the city of Mogila they slaughtered 800 nobles together with their wives and children as well as 700 Jews, also with wives and children. Some were cut into pieces, others were ordered to dig graves into which Jewish women and children were thrown and buried alive."
[455] https://foreignpolicy.com/2018/04/09/the-right-to-kill-brazil-infanticide/
[456] Николов, Борис Й. Вътрешна македоно-одринска революционна организация. Войводи и ръководители (1893–1934). Биографично-библиографски справочник, София, 2001, стр. 89 – 90.

[457] *Chang* (1997)
[458] Администрация (2008) ЙОРЦАЙТ http://holocaust-museum.org.ua/articles/arkhiv-nomerov-za-2008-god/sentyabr-2008-god-9-110/article-204.htm
[459] Sciolino (2007) A Priest Methodically Reveals Ukrainian Jews' Fate https://www.nytimes.com/2007/10/06/world/europe/06priest.html?pagewanted=all&_r=0:"Other witnesses described how the German were allowed only one bullet to the back per victim and that the Jews sometimes were buried alive."
[460] Yad Vashem Killing Sites: Stalino Region, 1941–1942 http://www.yadvashem.org/yv/en/about/institute/killing_sites_catalog_details_full.asp?region=Stalino January 11, 1942: "About 1,244 Jews (max. 3,000) were shot to death or buried alive; the little children were poisoned."
[461] Arem, Bock (2003) My Family Trip to Belarus http://www.jewishgen.org/belarus/newsletter/aremfamilytrip.htm Witness from Urechye: Mikhail remembered that in 1942, people who the Nazis thought wouldn't be helpful to them were marched to the forest and shot. Meyer Zalman and his family would be amongst the 625 families that shared this fate. In 1943 the remaining 93 Jewish families were buried alive. The ground moved for three days afterwards, but the Nazis heavily guarded the site.
[462] Witness Manie Feinholtz: On the morning of September 21, 1941, all the Jews were collected and sent out to work. During the course of the day, they discovered that some of them had been sent to dig a pit. More than a thousand of people were buried alive. World Holocaust Forum Uman. Memoirs of Manie Feinholtz http://www.worldholocaustforum.org/eng/persons/1/
[463] Cheong (2011), wordpress blog The Killing Fields – Pol Pot and the Khmer Rouge http://scheong.wordpress.com/2011/11/17/the-killing-fields-pol-pot-and-the-khmer-rouge/
[464] Chang, Jung. *The Unknown Story of Mao*. Anchor Books (2005) p. 170
[465] *Mysterious People* Mind Power – Strange Cases of Suspended Animation http://www.mysteriouspeople.com/suspended_animation.htm
[466] *BBC News* (2011) Russian who buried himself alive dies by mistake https://www.bbc.co.uk/news/world-europe-13623938
[467] *MacLeod Banks* (1931), pp.55-60
[468] *Bondeson* (2001), pp.35-50
[469] MythBusters.Season 1: Episode 5, "Buried Alive", Original airdate: October 24, 2003.
[470] https://books.google.com/books?id=1qFWAAAAcAAJ
[471] https://books.google.com/books?id=6PFCAAAAcAAJ
[472] https://books.google.com/books?id=r8YnAAAAMAAJ
[473] //www.worldcat.org/oclc/462909742
[474] https://books.google.com/books?id=x6BSAAAAcAAJ
[475] https://books.google.com/books?id=G0MUAAAAQAAJ
[476] https://books.google.com/books?id=rUqU5305GxEC
[477] https://books.google.com/books?id=YWE7AAAAcAAJ
[478] https://books.google.com/books?hl=no&id=MQpBAAAAcAAJ
[479] https://books.google.com/books?id=gF4DAAAAQAAJ
[480] https://books.google.com/books?id=P9pUAAAAcAAJ
[481] https://books.google.com/books?id=2X8AAAAAcAAJ
[482] https://books.google.com/books?id=TodPAAAAcAAJ
[483] https://www.bbc.co.uk/news/world-europe-13623938
[484] https://calgaryherald.com/Pakistani+police+arrest+accused+burying+alive+newborn+daughter/6935003/story.html
[485] http://www.dailymail.co.uk/news/article-2173837/Newborn-girl-buried-alive-father-Pakistan-deformed.html
[486] //www.jstor.org/stable/1256410
[487] https://timesmachine.nytimes.com/timesmachine/1885/02/21/109780353.pdf
[488] https://timesmachine.nytimes.com/timesmachine/1886/01/19/103950202.pdf
[489] https://books.google.com/books?id=a4bVAAAAMAAJ
[490] http://www.medicinae.org/e16
[491] http://www.jewishgen.org/belarus/newsletter/aremfamilytrip.htm
[492] http://holocaust-museum.org.ua/articles/arkhiv-nomerov-za-2008-god/sentyabr-2008-god-9-110/article-204.htm

[493] http://www.newadvent.org/cathen/15486a.htm
[494] http://scheong.wordpress.com/2011/11/17/the-killing-fields-pol-pot-and-the-khmer-rouge/
[495] http://www.medterms.com/script/main/art.asp?articlekey=11719
[496] http://www.snopes.com/horrors/gruesome/buried.asp
[497] http://www.mysteriouspeople.com/suspended_animation.htm
[498] http://www.heiligenlexikon.de/BiographienC/Castulus_Kastulus.htm
[499] http://penelope.uchicago.edu/Thayer/E/Roman/Texts/Plutarch/Lives/
[500] https://www.jewishvirtuallibrary.org/jsource/vjw/ukraine.html
[501] https://www.nytimes.com/2007/10/06/world/europe/06priest.html?pagewanted=all&_r=1&
[502] http://www.worldholocaustforum.org/eng/persons/1/
[503] http://www.yadvashem.org/yv/en/about/institute/killing_sites_catalog_details_full.asp?region=Stalino
[504] http://www.poenightmares.com/
[505] http://www.bbc.co.uk/northernireland/yourplaceandmine/armagh/mccall_grave.shtml
[506] *Murphy* (2012), pp. 67–68 https://books.google.com/books?id=tXywBrmhPTUC&pg=PA67
[507] *Roth* (2010), p. 5 https://books.google.com/books?id=awrOHv-gtqQC&pg=PA5
[508] *Wilkinson* (2011): Senusret I incident, p. 169 https://books.google.com/books?id=P07rgiJjsk4C&pg=PA169 Osorkon incident, p. 412 https://books.google.com/books?id=P07rgiJjsk4C&pg=PA412
[509] *White* (2011), p. 167 https://books.google.com/books?id=GVhQ_lDWq0EC&pg=PA167
[510] Diodorus Siculus, 1.77.8 http://penelope.uchicago.edu/Thayer/E/Roman/Texts/Diodorus_Siculus/1D*.html, accessed at LacusCurtius http://penelope.uchicago.edu/Thayer/E/Roman/home.html
[511] *Schneider* (2008), p. 154 https://books.google.com/books?id=4hHLe60cYBcC&pg=PA154
[512] *Olmstead* (1918) p. 66 https://www.jstor.org/stable/1946342
[513] *Reeder* (2012), p. 82 https://books.google.com/books?id=PiNSpBdtsCgC&pg=PA82
[514] Full list in *Quint* (2005), p. 257 https://books.google.com/books?id=2nEZQXWsXG4C&pg=PA257
[515] Quotation from *Ben-Menahem, Edrei, Hecht* (2012), p. 111 https://books.google.com/books?id=J-ZE_BJpJnIC&pg=PA111
[516] On this view, see for example, *Zvi Gilat, Lifshitz* (2013), p. 62, footnote 73 https://books.google.com/books?id=4h8iAQAAQBAJ&pg=PA62
[517] See *Watson* (1998) **Ulpian**, section 48.19.8.2, p. 361. **Callistratus**, sections 48.19.28.11–12, p. 366
[518] *Kyle* (2002), p. 53 https://books.google.com/books?id=x4vekGBc_McC&pg=PA53
[519] Martyrdom of Polycarp http://www.ccel.org/ccel/schaff/anf01.iv.iv.html
[520] Juvenal has an extended description of the tunica molesta, the punishment as meted out by Emperor Nero as contained in Tacitus matches the concept. See, for example *Pagán* (2012), p. 53 https://books.google.com/books?id=bHzMYrWHjVoC&pg=PA53
[521] *Miley* (1843), pp. 223–224 https://books.google.com/books?id=iSsLAAAAYAAJ&pg=PA223
[522] Law text found in *Pharr* (2001), pp. 244–245 https://books.google.com/books?id=-ROBb7SIvYgC&pg=PA244 The full law was changed in context to the penalties just 20 years later by Constantine's son, Constantius II, for free citizens aiding and abetting in the abduction, to an unspecified "capital punishment". The full severity of the law was to be kept, however, for slaves. p. 245 https://books.google.com/books?id=-ROBb7SIvYgC&pg=PA245, *ibidem*
[523] Law text in Codex Justinianus 9.11.1, as referred to in *Winroth, Müller, Sommar* (2006), p. 107 https://books.google.com/books?id=4smZ4JjGJcsC&pg=PA107
[524] *Pickett* (2009), p. xxi https://books.google.com/books?id=XH-SMq-NKf0C&pg=PR21
[525] On ritual description, Plutarch, and in general, see *Markoe* (2000), pp. 132–136 https://books.google.com/books?id=smPZ-ou74EwC&pg=PA132 On Diodorus, see *Schwartz, Houghton, Macchiarelli, Bondioli* (2010), Skeletal remains..do not support http://www.plosone.org/article/info:doi/10.1371/journal.pone.0009177 on phrase "the act of laughing", see for example, *Decker* (2001), p. 3 http://ancienthistory.about.com/library/bl/uc_decker_carthre13.htm
[526] **Generally accepting** the tradition of child sacrifice, see *Markoe* (2000), pp. 132–136 https://books.google.com/books?id=smPZ-ou74EwC&pg=PA132 **Generally skeptical**, see *Schwartz,*

Houghton, Macchiarelli, Bondioli (2010), Skeletal remains..do not support http://www.plosone.org/article/info:doi/10.1371/journal.pone.0009177

[527] *Julius Caesar, McDevitt, Bohn* (1851) **On penalty for conspiracy**, p. 4 https://books.google.com/books?hl=no&id=7FsIAAAAQAAJ&pg=PA4 **On criminals in large wicker frames**, p. 149 https://books.google.com/books?hl=no&id=7FsIAAAAQAAJ&pg=PA149 **On funeral human sacrifice**, pp. 150–151 https://books.google.com/books?hl=no&id=7FsIAAAAQAAJ&pg=P150

[528] This case, and a number of others in *Pluskowski* (2013), pp. 77–78 https://books.google.com/books?id=-8NykshHHesC&pg=PA77

[529] *Hamilton, Hamilton, Stoyanov* (1998), p. 13, footnote 42 https://books.google.com/books?id=uH-8AAAAIAAJ&pg=PA13

[530] *Haldon* (1997), p. 333, footnote 22 https://books.google.com/books?id=pSHmT1G_5T0C&pg=PA333

[531] *Trenchard-Smith, Turner* (2010), p. 48, footnote 58 https://books.google.com/books?id=2ombkgpGt_AC&pg=PA48

[532] Sumner, William Graham, 1840-1910. Folkways, a study of the sociological importance of usages, manners, customs, mores, and morals. p.247 (Publ. 1906); https://archive.org/stream/folkwaysastudys01sumngoog#page/n256/mode/2up

[533] Both incidents in *Weiss* (2004), [p. 104]

[534] *Prager, Telushkin* (2007), [p. 87]

[535] *Kantor* (2005) [p. 203]

[536] *Bülau* (1860), [pp. 423–424]

[537] *Richards* (2013), pp. 161–163 https://books.google.com/books?id=saXbAAAAQBAJ&pg=PA161

[538] *John, Pope* (2003), p. 177 https://books.google.com/books?id=-_fnv5pmECsC&pg=PA177

[539] *Smirke* (1865), pp. 326–331 https://books.google.com/books?id=G4dbAAAAQAAJ&pg=PA326

[540] Henry Kamen, *The Spanish Inquisition: A Historical Revision.*, p. 62, (Yale University Press, 1997).

[541] On mercy, and 50,000 estimate, for Marranos *Telchin* (2004), p. 41 https://books.google.com/books?id=4K7QH76_HdIC&pg=PA41 On 30,000 estimate of Marranos *killed*, see *Pasachoff, Littman* (2005), p. 151 https://books.google.com/books?id=z4eaj09hscAC&pg=PA151

[542] These information are included in the appendix, "Historical Notes" to the novel "The Hidden Scroll" *Anouchi* (2009), p. 471 https://books.google.com/books?id=pbP-yZL00eAC&pg=PT471

[543] *Cipolla* (2005), p. 91 https://books.google.com/books?id=Sggys-_O-2cC&pg=PA91

[544] *Stillman, Zucker* (1993) **On the Río de la Plata incident**, see *Matilde Gini de Barnatan*, p. 144 https://books.google.com/books?id=yq7VUKWz5dwC&pg=PA144, **on Mexico City incident**, see *Eva Alexandra Uchmany*, p. 128 https://books.google.com/books?id=yq7VUKWz5dwC&pg=PA128

[545] *Carr* (2009), p. 101 https://books.google.com/books?id=netlOtzI6R8C&pg=PA101

[546] *Kamen* (1997)The Spanish Inquisition - A Historical Revision FOURTH EDITION By Henry Kamen#page/n1355 https://archive.org/stream/spanishinquisition2/

[547] List And Analysis of State Papers Foreign, Jul 1593 – Dec 1594. v.5; p.444 (595): by Public Record Office ()

[548] *Matar* (2013), p. xxi https://books.google.com/books?id=z2QRd_rbWu8C&pg=PR21

[549] In Majorca, Atoning for the Sins of 1691 https://www.nytimes.com/2011/05/07/world/europe/07iht-spain07.html

[550] Nachman Seltzer,*Incredible*, Shaar Press, 2016

[551] Already noted originally by *Hunter* (1886), pp. 253–254 https://books.google.com/books?id=Vdv7AQAAQBAJ&pg=PA253, see also *Salomon, Sassoon, Saraiva* (2001), pp. 345–347

[552] See extensive table at Portuguese Inquisition, *de Almeida* (1923), in particular p. 442

[553] See for **first time** *Heng* (2013), p. 56 https://books.google.com/books?id=pRXvHbNLPQ0C&pg=PA56 on **option of public repentance** *Puff, Bennett, Karras* (2013), p. 387 https://books.google.com/books?id=QThLAAAAQBAJ&pg=PA387

[554] *Pickett* (2009), p. 178 https://books.google.com/books?id=XH-SMq-NKf0C&pg=PA178

[555] **On Geneva and Venice**, see *Coward, Dynes, Donaldson* (1992), p. 36 https://books.google.com/books?id=y8_Ya2s3zN8C&pg=PA36
[556] *Crompton* (2006), p. 450 https://books.google.com/books?id=TfBYd9xVaXcC&pg=PA450
[557] *Lithgow* (1814), p. 305 https://books.google.com/books?id=whMwAAAAYAAJ&pg=PA305
[558] *Osenbrüggen* (1860), p. 290 https://books.google.com/books?id=X9NCAAAAcAAJ&pg=PA290
[559] specified as men or women found guilty of same-sex sexual behaviour or guilty of having had sex with animals.
[560] As late as in 1730 Posen, a church robber had his right hand cut off, and the stump covered in pitch. Then, the pitch was ignited, and the person was burnt alive on a pyre as well. *Oehlschlaeger* (1866), p. 55 https://books.google.com/books?id=F41aAAAAcAAJ&pg=PA55
[561] No fixed penalty was placed on performing acts of witchcraft that had caused no harm
[562] All in *Koch* (1824) **Coin forgers**: Article 111, p. 52 https://books.google.com/books?id=nBZDAAAAcAAJ&pg=PA52, **Malevolent witchcraft**: Article 109, p. 55 https://books.google.com/books?id=nBZDAAAAcAAJ&pg=PA55 **Sexual acts contrary to nature**: Article 116, p. 58 https://books.google.com/books?id=nBZDAAAAcAAJ&pg=PA58, **Arson**: Article 125, p. 61 https://books.google.com/books?id=nBZDAAAAcAAJ&pg=PA61, **Theft of sacred objects**: Article 172, p. 84 https://books.google.com/books?id=nBZDAAAAcAAJ&pg=PA84
[563] *Osenbrüggen* (1854), p. 21 https://books.google.com/books?id=C-4PAAAAYAAJ&pg=PA21 For a similar, more modern assessment, as well as locating the incident to Hötzelsroda, see Dietze (1995)
[564] Last name "Mothas" used in extended account in *Bischoff, Hitzig* (1832), real name "Thomas" given in *Herden* (2005), p. 89 https://books.google.com/books?id=wVNuf9VEhGkC&pg=PA89
[565] On the manner of execution according to the original account, see *Bischoff, Hitzig* (1832), p. 178 https://books.google.com/books?id=88dCAAAAcAAJ&pg=PA178 Contemporary newspaper notice, *Hübner* (1804), p. 760, column 2 https://books.google.com/books?id=jyVEAAAAcAAJ&pg=PT964
[566] **Original account** by investigating police officer Heinrich L. Hermann, *Hermann* (1818) **Gustav Rudbrach's mention** *Rudbrach* (1992), p. 247 https://books.google.com/books?id=3JOVbGPdrjYC&pg=PA247 **Precise moment of strangulation** *Gräff* (1834), p. 56 https://books.google.com/books?id=v8ZDAAAAcAAJ&pg=PA56 **Modern newspaper article** *Springer* (2008), Das Letzte Feuer http//www.yasni.de
[567] *Osenbrüggen* (1854), pp. 21–22, footnote 83 https://books.google.com/books?id=C-4PAAAAYAAJ&pg=PA21
[568] *Thurston* (1912) Witchcraft http://www.newadvent.org/cathen/15674a.htm%20New%20Advent, 2010 web resource.
[569] Professional researchers in the 19th, and early 20th century tended to *refuse* giving any quantification at all but, when pushed, typically landed on about 100,000 to 1 million victims
[570] A lowest bound of 30,000 and a highest upper bound of 100,000 still within acceptability, but with a minority of professional researchers supporting either of them.
[571] See Wolfgang Behringer (1998) on the history of witch-counting, and on specialist academic consensus, Neun Millionen Hexen http://www.historicum.net/themen/hexenforschung/thementexte/rezeption/art/Neun_Millionen/html/ca/0e43e9dea3a4144c50997da6aa74bd34/ Originally published in GWU 49 (1998) pp. 664–685, web publication 2006
[572] Contemporary description of the burning at Ile-des-Javiaux in *Barber* (1993), p. 241 https://books.google.com/books?id=GEu58-OIT1MC&pg=PA241
[573] Extracts of eyewitness report at website of Columbia University, *Peter from Mladonovic* (2003), How was executed Jan Hus http://www.columbia.edu/~js322/misc/hus-eng.html
[574] Reconstruction of Joan of Arc's death scene in *Mooney, Patterson* (2002), pp. 1–2 https://books.google.com/books?id=0hYWzuecyHMC&pg=PA1 excerpt from *Mooney* (1919)
[575] Eyewitness account provided in *Landucci, Jarvis* (1927), pp. 142–143 https://archive.org/stream/ldpd_10273453_000#page/n169/mode/2up
[576] According to eyewitness Alexander Ales, Hamilton entered the pyre at noon, and died after six hours burning, see *Tjernagel* (1974, web reprint), p. 6 http://www.wlsessays.net/node/1535

[577] Description of John Frith's death in *Foxe, Townsend, Cattley* (1838), p. 15 https://books.google.com/books?id=5hA5AQAAMAAJ&pg=PA15

[578] Detailed description of Servetus' death at *Kurth* (2002) Out of the Flames http://www.salon.com/2002/11/12/goldstone/

[579] A perfunctory official notice of the manner of his death 17 February 1600, is contained in *Rowland* (2009), p. 10 https://books.google.com/books?id=Gus_rugtLN0C&pg=PA10

[580] Apparently, Grenadier had been promised to be strangled prior to his burning, but his executioners reneged on that promise as he was fastened to the stake. See **modern monograph** *Rapley* (2001), in particular pp. 195–198 https://books.google.com/books?id=lxlHuai91ZsC&pg=PA195, for a **classic description**, see Alexandre Dumas on the execution details in *Dumas* (1843), pp. 424–426 https://books.google.com/books?id=t64SAQAAMAAJ&pg=PA424

[581] Alan Wood describes Avvakum's execution as follows: *Avvakum and three fellow prisoners were led from their icy cells to an elaborate pyre of pinewood billets and there burned alive. The tsar had finally rid himself of "this turbulent priest"*, Wood (2011), p. 44 https://books.google.com/books?id=VZZLAQAAQBAJ&pg=PA44

[582] *Foxe, Milner, Cobbin* (1856), pp. 608–609 https://books.google.com/books?id=t1pIAAAAYAAJ&pg=PA608

[583] *Foxe, Milner, Cobbin* (1856), pp. 864–865 https://books.google.com/books?id=t1pIAAAAYAAJ&pg=PA864

[584] *Foxe, Milner, Cobbin* (1856), pp. 925–926 https://books.google.com/books?id=t1pIAAAAYAAJ&pg=PA925

[585] For Denmark, see for example, *Burns* (2003), pp. 64–65 https://books.google.com/books?id=Qr6_q-chR6MC&pg=PA64

[586] John Foxe is particularly mentioned in being assiduous at documenting such cases of persecutions. See, *Miller* (1972), p. 72 https://books.google.com/books?id=3S89AAAAIAAJ&pg=PA72

[587] For claim of being last heretic burned at the stake, see for example, *Durso* (2007), p. 29 https://books.google.com/books?id=68jfRYQo3zsC&pg=PA29

[588] *Sayles* (1971) p. 31 https://books.google.com/books?id=HVQLAAAAIAAJ&pg=PA31

[589] *Richards* (1812), p. 1190 https://books.google.com/books?id=JRkwAAAAYAAJ&pg=PA1190

[590] *Willis-Bund* (1982), p. 95 https://books.google.com/books?id=2gA9AAAAIAAJ&pg=PA95

[591] Direct citation in *McLynn* (2013), p. 122 https://books.google.com/books?id=Ylf8t7uSGJEC&pg=PA122

[592] *McLynn* (2013), p. 122 https://books.google.com/books?id=Ylf8t7uSGJEC&pg=PA122

[593] Comprehensive list at capitalpunishmentuk.org, Burning at the stake http://www.capitalpunishmentuk.org/burning.html.

[594] *O'Shea* (1999), p. 3 https://books.google.com/books?id=YvdKyEJo0osC&pg=PA3

[595] See website article, The Case of Catherine Hayes http://rictornorton.co.uk/grubstreet/hayes.htm at rictornorton.co.uk http://rictornorton.co.uk/ See also the detailed synthesis at capitalpunishmentuk.org, Catherine Hayes burnt for Petty Treason http://www.capitalpunishmentuk.org/hayes.html

[596] "Some time in the 1590s, Anne became a Roman Catholic." *Wilson* (1963), p. 95 "Some time after 1600, but well before March 1603, Queen Anne was received into the Catholic Church in a secret chamber in the royal palace" *Fraser* (1997), p. 15 "The Queen ... [converted] from her native Lutheranism to a discreet, but still politically embarrassing Catholicism which alienated many ministers of the Kirk" *Croft* (2003), pp. 24–25 "Catholic foreign ambassadors—who would surely have welcomed such a situation—were certain that the Queen was beyond their reach. 'She is a Lutheran', concluded the Venetian envoy Nicolo Molin in 1606." *Stewart* (2003), p. 182 "In 1602 a report appeared, claiming that Anne ... had converted to the Catholic faith some years before. The author of this report, the Scottish Jesuit Robert Abercromby, testified that James had received his wife's desertion with equanimity, commenting, 'Well, wife, if you cannot live without this sort of thing, do your best to keep things as quiet as possible.' Anne would, indeed, keep her religious beliefs as quiet as possible: for the remainder of her life—even after her death—they remained obfuscated." *Hogge* (2005), pp. 303–304

[597] *Pavlac* (2009), p. 145 https://books.google.com/books?id=KCjlptFEMZsC&pg=PA145

[598] de Ledrede, Wright (1843)
[599] de Ledrede, Davidson, Ward (2004)
[600] Story of flight in contemporary chronicle Gilbert (2012), p. cxxxiv https://books.google.com/books?id=R_w-CZ0eXnYC&pg=PR134
[601] McCullough (2000), The Fairy Defense https://query.nytimes.com/gst/fullpage.html?res=9D0CE4D91E3AF93BA35753C1A9669C8B63
[602] Scott (1940) p. 41
[603] CelebrateBoston.com (2014), "Maria, Burned at the Stake" http://www.celebrateboston.com/crime/puritan-burned-at-stake-maria.htm
[604] Mark and Phillis Executions http://www.celebrateboston.com/crime/puritan-mark-and-phillis-executions.htm (2014)
[605] Marie-Joseph Angélique
[606] McManus (1973), p. 86 https://books.google.com/books?id=2H3S1OLtmagC&pg=PA86
[607] Hoey (1974), Terror in New York–1741 http://www.americanheritage.com/content/terror-new-york--1741
[608] De las Casas (1974), pp. 34–35 https://books.google.com/books?id=krP0qAvXK4QC&pg=PA34
[609] Carvacho (2004), p. 62 https://books.google.com/books?hl=no&id=P30WGMWwsqMC&pg=PA62 "y que habiendo llegado el caso de practicar lo determinado por el Consejo en auto de 4 de febrero de 1732, ... acordaron, después de revisar la causa de Mariana de Castro y lo determinado por la Suprema el 4 de febrero de 1732"
[610] Waddell (1863), p. 19 https://books.google.com/books?id=bt71nHmVezMC&pg=PA19
[611] Blake (1857), pp. 154–155 https://books.google.com/books?id=Z6lDAQAAIAAJ&pg=PA154
[612] Woblers (1855), p. 205 https://books.google.com/books?id=WqcNAAAAQAAJ&pg=PA205
[613] William St Clair, *That Greece Might Still Be Free* (2008) Hydra incident, p. xxiv, *those suspected of hiding money*, p. 45, *the three Turkish children*, p. 77, *baked in ovens*, p. 81
[614] Zurkhana, Houtsma (1987), p. 830 https://books.google.com/books?id=wpM3AAAAIAAJ&pg=PA830
[615] Digby (1853), pp. 342–345 https://books.google.com/books?id=4K06AQAAMAAJ&pg=PA342
[616] De Thevenot, Lovell (1687), p. 69 https://books.google.com/books?jtp=69&id=6q9EAAAAcAAJ
[617] Moryson, Hadfield (2001), p. 171 https://books.google.com/books?id=fl6gkL5h6A0C&pg=PA171
[618] Braithwaite(1729)On apostates citation, see p. 366 https://books.google.com/books?jtp=366&id=iJA_AAAAMAAJ, on the conditional fate of non-Muslims, see p. 355 https://books.google.com/books?jtp=355&id=iJA_AAAAMAAJ
[619] Shaw (1757), p. 253 https://books.google.com/books?id=0c4GAAAAQAAJ&pg=PA253
[620] Stillman (1979), pp. 310–311 https://books.google.com/books?id=bFN2ismyhEYC&pg=PA310
[621] Kantor (1993), p. 230 https://books.google.com/books?id=1SD_AQAAQBAJ&pg=PA230
[622] JOS Calendar Conversion Results http://data.jewishgen.org/wconnect/wc.dll?jg~jgsys~josdates, Hirschberg (1981), p. 20 https://books.google.com/books?id=g_mh5fuel0QC&pg=PA20
[623] Tully (1817), p. 365 https://books.google.com/books?id=QBkQAQAAMAAJ&pg=PA365
[624] Ferrier (1996), p. 94 https://books.google.com/books?id=5CLkDgmVs1QC&pg=PA94
[625] Wills (1891), p. 204 http://openlibrary.org/books/OL7180554M/In_the_land_of_the_lion_and_sun
[626] Grote (2013), p. 305, footnote 1 https://books.google.com/books?id=62HlSNN2lqQC&pg=PA305
[627] Quote and extrapolation to be found in *Collins* (2004), p. 35
[628] Encycl. Perth. (1816), p. 131, column 1 https://books.google.com/books?id=VoJnKgmUH54C&pg=PA131
[629] Klein (1833), p. 351 https://books.google.com/books?id=ppwAAAAcAAJ&pg=PA351

[630] *Stevens* (1764), pp. 522–523 https://books.google.com/books?id=DIsfAAAAMAAJ&pg=PA522
[631] For full title and provenance, see item 357 in *Nassau* (1824), p. 17 https://books.google.com/books?id=MDlbAAAAQAAJ&pg=RA1-PA17
[632] *Steel* (2013), p. 98 https://books.google.com/books?id=Ae63Gjp21SgC&pg=PA98
[633] Marcus Licinius Crassus
[634] *Saunders* (2001), p. 57 https://books.google.com/books?id=nFx3OlrBMpQC&pg=PA57 According to the 13th-century historian al-Nasawi, the governor Inal Khan (who had assassinated the Mongol ambassadors and thus given Genghis Khan cause to invade), had the molten gold poured into his eyes and ears, rather than down his throat. *Cameron, Sela* (2010), p. 128 https://books.google.com/books?id=SAX5ohFkcVgC&pg=PA128
[635] Crawford regards the Hulagu story as a legend *Crawford* (2003), p. 149 https://books.google.com/books?id=BfNqgYlo9fMC&pg=PA149
[636] *Cummins, Cole, Zorach* (2009), p. 99 https://books.google.com/books?id=IUKBQfzKlIYC&pg=PA99
[637] *Begbie* (1834), p. 447 https://books.google.com/books?id=0MwNAAAAQAAJ&pg=PA447
[638] *Eaton* (2005), p. 121 https://books.google.com/books?id=DNNgdBWoYKoC&pg=PA121
[639] *Peletz* (2002), p. 28 https://books.google.com/books?id=q4TA4hjqjJ0C&pg=PA28
[640] *Buckingham* (1835), p. 250 https://books.google.com/books?id=qrhHAQAAIAAJ&pg=PA250
[641] *Berger, Sicker* (2009), p. 6 https://books.google.com/books?id=4jjhnbu8ytEC&pg=PA6
[642] *Sharma, Srivastava* (1981), p. 361 https://books.google.com/books?id=nKJiBUFrmfoC&pg=PA361
[643] *Benn* (2007), p. 3 https://books.google.com/books?id=dWL6EEkL8goC&pg=PA3
[644] *Benn* (2007), pp. 198–199 https://books.google.com/books?id=dWL6EEkL8goC&pg=PA198
[645] *Lee* (2010), pp. 121–122 https://books.google.com/books?id=LKj2B9vd7HsC&pg=PA121
[646] *Matsumoto* (2009), p. 73 https://books.google.com/books?id=kF1sTidtP_sC&pg=PA73
[647] *Perckmayr* (1738), p. 628 https://books.google.com/books?id=3lpBAAAAcAAJ&pg=PA628
[648] *Calvert, Rowe* (1858), p. 258 https://books.google.com/books?id=Ov1EAAAAIAAJ&pg=PA258
[649] See *Hogg* (1980)
[650] Shakuntala Rao Shastri, *Women in the Sacred Laws*—the later law books (1960), also reproduced online at http://www.hindubooks.org/women_in_the_sacredlaws/ .
[651] *Sashi* (1996), p.115
[652] For Yang's full discussion back and forth, see *Yang, Sarkar, Sarkar* (2008), pp.21-23 http://books.google.no/books?id=GEPYbuzOwcQC&pg=PA21
[653] S.M. *Ikram, Embree* (1964) XVII. "Economic and Social Developments under the Mughals" http://www.columbia.edu/itc/mealac/pritchett/00islamlinks/ikram/part2_17.html This page maintained by Prof. Frances Pritchett, Columbia University
[654] These statistics are further researched and discussed by other scholars, for their reliability (in particular, *objections* to that) and representation, see **For detailed official statistical information 1815-1829**,*Yang, Sarkar, Sarkar* (2008), pp.23-25 http://books.google.no/books?id=GEPYbuzOwcQC&pg=PA23 see pages 24 and 25 in particular, history behind them, p.23
[655] For notice of estimate of last time, see *Schulte Nordholt* (2010), pp. 211–212, footnote 56 https://books.google.com/books?id=ZUVlAAAAQBAJ&pg=PA211 For estimate of restriction to royal widows, see *Wiener* (1995), p. 267 https://books.google.com/books?id=GE1uc1UNXNYC&pg=PA267
[656] *Mittra, Kumar* (2004), p. 200 https://books.google.com/books?id=hYEQGam5hVgC&pg=PA200
[657] Biographical entry of C.H.L. Hahn at BIOGRAPHIES OF NAMIBIAN PERSONALITIES http://www.klausdierks.com/Biographies/Biographies_H.htm
[658] *Hahn* (1966), p. 33 https://books.google.com/books?id=Z8Z3FQXOiNEC&pg=PA33
[659] *Wilson* (1853), p. 4 https://books.google.com/books?id=JdkHAAAAQAAJ&pg=PA4
[660] *Hofmann* (2013), p. 86 https://books.google.com/books?id=JXZzAQAAQBAJ&pg=PA86

[661] Wilfried F. Schoeller: *Rückkehr in die verschollene Geschichte* http://www.deutschlandfunk.de/rueckkehr-in-die-verschollene-geschichte.700.de.html?dram:article_id=83403 Deutschlandfunk.de, 16 December 2007.
[662] Gernot Facius: *Kleines Wunder an der Moldau* https://www.welt.de/debatte/kolumnen/Meine-Woche/article6060701/Kleines-Wunder-an-der-Moldau.html Welt.de, 10 November 2008.
[663] *Grellet* (2010) Autorizado a visitar família.. http://www1.folha.uol.com.br/cotidiano/740136-autorizado-a-visitar-familia-condenado-por-morte-de-tim-lopes-foge-da-prisao.shtml
[664] *França* (2002), Como na Chicago de Capone http://veja.abril.com.br/300102/p_094.html
[665] *Paige* (1983), pp. 699–737
[666] *Garrard-Burnett* (2010), p. 141 https://books.google.com/books?id=BXWwm7jo-hEC&pg=PA141
[667] http://www.cnn.com/2015/05/27/americas/guatemala-girl-burned-mob/index.html
[668] ANNUAL REPORT OF THE INTER-AMERICAN COMMISSION ON HUMAN RIGHTS, 1987–1988. Case # 01a/88; Case 9755. Chile, 12 September 1988.
[669] *DuBois* (1916), pp. 1–8 http://dl.lib.brown.edu/pdfs/1292363091648500.pdf (Archive https://www.webcitation.org/6FXqUzw4u?url=http://dl.lib.brown.edu/pdfs/1292363091648500.pdf)
[670] Goodwyn, Wade. " Waco Recalls a 90-Year-Old 'Horror' https://www.npr.org/templates/story/story.php?storyId=5401868." *National Public Radio*. 13 May 2006. (Transcript of radio story https://www.npr.org/templates/transcript/transcript.php?storyId=5401868)
[671] Victor Suvorov (1995)
[672] Echo of Moscow webpage http://www.echo.msk.ru/programs/hrushev/655886-echo
[673] Suvorov profile https://www.scribd.com/doc/46398733/Suvorov-Aquarium-The-Career-and-Defection-of-a-Soviet-Spy-1985, scribd.com
[674] North Korean official 'executed by flame-thrower' - Telegraph https://www.telegraph.co.uk/news/worldnews/asia/northkorea/10750082/North-Korean-official-executed-by-flame-thrower.html
[675] U.S. Sanctions against South Africa, 1986 http://www.etsu.edu/cas/history/docs/southafrica.htm , College of Arts and Sciences, *East Tennessee State University*; retrieved 14 October 2007.
[676] Hilton, Ronald. worksmerica_latinamerica03102004.htm "Latin America http://wais.stanford.edu/LatinAmerica/latinaDerivative", World Association of International Studies, *Stanford University*; retrieved 14 October 2007.
[677] *Kanina* (2008) "Mob burns to death 11 Kenyan 'witches'" https://www.reuters.com/article/latestCrisis/idUSL21301127
[678] *BBC News* (1999) Missionary widow continues leprosy work http://news.bbc.co.uk/2/hi/asia-pacific/264326.stm
[679] *Sangvi* (1999) A Kill Before Dying http://www.rediff.com/news/1999/feb/08vir.htm
[680] http://www.highbeam.com/doc/1G1-180493576.html
[681] BBC:Jordan pilot hostage Moaz al-Kasasbeh 'burned alive' https://www.bbc.com/news/world-middle-east-31121160
[682] The victims are shown burning to death in the last three minutes of the film.
[683] *Feek* (2011), Burnt body victim named http://www.stuff.co.nz/national/4573912/Burnt-body-victim-named-as-search-goes-offshore
[684] https://books.google.com/books?id=XxUvfIko1TUC
[685] https://books.google.com/books?id=pbP-yZL00eAC
[686] https://books.google.com/books?id=GEu58-OIT1MC
[687] http://news.bbc.co.uk/2/hi/asia-pacific/264326.stm
[688] https://books.google.com/books?id=0MwNAAAAQAAJ
[689] http://www.historicum.net/themen/hexenforschung/thementexte/rezeption/art/Neun_Millionen/html/ca/0e43e9dea3a4144c50997da6aa74bd34/
[690] https://books.google.com/books?id=J-ZE_BJpJnIC
[691] https://books.google.com/books?id=dWL6EEkL8goC
[692] https://books.google.com/books?id=4jjhnbu8ytEC
[693] https://books.google.com/books?id=88dCAAAAcAAJ&pg=PA109
[694] https://books.google.com/books?id=Z6lDAQAAIAAJ&pg=PA154
[695] https://books.google.com/books?id=qrhHAQAAIAAJ
[696] https://books.google.com/books?id=z4YBAAAAQAAJ

[697] https://books.google.com/books?id=Qr6_q-chR6MC
[698] https://books.google.com/books?id=Ov1EAAAAIAAJ
[699] https://books.google.com/books?id=SAX5ohFkcVgC
[700] https://books.google.com/books?id=IfADAAAAQAAJ
[701] https://books.google.com/books?id=netlOtzI6R8C
[702] https://books.google.com/books?id=P30WGMWwsqMC
[703] https://books.google.com/books?id=krP0qAvXK4QC
[704] https://books.google.com/books?id=iJA_AAAAMAAJ
[705] https://books.google.com/books?id=Sggys-_O-2cC
[706] https://books.google.com/books?id=y8_Ya2s3zN8C
[707] https://books.google.com/books?id=BfNqgYlo9fMC&pg=PA149
[708] https://books.google.com/books?id=TfBYd9xVaXcC
[709] https://books.google.com/books?id=IUKBQfzKlIYC&pg=PA99
[710] https://books.google.com/books?id=rQa43r1GyicC
[711] http://ancienthistory.about.com/library/bl/uc_decker_carthrel3.htm
[712] https://books.google.com/books?id=4K06AQAAMAAJ
[713] http://dl.lib.brown.edu/pdfs/1292363091648500.pdf
[714] https://books.google.com/books?id=t64SAQAAMAAJ
[715] https://books.google.com/books?id=68jfRYQo3zsC
[716] https://books.google.com/books?id=VoJnKgmUH54C
[717] https://books.google.com/books?id=DNNgdBWoYKoC
[718] https://books.google.com/books?id=te1sqTzTxD8C
[719] http://www.stuff.co.nz/national/4573912/Burnt-body-victim-named-as-search-goes-offshore
[720] https://books.google.com/books?id=5CLkDgmVs1QC
[721] https://books.google.com/books?id=5hA5AQAAMAAJ
[722] https://books.google.com/books?id=t1pIAAAAYAAJ&pg=PA608
[723] http://veja.abril.com.br/300102/p_094.html
[724] https://books.google.com/books?id=BXWwm7jo-hEC
[725] https://books.google.com/books?id=R_w-CZ0eXnYC
[726] https://books.google.com/books?id=v8ZDAAAAcAAJ
[727] http://www1.folha.uol.com.br/cotidiano/740136-autorizado-a-visitar-familia-condenado-por-morte-de-tim-lopes-foge-da-prisao.shtml
[728] https://books.google.com/books?id=62HlSNN2lqQC
[729] https://books.google.com/books?id=pSHmT1G_5T0C
[730] https://books.google.com/books?id=uH-8AAAAIAAJ
[731] https://books.google.com/books?id=Z8Z3FQXOiNEC&pg=PA1
[732] https://books.google.com/books?id=pRXvHbNLPQ0C
[733] https://books.google.com/books?id=wVNuf9VEhGkC
[734] https://books.google.com/books?id=g_mh5fuel0QC
[735] //www.worldcat.org/issn/0002-8738
[736] https://books.google.com/books?id=JXZzAQAAQBAJ
[737] https://books.google.com/books?id=jyVEAAAAcAAJ&pg=PT964
[738] https://books.google.com/books?id=Vdv7AQAAQBAJ
[739] https://books.google.com/books?id=-_fnv5pmECsC
[740] https://books.google.com/books?id=7FsIAAAAQAAJ
[741] https://www.reuters.com/article/latestCrisis/idUSL21301127
[742] https://books.google.com/books?id=1SD_AQAAQBAJ
[743] https://books.google.com/books?id=6uK5pa3R4d8C&pg=PA203
[744] https://books.google.com/books?id=ppwAAAAAcAAJ
[745] https://books.google.com/books?id=nBZDAAAAcAAJ
[746] http://www.salon.com/2002/11/12/goldstone/
[747] https://books.google.com/books?id=x4vekGBc_McC
[748] https://archive.org/stream/ldpd_10273453_000
[749] https://www.theguardian.com/world/2007/dec/13/gender.iraq
[750] https://books.google.com/books?id=PQYQruNKzaYC&pg=PA216
[751] https://books.google.com/books?id=Dz07AQAAMAAJ

[752] https://books.google.com/books?id=LKj2B9vd7HsC
[753] https://books.google.com/books?id=whMwAAAAYAAJ
[754] https://query.nytimes.com/gst/fullpage.html?res=9D0CE4D91E3AF93BA35753C1A9669C8B63
[755] https://books.google.com/books?id=Ylf8t7uSGJEC
[756] https://books.google.com/books?id=2H3S1OLtmagC
[757] https://books.google.com/books?id=1blZAAAAMAAJ
[758] https://books.google.com/books?id=smPZ-ou74EwC
[759] https://books.google.com/books?id=z2QRd_rbWu8C
[760] https://books.google.com/books?id=kF1sTidtP_sC
[761] https://books.google.com/books?id=iSsLAAAAYAAJ&pg=PA223
[762] https://books.google.com/books?id=3S89AAAAIAAJ
[763] https://books.google.com/books?id=hYEQGam5hVgC
[764] https://books.google.com/books?id=0hYWzuecyHMC
[765] https://books.google.com/books?id=fl6gkL5h6A0C&pg=PA166
[766] https://books.google.com/books?id=tXywBrmhPTUC
[767] https://books.google.com/books?id=MDlbAAAAQAAJ
[768] https://books.google.com/books?id=F41aAAAAcAAJ
[769] //www.worldcat.org/issn/0003-0554
[770] //www.jstor.org/stable/1946342
[771] https://books.google.com/books?id=C-4PAAAAYAAJ
[772] https://books.google.com/books?id=X9NCAAAAcAAJ
[773] https://books.google.com/books?id=YvdKyEJo0osC
[774] https://books.google.com/books?id=bHzMYrWHjVoC
[775] https://deepblue.lib.umich.edu/bitstream/2027.42/43640/1/11186_2004_Article_BF00912078.pdf
[776] //doi.org/10.1007%2Fbf00912078
[777] //www.worldcat.org/issn/0304-2421
[778] https://books.google.com/books?id=z4eaj09hscAC
[779] https://books.google.com/books?id=KCjlptFEMZsC
[780] https://books.google.com/books?id=q4TA4hjqjJ0C
[781] https://books.google.com/books?id=3lpBAAAAcAAJ
[782] http://www.columbia.edu/~js322/misc/hus-eng.html
[783] //www.worldcat.org/issn/1093-2887
[784] https://books.google.com/books?id=-ROBb7SIvYgC
[785] https://books.google.com/books?id=XH-SMq-NKf0C
[786] https://books.google.com/books?id=-8NykshHHesC
[787] https://books.google.com/books?id=VK0llzUqQ2YC
[788] https://books.google.com/books?id=QThLAAAAQBAJ
[789] https://books.google.com/books?id=2nEZQXWsXG4C
[790] https://books.google.com/books?id=3JOVbGPdrjYC&pg=PA246
[791] https://books.google.com/books?id=lxlHuai91ZsC
[792] https://books.google.com/books?id=PiNSpBdtsCgC
[793] https://books.google.com/books?id=saXbAAAAQBAJ
[794] https://books.google.com/books?id=JRkwAAAAYAAJ
[795] https://books.google.com/books?id=awrOHv-gtqQC
[796] https://books.google.com/books?id=Gus_rugtLN0C&pg=PA10
[797] http://www.rediff.com/news/1999/feb/08vir.htm
[798] https://books.google.com/books?id=nFx3OlrBMpQC
[799] https://books.google.com/books?id=HVQLAAAAIAAJ&pg=PA28
[800] //www.worldcat.org/issn/0003-049X
[801] https://books.google.com/books?id=4hHLe60cYBcC
[802] https://books.google.com/books?id=ZUVlAAAAQBAJ
[803] http://www.plosone.org/article/info:doi/10.1371/journal.pone.0009177
[804] http://adsabs.harvard.edu/abs/2010PLoSO...5.9177S
[805] //doi.org/10.1371%2Fjournal.pone.0009177

[806] //www.ncbi.nlm.nih.gov/pmc/articles/PMC2822869
[807] //www.ncbi.nlm.nih.gov/pubmed/20174667
[808] https://books.google.com/books?id=nKJiBUFrmfoC&pg=PA361
[809] https://books.google.com/books?id=0c4GAAAAQAAJ&pg=PA253
[810] https://books.google.com/books?id=G4dbAAAAQAAJ&pg=PA326
[811] //doi.org/10.1080%2F00665983.1865.10851326
[812] https://www.telegraph.co.uk/news/worldnews/asia/northkorea/1464413/Train-blast-was-a-plot-to-kill-North-Koreas-leader.html
[813] http//www.yasni.de
[814] https://books.google.com/books?id=NphFnF2RRKUC
[815] https://books.google.com/books?id=Ae63Gjp21SgC&pg=PA98
[816] https://books.google.com/books?id=DIsfAAAAMAAJ
[817] https://books.google.com/books?id=bFN2ismyhEYC
[818] https://books.google.com/books?id=yq7VUKWz5dwC
[819] https://books.google.com/books?id=DoY-tEMgJ8UC
[820] https://books.google.com/books?id=4K7QH76_HdIC
[821] https://books.google.com/books?id=6q9EAAAAcAAJ
[822] http://www.newadvent.org/cathen/15674a.htm
[823] https://web.archive.org/web/20100707174042/http://www.wlsessays.net/node/1535
[824] //www.worldcat.org/issn/0362-5648
[825] http://www.wlsessays.net/node/1535
[826] https://books.google.com/books?id=2ombkgpGt_AC
[827] https://books.google.com/books?id=QBkQAQAAMAAJ
[828] http://bahai-library.com/uhj_applicability_laws_aqdas
[829] https://books.google.com/books?id=bt71nHmVezMC&pg=PA19
[830] https://books.google.com/books?id=3wPthVcxWGkC
[831] https://books.google.com/books?id=oJOvpkHg7msC
[832] https://books.google.com/books?id=GVhQ_lDWq0EC
[833] https://books.google.com/books?id=GE1uc1UNXNYC
[834] https://books.google.com/books?id=P07rgiJjsk4C
[835] https://books.google.com/books?id=2gA9AAAAIAAJ
[836] //www.amazon.com/dp/B0029U3KWY
[837] http://openlibrary.org/books/OL7180554M/In_the_land_of_the_lion_and_sun
[838] https://books.google.com/books?id=JdkHAAAAQAAJ
[839] https://books.google.com/books?id=4smZ4JjGJcsC
[840] https://books.google.com/books?id=WqcNAAAAQAAJ
[841] https://books.google.com/books?id=VZZLAQAAQBAJ&pg=PA44
[842] https://books.google.com/books?id=wpM3AAAAIAAJ
[843] https://books.google.com/books?id=GEPYbuzOwcQC
[844] https://books.google.com/books?id=4h8iAQAAQBAJ&pg=PA62
[845] http://www.capitalpunishmentuk.org/burning.html
[846] http://www.monkeychicken.com/fir.htm
[847] LSJ apotumpanizo http://www.perseus.tufts.edu/hopper/text?doc=Perseus%3Atext%3A1999.04.0057%3Aentry%3Da)potumpani%2Fzw&highlight=crucify ἀποτυμπα^ν-ίζω (later ἀποτύμπα^ν-τυπ- UPZ119 (2nd century BC), POxy.1798.1.7), A. crucify on a plank, D. 8.61,9.61:—Pass., Lys.13.56, D.19.137, Arist. Rh. 1383a5, Beros. ap. J.Ap.1.20. 2. generally, destroy, Plu.2.1049d.
[848] LSJ anastauro ἀνασταυρ-όω, = foreg., Hdt.3.125, 6.30, al.; identical with ἀνασκολοπίζω, 9.78:—Pass., Th. 1.110, Pl.Grg.473c. II. in Rom. times, affix to a cross, crucify, Plb. 1.11.5, al., Plu.Fab.6, al. 2. crucify afresh, Ep.Hebr.6.6.
[849] Plutarch Fabius Maximus 6.3 "Hannibal now perceived the mistake in his position, and its peril, and crucified the native guides who were responsible for it."
[850] Polybius 1.11.5 [5] Historiae https://archive.org/details/polybioyistoriai00polyuoft. Polybius. Theodorus Büttner-Wobst after L. Dindorf. Leipzig. Teubner. 1893-.
[851] Charlton T. Lewis, Charles Short, *A Latin Dictionary*: http://www.perseus.tufts.edu/hopper/text?doc=Perseus%3Atext%3A1999.04.0059%3Aentry%3Dcrux crux, ŭcis, f. (m., Enn.

ap. Non. p. 195, 13; Gracch. ap. Fest. s. v. masculino, p. 150, 24, and 151, 12 Müll.) [perh. kindred with circus]. I. Lit. A. In gen., a tree, frame, or other wooden instruments of execution, on which criminals were impaled or hanged, Sen. Prov. 3, 10; Cic. Rab. Perd. 3, 10 sqq.— B. In partic., a cross, Ter. And. 3, 5, 15; Cic. Verr. 2, 1, 3, § 7; 2, 1, 4, § 9; id. Pis. 18, 42; id. Fin. 5, 30, 92; Quint. 4, 2, 17; Tac. A. 15, 44; Hor. S. 1, 3, 82; 2, 7, 47; id. Ep. 1, 16, 48 et saep.: "dignus fuit qui malo cruce periret, Gracch. ap. Fest. l. l.: pendula", the pole of a carriage, Stat. S. 4, 3, 28.

[852] {{cite weblurl=http://webcache.googleusercontent.com/search?q=cache:www.thelatinlibrary.com/sen/sen.consolatione2.shtml+stipitem+patibul0ltitle=Dialogue "To Marcia on Consolation", 6.20.3] at The Latin Library in [[Latin]|author=|date=|website=googleusercontent.com}}

[853] Mishna, Shabbath 6.10: see David W. Chapman, *Ancient Jewish and Christian Perceptions of Crucifixion* https://books.google.com/books?id=EdbdQ-5fMr0C&pg=PA182 (Mohr Siebeck 2008), p. 182

[854] Seneca, Dialogue "To Marcia on Consolation", in *Moral Essays*, 6.20.3, trans. John W. Basore, The Loeb Classical Library (Cambridge, Mass.: Harvard University Press, 1946) 2:69

[855] (citing Cicero, *pro Rabirio Perduellionis Reo* 5.16 http://perseus.uchicago.edu/perseus-cgi/citequery3.pl?dbname=PerseusLatinTexts&getid=1&query=Cic.%20Rab.%20Perd.%2019).

[856] Justus Lipsius: *De cruce*, p. 47

[857] "The ... oldest depiction of a crucifixion ... was uncovered by archaeologists more than a century ago on the Palatine Hill in Rome. It is a second-century graffiti scratched into a wall that was part of the imperial palace complex. It includes a caption — not by a Christian, but by someone taunting and deriding Christians and the crucifixions they underwent. It shows crude stick-figures of a boy reverencing his 'God', who has the head of a jackass and is upon a cross with arms spread wide and with hands nailed to the crossbeam. Here we have a Roman sketch of a Roman crucifixion, and it is in the traditional cross shape." Clayton F. Bower, Jr. "Cross or Torture Stake?" http://www.catholic.com/thisrock/1991/9110fea1.asp

[858] Epistle of Barnabas, Chapter 9. The document no doubt belongs to the end of the 1st or beginning of the 2nd century.http://www.earlychristianwritings.com/barnabas-intro.html

[859] "The very form of the cross, too, has five extremities, two in length, two in breadth, and one in the middle, on which [last] the person rests who is fixed by the nails" (Irenaeus (c. 130–202), *Adversus Haereses* II, xxiv, 4 http://www.newadvent.org/fathers/0103224.htm).

[860] Justin Martyr (c. 100–165) Dialogue with Trypho "Chapter XC – The stretched-out hands of Moses signified beforehand the cross" http://www.ccel.org/ccel/schaff/anf01.viii.iv.xc.html, "Chapter XCI" http://www.ccel.org/ccel/schaff/anf01.viii.iv.xci.html "For the one beam is placed upright, from which the highest extremity is raised up into a horn, when the other beam is fitted on to it, and the ends appear on both sides as horns joined on to the one horn." "Chapter CXI" http://www.ccel.org/ccel/schaff/anf01.viii.iv.cxi.html "stretching out his hands, remained till evening on the hill, his hands being supported; and this reveals a type of no other thing than of the cross"

[861] http://bible.oremus.org/?passage=John+20:25–20:25&version=nrsv

[862] In the Homeric Greek of the Iliad XX, 478–480, a spear-point is said to have pierced the χεῖρ "where the sinews of the elbow join" (ἵνα τε ξενέχουσι τένοντες / ἀγκῶνος, τῇ τόν γε φίλης διὰ χειρὸς ἔπειρεν / αἰχμὴ χαλκείη).

[863] David W. Chapman, Ancient Jewish and Christian perceptions of crucifixion https://books.google.com/books?id=EdbdQ-5fMr0C (Mohr Siebeck, 2008), p. 86–89

[864] The Life Of Flavius Josephus http://www.ccel.org/j/josephus/works/autobiog.htm, 75.

[865] Tzaferis, V. 1970 Jewish Tombs at and near Giv'at ha-Mivtar. Israel Exploration Journal Vol. 20 pp. 18-32.

[866] Haas, Nicu. "Anthropological observations on the skeletal remains from Giv'at ha-Mivtar", Israel Exploration Journal 20 (1-2), 1970: 38-59; Tzaferis, Vassilios. "Crucifixion – The Archaeological Evidence", *Biblical Archaeology Review* 11 (February, 1985): 44–53; Zias, Joseph. "The Crucified Man from Giv'at Ha-Mivtar: A Reappraisal", *Israel Exploration Journal* 35 (1), 1985: 22–27; Hengel, Martin. *Crucifixion in the ancient world and the folly of the message of the cross* (Augsburg Fortress, 1977). See also Spectacles of Death in Ancient Rome, by Donald G. Kyle https://books.google.com/books?id=__IOAAAAQAAJ p. 181, note 93

[867] Stavros, Scolops (σταυρός, σκόλοψ). The cross; http://www.mlahanas.de/Greeks/LX/Stavros.html encyclopedia Hellinica

[868] Translation by Aubrey de Selincourt. The original, "σανίδα προσπασσαλεύσαντες, ἀνεκρέμασαν ... Τούτου δὲ τοῦ Ἀρταύκτεω τοῦ ἀνακρεμασθέντος ...", is translated by Henry Cary (Bohn's Classical Library: *Herodotus Literally Translated*. London, G. Bell and Sons 1917, pp. 591–592) as: "They nailed him to a plank and hoisted him aloft ... this Artayctes who was hoisted aloft".

[869] W.W. How and J. Wells, *A Commentary on Herodotus* (Clarendon Press, Oxford 1912), vol. 2, p. 336

[870] http://bible.oremus.org/?passage=Galatians+3:13–3:13&version=nrsv

[871] http://bible.oremus.org/?passage=Deuteronomy+21:22–23:22&version=nrsv

[872] See Mishnah, Sanhedrin 7:1, translated in Jacob Neusner, The Mishnah: A New Translation 591 (1988), supra note 8, at 595-96 (indicating that court ordered execution by stoning, burning, decapitation, or strangulation only)

[873] Levi,*Aramaic Testament of Levi* 4Q541 column 6 http://www.bibliotecapleyades.net/scrolls_deadsea/uncovered/uncovered05.htm

[874] Quintus Curtius Rufus, *History of Alexander the Great of Macedonia* 4.4.21 http://www.livius.org/aj-al/alexander/alexander_t09.html

[875] Herodotus, *Histories*, ("Having killed him in some way not fit to be told, Oroetes then crucified him")

[876] After quoting a poem by Maecenas that speaks of preferring life to death even when life is burdened with all the disadvantages of old age or even with acute torture ("vel acuta si sedeam cruce"), Seneca disagrees with the sentiment, saying death would be better for a crucified person hanging from the patibulum: "I should deem him most despicable had he wished to live to the point of crucifixion ... Is it worth so much to weigh down upon one's own wound, and hang stretched out from a patibulum? ... Is anyone found who, after being fastened to that accursed wood, already weakened, already deformed, swelling with ugly weals on shoulders and chest, with many reasons for dying even before getting to the cross, would wish to prolong a life-breath that is about to experience so many torments?" ("Contemptissimum putarem, si vivere vellet usque ad crucem ... Est tanti vulnus suum premere et patibulo pendere districtum ... Invenitur, qui velit adactus ad illud infelix lignum, iam debilis, iam pravus et in foedum scapularum ac pectoris tuber elisus, cui multae moriendi causae etiam citra crucem fuerant, trahere animam tot tormenta tracturam?" - Letter 101, 12-14 http://www.thelatinlibrary.com/sen/seneca.ep17-18.shtml)

[877] Titus Maccius Plautus *Miles gloriosus* Mason Hammond, Arthur M. Mack - 1997 Page 109, "The patibulum (in the next line) was a crossbar which the convicted criminal carried on his shoulders, with his arms fastened to it, to the place for ... Hoisted up on an upright post, the patibulum became the crossbar of the cross"

[878] Dictionary of Images and Symbols in Counselling By William Stewart https://books.google.com/books?id=GGJmFIf6mtIC 1998 , p. 120

[879] ' ' '

[880] Tacitus. *Annals*, Book 14, 42-45.

[881] It is a graffito found in a taberna (hostel for wayfarers) in Puteoli, dating to the time of Trajan or Hadrian (late 1st century to early 2nd century AD). An inscription over the person's left shoulder reads "Ἀλκίμιλα" (Alkimila), a female name. It is not clear, however, whether the inscription was written by the same person who drew the picture, or added by another person later. It is also not known whether the grafitto is intended to depict an actual event, as distinguished from, perhaps, the writer's desire for someone to be crucified, or as a jest. As such, the grafitto does not itself provide conclusive evidence of female crucifixion.

[882] Macall believes that the person would be given back his or her clothing following the scourging.

[883] Justin Martyr *Dialogue with Trypho, a Jew* 91

[884] Irenaeus *Against Heresies* II.24

[885] Tertullian *To the Nations* I.12

[886] Barbet, 45; Zugibe, 57; Vassilios Tzaferis, "Crucifixion—The Archaeological Evidence," *Biblical Archaeology Review* 11.1 (Jan./Feb. 1985), 44-53 (p. 49)

[887] Max Hastings, *Armageddon: the Battle for Germany 1944–45*,

888 " Saudi Arabia must immediately halt execution of children – UN rights experts urge http://www.ohchr.org/en/NewsEvents/Pages/DisplayNews.aspx?NewsID=16487&LangID=E". Office of the United Nations High Commissioner for Human Rights. 22 September 2015. Retrieved 3 November 2017.

889 " When Beheading Won't Do the Job, the Saudis Resort to Crucifixion https://www.theatlantic.com/international/archive/2015/09/saudi-arabia-beheading-crucifixion-nimr/407221/". *The Atlantic.* 24 September 2015. Retrieved 3 November 2017.

890 The Sanctions of the Islamic Criminal Law http://revcurentjur.ro/arhiva/attachments_201003/recjurid103_13F.pdf

891 Death Penalty Worldwide: Sudan http://www.deathpenaltyworldwide.org/country-search-post.cfm?country=Sudan

892 Directory on Popular Piety 144 http://www.vatican.va/roman_curia/congregations/ccdds/documents/rc_con_ccdds_doc_20020513_vers-direttorio_en.html

893 *Annals,* 15.44.

894 //web.archive.org/web/20040402184621/http://www.e-forensicmedicine.net/Turin2000.htm

895 http://www.konnections.com/Kcundick/crucifix.html

896 https://web.archive.org/web/20120212185552/http://www.joezias.com/CrucifixionAntiquity.html

897 http://media.wix.com/ugd/3089fd_df7187c57460442db5fc6d6ae7996df9.pdf

898 http://jewishencyclopedia.com/view.jsp?artid=905&letter=C

899 http://thecrucifixions.blogspot.com/2007/02/crucifix-of-joachim-of-nizhny.html

900 Summerson, Henry (1983). "The Early Development of Peine Forte et Dure."

901 *Law, Litigants, and the Legal Profession: Papers Presented to the Fourth British Legal History Conference at the University of Birmingham 10–13 July 1979* ed E. W. Ives & A. H. Manchester, 116-125. Royal Historical Society Studies in History Series 36. London: Humanities Press.

902 Sir Frederick Pollock and Frederic William Maitland, *The History of English Law,* v. 2, pp. 650–651 (Cambridge; 1968;)

903 See generally, William Blackstone, *Commentaries on the Laws of England* (1769), vol. 4, pp. *319-324

904 Drug Control and Asset Seizures: a review of the history of forfeiture in England and colonial America http://www.fsu.edu/~crimdo/forfeiture.html

905 Curiosities of Cowell's "Interpreter" https://books.google.com/books?id=veURAAAAYAAJ&pg=PA219&dq=%22laid+in+some+low+dark+house%22#PPA218,M1

906 The enterprising and tenacious Guy Miège: four dictionaries from 1677 to 1688 http://ora.ox.ac.uk/objects/uuid:ed89c430-0517-4065-b717-0243fd11b368

907 Miege, G.:" The present state of Great-Britain and Ireland https//books.google.no" London 1715, p.294

908 https://archive.is/20120801195952/www.historycooperative.org/journals/lhr/23.2/mckenzie.html

909 https://web.archive.org/web/19970428075512/http://www.fsu.edu/~crimdo/forfeiture.html

910 http://www.oldbaileyonline.org/browse.jsp?path=sessionsPapers%2F16760823.xml

911 For details of the Pogrom itself, see volume I, pp. 363–400.

912 For a number of such ordinances, see * **German original:** " und wo der begriffen wird, der einen stehenden baum schälet, dem wäre gnad nützer dan recht u. wann man deme sol recht thun, soll man ihm seinen nabel bei seinem bauch aufschneiden u. ein darm daraus thun, denselbigen nageln an den stamm u. mit der person herumgehen, so ‚lang er ein darm in seinem leib hat"

913 **i)** General comment, with connotations of this being a type of human sacrifice , **ii)** 8th century description from 772-73, , **iii)** Danish 1096 retaliation on Wends, by like execution method, , **iv)** 1131 pagan attacks on Christians by Wends,

914 Forty years earlier, in 1555 Seidenberg (nowadays Zawidow), a woman who had become pregnant by another man than her (absent) husband sought to preserve her honour by cutting out the fetus. Having pulled it out, along with much else, she began screaming of pain, but no one could help her, and she died three days later.

915 For status as municipality, see:

[916] Battuta, " The travels of Ibn Battuta https//books.google.com", transl. Lee, S, London 1829, pp. 146–47

[917] German original "Zu der Viertheylung: Durch seinen gantzen Leib zu vier stücken zu schnitten und zerhawen, und also zum todt gestrafft werden soll, und sollen solche viertheyl auff gemeyne vier wegstrassen offentlich gehangen und gesteckt werden"

[918] See also the 3-day long torture and execution method of Peter Niers, who was executed in 1581 for 544 murders, including the murder of 24 women and their fetuses, the latter to be used in rituals of black magic.

[919] Robert B.M. Binning http://www.docs.is.ed.ac.uk/docs/lib-archive/bgallery/Gallery/records/eighteen/binning.html

[920] Saudi Arabia chops off hand of Egyptian for theft http://www.monstersandcritics.com/news/middleeast/news/article_1371270.php/Saudi_Arabia_chops_off_hand_of_Egyptian_for_theft , 5 November 2007

[921] Described in

[922] Cited in

[923] Internet History Sourcebooks, Medieval Sourcebook: The Life of St. Columban, by the Monk Jonas, (7th Century) http://www.fordham.edu/halsall/basis/columban.asp, paragraph 58

[924] Secundus, Carpophorus, Victorinus und Severianus http://www.heiligenlexikon.de/BiographienS/Secundus_Carpophorus_Victorinus_Severianus.html

[925] Martyrdom of Shamuna, Guria and Habib http://www.newadvent.org/fathers/0858.htm

[926] "The Little Flat of Horrors" http://www.time.com/time/magazine/article/0,9171,973550-1,00.html, *Time*, 5 August 1991

[927] "*Rex eum, quasi regiae majestatis (occisorem), membratim laniatum equis apud Coventre, exemplum terribile et spectaculum comentabile praebere (iussit) omnibus audentibus talia machinari. Primo enim distractus, postea decollatus et corpus in tres partes divisum est.*"<ref>

[928] Treason before 1351 was defined by Alfred the Great's Doom book. As Patrick Wormald wrote, "if anyone plots against the king's life ... [*or* his lord's life], he is liable for his life and all that he owns ... or to clear himself by the king's [lord's] wergeld."<ref>

[929] Women were considered the legal property of their husbands,<ref>

[930] "And because that many other like cases of treason may happen in time to come, which a man cannot think nor declare at this present time; it is accorded, that if any other case supposed treason, which is not above specified, doth happen before any justice, the justice shall tarry without going to judgement of treason, till the cause be shewed and declared before the king and his parliament, whether it ought to be judged treason or other felony." Edward Coke<ref>

[931] Smith, Lacey, B. (1954) *English Treason Trials and Confessions in the Sixteenth Century*, Journal of the History of Ideas, Vol. 15, No. 4 (Oct., 1954), pp. 471-498 Published by: University of Pennsylvania Press, p. 484.

[932] For an explanation of "corruption of blood", see Attainder.

[933] Harrison's sentence was "That you be led to the place from whence you came, and from thence be drawn upon a hurdle to the place of execution, and then you shall be hanged by the neck and, being alive, shall be cut down, and your privy members to be cut off, and your entrails be taken out of your body and, you living, the same to be burnt before your eyes, and your head to be cut off, your body to be divided into four quarters, and head and quarters to be disposed of at the pleasure of the King's majesty. And the Lord have mercy on your soul."<ref>

[934] In the case of Hugh Despenser the Younger, Seymour Phillips writes: "All the good people of the realm, great and small, rich and poor, regarded Despenser as a traitor and a robber; for which he was sentenced to be hanged. As a traitor he was to be drawn and quartered and the quarters distributed around the kingdom; as an outlaw he was to be beheaded; and for procuring discord between the king and the queen and other people of the kingdom he was sentenced to be disembowelled and his entrails burned; finally he was declared to be a traitor, tyrant and renegade."<ref>

[935] Lewis 2008, pp. 113–124

[936] Kenny, C. *Outlines of Criminal Law* (Cambridge University Press, 1936), 15th edition, p. 318

[937] In 1534, a woman's head adorned the bridge; Elizabeth Barton, a domestic servant and later nun who forecast the early death of Henry VIII, was drawn to Tyburn, and hanged and beheaded.<ref>

[938] Although women were usually burned only after they had first been strangled to death, in 1726 Catherine Hayes's executioner botched the job and she perished in the flames, the last woman in England to do so."*Rex eum, quasi regiae majestatis (occisorem), membratim laniatum equis apud Coventre, exemplum terribile et spectaculum comentabile praebere (iussit) omnibus audentibus talia machinari. Primo enim distractus, postea decollatus et corpus in tres partes divisum est.*"<ref>

[939] Kenny, p. 319

[940] Forster's first attempt passed through both Houses of Parliament without obstruction, but was dropped following a change of government.<ref>

[941] Statute Law (Repeals) Act 1973 (c. 39), Sch. 1 Pt. V.

[942] Thomas Allen. *Tories: Fighting for the King in America's First Civil War*. New York, Harper, 2011.

[943] Peter J. Albert (ed.). *An Uncivil War: The Southern Backcountry During the American Revolution*. Charlottesville: University of Virginia Press, 1985.

[944] Alfred Young (ed.). *The American Revolution: Explorations in the History of American Radicalism*. DeKalb: Northern Illinois University Press, 1976.

[945] Armitage, David. Every Great Revolution Is a Civil War https://scholar.harvard.edu/files/armitage/files/scripting_revolutions.pdf . In: Keith Michael Baker and Dan Edelstein (eds.). *Scripting Revolution: A Historical Approach to the Comparative Study of Revolutions*. Stanford: Stanford University Press, 2015. According to Armitage, "The renaming can happen relatively quickly: for example, the transatlantic conflict of the 1770s that many contemporaries saw as a British "civil war" or even "the American Civil War" was first called "the American evolution" in 1776 by the chief justice of South Carolina, William Henry Drayton."

[946] https://books.google.com/books?id=Mp4DAAAAQAAJ
[947] https://books.google.com/books?id=46sDAAAAQAAJ
[948] https://books.google.com/books?id=jStcAAAAQAAJ
[949] https://books.google.com/books?id=CQdOF2zxlGgC
[950] https://books.google.com/books?id=hhsY0Yq8sWEC
[951] https://books.google.com/books?id=PPpBAAAAYAAJ
[952] https://books.google.com/books?id=wlonYyuDZS4C
[953] https://books.google.com/books?id=9XYe9l2aScgC
[954] https://books.google.com/books?id=k-r1XjsK1fwC
[955] https://books.google.com/books?id=_A8bAAAAYAAJ
[956] https://books.google.com/books?id=oH1DAAAAcAAJ
[957] https://books.google.com/books?id=8aXIm4ELnWwC
[958] https://books.google.com/books?id=DYvg1WipNX0C
[959] https://books.google.com/books?id=cjdbRF8PXhUC
[960] https://books.google.com/books?id=48sxAQAAIAAJ
[961] https://books.google.com/books?id=pg2Jx5LkGg0C
[962] https://books.google.com/books?id=mqG8a74SkRMC
[963] https://books.google.com/books?id=SCQLAAAAYAAJ
[964] https://books.google.com/books?id=6qQ0AAAAMAAJ
[965] https://books.google.com/books?id=f5AOAAAAQAAJ
[966] https://books.google.com/books?id=AIHtJKk8ejEC
[967] https://reading.academia.edu/MaryLewis/Papers/144764/A_Traitors_Death_The_identity_of_a_drawn_hanged_and_quartered_man_from_Hulton_Abbey_Staffordshire
[968] https://books.google.com/books?id=sXBdNsDxJ_cC
[969] https://books.google.com/books?id=OLUKAAAAYAAJ
[970] https://openlibrary.org/books/OL7037018M/The_Chronicle_of_Lanercost_1272-1346
[971] https://books.google.com/books?id=BVxcMtCxfdsC
[972] https://books.google.com/books?id=w8nYiyH-S_YC
[973] https://books.google.com/books?id=OHYOAAAAQAAJ
[974] https://books.google.com/books?id= opBt15kOE0C
[975] https://openlibrary.org/books/OL23354143M/Unpublished_documents_relating_to_the_English_martyrs
[976] https://books.google.com/books?id=JdisvDaHiIMC

[977] https://books.google.com/books?id=1dvep-L_iTUC
[978] https://books.google.com/books?id=WlnNUCS4R_MC
[979] https://books.google.com/books?id=5AM-AAAAcAAJ
[980] https://books.google.com/books?id=uY08aQoDx3gC
[981] https://books.google.com/books?id=T_ijDrLo9RMC
[982] https://books.google.com/books?id=THzwtbxEszoC
[983] https://books.google.com/books?id=Q9o8AAAAIAAJ
[984] https://books.google.com/books?id=mbNl_T-bFzcC
[985] https://books.google.com/books?id=ldT9Qu29phwC
[986] https://books.google.com/books?id=bfjHCrifKyMC
[987] https://books.google.com/books?id=R3fK0ewDbOcC
[988] https://books.google.com/books?id=rw3p-PS2upAC
[989] https://books.google.com/books?id=HC1D3K6EDv0C
[990] https://archive.org/details/oldtimepunishmen00andruoft
[991] https://books.google.com/books?id=bMjcCNND9AkC
[992] Pericles Collas (n.d.). *A Concise Guide of Delphi* https://archive.org/stream/conciseguideofde00colluoft#page/8/mode/2up, pp8. Athens. Cacoulides.
[993] News Scan Briefs: Killer Smile http://www.scientificamerican.com/article.cfm?id=in-brief-aug-09, Scientific American, August 2009
[994] Platner (1929). *A Topographical Dictionary of Ancient Rome* http://penelope.uchicago.edu/Thayer/E/Gazetteer/Places/Europe/Italy/Lazio/Roma/Rome/_Texts/PLATOP*/home*.html, Tarpeius Mons http://penelope.uchicago.edu/Thayer/E/Gazetteer/Places/Europe/Italy/Lazio/Roma/Rome/_Texts/PLATOP*/Tarpeius_Mons.html, pp509-510. London. Oxford University Press.
[995] Suetonius, *The Lives of Twelve Caesars*, Life of Tiberius 61.2 http://penelope.uchicago.edu/Thayer/E/Roman/Texts/Suetonius/12Caesars/Tiberius*.html#61.2
[996] Suetonius, *The Lives of Twelve Caesars*, Life of Tiberius 62.2 http://penelope.uchicago.edu/Thayer/E/Roman/Texts/Suetonius/12Caesars/Tiberius*.html#62.2
[997] Iran: UA 17/08 - Fear of imminent execution/ flogging | Amnesty International https://www.amnesty.org/en/library/info/MDE13/010/2008/en
[998] Death Sentences in Iran http://www.ambafrance-ir.org/article.php3?id_article=620
[999] Adam Withnall, Isis throws 'gay' men off tower, stones woman accused of adultery and crucifies 17 young men in 'retaliatory' wave of executions https://www.independent.co.uk, *The Independent*, 18 January 2015
[1000] p.69 *Kleine Kulturgeschichte der Haut* https://books.google.com/books?id=LAnRRHPMmlcC&pg=PA69. p. 69. Ernst G. Jung (2007).
[1001] Paragraph based on the essay "*Von Ursprung des Schindens in Assyrien*" in *Jung* (2007), p. 67-70 https://books.google.com/books?id=LAnRRHPMmlcC&pg=PA67
[1002] Rassam Cylinder. The British Museum. & 636BC, pp. Col.1, L.52 to Col.2, L. 27.
[1003] Wall, J. Charles (1912), *Porches and Fonts*. Wells Gardner and Darton, London. pp. 41-42.
[1004] 中国死刑观察 —中国的酷刑 http://www.chinamonitor.org/article/kuxing/zgkx.htm
[1005] 罩垔曬皮 http://fjtct.now.cn:7751/zjjxs.com/msfq/msfq/msfq-6.htm
[1006] 陈学霖 (2001). 史林漫识 . China Friendship Publishing Company.
[1007] History of Ming, vol.94
[1008] 魯迅 . 且介亭雜文 ·病後雜談
[1009] http://www.mystudios.com/art/italian/titian/titian-flaying-of-marsyas.jpg
[1010] *Oxford English Dictionary*, 11th Ed: **garrotte** is normal British English spelling, with single r alternate. Article title is US English spelling variant.
[1011] Newquist, H.P. and Maloof, Rich, *This Will Kill You: A Guide to the Ways in Which We Go*, New York: St. Martin's Press, (2009), pp. 133-6
[1012] Whittaker, Wayne, *Tough Guys*, Popular Mechanics, February 1943, Vol. 79 No. 2, pp. 44
[1013] Steele, David E., *Silent Sentry Removal*, Black Belt Magazine, August 1986, Vol. 24 No. 8, pp. 48-49
[1014] *garrote* http://buscon.rae.es/drael/SrvltGUIBusUsual?TIPO_HTML=2&TIPO_BUS=3&LEMA=garrote#0_7, 7th sense, *Diccionario de la Real Academia Española*.

[1015] El director de cine Manuel Huerga presenta el libro «Cómo se hizo: Salvador» http://www.lavozdegalicia.es/ed_corunia/noticia.jsp?CAT=127&TEXTO=5302415. *La Voz de Galicia*, 21 November 2006.
[1016] Oxford English Dictionary, 3rd Ed., Oxford University. Electronic CD edition.
[1017] Hanging in Chains By Albert Hartshorne, pp. 73–75, ,
[1018] Deuteronomy 21:22-23.
[1019] Seneca the Younger, Dialogue, Ad Marciam, De consolatione, 6.20.3
[1020] *The golden age of Islam* by Maurice Lombard, p. 152, ,
[1021] *Every Day Life in the Massachusetts Bay Colony* by George Francis Dow
[1022] Congressional series of United States public documents, vol. 936. 35th Congress, 1st session. Misc. doc. #207., Memorial of Lawrence Kearney..., Pg. 3. Published 2012 by US Congress.
[1023] http://www.law.mq.edu.au/sctas/html/1837cases/RvMcKay,1837.htm
[1024] Dr D. R. Johnson, Introductory Anatomy http://www.leeds.ac.uk/chb/lectures/anatomy1.html, Centre for Human Biology, (now renamed Faculty of Biological Sciences http://www.fbs.leeds.ac.uk/, Leeds University), Retrieved 17 November 2008
[1025] Retrieved 31 August 2017
[1026] Napier, William. (1851) *History Of General Sir Charles Napier's Administration Of Scinde*. (p. 35). London: Chapman and Hall https://books.google.com/books?id=d84BAAAAMAAJ&vq=suttee&dq=History%20of%20the%20Administration%20of%20Scinde&pg=PA35#v=onepage&q&f=false at books.google.com, accessed 10 July 2011
[1027] Definition of Immurement http://dictionary.reference.com/browse/immure
[1028] *Smith*, (1846), p.353 https://books.google.com/books?id=PeYRAAAAYAAJ&pg=PA353
[1029] *Dowling* (2001), Vestal Virgins-Chaste keepers of the flame http://members.bib-arch.org/publication.asp?PubID=BSAO&Volume=4&Issue=1&ArticleID=14
[1030] *Hume-Griffith* (1909), p.138-139 https://archive.org/stream/behindveilinpers00humeuoft#page/138/mode/2up
[1031] *Tavernier, Phillips* (1678), p.233 https://archive.org/stream/sixvoyagesJohnB00Tave#page/232/mode/2up
[1032] John Fryer http://www.iranicaonline.org/articles/freyer-john-writer-and-doctor
[1033] *Fryer* (1698), p.318 https://books.google.com/books?id=CrYIAAAAQAAJ&pg=PA318
[1034] *Eastwick* (1864), p.186 https://books.google.com/books?id=PVYOAAAAQAAJ&pg=PA186
[1035] *Browne* (2013), p.117-118 https://books.google.com/books?id=BerYAQAAQBAJ&pg=PA118
[1036] *New Zealand Herald* (1914), p.7 http://paperspast.natlib.govt.nz/cgi-bin/paperspast?a=d&d=NZH19140217.2.66
[1037] *Kurkijan* (2008), p.17 https://books.google.com/books?id=Z-xEyetzPPEC&pg=PA17
[1038] *Thucydides*, 3.81.5 http://perseus.mpiwg-berlin.mpg.de/GreekScience/Thuc.+3.69-85.html%20Thuc.%203.69-85:Civil%20War%20at%20Corcyra
[1039] *Varner* (2004), p.93-94 https://books.google.com/books?id=5IpPhTqnDJkC&pg=PA93
[1040] Peter Sarris opts for freezing to death, rather than death by starvation *Sarris* (2011), p.252 https://books.google.com/books?id=d6OMefsyv_EC&pg=PT252
[1041] Evagrius (2000), p.143, footnote 31 https://books.google.com/books?id=YP9cuh3KX3wC&pg=PA143
[1042] *Procopius* (2007), p.71 https://books.google.com/books?id=iH1L6UE5_e4C&pg=PA71
[1043] *Rohrbacher* (2013), p.89 https://books.google.com/books?id=VnaF58VDxzAC&pg=PA89
[1044] *Hübner* (1700), p.590 https://books.google.com/books?id=kN4GAAAAcAAJ&pg=PP718
[1045] Histoire des Ducs de Normandie et des Rois d'Angleterre, pp.112-5
[1046] *Wekebrod* (1814), p.118-119 https://books.google.com/books?id=djECAAAAcAAJ&pg=PA118
[1047] *Osenbrüggen* (1860), p.290 https://books.google.com/books?id=X9NCAAAAcAAJ&pg=PA290
[1048] Carlo Ginzburg, *Ecstasies*, 43
[1049] *Bernier* (1916), p.114-115 https://archive.org/stream/travelsinmogulem00bernuoft#page/114/mode/2up
[1050] *de Tott* (1786), p.97 https://books.google.com/books?id=6oc2AAAAMAAJ&pg=PA97
[1051] *Lerner* (1986), p.60 https://books.google.com/books?id=szm-8WgGjWgC&pg=PA60

[1052] Taylor (2009), p.25 https://books.google.com/books?id=63tYpCw4nIYC&pg=PA25
[1053] Batuta, Lee (1829), p.220 https://books.google.com/books?jtp=220&id=wjAtGKM_-WIC
[1054] Bindloss (1898), p.169 https://archive.org/stream/innigercountry00bind#page/168/mode/2up
[1055] French (2000), p.78 https://books.google.com/books?id=_ACqBJczrO8C&pg=PA78
[1056] O'Reilly (2000), p.180 https://books.google.com/books?id=T-9vsaISVKsC&pg=PA180
[1057] Lea (2012), p.487 http://www.gutenberg.org/files/39451/39451-h/39451-h.htm#FNanchor_444_444
[1058] Lea (2012), footnote 444 http://www.gutenberg.org/files/39451/39451-h/39451-h.htm#Footnote_444_444
[1059] Scott (1833), p.392 https://books.google.com/books?id=Sk9AAAAAYAAJ&pg=PA392
[1060] Medioli, Schutte, Kuehn, Menchi (2001), p.170-171 https://books.google.com/books?id=1TVrePw1sq4C&pg=PA170
[1061] Durkheim (2010), p.224 https://books.google.com/books?id=v23YleX1UskC&pg=PA224
[1062] Olavinlinna Legends http://www.nba.fi/en/olavinlinna_legends
[1063] The Immured Lady http://www.haapsalu.ee/index.php?lk=270&show=375
[1064] The immured knight http://www.aulik.se/Baltikumresan/Kuressaare/ppages/ppage6.htm
[1065] "*Legend has it that a girl was immured in the wall of the church in a kneeling position and thus the place came to be called Põlva* (the Estonian word põlv means knee in English). " Põlva linn http://www.polva.ee/tourism
[1066] *..is the Maiden's Tower (Jungfrutornet), in which legend has it that the daughter of a Visby goldsmith was walled up alive for betraying the town to the Danes out of love for the Danish king Valdemar Atterdag.* Visby Tourist Attractions http://www.planetware.com/tourist-attractions-/visby-s-gtl-vis.htm
[1067] On Anarkali legend and tomb, Anarkali's Tomb https://www.ualberta.ca/~rnoor/tomb_anarkali.html
[1068] Tappe (1984), A Rumanian Ballad and its English Adaptation https://www.jstor.org/discover/10.2307/1259765?uid=3738744&uid=2129&uid=2&uid=70&uid=4&sid=21103113155813
[1069] Examples of Bulgarian songs: *Three Brothers Were Building a Fortress* http://liternet.bg/folklor/sbornici/bnt/8/212.htm recorded near Smolyan, *Immured Bride* http://liternet.bg/folklor/sbornici/bnt/4/119.htm recorded in Struga.
[1070] Called "Clemens" in *Eliade, Dundes* (1996), p.77 https://books.google.com/books?id=MDmGX5y40IwC&pg=PA77
[1071] On the sacrifice, with ashes immured, see for example:*Mallows* (2013), p.219 https://books.google.com/books?id=Yt1M3egMbWMC&pg=PA219
[1072] Eliade, Dundes (1996), p.75-76 https://books.google.com/books?id=MDmGX5y40IwC&pg=PA75
[1073] Pozemovskis, Kā cēlies Madlienas nosaukums http://www.pasakas.net/teikas/vietas/k/ka-celies-madlienas-nosaukums/%20
[1074] Grimm (1854), p.1095 https://books.google.com/books?id=jT0CAAAAQAAJ&pg=PA1095
[1075] Dodsley (1744), p.103 https://books.google.com/books?id=m29bAAAAQAAJ&pg=PA103. On suspicion of it being the remains of the fourteenth abbot, Thornton Abbey; and its "immured" Abbot http://www.mspong.org/picturesque/thornton_abbey.html
[1076] Urban (1755), p.211 https://books.google.com/books?id=h3VIAAAAYAAJ&pg=PA211
[1077] Hupel (1782), p.197 https://books.google.com/books?id=86lKAAAAcAAJ&pg=PA197
[1078] Tiefburg
[1079] Schreiber (1811), p.212 https://books.google.com/books?id=E34AAAAAcAAJ&pg=PA212
[1080] Wraxall p.65-66 https://books.google.com/books?id=Bo1CAAAAcAAJ&pg=PA65
[1081] Miesegaes (1829), p.182-183 https://books.google.com/books?id=VSLTAAAAMAAJ&pg=PA182
[1082] Blumenbach, Spangenberg (1828), p.268-282 https://books.google.com/books?id=uGcAAAAAcAAJ&pg=PA268
[1083] Sophocles, Burian, Shapiro (2010), p.17 https://books.google.com/books?id=Fody0Nubm0AC&pg=PA17
[1084] See, for example, *Fumagalli* (2001), p.94 https://books.google.com/books?id=_2wSxSWT834C&pg=PA94

[1085] See both stanza and note at, for example, *Scott* (1833), p.392 https://books.google.com/books?id=Sk9AAAAAYAAJ&pg=PA392
[1086] For the Poe stories, see for example, *Hayes* (2012), p.101 https://books.google.com/books?id=A5i95b_FHvoC&pg=PA101
[1087] See, for example, *Wilde, Murray* (1998), p.77 https://books.google.com/books?id=__pdWkR_WXQC&pg=PA77
[1088] See, for example, relevant excerpt from Twain in *Brown* (2004), p.14-15 https://books.google.com/books?id=3CEvE-jRmQ0C&pg=PA14
[1089] See, for example, *Krehbiel* (2006), p.156 https://books.google.com/books?id=v12CCw-1R0gC&pg=PA156
[1090] https://books.google.com/books?id=VYG4K0yYHQgC
[1091] https://web.archive.org/web/20131203100622/http://www.aulik.se/Baltikumresan/Kuressaare/ppages/ppage6.htm
[1092] http://www.aulik.se/Baltikumresan/Kuressaare/ppages/ppage6.htm
[1093] https://books.google.com/books?jtp=220&id=wjAtGKM_-WIC
[1094] https://books.google.com/books?id=V0YWAAAAYAAJ
[1095] https://archive.org/stream/travelsinmogulem00bernuoft
[1096] https://archive.org/stream/innigercountry00bind
[1097] https://books.google.com/books?id=uGcAAAAAcAAJ
[1098] https://books.google.com/books?id=3CEvE-jRmQ0C
[1099] https://books.google.com/books?id=BerYAQAAQBAJ
[1100] https://books.google.com/books?id=Fody0Nubm0AC
[1101] https://books.google.com/books?id=sowAAAAAcAAJ
[1102] https://books.google.com/books?id=m29bAAAAQAAJ
[1103] http://members.bib-arch.org/publication.asp?PubID=BSAO&Volume=4&Issue=1&ArticleID=14
[1104] https://books.google.com/books?id=v23YleX1UskC
[1105] https://books.google.com/books?id=MDmGX5y40IwC
[1106] https://books.google.com/books?id=PVYOAAAAQAAJ
[1107] https://books.google.com/books?id=YP9cuh3KX3wC
[1108] http://www.executedtoday.com/category/how/starved/immured/
[1109] https://books.google.com/books?id=_ACqBJczrO8C
[1110] https://books.google.com/books?id=CrYIAAAAQAAJ
[1111] https://books.google.com/books?id=_2wSxSWT834C
[1112] https://books.google.com/books?id=jT0CAAAAQAAJ
[1113] https://web.archive.org/web/20090819143501/http://www.haapsalu.ee/index.php?lk=270&show=375
[1114] http://www.haapsalu.ee/index.php?lk=270&show=375
[1115] https://books.google.com/books?id=A5i95b_FHvoC
[1116] https://books.google.com/books?id=kN4GAAAAcAAJ
[1117] https://archive.org/stream/behindveilinpers00humeuoft
[1118] https://books.google.com/books?id=86IKAAAAcAAJ
[1119] http://www.pasakas.net/teikas/vietas/g/grobinas-pils/
[1120] https://books.google.com/books?id=v12CCw-1R0gC
[1121] https://books.google.com/books?id=Z-xEyetzPPEC
[1122] http://www.gutenberg.org/files/39451/39451-h/39451-h.htm
[1123] https://books.google.com/books?id=szm-8WgGjWgC
[1124] https://books.google.com/books?id=X-83AAAAIAAJ
[1125] https://books.google.com/books?id=Yt1M3egMbWMC
[1126] https://books.google.com/books?id=1TVrePw1sq4C
[1127] https://books.google.com/books?id=VSLTAAAAMAAJ
[1128] http://liternet.bg/publish/tmollov/troica.htm
[1129] https://books.google.com/books?id=Po2BO-TsMosC
[1130] http://paperspast.natlib.govt.nz/cgi-bin/paperspast?a=d&d=NZH19140217.2.66
[1131] https://www.ualberta.ca/~rnoor/tomb_anarkali.html
[1132] https://books.google.com/books?id=T-9vsaISVKsC

[1133] https://books.google.com/books?id=X9NCAAAAcAAJ
[1134] http://www.planetware.com/tourist-attractions-/visby-s-gtl-vis.htm
[1135] http://www.polva.ee/tourism
[1136] http://www.pasakas.net/teikas/vietas/k/ka-celies-madlienas-nosaukums/
[1137] https://books.google.com/books?id=iH1L6UE5_e4C
[1138] http://www.weitersfelden.ooe.gv.at/system/web/zusatzseite.aspx?detailonr=229725
[1139] https://books.google.com/books?id=VnaF58VDxzAC
[1140] https://books.google.com/books?id=d6OMefsyv_EC
[1141] http://liternet.bg/folklor/sbornici/bnt/8/212.htm
[1142] http://liternet.bg/folklor/sbornici/bnt/4/119.htm
[1143] https://books.google.com/books?id=E34AAAAAcAAJ
[1144] https://books.google.com/books?id=Sk9AAAAAYAAJ
[1145] https://books.google.com/books?id=PeYRAAAAYAAJ
[1146] https://www.jstor.org/discover/10.2307/1259765?uid=3738744&uid=2129&uid=2&uid=70&uid=4&sid=21103113155813
[1147] //doi.org/10.1080%2F0015587x.1984.9716302
[1148] //www.worldcat.org/issn/0015-587X
[1149] https://archive.org/details/sixvoyagesJohnB00Tave
[1150] https://books.google.com/books?id=63tYpCw4nIYC
[1151] https://news.google.com/newspapers?nid=38&dat=19060908&id=Syg1AAAAIBAJ&sjid=SikDAAAAIBAJ&pg=3044,4436382
[1152] http://perseus.mpiwg-berlin.mpg.de/GreekScience/Thuc.+3.69-85.html
[1153] https//books.google.com
[1154] https://books.google.com/books?id=h3VIAAAAYAAJ
[1155] https://books.google.com/books?id=5IpPhTqnDJkC
[1156] https://books.google.com/books?id=djECAAAAcAAJ
[1157] https://books.google.com/books?id=__pdWkR_WXQC
[1158] https://books.google.com/books?id=Bo1CAAAAcAAJ
[1159] *Thévenot* (1687) p. 259 https://books.google.com/books?jtp=259&id=6q9EAAAAcAAJ Other highly detailed accounts on methods are: 1. Extremely detailed description of the execution of Archbishop Serapheim in 1601. *Vaporis* (2000), pp. 101–102 https://books.google.com/books?id=wTdz-34tZ4sC&pg=PA101 2. Jean Coppin's account from 1640s Cairo, very similar to Thévenot's, *Raymond* (2000), p. 240 https://books.google.com/books?id=tdLALt9AbQQC&pg=PA240 3. Stavorinus (1798) p. 288–291 https://books.google.com/books?jtp=288&id=Ci0LAAAAYAAJ 4. von Taube (1777) footnote ** p. 70–71 https://books.google.com/books?jtp=70&id=gK8AAAAAcAAJ 5. The regrettably highly partisan "Aiolos (2004)" http://www.metopo.gr/article.php?id=5009, notes on methods partly from Guer, see for example, *Guer* (1747), p. 162 https://books.google.com/books?jtp=162&id=hI08AAAAcAAJ#v=onepage&q=empale&f=false 6. *d'Arvieux* (1755), p. 230–31 https://books.google.com/books?id=21ooAAAAYAAJ&pg=PA230 7. Recollection 20 years after second-hand narration, *Massett* (1863), p. 88–89 https://books.google.com/books?id=flsSAAAAYAAJ&pg=PA88 8. Ivo Andric's novel "The Bridge on the Drina", follows Serapheim execution (1.) closely. Excerpt: The Bridge on the Drina http://www.thefreelibrary.com/The+Bridge+on+the+Drina+%28excerpts%29.-a0165021314 9. A literary rendition in The Casket, from 1827, *Purser* (1827), p. 337 https://books.google.com/books?id=iHEEAAAAQAAJ&pg=PA337 10. *Koller* (2004), p. 145–46 https://books.google.com/books?id=cz9abClMbr8C&pg=PA145
[1160] **2 died during impalement process**, *Blount* (1636), p. 52 https://books.google.com/books?id=f1ZzqBTjDVcC&pg=PA52 **9 minutes**, 1773 case, Hungary: *Korabinsky* (1786) p. 139 https://books.google.com/books?jtp=139&id=gpEAAAAAcAAJ
[1161] 1800 assassin of General Kleber **a few hours** *Shepherd* (1814) p. 255 https://books.google.com/books?jtp=255&id=R3QDAAAAYAAJ, **six hours** *Hurd* (1814), p. 308 https://books.google.com/books?jtp=308&id=YnEAAAAMAAJ
[1162] **fifteen hours** *Bond* (1856) p. 172–73 https://books.google.com/books?jtp=172&id=jRcRAQAAIAAJ **24+ hours** *von Taube* (1777), footnote ** p. 70–71 https://books.google.com/books?jtp=70&id=gK8AAAAAcAAJ, *Hartmann* (1799) p. 520 https:

//books.google.com/books?jtp=520&id=bfFCAAAAcAAJ, **two to three days** *von Troilo http://de.wikisource.org/wiki/ADB:Troilo,_Franz_Ferdinand_von* (1676) p. 45 https://books.google.com/books?jtp=45&id=F3FBAAAAcAAJ, *Hueber* (1693) p. 480 https://books.google.com/books?jtp=480&id=PHJAJ-lTnDQC, *Dampier* (1729) p. 140 https://books.google.com/books?jtp=140&id=NCdDAAAAcAAJ, "Aiolos (2004)" http://www.metopo.gr/article.php?id=5009, *d'Arvieux* (1755), p. 230–31 https://books.google.com/books?id=2l0OAAAAYAAJ&pg=PA230, *Moryson, Hadfield* (2001), pp. 170–171 https://books.google.com/books?id=fl6gkL5h6A0C&pg=PA170 **two to three days in warm weather, dead by midnight in cold**, *Mentzel, Allemann* (1919), p. 102 https://books.google.com/books?id=t0Juf6TAqBoC&pg=PA102

[1163] *de Pages http://www.tshaonline.org/handbook/online/articles/fpa09* (1791) p. 284 https://books.google.com/books?jtp=284&id=B2EUAAAAQAAJ

[1164] *Stavorinus* (1798) p. 288–291 https://books.google.com/books?jtp=288&id=Ci0LAAAAYAAJ

[1165] **For following the spine:** *von Taube* (1777), footnote ** p. 70–71 https://books.google.com/books?jtp=70&id=gK8AAAAAcAAJ, *Stavorinus* (1798). p. 288–291 https://books.google.com/books?jtp=288&id=Ci0LAAAAYAAJ Another description, using a 15 cm thick stake, let it pass between the liver and the rib cage, *Koller* (2004), p. 145 https://books.google.com/books?id=cz9abClMbr8C&pg=PA145

[1166] *von Meyer von Knonau* (1855) p. 176, column 2 https://books.google.com/books?jtp=175&id=wEkAAAAAcAAJ, Example of thrusting a roasting spit through the stomach on orders of 16th Central Asian ruler Mirza Abu Bakr Dughlat upon his own nephew, *Elias, Ross* (1898), p. 227 https://archive.org/stream/TheTarikh-i-rashidi/TheTarikh-i-rashidiVer1.0#page/n227/mode/2up

[1167] For extra-cardial chest impalement *Döpler http://www.theatra.de/repertorium/ed000062.pdf* (1697) p. 371 https://books.google.com/books?jtp=371&id=LZlBAAAAcAAJ

[1168] *Roch* (1687) pp. 350–51 https://books.google.com/books?jtp=350&id=0rgAAAAAcAAJ

[1169] A possible case of 16th century dorsal-to-front impalement is given by *di Varthema* (1863) p. 147 https://books.google.com/books?jtp=147&id=MAcVAAAAQAAJ See also wood block print in Dracula subsection. In addition, the alleged "bamboo torture" seems to presume a dorsal-to-front impalement, see specific sub-section

[1170] *Wagner* (1687), p. 55 https://books.google.com/books?id=PJJOAAAAcAAJ&pg=PT51 NOTE: The German word "Pfahl" (with the associated verb "zu pfählen") refers to a *wooden stake*, and is the word used in influential law texts like the 1532 Constitutio Criminalis Carolina, so the reader should not assume that the use of a heated metal rod was the standard procedure. For 1532 law text, see for example, *Koch http://de.wikisource.org/wiki/ADB:Koch,_Johann_Christoph* (1824) p. 63 https://books.google.com/books?jtp=63&id=nBZDAAAAcAAJ#v=onepage&q=verzweiffelung&f=false

[1171] *de Tournefort* (1741) p. 98–100 https://books.google.com/books?jtp=98&id=nbLip5edYDQC A detailed description of the apparatus and procedure of gaunching can be found in *Mundy* (1907), pp. 55–56 https://archive.org/stream/travelsofpetermu01mund#page/n127/mode/2up and in *Moryson, Hadfield* (2001), pp. 170–171 https://books.google.com/books?id=fl6gkL5h6A0C&pg=PA170

[1172] *Thévenot* (1687) p. 68–69 https://books.google.com/books?jtp=68&id=6q9EAAAAcAAJ. For a fourth description plus drawing, see *Schweigger* (1613), p. 173 https://books.google.com/books?id=cl5OAAAAcAAJ&pg=RA2-PA75 Schweigger adds that many times, people are allowed to shorten the gaunched individual's time of misery by cutting his throat or decapitating him. Alexander Russell, from 1740s Aleppo knew of instances of "gaunching", but said those were rare, compared with other types of capital punishment.*Russell* (1794) p. 334 https://books.google.com/books?jtp=334&id=7PfaAAAAMAAJ

[1173] Breuning von Buchenbach, Hans Jakob https://de.wikisource.org/wiki/ADB:Breuning_von_Buchenbach,_Hans_Jakob

[1174] *Buchenbach* (1612), pp. 86–87 https://books.google.com/books?id=rlVEAAAAcAAJ&pg=PA86

[1175] Thomas Shaw http://www.vintage-maps.com/shop_content.php?language=en&coID=15&manID=108%20

[1176] *Shaw* (1757) p. 253–254 https://books.google.com/books?jtp=253&id=0c4GAAAAQAAJ Shaw's contemporary John Braithwaite reports impalement and throwing onto hooks for Morocco as well, *Braithwaite* (1729) p. 366 https://books.google.com/books?jtp=366&id=iJA_AAAAMAAJ On Morocco and Fez, see also the travel account by Sieur Mouette, who was captive there from 1670 to 1682, *Stevens* (1711), p. 69 https://books.google.com/books?id=VX4BAAAAQAAJ&pg=RA2-PA69

[1177] *Morgan* (1729) p. 392 https://books.google.com/books?jtp=392&id=ElZBAAAAcAAJ#v=onepage&q&f=false

[1178] in one of his acerbic comments and footnotes to translated accounts from Catholic priests' narratives of the redemption of slaves. Examples of other such acerbic notes: *Boyde* (1736) p. 3 https://books.google.com/books?id=hWI_AAAAMAAJ&pg=PA3, p. 25 https://books.google.com/books?id=hWI_AAAAMAAJ&pg=PA25, p. 35 https://books.google.com/books?id=hWI_AAAAMAAJ&pg=PA35, p. 44 https://books.google.com/books?id=hWI_AAAAMAAJ&pg=PA44 (compares French and Algerine slavery), p. 45 https://books.google.com/books?id=hWI_AAAAMAAJ&pg=PA45, p. 51 https://books.google.com/books?id=hWI_AAAAMAAJ&pg=PA51, p. 52 https://books.google.com/books?id=hWI_AAAAMAAJ&pg=PA52

[1179] *Boyde* (1736) p. 75, footnote https://books.google.com/books?jtp=75&id=hWI_AAAAMAAJ

[1180] *Osborne* (1745), p. 478 https://books.google.com/books?id=LbCs0L59DhkC&pg=PA478#v=onepage&q&f=false

[1181] *Koller* (2004), p. 146 https://books.google.com/books?id=cz9abClMbr8C&pg=PA146

[1182] *Stedman* (1813) p. 116 https://books.google.com/books?jtp=116&id=mywAAAAAQAAJ

[1183] As an example of popular promotion of this horror story, see for example: *WW2 People's War* JAPANESE TORTURE TECHNIQUES http://www.bbc.co.uk/history/ww2peopleswar/stories/37/a4865637.shtml

[1184] Middle chronology is used here

[1185] Article 153 in: *Harper* (1904), The Code of Hammurabi

[1186] *Tetlow* (2004) p. 34 https://books.google.com/books?id=ONkJ_Rj1SS8C&pg=PA34

[1187] *Hamblin* (2006), p. 208 https://books.google.com/books?id=h5IQQir5eFEC&pg=PA208

[1188] *Herrenschmidt, Bottéro* (2000), p. 84 https://books.google.com/books?id=wwoPiWG3-LQC&pg=PA84

[1189] *Mayer, ed.* (2005), p. 141 https://books.google.com/books?id=RhIayTaTwAcC&pg=PA141

[1190] http://ifpeakoilwerenoobject.blogspot.co.uk/2012/02/impalements-in-antiquity-2.html

[1191] *Ussishkin, Amit* (2006), p. 346 https://books.google.com/books?id=Ku4OKVrEd4MC&pg=PA346

[1192] Ekron incident from Sennacherib's own self-glorification, see *Callaway* (1995), p. 169 https://books.google.com/books?id=8F4oDF9dJvUC&pg=PA169

[1193] Relief and text in *Eph'al* (2009), p. 51–52 https://books.google.com/books?id=QdbVQ8OGfG4C&pg=PA51

[1194] Relative to *later* impalement practices, at least

[1195] *Layard* (1850) p. 374 https://books.google.com/books?jtp=374&id=z0CKptoRT3sC

[1196] *Olmstead* (1918), p. 66

[1197] Paul Kern http://www.iun.edu/~nwacadem/hppr/faculty/pkern.shtml

[1198] *Kern* (1999), p. 68–76 https://books.google.com/books?id=FBTesdgIbcsC&pg=PA68, Relative to impalement, for example, Ashurnasirpal II is credited with 5 distinct incidents, Shalmaneser III (r. 858–824 BC). For a number of examples of impalement of rebels and subjugated people under Neo-Assyrian king Shalmaneser III, see *Olmstead* (1921), **Battle at Sugania** p. 348, **Siege of Til Bashere** p. 354, **Battle of Arzashkun** p. 360, **Battle of Kulisi** p. 368, **Battle of Kinalua** p. 378 For the last, see also *Bryce* (2012), p. 244 https://books.google.com/books?id=k0dbRu1TOguC&pg=PA244 Tiglath-Pileser III (r. 745–727), For some specifics on Tiglath-Pileser's policy, see for example, *Crouch* (2009), p. 39–41 https://books.google.com/books?id=EODNwjxJxmoC&pg=PA39 and Ashurbanipal (r.668-627 BC), Ashurbanipal congratulates himself once over having impaled fleeing survivors from towns he has burnt down, *Ehrlich* (2004), p. 5 https://books.google.com/books?id=H1q1tAnYMY0C&pg=PA5

[1199] where Ashur-uballit I was king at that time

1200 *Kuhrt* (1995), p. 292 https://books.google.com/books?id=V_sfMzRPTgoC&pg=PA292 and *Gadd* (1965), p. 9 https://books.google.com/books?id=MRs7AAAAIAAJ&pg=PA9
1201 *Richardson, Laneri* (2007), p. 197
1202 *Schroeder* (1920), Keilschrifttexte aus Assur verschiedenen Inhalts https://archive.org/details/keilschrifttexte00schr
1203 *Jastrow* (1921), p. 48–49
1204 *Herodotus: A New and Literal Version from the Text of Baehr by Henry Cary*, page 236 https//books.google.com
1205 Pierre Briant, *From Cyrus to Alexander: A History of the Persian Empire*, p. 123 https//books.google.com
1206 Haman conspired to have all the Jews in the empire killed, the Book of Esther tells that story, and how Haman's plan was thwarted, and he was given the punishment he had thought to mete out to Mordecai
1207 Book of Esther, ESV Bible edition http://www.biblegateway.com/passage/?search=Esther+5&version=ESV
1208 Book of Esther, NIRV Bible edition http://www.biblica.com/bibles/chapter/?verse=Esther+5&version=nirv
1209 *Haupt* (1908), p. 122, 152, 154, 170
1210 *Shaw* (2012), Was Haman Hanged or Impaled? http://www.ligonier.org/blog/was-haman-hanged-or-impaled/
1211 The theologian Adam Clarke was deeply suspicious of whether this passage ought to be regarded as part of the original Biblical text, and wrote: "The definition of יָקַע (YaQ'a) in Strong's: 'a prim. primitive root; prop. properly to sever oneself, i.e. (by impl. implication) to be dislocated; fig. to abandon; causat. causatively to impale (and thus allow to drop to pieces by rotting):- be alienated, depart, hang (up), be out of joint'. The seven sons of Saul, mentioned here, [II Samuel 21:9], are represented as a sacrifice required by God, to make an atonement for the sin of Saul. Till I get farther light on the subject, I am led to conclude that the whole chapter is not now what it would be coming from the pen of an inspired writer; and that this part of the Jewish records has suffered much from rabbinical glosses, alterations, and additions." *Clarke* 1831, Bible ed. p. II 267
1212 *Crucifixion in the Mediterranean World* by John Granger Cook, 2014, published by Mohr Siebeck,
1213 For law text, *Koch* http://de.wikisource.org/wiki/ADB:Koch,_Johann_Christoph (1824) p. 63 https://books.google.com/books?jtp=63&id=nBZDAAAAcAAJ#v=onepage&q=verzweiffelung&f=false
1214 *Engel, Jacob* (2006), p. 75 https://books.google.com/books?id=OP3hhD7_T6QC&pg=PA75 A similar punishment of the couple by impalement for adultery if caught in the act is mentioned in Bavarian sources as well, see *His* (1928), p. 150
1215 *Schwetschke* (1789), col. 692 https://books.google.com/books?id=hytRAAAAYAAJ&pg=PT351
1216 *Ehrlich* (2005), p. 42
1217 *Fick* (1867), p. 14 https://books.google.com/books?id=b8JCAAAAcAAJ&pg=PA14
1218 *Engelmann* (1834) p. 158 https://books.google.com/books?jtp=158&id=KOAAAAAAcAAJ
1219 *Osenbrüggen* (1868), p. 297 https://books.google.com/books?id=YWE7AAAAcAAJ&pg=PA297
1220 Schwab (1827), p. 256 https://books.google.com/books?id=ubmr9w0g9GAC&pg=PA256
1221 *Gottfried, van Hulsius* (1633), p. 462 https://books.google.com/books?id=HItOAAAAcAAJ&pg=PA462
1222 *Han* (1669), p. 203 https://books.google.com/books?id=KIZBAAAAcAAJ&pg=RA2-PT55
1223 *Beer* (1713), p. 127 https://books.google.com/books?id=UT5VAAAAcAAJ&pg=PA127
1224 *von Loen* (1751), p. 420–422 https://books.google.com/books?id=tTUXAAAAYAAJ&pg=PA420
1225 *von Imhoff* (1736), p. 1051 https://books.google.com/books?id=uI.h5cjzNpz4C&pg=PA1051
1226 *Mannheimer Zeitung* (1784), p. 638 https://books.google.com/books?id=1BpEAAAAcAAJ&pg=PA631

[1227] *Vehse, Demmler* (1856), p. 318 https://books.google.com/books?id=vZVHAAAAIAAJ&pg=PA318
[1228] *Woltersdorf* (1812) p. 267 https://books.google.com/books?jtp=267&id=X8U3AAAAYAAJ
[1229] *Daschitsky* (1570), [https://books.google.com/books?id=h_xXAAAAcAAJ&pg=PA12 p. 1
[1230] *Wiltenburg* (2012), pp. 124–125 https://books.google.com/books?id=SAXvt1_0KL4C&pg=PT124
[1231] *Bastian* (1860), p. 105 https://books.google.com/books?id=17tSAAAAcAAJ&pg=PA105
[1232] *Muir* (1997), pp. 110–111 https://books.google.com/books?id=pvc1BT8yM6sC&pg=PA110
[1233] *Roch* (1687), p. 249 https://books.google.com/books?id=0rgAAAAAcAAJ&pg=PA249
[1234] Reid, (2000), p. 440
[1235] *Florescu* (1999)
[1236] "er liess kinnder praten die musten ire mütter essen. Und schneyd den frawen den prüst ab den musten ire man essen. Darnach liess er sie all spissen.", *Gutknecht http://www.deutsche-biographie.de/sfz24799.html* (1521), p. 7 https://books.google.com/books?id=mqJSAAAAcAAJ&pg=PA7
[1237] *Philippides, Hanak* (2011), p. 587 https://books.google.com/books?id=qvvdVXckfqQC&pg=PA587
[1238] *Runciman* (1965), p. 67 https://books.google.com/books?id=BAzntP0lg58C&pg=PA67
[1239] Pears, (2004), p. 253 https://books.google.com/books?id=NMQ7X6fe5CwC&pg=PA253
[1240] *de La Mottraye* p. 188 https://books.google.com/books?jtp=188&id=x3dUAAAAYAAJ
[1241] *Russell* (1794) p. 331 https://books.google.com/books?jtp=331&id=7PfaAAAAMAAJ
[1242] See *de Thévenot*(1687), p. 68–69 https://books.google.com/books?jtp=68&id=6q9EAAAAcAAJ and p. 259 https://books.google.com/books?jtp=259&id=6q9EAAAAcAAJ
[1243] Late Ottoman cases in 1830s Balkans, i) Some five case reported 1833, *M***r* (1833) p. 440–41 columns 2 https://books.google.com/books?jtp=440&id=Jow0AQAAMAAJ ii) 1834, Two such corpses, close to the village Paracini in the vicinity of Jagodina, see: *Burgess* (1835) p. 275 https://books.google.com/books?jtp=275&id=hr_0VHlDUjwC iii) Rarity of such cases in the 1830s,*Goodrich* (1836) p. 308 https://books.google.com/books?id=edABAAAAYAAJ 1835, Retaliative cycle Turkish authorities relative Kurdish "robbers", *Slade* (1837) p. 191 https://books.google.com/books?jtp=191&id=hVMEAAAAQAAJ
[1244] Stephen Massett http://www.maritimeheritage.org/vips/massettStephen.html
[1245] *Massett* (1863), p. 88–89 https://books.google.com/books?id=flsSAAAAYAAJ&pg=PA88
[1246] *Layard* (1871), p. 307 https://books.google.com/books?id=t2RHAAAAYAAJ&pg=PA307
[1247] *Ranft* (1769), p. 345 https://books.google.com/books?id=epZAAAAAcAAJ&pg=PA345
[1248] missing
[1249] "Aiolos (2004)" http://www.metopo.gr/article.php?id=5009
[1250] *Dumas* (2008), volume 8, chapter 3
[1251] *Hughes* (1820) p. 454 https://books.google.com/books?jtp=454&id=qy3RAAAAMAAJ, see also, on roasting incident: *Holland* (1815) p. 194 https://books.google.com/books?jtp=194&id=3D9MAAAAMAAJ
[1252] J.W.A.Streit, Constantinopel im Jahr 1821, oder Darstellung der blutigen und höchst schauderhaften Begebenheiten ... Leipzig, 1822, pp. 30, 31, 42–45. Cited by Kyriakos Simopoulos, "How Foreigners saw the Greece of the 1821 Revolution", Athens, 2004 (5th edition), vol. 1, pp. 153, 154, in Greek language.
[1253] Pouqueville Fr., Histoire de la régénération de la Grèce, Paris, 1825, vol. 2, p. 580 https//books.google.com
[1254] Makrygiannis Yannis, Memoirs, p. 27. (In Greek language) http://www.24grammata.com/wp-content/uploads/2010/12/apomnimon.pdf Yannis Makrygiannis (1797–1864) was a general and politician, hero of the Greek Revolution.
[1255] *Paroulakis* (1984)
[1256] **Turkish reprisals on Greek War of independence**, **i)** 2.June 1821, 10 Greeks at Bucharest, *Fick* (1821) p. 254 https://books.google.com/books?jtp=254&id=ExtEAAAAcAAJ#v=snippet&q=lebendig%20t%C3%BCrken%20schaar&f=false **ii)** During the massacre at Crete around 24 June 1821, most are said to have been impaled: *Siegman* (1821) p. 988, column 1 https://books.google.com/books?jtp=988&id=CZtHAQAAIAAJ **iii)** 36

Greek hostages, including 7 bishops at onset of Siege of Tripolitsa *Colburn* (1821) p. 56 https://books.google.com/books?jtp=56&id=UDMaAQAAIAAJ **iv**) In conjunction with the Chios Massacre in 1822, several Chiote merchants were detained and executed at Constantinople, 6 of whom were impaled alive: *Hughes* (1822) p. 169 https://books.google.com/books?jtp=169&id=nfYaAAAAYAAJ **v**) Omer Vrioni organizing in 1821 *Greek hunts* where civilians were, at least in one instance, impaled on his orders.*Waddington* (1825) p. 52–54 https://books.google.com/books?jtp=52&id=SX82AAAAMAAJ **vi**) In early 1822 Cassandreia, some 300 civilians massacred, several reported to have been impaled, *Grund* (1822) p. 4 https://books.google.com/books?id=xowpAAAAYAAJ&pg=PT329 **vii**) During the last Siege of Missolonghi, in 1826, the Ottoman besiegers offered opportunity for capitulation for the besieged, while they also sent a message of consequences for refusal by impaling alive a priest, two women and several children in front of the line. The offer of capitulation was declined by the besieged Greeks. *Alison*(1856), p. 206 https://books.google.com/books?id=bv0KAAAAYAAJ&pg=PA206

[1257] George Waddington, "A visit to Greece in 1823 and 1824", 2nd ed., London, 1825, p. 52 https://archive.org/stream/gri_000033125010873152#page/n133/mode/2up

[1258] 20-50 "daily" brought in, most impaled *Urban* (1810) p. 74 https://books.google.com/books?jtp=74&id=qg83AAAAYAAJ

[1259] *Sowards* (2009) The Serbian Revolution and the Serbian State http://staff.lib.msu.edu/sowards/balkan/lecture5.html

[1260] Obituary James Reid http://armenianstudies.csufresno.edu/hye_sharzhoom/vol28/oct06/dr_reid.aspx

[1261] *Reid* (2000), p. 441 https://books.google.com/books?id=Zgg6c_Ndtu4C&pg=PA441

[1262] "Sees Bolshevism as Hideous Religion" https://timesmachine.nytimes.com/timesmachine/1920/08/02/102879148.pdf, *The New York Times*, August 2, 1920

[1263] *Erish* (2012) p. 212 https://books.google.com/books?id=TKskLkvWnDgC&pg=PA212

[1264] *Shahbaz* (1918), p. 142 https://archive.org/stream/rageofislamaccou00shah#page/142/mode/2up

[1265] https://books.google.com/?id=bv0KAAAAYAAJ

[1266] http://www.thefreelibrary.com/The+Bridge+on+the+Drina+%28excerpts%29.-a0165021314

[1267] https://books.google.com/?id=210oAAAAYAAJ

[1268] https://books.google.com/books?id=17tSAAAAcAAJ

[1269] https://books.google.com/books?id=UT5VAAAAcAAJ

[1270] https://books.google.com/?id=f1ZzqBTjDVcC

[1271] https://books.google.com/?id=jRcRAQAAIAAJ

[1272] https://books.google.com/?id=hWI_AAAAMAAJ

[1273] https://books.google.com/?id=iJA_AAAAMAAJ

[1274] https://books.google.com/books?id=k0dbRu1TOgUC

[1275] https://books.google.com/?id=rlVEAAAAcAAJ

[1276] https://books.google.com/?id=hr_0VHlDUjwC

[1277] https://books.google.com/books?id=8F4oDF9dJvUC

[1278] https://books.google.com/books?id=EODNwjxJxmoC

[1279] https://books.google.com/?id=NCdDAAAAcAAJ

[1280] https://books.google.com/books?id=h_xXAAAAcAAJ

[1281] https://books.google.com/?id=LZIBAAAAcAAJ

[1282] https://books.google.com/books?id=H1q1tAnYMY0C

[1283] https://archive.org/details/TheTarikh-i-rashidi

[1284] https://books.google.com/books?id=OP3hhD7_T6QC

[1285] https://books.google.com/books?id=QdbVQ8OGfG4C

[1286] https://books.google.com/books?id=TKskLkvWnDgC

[1287] https://books.google.com/books?id=b8JCAAAAcAAJ

[1288] https://books.google.com/books?id=MRs7AAAAIAAJ

[1289] https://books.google.com/?id=edABAAAAYAAJ

[1290] https://books.google.com/books?id=HItOAAAAcAAJ

[1291] https://books.google.com/?id=8MopwCROkrUC

[1292] https://books.google.com/?id=hI08AAAAcAAJ

[1293] https://books.google.com/?id=mqJSAAAAcAAJ
[1294] https://books.google.com/books?id=h5IQQir5eFEC
[1295] https://books.google.com/books?id=KlZBAAAAcAAJ
[1296] https://books.google.com/?id=bfFCAAAAcAAJ
[1297] https://books.google.com/books?id=wwoPiWG3-LQC
[1298] //www.amazon.com/dp/B0000BRMK3
[1299] https://books.google.com/?id=3D9MAAAAMAAJ
[1300] https://books.google.com/?id=PHJAJ-lTnDQC
[1301] https://books.google.com/?id=qy3RAAAAMAAJ
[1302] https://books.google.com/books?id=uLb5cjzNpz4C
[1303] https://books.google.com/books?id=FBTesdgIbcsC
[1304] https://books.google.com/?id=nBZDAAAAcAAJ
[1305] https://books.google.com/books?id=cz9abClMbr8C
[1306] https://books.google.com/?id=gpEAAAAAcAAJ
[1307] https://books.google.com/books?id=V_sfMzRPTgoC
[1308] https://books.google.com/?id=x3dUAAAAYAAJ
[1309] https://books.google.com/?id=z0CKptoRT3sC
[1310] https://books.google.com/?id=t2RHAAAAYAAJ
[1311] https://books.google.com/books?id=tTUXAAAAYAAJ
[1312] https://books.google.com/?id=flsSAAAAYAAJ
[1313] https://books.google.com/books?id=t0Juf6TAqBoC
[1314] https://books.google.com/books?id=Q-lr20SuvfIC
[1315] https://books.google.com/?id=ElZBAAAAcAAJ
[1316] https://books.google.com/books?id=fl6gkL5h6A0C
[1317] https://books.google.com/books?id=pvc1BT8yM6sC
[1318] https://archive.org/details/travelsofpetermu01mund
[1319] https://books.google.com/?id=LbCs0L59DhkC
[1320] https://books.google.com/?id=YWE7AAAAcAAJ
[1321] https://books.google.com/?id=B2EUAAAAQAAJ
[1322] https://books.google.com/books?id=NMQ7X6fe5CwC
[1323] https://books.google.com/books?id=qvvdVXckfqQC
[1324] https://books.google.com/books?id=tdLALt9AbQQC
[1325] https://books.google.com/?id=Zgg6c_Ndtu4C
[1326] https://books.google.com/?id=0rgAAAAAcAAJ
[1327] https://books.google.com/books?id=BAzntP0lg58C
[1328] https://books.google.com/?id=7PfaAAAAMAAJ
[1329] https://books.google.com/?id=NphFnF2RRKUC
[1330] https://archive.org/details/keilschrifttexte00schr
[1331] https://books.google.com/books?id=ubmr9w0g9GAC
[1332] https://books.google.com/?id=cl5OAAAAcAAJ
[1333] https://archive.org/details/rageofislamaccou00shah
[1334] https://books.google.com/?id=0c4GAAAAQAAJ
[1335] https://books.google.com/books?id=R3QDAAAAYAAJ
[1336] https://books.google.com/?id=hVMEAAAAQAAJ
[1337] https://books.google.com/?id=Ci0LAAAAYAAJ
[1338] https://books.google.com/?id=mywAAAAAQAAJ
[1339] https://books.google.com/?id=VX4BAAAAQAAJ
[1340] https://books.google.com/?id=gK8AAAAAcAAJ
[1341] https://books.google.com/books?id=ONkJ_Rj1SS8C
[1342] https://books.google.com/?id=6q9EAAAAcAAJ
[1343] https://books.google.com/?id=nbLip5edYDQC
[1344] https://books.google.com/?id=F3FBAAAAcAAJ
[1345] https://books.google.com/books?id=Ku4OKVrEd4MC
[1346] https://books.google.com/books?id=wTdz-34tZ4sC
[1347] https://books.google.com/?id=MAcVAAAAQAAJ
[1348] https://books.google.com/books?id=vZVHAAAAIAAJ

[1349] https://books.google.com/?id=SX82AAAAMAAJ
[1350] https://books.google.com/books?id=SAXvt1_0KL4C
[1351] https://books.google.com/books?id=PJJOAAAAcAAJ
[1352] https://books.google.com/?id=X8U3AAAAYAAJ
[1353] https://books.google.com/?id=UDMaAQAAIAAJ
[1354] https://books.google.com/?id=6VwAAAAAYAAJ
[1355] https://books.google.com/?id=KOAAAAAAcAAJ
[1356] https://books.google.com/?id=ExtEAAAAcAAJ
[1357] https://books.google.com/?id=xowpAAAAYAAJ
[1358] //www.worldcat.org/issn/1062-0516
[1359] //www.jstor.org/stable/527925
[1360] https://books.google.com/?id=nfYaAAAAYAAJ
[1361] //doi.org/10.2307%2F593702
[1362] //www.worldcat.org/issn/0003-0279
[1363] //www.jstor.org/stable/593702
[1364] https://books.google.com/?id=Jow0AQAAMAAJ
[1365] https://books.google.com/books?id=1BpEAAAAcAAJ&pg=PA630
[1366] https://books.google.com/books?id=RhIayTaTwAcC
[1367] https://books.google.com/?id=wEkAAAAAcAAJ
[1368] //www.worldcat.org/issn/0003-0554
[1369] //www.jstor.org/stable/1946342
[1370] //doi.org/10.2307%2F593746
[1371] https://books.google.com/?id=OxAEAAAAQAAJ
[1372] https://books.google.com/?id=iHEEAAAAQAAJ
[1373] https://books.google.com/?id=epZAAAAAcAAJ
[1374] https://books.google.com/?id=hytRAAAAYAAJ
[1375] https://books.google.com/?id=CZtHAQAAIAAJ
[1376] https://books.google.com/?id=qg83AAAAYAAJ
[1377] https://web.archive.org/web/20150113024717/http://www.metopo.gr/article.php?id=5009
[1378] http://www.stanford.edu/group/rsa/_content/_public/_htm/dracula.shtml
[1379] http://www.biblegateway.com/passage/?search=Esther+5&version=ESV
[1380] http://www.biblica.com/bibles/chapter/?verse=Esther+5&version=nirv
[1381] http://en.wikisource.org/wiki/The_Code_of_Hammurabi_%28Harper_translation%29
[1382] http://www.ligonier.org/blog/was-haman-hanged-or-impaled/
[1383] http://staff.lib.msu.edu/sowards/balkan/lecture5.html
[1384] http://www.bbc.co.uk/history/ww2peopleswar/stories/37/a4865637.shtml
[1385] H. A. Ormerod, Piracy in the Ancient World (New York: Dorset Press, 1987), 54-56.
[1386] Boteler's Dialogues, ed Perrin 11-25
[1387] Nicholas A. M. Rodger, 2017 Personal communication
[1388] NAVY—ALLEGED INSTANCE OF "KEEL-HAULING." HC Deb 04 September 1880 vol 256 c1275 https://api.parliament.uk/historic-hansard/commons/1880/sep/04/navy-alleged-instance-of-keel-hauling api.parliament.uk/historic-hansard, accessed 8 August 2018.
[1389] The Dutch navy of the seventeenth and eighteenth centuries, Jaap R. Bruijn
[1390] An Universal Dictionary of the Marine, W. Falconer, 1784
[1391] 'Ducking' at the main yard arm is, when a malefactor by having a rope fastened under his arms and about his middle, and under his breech, is thus hois[t]ed up to the end of the yard; from whence he is again violently let fall into the sea, sometimes twice, sometimes three several times one after another; and if the offence be very foul, he is also drawn under the very keel of the ship... Dialogical Discourse of Marine affairs, Nathaniel Boteler (1685)
[1392] http://www.bruzelius.info/Nautica/Etymology/German/Roeding(1793)/Kielholen.html
[1393] http://www.straightdope.com/classics/a4_239.html
[1394] Richard A. Bauman (2005), *Crime and Punishment in Ancient Rome*, London & New York: Routledge, reprint of 1996 edition, , p. 23.
[1395] *Mommsen* (1899), pp. 921–923 https://archive.org/stream/rmischesstrafre00mommgoog#page/n943/mode/2up

[1396] See, in particular, *Watson, Robinson* (1998), p.336 and for example, "blood-red rods" in *Gaughan* (2010), p.85 https://books.google.com/books?id=JN4-lPYKCxIC&pg=PT105

[1397] *Cicero, Yonge* (1852), p.369 https://books.google.com/books?id=59sIAAAAQAAJ&pg=PA369 and, on wine sack, *Francesce* (2007), pp. 184–185 https://books.google.com/books?id=gl5T47CvuDsC&pg=PA184

[1398] *Radin* (1920), p.119 https://www.jstor.org/stable/295798

[1399] *Caplan* (1954), pp. 41–43 https://archive.org/stream/adcherenniumdera00capluoft#page/40/mode/2up

[1400] *Livy, Baker* (1797), p.338 https://books.google.com/books?id=19w_AAAAYAAJ&pg=PA338

[1401] working primarily under emperors Augustus (r. 27 BCE – 14 CE) and Tiberius (r. 14 – 37 CE), respectively

[1402] *Valerius, Walker* (2004), p.6 https://books.google.com/books?id=5imDC6VN-FcC&pg=PA6 and *Dionysius, Spelman* (1758), p.262 https://books.google.com/books?id=ZAEMAAAAYAAJ&pg=PA262

[1403] *Plutarch, Dryden* (2008), p.55 https://books.google.com/books?id=9O1-c6BF9VEC&pg=PA55

[1404] For this shift, see for example, *Lintott* (1999), p.38 https://books.google.com/books?id=QIKEpOP4lLIC&pg=PA38

[1405] See footnote 86 reference to Cloud in *Robinson* (2007), p.45 https://books.google.com/books?id=SOz_W0X9BzoC&pg=PA45

[1406] *Plutarch, Stadter* (1999), p.99 https://books.google.com/books?id=WViVSiCfmlEC&pg=PA99

[1407] *Long* (1855), p.55 https://books.google.com/books?id=uokvAAAAYAAJ&pg=PA55

[1408] *Watson, Robinson* (1998), p.335

[1409] A type of banishment/exile, see for example, Exsilium http://penelope.uchicago.edu/Thayer/E/Roman/Texts/secondary/SMIGRA*/Exsilium.html at LacusCurtius website

[1410] *Kyle* (2012), p.231, footnote 20 https://books.google.com/books?id=F2DkmT79JeMC&pg=PA231

[1411] Translation by Berry (2000), quoted in *Bradley* (2012), pp. 131–132 https://books.google.com/books?id=xdVhSEdsvqYC&pg=PA131

[1412] *Cicero, Watson* (1871), p.24 https://books.google.com/books?id=eCMBAAAAMAAJ&pg=PA24

[1413] *Suetonius, Hurley* (2011), p.70 https://books.google.com/books?id=-0EtPxT_z4gC&pg=PA70

[1414] *Francesce* (2007), p. 184–185 https://books.google.com/books?id=gl5T47CvuDsC&pg=PA184

[1415] But, serpents only, cf. *Robinson* (2007), footnote 91, p.46 https://books.google.com/books?id=SOz_W0X9BzoC&pg=PA46

[1416] Satire 13, "*Or those, who in a raw ox-hide are bound, And, with an ill-starr'd ape, poor sufferer! drown'd?*", in *Juvenal, Gifford, Nuttall* (1836), p.152 https://books.google.com/books?id=LdgNAAAAQAAJ&pg=PA152

[1417] "*Nero, for whose chastisement no single ape or adder, no solitary sack, should have been provided*" Satire 8, cited in *Kahn* (2005), p.85 https://books.google.com/books?id=Lrumt0Syn1sC&pg=PA85

[1418] On this interpretation, see *Varner* (2004), p.47 https://books.google.com/books?id=5IpPhTqnDJkC&pg=PA47

[1419] Suetonius reference in *Elliott, Reasoner* (2011), pp. 152–153 https://books.google.com/books?id=x4bNGIM-K94C&pg=PA153

[1420] *Watson, Robinson* (1998), p.336. *S.P. Scott* (1911) translates "virgis sanguinis" as "rods stained with his own blood", see Translation of Digest 48.9.9 http://droitromain.upmf-grenoble.fr/Anglica/D48_Scott.htm#IX

[1421] On Dositheus and Paulus references, see *Mommsen* (1899), footnotes at p.922 and p.923 https://archive.org/stream/rmischesstrafre00mommgoog#page/n943/mode/2up, respectively

[1422] *Eusebius, Cureton* (1861), pp. 59–60 https://books.google.com/books?id=t43JGL9O0mAC&pg=PA59

[1423] On feast day and date of martyrdom, Who was a Christian in the Holy Land? http://www.christusrex.org/www1/ofm/sbf/escurs/wwc/u.html

[1424] That is, for example, the view of Mommsen. A more modern historian, Connie Scarborough, notes that at the times of Paulus, parricides were generally burnt, and that the particular punishment of *poena cullei* was certainly obsolete at the tom of Constantine's accession. Scarborough, Classen, Scarborough (2012), p.229 https://books.google.com/books?id=BxmTcMMfLpIC&pg=PA229

[1425] Translation by Justice Blume http://www.uwyo.edu/lawlib/blume-justinian/_files/docs/book-9pdf/book9-17.pdf

[1426] 1911 translation Institutes by J.B. Moyle http://amesfoundation.law.harvard.edu/digital/CJCiv/JInst.pdf

[1427] Robinson (2007), footnote 100, p.46 https://books.google.com/books?id=SOz_W0X9BzoC&pg=PA46

[1428] *Trenchard-Smith, Turner* (2010), p.48 https://books.google.com/books?id=2ombkgpGt_AC&pg=PA48

[1429] Johann von Buch http://www.hrgdigital.de/id/johann_von_buch_um_1290_um_1356/stichwort.html

[1430] *Böhmer* (1820), p. 377–378 https://books.google.com/books?id=SVsTAAAAQAAJ&pg=PA377

[1431] Original story in *Weck* (1680), p.482 https://books.google.com/books?id=fz9JAAAAcAAJ&pg=PT584

[1432] See, for assertion of 1734 as last case, *Auler* (2012), p.453 https://books.google.com/books?id=V-W9IElqv7EC&pg=PA453 The standard reference to the 1734 case is *Grimm* (1828), p.697 https://books.google.com/books?id=6gAuAAAAQAAJ&pg=PA697, but Grimm merely says there happened a case in 1734, not that it was the last one.

[1433] *Pescheck* (1837), p.189 https://books.google.com/books?id=BcFRAAAAcAAJ&pg=PA189 According to Pescheck at that page, as many as 6 cases of sacking are recorded in Zittau in the 18th century: in 1712, 1713, 1714, 1718, 1726 and 1749

[1434] *Böhmer* (1820), p. 377–378 https://books.google.com/books?id=SVsTAAAAQAAJ&pg=PA377 Original rescript by Prince Elector Friedrich August in *Weiske* (1833), p.98 https://books.google.com/books?id=UzBRAAAAcAAJ&pg=PA98

[1435] https://books.google.com/books?id=V-W9IElqv7EC
[1436] https://books.google.com/books?id=xdVhSEdsvqYC
[1437] https://books.google.com/books?id=SVsTAAAAQAAJ
[1438] https://archive.org/details/adcherenniumdera00capluoft
[1439] https://books.google.com/books?id=eCMBAAAAMAAJ
[1440] https://books.google.com/books?id=59sIAAAAQAAJ
[1441] https://books.google.com/books?id=ZAEMAAAAYAAJ
[1442] https://books.google.com/books?id=x4bNGIM-K94C
[1443] https://books.google.com/books?id=t43JGL9O0mAC
[1444] https://books.google.com/books?id=gl5T47CvuDsC
[1445] https://books.google.com/books?id=JN4-1PYKCxIC
[1446] https://books.google.com/books?id=6gAuAAAAQAAJ
[1447] https://books.google.com/books?id=LdgNAAAAQAAJ
[1448] https://books.google.com/books?id=Lrumt0Syn1sC
[1449] https://books.google.com/books?id=F2DkmT79JeMC
[1450] https://books.google.com/books?id=QIKEpOP4lLIC
[1451] https://books.google.com/books?id=19w_AAAAYAAJ
[1452] https://books.google.com/books?id=uokvAAAAYAAJ
[1453] https://archive.org/stream/rmischesstrafre00mommgoog#page/n943/mode/2up
[1454] https://books.google.com/books?id=BcFRAAAAcAAJ
[1455] https://books.google.com/books?id=9O1-c6BF9VEC
[1456] https://books.google.com/books?id=WViVSiCfmlEC
[1457] //doi.org/10.2307%2F295798
[1458] //www.worldcat.org/issn/0075-4358
[1459] //www.jstor.org/stable/295798

[1460] https://books.google.com/books?id=SOz_W0X9BzoC
[1461] https://books.google.com/books?id=ZxY_pgPTW0EC
[1462] https://books.google.com/books?id=BxmTcMMfLpIC
[1463] https://books.google.com/books?id=-0EtPxT_z4gC
[1464] https://books.google.com/books?id=2ombkgpGt_AC
[1465] https://books.google.com/books?id=5imDC6VN-FcC
[1466] https://books.google.com/books?id=5IpPhTqnDJkC
[1467] https://books.google.com/books?id=fz9JAAAAcAAJ
[1468] https://books.google.com/books?id=UzBRAAAAcAAJ
[1469] http://www.uwyo.edu/lawlib/blume-justinian/
[1470] http://www.christusrex.org/www1/ofm/sbf/escurs/wwc/
[1471] http://amesfoundation.law.harvard.edu/digital/CJCiv/JInst.pdf
[1472] http://droitromain.upmf-grenoble.fr/Anglica/D48_Scott.htm#IX
[1473] //doi.org/10.7767%2Fzrgra.1971.88.1.1
[1474] //www.worldcat.org/issn/0323-4096
[1475] //www.worldcat.org/issn/1874-6292
[1476] //www.jstor.org/stable/30222199
[1477] //www.worldcat.org/oclc/492555150
[1478] http://apps.who.int/classifications/icd10/browse/2016/en#/Xxx.x
[1479] http://www.icd9data.com/getICD9Code.ashx?icd9=xxx
[1480] defined by Christiaan Huygens: , Part 4, Definition 3, translated July 2007 by Ian Bruce
[1481] , p.188-194
[1482] A "small" swing is one in which the angle θ is small enough that sin(θ) can be approximated by θ when θ is measured in radians
[1483] includes a derivation
[1484] , Part 4, Proposition 5
[1485] Huygens (1673) Horologium Oscillatorium http://www.17centurymaths.com/contents/huygenscontents.html, Part 4, Proposition 20
[1486] Morton, W. Scott and Charlton M. Lewis (2005). China: Its History and Culture. New York: McGraw-Hill, Inc., p. 70
[1487] Needham, Volume 3, 627-629
[1488] La Lampada di Galileo https://books.google.com/books?id=wq1aAAAAYAAJ, by Francesco Malaguzzi Valeri, for Archivio storico dell'arte, Volume 6 (1893); Editor, Domenico Gnoli; Publisher Danesi, Rome; Page 215-218.
[1489] Drake 2003 https://books.google.com/books?id=OwOlRPbrZeQC&pg=PA20, p.419–420
[1490] although there are unsubstantiated references to prior pendulum clocks made by others:
[1491] Milham 1945, p.145
[1492] cited in Lenzen & Multauf, 1964 https://books.google.com/books?id=A1IqAAAAMAAJ&pg=RA2-PA307, p.307
[1493] Lenzen & Multauf, 1964 https://books.google.com/books?id=A1IqAAAAMAAJ&pg=RA2-PA307, p.307
[1494] The constellation of Horologium was later named in honor of this book.
[1495] Huygens, Horologium Oscillatorium http://www.17centurymaths.com/contents/huygens/horologiumpart2b.pdf, Part 2, Proposition 25
[1496] gives a detailed description of Huygen's methods
[1497] "...it is affected by either the intemperance of the air or any faults in the mechanism so the crutch QR is not always activated by the same force... With large arcs the swings take longer, in the way I have explained, therefore some inequalities in the motion of the timepiece exist from this cause...", , translation by Ernest L. Edwardes (December 1970) Antiquarian Horology, Vol. 7, No.1
[1498] Andrewes, W.J.H. Clocks and Watches: The leap to precision https://books.google.com/books?id=F7wNQk219KMC&pg=PA126&sig=v3OGcBZ9yAuEx-hfdTfUWnBfiFQ in
[1499] Usher, 1988 https://books.google.com/books?id=xuDDqqa8FlwC&pg=PA312&sig=J5ajZWdvRQER-CD4CFSHP2mXu6s, p.312
[1500] cited in
[1501] Amir Aczel (2003) Leon Foucault: His life, times and achievements, in

[1502] Milham 1945, p.334
[1503] calculated from equation (1)
[1504] Mattheys, 2004, p. 13 https://books.google.com/books?id=_78S_w3EBmAC&pg=PA13&dq=matthys+%22common+bob+size
[1505] Matthys 2004 https://books.google.com/books?id=Lx0v2dhnZo8C&pg=PA91, p.91-92
[1506] Beckett 1874 https://books.google.com/books?id=OvQ3AAAAMAAJ&pg=PA48, p.48
[1507] Beckett 1874 https://books.google.com/books?id=OvQ3AAAAMAAJ&pg=PA43, p.43
[1508] Glasgow 1885 https://books.google.com/books?id=9wUFAAAAQAAJ&pg=PA282, p.282
[1509] Matthys 2004 https://books.google.com/books?id=Lx0v2dhnZo8C&pg=PA3&sig=yYIWqaccL-YA2Mrigw4sFw5k-tk, p.3
[1510] , translation by Ernest L. Edwardes (December 1970) *Antiquarian Horology*, Vol.7, No.1
[1511] Picard, Jean, *La Mesure de la Terre* [The measurement of the Earth] (Paris, France: Imprimerie Royale, 1671), p. 4. http://gallica.bnf.fr/ark:/12148/btv1b7300361b/f14.item.zoom Picard described a pendulum consisting of a copper ball which was an inch in diameter and was suspended by a strand of *pite*, a fiber from the aloe plant. Picard then mentions that temperature slightly effects the length of this pendulum: *"Il est vray que cette longueur ne s'est pas toûjours trouvées si précise, & qu'il a semblé qu'elle devoit estre toûjours un peu accourcie en Hyver, & allongée en esté; mais c'est seulement de la dixieme partie d'une ligne ... "* (It is true that this length [of the pendulum] is not always found [to be] so precise, and that it seemed that it should be always a bit shortened in winter, and lengthened in summer; but it is only by a tenth part of a line [1 *ligne* (line) = 2.2558 mm] ...)
[1512] Matthys 2004 https://books.google.com/books?id=Lx0v2dhnZo8C&pg=PA7&sig=yYIWqaccL-YA2Mrigw4sFw5k-tk, p.7-12
[1513] Milham 1945, p.335
[1514] Milham 1945, p.331-332
[1515] Matthys 2004 https://books.google.com/books?id=Lx0v2dhnZo8C&pg=PA153&sig=yYIWqaccL-YA2Mrigw4sFw5k-tk, Part 3, p.153-179
[1516] Poynting & Thompson, 1907, p.13-14 https://books.google.com/books?id=TL4KAAAAIAAJ&pg=PA13#
[1517] p.39
[1518] has an excellent comprehensive discussion of the controversy over the applicability of Q to the accuracy of pendulums.
[1519] Matthys, 2004, p.32, fig. 7.2 and text https://books.google.com/books?id=Lx0v2dhnZo8C&pg=PA32&sig=yYIWqaccL-YA2Mrigw4sFw5k-tk
[1520] Matthys, 2004, p.81 https://books.google.com/books?id=Lx0v2dhnZo8C&pg=PA81&sig=yYIWqaccL-YA2Mrigw4sFw5k-tk
[1521] Milham 1945, p.615
[1522] Beckett 1874 https://books.google.com/books?id=OvQ3AAAAMAAJ&pg=PA75, p.75-79
[1523] The value of "g" (acceleration due to gravity) at the equator is 9.780 m/s^2 and at the poles is 9.832 m/s^2, a difference of 0.53%.
[1524] Poynting & Thompson 1907, p.9 https://books.google.com/books?id=TL4KAAAAIAAJ&pg=PA9
[1525] Poynting & Thompson, 1907, p.10 https://books.google.com/books?id=TL4KAAAAIAAJ&pg=PA10
[1526] Poynting & Thomson 1904, p.23 https://books.google.com/books?id=TL4KAAAAIAAJ&pg=PA23
[1527] Lenzen & Multauf 1964, p.320 https://books.google.com/books?id=A1IqAAAAMAAJ&pg=RA2-PA320
[1528] Poynting & Thompson 1907, p.18 https://books.google.com/books?id=TL4KAAAAIAAJ&pg=PA18
[1529] Lenzen & Multauf 1964, p.324 https://books.google.com/books?id=A1IqAAAAMAAJ&pg=RA2-PA324
[1530] Lenzen & Multauf 1964, p.329 https://books.google.com/books?id=A1IqAAAAMAAJ&pg=RA2-PA329
[1531] Lenzen & Multauf 1964, p.336, fig.28 https://books.google.com/books?id=A1IqAAAAMAAJ&pg=RA2-PA336

[1532] cited in
[1533] quoted in
[1534] Zupko, 1990, p.131 https://books.google.com/books?id=twUNAAAAIAAJ&pg=PA131&source=gbs_selected_pages&cad=0_1
[1535] Zupko, 1990, p.140-141 https://books.google.com/books?id=twUNAAAAIAAJ&pg=PA131&source=gbs_selected_pages&cad=0_1
[1536] Zupko, 1990, p.93 https://books.google.com/books?id=twUNAAAAIAAJ&pg=PA131&source=gbs_selected_pages&cad=0_1
[1537] A.L. Fradkov and B. Andrievsky, "Synchronization and phase relations in the motion of two-pendulum system", International Journal of Non-linear Mechanics, vol. 42 (2007), pp. 895–901.
[1538] I.I. Blekhman, "Synchronization in science and technology", ASME Press, New York, 1988, (Translated from Russian into English)
[1539] An interesting simulation of thurible motion can be found at this site http://www.sciences.univ-nantes.fr/physique/perso/gtulloue/Meca/Oscillateurs/botafumeiro.html#manip.
[1540] http://adsabs.harvard.edu/abs/2004Sc&Ed..13..261M
[1541] //doi.org/10.1023%2Fb%3Asced.0000041867.60452.18
[1542] http://adsabs.harvard.edu/abs/1986AmJPh..54..112N
[1543] //doi.org/10.1119%2F1.14703
[1544] *Schild* (1997) p. 44 ff.
[1545] *Scott* (1995), p.142
[1546] *Busnot* (1717), pp.167-70 https://books.google.com/books?id=yiNSAAAAcAAJ&pg=PA167
[1547] *Geyer* (1738) p.631 https://books.google.com/books?id=o2VCAAAAcAAJ&pg=PA631
[1548] *Osborne* (1744), p.179 https://books.google.com/books?id=afRSAAAAcAAJ&pg=PA179
[1549] *Osborne* (1747), p.266 https://books.google.com/books?jtp=266&id=Y9gGAAAAcAAJ
[1550] *Dignas; Winter* (2007) p.42
[1551] *Osborne* (1742), p.535 https://books.google.com/books?jtp=535&id=tfJSAAAAcAAJ
[1552] *Head; Heath* (1982), p. 51, *Webber; McBride* (2001): "Perhaps the prospect of getting to the spoils explains Thucydides VII, 29: 'For the Thracian race, like all the most bloodthirsty barbarians, are always particularly bloodthirsty when everything is going their own way", p.1
[1553] *Diodorus Seculus* (1840), p.2450 https://books.google.com/books?id=LFg-AAAAcAAJ&pg=PA2450
[1554] For Gellius' statement, see, *Rosenmüller* (1820), p.95 https://books.google.com/books?id=dk8_AAAAcAAJ&pg=PA95
[1555] *Coleman-Norton* (1948)) The Twelve Tables https://archive.org/stream/thetwelvetables14783gut/14783.txt
[1556] Suet. Calig. 27: multos [...] medios serra dissecuit - , Vita Caligulae http://penelope.uchicago.edu/Thayer/L/Roman/Texts/Suetonius/12Caesars/Caligula*.html "Many..had them sawn asunder" Life of Caligula http://penelope.uchicago.edu/Thayer/E/Roman/Texts/Suetonius/12Caesars/Caligula*.html
[1557] *Gibbon* (1776), Appendix, p.lxxvi https://books.google.com/books?id=aLcWAAAAQAAJ&pg=PR76
[1558] *Sozomen* (1846), p.262 https://books.google.com/books?id=lDmxf3_Ju1sC&pg=PA262
[1559] *Warnekros* (1832), p.368 https://books.google.com/books?id=P4hAAAAAcAAJ&PA=711
[1560] *Du Pin* (1699), p.115 https://books.google.com/books?id=VzZWAAAAYAAJ&pg=PA115
[1561] *Schmauss* (1719), p.69 https://books.google.com/books?id=e6VMAAAAcAAJ&pg=PA69
[1562] *Foxe* (1840), p.5 https://books.google.com/books?jtp=5&id=IeLq-CNyOcIC
[1563] Symphorosa http://www.newadvent.org/cathen/14379a.htm at the Catholic Encyclopedia
[1564] *Deinl* (1850), p.42 https://books.google.com/books?id=MhJNAAAAcAAJ&pg=PA42
[1565] St. Tarbula http://www.catholic.org/saints/saint.php?saint_id=1909
[1566] *Chateaubriand* (1812), p.143 https://books.google.com/books?id=3uFBAAAAIAAJ&pg=PA143
[1567] *Yates* (1843), p.123 https://books.google.com/books?id=7WRCAAAAcAAJ&pg=PA123 More on this governor and his assassination in 1840 in *Gliddon* (1841), p.70-72, footnote https://books.google.com/books?id=YWQGAAAAQAAJ&pg=PA70
[1568] fr:Dominique Busnot
[1569] *Rhodes* (1706), p.46 https://books.google.com/books?id=bwALAQAAMAAJ&pg=PA46

[1570] *Busnot* (1716), p.66-67 https://books.google.com/books?id=yiNSAAAAcAAJ&pg=PA167
[1571] *Windus* (1725), p.156-57 https://books.google.com/books?id=rmRCAAAAcAAJ&pg=PA156
[1572] On French publication date and biographical details of Bossu, see: Jean Bernard Bossu (1720–1792) http://www.encyclopediaofarkansas.net/encyclopedia/entry-detail.aspx? entryID=5922 at the website: " Encyclopedia of Arkansas History&Culture http://www.encyclopediaofarkansas.net/". On relevant excerpt, see *Forster* (1771), p.324-325 https://books.google.com/books?id=QiYVAAAAYAAJ&pg=PA324
[1573] *Lewis, Arnold* (1998), footnote 11, p.200 https://books.google.com/books?id=h2tGe9U39UIC&pg=PA200
[1574] *Forster* (1771), p.324 https://books.google.com/books?id=QiYVAAAAYAAJ&pg=PA324
[1575] " Whatever the rights and wrongs of a particular case might be, the Swiss were not to be treated as an independent unit and their officers must be subordinate to the French commandant", at The Administration Of Justice At The Fortress Of Louisbourg (1713-1758) http://fortress.cbu.ca/justice/Karrer.htm, excerpted from Greer (1976), "The Soldiers of Isle Royale, 1720-1745"
[1576] *Knonau* http://de.wikisource.org/wiki/ADB:Meyer_von_Knonau,_Gerold_%28Archivar%29 (1846) p.335 https://books.google.com/books?jtp=335&id=4xRMAAAAYAAJ
[1577] *Censer and Hunt* (2001), p.124
[1578] *Edwards* (1819), p.79 https://books.google.com/books?id=TcI-AAAAYAAJ&pg=PA79
[1579] *Collins* (1812), p.220 https://books.google.com/books?id=YhIwAAAAYAAJ&pg=PA220
[1580] *Benjamin of Tudela* (1858), p.10 https://books.google.com/books?id=LR09AAAAcAAJ&pg=PA10
[1581] *Salisbury* (1830), p.225 https://books.google.com/books?id=24BUAAAAYAAJ&pg=PA225
[1582] *Pouqueville* (1813), p.82 https://books.google.com/books?id=Ar9BAAAAYAAJ&pg=PA82
[1583] *Grumeza* (2010), p.8 https://books.google.com/books?id=DTxu6RxdecUC&pg=PA8
[1584] *Fallmerayer* (1836), p.420 https://books.google.com/books?id=Z2xKAAAAYAAJ&pg=PA420
[1585] *Mignot* (1787), p.162 https://books.google.com/books?id=2eApAAAAYAAJ&pg=PA162
[1586] *Setton* (1978), p.238 https://books.google.com/books?id=0Sz2VYI0l1IC&pg=PA238
[1587] *Watkins* (1806), p.366 https://books.google.com/books?id=Sxs2AAAAMAAJ&pg=PT366
[1588] a)For dating and place of capture, *Lempriere* (1825), p.99 https://books.google.com/books?id=nHRkAAAAMAAJ&pg=PA99" b) For interview between Anthony and sultan, see: *von Kreckwitz* (1654), p.240 https://books.google.com/books?id=Py9RAAAAcAAJ&pg=PA240"
[1589] 11.000, by "traditional" count, see for example *Smedley* (1832), p.110 https://books.google.com/books?id=QHI2AAAAMAAJ&pg=PA110
[1590] *Reider* (1841), p.125 https://books.google.com/books?id=ax88bYJY4CcC&pg=PA125
[1591] *Hughes* (1820), p.22 https://books.google.com/books?id=cpvOAAAAMAAJ&pg=PA22
[1592] CONSTANTINE RHIGAS http://www.theodora.com/encyclopedia/r/constantine_rhigas.html
[1593] See, for example: *Wigand* (1844) p.307 https://books.google.com/books?id=uQVIAAAAcAAJ&pg=PA307
[1594] *Aurach* (1859), p.82 https://books.google.com/books?id=tKdBAAAAcAAJ&pg=PA82
[1595] *Singha* (2000), p.142 https://books.google.com/books?id=gqIbJz7vMn0C&pg=PA142
[1596] *Murray* (1829), p.44 https://books.google.com/books?id=DAussrqql4AC&pg=PA44
[1597] For eyewitness report disembowelment *Judson* (1823), p.84-86 https://books.google.com/books?id=J00RAQAAMAAJ&pg=PA84
[1598] *Knowles* (1830) " p.167-68 https://books.google.com/books?id=Dz4XAAAAYAAJ&pg=PA167
[1599] St. Domingo Nicolas Dat Dinh http://www.catholic.org/saints/saint.php?saint_id=5837
[1600] *Sadler* (1858), p.356 https://books.google.com/books?id=yvC4swXcfw0C&pg=PA356 *Pachtler* (1861), p.353 https://books.google.com/books?id=tyM3AAAAMAAJ&pg=PA353
[1601] *Inderbitzi* (1840), p.548 https://books.google.com/books?id=tJ0AAAAAcAAJ&pg=PA548" *Hahn* (1860), p.120-21 https://books.google.com/books?id=fKkAAAAAcAAJ&pg=PA120
[1602] *Inst. Prop. Faith* (1840), p.559-60 https://books.google.com/books?id=z5AAAAAAcAAJ&pg=PA559
[1603] *Asiat. Journ.* (1840), p.120 https://books.google.com/books?id=vysYAAAAYAAJ&pg=RA1-PA120
[1604] *Abbott* (2004)

[1605] *Bridgman* (1841), p.141 https://books.google.com/books?id=eJYZAAAAYAAJ&pg=PA148
[1606] *Günther* (1856), p.20 https://books.google.com/books?id=sBRKAAAAcAAJ&pg=PA20
[1607] *de Ferreras* (1760), p.89 https://books.google.com/books?id=CCRDAAAAcAAJ&pg=PA89
[1608] *Napier* (1862), p.88 https://books.google.com/books?id=7m8PAAAAYAAJ&pg=PA88
[1609] *Napier* (1839), p.73 https://books.google.com/books?id=pxBAAAAAcAAJ&pg=PA73
[1610] *Foy* (1827), p.192 https://books.google.com/books?id=Ufbi8fQ8mm4C&pg=PA192
[1611] *Heyne* (1840) p.386 https://books.google.com/books?id=otNBAAAAcAAJ&pg=PA386
[1612] *Anon* (1850), p.50 https://books.google.com/books?id=MTYsAAAAYAAJ&pg=RA1-PA50
[1613] *Majer* (1804), p.346 https://books.google.com/books?id=R-JAAAAAcAAJ&pg=346
[1614] *Lay* (1841), p.195 https://books.google.com/books?id=5T8PAQAAMAAJ&pg=PA195
[1615] *Grimm* (1835) p.453 https://books.google.com/books?id=OhIWAAAAYAAJ&pg=PA453
[1616] https://books.google.com/books?id=MTYsAAAAYAAJ
[1617] https://books.google.com/books?id=vysYAAAAYAAJ
[1618] https://books.google.com/books?id=tKdBAAAAcAAJ
[1619] https://books.google.com/books?id=LR09AAAAcAAJ
[1620] https://books.google.com/books?id=eJYZAAAAYAAJ
[1621] https://books.google.com/books?id=yiNSAAAAcAAJ
[1622] https://books.google.com/books?id=3uFBAAAAIAAJ
[1623] https://archive.org/stream/thetwelvetables14783gut/14783.txt
[1624] //www.amazon.com/dp/B0007HKWAO
[1625] https://books.google.com/books?id=YhIwAAAAYAAJ
[1626] https://books.google.com/books?id=MhJNAAAAcAAJ
[1627] https://books.google.com/books?id=LFg-AAAAcAAJ
[1628] https://books.google.com/books?id=VzZWAAAAYAAJ
[1629] https://books.google.com/books?id=TcI-AAAAYAAJ
[1630] https://books.google.com/books?id=Z2xKAAAAYAAJ
[1631] https://books.google.com/books?id=CCRDAAAAcAAJ
[1632] https://books.google.com/books?id=QiYVAAAAYAAJ
[1633] https://books.google.com/books?id=IeLq-CNyOcIC
[1634] https://books.google.com/books?id=Ufbi8fQ8mm4C
[1635] https://books.google.com/books?id=o2VCAAAAcAAJ
[1636] https://books.google.com/books?id=aLcWAAAAQAAJ
[1637] https://books.google.com/books?id=YWQGAAAAQAAJ
[1638] https://books.google.com/books?id=OhIWAAAAYAAJ
[1639] https://books.google.com/books?id=DTxu6RxdecUC
[1640] https://books.google.com/books?id=sBRKAAAAcAAJ
[1641] https://books.google.com/books?id=fKkAAAAAcAAJ
[1642] https://books.google.com/books?id=otNBAAAAcAAJ
[1643] https://books.google.com/books?id=cpvOAAAAMAAJ
[1644] https://books.google.com/books?id=tJ0AAAAAcAAJ
[1645] https://books.google.com/books?id=z5AAAAAAcAAJ
[1646] https://books.google.com/books?id=J00RAQAAMAAJ
[1647] https://books.google.com/?id=4xRMAAAAYAAJ
[1648] https://books.google.com/books?id=Dz4XAAAAYAAJ
[1649] https://books.google.com/books?id=Py9RAAAAcAAJ
[1650] https://books.google.com/books?id=5T8PAQAAMAAJ
[1651] https://books.google.com/books?id=nHRkAAAAMAAJ
[1652] https://books.google.com/books?id=h2tGe9U39UIC
[1653] https://books.google.com/books?id=R-JAAAAAcAAJ
[1654] https://books.google.com/books?id=2eApAAAAYAAJ
[1655] https://books.google.com/books?id=DAussrqql4AC
[1656] https://books.google.com/books?id=7m8PAAAAYAAJ
[1657] https://books.google.com/books?id=pxBAAAAAcAAJ
[1658] https://books.google.com/books?id=tfJSAAAAcAAJ
[1659] https://books.google.com/books?id=afRSAAAAcAAJ
[1660] https://books.google.com/books?id=Y9gGAAAAcAAJ

[1661] https://books.google.com/books?id=tyM3AAAAMAAJ
[1662] https://books.google.com/books?id=Ar9BAAAAYAAJ
[1663] https://books.google.com/books?id=ax88bYJY4CcC
[1664] https://books.google.com/books?id=bwALAQAAMAAJ
[1665] https://books.google.com/books?id=dk8_AAAAcAAJ
[1666] https://books.google.com/books?id=yvC4swXcfw0C
[1667] https://books.google.com/books?id=24BUAAAAYAAJ
[1668] https://books.google.com/books?id=e6VMAAAAcAAJ
[1669] https://books.google.com/books?id=0Sz2VYI0l1IC
[1670] https://books.google.com/books?id=gqIbJz7vMn0C
[1671] https://books.google.com/books?id=QHI2AAAAMAAJ
[1672] https://books.google.com/books?id=lDmxf3_Ju1sC
[1673] https://books.google.com/books?id=P4hAAAAAcAAJ
[1674] https://books.google.com/books?id=Sxs2AAAAMAAJ
[1675] https://books.google.com/books?id=uQVIAAAAcAAJ
[1676] https://books.google.com/books?id=rmRCAAAAcAAJ
[1677] https://books.google.com/books?id=7WRCAAAAcAAJ
[1678] http://penelope.uchicago.edu/Thayer/E/Roman/Texts/Suetonius/12Caesars/home.html
[1679] http://www.catholic.org/saints/saint.php?saint_id=1909
[1680] http://www.theodora.com/encyclopedia/r/constantine_rhigas.html
[1681] http://www.catholic.org/saints/saint.php?saint_id=5837
[1682] The sources only refer to the victim as male, i.e. an enemy soldier.
[1683] Burn A.R. Persia and the Greeks. Duckworth. London. 1984. As quoted by Peter Frederick Barker, FROM THE SCAMANDER TO SYRACUSE. STUDIES IN ANCIENT LOGISTICS, page 9, chapter 1. http://uir.unisa.ac.za/bitstream/handle/10500/1740/00dissertation.pdf?sequence=2
[1684] Lucian, *A True Story*, 2.31
[1685] "Ctesias and the Importance of his Writings Revisited", ELECTRUM * Vol. 19 (2012): 9–40 doi:10.4467/20843909EL.12.001.0742 http://www.ejournals.eu/pliki/art/73/l
[1686] https://archive.org/details/torturesettourments00galluoft
[1687] http://words.fromoldbooks.org/Brewer-DictionaryOfPhraseAndFable/s/scaphism.html
[1688] https://web.archive.org/web/20050903181149/http://www.4literature.net/Plutarch/Artaxerxes/4.html
[1689] http://www.uni-mannheim.de/mateo/camenaref/hofmann/hof4/s0213b.html
[1690] http://www.fromoldbooks.org/Gallonio-TorturesAndTorments/text-chapter1/section12.html
[1691] Hongwu Emperor. 大誥 [*Letters Patent*]
[1692] 文秉 [Wen Bing]. 先撥志始 [Volume One of the History]
[1693] 王世貞 [Shizhen (1526–90)]. 弇山堂別集 [*Yanshan Hall Collection*], vol. 97
[1694] 劉若愚 [Liu Ruoyu (1584–?)]. 酌中志 [*Discretion in Chi*], vol. 2
[1695] Elkins, James, *The Object Stares Back: On the Nature of Seeing*, New York: Simon and Schuster, 1996
[1696] Guan, Hanqing. *The Injustice to Dou E.*
[1697] Deng, Zhicheng (鄧之誠). *Gu Dong Xu Ji* (骨董續記), vol. 2.
[1698] *Yu Qiao Hua Zheng Ben Mo* (漁樵話鄭本末)
[1699] Shen, Defu (沈德符). *Wan Li Ye Huo Bian* (萬曆野獲編), vol. 28.
[1700] Zhang, Wenlin (張文麟). *Duan Yan Gong Nian Pu* (端巖公年譜).
[1701] Death of the Taiwanese eunuch Lin Biao (台灣籍太監林表之死) http//dspace.xmu.edu.cn
[1702] Yanbei Laoren (燕北老人). *Qingdai Shisan Chao Gongwei Mishi* (清代十三朝宮闈秘史).
[1703] Xu, Ke (徐珂). *Qing Bai Lei Chao* (清稗類鈔).
[1704] Lingchi - The Most Dreaded Form of Execution (Enter with Caution) (「凌遲」最駭人的死刑 5 (慎入)) http://lin61930726.pixnet.net/blog/post/30987636 . Pixnet (22 April 2010). Retrieved 20 May 2012.
[1705] Ji, Liuqi (計六奇). *Ming Ji Bei Lue* (明季北略), vol. 5.
[1706] Ji, Liuqi (計六奇). *Ming Ji Bei Lue* (明季北略), vol. 15.
[1707] Roberts, p. 60, footnote 8.

[1708] 清华大学教授刘书林 ——中国第一汉奸曾国藩 http://www.peacehall.com/cgi-bin/news/gb_display/print_version.cgi?art=/gb/pubvp/2006/03&link=200603030452.shtml
[1709] Shen, Jiaben. *Ji Yi Wen Cun - Zou Yi - Shan Chu Lü Li Nei Zhong Fa Zhe* (寄簃文存 ·奏議 · 刪除律例內重法折).
[1710] Turandot: Chinese Torture/Supplice chinois http://turandot.chineselegalculture.org/Textual.php?ID=3&CF=2&Fa=5. CNRS. Retrieved 20 May 2012.
[1711] Turandot: Chinese Torture/Supplice chinois http://turandot.chineselegalculture.org/Event.php?ID=1. CNRS. Retrieved 20 May 2012.
[1712] 史学研究向下延伸的道路能走多久 mm读《狼烟北平》有感 http://data.tv.sohu.com/movie/data/24054/. Sohu. Retrieved 20 May 2012.
[1713] //doi.org/10.1017%2FS0026749X03004050
[1714] Rollin, C.:" The ancient history of the Egyptians, Carthaginians, Assyrians ..., Volume 3 https://books.google.com/books?id=WQ8PAAAAYAAJ&pg=PA398, London 1735, p.396-98"
[1715] For Maccabee description, see: George D'Oyly and Richard Mant: " The Holy Bible: With Notes, Explanatory and Practical... Together ..., Volum 2 https//books.google.com" Oxford 1818, page xcvii and xvii
[1716] Kitto, J. " Palestine: the Bible History of the holy land https://books.google.com/books?id=wd0- AAAAcAAJ&pg=PR98-IA43" London 1841, p.657
[1717] Ida Lichter, Muslim Women Reformers: Inspiring Voices Against Oppression, , p. 189
[1718] http://bible.oremus.org/?passage=Exodus+19:13–19:13&version=nrsv
[1719] http://bible.oremus.org/?passage=Exodus+21:28–21:28&version=nrsv
[1720] http://bible.oremus.org/?passage=Numbers+15:32–15:32&version=nrsv
[1721] http://bible.oremus.org/?passage=Leviticus+20:2–20:2&version=nrsv
[1722] http://bible.oremus.org/?passage=Leviticus+20:27–20:27&version=nrsv
[1723] http://bible.oremus.org/?passage=Deuteronomy+13:7–13:7&version=nrsv
[1724] http://bible.oremus.org/?passage=Leviticus+24:10–24:10&version=nrsv
[1725] http://bible.oremus.org/?passage=Deuteronomy+21:18–21:18&version=nrsv
[1726] http://bible.oremus.org/?passage=Deuteronomy+22:13–22:13&version=nrsv
[1727] http://bible.oremus.org/?passage=Deuteronomy+22:23–22:23&version=nrsv
[1728] http://bible.oremus.org/?passage=Deuteronomy+22:25–22:25&version=nrsv
[1729] Deuteronomy 13:6–10 http://www.apostolic-churches.net/bible/search/list/?search_book=Deuteronomy&search_chapter_verse=13&varchapter_verse=13:6
[1730] Sanhedrin Chapter 7, p. 53a https://www.jewishvirtuallibrary.org/jsource/Talmud/sanhedrin7.html, in Hebrew: http://www.mechon-mamre.org/b/l/l4407.htm
[1731] Jerusalem Talmud (Sanhedrin 41 a)
[1732] makkot 1:10 March 11, 2008
[1733] Moses Maimonides, Sefer Hamitzvot, Negative Commandment no. 290.
[1734] Moses Maimonides, *The Commandments, Neg. Comm. 290*, at 269–71 (Charles B. Chavel trans., 1967).
[1735]
[1736] ,, Hadith Muslim 17:4192. Also, see the following: Bukhari 6:60:79, Bukhari 83:37, Muslim 17:4196, Muslim 17:4206, Muslim 17:4209, Ibn Ishaq 970.
[1737] Rafed.net http://www.rafed.net/books/hadith/wasael-20/v16.html
[1738] Islamonline.net http://www.islamonline.net/servlet/Satellite?pagename=IslamOnline-Arabic-Ask_Scholar/FatwaA/FatwaA&cid=1122528602718
[1739]
[1740]
[1741] KB Khan (2014), Versions and Subversions of Islamic Cultures in the Film The Stoning of Soraya, Journal of Literary Studies, 30(3), pp. 149-167
[1742] Z Maghen (2005), Virtues Of The Flesh: Passion and Purity In Early Islamic Jurisprudence, Studies in Islamic Law and Society, Brill Academic, , pp 155
[1743] http://cmje.usc.edu/religious-texts/hadith/bukhari/050-sbt.php#003.050.885
[1744] http://cmje.usc.edu/religious-texts/hadith/bukhari/049-sbt.php#003.049.860
[1745] http://cmje.usc.edu/religious-texts/hadith/bukhari/082-sbt.php#008.082.842
[1746] http://cmje.usc.edu/religious-texts/hadith/bukhari/089-sbt.php#009.089.303
[1747] http://cmje.usc.edu/religious-texts/hadith/bukhari/082-sbt.php#008.082.824

[1748] http://cmje.usc.edu/religious-texts/hadith/bukhari/082-sbt.php#008.082.809
[1749] http://cmje.usc.edu/religious-texts/hadith/bukhari/092-sbt.php#009.092.432
[1750] http://cmje.usc.edu/religious-texts/hadith/muslim/008-smt.php#008.3435
[1751] http://cmje.usc.edu/religious-texts/hadith/muslim/017-smt.php#017.4216
[1752] http://cmje.usc.edu/religious-texts/hadith/muslim/017-smt.php#017.4191
[1753] http://cmje.usc.edu/religious-texts/hadith/muslim/017-smt.php#017.4212
[1754] Ismail Poonwala (2004), The Pillars of Islam: Laws pertaining to human intercourse, Oxford University Press, Oxford University Press, pp. 448-457
[1755] A. Quraishi (1999), Her honour: an Islamic critique of the rape provisions in Pakistan's ordinance on zina, *Islamic studies*, Vol. 38, No. 3, pp. 403-431
[1756] DeLong-Bas, *Wahhabi Islam*, 2004: 89-90
[1757] Joseph Schacht, *An Introduction to Islamic Law* (Oxford: Clarendon Press, 1973), pp. 178–181
[1758] Quran 24:6-9, Quote - "And for those who launch a charge against their spouses, and have (in support) no evidence but their own— their solitary evidence (can be received) if they bear witness four times (with an oath) by Allah that they are solemnly telling the truth; And the fifth (oath) (should be) that they solemnly invoke the curse of Allah on themselves if they tell a lie. But it would avert the punishment from the wife, if she bears witness four times (with an oath) by Allah, that (her husband) is telling a lie; And the fifth (oath) should be that she solemnly invokes the wrath of Allah on herself if (her accuser) is telling the truth. "
[1759] Al-Muwatta
[1760]
[1761]
[1762] Rudolph Peters, Crime and Punishment in Islamic Law, Cambridge University Press, , pp. 37
[1763]
[1764] Nisrine Abiad (2008), Sharia, Muslim States and International Human Rights Treaty Obligations, British Institute of International and Comparative Law, , pp. 24-26
[1765] The Hindu, "Taliban stones couple to death in northern Afghanistan", August 16, 2010, thehindu.com http://www.thehindu.com/news/international/article574389.ece
[1766] Katie Hamann Aceh's Sharia Law Still Controversial in Indonesia http://www.voanews.com/english/news/Acehs-Sharia-Law-Still-Controversial-in-Indonesia-80257482.html *Voice of America* 29 December 2009, and: In Enforcing Shariah Law, Religious Police in Aceh on Hemline Frontline http://jakartaglobe.beritasatu.com/archive/in-enforcing-shariah-law-religious-police-in-aceh-on-hemline-frontline/ Jakarta Globe, December 28, 2009
[1767] Aceh Stoning Law Hits a New Wall http://jakartaglobe.beritasatu.com/archive/aceh-stoning-law-hits-a-new-wall/ The Jakarta Globe, 12th October 2009
[1768] Aceh Government Removes Stoning Sentence From Draft Bylaw http://jakartaglobe.beritasatu.com/news/aceh-government-removes-stoning-sentence-from-draft-bylaw/, Jakarta Globe 12 March 2013
[1769] Iran executes two men by stoning http://news.bbc.co.uk/2/hi/middle_east/7826018.stm BBC News (January 13, 2009)
[1770] «سنگسار» در شرع حذف شدنی نیست http://rc.majlis.ir/fa/news/show/831790 Persian document; Translation - "Muhammad Ali Asfnany spokesman for the Judicial Committee of the Parliament said Rajm is not being listed in the legislation, but the punishment per the law will be practically the same as the rest of the rules are valid in Islamic law. Asfnany said Western media makes noise against the implementation of Islamic law in Iran, a sentiment that is rooted in Western enmity with us, when their excuse is to change our rules."
[1771] Amnesty International (2008), Iran - End executions by Stoning https://www.amnesty.org/en/documents/MDE13/001/2008/en/
[1772] English Translation of Regulatory Code on Sentences of Qisas, Stoning, Crucifixion, Execution, and Flogging http//www.iranhrdc.org Iran Human Rights Documentation Center (2013)
[1773]
[1774]
[1775] National Laws - Iran http://www.ecoi.net/iran/nationallaw (2014)
[1776] Islamic State militants stone man to death in Iraq: witness https://www.reuters.com/article/2014/08/22/us-iraq-security-stoning-idUSKBN0GM0Q820140822 Reuters (August 22, 2014)
[1777] file:///C:/Users/mohammedf/Downloads/ACT5057402017ENGLISH%20(1).PDF

[1778] Memri TV: "#4558 Woman Stoned to Death by ISIS in Syria" http://www.memritv.org/clip/en/4558.htm October 21, 2014

[1779] Invitation to a Stoning http://reason.com/archives/1998/11/01/invitation-to-a-stoning, Reason.com, Walter Olson, November 1998. Retrieved May 1, 2014.

[1780] Retrieved 1 May 2014.

[1781] http://www.stopstoning.net/IMG/article_PDF/article_20.pdf

[1782] "Sharia court frees Nigerian woman" http://news.bbc.co.uk/2/hi/africa/1891395.stm, 25 March 2002, BBC News

[1783] http://bible.oremus.org/?passage=Leviticus+24:10–23:10&version=nrsv

[1784] http://bible.oremus.org/?passage=Numbers+15:32–36:32&version=nrsv

[1785] http://bible.oremus.org/?passage=Joshua+7–7&version=nrsv

[1786] http://bible.oremus.org/?passage=1+Kings+12:18–12:18&version=nrsv

[1787] http://bible.oremus.org/?passage=1+Kings+21–21&version=nrsv

[1788] http://bible.oremus.org/?passage=2+Chronicles+24:20–21:20&version=nrsv

[1789] http://bible.oremus.org/?passage=Matthew+23:35–23:35&version=nrsv

[1790] http://bible.oremus.org/?passage=Acts+6:8–14:8&version=nrsv

[1791] http://bible.oremus.org/?passage=Acts+7:58–60:58&version=nrsv

[1792] http://bible.oremus.org/?passage=Acts+14:19–14:19&version=nrsv

[1793] Bruce Chilton, Craig A. Evans *Studying the historical Jesus* 1998 Page 447 "There are three among these that merit some attention: (1) "And it is tradition: On the eve of Passover ... And the herald went forth before him for forty days, 'Yeshu ha-Nosri is to be stoned, because he has practiced magic and enticed and led Israel astray. Any one who knows anything in his favor, let him come and speak concerning him."

[1794] http://bible.oremus.org/?passage=Exodus+17:4–17:4&version=nrsv

[1795] http://bible.oremus.org/?passage=Numbers+14:6–10:6&version=nrsv

[1796] http://bible.oremus.org/?passage=1+Samuel+30:6–30:6&version=nrsv

[1797] http://bible.oremus.org/?passage=John+8:59–8:59&version=nrsv

[1798] http://bible.oremus.org/?passage=John+10:31–10:31&version=nrsv

[1799] http://bible.oremus.org/?passage=Acts+5:26–5:26&version=nrsv

[1800] http://bible.oremus.org/?passage=Acts+14:4–14:4&version=nrsv

[1801] https://web.archive.org/web/20141129025158/http://www.violenceisnotourculture.org/faq_stoning

[1802] http://www.violenceisnotourculture.org/node/10

[1803] http://www.violenceisnotourculture.org/node/13

[1804] https://web.archive.org/web/20080103135235/http://www.usc.edu/dept/MSA/fundamentals/hadithsunnah/muslim/017.smt.html

[1805] http://www.khaleejtimes.com/DisplayArticle.asp?xfile=data/theuae/2006/June/theuae_June301.xml&section=theuae

[1806] https://web.archive.org/web/20080215221459/http://www.progressivemuslims.org/sub/stoning.htm

[1807] http://www.quranicpath.com/misconceptions/adultery_punishment.html

[1808] http://apostatesofislam.com/media/video/stoning-original.wmv

[1809] http://www.iran-e-azad.org/stoning/video.html

[1810] http://news.nationalpost.com/2010/11/20/graphic-anatomy-of-a-stoning/

[1811] https://www.amnesty.org/en/news-and-updates/report/campaigning-end-stoning-iran-20080115

[1812] Ernoehazy, William; Ernoehazy, WS. Hanging Injuries and Strangulation http://www.emedicine.com/emerg/topic227.htm. *www.emedicine.com*. URL last accessed March 3, 2006.

[1813] Strack, Gael; McClane, George. How to Improve Investigation and Prosecution of Strangulation Cases https://archive.is/20130104140337/http://www.polaroid.com/global/printer_friendly.jsp?PRODUCT%3C%3Eprd_id=845524441760370. *www.polaroid.com*. URL last accessed March 3, 2006.

[1814] Jones, Richard. Asphyxia http://www.forensicmed.co.uk/asphyxia.htm , Strangulation http://www.forensicmed.co.uk/strangulation.htm . *www.forensicmed.co.uk*. URL last accessed February 26, 2006.

[1815] Koiwai, Karl. How Safe is Choking in Judo? http://judoinfo.com/chokes5.htm. *judoinfo.com*. URL last accessed March 3, 2006.

[1816] Reay, Donald; Eisele, John. Death from law enforcement neck holds http://www.charlydmiller.com/LIB/1982neckholds.html. *www.charlydmiller.com*.URL last accessed March 3, 2006

[1817] Gunther, Wendy. On Chokes (Medical) http://www.aikiweb.com/techniques/gunther1.html, with quotations from Spitz and Fisher's *Medicolegal Investigation of Death: Guidelines for the Application of Pathology to Crime Investigation*. *www.aikiweb.com*. URL last accessed March 3, 2006.

[1818] Passig, K. Carotid Sinus reflex death - a theory and its history http://www.datenschlag.org/howto/atem/english/csr.html. *www.datenschlag.org*. URL last accessed February 28, 2006.

[1819] Koiwai, Karl. Deaths Allegedly Caused by the Use of "Choke Holds" (Shime-Waza) http://judoinfo.com/chokes6.htm. *judoinfo.com* URL last accessed March 3, 2006.

[1820] *Culloden*. BBC Drama Documentary, 1964.

[1821] Turvey, Brent (1996). A guide to the physical analysis of ligature patterns in homicide investigations http://www.corpus-delicti.com/ligature.html. Knowledge Solutions Library, Electronic Publication. *www.corpus-delicti.com*. URL last accessed March 1, 2006.

[1822] University of Dundee, Forensic Medicine. Asphyxial Deaths http://www.dundee.ac.uk/forensicmedicine/llb/deaths.htm#Stages. *www.dundee.ac.uk*. URL last accessed March 3, 2006.

[1823] Reston, James Jr. *Dogs of God: Columbus, the Inquisition, and the Defeat of the Moors*. Doubleday, 2005.

[1824] http://judounleashed.com

Article Sources and Contributors

The sources listed for each article provide more detailed licensing information including the copyright status, the copyright owner, and the license conditions.

Capital punishment *Source:* https://en.wikipedia.org/w/index.php?oldid=864548296 *License:* Creative Commons Attribution-Share Alike 3.0 *Contributors:* 42800141, Aaronruddock, Adavidb, Adithya harish pergade, Al-Andalus, AlHazen, Alexb102072, ApprenticeFan, Ashbeckjonathan, Aubreybardo, AusLondonder, BananaCarrot152, Bbx118, Begoon, Bel-Shamharoth, CH1109, Captain Cornwall, Cherkash, Coltsfan, Cpt.a.haddock, Cvthnyfzrfpym, DA1, Dale Arnett, Daniel Staudenmann, Davide King, Dl2000, Dmartin969, Dragfyre, Dwo, Eagle4000, Edgar181, Edison, Edrussia567, EllenCT, Eperoton, Equinox, Eric Corbett, Examplar, Facts707, Felicia777, FilBenLeafBoy, Finnusertop, Forthrunner, Fountainoffacts, Francis Neary, FreeKnowledgeCreator, GHcool, GaryGill, Gdeblois19, God's Godzilla, Goldencheesepie, Hairy Dude, Harry1835, Here2help, Hubon, Hyperbolick, Iloveredhair, ImYourTurboLover, Indyguy, Inter&anthro, J 1982, Jackflann, Janeyleeme, Jarble, JayCoop, Jmarchn, Joefromrandb, JoeyRuss, John, John Paul Parks, Joreberg, Josebarbosa, Kaiketsu, KaiserDog21, KaplanAL, Kate Phaye, Kelisi, Kku, Kndimov, Krakkos, LarryPate, LeRoiDesRois, Leftwinguy92, Leugen9001, Level C, Lightlowemon, Lindsay658, Lonnez, Luciano.nyc, Madacs, Madreterra, Mandruss, Manu1400, Markelele, Master of Time, Max.Moore, Mccapra, MediaKill13, Moogsi, Moonraker, Moxy, Mr Serjeant Buzfuz, Nat965, Natg 19, Neun-x, Nick-D, Nightsturm, Nikoo.Amini, Onel5969, Oneultralamewhiteboy, Only in death, Oranjelo100, Otr500, OwenBlacker, Pedro8790, Pgallert, Pincrete, Pofka, Polmandc, QubecMan, Rathfelder, Rfc1394, Rjwilmsi, Robertgombos, Robertinventor, Roger 8 Roger, Roscelese, Rupert loup, Sanathkumaradoor, Seraphim System, Signedzzz, Sion8, Smasongarrison, Smeagol 17, Sohale, Sophivorus, Spacecowboy420, Spintendo, Srich32977, Stevietheman, Surachit, TRAVIS1890, Terrorist96, The Wonkers, Tlhslobus, Tobby72, Tonneduroc, Torygreen84, Turnless, Twin Bird, Vahurzpu, Varavour, Vijay rath, Vmavanti, W33dscoper, WCIDFS, Waldir ... 1

Hanging *Source:* https://en.wikipedia.org/w/index.php?oldid=864202674 *License:* Creative Commons Attribution-Share Alike 3.0 *Contributors:* Albatross8000, Allforrous, Anaxial, Anonimski, Arildnordby, Arunsingh16, Austrianbird, Avochelm, BD2412, Balon Greyjoy, Bender235, Benqish, Bossrat, Brandmeister, Bri, Captain Cornwall, Carewolf, Carrite, CharlesHBennett, Chris Howard, Chrismorey, ClueBot NG, Cooltrainer Hugh, Cyberbot II, DARRIN01, DVdm, DagosNavy, Danechip, Dawn Bard, Dawnseeker2000, Dcirovic, DeNoel, Deisenbe, Denisarona, Denniscabrams, Derek R Bullamore, Dewritech, Diannaa, DivermanAU, Doc James, Donner60, Drewmutt, DuncanHill, Eagleash, Ego White Tray, ExpatSalopian, Favonian, Flyer22 Reborn, Frederick crowe, Frietjes, G S Palmer, GSS, Gadfium, Gareth2003, Geo Swan, George.N.Harris, Gimere, Gkml, Goat1101, Gourami Watcher, Ground Zero, Grubbybest, GünniX, Hairy Dude, Hansmuller, Harry1835, Hillbillyholiday, Home Lander, Honzula, I dream of horses, IsUnsigned, JSquish, Jackfork, Janko, Jax 0677, Jayjg, Jessicapierce, Jim1138, Joefromrandb, John, Joseph Moraña, Julesd, KConWiki, Kablammo, Ketiltrout, Kuru, Logan157, Lotje, Luv2Write MC, Materialscientist, Mattythewhite, Mevagiss, Mike Mounier, Mitchumch, Mogism, Mohammad Abulhassan, Moozipan Cheese, Mx. Granger, NebY, NeilN, NewTestLeper79, Num1dgen, Ohconfucius, Omnipaedista, OnBeyondZebrax, OttRider, Pdeck2013, Pinethicket, Pipetricker, Prestonmag, Red Jay, Redzimus, RicHard-59, Richard27182, Roger.lee, Rorymcl24, Royroydeb, Sadads, Saqib, Schwerdf, Serial Number 54129, Serols, Shannon Alther, Shellwood, Shenme, Sir Liu(the first), Smyth, Snori, Someone Not Awful, Spartay, Stevietheman, The Old Pueblo, TheGreatConsultingDetective, ThomasHarrisGrantsPass, ToBeFree, Tobby72, Tomolobla, Topboy enterprice, Toshinoukyouko, Tothmetres, Trovatore, UglowT, Vermont, Virshul, VladGerp, Waldhorn, Wannabemodel, Wbm1058, Wiae, Widr, Wikizard1991, Wtmitchell, XXzoonamiXX, Xander Lindnor, 195 anonymous edits ... 37

Execution by shooting *Source:* https://en.wikipedia.org/w/index.php?oldid=862673418 *License:* Creative Commons Attribution-Share Alike 3.0 *Contributors:* Aabicus, Alistair1978, AllenZh, Altenmann, Andy80586, Anthony Appleyard, Antwon Bob, Aridd, Banedon, BeeTea, Blaylockjam10, Brian Geppert, Canterbury Tail, Celia Homeford, CharlotteWebb, ClueBot NG, CompliantDrone, DXRAW, DarkUniverse121, Darylgolden, Doc James, DonChris, Donner60, Drea0284, Dynaflow, El C, Faceless Enemy, Fish storm, Fogelstrom, Gidev, Gladamas, GlasGhost, Gracenotes, GregorStocks, Hairy Dude, HastyDeparture, Hayden120, I need to read V for Vendetta, IvoShandor, Ixfd64, JRayD123, Janneman666, Japanese Searobin, Jmlk17, Joefromrandb, John Crowfoot, Jpgoelz, JzG, Kaba, Khathi, KimChee, Kintetsubuffalo, Kuru, Lapin rossignol, Leeyc0, Luriflax, MBob, Metalhead94, NEMT, NebY, Nick19thind, Nneonneo, NonNobisSolum, Olegwiki, OnBeyondZebrax, Pajfarmor, Paris1127, PaulVIF, Paulrach, Peeweebee, RatWeazle, Rebbing, Rex480, Rigley, Rossami, Selket, Sericea, Shmurak, Skellious, Susan Davis, Tabletop, Takamaxa, TenthEagle, TheStrayCat, Tripleahg, Trumpet marietta 45750, Unigolyn, Unused000705, Viciarg, Werieth, Ykhwong, Z10x, Zeus, 81 anonymous edits ... 67

Lethal injection *Source:* https://en.wikipedia.org/w/index.php?oldid=863383313 *License:* Creative Commons Attribution-Share Alike 3.0 *Contributors:* 1779Days, Aidanriggansss, Albany NY, Alvin Seville, Amire80, BD2412, Banditgeneral4, Bangalamania, Bender235, Bgwhite, Bridies, Brit321, Bumm13, Captain Cornwall, Catsmeat, Cavedivr, Chensixiao, ChiIsKool, ClueBot NG, Ctxppc, Cyberbot II, DBZFan30, Damien Linnane, DavidIvar, Dawnseeker2000, Diannaa, Doc James, Donner60, DrStrauss, Drmies, ElSaxo, Epicgenius, EronMain, Evasivo, Excirial, Fabiwanne, Factsearch, Farrellla11, Flyer22 Reborn, Funcrunch, Gdeblois19, Gidev, Gilliam, Giraffedata, Gloop899, Gplayaccon, Gringo300, GünniX, Harry1835, Heiwa Yagi, Huggums537, Huntster, Iqseo, JaconaFrere, Janko, Jarble, Jasper Deng, Jerzy, Jidanni, Jlivewell, John, John of Reading, Jravid, Karrie Cole, Kay2916, Lethalinjection4, Level C, Makyen, Mamathomas, MarnetteD, Martinlw, MattDuckPhpMaster, Maximumpyro, Me, Myself, and I are Here, Mean as custard, Medic-ben, Mehow98, Metallichris17, Mike Mounier, Modanung, Mress2, Name goes here, Narky Blert, Nick Fisher, Nthep, OctaviusPublius, OliviaSimmons13, OnBeyondZebrax, Onel5969, Paulscrawl, Pgallert, Proxima Centauri, PurpleChez, Qwertyxp2000, Rebbing, RikoTzac, Rjwilmsi, Rodw, Rsrikanth05, Sanket Edits Wiki, Sara Mayorga, SeanGauld, Serols, Sheenanigans707, Shellwood, Sigmund2018, SolomonZacharyLawrence, Stardxm-, Stephencdickson, StevM8, Stevietheman, SuperEmbracer, Symphonyinpeach, Tdslk, Thomas419ca, Tonedeafyodler, Tornado chaser, Trappist the monk, Vandalism destroyer, Voxadam, Wbm1058, WhisperToMe, Whitecliff, Widr, Wzrd1, Xander Lindnor, YSSYguy, 七战功成 , 178 anonymous edits ... 71

Electric chair *Source:* https://en.wikipedia.org/w/index.php?oldid=863253812 *License:* Creative Commons Attribution-Share Alike 3.0 *Contributors:* 5 albert square, Aarp65, AlexanderHaas, Amiaheroyet, Ammodramus, Andrewpmk, Anthony22, Archanian, Avoided, Baderrisch, Balon Greyjoy, Beetstra, Bender235, C.Fred, CaSJer, Caballero1967, Carrite, CatcherStorm, Cfelicione, Chattering pie, CheyenneF0186, Chris the speller, Chrismorey, Clarkcj12, Claycrow, ClueBot NG, Colt0419, Comedyguy2012, Cyberbot II, Dark-World25, Doc James, DocWatson42, Donner60, Dr.K., Drewr2002, DudeWithAFeud, EEng, Esrever, EurovisionNim, Evans1982, Excirial, Factsearch, Finnusertop, Fountains of Bryn Mawr, Furrykef, GLG GLG, Garik, Gdeblois19, George.N.Harris, Gulumeemee, Hallsville3, Harchjuh hy, Harry1835, Hiddenstranger, Howcheng, Huntster, Hydrargyrum, IAmColossus, Idfah, JackofOz, Jamespfeffer, JessicaFaith84, Jim1138, Jmowreader, John, Jonbrownfromeaton, Joshiswak21, K6ka, Kalamed, Katieh5584, Kelisi, Khazar2, KylieTastic, LilHelpa, Lotje, Lugia2453, M Alan Thomas, Mark Arsten, Martarius, Materialscientist, Mdnavman, Mean as custard, Men with no name, Menah the Great, MithrandirAgain, Mtaylor848, Mx. Granger, My Chemistry romantic, NebY, Niharlayek, Nihiltres, Nonstopdrivel, OwenBlacker, PMLawrence, Paris1127, Pbrower2a, Piguy101, Piledhigheranddeeper, Professor2789, PuffMuff, Quisqualis, Qzd, Qzekrom, Redd Foxx 1991, RicHard-59, Rothorpe, Rsrikanth05, Sailee5, Sakura Cartelet, SamWinchester000, Samf4u, Shellwood, Stevietheman, Telfordbuck, The Rambling Man, This lousy T-shirt, Tobby72, Valenciano, Velella, VeryCrocker, Weezow, WelcomeToTheUSA1988, Wildcatsquid, WilliamJE, Wolfita, WoodsieGirl, XXzoonamiXX, Xpnc, 196 anonymous edits ... 92

Gas chamber *Source:* https://en.wikipedia.org/w/index.php?oldid=863253625 *License:* Creative Commons Attribution-Share Alike 3.0 *Contributors:* 5WayRevenge, 7mike5000, AVand, Acroterion, Addshore, Alepik, Alexb102072, Altenmann, Ammodramus, Anonymousman001, Anthony Appleyard, Apokrif, Ashphalt, Ask123, Awesomewiki64, B12nd0n, BD2412, BOTarate, Bacchus87, Baltutej, Bearcat, Bender235, Bermicourt, Beyond My Ken, Binksternet, BlackcurrantTea, Bobo192, Brewcrewer, Britannic124, CPMcE, CableCat, Callinus, Catsmeat, Chaheel Riens, Chetvorno, Citation bot 1, Cliftonian, Cloud200, CommonsDelinker, Consequences2, CowboySpartan, Cyan22, Cyberbot II, Czolgolz, Darth Panda, Defender of torch, Deor, DerHexer, Derwyddcymraeg, Detruncate, Doc James, Dolfrog, Drcampbell, Dreadstar, Dthomsen8, DuLithgow, Dzordzm, EEng, Editor2020, EdwinHJ, Element16, Epa101, Equendil, Erik Wannee, EronMain, Esrever, Etineskid, FarnuBak, Fences and windows, Fish and karate, Flix11, Furry-friend, Gabbe, Gaius Cornelius, George100, Ghostwriter13, Good Olfactory, GregorB, Grubel, GuyHimGuy, Hadding, Helopticor, Historicist, Hklkk2015, Hohum, Howcheng, II MusLiM HyBRiD II, Injust, Iridescent, J.delanoy, J04n, Jaq2013, Jarble, Jayjg, Jeff5102, Jimgerbig, Jnocook, John, John Paul Parks, Jpgordon, Julietdeltalima, Kaiketsu, Kelisi, Kierzek, KimChee, Kiruning, Kuru, LL221W, Laberkiste, Lambdalix, Lbthomsen, Level C, Lightmouse, Lihaas, Lokal Profil, Magioladitis, MarcusBritish, MerillLeroy, Mjsa, MorbidEntree, MrX, Mrceleb2007, Muadd, My very best wishes, Nazgul02, Nbanic, Newyork1501, Nicholas Tan, Noozgroop, Nparlante, OjdvQ9fNJWl, Olgerd, One cookie, Pediainsight, Peridon, Phantom in ca, Pharos, Pingveno, Poeticbent, PostalDude96, Professional Assassin, Quebec99, Raquel Baranow, Raspi Fly, Reich68686, Renata3, Richard Keatinge, Richard27182, Rjwilmsi, Robvhoorn, Rsrikanth05, Rupert loup, Signalhead, Sjones23, Slatersteven, SoledadKabocha, Solitaire2006, Southernchristian06, SparklingPessimist, Stanton13, Stapmoshun, Steven Crossin, Steven J. Anderson, StillTrill, THEN WHO WAS PHONE?, Tcncv, Tehsnyder, The Thing That Should Not Be, Thingg, Thriley, Tiddly Tom, Tiptopper, TitaniumCarbide, Tizzomi the all knowing, Train2104, Trovatore, VanishedUser sdu9aya9fasdsopa, Varnav, Vidor, Vikedal, Vikiçizer, Waldir, WhiteArcticWolf, WilliamH, Wjejskenewr, Woody, XXzoonamiXX, Yamamoto Ichiro, Yunshui, ZappaOMati, 92 anonymous edits ... 104

Decapitation *Source:* https://en.wikipedia.org/w/index.php?oldid=863590967 *License:* Creative Commons Attribution-Share Alike 3.0 *Contributors:* 23 editor, ADP1998, AKS.9955, All4trutheng, Andreaseksted, Anuchikibrikiivdamke, Apokrif, Ashleyaubele, Austin754, BD2412, Banedon, Batternut, Bender235, Bgwhite, Big Wang, BlueResistance, Bongwarrior, BoogaLouie, BrxBrx, CKBrown1000, Camusot, CanadianLinuxUser, Captain Cornwall, Carolus, Catlemur, Cerabot～enwiki, ChamithN, ClueBot NG, Colonies Chris, Correctiator, Cramyourspam, Curly Turkey, DGG, Dadofsam, Darkwind, Dawnseeker2000, Deepspace9odo, Deskana, Dl2000, Doc James, Doremo, DragonflySixtyseven, Dweller, EEng, Ebehn, Emefie, Eperoton, EtienneDolet, Excirial, Fragglet, Frietjes, GoingBatty, GundlachJ, HCPUNXKID, Hl, I dream of horses, Ianmacm, ImHere2015, InedibleHulk, Ira Leviton, Jdad6901, JeannieAllergy, Jej1997, JesseRafe, Jim1138, Jmrowland, JoergenB, K6ka, KConWiki, Kablammo, Kaiketsu, Kalamed, Kdiepholz, Kmccargo, Kurtis, Kuru, Kylesenior, Laberkiste, LilHelpa, Lilyb283, LlywelynII, Lotje, MRD2014, Magioladitis, MehrdadFR, Michaelsbll, Misconceptions2, Missvain,

Monochrome Monitor, Muhammed Kabir, NebY, Neuroforever, NewEnglandYankee, Nick2crosby, Nonstopdrivel, Notreallydavid, Okstfan03, Orphan Wiki, Pajfarmor, Pedrampl77, Piledhigheranddeeper, Raquel Baranow, Red Jay, Regulov, Retardednamingpolicy, Reza luke, Rich Farmbrough, Richwales, Roxy the dog, Rpot2, Ruhoff, Sabar, Scwlong, ShulMaven, SimonTrew, Sjö, Staglit, Strauss MAE-USP, Surtsicna, THEWULFMAN, TJRC, TRUEandHONESTuser, Tbanderson, Thine Antique Pen, Tony.ganchev, Tutelary, VladGerp, Vycl1994, Werldwayd, Wetman, Wilhelm666666, Yardfridge, Zmetzger11, ÄDA - DÄP, 210 anonymous edits 111

Execution by elephant *Source:* https://en.wikipedia.org/w/index.php?oldid=855558276 *License:* Creative Commons Attribution-Share Alike 3.0 *Contributors:* 100110100, 123957a, 99of9, AaRH, Ahoerstemeier, Ajsimas, Alansohn, Albany NY, Andreas Kaganov, Andy85719, Antandrus, Aphhamra, Apostrophe, Arildnordby, Atakdoug, BOTarate, Bender235, Besselfunctions, Bri, Brighterorange, Brookie, CASSIOPEIA, CanOfWorms, Causa sui, Cedrus-Libani, Ceoil, Charles Matthews, ChrisO∼enwiki, ClueBot NG, Cntras, Colonel Warden, Cornersss, Crazy87(smeltingaccedent), Ctesiphon7, Cybercobra, DA1, DVdm, DaGizza, Dasfreedomfighters, Deckiller, Ding78, Doc James, Donlammers, Donreed, Dougofborg, Dr.weez, DrKay, DrSaturn, Drsavage84, E-Kartoffel, Eddy Tor, Edwardnine, El bot de la dieta, Enerelt, Enuja, Feminist, Feureau, Finerpointsoflife, Finnusertop, GB fan, Gegnome, Gemini1980, Gilliam, Gimmetrow, Gnanapiti, Gnangarra, Gobonobo, Graham87, GrittyLobo441, Grrahnbahr, Hadrian89, Hairy Dude, Harthacnut, Hasafienda, Hijiri88, Ifny, Indon, InverseHypercube, IvoShandor, Jack.goat, Jackrm, Jacob Finn, Jarble, Joefromrandb, Johnbod, Jovianeye, KP Botany, Kamolan, Kozuch, KrakatoaKatie, L337p4wn, Lalbe4, Landon1980, Le Anh-Huy, LittleOldMe, Littleghostboo, Lykzomg, MIDI, Marskell, Martinlc, Mgiganteus1, Moez, Mohanazadeh25, Mootros, N8mitchell9655, Netscott, Newyork1501, Niceguyedc, Nikkimaria, Nohat, Nyttend, Pagrashtak, Panser Born, PhoenixRevealed, Pikazilla, Piratedan, Pitke, Pokajanje, Portillo, Prioryman, Ptbotgourou, Purplebackpack89, QDK01, Random Hero 791, Randomblue, Redtigerxyz, Reywas92, Rikker04, Rm w a vu, Rnickel, RobertG, Rosalina2427, RoyBoy, SUM1, Sadads, SamuelTheGhost, Schekinov Alexey Victorovich, SchfiftyThree, Sd31415, Seduisant, Ser Amantio di Nicolao, Shadowlink1014, SheepNotGoats, Shyamsunder, Smalljim, Spawn Man, Staszek Lem, Stesmo, Storkk, Suruena, Swf20, TYelliot, Tamfang, Targaryen, Tavix, Terryeo, The Bangsawan, The Messenger 4321, The ed17, TheReferenceProvider, TheXenocide, Tholme, Tide rolls, Toyokuni3, Valentinian, Vanished user qwqwijr8hwrkjdnvkanfoh4, WODUP, WissensDürster, Woohookitty, Writtenonsand, Yogesh Khandke, Yvwv, Zafiroblue05, Σ, 127 anonymous edits 135

Blowing from a gun *Source:* https://en.wikipedia.org/w/index.php?oldid=861968692 *License:* Creative Commons Attribution-Share Alike 3.0 *Contributors:* A2soup, Andy Smith, Arildnordby, Avskbhatta, Blaylockjam10, Charles Matthews, Citizen Canine, Colonies Chris, DHBirr, David Charles, Davidbrookesland, Dewritech, Dl2000, Doc James, Drewmutt, Dubmill, Epicgenius, ExpatSalopian, Faizhaider, Felviper, Gatoclass, Geoffb91, Graham87, Groyolo, Hairy Dude, I am One of Many, Ibensis, IgnorantArmies, Jarble, Jeff3000, Jimurphy, Joefromrandb, John of Reading, Jonathandore, Jossi2, Kerry Raymond, Konstantin.V.Azarov, Magioladitis, Mogism, Mr Stephen, NebY, Nihiltres, Nnemo, North8000, Nowthis, Nyttend, Ohconfucius, Oreo Priest, Ost316, Peterbruce01, Preethikasanilwiki, Rhododendrites, SchreiberBike, Snori, Speaklanguages, Superdupersmartdude, Tabletop, Telfordbuck, U. E. Aduan, Whoop whoop pull up, Wraithful, 57 anonymous edits 145

Blood eagle *Source:* https://en.wikipedia.org/w/index.php?oldid=845748457 *License:* Creative Commons Attribution-Share Alike 3.0 *Contributors:* 61mei31, AGS, AWhiteC, Agamemnon2, Agricolae, Andy5421, AshLin, Auric, BD2412, Bennybp, Benwildeboer, Berig, Bgwhite, Bill52270, Billinghurst, Bloodofox, Bookluva323, Brianann MacAmhlaidh, Briangotts, Cat-five, Ccdesan, Celtus, Cerdic, Cesue, ClueBot NG, CompliantDrone, Creuzbourg, Crimson JT, Daf, Dante Alighieri, Davepain, Dbachmann, Dcinamon, Deanlaw, Deenoe, Denisarona, Deuxentre, Discospinster, Doc James, DocWatson42, Dr. Hannibal Lecter, DrKay, Drkoop, EmanWilm, Eric Yurken, Ethan Mitchell, EvergreenFir, Faizan, Fireflash1536, Franz-kafka, Froglich, Froid, Frymaster, Ghirlandajo, Gilliam, Giraffedata, Goodnightmush, Gracenotes, Gwern, Hairy Dude, Holt, Hornean, Igiffin, Ipoellet, JDspeeder1, Jamoche, Jaysel, Jehnidiah, Kcxmx, Klausok, Klemen Kocjancic, Krakkos, Londonclanger, Materialscientist, Mbell, Mcc1789, Mikelines, Mleskin, Mothicus, NebY, Netkinetic, Nightscream, Nynewart, Outboardtech, OwenBlacker, Pastbury, Patricksmithjournalist, Paul A, Persian Poet Gal, Piratedan, Pontificalibus, Quirk, RA0808, ReaderofthePack, Repku, Reyk, Rhytre, Rich Farmbrough, Richard75, Roidenavarre, Rsrikanth05, Saddhiyama, Sadistik, Septegram, Shadowlink1014, Slayer12317, SloughFeg, Smile a While, Snorri2, SolInvictus, Solenoc, Springhill40, Steelion, Sun Creator, Svartalf, Tamfang, Tassedethe, Tawkerbot4, The Man in Question, TheLateDentarthurdent, TyronePower17, Ugur Basak, V2Blast, Voidian, Walgamanus, Wetman, WikiTryHardDieHard, Woohookitty, Xanzzibar, Yintan, Yojimbo1941, Yvonnelouise, Zantolak, Zinnmann, 216 anonymous edits 160

Death by boiling *Source:* https://en.wikipedia.org/w/index.php?oldid=863228502 *License:* Creative Commons Attribution-Share Alike 3.0 *Contributors:* *Kat*, Aarp65, Adûnâi, Aelffin, Alansohn, Aldaron, Alexusaxus, American Starkiller, Ammodramus, Apwith, Arildnordby, Art LaPella, Barrywise, Bladesmulti, Blazotron, Bogdanb, Boneyard90, Brendandh, Brideshead, Brycehughes, Canterbury Tail, Carbon Caryatid, Clegs, CowboySpartan, Dan Koehl, DarkUniverse121, DavidBrooks, DavidBrooks-AWB, Deacon of Pndapetzim, Doc James, Doksum, Dominus, Doug butler, Dylanfromthenorth, EEng, EaZy87, Eebahgum, Emperor, Evilgidgit, FT2, Finetooth, Flavio.brandani, Freestylefrappe, Furrykef, Fyrael, Galootius, Gothica36, Gpvos, GrahamHardy, Gwinva, HandsomeFella, Harachte, Hardyplants, HarmonicFeather, Herostratus, Hippo43, Hvn0413, I am One of Many, ITSAMENICK, JForget, Jagged 85, Jakoboleson, Jibi44, Joe Schmedley, John, John Nevard, Jpgordon, Keepin' It Real 24.7, Kendite, Khazar2, Kilowattradio, Kommodorekerz, Leeyc0, Lewis Goudy, Lexicality, Lightmouse, Logflume12, Lowellian, Matt Crypto, Max Naylor, Mike0001, MisfitToys, Mr pand, Mschel, Mvdleeuw, Narky Blert, NebY, Ngchen, Nymetsfan1027, Olegwiki, Omeganian, Pablomartinez, Pahari Sahib, Pajfarmor, Paul Magnussen, Peter B., Piano non troppo, Polylepsis, Portillo, Pozytyv, ProhibitOnions, Reyk, Reza789, Rigley, Risk one, RobertLunaIII, Robofish, Ruakh, Sailmaker, Schneelocke, Shadowlink1014, Sheitan, SheriffIsInTown, Sherurcij, Sirveaux, Slightsmile, Smasongarrison, Solomonfromfinland, Staticshakedown, StevenMario, TheMadBaron, Thebummerblitz, Theopolisme, Tktktk, UKoch, Unisonus, Urgos, Vanished user 8jq3ijalkdjhviewrie, VanishedUser sdu9aya9fasdsopa, Varlaam, Vertium, Vess, Whoop whoop pull up, Witan, Xaosflux, Yugyug, Ze miguel, Île flottante, Švitrigaila, 206 anonymous edits 163

Brazen bull *Source:* https://en.wikipedia.org/w/index.php?oldid=863284201 *License:* Creative Commons Attribution-Share Alike 3.0 *Contributors:* A3RO, Aarondminnick, Adashiel, Afernand74, Ahmer Jamil Khan, Aitch & Aitch Aitch, Anne McDermott, Anonymous from the 21st century, BD2412, Bassington, BenFrantzDale, Blackguard SF, BrayLockBoy, CASSIOPEIA, CSZero, Carlmcg, Chris4315, Clarityfiend, ClueBot NG, Conphucius, Craftyminion, CrossHouses, Ctitoyoung, Czolgolz, DadaNeem, Dbachmann, Dbrodbeck, Doc James, Dr.K., El C, Error, Eskandarany, Esrever, Feudonym, Fratrep, Futuristcorporation, Fyyer, Gamaliel, GateKeeper, Govgovgov, Grafen, Greg Holden 08, Gustavo Rubén, Heroic665, JTtheOG, Jim1138, Jimbo1uk, JoJan, Jodosma, Jusdafax, JustinFranks, Klemen Kocjancic, Kstone999, Kvn8907, Larryv, Legobot II, Lerdthenerd, LokiClock, LouriePieterse, Lx 121, Madhero88, Madreterra, Malleus Fatuorum, Mannanan51, Marcuslx, Markunit23, Markus451, Materialscientist, Math321, Matt Gies, MedicMedia, Meursault2004, Mike Rosoft, Miles Edgeworth, Mindmatrix, Mogism, Moonriddengirl, Mr Stephen, MusikAnimal, Naagin who, Nashhinton, NawlinWiki, NebY, NilesG, Optimale, Oreo Priest, Ost316, PaleoNeonate, Penitence, Phil Boswell, Philip Taron, Philip of Montferrat, Plethora of ducks, Pollinosisss, Primefac, Pseudonymo, Puffin, Qoncept, Quibik, Raginghamsterx, Reepnorp, Rehnn83, Rjwilmsi, Robertgreer, Rotational, Rubinia, Scalhotrod, Shabidoo, SheriffIsInTown, Sigehelmus, Smeat75, Spandox, SquarePeg, SummerPhD, T0mpr1c3, TPIRFanSteve, TallNapoleon, TenPoundHammer, The Man in Question, TheDragonFire300, TheGuyWhoDoesThings, Thorwald, Tide rolls, Tmangray, Triterion, Urgos, Vanstrat, Vermont, WTucker, WikiWhatWho, WilPwr, Xanzzibar, Zimriel, Ὁ οἶστρος, 236 anonymous edits 167

Breaking wheel *Source:* https://en.wikipedia.org/w/index.php?oldid=860323317 *License:* Creative Commons Attribution-Share Alike 3.0 *Contributors:* Aircorn, Alansohn, Aleksandr Grigoryev, Anagoria, Anamdas, Andrei Stroe, Anescient, ArglebargleIV, Arildnordby, Asarelah, Base, Beaner445, Becelespara, Bellroth, Bender235, BillC, BlueOrb, BlueUndigoFuckerNebY2, Bobrayner, Braincricket, BrokenSphere, Caidh, Cbbkr, Chaosdruid, Chatfecter, Cherkash, Chris the speller, ChrisGualtieri, Chzz, ClueBot NG, Codrinb, Crusoe8181, Daddyman1962, Dany44, David Edgar, DavidBrooks-AWB, Dcirovic, Deb, Deipnosophista, Delusion23, Doc James, DonFB, Donfbreed, Dr. Dan, EDVos, Elizium23, Examplar, Faulty, Finnusertop, FlyingMeeces, Franknotes, Frecklefoot, Gergis, GoingBatty, Graham87, Gui le Roi, Hairy Dude, Haymouse, Hellbus, Helterskelter80, Here2help, Hlucho, Htplus, Hushpuckena, Hydrargyrum, Ibadibam, Ilikepie678, Ionutzmovie, JMCC1, Jacob Lundberg, Jason Quinn, Javelin98, Jaydec, Jayme, Jfmantis, Jmcw37, Jmontouliu, John, John Paul Parks, Johnbod, Jontel, Josve05a, Katalaveno, Kelisi, Kwamikagami, L1A1 FAL, L235, LlywelynII, Lotje, LoveActresses, Magioladitis, Man vyi, Martin451, Matthias Blazek, Mercurywoodrose, Midnight1131, Mogism, MrBlueSky, Mushlack, Mycomp, NebY, Newyork1501, Nightsturm, NorwegianBlue, NotAnonymous0, Oranjelo100, PBS-AWB, Paleface Jack, Paulc206, Peter Isotalo, Philly jawn, Pigsonthewing, Place Clichy, Plamoa, Pmj, Quebec99, R'n'B, RevZoe, RickinBaltimore, Rjwilmsi, Rnickel, Rockhoppr, Rontrigger, Rosser1954, Rsandu, SHCarter, Scrooke, Serial Number 54129, Serols, SiJayGreen, SilverbackNet, SimonTrew, Sitush, Skittleys, Spicemix, StevenMario, Stevencoulthard, Stratman07, TallNapoleon, Targaryen, Taylornate, Telfordbuck, Textorus, The Man in Question, The Uncyclopedian, TheOldJacobite, Thecurran, Thomas Blomberg, Tjbird9675, Tobby72, Toddcs, Tpbradbury, Trackteur, Tragic romance, TransJames, Trappist the monk, Varlaam, Vihelik, W.stanovsky, WOSlinker, Walshga, WhisperToMe, Whoop whoop pull up, Widr, Woohookitty, Yone Fernandes, Zajacik99, 186 anonymous edits 171

Premature burial *Source:* https://en.wikipedia.org/w/index.php?oldid=863734736 *License:* Creative Commons Attribution-Share Alike 3.0 *Contributors:* 45ossington, 777sms, Alan Liefting, Albany NY, Allthefoxes, Americus55, AndreasPraefcke, AngelSaciel, Arildnordby, Arny, Ashphalt, Athomeinkobe, Auric, AussieLegend, Banedon, Beao, Bender235, Bgwhite, Blainster, Blanche of King's Lynn, BobNesh, Boneyard90, Boomer Vial, Carbon Caryatid, Checkingfax, Citizen Canine, ClueBot NG, Colapeninsula, CompliantDrone, Curb Chain, Cymru.lass, Dawidels23, Dlabtot, Doc James, Dogman15, Eastmain, Elockid, Erik, Evangeline, Evileel, FT2, FergusM1970, Ferret, Feudonym, Francois, Ginkgo100, Gothaparduskerialldrapolatkh, Graham87, Greg Holden 08, HandsomeFella, Hoponpop69, Iridescent, Isque, IvyVine, Iwavns, JHunterJ, Jason Quinn, Jeffq, Jeffzedit, Jeremy112233, Jikybebna, Jnestorius, John of Reading, Jon Kolbert, Jprg1966, Julianhall, K-pachs, Keepin' It Real 24.7, LanthanumK, Lawrencegordon, LilHelpa, M.O.X, Malleus Fatuorum, Maproom, Marcel miller, Matchups, MattSucci, Matth23, Microchip08, Mike Mounier, Milowent, Mjasfea, Mjhtcarfan, Mogism, Mulvenea, Musska, Mx. Granger, Narky Blert, Niceguyedc, Nloveladyallen, Omnipaedista, Oxford pictionary, Parmadil, Pattette, Pinethicket, Popcornduff, Primergrey, Quisquiliae, Rich Farmbrough, Richard Arthur Norton (1958-), Rjwilmsi, Rusted AutoParts, Satellizer, Saturn comes back around, Ser Amantio di Nicolao, Shellwood, Smw0985, Snow Blizzard, Stephanie Lahey, Syzygy, TJRC, Taistelu-Jaska, ThePlatypusofDoom, This lousy T-shirt, Tjmayerinsf, Tobby72, Tpbradbury, Trunks ishida, Vadon Mich, Vranak, Wavelength, Webclient101, WhisperToMe, Whoop whoop pull up, XP1, Xx-morgan-lee-xx, Yilloslime, 123 anonymous edits 187

Death by burning *Source:* https://en.wikipedia.org/w/index.php?oldid=864559570 *License:* Creative Commons Attribution-Share Alike 3.0 *Contributors:* 72, 786wiki, A35821361, Abed J Mattar, Adûnâi, Alpha3031, Anarchangel, Anassjerjawi, Anthony Appleyard, Athene cheval, Awien, BD2412, Bender235, Bgwhite, BillC, Bilsonius, Bladesmulti, Blanche of King's Lynn, Brenont, Brob, Cashewnøtt, Catriona, Ch'marr, Citizen Canine, Clarityfiend, ClueBot NG, Colonies Chris, Cpt Wise, Cramyourspam, Cuddly Visionary, Cuñado, Cyberbot II, Daask, Damián A. Fernández Beanato, DarkUniverse121, Darkness Shines, DemocraticLuntz, Dentren, Dl2000, Dmol, Doc James, Doremo, Dragfyre, Dubmill, EEng, Editor2020, Ender's Shadow Snr, Eve

Teschlemacher, Famaouz, Faze Ninja, Fraytel, Gilliam, Gillyweed, Gobonobo, God-Himself, Graham87, Hairy Dude, HarryHenryGebel, Haveitmade, Heliotom, IjonTichyIjonTichy, ImHere2015, Inexpiable, Iridescent, Jim1138, JimVC3, Jjfredregill, Joe2719, Jonesey95, Josve05a, JzG, K.e.coffman, K6ka, Kaiketsu, Katolophyromai, Kelapstick, Kind Tennis Fan, Labtek00, LakesideMiners, Lawrencegordon, LilyKitty, LoneWolf1992, Macrakis, Makaioisfree, Malcolmmwa, Manxruler, Markbellis, Materialscientist, Me, Myself, and I are Here, Mike Mounier, Mikedelsol, Mogism, Mspritch, Nazgul02, NebY, Nowa, Nyttend, Onel5969, Optakeover, Orientls, Oshwah, Patapsco913, Piledhigheranddeeper, Plantdrew, PlyrStar93, Prayer for the wild at heart, Proxyma, R'n'B, Redaktor, Rjwilmsi, Rockhoppr, Roger 8 Roger, Roxy the dog, Salsabeel Zeineddin, Scandiescot, Sealle, SiJayGreen, Smasongarrison, Spencer, Stamptrader, StarSword, Sugrammr, Supreme Dragon, Suriel1981, TJRC, The blue dancing cat, Thrownshadows, Tongtongtta, Victor Lopes, Wnt, Yopie, Zuko Halliwell, Île flottante, 171 anonymous edits 200

Crucifixion *Source:* https://en.wikipedia.org/w/index.php?oldid=863485437 *License:* Creative Commons Attribution-Share Alike 3.0 *Contributors:* Abelmoschus Esculentus, Ammodramus, Anomalocaris, Anonimeco, Arjayay, Ashbeckjonathan, Atvica, BD2412, Banjohunter, Beland, Bender235, Bgwhite, Biografer, Bishop Morehouse, CLCStudent, Chrism, CityOfSilver, ClueBot NG, Cricketfan05, Curly Turkey, DPdH, DVdm, Dale Arnett, Dbachmann, Dcirovic, DivermanAU, Dkspartan1835, Dmol, Doc James, Donner60, Doug Weller, Drm310, DybrarH, Eperoton, Eteethan, Ethan817, Evant939012, Favonian, Feature87, Fidulario, Finleydl, Finuaz, Frietjes, Gaioa, Gavriil Khipés, Gorgon55, Graeme Bartlett, Grassynoel, HD86, Hairy Dude, Hornesid37, HowlingAngel, Ilovefinnigan, Isaac Samuel 2003 2012, J 1982, Jac16888, Jessicapierce, Jim1138, Jmrowland, Jpbrenna, Jveeds, Kahtar, Kazvorpal, Kmote, KylieTastic, LittleDipper, Macedonian, MagicatthemovieS, Manul, Marcocapelle, Marvixo, Materialscientist, Mauro Lanari, Mikeblas, Mkweise, Mx. Granger, Mytwocents, Naraht, Narky Blert, NebY, NewEnglandYankee, Ohnoitsjamie, Onel5969, Oshwah, Peacewise, Plandu, Porterhse, Pureness5, Rich Farmbrough, RickinBaltimore, Rjwilmsi, Rui Gabriel Correia, Rupert loup, Sapphique9, Sebitasguerrero, Serols, Shellwood, SheriffIsInTown, Shrek33sander, Sizeofint, Slightsmile, Smeat75, Super ninja2, Supernova1235, TAnthony, TJRC, Tachs, Talal.itani, The New Classic, The.Editor04, TheBlinkster, Theroadislong, Tom.Reding, Ttwaring, TwoTwoHello, VirginiaLeontaridou, Vmelkon, WQUlrich, Yopienso, 158 anonymous edits ... 250

Crushing (execution) *Source:* https://en.wikipedia.org/w/index.php?oldid=859992043 *License:* Creative Commons Attribution-Share Alike 3.0 *Contributors:* 2over0, 777sms, A8UDI, Acetotyce, Adoniscik, Arcadian, Arildnordby, Ashmoo, Ask123, Awilko89, Bobblewik, BobbyDude13, Bobet, Bryan Derksen, CDN99, Canek, Cassowary, Charleys2004, ClueBot NG, Colonies Chris, CommonsDelinker, Crasshopper, Cs302b, Curlingpro47, Cyan, Cybercobra, Danceswithzerglings, Destynova, Dl2000, Doc James, Donreed, Dr Gangrene, E-Kartoffel, Emperorbma, Equazcion, Esrever, Evrik, Fastifex, Fconaway, Fede.Campana, Flockmeal, Fluffernutter, Fr33kman, Fuortu, Gabbe, Gaius Cornelius, Gamer Eek, GoingBatty, Hibernian, Hotlorp, I am One of Many, Iamthedeus, Ihcoyc, Int21h, Iridescent, Jigaro Kano, John, JosephBarillari, Julesd, KJK::Hyperion, Karada, Kasper2006, Kelvinc, Klacquement, KnowledgeOfSelf, Kwertii, Latimermartyrs, LilHelpa, Luwilt, M.thoriyan, MBisanz, Macrakis, Malleus Fatuorum, Marek69, Mark Taylor, Matthew Stannard, McAusten, Mdnavman, Mediatech492, MesserWoland, Michael Hardy, Mikem, Mikeo, Mitrius, Montrealais, MrBlueSky, NebY, Nihiltres, Nunh-huh, Ogram, OrenBochman, PFHLai, Paulromney, Piano non troppo, Ponkywatts, Promking, Qdiderot, Qsaw, RandomCritic, Richard75, Ripley Crouch, Ruakh, Schnurrbart, Scott, SeanDuggan, Securiger, Septegram, Ser Amantio di Nicolao, Sfan00 IMG, Shadowlink1014, Shai-kun, SheldonPHDkuthropolly, Sherurcij, SlamDiego, Smasongarrison, Snoyes, Someone else, Spoonkymonkey, Staxringold, StevenMario, Targaryen, The Anome, Toddy1, Tomchiukc, Tomixdf, Transmissionelement, Ubergeekguy, Uvaduck, Victor Gijsbers, Wiki alf, Wikiain, Winchelsea, Ze miguel, 136 anonymous edits 275

Disembowelment *Source:* https://en.wikipedia.org/w/index.php?oldid=864135109 *License:* Creative Commons Attribution-Share Alike 3.0 *Contributors:* 100110100, A520, Abbeyhb86, Adam Field, Alphaboi867, Amber388, AndperseAndy, Andycjp, Anir1uph, Anonymous from the 21st century, Arildnordby, Asarelah, Athenapyros, Azathar, BananaBork, Blackhawk charlie2003, Bloodbath 87, Boneyard90, Brandon5485, Brianski, Calousrm, Captain Cornwall, Certes, Chzz, ClueBot NG, Cnwilliams, Coastergeekperson04, CoreyEdwards, Cramyourspam, CrazyChemGuy, Crazycomputers, D6, Dan Koehl, Darter, Darth Panda, David Kernow, Dean1954, Dewritech, Doc James, Donner60, ElementFire, Elkman, Enric Naval, Epipelagic, Ettrig, Euchiasmus, Feedintm, Frecklefoot, Frotz, GQsm, Gilliam, GimliDotNet, GorgeCustersSabre, Graham87, Green caterpillar, GregorB, Gurch, HARTPOINTER1, Hiddekel, Inter16, Ixat, James g2, Jeremiahtabbada27, Jjkkllmnocum, John, Joseph A. Spadaro, Jpatokal, Jtanadi, Juliancolton, Kelvinc, Khazar2, Koavf, Kwesiidun91, KylieTastic, Legobot II, LeinaD natipaC, Liempt, LilHelpa, Limxzero, Locos epraix, Mac Davis, Magioladitis, Mahagaja, Mandarax, Maxmizerski2000, Mdebets, Meachly, Michael Daly, Msignor, Narahasphael, Neils51, Neutrality, Nishkid64, Nlaporte, Noushif, NuclearWarfare, Old Moonraker, Ollie the Magic Skater, Onejaguar, Onomou, PacificBoy, Pashute, Pawyilee, Philip Trueman, Pinethicket, Porkins8888, PraetorianFury, Quicksilvre, Rjwilmsi, Rm1271, Roboshed, SMcCandlish, SaMaDaMordor, Sacre, Shadowlink1014, Shultz, Sivart345, Slabsky, Socommk23, SomeUsr, Srich32977, Stenen Bijl, Stevetursi, Str1977, TalibKweli123, TallulahBelle, Tassedethe, Teeninvestor, Teratix, The Anome, The Thing That Should Not Be, The Wiki ghost, TheMadBaron, Theelf29, Tide rolls, Tiggerjay, TimSE, Toyokuni3, VAcharon, Volunteer1234, Vranak, Vrenator, Vsmith, Wbm1058, Webclient101, Whoop whoop pull up, Widr, Wifione, Worch, Wtmitchell, Xxxxzickxxxx, Yossarian, Ze miguel, 211 anonymous edits 279

Dismemberment *Source:* https://en.wikipedia.org/w/index.php?oldid=864207824 *License:* Creative Commons Attribution-Share Alike 3.0 *Contributors:* 777sms, Abt7217tc, Ainlina, Angel ivanov angelov, Arichang, Arildnordby, Ashphalt, Atakdoug, BD2412, Benjamin "Jeffrey" Powell, Bernardoni, Bgwhite, Binksternet, Boneyard90, Buchraeumer, Captain Cornwall, Chasingsol, ChrisGualtieri, ChrisHodgesUK, ClueBot NG, Coccyx Bloccyx, Colonies Chris, DO11.10, Dan Murphy, DanielC46, Denisarona, Dexter prog, Doc James, Ebfh, EdMcMahon, Editorjr101, Egsan Bacon, Evanherk, Froid, FunkyFoves19, Georgeharrrison, Georgejmyersjr, Gilliam, God-Himself, HistOry neRd 3850, Holme053, Husond, Insanity Incarnate, Jhon montes24, Jmrowland, Jonesey95, Joshua Server, Jusdafax, Jwilson1891, Kafziel, Khunglongcon, KimChee, Kmaster, L3X1, Lds, Leeyc0, LilHelpa, Linguist111, Mani1, Martinevans123, Materialscientist, Mcc1789, Mike Mounier, Mliu92, Moe Epsilon, Mogism, Mr pand, Mtcv, NTsilakis, Naraht, Nihiltres, Noctibus, Omnipaedista, Ontheclosedcircuit, Owlpamy, Pete unseth, Pseudomonas, Pyams, Racerspeed, Reyk, Rjwilmsi, Rlest, Rodw, Scewing, ScottSteiner, Seejyb, Serols, Shadowlink1014, ShelfSkewed, Sloewen, Sláine mac Dela, Solomonfromfinland, Srednuas Lenoroc, Ssall, SuperHypercane, TacitSilence, Taschenrechner∼enwiki, Tassedethe, Tcpp, Test piggy, Tiria, Tony1, Toquinha, Underbar dk, Viril2000, Vranak, WaterCrane, Whoop whoop pull up, Womblytom, Wraithful, XXnateXX55, Yhljjang, ZappaOMati, 219 anonymous edits 286

Hanged, drawn and quartered *Source:* https://en.wikipedia.org/w/index.php?oldid=864551798 *License:* Creative Commons Attribution-Share Alike 3.0 *Contributors:* Acad Ronin, Acetotyce, Adirlanz, AgadaUrbanit, Amandajm, Anupmehra, Arildnordby, BD2412, Bender235, Blanche of King's Lynn, Bongwarrior, Boubsterama, Brenont, Callanecc, Cassianto, Charles Matthews, ChouxMonster, Ciphergoth, ClueBot NG, Colonies Chris, Crystallizedcarbon, Cyberbot II, DAFMM, Dan100, DazzleXWEdwards, Demiurge1000, Diannaa, Dilidor, DrKay, Drdpw, Dubmill, Ealdgyth, Edison, Elizium23, Epicgenius, Eric Corbett, Esrever, Favonian, Gargleyark, Gerda Arendt, Ginkgo100, Gledakronen, GorillaWarfare, Gpaetz, GreenRunner0, Hairy Dude, Hchc2009, Hebel, Helmfr00, Henry plantagenet ii, IAmNitpicking, IJBall, Ian Rose, Iavila, Ifnord, Inglok, Iridescent, Iridescent 2, Jack Frost, JamesBWatson, Jayman4426, Jayron32, Jean Po, Jim1138, John, Kablammo, Laser brain, Lenin and McCarthy, Level C, Longhair, Lotje, Lugia2453, Malleus Fatuorum, Mandorix, Materialscientist, Meddling meddler, Michael Devore, Mikedelsol, MusikAnimal, Nev1, Niceguyedc, Nikkimaria, NorthCoastReader, Nthep, Oiyarbepsy, Oli.reeves, Oshwah, Ost316, PBS, Parrot of Doom, PatGallacher, Peter Isotalo, Pierre M Aronnax, Piledhigheranddeeper, Pincrete, Portillo, Psyzzlewazzle, Qwerty Binary, RGCorris, RS-Fighter, Rachelmc2, Redrose64, Regicide1649, Reubenburgess13, Richard75, Richardisnotcool, Rjwilmsi, RobinClay, Rrostrom, Sagaciousphil, SamX, SarahTehCat, Shenme, Slashme, Slightsmile, Springnuts, SulfuricRed, Surtsicna, TBNRBlakeus, TX55, Taco Viva, Terry3439, The Blade of the Northern Lights, The C of E, Tobby72, TomBulweed6536, Tropicalkitty, Ulenspegel, Urselius, User000name, VQuakr, Vanished user 31lk45mnzx90, Vegasrunaway, Vgy7ujm, Websterwebfoot, Werldwayd, Whoop whoop pull up, William Avery, Wisdom89, Wkitty42, Writ Keeper, X aimzzzzz, Yavorpenchev, Zentomologist, ZfJames, 112 anonymous edits 298

Falling (execution) *Source:* https://en.wikipedia.org/w/index.php?oldid=801631285 *License:* Creative Commons Attribution-Share Alike 3.0 *Contributors:* -wuppertaler, Andrewjlockley, Bender235, Citation bot 1, Dcirovic, Doc James, EagleFan, Ego White Tray, GCarty, GrahamSmith, Ian Spackman, J 1982, Martina Moreau, Muhammed Kabir, Nyttend, PhnomPencil, Schnurrbart, ThiagoRuiz, Viper426, 8 anonymous edits 316

Flaying *Source:* https://en.wikipedia.org/w/index.php?oldid=861937022 *License:* Creative Commons Attribution-Share Alike 3.0 *Contributors:* 1812ahill, 4twenty42o, Adûnâi, Ahecht, Alarics, Allmyevilbunnies, Anaxial, AndrewHowse, Anna678, Anonymous from the 21st century, Arildnordby, Atakdoug, Atchom, Attilios, BD2412, Bender235, Big Bird, Blaylockjam10, Briangotts, Calm, Cannibalicious!, Catholic nerd, Charles Matthews, Chasingsol, Chianti, Chonanh, ClueBot NG, Colbey84, Commissarvan, Contract Murder, Cplakidas, DBigXray, DWorley, DagosNavy, DarkUniverse121, Darklilac, Dayana Hashim, Dekimasu, DivermanAU, Doc James, Donreed, Drmies, Dweller, Eagleash, Eastlaw, Ecomism, EdwardZhao, Eeosalel, Elkman, Enviroboy, Euryalus, Fastifex, Fedayee, Filippo83, Flyer22 Reborn, ForestAngel, Froid, Gaganaut, Geekdiva, General chi, Glishev, Gonzalo84, Good Olfactory, HRW in 1899, Heathermcphrsn, Hmains, HolidayInGibraltar, Ignus, InternetMeme, Iridescent, J.delanoy, Jagnor, Jarble, Jarekt, Jayron32, Jim1138, Jmabel, Jmrowland, Johnbod, JorgePeixoto, Joseph A. Spadaro, Kablammo, Khorshid, KuroiShiroi, KylieTastic, LP-mn, Leoger, Lotje, MSUGRA, Major Bonkers, MarnetteD, Mathrick, Matthau, Mddombrowski, Miborovsky, Mogism, Mompati Dikunwane, Mordicai, Neelix, Nihiltres, Nipsonanomhmata, Noca2plus, Ntsimp, Nv02migu, Oatmeal batman, Onel5969, Patar knight, Peter Horn, Picus viridis, Pikazilla, Pinethicket, Polylerus, Portillo, Qwerty Binary, RandyBirch, Reptilian Humanoid, Rich Farmbrough, Rosser1954, SJ Defender, SMcCandlish, STBotD, Sappulibedumisifa, Scrabbleship1, Scriberius, Scythian1, Seelie, Simon Burchell, Smjg, Smk65536, Snakemike, Solarra, Splintax, StevenMario, Subsume, Supertouch, Switchiedagger, Tabletop, Tachs, TallNapoleon, The Land, TheAwesomeWrath, Tim1357, Tiny plastic Grey Knight, Tobby72, Tomchiukc, Toystars, UKER, Urcounterclockwise, Vcena, WLU, William Avery, Woohookitty, Xezbeth, Yogesh Khandke, Zenswashbuckler, ZjarriRrethues, 226 anonymous edits 318

Garrote *Source:* https://en.wikipedia.org/w/index.php?oldid=863525580 *License:* Creative Commons Attribution-Share Alike 3.0 *Contributors:* A glimpse of the past, Ad Orientem, Afoxtrotn00b, Againme, Andy Dingley, Anonymous from the 21st century, Arancaytar, Arthur Ellis, Asqueladd, Aza-Toth, Azumanga1, BarrelProof, Bgwhite, Bielle, Biruitorul, Blackhawk charlie2003, Bobanny, Brad Eleven, Bri, BrokenSphere, CKCortez, Calliopejen1, Cap10xb1s, Carmichael, Cheluco, Chris Capoccia, Chris9086, Christofer C. Bell, ClueBot NG, CommonsDelinker, DagosNavy, Daniel Olsen, Daniellagreen, Dcandeto, DeepCurl, Dellant, DeltaQuad, DerHexer, DickyP, Dirk Chivers, DiverDave, Doc James, Dr. Mott, Ealy, Ed558, EdgarCabreraFariña, Eliz81, Emuman423, Enviroboy, Epbr123, Equinox, Eugene-elgato, Francomassaro, Fru1tbat, Gilliam, Giraffedata, Gogo Dodo, Good Olfactory, Greasycaesar, Gunsfornuns, Gurch, Hairy Dude, HalfShadow, Hooperbloob, IrishPete, It Is Me Here, Ithinkicahn, JIP, JackFarias, JaconaFrere, Jarble, Javascap, Jaxoun, Jbawasanta, Jeffrey Zimmerman, Jonathan.s.kt, JonathanCoyle, Joseph Solis in Australia, Jrundin, Jtk13, Kaare, Kalaong, Kelisi, Kelly Martin, Kent Wang, Kgrad, Knowledge-is-power, LafinJack, Larry Hockett, LexLata, Longhair, Lotje, Luisdelafuente, M.nelson, Madalibi, Magioladitis, Malleus Fatuorum, Malo, Manu Lop, MarioProtIV, Markussep, Materialscientist, Mboverload, Mcknockiterp, Mghabmw, Mike.lifeguard, Mixetmurri, Mootros, Mortice, Murderbike, Mutt Lunker, Mvdejong, Mycroft.Holmes, Nancy, NapoleonB, Ndrwzheng, Nellis, Neuralwarp, Newyorkbrad, Noctibus, Ollie, Omnipaedista,

Pepperpop11, Peter AUDEMG, Pinethicket, Pjacobi, Prari, Prof. Mc, Purestgreen, Qviri, Rahulghose, Ranveig, Recury, Regulov, Renamed user ixgysjijel, Richwales, RickyCourtney, Rjwilmsi, Rob Pommer, Roboto de Ajvol, Roman à clef, Ruakh, Ryanbstevens, SchuminWeb, Serols, Shadowlink1014, ShelfSkewed, Sherurcij, Snoozehard, SoWhy, TJRC, The Rumour, Themoodyblue, Theopolisme, Tide rolls, Tomason33, Tony Myers, Travis.Thurston, Tustin2121, TwoTwoHello, VoABot II, VonWoland, Vranak, WhatsUpWorld, Yone Fernandes, ZPM, Zzuuzz, ♡Golf, 232 anonymous edits 325

Gibbeting *Source:* https://en.wikipedia.org/w/index.php?oldid=863780483 *License:* Creative Commons Attribution-Share Alike 3.0 *Contributors:* A loose noose, Aerach, Aescwyn, Aetheling, AjaxSmack, Albany NY, Alexb102072, Arbitershadow, Audaciter, AuthorityTam, BD2412, BaldBoris, BeatrixBelibaste, Benandorsqueaks, Bender235, Benw, Bezapt, Branddobbe, Brenont, BrownHairedGirl, Chase me ladies, I'm the Cavalry, Chaser, Cheesy mike, Chkno, Chris troutman, Cjwright79, Claireislovely, ClueBot NG, Cluneslife, Cyberbot II, Darklilac, Defaultdotxbe, Deflective, DferDaisy, Dhodges, Dilidor, Dl2000, Docu, Donfbreed, DrJos, Drilnoth, Dtgm, Edmund Patrick, Elronxenu, Epbr123, Fuhvah, Furrykef, Furshur, GBH, General Ization, Girlwithgreeneyes, Good Olfactory, Graham87, Gregorydavid, Halavais, Halifaxpier, Harlem Baker Hughes, Hermione is a dude, Hertz1888, IGeMiNix, Il fugitivo, Iloveinter, Inclusivedisjunction, Inhighspeed, Jabberjaw, Jackfork, JamesMLane, Jeppi, Jeremy Bolwell, JohnnyCalifornia, Joseph Solis in Australia, Josve05a, Julesd, KFP, Kablammo, Kchishol1970, Kelisi, KnutHj, Kwonbbl, Legacypac, Legobot II, Lokiloki, Lyricist99, Macr237, Macrakis, Malleus Fatuorum, Mandorix, MarkinBoston, Mathrick, Me and, Micahbrwn, Michael Hardy, Moozipan Cheese, Mrgibbets, Necrothesp, Niceguyedc, Noah Salzman, Nono64, Nyttend, Oatmeal batman, Omni5cience, PBS, Paul W, Peaceray, Pebkac, Pekaje, Peruvianllama, Pigsonthewing, Pinethicket, Plot Spoiler, Postdlf, Preczewski, Primergrey, Rachelbennett1989, Rjwilmsi, Robertgreer, RossRSmith, Rosser1954, Rotlink, SchreiberBike, Scottperry, Searchme, Seduisant, SheriffIsInTown, Simple Bob, Slashme, Soap, Solipsist, Somercet, Spoonkymonkey, SteveSims, Stumps, Suriel1981, Syzygy, TGC55, Talskiddy, TheScarletRogue, Thewalrus, Timothy Titus, Tmopkisn, Todd661, Troglo, Turgan, Usernameenteredalreadyinusetoo, Varlaam, Vernon39, VoABot II, Werieth, Wetman, Widr, Wilfridselsey, Wuerzele, Ze miguel, 176 anonymous edits 330

Immurement *Source:* https://en.wikipedia.org/w/index.php?oldid=863478361 *License:* Creative Commons Attribution-Share Alike 3.0 *Contributors:* Acjelen, Amerias, Arildnordby, Ashanda, Audaciter, Auric, BD2412, Bignolles, Boneyard90, Cariaso, Ceosad, Ceplm, Chris troutman, Cingu23, Coinmanj, DeNoel, Dewritech, Doc James, Doormatt00, Doug Weller, Ehrenkater, Elendil's Heir, Frietjes, Ghostgate2001, Haeinous, HaileJones, Hazelares, Hickok45, Hospy, Hushpuckena, Ileanadu, Jasper Deng, Jdlankin, Jellyfish10, John of Reading, Jonesey95, Just Chilling, K9re11, Khazar2, KylieTastic, Ljgua124, Lojbanist, Lord Roem, Lynsmi, Macofe, Magedalmaged, Mathiastck, Me and, Me, Myself, and I are Here, Midas02, Mogism, Mozzie, Mr Xaero, Mr. Laser Beam, Neitrāls vārds, Nikkimaria, Nikola Smolenski, Omnipaedista, Orenburg1, Paris1127, Pleiotrop3, Popcornduff, Primergrey, Primium mobile, Quindraco, Qwerty Binary, Regulov, Reynardo, Rjwilmsi, Scwlong, Septegram, Seraphimblade, SidP, Srednuas Lenoroc, Stevenmitchell, Succubus MacAstaroth, TAnthony, Tabletop, Tar-Elessar, Tegrenath, Thor Dockweiler, WOSlinker, Wavelength, Xaosflux, 105 anonymous edits 340

Impalement *Source:* https://en.wikipedia.org/w/index.php?oldid=862614582 *License:* Creative Commons Attribution-Share Alike 3.0 *Contributors:* A Georgian, Anomalocaris, Anotherclown, Aquila89, Arildnordby, BD2412, Bazza 7, Bealtainemí, Bender235, Bgwhite, Bingobingy, Blackguard SF, Blanche of King's Lynn, Boneyard90, Callanecc, Charles Matthews, Cliquot, ClueBot NG, DGG, DPdH, Denisarona, Dewritech, Doc James, Dolkungbighead, DuncanHill, Euzen, Fishycow, God's Godzilla, GraemeLeggett, Hairy Dude, Hilmorel, I am One of Many, Iridescent, JeremiahY, Jon Kolbert, Jonesey95, Joy, Ks0stm, KylieTastic, Laero, Laszlo Panaflex, LilHelpa, Little Mountain 5, Magioladitis, Medevam, Mike Mounier, Mild Bill Hiccup, Mogism, Mr. Stradivarius, NMaia, Niceguyedc, OcarinaOfTime, OccultZone, PJeganathan, Redmustang01, Rickremember, Rjwilmsi, SJ Defender, Semidimes, Skylax30, TBoaN, The PIPE, Tiemianwusi, Tobby72, TwoTwoHello, Tóraí, Ullierlich, Vanisaac, Wavelength, Wetman, Whynowagain2, Wiki841, Wikimandia, Wtmitchell, Ymblanter, Zuligin, Удивленный1, 105 anonymous edits 364

Keelhauling *Source:* https://en.wikipedia.org/w/index.php?oldid=862351049 *License:* Creative Commons Attribution-Share Alike 3.0 *Contributors:* 87gabalfa, Aaron Brenneman, Alarics, Alcmaeonid, Alexpillar, Amberrock, Amcbride, AndrewWTaylor, Andyhowlett, Antandrus, Anthony Appleyard, Aoidh, Arrivisto, Askanius∼enwiki, Auralrothko, Barneca, Barque, Bigturtle, BoH, Brandizzi, Bri, Brianeames, BrownHairedGirl, Calvinballing, Canis Lupus, CannedMan, CapitalR, ChrJahnsen, ClueBot NG, Dabbler, David Stewart, Dbachmann, Diannaa, Dlohcierekim, DrFrench, Driscolj, Eagle4000, Emcnie, Fastifex, Flip260z, Fluffy444, Fluzwup, Fourthords, Furrykef, Gavron, Gerhard51, Ghirlandajo, Goldman60, Groyolo, Haggawaga - Oegawagga, Hebrides, Hmains, Hq3473, Hugh Manatee, Ibadibam, Inkington, Jack Merridew, Jbening, Jivecat, John of Reading, Johnpacklambert, Joyous!, Kablammo, Kelisi, Knellotron, Kyuss-Apollo, Life of Riley, Link2006155, Lots42, MHansen, Madripper, Magioladitis, Magnet For Knowledge, MagnusA, MattDP, Mean as custard, Mh26, Mikael.argelius, MileyDavidA, Multichill, O-Qua-Tangin-Wann 2015, O467123, Oranjelo100, Orav∼enwiki, PFHLai, Pedta, Peter Isotalo, Pinethicket, Pjbflynn, Pladask, PohranicniStraze, Polyamorph, Quark1005, Rama, Ramaksoud2000, Randi75, RedWolf, Rex Germanus, RupertMillard, Sandyk67, Satellizer, Scipius, Scottperry, Serial Number 54129, ShelfSkewed, Sluzzelin, Smyth, Snowfalcon, Sonett72, Spoonkymonkey, Swartd, TaintedMustard, TenebrisFerre, The Anome, The Rambling Man, The snare, Thief12, Timo Honkasalo, Trovatore, USN1977, Ulflarsen, Unschool, V2Blast, Vardion, Wintermourn∼enwiki, Wolfox4777, Wyddgrug, Xmrc85x, Yadsalohcin, Ze miguel, 180 anonymous edits 391

Poena cullei *Source:* https://en.wikipedia.org/w/index.php?oldid=863552130 *License:* Creative Commons Attribution-Share Alike 3.0 *Contributors:* AmericanLemming, Ammarpad, AngryEpaminondas, Arildnordby, Awien, Bahudhara, Carlstak, Chris the speller, ChrisGualtieri, Complainer, Cynwolfe, Demiurge1000, DudeWithAFeud, Fitindia, GiantSnowman, Gilliam, Iselilja, Jason Quinn, John of Reading, KLBot2, Kahtar, Lightlowemon, Marcocapelle, Mdann52, Mild Bill Hiccup, Mindmatrix, Mr Stephen, MrTree, Nikkimaria, PériclesofAthens, Philafrenzy, Qzd, Rjwilmsi, Robfenix, Sebarsetian, Snori, ThaddeusB, William Avery, 24 anonymous edits 394

Poisoning *Source:* https://en.wikipedia.org/w/index.php?oldid=846726861 *License:* Creative Commons Attribution-Share Alike 3.0 *Contributors:* Arjayay, Doc James, John P. Sadowski (NIOSH), Piperh, Quercus solaris, Rathfelder, Sahehco, Wouterstomp, 1 anonymous edits 410

Pendulum *Source:* https://en.wikipedia.org/w/index.php?oldid=858298510 *License:* Creative Commons Attribution-Share Alike 3.0 *Contributors:* 22merlin, Alex123101, AlexiusHoratius, Amlanjyoti Roy, Anrnusna, BD2412, Bernd2015, Bgwhite, Biruxx, Bmazzoni27, Charles Matthews, Chetvorno, Civlover, ClueBot NG, Crowsnest, Cuzkatzimhut, DBlomgren, DOwenWilliams, DadaNeem, Dbfirs, Dcirovic, EdJohnston, Eleassar, Eustachiusz, Flyer22 Reborn, Fmadd, Forbes72, Gaius Cornelius, Gap9551, Gilliam, Ginsuloft, Gob Lofa, Gravyboi, Headbomb, Hhhippo, Home Lander, Hugozair, Iridescent, Ixfd64, J20160628, J991, JaconaFrere, Jennica, Jiten D, Joelei18, Jrogers28, JustBerry, Keleste, Khazar2, Kku, Lemnaminor, LuK3, Mad666paul, Majora4, Mandarax, Manoguru, MaoGo, Maproom, Mark Arsten, MarnetteD, Martinvl, Maschen, Materialscientist, Mathnerd314159, Mjs1991, Myasuda, N0n3up, OcarinaOfTime, Onel5969, Oshwah, PaleoNeonate, Pbfy0, Pbosque, Pinethicket, Poco a poco, Prajaman, Prhartcom, Questionefisica, Raycheng200, Reatlas, Rjwilmsi, Roberticus, Rococo1700, Roly Williams, Rrburke, SassygalJoanne, Satellizer, Septrillion, Serols, Shellwood, Simiprof, Simplexity22, Sol1, Stesmo, TCMemoire, TYelliot, Tecsie, Thebassangler, Thomas H. White, ThomasEdistar, Tigraan, Tomasz59, Tornado chaser, Transmit-receive, Trappist the monk, Velella, VexorAbVikipædia, Vycl1994, Widr, Wikipelli, Za dom spremi, Zingvin, 178 anonymous edits 411

Death by sawing *Source:* https://en.wikipedia.org/w/index.php?oldid=858915572 *License:* Creative Commons Attribution-Share Alike 3.0 *Contributors:* Acabashi, All hail cale, Altenmann, Anastrophe, Arildnordby, Ben Ben, Boneyard90, Bryan Derksen, C777, CambridgeBayWeather, Carnildo, Chzz, Cirxe, ClueBot NG, Cmdrjameson, Colonies Chris, CommonsDelinker, Damouns, DeadEyeArrow, Dewritech, DigitalEnthusiast, Doc James, Dweller, E-Kartoffel, Exceedingly Rare, Fibonacci, FirstPrinciples, Fluzwup, Francosalo, Frazzydee, Gdo01, Ghostrider, Glane23, Graham87, Grrahnbahr, Grutness, InedibleHulk, IronGargoyle, J'raxis, Jetmysterydino, Jibi44, Joefromrandb, John of Reading, Jojit fb, Julesd, KGirlTrucker81, Keshad2, Kingpin13, Kjkolb, Krakkos, LOTRrules, LakesideMiners, Lectonar, Lemarksmen, Lights, LilHelpa, Mark Schierbecker, Marudubshinki, Maxis ftw, Mentifisto, Mogism, Monstar1, Munich1158, Mx. Granger, Nick Number, Nick363, Ninetailsgirl, Nonstopdrivel, Nyttend, Oxymoron83, Pinethicket, PohranicniStraze, Pp.paul.4, Queenmomcat, Racerspeed, RainbowOfLight, Renamed user KdYpUvMgT, Rettetast, Rich Farmbrough, Richard D. LeCour, Rls, Rp3131, Serols, Shadowlink1014, SkyWarrior, StuartDouglas, The Rambling Man, TheConduqtor, Tobymanchee, Tom.Reding, Versus22, WhisperToMe, Whoop whoop pull up, Wknight94, Xaosflux, Z10x, Ze miguel, 111 anonymous edits 452

Scaphism *Source:* https://en.wikipedia.org/w/index.php?oldid=861961101 *License:* Creative Commons Attribution-Share Alike 3.0 *Contributors:* Agathoclea, Alarics, Alcmaeonid, Alexius08, Anexpertpersonphd, Anonymous from the 21st century, Arrivisto, BD2412, Banedon, Barefootliam, Barek, Bdwilner, Bennie Noakes, BillySpradlee, Blanchardb, Bodyservant, Bonadea, Bongwarrior, Brookie, Burpen, CMBJ, Carsrac, Closedmouth, Clpo13, ClueBot NG, Dcirovic, Denniscabrams, Dewritech, Diddims, Doc James, Doug Weller, DrRogla, Drmies, Dvmlny, Dysmorodrepanis∼enwiki, EamonnPKeane, El C, Embram, Emmette Hernandez Coleman, Endovior, Epicgenius, Eric980816, FT2, Falsafeh, Fesh0r, Fibonacci, Fraggle81, Free11hunter, Frosty, Furrykef, G-my, Gareth Griffith-Jones, Gdr, Geoff B, Gilliam, Gillyweed, Gjaida, GoingBatty, Gssq, Hall Monitor, Hmainsbot1, Hoboperson456, Hooona, HorsePunchKid, Iamozy, Ian Page, Infixskis, JacksonBaggs∼enwiki, Joe Vitale 5, Joefromrandb, Jonathandeamer, Jondray, K k Martin, LeJC, Lectonar, Loonball5, Lowellian, MC10, Magioladitis, Magnet For Knowledge, Materialscientist, Matt Crypto, MatthewVanitas, Me, Myself, and I are Here, Mentifisto, Mike hayes, Mogism, Mohammad r nazari, Mononomic, MrBill3, MrKIA11, MrSampson, Mrwojo, Nakon, NewEnglandYankee, NightWolf1298, Ninad023, Octane, OlEnglish, Omnipaedista, Opencooper, P Aculeius, PMLawrence, Paul2520, Philafrenzy, PiCo, Pinethicket, Pjacobi, Pompilos, Primergrey, QuentinUK, RafaelS1979, Renamed user KdYpUvMgT, RexNL, Rich Farmbrough, Rp3131, Rpyle731, Rrburke, Sdca97, Seahawksdude12, Seduisant, Shadowlink1014, Shadowxfox, Snori, TJRC, Thaagenson, Thatguywael, The Man in Question, TheMadBaron, Tone, Varlaam, Vorziblix, WadeSimMiser, Waggie, Wetman, WhisperToMe, Whoop whoop pull up, Wikipelli, William Avery, Woohookitty, Yca.zuback, Yourmanstan, Zaphod Beeblebrox, Ze miguel, Zilkane, 232 anonymous edits 474

Lingchi *Source:* https://en.wikipedia.org/w/index.php?oldid=863029825 *License:* Creative Commons Attribution-Share Alike 3.0 *Contributors:* 14kparrett, 777sms, Abw1989, Agnamaracs, Alvin Seville, AmbivalentLife, Amys eye, Andreas Kaganov, Anthony Appleyard, Arjayay, Arthur Rubin, Atakdoug, BD2412, Barsoomian, Bender235, Boneyard90, Broadwaygenius, CCH1234, CRGreathouse, CWH, Calabe1992, Captain Cornwall, Chris the speller, CiaPan, ClueBot NG, Comp.arch, Confuzion, Crito10, DPS145192, DReifGalaxyM31, Dalliance, Delusion23, Denny, Derek R Bullamore, Destynova, Dhtwiki, Doc James, Doprendek, Edward130603, Emperor, EoGuy, Erkan Yilmaz, Esiymbro, Esowteric, Eve Teschlemacher, Everyking, Felix Folio Secundus, Finnusertop, Fixer88, Fustos, Gaius Cornelius, Geekdiva, George Ho, Gongshow, Greg Holden 08, Groyolo, HRW in 1899, Huodaxia, Immunize, Jade Phoenix Pence, Jdb00, Jim1138, Joefromrandb, Johannes Rohr, John, Julcad, Jusdafax, JustAGal, K.eight.a, Kamek98, Kartoffelsalat275, Kay Dekker, Kayau, Kintetsubuffalo, Klemen Kocjancic, Ktr101, Lds, Lgfcd, LilyKitty, Limxzero, Lo Ximiendo, Lowellian, Loyalist Cannons, LukusAreulius, MarB4, Martarius, Mediation4u, Milktaco, Mimihitam, Moe Epsilon, NawlinWiki, Neo-Jay, Niceguyedc, Nivekin, Nyttend, Ohconfucius, OlEnglish, PMLawrence, Penom, Perriguez, Philg88, Player-23, Portillo, Primergrey, Punchomatic, Qrfqr, Quebec99, Radh, Ravenswing, Rich Farmbrough, Rolfmueller, Rubbish computer, Rédacteur Tibet, Seduisant, Ser Amantio di Nicolao, Sheitan, Shujenchang, Sladen, Smasongarrison, SnowFire, Solomonfromfinland,

Stephen B Streater, Sudheerulz, Sundostund, Talon Allen, Tassedethe, Thumperward, Tobby72, Tolly4bolly, Tono Fonseca, Trigaramus, UKER, Underbar dk, Varlaam, Viril2000, WhisperToMe, White whirlwind, Widefox, Widr, Wikievil666, Woohookitty, XP1, Zzuuzz, 143 anonymous edits 476

Suffocation in ash *Source:* https://en.wikipedia.org/w/index.php?oldid=822705510 *License:* Creative Commons Attribution-Share Alike 3.0 *Contributors:* Arildnordby, Audacityxrose, Auric, Certes, Charles Matthews, Doc James, Frietjes, Martarius, Mogism, Oxfordwang, Paradies, PiusImpavidus, Trivialist, WereSpielChequers, 9 anonymous edits 486

Stoning *Source:* https://en.wikipedia.org/w/index.php?oldid=864505983 *License:* Creative Commons Attribution-Share Alike 3.0 *Contributors:* Acalycine, Adavidb, Adrian J. Hunter, Adûnâi, Aetheling, Alexb102072, AllGloryToTheHypnotoad, Anomalocaris, Anti-backwards 21 century homo sapiens civilization, Arrivisto, Bahram.zahir, Basitsheikh, Bender235, Bgwhite, Bishonen, Bishop Morehouse, BobKilcoyne, Callinus, CambridgeBayWeather, Chad j thundercock, Chefassassin, Chris the speller, Closeapple, ClueBot NG, Cold-scarface, Coreybchapman, Cplakidas, DMacks, David.moreno72, Davidmerfield, DeNTisTaWy, Dewritech, Disciple4lif, Doc James, Donner60, Dorpater, Dwo, Eperoton, Equinox, Eric Kvaalen, EvergreenFir, Faizan, Flyer22 Reborn, Gejyspa, Gilliam, Gnostics, GrahamZC, HaeB, Haminoon, Hippo43, Home Lander, Human10.0, IOHANNVSVERVS, IRISZOOM, Ilham Jenor, InedibleHulk, InfoFlaminjo, Iridescent, Jeff5102, Jessicapierce, Jimw338, Jodosma, Joefromrandb, JzG, KTo288, Khoshhat, Kku, Krzyhorse22, L3X1, LilHelpa, LouisAragon, Lumpasina, MagicatthemovieS, Magioladitis, MarginalCost, Markos37, MehrdadFR, Mizzymaaz, Mogism, Motivação, Mr. Yondris Ferguson, Muhammed Kabir, My Chemistry romantic, Narky Blert, NebY, NinjaRobotPirate, Onel5969, Oranjelo100, Ottawahitech, PaleoNeonate, Patapsco913, Pincrete, Prof. Mc, QPT, Qizilbash123, RLoutfy, Rarevogel, Redmat85, Regulov, Rentier, Rupert loup, ScrapIronIV, Seraphimblade, Sheila Ki Jawani, Sheila1988, Shellwood, Signedzzz, Spacecowboy420, Spudst3r, Stevenmitchell, SummerPhD, SuperHamster, Tassedethe, Underlying lk, Valley2city, Wavelength, Widr, Yamaguchi先生 , Youmehim, Zimmygirl7, 130 anonymous edits 487

Strangling *Source:* https://en.wikipedia.org/w/index.php?oldid=863968196 *License:* Creative Commons Attribution-Share Alike 3.0 *Contributors:* -Marcus-, 16@r, Adeliine, Andries, Aoi is great for rectal probing, Arcadian, AzaToth, BD2412, Barticus88, Beach drifter, Bhadani, Boneyard90, Bubbajaxn, Chris Bulgin, ClueBot NG, Ctxppc, Dagonet, Daniellagreen, Danthemango, DerHexer, DocWatson42, Donfbreed, Donreed, Drmies, EEng, ESkog, Esowteric, Evercat, Ex nihil, FFXFan1991, Falcon8765, Fifth Rider, Finnancier, Flyer22 Reborn, Formol, Gadget850, Gaius Cornelius, GreenC, Groovenstein, Gunmetal Angel, Gwern, Hairy Dude, Harvey Milligan, Hux, Imransabri, Ithinkicahn, J04n, JJL, JakobSteenberg, Jarble, Jarke, Jim1138, Jmlk17, Jodosma, JoeBlogsDord, John, Jrgorilla1, Jtle515, Kant66, Kauczuk, Kayau, Kennethmaage, KnowledgeOfSelf, Le Deluge, Lean n mean, Leeroy1981, Ligulem, Lotusflower77, Mariomassone, Montanabw, Mooncow, Mumbo-jumbophobe, Nathanael Bar-Aur L., NellieBly, Onorem, Paul 1953, Petter Haggholm, Picus viridis, Plutonium27, Pol098, Puldis, Qnc, Qwertyxp2000, Ranze, Richard3120, Rmashhadi, Robyn.oster44, Ronhjones, SNIyer12, Sarah Goldberg, SchfiftyThree, Sesesq, Shanes, SimonTrew, Skomorokh, SkyWalker, Soumyasch, TAnthony, TaintedMustard, Tbhotch, The Thing That Should Not Be, Timpo, Vegetarianwikiaddict, Vidor, Wayne Miller, ΨΦΘ, 自扰庸人 , 130 anonymous edits 512

Image Sources, Licenses and Contributors

The sources listed for each image provide more detailed licensing information including the copyright status, the copyright owner, and the license conditions.

Image *Source:* https://en.wikipedia.org/w/index.php?title=File:Padlock-silver.svg *Contributors:* AzaToth, BotMultichill, BotMultichillT, Gurch, Jarekt, Kallerna, Multichill, Perhelion, Rd232, Riana, Sarang, Siebrand, Steinsplitter, 4 anonymous edits 1

Figure 1 *Source:* https://en.wikipedia.org/w/index.php?title=File:Auguste_Vaillant_execution.jpg *License:* Public Domain *Contributors:* Koroesu 3

Figure 2 *Source:* https://en.wikipedia.org/w/index.php?title=File:Jean-Léon_Gérôme_-_The_Christian_Martyrs'_Last_Prayer_-_Walters_37113.jpg *Contributors:* .js, Austriacus, Be..anyone, Boo-Boo Baroo, BotMultichill, Chapeaumelon∼commonswiki, Chatsam, Engelberthumperdink, File Upload Bot (Kaldari), Jarekt, Jed, Johnbod, Leo1pard, Mattes, Mel22, Micione, Oursana, Shakko, Soerfm, Turris Davidica, TwoWings, Túrelio, Wmpearl, Yann, Zolo, 3 anonymous edits 5

Figure 3 *Source:* https://en.wikipedia.org/w/index.php?title=File:Lingchi_(cropped).jpg *License:* Public Domain *Contributors:* Badzil, Camilo324, DivadH, Foroa, Sheitan, Trijnstel, Underwaterbuffalo, Varlaam, WhisperToMe, Wikieditoroftoday, Yann, 維基小霸王 , 13 anonymous edits 6

Figure 4 *Source:* https://en.wikipedia.org/w/index.php?title=File:Rohrbach-verbrennung-1525.jpg *License:* Public Domain *Contributors:* AnRo0002, Auntieruth55, Bohème, FA2010, Julien Demade, Man vyi, Off-shell, Pp.paul.4, Rosenzweig, Schmelzle, Shakko, Werieth, Wieralee, Wst, Wuselig, ペーター 8

Figure 5 *Source:* https://en.wikipedia.org/w/index.php?title=File:Lamanie_kolem_L_001xx.jpg *License:* Public Domain *Contributors:* pl:Pierre Larousse; Original uploader was Dixi at pl.wikipedia 8

Figure 6 *Source:* https://en.wikipedia.org/w/index.php?title=File:Beccaria_-_Dei_delitti_e_delle_pene_-_6043967_A.jpg *Contributors:* Beccaria, Cesare 9

Figure 7 *Source:* https://en.wikipedia.org/w/index.php?title=File:Mexican_execution,_1914.jpg *License:* Public Domain *Contributors:* Hilohello, Quibik, Skimel, Struthious Bandersnatch, Thelmadatter 10

Figure 8 *Source:* https://en.wikipedia.org/w/index.php?title=File:German_announcement_General_Government_Poland_1944.jpg *License:* Public Domain *Contributors:* German nazi security police (de: Sicherheitspolizei, SiPo) 11

Figure 9 *Source:* https://en.wikipedia.org/w/index.php?title=File:Antanas_Smetona_2.jpg *License:* Creative Commons Attribution-Sharealike 2.5 *Contributors:* Owned by the National Museum of Lithuania 12

Figure 10 *Source:* https://en.wikipedia.org/w/index.php?title=File:SQ_Lethal_Injection_Room.jpg *License:* Public Domain *Contributors:* CACorrections () 14

Figure 11 *Source:* https://en.wikipedia.org/w/index.php?title=File:Leopold_II_as_Grand_Duke_of_Tuscany_by_Joseph_Hickel_1769.jpg *License:* Public Domain *Contributors:* Joseph Hickel 15

Figure 12 *Source:* https://en.wikipedia.org/w/index.php?title=File:Capital_punishment_in_the_world.svg *Contributors:* AKS471883, Ciaurlec, Dank Chicken, Delusion23, Forthrunner, Harry1835, Jedi Friend, LeRoiDesRois, Red Icarus of Jakarta, Sarang, TU-nor, Terrorist96, Turnless, 1 anonymous edits 17

Image *Source:* https://en.wikipedia.org/w/index.php?title=File:Flag_of_the_People's_Republic_of_China.svg *License:* Public Domain *Contributors:* Drawn by User:SKopp, redrawn by User:Denelson83 and User:Zscout370 Recode by cs:User:-xfi- (code), User:Shizhao (colors 18

Image *Source:* https://en.wikipedia.org/w/index.php?title=File:Flag_of_Iran.svg *License:* Public Domain *Contributors:* Various 18

Image *Source:* https://en.wikipedia.org/w/index.php?title=File:Flag_of_Saudi_Arabia.svg *License:* Public Domain *Contributors:* Alhadramy Alkendy, Alkari, Ancintosh, Anime Addict AA, AnonMoos, Bobika, Brian Ammon, CommonsDelinker, Cycn, Denelson83, Duduziq, Ekabhishek, Er Komandante, FDRMRZUSA, Fabioravanelli, File Upload Bot (Magnus Manske), Fry1989, Gazimagomedov, Herbythyme, Homo lupus, INeverCry, Itsemurhaja, Jeff G., Klemen Kocjancic, Lokal Profil, Love Krittaya, Love monju, Mattes, Menasim, Meno25, Mnmazur, Mohammed alkhater, Nagy, Nard the Bard, Nightstallion, Palosirkka, Pitke, Pmsyyz, Ranveig, Ratatosk, Reisio, Ricordisamoa, Saibo, Sarang, SiBr4, Wouterhagens, Zscout370, Zyido, 17 anonymous edits 18

Image *Source:* https://en.wikipedia.org/w/index.php?title=File:Flag_of_Iraq.svg *License:* Public Domain *Contributors:* User:Hoshie, User:Militaryace 18

Image *Source:* https://en.wikipedia.org/w/index.php?title=File:Flag_of_Pakistan.svg *License:* Public Domain *Contributors:* User:Zscout370 ... 18

Image *Source:* https://en.wikipedia.org/w/index.php?title=File:Flag_of_Egypt.svg *License:* Public Domain *Contributors:* Open Clip Art 18

Image *Source:* https://en.wikipedia.org/w/index.php?title=File:Flag_of_the_United_States.svg *License:* Public Domain *Contributors:* Anomie, Jo-Jo Eumerus, MSGJ, Mr. Stradivarius 18

Image *Source:* https://en.wikipedia.org/w/index.php?title=File:Flag_of_Somalia.svg *License:* Public Domain *Contributors:* see upload history . 18

Image *Source:* https://en.wikipedia.org/w/index.php?title=File:Flag_of_Bangladesh.svg *License:* Public Domain *Contributors:* User:SKopp ... 18

Image *Source:* https://en.wikipedia.org/w/index.php?title=File:Flag_of_Malaysia.svg *Contributors:* , and 18

Image *Source:* https://en.wikipedia.org/w/index.php?title=File:Flag_of_Afghanistan.svg *Contributors:* 5ko, Aaxelpediaa, Ahmad2099, Alex Great, Alkari, Amateur55, Andres gb.ldc, Ankry, Antonsusi, Avala, Bastique, BotMultichill, BotMultichillT, Cycn, Dancingwombatsrule, Dbenbenn, Denelson83, Denniss, Domhnall, Duduziq, Erlenmeyer, F l a n k e r, Farhod, Frigotoni, Fry1989, Gast32, Golden Bosnian Lily, GoldenRainbow, Happenstance, Henriquebachelor, Herbythyme, Homo lupus, Ilfga, Illegitimate Barrister, Jarekt, Jebulon, JoaoPedro10029, Khwahan, Klemen Kocjancic, Koefbac, Kookaburra, Lokal Profil, Ludger1961, Lumia1234, MPF, Mattes, MrPanyGoff, Myself488, Neq00, Nersy, Nightstallion, O, Orange Tuesday, Palosirkka, Prev, RainbowSilver, Rainforest tropicana, Reisio, Ricordisamoa, Rocket000, Sangjinhwa, Sarang, Sarilho1, SiBr4, Smaug the Golden, Smooth O, Sojah, Solar Police, Stasyan117, SteveGOLD, Stewi101015, Supreme Dragon, TFerenczy, Tabasco∼commonswiki, Tcfc2349, Unma.af, VulpesVulpes42, Zscout370, \\'arrior 786, Şêr, ייחל'ייושמר, 李煊洋 567, 33 anonymous edits 18

Image *Source:* https://en.wikipedia.org/w/index.php?title=File:Flag_of_Belarus.svg *License:* Public Domain *Contributors:* Zscout370 18

Image *Source:* https://en.wikipedia.org/w/index.php?title=File:Flag_of_Indonesia.svg *License:* Public Domain *Contributors:* User:SKopp 18

Image *Source:* https://en.wikipedia.org/w/index.php?title=File:Flag_of_Singapore.svg *License:* Public Domain *Contributors:* Various 18

Image *Source:* https://en.wikipedia.org/w/index.php?title=File:Flag_of_Japan.svg *License:* Public Domain *Contributors:* Anomie, Jo-Jo Eumerus 18

Image *Source:* https://en.wikipedia.org/w/index.php?title=File:Flag_of_Nigeria.svg *License:* Public Domain *Contributors:* User:Jhs 18

Image *Source:* https://en.wikipedia.org/w/index.php?title=File:Flag_of_Palestine.svg *License:* Public Domain *Contributors:* Orionist, previous versions by Makaristos, Mysid, etc. 18

Image *Source:* https://en.wikipedia.org/w/index.php?title=File:Flag_of_Sudan.svg *License:* Public Domain *Contributors:* Vzb83 19

Image *Source:* https://en.wikipedia.org/w/index.php?title=File:Flag_of_Botswana.svg *License:* Public Domain *Contributors:* Andres gb.ldc, Antemister, Benzoyl, Blackcat, Cathy Richards, Charlesjsharp, Cycn, Denelson83, Fry1989, Gabbe, GoldenRainbow, HoheHoffnungen, Ilfga, Klemen Kocjancic, Koefbac, Madden, Mattes, Neq00, Reisio, Rodejong, SKopp, Sangjinhwa, Sarang, Smaug the Golden, Stasyan117, TFerenczy, ThomasPusch, Torstein, Xoristzatziki, Zscout370, 1 anonymous edits 19

Image *Source:* https://en.wikipedia.org/w/index.php?title=File:Flag_of_the_Republic_of_China.svg *License:* Public Domain *Contributors:* User:SKopp 19

Image *Source:* https://en.wikipedia.org/w/index.php?title=File:Flag_of_North_Korea.svg *License:* Public Domain *Contributors:* Anime Addict AA, Bodhisattwa, EugeneZelenko, FDRMRZUSA, FSII, Fastily, FieldMarine, Fred J, Fry1989, Haha169, HapHaxion, Homo lupus, Hongtiezhu, Illegitimate Barrister, Kleinstein95, Klemen Kocjancic, LoveToGamer, Ludger1961, MAXXX-309, Mattes, Metrónomo, Neq00, Pjotr Ligthart, R-41∼commonswiki, RainbowSilver2ndBackup, Ricordisamoa, Rory096, Sarang, SiBr4, SomeDudeWithAUserName, ThomasPusch, Toben, Trijnstel, Túrelio, VAIO HK, Valentim, Waddie96, Zscout370, 42 anonymous edits 19

Image *Source:* https://en.wikipedia.org/w/index.php?title=File:Flag_of_South_Sudan.svg *License:* Public Domain *Contributors:* User:Achim1999 19

Image *Source:* https://en.wikipedia.org/w/index.php?title=File:Flag_of_Vietnam.svg *License:* Public Domain *Contributors:* Lưu Ly vẽ lại theo nguồn trên 19

Figure 13 *Source:* https://en.wikipedia.org/w/index.php?title=File:Death_penalty_in_the_United_States.svg *Contributors:* User:JayCoop 20

Figure 14 *Source:* https://en.wikipedia.org/w/index.php?title=File:CKS_Airport_drugs_sign.JPG *License:* Public Domain *Contributors:* User:Jiang 24

Figure 15 *Source:* https://en.wikipedia.org/w/index.php?title=File:Karl_Morgenschweis_prays_for_Franz_Strasser.jpg *License:* Public Domain *Contributors:* US Army photographers on behalf of the OCCWC 26

Figure 16 *Source:* https://en.wikipedia.org/w/index.php?title=File:Timothy_Evans_Grave.JPG *License:* Public Domain *Contributors:* Adebarry∼enwiki, Nabokov, Stevingtonian, 1 anonymous edits 28

Figure 17 *Source:* https://en.wikipedia.org/w/index.php?title=File:04CFREU-Article2-Crop.jpg *License:* Creative Commons Attribution 3.0 *Contributors:* Trounce 29

Figure 18 *Source:* https://en.wikipedia.org/w/index.php?title=File:ICCPR-OP2_members.svg *Contributors:* User:Forthrunner 30
Image *Source:* https://en.wikipedia.org/w/index.php?title=File:Wikinews-logo.svg *License:* Creative Commons Attribution-Sharealike 3.0 *Contributors:* Vectorized by Simon 01:05, 2 August 2006 (UTC) Updated by Time3000 17 April 2007 to use official Wikinews colours and ap 32
Image *Source:* https://en.wikipedia.org/w/index.php?title=File:Commons-logo.svg *License:* logo *Contributors:* Anomie, Callanecc, CambridgeBay-Weather, Jo-Jo Eumerus, RHaworth 32
Image *Source:* https://en.wikipedia.org/w/index.php?title=File:Wikiquote-logo.svg *License:* Public Domain *Contributors:* Rei-artur 32
Image *Source:* https://en.wikipedia.org/w/index.php?title=File:Wikisource-logo.svg *License:* Creative Commons Attribution-Sharealike 3.0 *Contributors:* ChrisiPK, Guillom, INeverCry, Jarekt, JuTa, Leyo, Lokal Profil, MichaelMaggs, NielsF, Rei-artur, Rocket000, Romaine, Steinsplitter 36
Figure 19 *Source:* https://en.wikipedia.org/w/index.php?title=File:Execution_of_Henry_Wirz.jpg *Contributors:* Bohème, Calliopejen1, Catsmeat, Eoghanacht, Evrik, Ibagli, Jmabel, Man vyi, Mangoman88, Martin H., Mjrmtg, Mtsmallwood, Slowking4, TheDJ 38
Figure 20 *Source:* https://en.wikipedia.org/w/index.php?title=File:Pisanello_010.jpg *License:* Public Domain *Contributors:* Aavindraa, Andrea-sPraefcke, File Upload Bot (Eloquence), GMLSX, Infrogmation, Jbribeiro1, Mattes, OrbiliusMagister, Sailko, StromBer, Warburg, Wolfmann, Zhuyifei1999 38
Figure 21 *Source:* https://en.wikipedia.org/w/index.php?title=File:Biskupia_Gorka_executions_-_14_-_Barkmann,_Paradies,_Becker,_Klaff,_Steinhoff_(left_to_right).jpg *License:* Public Domain *Contributors:* Austrianbird, Gkml, Spiritus Rector, Tm 39
Figure 22 *Source:* https://en.wikipedia.org/w/index.php?title=File:Hromadná_poprava_Srbů.jpg *Contributors:* Anonimski, Boris Dimitrov, John commons, Lotje, Marcus Cyron, Miaow Miaow, Nameless23, Niklas 555, Sorabino, Zoupan, 4 anonymous edits 40
Figure 23 *Source:* https://en.wikipedia.org/w/index.php?title=File:KetchumDecapitated.jpg *License:* Public Domain *Contributors:* Crusoe8181, File Upload Bot (Magnus Manske), Jcb, OgreBot 2, Quadell, The Man in Question, Themightyquill, 2 anonymous edits 42
Figure 24 *Source:* https://en.wikipedia.org/w/index.php?title=File:Karl_Morgenschweis_prays_for_Franz_Strasser.jpg *License:* Public Domain *Contributors:* US Army photographers on behalf of the OCCWC 42
Figure 25 *Source:* https://en.wikipedia.org/w/index.php?title=File:Giotto_-_Scrovegni_-_-47-_-_Desperation.jpg *License:* Public Domain *Contributors:* Andreagrossmann, AndreasPraefcke, Bukk, Eusebius, G.dallorto, Goldfritha~commonswiki, Graphium, Hekerui, Mattes, Oldrydalian, Olivier, Petrusbarbygere, Sailko, Un1c0s bot~commonswiki, Wst, 3 anonymous edits 44
Figure 26 *Source:* https://en.wikipedia.org/w/index.php?title=File:Anoxicbraininjury.png *Contributors:* User:Doc James 45
Figure 27 *Source:* https://en.wikipedia.org/w/index.php?title=File:Hanged,_drawn_and_quartered.jpg *License:* Public Domain *Contributors:* Gugganji, Jibi44, QWerk, 2 anonymous edits 47
Figure 28 *Source:* https://en.wikipedia.org/w/index.php?title=File:The_Hanging_by_Jacques_Callot.jpg *License:* Public Domain *Contributors:* Botaurus, Brackenheim, Hello world, Johnbod, Merkið, P. S. Burton, Slowking4, Vincent Steenberg 48
Figure 29 *Source:* https://en.wikipedia.org/w/index.php?title=File:WWII_Krakow_-_04.jpg *License:* Public Domain *Contributors:* "Ze zbiorow prywatnych" 50
Figure 30 *Source:* https://en.wikipedia.org/w/index.php?title=File:Bundesarchiv_Bild_101I-031-2436-03A,_Russland,_Hinrichtung_von_Partisanen.jpg *License:* Creative Commons Attribution-Sharealike 3.0 Germany *Contributors:* BotMultichill, Origamiemensch, Poeticbent, RMHED, Thgoiter, Thorjoetunheim, Timeshifter, 1 anonymous edits 51
Figure 31 *Source:* https://en.wikipedia.org/w/index.php?title=File:The_hanging_of_two_participants_in_the_Indian_Rebellion_of_1857..jpg *License:* Public Domain *Contributors:* Denniss, JMCC1, Primaler, Roland zh, Sridhar1000 52
Figure 32 *Source:* https://en.wikipedia.org/w/index.php *License:* Attribution *Contributors:* Edoderoo, Hansmuller, PawełMM 55
Figure 33 *Source:* https://en.wikipedia.org/w/index.php?title=File:Eli_Cohen.jpg *License:* Public Domain *Contributors:* Bohème, BotMultichill, Chesdovi, Lotje, Sanandros, Tarawneh, Zero0000, Ö, חובבשירה 57
Figure 34 *Source:* https://en.wikipedia.org/w/index.php?title=File:Witches_Being_Hanged.jpg *License:* Public Domain *Contributors:* Unknown. 59
Figure 35 *Source:* https://en.wikipedia.org/w/index.php?title=File:Balvenie_Pillar_2017-05-27.jpg *Contributors:* User:Schwerdf 59
Figure 36 *Source:* https://en.wikipedia.org/w/index.php?title=File:ExecutionNoose.JPG *License:* Creative Commons Attribution-Sharealike 3.0 *Contributors:* Nabokov (talk). 60
Figure 37 *Source:* https://en.wikipedia.org/w/index.php?title=File:Execution_Lincoln_assassins.jpg *Contributors:* 1Veertje, Ashkan P., BotMultichill, CommonsDelinker, Dinosaurioamarillo, Diwas, GDK, Groupsixty, Hansmuller, Howcheng, Jebulon, Jupiter-Perfect, Marc Kupper, Mogelzahn, Nis Hoff, Nnhyttin, Sammyday, SecretName101, Wstrwald, 2 anonymous edits 61
Figure 38 *Source:* https://en.wikipedia.org/w/index.php?title=File:Picture_of_inverted_hanging.png *Contributors:* Johann Stumpf (Life time: fl 1589) 62
Figure 39 *Source:* https://en.wikipedia.org/w/index.php?title=File:Blake_after_John_Gabriel_Stedman_Narrative_of_a_Five_Years_copy_2_object_2-detail.jpg *License:* Public Domain *Contributors:* Dmitrismirnov, Sadads 66
Figure 40 *Source:* https://en.wikipedia.org/w/index.php?title=File:BatistaFireSquad.jpg *License:* Public Domain *Contributors:* Unknown photographer, now held by Imagno. 68
Figure 41 *Source:* https://en.wikipedia.org/w/index.php?title=File:Map_of_US_lethal_injection_usage.svg *License:* Creative Commons Attribution-Sharealike 2.5 *Contributors:* Blackfish, Huntster, Ibagli, Jatkins, Lokal Profil, MissMJ, Sarang, Timeshifter, Wknight94, Xnux, 5 anonymous edits 75
Figure 42 *Source:* https://en.wikipedia.org/w/index.php?title=File:SQ_Lethal_Injection_Room.jpg *License:* Public Domain *Contributors:* CACorrections () 75
Figure 43 *Source:* https://en.wikipedia.org/w/index.php?title=File:National_Museum_of_Crime_and_Punishment_-_Delaware_lethal_injection_machine_(2868729627).jpg *License:* Creative Commons Attribution 2.0 *Contributors:* David from Washington, DC 76
Figure 44 *Source:* https://en.wikipedia.org/w/index.php?title=File:Florida_electric_chair.jpg *License:* Public Domain *Contributors:* Oaktree b, OgreBot 2 93
Figure 45 *Source:* https://en.wikipedia.org/w/index.php *License:* Public Domain *Contributors:* Fountains of Bryn Mawr, OgreBot 2 93
Figure 46 *Source:* https://en.wikipedia.org/w/index.php?title=File:Harold_Pitney_Brown_edison_electrocute_horse_1888_New_York_Medico-Legal_Journal_vol_6_issue_4.png *License:* Public Domain *Contributors:* Fountains of Bryn Mawr, OgreBot 2 96
Figure 47 *Source:* https://en.wikipedia.org/w/index.php?title=File:Kemmler_exécuté_par_l'électricité.jpg *Contributors:* Jospe 97
Figure 48 *Source:* https://en.wikipedia.org/w/index.php?title=File:Map_of_US_electric_chair_usage.svg *License:* Creative Commons Attribution-Sharealike 2.5 *Contributors:* Ibagli, Laberkiste, Lokal Profil, MissMJ, Sarang, Shadowlink1014~commonswiki, Timeshifter, Wikieditoroftoday, 1 anonymous edits 99
Figure 49 *Source:* https://en.wikipedia.org/w/index.php?title=File:RedHatsExecutionChamber.jpg *License:* Creative Commons Attribution-Sharealike 2.0 *Contributors:* Lee Honeycutt from Angola, LA, USA 100
Figure 50 *Source:* https://en.wikipedia.org/w/index.php?title=File:Majdanek_Komora_Gazowa.JPG *License:* Creative Commons Attribution-Share Alike *Contributors:* Cezary p 105
Figure 51 *Source:* https://en.wikipedia.org/w/index.php?title=File:Map_of_US_gas_chamber_usage.svg *License:* Creative Commons Attribution-Sharealike 2.5 *Contributors:* Laberkiste, Lokal Profil, MissMJ, Sarang, Timeshifter, 1 anonymous edits 107
Figure 52 *Source:* https://en.wikipedia.org/w/index.php?title=File:PostFurmanUSGasChamber.gif *License:* Public Domain *Contributors:* Darth Kalwejt 107
Figure 53 *Source:* https://en.wikipedia.org/w/index.php?title=File:Santa_Fe_gas_chamber.jpg *License:* Creative Commons Attribution 3.0 *Contributors:* Shelka04 at en.wikipedia 109
Figure 54 *Source:* https://en.wikipedia.org/w/index.php?title=File:Gaschamber.jpg *License:* Public Domain *Contributors:* California Department of Corrections 110
Image *Source:* https://en.wikipedia.org/w/index.php?title=File:Decapitación_de_San_Pablo_-_Simonet_-_1887.jpg *License:* Public Domain *Contributors:* Auric, BotMultichill, Carolus, Deskana, Frank C. Müller, Ixtzib, Jbribeiro1, Smnt, Tiberioclaudio99, Tm, 5 anonymous edits 111
Figure 55 *Source:* https://en.wikipedia.org/w/index.php?title=File:Froissart_Chronicles,_execution.jpg *License:* Public Domain *Contributors:* Albedo-ukr, Alonso de Mendoza, DieBuche, Frank C. Müller, Il Dottore, Jheald, MGA73, Mel22, Shakko, Themightyquill, William Jexpire, 1 anonymous edits 112
Figure 56 *Source:* https://en.wikipedia.org/w/index.php?title=File:Lapa_do_Santo_-_Sepultamento_26_-_Visualizacao_esquematica_da_decapitação.jpg *Contributors:* Joalpe 112
Figure 57 *Source:* https://en.wikipedia.org/w/index.php?title=File:Traditional_Ethiopian_picture.jpg *License:* Public Domain *Contributors:* Frank C. Müller, G.dallorto, Janweh64, Johnbod, Llywrch, Ranveig, Shakko, Themightyquill, Zheim~commonswiki 113
Figure 58 *Source:* https://en.wikipedia.org/w/index.php?title=File:Beheading.jpg *License:* Public Domain *Contributors:* Alonso de Mendoza, Bukk, Frank C. Müller, Kocio, RobertLechner, Shakko, Themightyquill 114
Figure 59 *Source:* https://en.wikipedia.org/w/index.php?title=File:Anne_Boleyn_London_Tower.jpg *License:* Public Domain *Contributors:* Alonso de Mendoza, Aylaross, Bohème, BotMultichillT, Bukk, Cathy Richards, Hilohello, Mattes, Otourly, Shakko, Verica Atrebatum, 2 anonymous edits 114
Figure 60 *Source:* https://en.wikipedia.org/w/index.php?title=File:CosmasDamianfraangelico.jpg *License:* Public Domain *Contributors:* Bohème, Mauro do Carmo~commonswiki, OgreBot 2, Shakko, Xenophon 116
Figure 61 *Source:* https://en.wikipedia.org/w/index.php?title=File:Heads_on_pikes.jpg *License:* Public Domain *Contributors:* ChrisO~enwiki, Tomas Tso, 1 anonymous edits 118

Figure 62 *Source:* https://en.wikipedia.org/w/index.php?title=File:Auguste_Vaillant_execution.jpg *License:* Public Domain *Contributors:* Koroesu 120

Figure 63 *Source:* https://en.wikipedia.org/w/index.php?title=File:Ambrogio_Lorenzetti_005.jpg *License:* Public Domain *Contributors:* Aavindraa, AndreasPraefcke, Aotake, Carolus, Diligent, File Upload Bot (Eloquence), G.dallorto, Jbribeiro1, MGA73bot2, Mattes, Pablo Busatto, Wst, Zhuyifei1999, 1 anonymous edits ... 121

Figure 64 *Source:* https://en.wikipedia.org/w/index.php?title=File:Caishikou_Beheaded_Corpses2.jpeg *License:* Public Domain *Contributors:* Cia-Pan, Da Vynci~commonswiki, Olybrius, Popolon, Rédacteur Tibet, Takabeg, Underwaterbuffalo, Wieralee, 1 anonymous edits ... 122

Figure 65 *Source:* https://en.wikipedia.org/w/index.php?title=File:Japanese_Beheading_1894.jpg *License:* Public Domain *Contributors:* Frank C. Müller, Heckenreuter~commonswiki, Hiart, Hilohello, Jjok, PawełMM, Primaler, Ruthven, Shakko, Themightyquill, Y.haruo, 2 anonymous edits ... 123

Figure 66 *Source:* https://en.wikipedia.org/w/index.php?title=File:LeonardGSiffleet.jpg *License:* Public Domain *Contributors:* Ajtnk~commonswiki, Albval, Benzoyl, Brandmeister~commonswiki, ChrisiPK, Cobatfor, Docu, File Upload Bot (Magnus Manske), Hohoho, Hohum, Humboldt, Illegitimate Barrister, JPwargamez, Kl833x9~commonswiki, Manxruler, McZusatz, Morio, Movieevery, Nard the Bard, OgreBot 2, Pa3ems, Royalbroil, Schekinov Alexey Victorovich, Takabeg, Túrelio, Wikieditoroftoday, Worldantiques, 3 anonymous edits ... 124

Figure 67 *Source:* https://en.wikipedia.org/w/index.php?title=File:Beheading_duke_somerset.jpg *License:* Public Domain *Contributors:* Auntof6, Bukk, Cnyborg, Dake~commonswiki, Frank C. Müller, Henxter, Javierme, Mathsci, Mel22, Shakko, Themightyquill, Thomas Gun, Verica Atrebatum, 1 anonymous edits ... 129

Figure 68 *Source:* https://en.wikipedia.org/w/index.php?title=File:BeheadingPanelSBCTajin.JPG *License:* Creative Commons Attribution-Share Alike *Contributors:* AlejandroLinaresGarcia ... 130

Figure 69 *Source:* https://en.wikipedia.org/w/index.php?title=File:Adahoonzou-1793.jpg *License:* Public Domain *Contributors:* Archibad Dalzel 131

Figure 70 *Source:* https//en.wikipedia.org *Contributors:* User:Neuroforever ... 133

Image *Source:* https://en.wikipedia.org/w/index.php?title=File:PD-icon.svg *License:* Public Domain *Contributors:* Alex.muller, Anomie, Anonymous Dissident, CBM, Jo-Jo Eumerus, MBisanz, PBS, Quadell, Rocket000, Strangerer, Timotheus Canens, 1 anonymous edits ... 133

Figure 71 *Source:* https://en.wikipedia.org/w/index.php?title=File:Jamal_al-Din_Husayn_Inju_Shirazi_-_Two_Folios_from_the_Akbarnama_-_Walters_W684_-_Detail_A.jpg *Contributors:* Cpt.a.haddock, File Upload Bot (Kaldari), Gamaliel, Roland zh, Vivek Sarje, ZxxZxxZ ... 136

Figure 72 *Source:* https://en.wikipedia.org/w/index.php?title=File:Execution_by_elephant_distribution_map.svg *License:* Creative Commons Attribution-Sharealike 3.0,2.5,2.0,1.0 *Contributors:* World_map_blank_without_borders.svg: Crates derivative work: Abujoy (talk) ... 137

Figure 73 *Source:* https://en.wikipedia.org/w/index.php?title=File:Le_Toru_Du_MOnde.jpg *Contributors:* Cherubino, Infrogmation, Kneiphof, MilkyWei~commonswiki, Picus viridis, Ramaksoud2000, Shakko, Svajcr, Themightyquill, Un1c0s bot~commonswiki, Wst ... 140

Figure 74 *Source:* https://en.wikipedia.org/w/index.php?title=File:Crushed_by_elephant.png *License:* Public Domain *Contributors:* Robert Knox 141

Figure 75 *Source:* https://en.wikipedia.org/w/index.php?title=File:Execution_of_Prisonsers_Belgrade-Suleymanname.jpg *License:* Public Domain *Contributors:* Matrakci Nasuh ... 143

Image *Source:* https://en.wikipedia.org/w/index.php?title=File:Cscr-featured.svg *License:* GNU Lesser General Public License *Contributors:* Anomie ... 145

Image *Source:* https://en.wikipedia.org/w/index.php?title=File:Symbol_support_vote.svg *License:* Public Domain *Contributors:* Anomie, Fastily, Jo-Jo Eumerus ... 145

Figure 76 *Source:* https://en.wikipedia.org/w/index.php?title=File:Vereshchagin-Blowing_from_Guns_in_British_India.jpg *License:* Public Domain *Contributors:* Botaurus, Butko, Jusjih, Kritkitty, Man vyi, Shakko, Vadakkan, Vizu, 5 anonymous edits ... 151

Figure 77 *Source:* https://en.wikipedia.org/w/index.php?title=File:Sacrificial_scene_on_Hammars_(II).png *License:* Creative Commons Attribution-Sharealike 3.0 *Contributors:* Sacrificial_scene_on_Hammars_(I).JPG: Berig derivative work: The Man in Question (talk) ... 160

Figure 78 *Source:* https://en.wikipedia.org/w/index.php?title=File:Deventer_ketel.jpg *License:* Public Domain *Contributors:* Arch ... 164

Figure 79 *Source:* https://en.wikipedia.org/w/index.php?title=File:Excecution_of_Goemon_Ishikawa.jpg *License:* Public Domain *Contributors:* Aschroet, Daderot, Horst Gräbner, OlEnglish, Sangrila, SunOfErat, Worldantiques, 白拍子花子, 1 anonymous edits ... 165

Figure 80 *Source:* https://en.wikipedia.org/w/index.php?title=File:Pierre_Woeiriot_Phalaris.jpg *License:* Public Domain *Contributors:* Aavindraa, AndreasPraefcke, DenghiùComm, Rotational~commonswiki, Un1c0s bot~commonswiki, Wst ... 168

Figure 81 *Source:* https://en.wikipedia.org/w/index.php?title=File:Spisska_Hrad_048.jpg *License:* Creative Commons Attribution 3.0 *Contributors:* User:JoJan ... 168

Figure 82 *Source:* https://en.wikipedia.org/w/index.php?title=File:EustaceDeathFerdinandi.jpg *License:* Creative Commons Attribution 2.0 *Contributors:* Dickstracke ... 169

Figure 83 *Source:* https://en.wikipedia.org/w/index.php?title=File:17XX_Richtrad_anagoria.JPG *License:* Creative Commons Attribution 3.0 *Contributors:* Anagoria ... 172

Figure 84 *Source:* https://en.wikipedia.org/w/index.php?title=File:Klassisches_Radern.png *License:* Public Domain *Contributors:* Evrik, Lewenstein, Lupo, OgreBot 2, Richardkiwi, 10 anonymous edits ... 173

Figure 85 *Source:* https://en.wikipedia.org/w/index.php?title=File:Städtisches_museum_zittau_-_44.jpg *License:* Creative Commons Attribution-Sharealike 3.0 *Contributors:* User:Z thomas ... 173

Figure 86 *Source:* https://en.wikipedia.org/w/index.php?title=File:Klostermayr_Radbrechmaschine.jpg *License:* Public Domain *Contributors:* Dark Avenger~commonswiki, 7 anonymous edits ... 175

Figure 87 *Source:* https://en.wikipedia.org/w/index.php?title=File:Breaking_Wheel.jpg *License:* Public Domain *Contributors:* Ahellwig, Allforrous, Bellroth, DenghiùComm, DragonflySixtyseven, JMCC1, Ludger1961, OgreBot 2, Oursana, Shakko, StromBer, Syrthiss, Tasja~commonswiki, The Deceiver, Themightyquill, Бериллий, 9 anonymous edits ... 177

Figure 88 *Source:* https://en.wikipedia.org/w/index.php?title=File:Hinrichtung_durch_Rädern,_Skelett.jpg *License:* Creative Commons Attribution-ShareAlike 3.0 *Contributors:* suit verweis=Benutzer Diskussion:Suit ... 179

Figure 89 *Source:* https://en.wikipedia.org/w/index.php?title=File:Coa_Illustration_Cross_Of_St_Catherine.svg *License:* Creative Commons Zero *Contributors:* Madboy74 ... 181

Figure 90 *Source:* https://en.wikipedia.org/w/index.php?title=File:Waldburg-Gebetbuch_096.jpg *License:* Public Domain *Contributors:* AndreasPraefcke, Johnbod ... 181

Figure 91 *Source:* https://en.wikipedia.org/w/index.php?title=File:St-Catherines_College_Oxford_Coat_Of_Arms_(Motto).svg *License:* Creative Commons Attribution-Sharealike 3.0 *Contributors:* User:ChevronTango ... 182

Figure 92 *Source:* https://en.wikipedia.org/w/index.php?title=File:Coat_of_Arms_of_Kremnica.svg *License:* Public Domain *Contributors:* Peter Hanula ... 182

Figure 93 *Source:* https://en.wikipedia.org/w/index.php?title=File:Thetriumphofdeath_-_detail.jpg *License:* Public Domain *Contributors:* Aavindraa, DenghiùComm, Evrik, Ktotam, Mattes, Rocket000, Vincent Steenberg, Zhuyifei1999 ... 183

Figure 94 *Source:* https://en.wikipedia.org/w/index.php?title=File:Radern_(Variante_mit_Eisenstange).png *License:* Public Domain *Contributors:* Bestiasonica, Evrik, Lewenstein, Lupo, Merkið, Saviour1981 ... 184

Figure 95 *Source:* https://en.wikipedia.org/w/index.php?title=File:Kazn_kolesovaniem.jpg *License:* Public Domain *Contributors:* Base, DonaldDuck, Иван Московит ... 184

Figure 96 *Source:* https://en.wikipedia.org/w/index.php?title=File:Cartoucheroué.JPG *License:* Public Domain *Contributors:* Eurodyne, Florival fr, G.dallorto, Jdx, Phildij, 3 anonymous edits ... 185

Figure 97 *Source:* https://en.wikipedia.org/w/index.php?title=File:CalasChapbook.jpg *License:* Public Domain *Contributors:* Carcharoth, Kintetsubuffalo, Ludger1961, Mike Hayes, Olybrius, PawełMM, Rosiestep, Sherurcij, The Deceiver, Wst, 3 anonymous edits ... 185

Figure 98 *Source:* https://en.wikipedia.org/w/index.php?title=File:Hiesel-hinrichtung-1771.jpg *License:* Public Domain *Contributors:* J. G. Will, Augsburg (1771) ... 185

Figure 99 *Source:* https://en.wikipedia.org/w/index.php?title=File:Wiertz_burial.jpg *License:* Public Domain *Contributors:* Alonso de Mendoza, AndreasPraefcke, Bukk, Hekerui, J.delanoy, Jappalang, Javierme, Kilom691, Mattes, Micione, Verica Atrebatum, Wst, Yomangani, 2 anonymous edits 188

Figure 100 *Source:* https://en.wikipedia.org/w/index.php?title=File:Premature_Burial_Vault.JPG *License:* Public Domain *Contributors:* AndreasPraefcke, Askold Ingvarssen, Beao, BotMultichill, Pmcyclist, Verica Atrebatum ... 189

Figure 101 *Source:* https://en.wikipedia.org/w/index.php?title=File:Chinese_civilians_to_be_buried_alive.jpg *License:* Public Domain *Contributors:* User:File Upload Bot (Magnus Manske) ... 190

Figure 102 *Source:* https://en.wikipedia.org/w/index.php?title=File:Anneken_van_den_Hove_te_Brussel_levend_begraven_(Jan_Luyken,_1597).PNG *Contributors:* Jane023, Karmakolle, Kleon3, Lotje, Paulbe, Racconish, 1 anonymous edits ... 191

Figure 103 *Source:* https://en.wikipedia.org/w/index.php?title=File:Codice_Casanatense_Hindu_Burial.jpg *License:* Creative Commons Zero *Contributors:* Joseolgon, Macassar, Wareno ... 194

Figure 104 *Source:* https://en.wikipedia.org/w/index.php?title=File:Avvakum_by_Pyotr_Yevgenyevich_Myasoyedov.jpg *License:* Public Domain *Contributors:* Blacklake, BotMultichill, Deodar~commonswiki, Mattes, Meistaru 10, Schekinov Alexey Victorovich, Sealle, Shakko, VladiMens, Оркрист, Чрьный человек ... 201

Figure 105 *Source:* https://en.wikipedia.org/w/index.php?title=File:Bardo_National_Museum_tanit.jpg *License:* Creative Commons Attribution-Sharealike 2.0 *Contributors:* Sarah Murray ... 204

Figure 106 *Source:* https://en.wikipedia.org/w/index.php?title=File:Filip2_albigensti.jpg *License:* Public Domain *Contributors:* Acoma, Mel22 206

Figure 107 *Source:* https://en.wikipedia.org/w/index.php?title=File:Templars_Burning.jpg *License:* Public Domain *Contributors:* AndreasPraefcke, Andrew Gray, Bohème, Butko, Darsie, Elonka, G.dallorto, Jheald, Jibi44, Johnbod, Judithcomm, Lotje, Mattes, Mel22, Moeby1, Olivier, Paris 16, Pline, Quibik, Shakko, Siren-Com, Thuresson, Un1c0s bot~commonswiki, 1 anonymous edits 206
Figure 108 *Source:* https://en.wikipedia.org/w/index.php?title=File:Jews_burned_to_death_in_Strasbourg_Feb._14_1349_during_the_Black_Death.jpg *License:* Public Domain *Contributors:* Anonymous Medieval drawing (Life time: circa 1375) 207
Figure 109 *Source:* https://en.wikipedia.org/w/index.php?title=File:Witch-scene4.JPG *License:* Public Domain *Contributors:* BotMultichill, Brackenheim, Mu, PulkoCitron~commonswiki, 1 anonymous edits 209
Figure 110 *Source:* https://en.wikipedia.org/w/index.php?title=File:Burning_of_Sodomites.jpg *License:* Public Domain *Contributors:* Bernd Schwabe in Hannover, Bibi Saint-Pol, Caveman80, Dsmdgold, G.dallorto, GeorgHH, Jheald, Jibi44, Lysis~commonswiki, Mel22, Ophelia Bogner, Outsider80, Parpan05, Rd232, Shakko, Sidonius, SunOfErat, Un1c0s bot~commonswiki, Vg25es~commonswiki, Vinom, Wolfmann, Wuselig, 5 anonymous edits 211
Figure 111 *Source:* https://en.wikipedia.org/w/index.php?title=File:Augsburg-Perlachkirche.jpg *License:* GNU Free Documentation License *Contributors:* Dark Avenger~commonswiki, Kurpfalzbilder.de, MGA73bot2, NeverDoING, Olivier, Timo Beil, 1 anonymous edits 212
Figure 112 *Source:* https://en.wikipedia.org/w/index.php?title=File:Wickiana5.jpg *License:* Public Domain *Contributors:* Johann Jakob Wick 213
Figure 113 *Source:* https://en.wikipedia.org/w/index.php?title=File:Jan_Hus_at_the_Stake.jpg *License:* Public Domain *Contributors:* Janíček Zmilelý z Písku 214
Figure 114 *Source:* https://en.wikipedia.org/w/index.php?title=File:Stilke_Hermann_Anton_-_Joan_of_Arc's_Death_at_the_Stake.jpg *License:* Public Domain *Contributors:* Bohème, BotMultichillT, Jarekt, Mabrndt, Micione, Olivier, Olpl, Shakko, Slomox, Tangopaso, 1 anonymous edits 215
Figure 115 *Source:* https://en.wikipedia.org/w/index.php?title=File:Execution_of_Mariana_de_Carabajal.jpg *License:* Public Domain *Contributors:* Foroa, Hilohello, Liftarn, Marrovi, Nacasma, OgreBot 2, Tyk, 1 anonymous edits 218
Figure 116 *Source:* https://en.wikipedia.org/w/index.php?title=File:Modocs_Scalping_and_Torturing_Prisoners.jpg *License:* Public Domain *Contributors:* AnRo0002, File Upload Bot (Magnus Manske), OgreBot 2, 1 anonymous edits 219
Figure 117 *Source:* https://en.wikipedia.org/w/index.php?title=File:Pierre_Woeiriot_Phalaris.jpg *License:* Public Domain *Contributors:* Aavindraa, AndreasPraefcke, DenghiùComm, Rotational~commonswiki, Un1c0s bot~commonswiki, Wst 224
Figure 118 *Source:* https://en.wikipedia.org/w/index.php?title=File:GeorgheDoja.jpg *License:* Public Domain *Contributors:* AndreasPraefcke, CristianChirita, Hello world, Mutter Erde, OsamaK, Paul Barlow, Pe-Jo, Un1c0s bot~commonswiki, Wst 225
Figure 119 *Source:* https://en.wikipedia.org/w/index.php?title=File:A_Hindoo_Widow_Burning_Herself_with_the_Corpse_of_her_Husband.jpg *License:* Public Domain *Contributors:* Clusternote, Infrogmation, Ranveig, Yann, 2 anonymous edits 229
Figure 120 *Source:* https://en.wikipedia.org/w/index.php?title=File:Burning_of_a_Widow.jpg *License:* Public Domain *Contributors:* User:Immanuel Giel 230
Figure 121 *Source:* https://en.wikipedia.org/w/index.php?title=File:Christ_at_the_Cross_-_Cristo_en_la_Cruz.jpg *License:* Public Domain *Contributors:* Goose friend, Kokodyl, Lecen, Leyo, NeverDoING, Obbart, Shakko 251
Figure 122 *Source:* https://en.wikipedia.org/w/index.php?title=File:Santo_Spirito,_sagrestia,_crocifisso_di_michelangelo_04.JPG *License:* Creative Commons Attribution-ShareAlike 3.0 Unported *Contributors:* sailko 252
Image *Source:* https://en.wikipedia.org/w/index.php?title=File:Justus_Lipsius_Crux_Simplex_1629.jpg *License:* Public Domain *Contributors:* Pvasiliadis 254
Image *Source:* https://en.wikipedia.org/w/index.php?title=File:De_Cruci_Libres_Tres_47.jpg *License:* Public Domain *Contributors:* Justus Lipsius 254
Figure 123 *Source:* https://en.wikipedia.org/w/index.php?title=File:CrucifixionSt.Matts.jpg *License:* Creative Commons Attribution-Sharealike 3.0 *Contributors:* Cadetgray 255
Figure 124 *Source:* https://en.wikipedia.org/w/index.php?title=File:Burmese_Dacoits_Readied_for_Execution_by_WW_Hooper_c1880s.jpg *License:* Public Domain *Contributors:* Willoughby Wallace Hooper 257
Image *Source:* https://en.wikipedia.org/w/index.php?title=File:Alexorig.jpg *License:* Public Domain *Contributors:* BotMultichill, DenghiùComm, File Upload Bot (Magnus Manske), Jcb, OgreBot 2, Pieter Kuiper, Soerfm 261
Image *Source:* https://en.wikipedia.org/w/index.php?title=File:Alexamenos_trazo.png *License:* Public Domain *Contributors:* Al2, BotMultichill, DenghiùComm, Wst 261
Figure 125 *Source:* https://en.wikipedia.org/w/index.php?title=File:Japanese_Crucifixion.jpg *Contributors:* Botaurus, Cathy Richards, Daderot, Docu, JMCC1, Russavia, Saforrest, Scewing, TJRC, Tryptofish, 6 anonymous edits 264
Figure 126 *Source:* https://en.wikipedia.org/w/index.php?title=File:ChristianMartyrsOfNagasaki.jpg *License:* Public Domain *Contributors:* Japanese artist, unknown 265
Figure 127 *Source:* https://en.wikipedia.org/w/index.php?title=File:Your_Liberty_Bond_will_help_stop_this_Crisco_restoration_and_colours.jpg *License:* Public Domain *Contributors:* Fernando Amorsolo 267
Figure 128 *Source:* https://en.wikipedia.org/w/index.php?title=File:Punishment_china_1900.jpg *License:* Creative Commons Attribution-Sharealike 2.0 *Contributors:* Hawley C. White, uploaded by David Shapinsky from Washington, D.C., United States 268
Figure 129 *Source:* https://en.wikipedia.org/w/index.php?title=File:Construction_Crucifixion_Homage_to_Mondrian_crop.jpg *License:* Public domain *Contributors:* cropped by H Debussy-Jones (talk) 0645, 21 November 2009 (UTC) 269
Figure 130 *Source:* https://en.wikipedia.org/w/index.php?title=File:Sergey_Solomko_025.JPG *License:* Public Domain *Contributors:* Sergey Solomko (1855 — 1928) 270
Figure 131 *Source:* https://en.wikipedia.org/w/index.php?title=File:Sveti_Kriz_(Novine,_1933._IX._3.).JPG *License:* Public Domain *Contributors:* User:Doncsecz 271
Figure 132 *Source:* https://en.wikipedia.org/w/index.php?title=File:CarFloatLagosDoctores201103.jpg *License:* Creative Commons Attribution-Sharealike 3.0 *Contributors:* User:AlejandroLinaresGarcia 271
Figure 133 *Source:* https://en.wikipedia.org/w/index.php?title=File:18960415_antisemitic_political_cartoon_in_Sound_Money.jpg *License:* Public Domain *Contributors:* Watson Heston 272
Figure 134 *Source:* https://en.wikipedia.org/w/index.php?title=File:Protester_tied_to_a_cross_in_Washington_D.C_-_NARA_-_194675.tif *License:* Public Domain *Contributors:* Closeapple, DutchTreat, Esemono, Orrling, 1 anonymous edits 272
Figure 135 *Source:* https://en.wikipedia.org/w/index.php?title=File:Crucifixion_in_San_Fernando,_Pampanga,_Philippines,_easter_2006,_p-ad20060414-12h54m52s-r.jpg *License:* Creative Commons Attribution-ShareAlike 3.0 Unported *Contributors:* Baptiste Marcel 273
Figure 136 *Source:* https://en.wikipedia.org/w/index.php?title=File:Le_Toru_Du_MOnde.jpg *Contributors:* Cherubino, Infrogmation, Kneiphof, MilkyWei~commonswiki, Picus viridis, Ramaksoud2000, Shakko, Svajcr, Themightyquill, Un1c0s bot~commonswiki, Wst 276
Figure 137 *Source:* https://en.wikipedia.org/w/index.php?title=File:Giles_Corey_restored.jpg *License:* Public Domain *Contributors:* Uncle Azane, 1 anonymous edits 278
Figure 138 *Source:* https://en.wikipedia.org/w/index.php?title=File:Seppuku-2.jpg *License:* Public Domain *Contributors:* signed Kunikazu Utagawa (歌川 国員), pupil of Kunisada 280
Figure 139 *Source:* https://en.wikipedia.org/w/index.php?title=File:BNMsFr2643FroissartFol97vExecHughDespenser.jpg *License:* Public Domain *Contributors:* Loyset Liédet 282
Figure 140 *Source:* https://en.wikipedia.org/w/index.php?title=File:Nezahualcoyotl.jpg *Contributors:* Alexis Jazz, Gryffindor, Historym1468, Ptcamn~commonswiki, Usernameunique, Zanhe 283
Figure 141 *Source:* https://en.wikipedia.org/w/index.php?title=File:Dieric_Bouts_013.jpg *License:* Public Domain *Contributors:* Aavindraa, AndreasPraefcke, EDUCA33E, File Upload Bot (Eloquence), Gary Dee, KimChee, Leyo, Mabrndt, Mattes, Missvain, Oursana, Shakko, Stomme~commonswiki, TwoWings, Wolfmann, Wst, Xenophon, Zhuyifei1999, 2 anonymous edits 287
Figure 142 *Source:* https://en.wikipedia.org/w/index.php?title=File:Coyolxauhqui_4095977415_b89d64f008-2.jpg *License:* Creative Commons Attribution-Sharealike 2.0 *Contributors:* miguelão 287
Figure 143 *Source:* https://en.wikipedia.org/w/index.php?title=File:Execution_of_thomas_armstrong_1683.jpg *License:* Public Domain *Contributors:* & Jan Claesz ten Hoorn (printer) 288
Figure 144 *Source:* https://en.wikipedia.org/w/index.php?title=File:Tiradentes_escuartejado_(Tiradentes_supliciado)_by_Pedro_Américo_1893.jpg *License:* Public Domain *Contributors:* BotMultichillT, Bukk, DarwIn, GiFontenelle, Jacopo Werther, RickMorais, The Photographer, Zhuyifei1999, 1 anonymous edits 288
Figure 145 *Source:* https://en.wikipedia.org/w/index.php?title=File:Tupac_amaru_execution.jpg *License:* Public Domain *Contributors:* BotMultichill, Cambalachero, Damiens.rf, Ecummenic, Huhsunqu, Leyo, Skippan, TwoWings, 2 anonymous edits 292
Figure 146 *Source:* https://en.wikipedia.org/w/index.php?title=File:Brunhilda.jpg *License:* Public Domain *Contributors:* Blackcat, Cathy Richards, Cirt, Holt, Obersachse, OgreBot 2, Romain0, Tangopaso, Wst 293
Figure 147 *Source:* https://en.wikipedia.org/w/index.php?title=File:BNMsFr2643FroissartFol97vExecHughDespenser.jpg *License:* Public Domain *Contributors:* Loyset Liédet 299
Figure 148 *Source:* https://en.wikipedia.org/w/index.php?title=File:Drawing_of_William_de_Marisco.jpg *License:* Public Domain *Contributors:* 13th-century chronicler Matthew Paris 300
Figure 149 *Source:* https://en.wikipedia.org/w/index.php?title=File:King_Edward_III_from_NPG.jpg *License:* Public Domain *Contributors:* User:Dcoetzee 301

Figure 150 *Source:* https://en.wikipedia.org/w/index.php?title=File:Traitors_heads_on_old_london_bridge.jpg *License:* Public Domain *Contributors:* artist unknown ... 304
Figure 151 *Source:* https://en.wikipedia.org/w/index.php?title=File:Charles_I_execution,_and_execution_of_regicides.jpg *License:* Public Domain *Contributors:* Caravaggista, Kigsz, Parrot of Doom, 2 anonymous edits ... 305
Figure 152 *Source:* https://en.wikipedia.org/w/index.php?title=File:Execution_of_thomas_armstrong_1683.jpg *License:* Public Domain *Contributors:* & Jan Claesz ten Hoorn (printer) ... 307
Figure 153 *Source:* https://en.wikipedia.org/w/index.php?title=File:Jeremiah_Brandreths_head.jpg *License:* Public Domain *Contributors:* Neale? 309
Figure 154 *Source:* https://en.wikipedia.org/w/index.php?title=File:Last_judgement.jpg *License:* Public Domain *Contributors:* Aavindraa, Alonso de Mendoza, Amandajm, DenghiùComm, Docu, G.dallorto, Hellisp, Kilom691, Kramer Associates, Man vyi, Mattes, Oursana, Pe-Jo, Pko, Shakko, TwoWings, Un1c0s bot~commonswiki, Willemnabuurs, Winterkind, 2 anonymous edits ... 319
Figure 155 *Source:* https://en.wikipedia.org/w/index.php?title=File:Flaying_of_rebels.jpg *License:* Public Domain *Contributors:* DenghiùComm, Geekdiva, Årvasbåo ... 319
Figure 156 *Source:* https://en.wikipedia.org/w/index.php?title=File:Apollo_flaying_Marsyas_by_Antonio_Corradini_(1658-1752),_V&A.JPG *Contributors:* User:Stephencdickson ... 321
Figure 157 *Source:* https://en.wikipedia.org/w/index.php?title=File:Titian_-_The_Flaying_of_Marsyas_-_WGA22909.jpg *License:* Public Domain *Contributors:* Bukk, Marv1N, Mattes, Missvain, Shakko ... 322
Figure 158 *Source:* https://en.wikipedia.org/w/index.php?title=File:The_Judgment_of_Cambyses2_WGA.jpg *License:* Public Domain *Contributors:* AJim, Drewwiki ... 322
Figure 159 *Source:* https://en.wikipedia.org/w/index.php?title=File:Garrote_Execution_-_1901.png *License:* Public Domain *Contributors:* Underwood & Underwood ... 326
Figure 160 *Source:* https://en.wikipedia.org/w/index.php?title=File:Fomfr_garrote.jpg *License:* Creative Commons Attribution-ShareAlike 3.0 Unported *Contributors:* Flominator ... 326
Figure 161 *Source:* https://en.wikipedia.org/w/index.php?title=File:Pedro_Berruguete_Saint_Dominic_Presiding_over_an_Auto-da-fe_1495.jpg *License:* Public Domain *Contributors:* Aavindraa, Alonso de Mendoza, Balbo, BotMultichill, Bukk, Crisco 1492, Eandré, Eleassar, Eugene a, G.dallorto, GDK, JarrahTree, Leinad-Z~commonswiki, Mattes, Outisnn, Sailko, Scottperry, Shakko, Soerfm, Strakhov, Tiberioclaudio99, Túrelio, Zarateman, Лобачев Владимир, 10 anonymous edits ... 327
Figure 162 *Source:* https://en.wikipedia.org/w/index.php?title=File:Gallows_at_Caxton_Gibbet.jpg *License:* Creative Commons Attribution-Share Alike 2.0 Generic *Contributors:* Ardfern, Catsmeat, Crouch, Swale, Man vyi, Saga City, Solipsist~commonswiki ... 331
Figure 163 *Source:* https://en.wikipedia.org/w/index.php?title=File:Hanging_of_William_Kidd.jpg *License:* Public Domain *Contributors:* BeatrixBelibaste, File Upload Bot (Magnus Manske), Kenmayer, Lotje, Magog the Ogre, Man vyi, OgreBot 2, Rsteen ... 331
Figure 164 *Source:* https://en.wikipedia.org/w/index.php?title=File:Fomfr_cage.jpg *License:* Creative Commons Attribution-ShareAlike 3.0 Unported *Contributors:* Flominator ... 332
Figure 165 *Source:* https://en.wikipedia.org/w/index.php?title=File:Corciano-door-tower.jpg *License:* Creative Commons Attribution-Sharealike 3.0,2.5,2.0,1.0 *Contributors:* Fradevel1 ... 333
Figure 166 *Source:* https://en.wikipedia.org/w/index.php?title=File:Gibbet_of_La_Corriveau_(NYPL)_(cropped-2).jpg *License:* Public Domain *Contributors:* BeatrixBelibaste ... 335
Figure 167 *Source:* https://en.wikipedia.org/w/index.php?title=File:Execution_of_Cromwell,_Bradshaw_and_Ireton,_1661.jpg *License:* Public Domain *Contributors:* PeterSymonds, Wutsje, 2 anonymous edits ... 335
Figure 168 *Source:* https://en.wikipedia.org/w/index.php?title=File:Hinrichtung_Joseph_Süss_2.jpg *License:* Public Domain *Contributors:* Andys 336
Figure 169 *Source:* https://en.wikipedia.org/w/index.php?title=File:Combe_jibbet_jan_7_2007_128.jpg *License:* Public Domain *Contributors:* Simon Green eventful ... 338
Figure 170 *Source:* https://en.wikipedia.org/w/index.php?title=File:Mongolian_woman_condemned_to_die_of_starvation_(retouched).jpg *License:* Public Domain *Contributors:* Stéphane Passet (1875-after 1930), on behalf of Albert Kahn (1860-1940) ... 343
Figure 171 *Source:* https://en.wikipedia.org/w/index.php?title=File:Augsburg-Perlachkirche.jpg *License:* GNU Free Documentation License *Contributors:* Dark Avenger~commonswiki, Kurpfalzbilder.de, MGA73bot2, NeverDoING, Olivier, Timo Beil, 1 anonymous edits ... 345
Figure 172 *Source:* https://en.wikipedia.org/w/index.php?title=File:Die_eingemauerte_Nonne.jpg *License:* Public Domain *Contributors:* Achim55, Cecil, Shakko, Simonxag, WolfD59 ... 349
Figure 173 *Source:* https://en.wikipedia.org/w/index.php?title=File:Estonia_Immuration02.JPG *License:* Public Domain *Contributors:* Photograph taken by Mark A. Wilson (Department of Geology, The College of Wooster). ... 351
Figure 174 *Source:* https://en.wikipedia.org/w/index.php?title=File:Thornton_Abbey_Ruins.jpg *License:* Creative Commons Attribution-Share Alike 2.0 Generic *Contributors:* David Wright ... 354
Figure 175 *Source:* https://en.wikipedia.org/w/index.php?title=File:Cesvaine.jpg *License:* Creative Commons Attribution 3.0 *Contributors:* Jānis Sedols ... 355
Figure 176 *Source:* https://en.wikipedia.org/w/index.php?title=File:7sleepersmedievalmanuscript.jpg *License:* Public Domain *Contributors:* 1989, Polylerus, Shakko ... 357
Figure 177 *Source:* https://en.wikipedia.org/w/index.php?title=File:Empalement.jpg *License:* Public Domain *Contributors:* Ashashyou, Cirt, Crazy Ivan, Dencey, DenghiùComm, DocteurCosmos, Finavon, Infrogmation, JMCC1, Lamiot, Mattes, Ruff tuff cream puff, Themightyquill, Wst ... 365
Figure 178 *Source:* https//en.wikipedia.org *Contributors:* User:PJeganathan ... 366
Figure 179 *Source:* https://en.wikipedia.org/w/index.php?title=File:The_Gaunche,_Turkish_capital_punishment.jpg *License:* Public Domain *Contributors:* Joseph Pitton de Tournefort (Life time: 28 December 1708) ... 368
Figure 180 *Source:* https://en.wikipedia.org/w/index.php?title=File:Blake_after_John_Gabriel_Stedman_Narrative_of_a_Five_Years_copy_2_object_2-detail.jpg *License:* Public Domain *Contributors:* Dmitrismirnov, Sadads ... 369
Figure 181 *Source:* https://en.wikipedia.org/w/index.php?title=File:JudeanImpalement_Roaf185.jpg *License:* Public Domain *Contributors:* unknown (Assyrians) ... 371
Figure 182 *Source:* https://en.wikipedia.org/w/index.php?title=File:Impaled.gif *License:* Public Domain *Contributors:* Aavindraa, Ashashyou, Dahn, Dbachmann, File Upload Bot (Magnus Manske), Mhmrodrigues, OgreBot 2, Ruff tuff cream puff, Sphilbrick, Themightyquill ... 376
Figure 183 *Source:* https://en.wikipedia.org/w/index.php?title=File:Torture_of_captain_rosinsky_by_soldies_of_red_army.jpg *License:* Public Domain *Contributors:* CheloVechek, Globetrotter19, HOBOPOCC, Hilohello, Off-shell, OgreBot 2, Ruff tuff cream puff, Saectar, Túrelio, Удивленный1, 2 anonymous edits ... 380
Figure 184 *Source:* https://en.wikipedia.org/w/index.php?title=File:Woodcut_Print_of_Keelhauling.jpg *License:* Public Domain *Contributors:* Finavon, Gueneverey~commonswiki, Kameraad Pjotr, Rsteen, Toyota prius 2~commonswiki, Wouterhagens, Иван Дулин, 4 anonymous edits ... 392
Figure 185 *Source:* https://en.wikipedia.org/w/index.php?title=File:Het_kielhalen_van_de_scheepschirurgijn_van_admiraal_Jan_van_Nes_Rijksmuseum_SK-A-449.jpeg *License:* Public Domain *Contributors:* BotMultichill, Fæ, Revent, Spinster, Vincent Steenberg ... 392
Image *Source:* https://en.wikipedia.org/w/index.php?title=File:GHS-pictogram-skull.svg *License:* Public Domain *Contributors:* A.Spielhoff, Cathy Richards, DrTorstenHenning, Eugenio Hansen, OFS, Leyo, Perhelion, Pierpao, Semtall, Sponk, 2 anonymous edits ... 410
Figure 186 *Source:* https://en.wikipedia.org/w/index.php?title=File:Simple_gravity_pendulum.svg *License:* Public Domain *Contributors:* Chetvorno ... 412
Image *Source:* https://en.wikipedia.org/w/index.php?title=File:PenduloTmg.gif *License:* Creative Commons Attribution-Sharealike 3.0 *Contributors:* User:Ruryk ... 413
Image *Source:* https://en.wikipedia.org/w/index.php?title=File:Oscillating_pendulum.gif *License:* Creative Commons Attribution-Sharealike 3.0 *Contributors:* User:Ruryk ... 413
Image *Source:* https://en.wikipedia.org/w/index.php?title=File:Pendulum_30deg.gif *License:* Public Domain *Contributors:* Lucas V. Barbosa (Kieff) 413
Image *Source:* https://en.wikipedia.org/w/index.php?title=File:Pendulum_60deg.gif *License:* Public Domain *Contributors:* Lucas V. Barbosa (Kieff) 413
Image *Source:* https://en.wikipedia.org/w/index.php?title=File:Pendulum_120deg.gif *License:* Public Domain *Contributors:* Lucas V. Barbosa (Kieff) ... 414
Image *Source:* https://en.wikipedia.org/w/index.php?title=File:Pendulum_170deg.gif *License:* Public Domain *Contributors:* Lucas V. Barbosa (Kieff) ... 414
Figure 187 *Source:* https://en.wikipedia.org/w/index.php?title=File:EastHanSeismograph.JPG *License:* GNU Free Documentation License *Contributors:* Didym, Flickrworker, HenkvD, Lamiot, MGA73bot2, Miaow Miaow, Salsero35, Shizhao, Soerfm, Steinsplitter, WillemBK, Zhuyifei1999, 2 anonymous edits ... 416
Image *Source:* https://en.wikipedia.org/w/index.php?title=File:Huygens_first_pendulum_clock_-_front_view.png *License:* Public Domain *Contributors:* Chetvorno, Karel K., Mdd, Thib Phil ... 417
Image *Source:* https://en.wikipedia.org/w/index.php?title=File:Huygens_first_pendulum_clock.png *License:* Public Domain *Contributors:* Chetvorno, Karel K., Mdd ... 418

Figure 188 *Source:* https://en.wikipedia.org/w/index.php?title=File:Foucault_pendulum_animated.gif *License:* Creative Commons Attribution-ShareAlike 3.0 Unported *Contributors:* DemonDeLuxe (Dominique Toussaint) 420
Image Source: https://en.wikipedia.org/w/index.php?title=File:Grandfather_clock_pendulum.png *License:* Public Domain *Contributors:*   Charles H. Henderson and John F. Woodhull 421
Image Source: https://en.wikipedia.org/w/index.php?title=File:Gaine_Comtoise.jpg *License:* Creative Commons Attribution-Sharealike 3.0,2.5,2.0,1.0 *Contributors:* FrancoisFC 422
Image Source: https://en.wikipedia.org/w/index.php?title=File:Mercury_pendulum.png *License:* Public Domain *Contributors:*   Augustin-Privat Deschanel 422
Image Source: https://en.wikipedia.org/w/index.php?title=File:Tidens_naturlære_fig22.png *License:* Public Domain *Contributors:*   Morten Bisgaard 423
Image Source: https://en.wikipedia.org/w/index.php?title=File:Ellicott_pendulum.png *License:* Public Domain *Contributors:* Augustin-Privat Deschanel 423
Image Source: https://en.wikipedia.org/w/index.php?title=File:Riefler_clock_NIST.jpg *License:* Public Domain *Contributors:* Michael A. Lombardi, Thomas P. Heavner, Steven R. Jefferts 424
Figure 189 *Source:* https://en.wikipedia.org/w/index.php?title=File:Pendulum-with-Escapement.png *License:* Public Domain *Contributors:* Silas Ellisworth Coleman 424
Figure 190 *Source:* https://en.wikipedia.org/w/index.php?title=File:Anchor_escapement_animation_217x328px.gif *License:* Creative Commons Zero *Contributors:* User:Chetvorno 425
Figure 191 *Source:* https://en.wikipedia.org/w/index.php?title=File:Howard_astronomical_regulator_clock.png *License:* Public Domain *Contributors:*   Edward S. Holden 427
Figure 192 *Source:* https://en.wikipedia.org/w/index.php?title=File:BanjoPendulum.png *License:* Public Domain *Contributors:* Leonard G. .. 428
Figure 193 *Source:* https://en.wikipedia.org/w/index.php?title=File:Shortt_Synchronome_free_pendulum_clock.jpg *License:* Public Domain *Contributors:* Chetvorno, Geek3, Karel K. 431
Figure 194 *Source:* https://en.wikipedia.org/w/index.php?title=File:Pendulum2secondclock.gif *License:* Creative Commons Attribution-Sharealike 3.0 *Contributors:* User:Lookang 434
Figure 195 *Source:* https://en.wikipedia.org/w/index.php?title=File:Borda_and_Cassini_pendulum_experiment.png *License:* Public Domain *Contributors:* Jean-Charles de Borda and Jean-Dominique Cassini 435
Figure 196 *Source:* https://en.wikipedia.org/w/index.php?title=File:PenduloCaminos.jpg *License:* Creative Commons Attribution-Sharealike 3.0 *Contributors:* Chetvorno, Duke Q, Luiswqz, Rodelar, Tiberioclaudio99, 5 anonymous edits 437
Figure 197 *Source:* https://en.wikipedia.org/w/index.php?title=File:Kater_pendulum_use.png *License:* Public Domain *Contributors:* Henry Kater 437
Figure 198 *Source:* https://en.wikipedia.org/w/index.php?title=File:Kater_pendulum_vertical.png *License:* Public Domain *Contributors:*   William Watson 438
Figure 199 *Source:* https://en.wikipedia.org/w/index.php?title=File:Using_Kater_pendulum_in_India.png *License:* Public Domain *Contributors:* John Goldingham 439
Figure 200 *Source:* https://en.wikipedia.org/w/index.php?title=File:Repsold_pendulum.png *License:* Public Domain *Contributors:* Halsey Dunwoody 441
Figure 201 *Source:* https://en.wikipedia.org/w/index.php?title=File:Mendenhall_gravimeter_pendulums.jpg *License:* Public Domain *Contributors:*   G. R. Putnam 442
Figure 202 *Source:* https://en.wikipedia.org/w/index.php?title=File:Quartz_gravimeter_pendulums.jpg *License:* Public Domain *Contributors:* US Coast and Geodetic Survey 443
Figure 203 *Source:* https://en.wikipedia.org/w/index.php?title=File:Coupled_oscillators.gif *License:* Public Domain *Contributors:* Lucas V. Barbosa 448
Figure 204 *Source:* https://en.wikipedia.org/w/index.php?title=File:Huygens_synchronization_of_two_clocks_(Experiment).jpg *Contributors:* Tecsie 448
Figure 205 *Source:* https://en.wikipedia.org/w/index.php?title=File:Catedral_Metropolitana,_México,_D.F.,_México,_2013-10-16,_DD_89.JPG *License:* Creative Commons Attribution-Sharealike 3.0 *Contributors:* Ben P L, Look2See1, Poco a poco, WeltDerPhysik 449
Figure 206 *Source:* https://en.wikipedia.org/w/index.php?title=File:Die_Saege.JPG *License:* Public Domain *Contributors:* AndreasPraefcke, Francosalo, Jibi44, Markus3∼commonswiki, Petr Matas, WikipediaMaster, 1 anonymous edits 453
Figure 207 *Source:* https://en.wikipedia.org/w/index.php?title=File:Zersägen_des_Heiligen_Simon.png *License:* Public Domain *Contributors:* Lewenstein, Oursana, Perhelion, Tanzmariechen 455
Figure 208 *Source:* https://en.wikipedia.org/w/index.php?title=File:Bhai_Mati_Das.jpg *License:* Public domain *Contributors:* Bill william compton, OgreBot 2 462
Figure 209 *Source:* https://en.wikipedia.org/w/index.php?title=File:Martyrerp_2.jpg *License:* Public Domain *Contributors:*   Dunwich, FreCha, Happyseeu, Kokodyl, MichaelFrey, Olivier, Rédacteur Tibet, Türelio, Underwaterbuffalo, WhisperToMe, Wikieditoroftoday, 3 anonymous edits 478
Image Source: https://en.wikipedia.org/w/index.php?title=File:Lingchi_(Chinese_characters).svg *License:* Public Domain *Contributors:*   White whirlwind 476
Figure 210 *Source:* https://en.wikipedia.org/w/index.php?title=File:Martyrdom_of_Joseph_Marchand.jpg *License:* Creative Commons Attribution-Sharealike 3.0 *Contributors:* PHGCOM 481
Figure 211 *Source:* https://en.wikipedia.org/w/index.php?title=File:Marx_Reichlich_001.jpg *License:* Public Domain *Contributors:*   Aavindraa, AndreasPraefcke, Auntof6, BotMultichillT, Bukk, EDUCA33E, Emijrp, File Upload Bot (Eloquence), Joseolgon, Mattes, Revent, Sailko, Xenophon, Zhuyifei1999 488
Figure 212 *Source:* https://en.wikipedia.org/w/index.php?title=File:AMH-6977-KB_Virasundara_is_put_to_death.jpg *License:* Public Domain *Contributors:* Lotje 489
Figure 213 *Source:* https://en.wikipedia.org/w/index.php?title=File:Botticcelli,_Sandro_-_The_Punishment_of_Korah_and_the_Stoning_of_Moses_and_Aaron_-_1481-82.jpg *License:* Public Domain *Contributors:*   Adri08, Alonso de Mendoza, Eugene a, Mattes, Sailko, Slowking4 ... 491
Figure 214 *Source:* https://en.wikipedia.org/w/index.php?title=File:Amellie_-_Stoning_of_the_devil_2006_Hajj.jpg *License:* Creative Commons Attribution 2.0 *Contributors:*   Elonka, Grenavitar, Kallewirsch, Look2See1, Rafic.Mufid, Sanandros 493
Figure 215 *Source:* https://en.wikipedia.org/w/index.php?title=File:Sacrificio_azteca.jpg *License:* Public Domain *Contributors:*   Cathy Richards, FA2010, Gospodar svemira, MesserWoland, Türelio 499
Figure 216 *Source:* https://en.wikipedia.org/w/index.php?title=File:A_map_showing_countries_where_public_stoning_is_judicial_or_extrajudicial_form_of_punishment.SVG *Contributors:* User:RLoutfy 499
Figure 217 *Source:* https://en.wikipedia.org/w/index.php?title=File:St_stephen_stoning.jpg *License:* Public Domain *Contributors:* Jebulon .. 507
Figure 218 *Source:* https://en.wikipedia.org/w/index.php?title=File:Cheetah_with_impala.jpg *License:* Creative Commons Attribution 2.0 *Contributors:* Nick Farnhill 513
Figure 219 *Source:* https://en.wikipedia.org/w/index.php?title=File:Gray513.png *License:* Public Domain *Contributors:* Arcadian, Jarekt, Jmarchn, Lipothymia, Outriggr, Raymond, Valdis72, Was a bee, 3 anonymous edits 514
Image Source: https://en.wikipedia.org/w/index.php?title=File:Wiktionary-logo-en-v2.svg *Contributors:* User:Dan Polansky, User:Smurrayinchester 515

License

Creative Commons Attribution-Share Alike 3.0
//creativecommons.org/licenses/by-sa/3.0/

Index

Aaron, 510
Abadeh, 342
Abbasid, 9
Abd al-Rahman al-Awzai, 263
Abdomen, 124, 279, 367
Abdominal distension, 475
Aben Humeya, 464
Abolition, 16
Absolute monarchy, 135
Abu Hanifa, 263
Abū Ḥanīfa, 497
Abu Hurairah, 495
Academica Press, 315
Acceleration of gravity, 412, 414, 418, 430, 433, 444
Accelerometer, 412
Accession of Turkey to the European Union, 31
Accuracy of pendulums as timekeepers, 425
Aceh, 487
Acetylcholine, 79
Achaemenid Empire, 372, 453
Achaemenid Empire .28550.E2.80.93330 BC. 29, 475
Achaemenid Persia, 259
Achan (Bible), 509
Achan (biblical figure), 489
Acidosis, 256
Acolhua, 283, 486
Acquittal, 1
Action T4, 71
Act of Independence of Lithuania, 12
Act of Parliament, 299
Adam Clarke, 554
Adam of Bremen, 65
Adam of Melrose, 164
Adenosine triphosphate, 411
Adolescence, 20
Adolf Eichmann, 54
Adoniram, 509
Adultery, 4, 373, 500, 504
Aelius Marcianus, 398

Ælla of Northumbria, 160, 161

Afghanistan, 18, 153, 487, 500

Africa, 19
African elephant, 137
Afzal Guru, 51
Agapito García Atadell, 329
Age of Enlightenment, 444
Age of Majority, 20
Aggravating factor, 24
Agra, 152
Agrigento, 167
Agrigentum, 223
Agrippina Minor, 400
Ahmadnagar Sultanate, 227
Ahmed I, 461
Aida, 358
Ainslie Embree, 240
Air drag, 412
Air hunger, 514
Air resistance, 425, 430
Airway, 45, 514
Aisha, 496
Aisha Ibrahim Duhulow, 504
Ajmal Kasab, 51
Akbar, 136, 352
Akbarnama, 136
Akbar the Great, 136
Akhenaten, 370
Akira Mutō, 54
Aktion T4, 104
Alabama, 92, 101, 102
Al-Anfal Campaign, 53
Alaric II, 169
Alawite, 56
Albanian Mythology, 352
Albanians, 378
Albert A. Michelson, 442
Albert Camus, 26
Albert Pierrepoint, 43, 58
Albigensian, 327
Alcohol, 73
Alcuronium chloride, 81
Aleksotas, 105
Alexamenos graffito, 256, 261
Alexander Ales, 534
Alexander Falconer Murison, 314

585

Alexander Hamilton (sailor), 137, 138
Alexander II of Russia, 56
Alexander II of Scotland, 164
Alexander Jannaeus, 260
Alexander Pope, 180
Alexander the Great, 143, 260, 294
Alexandre Dumas, 535
Alexis Claude Clairaut, 435
Alfred P. Smyth, 528
Alfred P. Southwick, 92, 93
Alfred the Great, 545
Algeria, 119
Algiers, 222, 368
Alhóndiga de Granaditas, 131
Alice Blunden, 187
Alice Kyteler, 217
Ali Hassan al-Majid, 53
Ali Mohammed Baqir al-Nimr, 267
Ali Pasha of Ioannina, 378
Alkaloid, 79
Allan Quatermain, 475
Allen Lee Davis, 103
Allied-occupied Germany, 50
Alloy, 429
Almería, 464
Al-Mustasim, 226
Al-Mutadid, 9
Al-Numan III ibn al-Mundhir, 142
Aloeus, 321
Al-Shabaab (militant group), 504
Al-Shafii, 263
Altemio Sanchez, 515
Altena, 183
Alternate History, 154
Alternating current, 92, 95
Altiplano, 436
Altona Bloody Sunday, 127
Altona, Hamburg, 127
Ambala, 151
Ambrogio Lorenzetti, 121
American Civil Liberties Union, 25
American Civil War, 69
American Convention on Human Rights, 29
American mafia, 296, 515
American Medical Association, 82, 91
American University, 33
American War of Independence, 311
Amida Buddha, 350
Amina Lawal, 506, 509
Amish, 511
Ammonia, 109
Amnesia: The Dark Descent, 170
Amnesty International, 17, 23, 25–27, 89, 132, 268, 317, 503, 504, 506, 517
Amnesty International USA, 520
Amplitude, 411, 412, 414, 417

Amputation, 286
Amulets, 253
Amy Madison, 325
Amy Tan, 485
Anabaptist, 191, 192, 209, 336
Anal intercourse, 486
Anarkali, 352
Anarkali Bazaar, 352
Anatolia, 456
Anatomical plane, 452
Anchor escapement, 419, 424, 425
Anchorites, 348
Ancien regime, 446
Ancient Carthage, 275
Ancient Egypt, 201, 285
Ancient Greece, 5, 167
Ancient Macedonians, 143, 259
Ancient Rome, 5, 135, 260, 323, 394
Ancient world, 391
Andalusia, 458
Andes, 436
Andorra, 328
Andrei Chikatilo, 69
Andrew Bobola, 323
Andrew Harclay, 1st Earl of Carlisle, 300, 306
Andrey Vlasov, 56
Aneroid barometer, 430
Anesthesia, 80
Anesthesia awareness, 83
Anesthesiologist, 71
Anesthetic, 110
Angel Nieves Diaz, 86
Angle, 414
Anglo-Afghan War, 123
An Historical Relation of the Island Ceylon, 141
Aniene, 456
Animal, 410
Animal euthanasia, 80, 110
An Lushan, 480
An Lushan Rebellion, 6
Annals (Tacitus), 261
Anne Boleyn, 114
Anne of Denmark, 217
Antanas Smetona, 12
Anterior, 376
Anthony van Stralen, Lord of Merksem, 130
Antigone (Sophocles), 356
Antiochus V, 486
Antipas of Pergamum, 169
Antoine Wiertz, 188
Antonia Fraser, 313
Antonia Minor, 344
António José da Silva, 329
Aohan Banner, 483

A Pigeon Sat on a Branch Reflecting on Existence, 170
Apocryphal, 187
Apollo, 321
Apollo (mythology), 322
Apostasy, 504
Apostasy from Islam, 4
Apostasy from Judaism, 488
Apostasy in Islam, 25, 221
Apostles (Christian), 510
Appian Way, 274
Aquarium (Suvorov), 233
Arab Spring, 267
Arbor felix, 260
Archbishop of Armagh, 308
Archimedes principle, 429
Arc lamp, 93
Arcot, 526
Arizona, 43, 80, 108
Arkansas, 80, 92, 100, 102
Armenia, 3, 508
Armenian Genocide, 379
Armenians, 459
Army of the Republic of Bosnia and Herzegovina, 125
Arrack, 227
Arson, 171, 200
Arson in royal dockyards, 16
Artaxerxes II of Persia, 453
Artayctes, 259
Arthur Lucas, 43
As a devotional practice, 258
As a punishment in Islam, 291
Asceticism, 348
Ashurbanipal, 553
Ashur-bel-kala, 372
Ashurnasirpal II, 318, 343, 371
Ashur-uballit I, 553
Asia, 19, 163
Asia Minor, 399
Asian elephant, 135, 137
A Song of Ice and Fire, 324
Asphyxia, 47, 74, 109, 256, 262, 340, 513
Asphyxiant gas, 104, 106
Asphyxiation, 187, 250, 257, 486
Assassin, 529
Assassination of Abraham Lincoln, 60
Assassins, 460
Associated Press, 517
Assyria, 319
Assyrian genocide, 379
A Stoning in Fulham County, 511
Asuhurnasirpal II, 202
Asystole, 79
Atahualpa, 327, 329
Atefeh Sahaaleh, 52
Athanasios Diakos, 379
Athenian, 5
Athens, 167, 223
Atkins v. Virginia, 17
Atmospheric pressure, 421
Atomic clock, 430
Attainder, 164, 545
Attorneys in the United States, 108
Atwater Kent Museum of Philadelphia, 333
Auburn Correctional Facility, 94
Augsburg, 173, 191, 211, 345
Auguste Chapdelaine, 478, 482
Auguste Vaillant, 3, 120
Augusto Pinochet, 233
Augustus, 559
Augustus, Elector of Saxony, 213
Augustus III of Poland, 560
Aulus Gellius, 454
Aum Shinrikyo, 20
Aurangabad, Bihar, 147
Aurangabad, Maharashtra, 151
Aurangzeb, 147, 324, 346, 462
Aurelian, 294
Aurora Mardiganian, 379
Auschwitz, 128
Auschwitz concentration camp, 104
Austen Henry Layard, 378
Aus tiefer Not schrei ich zu dir, 404
Austin E. Lathrop, 97
Austria, 119
Austro-Hungarian, 40
Austro-Hungarian army, 40
Auto da fe, 327
Auto-da-fé, 200, 515
AutoMaidan, 269
Autonomic nervous system, 111
Autopsy, 101
Autos-da-fé, 208
Avenger of blood, 487
Avudaiyarkoil, 366
Avvakum, 201, 214
Awad Hamed al-Bandar, 53
Axe, 129
Ayah, 493
Azerbaijan, 3
Azerbaijani Armed Forces, 122
Azov Battalion, 269
Aztec, 287, 486, 498, 499
Aztec Empire, 275
Aztec mythology, 297, 321
Aztec Triple Alliance, 283

Baal Hammon, 203
Babak Khorramdin, 336
Babur, 147
Babylon, 143

Babylonia, 364
Babylonian King, 200
Babylonian revolt, 372
Baccano, 295
Bad date, 156, 382, 386
Baden, Switzerland, 213
Bad Wimpfen, 284
Bagdad Café, 166
Baghdad, 9
Bahrain, 69
Bahubali The Beginning (2015), 295
Bahubali The Conclusion (2017), 295
Bajrang Dal, 234
Balance wheel, 430, 432
Baldomero Fernández Ladreda, 329
Baldwin II of Jerusalem, 459
Bali, 230
Balkan Wars, 193
Balthasar Gérard, 281
Baltic Sea, 205
Baluchistan, 123
Baluchistan, Pakistan, 503
Bana Mura, 120
Banat, 465
Banda Singh Bahadur, 147
Bandwidth (signal processing), 430
Bangalore, 150
Bangladesh, 18, 21
Banned from Television, 232
Banners of Inner Mongolia, 483
Baptism, 201
Barbarian, 474
Barbary Coast, 458
Barbiturate, 71
Barcelona, 328
Bardhaman, 149
Barnacle, 391
Barnim X, Duke of Pomerania, 307
Baroda, 139
Barometric pressure, 430
Barrackpore, 149
Barrackpore Mutiny of 1824, 150
Barry Cunliffe, 524
Bartolomé de las Casas, 219
Barton Kay Kirkham, 61
Barzan Ibrahim, 53
Barzan Ibrahim al-Tikriti, 43
Basel, 114, 208
Basic Law for the Federal Republic of Germany, 50
Basilika, 403
Basiliscus, 344
Basingstoke, 187
Battle of Alamana, 379
Battle of Alcatraz, 106
Battle of Negropont, 461

Battle of Tewkesbury, 129
Bavaria, 171
Bayonet, 266
Baze v. Rees, 15, 82
BBC News, 91
BBC Online, 199
Bear, 135
Bearded axe, 115
Bee, 475
Beelitz, 208
Beginning of civilizations, 3
Beheading, 23, 375
Beheading video, 132
Behistun Inscription, 372
Beijing, 122, 483
Beirut, 346
Belarus, 18, 67
Belgrade, 143, 379
Bełżec extermination camp, 104
Beneficial organism, 411
Benefit of clergy, 164
Bengal, 229
Benigno Andrade, 329
Benin, 31
Benita von Falkenhayn, 128
Benito Mussolini, 57
Benjamin B. Ferencz, 231
Benjamin of Tudela, 460
Bergen, Lower Saxony, 63
Berkshire, 338
Berlin, 128
Berlin Observatory, 430
Bermuda, 334
Berwick-upon-Tweed, 300
Bessus, 294
Bestiality, 210, 496, 504
Bhai Dayala, 165
Bhai Mati Das, 462
Bible, 372
Biblical Sabbath, 487, 509
Bibliotheca historica, 167
Big Ben, 426
Bihar, 147
Billy Bailey, 61
Bioaccumulate, 410
Biomagnification, 410
Bird Island (Massachusetts), 337
Birds of prey, 147
Bishop of Ossory, 217
Bishops of Jerusalem, 274
Black Death, 172, 208
Black Death (film), 296
Black Death Jewish persecutions, 208
Black market, 50
Black Sun (occult symbol), 269
Blank cartridge, 76, 146

Blasphemy, 5, 488, 504
Blois, 207
Blood, 318
Blood Court, 174
Blood eagle, **160**
Blood libel, 207
Blood money (term), 4
Bloody Code, 10, 309
Blowing from a gun, 14, 69, **145**
Blow torch, 233
Bob (physics), 412, 425, 429
Body fluid, 318
Body snatching, 309
Body Worlds, 321
Bohemia, 192, 373
Boiling, 163
Bolsheviks, 380
Bone, 174
Bone Tomahawk, 296
Bonny, Nigeria, 348
Book of Deuteronomy, 487
Book of Esther, 554
Book of Exodus, 487
Book of Genesis, 202, 487
Book of Jubilees, 202
Book of Leviticus, 487
Book of Numbers, 487
Bosnian mujahideen, 125
Bosphorus, 377
Boston Harbor, 337
Botswana, 19
Boudica, 334
Bowels, 279
Bowling ball, 449
Boyar, 376
Bradycardia, 513
Brahmin, 146, 465
Brain damage, 116, 513
Braindead (film), 296
Brain death, 92
Brain ischemia, 116
Brain stem, 70
Brandenburg, 178
Brass, 428
Braveheart, 296
Brazen bull, **167**, 200, 223
Brazil, 68, 145
Breaking wheel, 3, 8, 64, 98, 139, **171**, 458
Bremen, 165, 356
Breslau, 63
Bride of Chucky, 296
Bridge of Arta, 353
Bridget Cleary, 217
Bristol, 330
Britain and Denmark, 439
British colonization of the Americas, 302

British Empire, 140
British Free Corps, 58
British Isles, 217
British Medical Association, 71
British Raj, 69, 145
Brno, 364
Broken on the wheel, 289, 375
Bronze, 167
Brunhilda of Austrasia, 292
Bruno Tesch (antifascist), 127
Brush (electric), 93
Brush Electrical Machines, 93
Buddhist, 227
Buffalo Bill (character), 324
Buffalo, New York, 92
Buffy the Vampire Slayer (TV series), 324
Buggery, 9
Buggery Act 1533, 9
Bulgarian music, 353
Buncombe County, North Carolina, 188
Buoyancy, 421
Burdunellus, 169, 224
Burglary, 49
Burial, 187
Buried alive, 347, 373
Buried Alive (performance), 195
Burkina Faso, 20
Burma, 137, 227, 266, 269
Burned alive, 394
Burn in effigy, 209
Burning at the stake, 217
Burning of Parliament, 447
Burning of women in England, 216, 298, 301
Burning to Death, 250
Burton Abbott, 106
Burton on Trent, 215
Burundi, 31
Buttocks, 318
Byzantine Empire, 142, 403
Byzantine law, 394
Byzantium, 404

Cabin Fever 2: Spring Fever, 296
Cable tie, 325
Caishikou Execution Grounds, 122
Caithness, 164
Cal Coburn Brown, 80
Calculus, 419
California, 14
California Administrative Procedure Act, 82
California Department of Corrections and Rehabilitation, 82
Caligula, 400, 452, 454
Caliph, 9
Callisthenes, 260
Callistratus (jurist), 203

Call of Duty: Black Ops, 298
Call of Duty: World at War, 298
Callwey Verlag, 472
Cambridge, Massachusetts, 218
Cambridgeshire, 331
Cambyses II of Persia, 323
Camilo José Cela, 328
Camp 22, 106
Camulodunum, 334
Canada, 43
Canadian Broadcasting Corporation, 266
Cannibalism, 121
Cannibals, 166
Cannon, 145
Canon law, 217
Canopic jars, 285
Cantonese, 477
Cantonment, 526
Canton of Zürich, 459
Capital and corporal punishment in Judaism, 490
Capital murder, 58
Capital offence, 59
Capital punishment, 1, **1**, 36, 37, 48, 51, 67, 71, 92, 111, 113, 118, 135, 160, 167, 190, 250, 275, 279, 316, 340, 364, 474, 486, 487
Capital Punishment Amendment Act 1868, 311
Capital punishment debate in the United States, 12
Capital punishment in Afghanistan, 22
Capital punishment in Australia, 12
Capital punishment in Bangladesh, 3
Capital punishment in Belarus, 12, 19, 23, 30, 31
Capital punishment in Botswana, 12
Capital punishment in Brazil, 12
Capital punishment in Canada, 12
Capital punishment in China, 3, 6, 71
Capital punishment in Egypt, 22
Capital punishment in Europe, 19
Capital punishment in Guatemala, 12, 23, 71
Capital punishment in India, 3, 12, 18, 22
Capital punishment in Indonesia, 3, 23, 69
Capital punishment in Iran, 22
Capital punishment in Iraq, 22
Capital punishment in Japan, 3, 12, 18, 22
Capital punishment in Kazakhstan, 30
Capital punishment in Latvia, 30
Capital punishment in Malaysia, 22
Capital punishment in Mongolia, 70, 342
Capital punishment in New Zealand, 12
Capital punishment in North Korea, 18, 23
Capital punishment in Oklahoma, 23
Capital punishment in Pakistan, 3, 13, 22

Capital punishment in Poland, 30
Capital punishment in Russia, 30
Capital punishment in Saudi Arabia, 23
Capital punishment in Singapore, 22
Capital punishment in South Africa, 12
Capital punishment in Sri Lanka, 3, 22
Capital punishment in Syria, 22
Capital punishment in Taiwan, 70, 71
Capital punishment in Thailand, 23, 71
Capital punishment in the Czech Republic, 41
Capital punishment in the Maldives, 71
Capital punishment in the Peoples Republic of China, 18, 23, 69
Capital punishment in the Philippines, 13, 71
Capital punishment in the Republic of China, 23
Capital punishment in the United States, 3, 12, 18, 23, 71, 106
Capital punishment in the USA, 22
Capital punishment in Turkey, 13
Capital punishment in Utah, 23
Capital punishment in Vietnam, 23, 71
Capital punishment in Washington, 22
Capital punishment in Yemen, 22, 23
Capitoline Hill, 316
Cappadocia, 344
Capri, 317
Captives in American Indian Wars, 218
Caravanserai, 379
Carbon dioxide, 104
Carbon monoxide, 104, 110
Carbon monoxide poisoning, 200
Cardiac arrest, 45, 74
Cardiac arrhythmia, 85
Cardiac muscle, 74
Cardioplegia, 87
Caribbean, 12, 19
Carl Bloch, 251
Carlos Frederick MacDonald, 96
Carmageddon, 298
Carmen Gloria Quintana, 233
Caroline Matilda of Great Britain, 115
Carotid arteries, 39, 45, 513–515
Carotid sinus, 47
Carotid sinus reflex, 513
Carotid sinus reflex death, 45, 47, 513
Carotid sinus stimulation, 513
Carpal tunnel, 256
Carriages, 171
Carrion, 163, 174, 317
Carthage, 135, 143, 260
Carthaginians, 203, 223, 259
Cassandreia, 556
Cassius Dio, 334, 344, 454
Castalian Spring, 316
Castellan, 460

Castrated, 323
Catacombs, 358
Category:Criminal defenses, 2
Caterina Tarongí, 210
Cathar, 349
Catharism, 206
Catherine Hayes (murderer), 216, 546
Catherine Murphy (counterfeiter), 216, 231, 309
Catherine of Alexandria, 180, 181
Catholic Church, 273, 299
Catholic Church in the Philippines, 273
Catholic Encyclopedia, 36, 563
Cat Island (Mississippi), 458
Cato Street Conspiracy, 310
Cato the Elder, 284
Cato the Younger, 284
Cattle car, 120
Caudillo, 328
Cauldron, 163, 165
Caxton Gibbet, 331
Cayenne, 418, 435
Cedar oil, 126
Celibacy, 191
Celle, 64
Celts, 126, 204
Censer, 449
Center of gravity, 437
Center of mass, 415
Center of percussion, 415, 419, 437
Central Europe, 177
Central Intelligence Agency, 280
Centre of mass, 427
Centrifugal force, 418, 435
Centurion, 262
Cephalophore, 126
Cerebral anoxia, 44
Cerebral hypoxia, 45
Cerebral ischemia, 47, 513
Cerebral oedema, 47
Certain accursed ones of no significance, 222
Cervical dislocation, 14
Cervical fracture, 41, 45
Cervical spine injury, 45
Cervical vertebrae, 43
Cesare Beccaria, 16
Cesare, Marquis of Beccaria, 10
Cesvaine Palace, 355
Ceylon, 141, 145, 148
Chalcis, 461
Châlus, 323
Champa, 137
Changeling, 217
Channel 4, 266
Chapter 9, 542
Charles A. Goodrich, 555

Charles Brooks, Jr., 72
Charles Dickens, 10
Charles Édouard Guillaume, 429
Charles II of England, 216
Charles I of England, 305, 307
Charles James Napier, 339
Charles Lane (journalist), 34
Charles Marie de la Condamine, 445
Charles Rollin, 567
Charlestown, Massachusetts, 337
Charles V, Holy Roman Emperor, 212, 289
Charles XII of Sweden, 177
Charlie Crist, 86
Charlotte Corday, 119
Charter of Fundamental Rights of the European Union, 2, 29
Chartism, 310
Chase (son of Ioube), 508
Chastity, 52
Chatrapati, 139
Cheetah, 513
Chełmno extermination camp, 104
Chemical warfare, 411
Chemistry, 410
Chest, 367
Chicken, 117
Child murder, 25
Child sacrifice, 203, 487
Chile, 233
Chilean Army, 233
China, 4, 18, 19, 122, 477
China Miéville, 404
Chinon, 208
Chios Massacre, 556
Chlothar II, 292
Chokehold, 514
Choking, 48
Choking game, 512
Chongzhen Emperor, 464
Christendom, 7, 32
Christiaan Huygens, 416, 418, 419, 445
Christian, 163, 265, 281, 323
Christian cross, 250
Christian Huygens, 411
Christianity, 169, 234, 250, 264, 356
Christian IV of Denmark, 215
Christianization of Scandinavia, 162
Christian missionaries, 166
Christian Reconstructionism, 504
Christman Genipperteinga, 172
Christopher Moltisanti, 297
Christopher Newton (criminal), 75
Christopher Wren, 445
Christoph Probst, 128
Chronica caesaraugustana, 169
Chronica Majora, 300

Chronological items, 22
Chuck Palahniuk, 285
Cicero, 127, 253, 395
Ciconian, 297
Cisatracurium, 73
Cistern, 348
CITEREFChisholm1911, 529
CITEREFLewis2008, 545
CITEREFRassam Cylinder. The British Museum.636BC, 547
Cities for Life Day, 16
City Lights Bookstore, 484
City of London, 57
City Primeval, 358
Ciudad Juárez, 508
Civil procedure, 2
Clairauts theorem, 435
Clan Kincaid, 176
Clarence Ray Allen, 90
Classical antiquity, 137, 171, 397
Classical liberalism, 450
Classic Veracruz culture, 130
Cleitarchus, 203
Cleomenes I, 283
Clinton Correctional Facility, 94
Clinton Duffy, 60
Clouds of Witness, 59
Club (weapon), 171, 514
C. Northcote Parkinson, 314
CNRS, 484
Coal oil, 233
Coatlicue, 297
Cochinchina, 138
Cockroach, 117
Code of Hammurabi, 5, 370
Codex Ixtlilxochitl, 283
Codex Justinianus, 401, 532
Códice Casanatense, 194
Coefficient of thermal expansion, 428, 429
Coldingham Priory, 350
Collective responsibility, 489
Colliery, 338
Cologne, 127
Colombo, 148
Colonial history of the United States, 69
Colorado, 108
Colosseum, 5
Colubrid, 403
Columbia University, 537
Coma, 78
Combat sport, 512, 514
Combe Gibbet, 338
Combustion, 200
Commentaries on the Laws of England, 544
Committee on the Rights of the Child, 268
Common law, 276, 301, 330

Commons:Category:Beheadings, 134
Commons:Category:Breaking wheels, 186
Commons:Category:Bronze Bull, 170
Commons:Category:Crucifixion, 275
Commons:Category:Death penalty, 32
Commons:Category:Dismemberment, 298
Commons:Category:Execution by elephant, 144
Commons:Category:Flaying, 325
Commons:Category:Garrote, 330
Commons:Category:Hanging, 67
Commons:Category:Impalement, 380
Commons:Category:Lingchi, 485
Commons:Category:Pendulums, 451
Commons:Category:Premature burial, 199
Commons:Category:Sawing (torture), 466
Commons:Category:Stonings, 512
Commonwealth, 16
Communism, 19
Communist Party of China, 482
Communists, 12
Communist state, 68
Commutation of sentence, 328
Compressive asphyxia, 276
Concise Oxford English Dictionary, 547
Confucianism, 477
Congress Poland, 56
Conical pendulum, 418
Conkers Bad Fur Day, 298
Connemara, 126
Conquest of Canaan, 489
Conservation of energy, 449
Consort Duan (Cao), 481
Constantine I, 260
Constantine-Silvanus, 508
Constantine the Great, 203, 255
Constantinople, 460
Constantinople massacre of 1821, 379
Constantius II, 532
Constitutio Criminalis Carolina, 192, 212, 213, 289, 373, 552
Constitution of Germany, 50
Constitution of Turkey, 31
Constructive treason, 302
Contract killing, 328
Control system, 447
Convention on the Rights of the Child, 21, 22
Convention protocols, 3
Conviction, 1
Copford, 320
Copts, 457
Corciano, 333
Corfu, 344
Coroner, 75
Corporal punishment, 4
Corpus Juris Civilis, 402

Corrosive substance, 410
Cosmas and Damian, 116
Cosmographia (Sebastian Münster), 114
Cossacks, 464
Coulter (agriculture), 176
Council of Constance, 207
Council of Europe, 2, 19, 30
Council of Nablus, 210
Counsel, 302
Counterfeit, 231
Counterfeiter, 165
Countess, 346
Count of Edessa, 459
County of Hainaut, 63
County of Tecklenburg, 175
County of Tyrol, 192
County Tipperary, 217
Coup de grâce, 171, 174, 479
Coupled oscillation, 447
Course of the war, 328
Court Martial, 515
Courts-martial, 4
Courts of Canada, 2
Courts of England and Wales, 2
Courts of Scotland, 2
Courts of the United Kingdom, 2
Courts of the United States, 2
Court TV, 90
Cowardice, 4, 11
Coyolxauhqui, 287, 297
Crassus, 260
Creep (deformation), 429
Crematorium, 233
Cretan, 324
Cretan Revolt (1866–1869), 379
Cretan War (1645–69), 374
Crete, 374, 555
Crime, 318
Crime and Disorder Act 1998, 58, 299, 311
Crimes against humanity, 2, 53, 54
Crimes against peace, 54
Criminal justice, 276
Criminal law, 2
Criminal procedure, 1
Criminology, 10, 286
Cross, 251
Crossbow, 323
Cross of St. Peter, 274
Crucifix, 250, 251
Crucifixion, 37, 127, 171, **250**, 323, 334, 379
Crucifixion in the Philippines, 273
Crucifixion of Jesus, 250, 274
Cruel and unusual punishment, 1, 15, 26, 98, 102, 108, 311, 506
Crusaders, 210
Crusader states, 461
Crusades, 460
Crushing (execution), 135, **275**
Crus (lower leg), 318
Crux simplex, 252
Cryonics, 111
Crystal oscillator, 421, 430, 432, 443
Ctesias, 474
Cuba, 68
Cubit, 143
Cuckolds Point, 332
Cultural definition, 18
Cultural Revolution, 11
Cumin, 307
Curare, 79
Curtea de Argeş Cathedral, 352
Custodial sentence, 1
Customary international law, 21
Cyanide, 411
Cyanosis, 47
Cycloid, 419
Cyclopædia, or an Universal Dictionary of Arts and Sciences, 133
Cyprus, 454
Cyrene, Libya, 454
Czechoslovakia, 41

Dabiq (magazine), 504
Dachau concentration camp, 105
Dacoit, 257
Dafydd ap Gruffydd, 300, 306
Dahomey, 131
Daimyō, 124
Damnatio ad bestias, 394
Damping, 432
Dangerous offender, 1
Daniel Bernoulli, 436
Daniel Pearl, 123
Danish language, 179
Dansai Bunri no Crime Edge, 295
Dante, 192, 357
Danube River, 376
Danzig, 165
Dara Singh (Hindu nationalist), 234
Darius I, 372
Darius II, 453, 486
Darius III, 294
Daskalogiannis, 324
David, 510
David B. Hill, 94
David Bruck, 108
David Herold, 60
David Hume, 115
David Paterson, 108
David Souter, 82
Deadbeat escapement, 433
Dead Island, 298

Dead Space (video game), 298
Death, 200, 281, 318, 512, 513, 523
Death by a Thousand Cuts (book), 485
Death by boiling, **163**, 200
Death by burning, 54, 98, **200**, 378
Death by sawing, 377, **452**
Death flights, 317
Death of Abigail Taylor, 284
Death of Ingrid Lyne, 295
Death penalty, 394
Death Penalty Information Center, 89
Death row, 27
Decapitation, 43, 45, **111**, 171, 178, 180, 279, 281, 298, 323, 330, 452
Deccan Plateau, 227
Decimation (Roman army), 11
Decius, 356, 357
Declaration of Geneva, 80
Decomposition, 316
De:Eduard Osenbrüggen, 554
Defecting, 374
Defendant, 276
De:Guido Kisch, 63
De heretico comburendo, 207
De:Hermann Stilke, 215
De:Hötzelsroda, 212
Dehydration, 174, 187, 257, 340
Dei delitti e delle pene, 10
De Inventione, 395
De:Judenstrafe, 62
De jure, 2
Delaware, 61, 75
Delhi, 138, 165
Delhi Sultanate, 138
Delphi, 316
Demetrios Palaiologos, 460
Democratic Republic of Congo, 21, 120
Demonism, 217
Denis, 126
Denmark, 129
Department of Health (Philippines), 273
Depolarization, 74
Dera Ghazi Khan District, 503
Derby Gaol, 310
Dermatologist, 318
Description, 258
Desertion, 4, 11
Despard Plot, 308
Despotate of the Morea, 460
Destruction of Jerusalem, 260
Deterrence (legal), 261, 281
Deterrence (prevention), 253
De:Tiefburg (Handschuhsheim), 549
Deuterocanonical books, 144
Deuteronomy, 259, 489, 548, 567
Deutschlandfunk, 538

Deva, Romania, 353
Deventer, 164, 165
Devil, 195
Dialogue with Trypho, 542
Diaphragm (anatomy), 74
Diazepam, 73
Diccionario de la Real Academia Española, 547
Diegylis, 454
Dieric Bouts, 287
Diesel engine, 104
Die Welt, 538
Digest (Roman law), 203, 398, 400
Digital object identifier, 32
Diocletian, 169, 281, 295, 456
Diodorus Siculus, 126, 167, 201, 204, 454
Dionysius of Halicarnassus, 396
Dionysius the Philosopher, 461
Dionysus, 144, 297
Diptych, 322
Direct current, 95
Directed verdict, 1
Dirty War, 317
Discharge (sentence), 1
Discipline and Punish, 320
Discrimination, 506
Disembowelment, 124, **279**, 296, 298, 463, 486
Dismembered, 281
Dismemberment, 174, **286**, 298, 374, 452, 478
District of Columbia, 17
Diyya, 52
DLB2004, 568
DNA evidence, 27
Dog, 147
Doge of Venice, 344
Domenico I Contarini, 344
Domitian, 169, 456
Donald Harding (murderer), 108
Donkey, 542
Donnie Brasco (film), 296
Doom book, 545
Doom (franchise), 298
Dooplaya District, 269
Dorsum (anatomy), 367, 376
Dortmund, 63
Dose–response relationship, 410
Dositheus Magister, 401
Dost Mohammad Khan, 146
Double jeopardy, 1, 102
Doublet (clothing), 342
Draco (lawgiver), 5
Dracula, 552
Dragging death, 292
Dresden, 403
Drown, 391
Drowning, 192

Drug interaction, 89
Drugs, 78
Drug trafficking, 4, 25, 56
Druid, 195
Drumhead court-martial, 11
Ducking-stools, 393
Duel, 4
Du'a Khalil Aswad, 508
Duke of Denver, 59
Duke of Dorset, 355
Durham, England, 338
Durrani Empire, 153
Dutch language, 179, 391
Dutch Revolt, 192
Duumviri, 396
Dwarf Fortress, 298
Dynamics (mechanics), 449
Dzhokhar Tsarnaev, 20

Early Modern era, 291
Early Modern Europe, 213
Early modern period, 171
Earth (1998 film), 296
Earthquake, 416
East Asia, 25
Eastern Europe, 177
Eastern Roman Empire, 344
East Germany, 120
East India Company, 290, 526
East Prussia, 266
East Timor, 12
Ebensee concentration camp, 231
Ecbatana, 294
ECG, 79
Echo of Moscow, 233
Edgar Allan Poe, 358, 450
Ed Gein, 324
Edinburgh, 118, 176
Edirne, 222
Edmund Beaufort, 4th Duke of Somerset, 129
Edmund Gennings, 304
Edo, 228
Edo period, 280

Édouard Cibot, 114

Eduard Henke, 192
Eduard Osenbrüggen, 192, 212
Edward Backhouse Eastwick, 342
Edward Charles Spitzka, 98
Edward Christian, 312
Edward Coke, 306, 312, 545
Edward Despard, 308
Edward Granville Browne, 342
Edward II, 330
Edward III of England, 301

Edward II of England, 301
Edward I of England, 300, 320
Edward James (martyr), 305
Edward Sabine, 445
Edward Stafford, 3rd Duke of Buckingham, 302
Edward VI of England, 164
Edward Wightman, 215
Edwin Davis (executioner), 97
Egypt, 18
Egyptian Jews, 144
Egyptian mythology, 297
Eighth Amendment to the United States Constitution, 81, 311
Einsatzgruppen, 104
Eisenach, 212
Ekron, 371
Elam, 370
Elbridge Thomas Gerry, 94
Electorate of Hesse, 171, 178
Electorate of Saxony, 394
Electric chair, 23, 71, 73, **92**, 103
Electric spark, 441
Electrocardiography, 74
Electrocution, 14, 92
Electrode, 92
Electrolyte, 79
Electrotherapy, 96
Elephant, 170
Eli Cohen, 56, 57
Elihu Thomson, 94
Elinvar, 429
Elisabeth Becker, 39
Elisabeth Volkenrath, 43
Elizabethan era, 299
Elizabeth Barton, 545
Elizabeth I, 65
Elizabeth I of England, 305
Ell, 367
Ellipticity, 435
Elmore Leonard, 358
Emasculated, 306
Emasculation, 281, 298
Embalming, 285
Emile Durkheim, 350
Emir, 459
Emir of Afghanistan, 153
Emo, 502
Emperor, 136
Emperor Augustus, 399
Emperor Claudius, 399
Emperor Constantine, 394, 401
Emperor Hadrian, 394, 400
Emperor Justinian, 402
Emperor Nero, 399
Emperor Renzong of Song, 480

Emperor Saga, 15
Emperor Shenzong of Song, 404, 480
Emperor Tianzuo of Liao, 480
Emperor Tiberius, 344
Emperor Wenxuan of Northern Qi, 480
Emperor Xuanzong of Tang, 6
Emperor Zhaozong of Tang, 463
En:Amazon Standard Identification Number, 249, 384, 467
En:Bibcode, 246, 451
Encyclopædia Britannica Eleventh Edition, 250, 462
En:Digital object identifier, 91, 244, 246, 247, 363, 389, 390, 406, 408, 409, 451, 485
Enemy of the people, 68
England, 281, 323, 331
English, 330
English common law, 217
En:International Standard Serial Number, 240, 243, 244, 246, 248, 363, 389, 390, 406, 408, 409
En:JSTOR, 198, 243, 389, 390, 406, 408, 409
En:OCLC, 196, 409
En:PubMed Central, 246
Enrique Simonet, 111
Ensisheim, 192
Entrail, 281
Entrainment (physics), 447
Enzyme, 411
Enzyme inhibitor, 411
Enzymes, 411
Ephraim Chambers, 133
Episode 5 – Buried Alive, 531
Epistle of Barnabas, 542
Epistle to Dr Arbuthnot, 180
Epistle to the Galatians, 259
Equations of motion, 413
Equator, 444, 562
Equilibrium point, 433
Erasmus of Formiae, 281
Ernst Kaltenbrunner, 41
Erotic asphyxia, 512
Escapement, 426, 431, 432
Escheat, 276
Espionage, 2, 4, 25, 101
Esquiline Gate, 253
Estonia, 351
Ethiopia, 113
Etomidate, 87
Eulalia of Barcelona, 274
Euphrates, 370
Europe, 19, 150, 163
European colonialism, 135
European Convention on Human Rights, 3, 29, 311
European Union, 2, 19, 29, 30, 73

Eusebius, 401
Euthanasia, 71, 81
Euthanasia machine, 81
Euxine Sea, 378
Eva Dugan, 43
Evan Mandery, 33
Evidence (law), 2
Evin Prison, 52
Ewa Paradies, 39
Excitotoxicity, 116
Exclusionary rule, 1
Executed, 200
Execution, 279, 340, 364, 411, 450, 477
Execution by elephant, **135**, 286
Execution by firing squad, 61, 67, 71, 73, 76, 77, 120
Execution by shooting, 23, **67**, 76
Execution Dock, 332
Executioner, 57, 97, 111, 171, 487
Executioners sword, 115
Execution (legal), 71, 163, 187, 318
Execution of Carey Dean Moore, 73
Execution of Clayton Lockett, 86
Execution of Rizana Nafeek, 22
Executions of Cossacks in Lebedin, 184
Execution warrant, 1
Exhaust gas, 104
Exile, 4
Exoneration, 2
Ex parte Quirin, 101
Expatriate, 57
Expatriates in the United Arab Emirates, 504
Expiation, 395
Expulsion of Germans from Czechoslovakia, 231
Extermination camp, 104
Extrajudicial, 234

Facsimile, 114
Fact-finding, 94
Fail-safe, 80
Fairy, 217
Fakir, 194
Falling (execution), **316**
Fall of Constantinople, 377, 460
Fallout (franchise), 298
Fallout: New Vegas, 285
Familiar spirit, 487
Famine and the Great Terror: 1932–1939, 11
Faqir, 150
Farmhand, 233
Faroe Islands, 129, 192
Farrukhsiyar, 147
Fasad, 4
Fascist, 57
Fatehgarh, 152

Fatigue (medical), 257
Fear of being buried alive, 187
Feature (archaeology), 178
February 2010 Sikh beheadings by Taliban, 123
Felony, 217
Female Genital Mutilation, 494
Fentanyl, 73
Ferdowsi, 452
Feud, 4
Field dressing (hunting), 324
Figure of the Earth, 418
Fiji, 166, 228
File:Kaarinan vaakuna.png, 183
Filial piety, 477
Financial crime, 4
Financier, 336
Finland, 115, 129
Fiqh, 496, 498
Fire and Faggot Parliament, 207
Firearms, 67
Fire of Moscow (1812), 464
Firing squad, 11, 68, 69, 119, 130
Firozpur, 146
First Anglo-Burmese War, 150
First Babylonian Dynasty, 370
First Sino-Japanese War, 123
First War of Indian Independence, 149
First World, 18
Five Dynasties, 480
Five Punishments, 481
Flagellants, 274
Flagellation, 257, 262, 273
Flamethrower, 233
Flashman in the Great Game, 154
Flaying, **318**, 374, 456, 484
Flaying of Marsyas (Titian), 322, 323
Flies, 475
Flogging, 492
Flogging round the fleet, 393
Florence Shoemaker Thompson, 60
Florentine Codex, 499
Florida, 92, 102
Florida Supreme Court, 86
Fluid mechanics, 429
Folha de S.Paulo, 239
Folk hero, 65
Folklore, 195, 346
Folklore of Romania, 353
Footpad, 171
Forced disappearance, 317
Fordham Urban Law Journal, 91
Forfeiture Act 1870, 125, 299, 311
Forfeiture (law), 311
Forger, 165
Forgery, 49

Formaldehyde, 411
Formic acid, 411
Fornication, 4
Fort McNair, 60
Fortunatus Hueber, 552
Forum Romanum, 127
Foucault pendulum, 420
Foxes Book of Martyrs, 215
Fra Angelico, 116
France, 119, 138
Francesco Carlini, 436
Francesco Ferdinandi, 169
Frances Pritchett, 537
Francis Bacon, 434
Franciscan, 265
Francisca Nuñez de Carabajal, 218
Francisco Barreto, 148
Francisco Castro Bueno, 329
Francisco de Almeida, 148
Francisco Franco, 328
Francisco Javier de Elío, 329
Francisco Otero González, 329
Francis Towneley, 308
Francois Bernier, 346
François Bernier, 138
François Henri de la Motte, 308
François Mignet, 523
François Mitterrand, 128
François Pouqueville, 379
François Ravaillac, 291
Francoist Spain, 328
Frankfurt am Main, 63
Franz Strasser, 42
Fr:Dominique Busnot, 563
Fred A. Leuchter, 75
Frederick II, Holy Roman Emperor, 205
Frederick Peterson, 95
Frederick Zugibe, 256, 257
Frederic William Maitland, 303, 314, 544
Freedom of the City of London, 59
Freedwoman, 261
Freiburg im Breisgau, 326
Freidoune Sahebjam, 510
French Academy of Sciences, 446
French Foreign Legion, 325
French Guiana, 418, 435
French language, 174
French Resistance, 324
French Revolution, 113, 118, 128
Frequency, 411, 414, 430, 444
Fresenius Kabi, 73
Friction, 412
Friday the 13th Part III, 296
Friederike Luise Delitz, 213
Friedrich Bessel, 440
Fritz Haarmann, 127

Fritz Klein, 43
Fr:Jean-Antoine Guer, 551
Froissart of Louis of Gruuthuse (BnF Fr 2643-6), 299
Fulgencio Batista, 68
Fumigation, 104
Funeral, 229
Funeral pyre, 229
Fur, 318
Furman v. Georgia, 17, 107
Fused quartz, 421, 429, 443
Fu Sheng, 320
Fynes Moryson, 221

Gabon, 31
Gabriel-Jules Thomas, 507
Gabriel Mouton, 445
Gainesville, Texas, 60
Gaius Marius, 127
Galileo Galilei, 411, 417
Gallipoli, 461
Gallows, 171, 330, 331
Gao Heng, 320
Garrote, 37, **325**, 512, 515
Garrotte, 130, 171, 175
Garry Wills, 127
Gary North (economist), 504
Gary Ridgway, 515
Gas chamber, 14, 23, 43, 71, **104**, 111, 411
Gas van, 104
Gathorne Hardy, 311
Gausss law for gravity, 440
Gaza Strip, 23
Gears of War 3, 298
Gedik Ahmed Pasha, 461
Gee Jon, 106
Gemonian stairs, 316
General anesthesia, 87
General Council of the Judiciary, 328
General Kleber, 551
Geneva, 210
Genghis Khan, 226
Genocide, 2, 24, 25, 104
Geodesy, 439
Geodetic surveying, 439
Geoffrey Chaucer, 517
Geographical pole, 444
George Airy, 433, 440
George Atzerodt, 60
George DOyly, 567
George Ernest Morrison, 479, 482
George Fell, 94, 97
George Graham (clockmaker), 427
George III of the United Kingdom, 231
George IV of the United Kingdom, 310
George Macartney, 1st Earl Macartney, 526

George MacDonald Fraser, 154
George Roerich, 483
George Ryley Scott, 483
George Sandys, 290
Georges Bataille, 484
George Skene Keith, 445
Georges-Louis Leclerc, Comte de Buffon, 139
George Waddington, 556
George Westinghouse, 95
Georgia (U.S. state), 80, 102
Gerard David, 322
Gerardus Johannes Geers, 524
Gerda Steinhoff, 39
German Democratic Republic, 50, 128
Germania, 190
German language, 179
German-occupied Europe, 119
German Peasants War, 8
Germans, 352
Germany, 119, 266
Ghilzai, 153
Giacomo Casanova, 291
Gibbet, 111, 150, 218, 254, 300, 323
Gibbeting, **330**
Gibbet Island, Bermuda, 334
Gibraltar, 458
Gilan, 508
Gilbert de Middleton, 306
Gilding, 355
Giles Corey, 277
Gillo Pontecorvo, 119
Giordano Bruno, 214
Girolamo Savonarola, 214
Giuseppe Verdi, 358
Givat ha-Mivtar, 256
Givat HaMivtar, 258
Glenbervie, 164
Glossip v. Gross, 15, 82
Goa, 139, 183, 210
Goa Inquisition, 210
God, 172
Godefroy Wendelin, 426
God of War (franchise), 298
Golden Legend, 169, 180
Gomoarius, 455
Good Friday, 273
Goodwin J. Knight, 106
Gospel, 274
Gospel of John, 510
Governor of New York, 108
Governor of Oklahoma, 109
Grado, Friuli-Venezia Giulia, 344
Graffiti, 542
Graham Staines, 234
Granada, 210
Grand Duchy of Finland, 56

Grand Duchy of Tuscany, 16
Grande Armée, 464
Grandfather clock, 414, 424, 426
Grand National Assembly of Turkey, 31
Grapeshot, 146
Grave robbery, 364
Gravimeter, 412, 418, 421, 433, 447
Gravimetry, 433, 439
Gravity, 411, 433
Greater Iran, 452
Great Northern War, 177
Great Purges, 68
Great Seal of the Realm, 302
Great Swamp Fight, 302
Great Trigonometric Survey, 439
Greece, 188
Greek language, 353, 474
Greek Macedonia, 188
Greek mythology, 297, 321
Greek War of Independence, 220, 379, 462
Green Knight, 126
Greensville Correctional Center, 103
Greenwich peninsula, 332
Gregg v. Georgia, 17, 101
Gregory of Tours, 174
Grey Friars Priory, 207
Gridiron pendulum, 419, 423, 428
Grobiņa Castle, 351
Groß Pankow (Prignitz), 178
Ground (electricity), 93
Guanajuato, 131
Guangzhou, 482, 483
Guan Hanqing, 566
Guatemala City, 232
Guatemalan Civil War, 232
Guelphs and Ghibellines, 357
Guerrilla, 378
Guerrilla warfare, 464
Guillotine, 14, 50, 111, 118, 119, 128, 330
Gulf War, 193
Gunpowder Plot, 306
Gunshot wounds, 43
Gun (video game), 298
Gupta Empire, 229
Gurney, 73
Guru Arjan, 166
Guru Gobind Singh, 347
Guru Nanak, 166
Guru Tegh Bahadur, 462
Gustav Radbruch, 213
Gutenberg:50460, 199
Guts, 285
Guy Fawkes, 306
Gwynne Owen Evans, 58
György Dózsa, 224
Gyroscope, 420, 447

Haapsalu, 351, 360
Habeas corpus, 98
Habibullāh Kalakāni, 153
Habsburg, 374
Habsburg Netherlands, 192
Hacktivist, 269
Hadd, 263, 267
Hadith, 263, 492, 493, 495, 496
Hadith of Umars ban on hadith, 493
Hadrian, 169, 254, 456, 543
Hai Rui, 320
Haiti, 231
Hajj, 493
Halfdan Halegs Death., 160
Halfdan Long-Leg, 161
Half-life, 78
Halifax Gibbet, 118, 330
Halifax, West Yorkshire, 118
Halle (region), 63
Halle (Saale), 208
Haman (Bible), 372
Hamas, 23
Hamath, 323
Hamida Djandoubi, 129
Hammer, 174
Hammurabi, 200, 370
Hanafi, 263, 497
Hanau, 63
Hanbali, 263, 498
Hand-to-hand combat, 514
Han dynasty, 290, 416
Hanged, 298
Hanged, drawn and quartered, 14, 122, 216, 281, **298**, 330, 332
Hanged, drawn, and quartered, 296
Hanging, 14, 22, **37**, 71, 92, 98, 111, 125, 132, 281, 323, 512, 515
Hanging, drawing and quartering, 125
Hanging, drawing, and quartering, 482
Hangmans fracture, 45
Hannibal, 135, 143, 397
Hannibal (Harris novel), 485
Hannover, 127
Hanoi, 280
Hans Scholl, 119, 128
Hanyu Pinyin, 477
Harald Fairhair, 161
Harburg (quarter), 356
Harmonic oscillator, 415, 417, 430, 449
Harold Edward Bindloss, 348
Harold P. Brown, 95
Harper, Liberia, 55
Harpers Weekly, 140, 482
Harry Allen (executioner), 57
Harry Band, 266
Harry Flashman, 154

Haruki Murakami, 324
Hassanal Bolkiah, 500
Haunted (Palahniuk novel), 285
H. Beam Piper, 154
Headhunting, 111, 126
Head hunting, 126
Head injury, 391
Headsman, 111
Head transplant, 118
Heart, 69, 92, 279, 411
Heart arrhythmia, 74, 256
Heatstroke, 200
Hebrew Bible, 487
Hector Munro, 8th of Novar, 149
Heidelberg, 355
Heimskringla, 161
Heinz Chez, 328, 329
Heitaro Kimura, 54
Helmuth Hübener, 128
Henri Félix Emmanuel Philippoteaux, 293
Henry Charles Lea, 349
Henry Charles Sirr, 141
Henry E. Sharp, 255
Henry III of England, 298, 299
Henry Kamen, 533
Henry Kater, 416, 420, 438
Henry VI, Holy Roman Emperor, 65
Henry VIII, 334
Henry VIII of England, 7, 163, 545
Henry V of England, 207
Henry Wirz, 38
Hephaestion, 260
Herat, 525
Herculanus of Perugia, 323
Hereditary peer, 59
Heresy, 200, 205, 215, 217, 323
Hermann Stilke, 215
Hernando del Pulgar, 209
Herodotus, 259, 260, 323
Herzegovina Uprising (1875–1878), 379
Hiberno-Norman, 217
Hideki Tojo, 54
High Middle Ages, 299
High Treason, 163, 216, 281, 290, 298, 478
High treason in the United Kingdom, 301
Highwayman, 330
Highwaymen, 171
Highway robbery, 364
Hill v. McDonough, 81
Hindu, 229
Hinduism, 146, 194
Hippolytus of Rome, 287
Hirabah, 4, 25
Hiroaki Hidaka, 54
History, 16
History of Anglo-Saxon England, 57

History of Iran, 486
History of Ming, 547
History of Song, 404
History of the Peloponnesian War, 344
Hizbul Islam, 504
Hizb ut-Tahrir, 166
Hjørring, 183
HM Prison Pentonville, 58
HMS Alexandra (1875), 393
Holy Roman Emperor, 374
Holy Roman Empire, 165, 171, 174, 191, 213, 289
Holy See, 119
Holy tradition in the Catholic and Orthodox Churches, 323
Holy Week, 274
Homer, 37
Homeric Greek, 542
Home Secretary, 310
Homicide, 25, 397, 515
Homicide Act 1957, 58
Homosexual, 486
Homosexuality, 52, 200, 317, 490, 504
Homosexuals, 211
Honey, 475
Hongwu Emperor, 320, 566
Hopscotch (Cortázar novel), 485
Horizon (BBC TV series), 34
Hormizd IV, 453
Horologium (constellation), 561
Horologium Oscillatorium, 419, 445
Horror film, 295
Horse, 135
Horsemonger Lane Gaol, 308
Horst Fischer, 128
Hospira, 80
Host desecration, 207, 208
Hôtel Terminus: The Life and Times of Klaus Barbie, 324
House of Commons of the United Kingdom, 152
House of Lords, 59, 309
HowStuffWorks, 90
Hradisko Monastery, 345
H. Rider Haggard, 475
Hudibras, 445
Hudood Ordinances, 502
Hudud, 4, 25, 501
Hugh Capet, 65
Hugh Despenser the Younger, 282, 299, 300, 545
Hugh Latimer, 214
Huginn, 162
Huitzilopochtli, 297
Hulagu Khan, 226
Hull (ship), 391

Human, 364, 411
Human body, 318
Humane society, 108
Human gastrointestinal tract, 279
Human head, 111, 126
Human rights, 11, 17, 26
Human Rights Act 1998, 58
Human Rights Watch, 31, 89, 506
Human sacrifice, 44, 162, 316, 340
Human skull, 333
Humayun, 138, 147
Humiliating, 261
Hungarian language, 346
Hungarian Revolution of 1848, 465
Hungarian Revolution of 1956, 51
Hurdle, 298, 303
Hurufi, 222, 323
Hurufiyya, 222
Húsavík, Faroe Islands, 192
Hu:Wesselényi Pál, 374
Hyampeia, 316
Hyder Ali, 146
Hydrogen cyanide, 104, 108
Hydromorphone, 80
Hyoid, 514
Hyoid bone, 48
Hypatia, 323
Hyperkalemia, 74, 79
Hypnotic, 15
Hypokalemia, 79
Hypotension, 513
Hypothermia, 187, 318
Hypovolemia, 200
Hypovolemic shock, 256
Hypoxia (medical), 512

Iain Overton, 266
Ian Mortimer (historian), 303
Iberian Peninsula, 223
Ibn Battuta, 138, 286
Ibn Batuta, 348
Ibn Hanbal, 263
Ibn Qudamah, 498
Ibn Yunus, 417
ICD-10, 134, 410
Iceland, 129
Idaho, 80
Idolatry, 488, 504
Ifrane, 222
Iglau, 373
Ignacio Allende, 130
II Samuel, 372
Ikebukuro, 54
Iliad, 542
Illiterate, 507
Imam, 138

Imamah (Shia doctrine), 495
Immanuel Kant, 25
Immortals (2011 film), 170
Immurement, 191, **340**
Impala, 513
Impalement, 37, 56, 252, 254, 262, 330, **364**, 458
Impalement (in myth and art), 364
Imprisonment, 1
Imre Nagy, 51
Inca culture, 348
Inca Empire, 327
Incense, 449
Incest, 4, 200, 490, 504
Inch, 446
Inch of mercury, 430
In Christianity, 203
Indefinite imprisonment, 1
India, 69, 135
Indiana, 102
Indian Muslims, 146
Indian Rebellion of 1857, 52, 145, 151
Indian subcontinent, 141, 229
Indigenous peoples of the Americas, 324
Indochina, 137
Indonesia, 18, 69, 487
Indore, 152
Industrial Revolution, 310
Inertia, 429
Inertial guidance system, 447
Inertial platform, 447
Infanticide, 373
Infection, 318
Inferno, 192
Infinite series, 414
In flagrante delicto, 374
Inhalational anesthetic, 87
Initial conditions, 415
Injun Joe, 358
Inner Hebrides, 195
Inner Mongolia, 483
Inquisition, 205
Institute of Electrical and Electronics Engineers, 522
Institutes of Justinian, 402
Insubordination, 4, 11
Intellectual disability, 17
Interferometer, 443
International Covenant on Civil and Political Rights, 21, 30
International Criminal Court, 24
International Criminal Tribunal for the former Yugoslavia, 125
International Standard Book Number, 32, 33, 67, 144, 145, 154–159, 170, 186, 196, 197, 235–250, 312–316, 325,

339, 359–364, 381–388, 404–409, 451, 466–468, 470, 472, 485, 515
International Statistical Classification of Diseases and Related Health Problems, 134, 410
Internet Encyclopedia of Philosophy, 34
Intravenous, 73
Intravenous therapy, 71, 73
Intubation, 88
Invar, 421, 424, 429, 432
Ioannina, 378, 461
Iona, 195
Iona Abbey, 195
Iowa, 61
Iran, 18, 21, 23, 267, 317, 456, 487
Iraq, 18, 21, 142, 487, 502, 508
Iraqi insurgency (Iraq War), 53
Iraqi Kurdistan, 508
Irenaeus, 542
Irma Grese, 43
Iron, 171
Iron Age, 44
Irwandi Yusuf, 500
Isaac Beeckman, 445
Isaac Newton, 418, 435
Isaiah, 455
Ishikawa Goemon, 165
ISIL, 504
Isin-Larsa, Old Babylonian and Shamshi-Adad I, 370
Iskandar Muda, 227
Islam, 18, 165, 323
Islam and blasphemy, 4, 25
Islamic Courts Union, 22
Islamic Emirate of Afghanistan, 500
Islamic State of Iraq and the Levant, 133, 193, 234, 268, 269, 317
Islamic terrorism, 268
Islamism, 504
Islam Karimov, 166
Ismail Ibn Sharif, 457
Ismailism, 460
Isochronism, 414
Isochronous, 419
Istanbul, 146
Italian resistance movement, 57
Iudaea province, 274
Ivančice, 375
Ivar the Boneless, 161
Ivo Andrić, 379
Iwane Matsui, 54
Ixcan, 232
Izanagi, 297
Izanami, 297

Jacinto Zamora, 329

Jack Bauer, 297
Jacob Grimm, 282, 353, 466
Jacobite Rising of 1745, 308
Jacobitism, 308
Jacques Callot, 48, 184
Jacques de Molay, 214
Jahangir, 138, 148
Jakarta, 366
Jalal Talabani, 54
Jamaica, 220
James Autry, 73
James Bell (priest), 305
James Elkins (art critic), 478
James Emerson Tennent, 141
James French (murderer), 101
James I of England, 217
James I of Scotland, 224
James Justinian Morier, 294
James Pratt and John Smith, 9
James Steuart (economist), 445
James the Just, 508
James T. Vaughn Correctional Center, 76
James VI of Scotland, 217
Jamie Hyneman, 195
Jamshid, 452
Janet Horne, 217
Jang Song-taek, 233
Jan Hus, 207, 214
Jan Janssen van Nes, 392
Jan Luyken, 191
Japan, 18, 19, 21, 123, 264, 279
Japanese castle, 279
Japanese Martyrs, 265
Japanese mythology, 297
Japji, 166
Jared Carter, 35
Jarrow, 338
Jaslyk Prison, 166
Jason Voorhees, 296
Jat people, 147
Jauhar, 230
Jay Chapman (physician), 71, 84
Jean Baptiste Tavernier, 341
Jean Bastien-Thiry, 128
Jean Bernard Bossu, 459
Jean Bernard Léon Foucault, 420
Jean Calas, 185
Jean-Charles de Borda, 436
Jean de Thevenot, 221, 365
Jean-Dominique Cassini, 436
Jean Froissart, 112
Jean-Jacques Rousseau, 480
Jean Kincaid, 176
Jean-Léon Gérôme, 5
Jean Picard, 427, 434, 445
Jean Richer, 418, 435

Jean Sasson, 510
Jeb Bush, 86
Jeffrey Dahmer, 295
Jehangir, 352
Jehohanan, 256, 258, 274
Jehovahs Witness, 255
Jenny-Wanda Barkmann, 39
Jeremiah Brandreth, 309, 310
Jeremy Beadle, 312
Jeremy Bentham, 10, 309
Jericho, 489
Jersey, 208
Jerusalem, 256
Jerusalem Talmud, 567
Jesse Washington lynching, 233
Jesuit, 323, 535
Jesus, 456, 510
Jesus and the woman taken in adultery, 510
Jesus Christ, 260
Jesus in the Talmud, 509
Jesus, King of the Jews, 274
Jesus of Nazareth, 274
Jewish, 9, 281
Jews, 104
Jezzar Pasha, 346
Jhelum, 151
Jiajing Emperor, 481
Jihlava, 373
Jim Crow laws, 62
Jimmy Lee Gray, 106
Joachim von Ribbentrop, 41
Joannes Zonaras, 474, 475
Joan of Arc, 214
Johan Alfred Ander, 129
Johan Filip Nordlund, 129
Johann Friedrich Struensee, 115
Johann Jakob Wick, 213
Johann Ludwig Burckhardt, 56
Johann Patkul, 177
Johann Reichhart, 119
Johann Reinhold Forster, 459
Johann Stumpf (writer), 62
John Allen Giles, 313
John Amery, 57
John Braithwaite (author), 222, 553
John Cooke (prosecutor), 306
John Crawfurd, 138
John David Duty, 80
John Duns Scotus, 187
John Evelyn, 307, 313
John Finch (martyr), 305
John Fisher, 163
John Foxe, 535
John Frith, 214
John Fryer (FRS), 342
John Gabriel Stedman, 66

John Harrison, 428
John Houghton (martyr), 306
John Hungerford Pollen (Jesuit), 314
John, King of England, 344
John Locke, 27
John Masters, 123
John Murray (publisher), 519
John Ogilvie (saint), 47
John Oldcastle, 207
John Payne (martyr), 305
John Riggs Miller, 446
John Roberts (historian), 480
John Rogers (Bible editor and martyr), 214
John Russell, 1st Earl Russell, 310
John Spenkelink, 101
John Stuart Mill, 27
John Wycliffe, 207
Joints, 171
Jon Haraldsson, 164
Jon Manchip White, 201
Jordan, 54
Joscelin I, Count of Edessa, 459
José Apolonio Burgos, 329
Josef Kramer, 43
José Luis Cerveto, 328
José María Jarabo, 328, 329
José Mariano Jiménez, 130
Joseon Dynasty, 290
Joseph Chitty, 312
Joseph Hickel, 15
Joseph Justus Scaliger, 307
Joseph Marchand, 481
Joseph Morgan (historian), 385
Joseph Pitton de Tournefort, 367
Joseph Süß Oppenheimer, 336
Josephus, 144, 253, 254, 258
Joshua, 489
Josif Rajačić, 465
Juan Aldama, 130
Juan Antonio Llorente, 450
Juan Díaz de Garayo, 329
Juan García Suárez, 329
Juan Vázquez Pérez, 329
Judah (biblical person), 202
Judaism, 487
Judeans, 371
Judge Dee, 485
Judicial corporal punishment, 26
Judiciary, 57
Judo, 514
Jugular vein, 39, 45
Jugular veins, 513
Jujutsu, 514
Julio Cortázar, 485
Julio López Guixot, 329
Julius and Ethel Rosenberg, 101

Julius Caesar, 204, 284
Julius Mount Bleyer, 71
Julius Paulus Prudentissimus, 401
Juraj Jánošík, 65
Jurisdiction, 276
Jury trial, 1
Jus cogens, 21
Justices of the peace, 207
Justinian, 394
Justinian I, 205
Justin Martyr, 542
Justus Lipsius, 254
Jutland, 215
Juvenal, 400, 532
Jyutping, 477

Kaarina, 183
Kabul, 500, 511
Kagutsuchi, 297
Kamakura period, 264
Kamuina Nsapu, 120
Kandy, 142
Kang Youwei, 480
Kappa (folklore), 285
Karachi, 152
Karakalpakstan, 166
Karamanli dynasty, 222
Kara Mustafa Pasha, 329
Karen people, 269
Karl Eugen, Duke of Württemberg, 336
Karl Hermann Frank, 41
Karl Marx, 10
Kashmir, 140
Katana, 124
Kater pendulum, 416
Katers pendulum, 420
Katherine Swynford, 180
Kaunas Fortress, 105
Kayin State, 269
Keel, 391
Keelhauling, **391**
Kenji Doihara, 54
Kenneth Biros, 80
Kenneth Setton, 461
Kenning, 163
Kentucky, 80, 92, 102
Kenya, 234
Keonjhar, 234
Kettle, 163
Kew Observatory, 440
Kgf, 43
Khaled Hosseini, 510
Khanaqin, 508
Kharijite, 498
Khartoum, 503
Khmelnytsky Uprising, 193

Khmer Rouge, 194
Khosrau II, 142
Khosrow I, 453
Khosrow II, 453
Khyber-Pakhtunkhwa, 123
Kidnapping, 5, 25, 56, 108, 504
Kidney, 89
Kiel, 374
Kiev, 269
Kilkenny, 217
Kill Bill, 296
Killing Fields, 194
Kincardineshire, 164
Kingdom of Afghanistan, 146
Kingdom of Great Britain, 276
Kingdom of Hungary, 346
Kingdom of Jerusalem, 210
Kingdom of Nagpur, 150
Kismayo, 504, 508
Kitab al-Kafi, 495
Kite (bird), 525
Kitos War, 454
Klaus Barbie, 324
Klepht, 378
Knights Hospitaller, 461
Knights Templar, 206
Knútsdrápa, 161
Kohat, 234
Kōki Hirota, 54
Konya, 456, 510
Košice, 367
Kraken: Tentacles of the Deep, 296
Kraków, 50
Krasny Bor Forest, Karelia, 68
Kremnica, 183
Kuldīga, 183
Kuressaare, 351
Kuressaare Castle, 351
Kurram Agency, 503
Kurram Valley, 487
Kyaram Sloyan, 122

Lady Gaga, 511
Lady with the Ring, 195
Laetare Sunday, 466
Lahore, 352, 503
Lakhipur, 149
Lamoral, Count of Egmont, 130
Lancaster Castle, 60
Landgraviate of Hesse, 192
Landrecht (medieval), 192
Landsberg am Lech, 50
Landsberg Prison, 42
Lansdowne, Pennsylvania, 508
Lapa do Santo, 112
Laryngopharynx, 513

Larynx, 327, 513, 514
Latin, 2, 251, 262
Latin America, 12
Latin language, 327, 394
Latitude, 418, 444
Lattakia, 56
Latvian people, 351
Laurence Shirley, 4th Earl Ferrers, 59
La Voz de Galicia, 548
Law, 10
Law Abiding Citizen, 296
Law code, 486
Law French, 276
Law of universal gravitation, 418
Lbf, 43
Lead, 410
Leeds University, 548
Left 4 Dead, 298
Legal burden of proof, 9
Leg bones, 171
Legislative Assembly (France), 128
Legitimacy (family law), 324
Leicester, 207, 339
Le Monde illustré, 478
Length, 414
Lent, 466
Leo Amery, 57
Leonardo Bravo (general officer), 329
Leonardo da Vinci, 417
Leonard Siffleet, 124
Leopold I, Holy Roman Emperor, 374
Leopold II, Holy Roman Emperor, 15, 16
Leprosy, 234
Lèse majesté, 323
Les Grandes Misères de la guerre, 48, 184
Lethal injection, 14, 23, 61, 70, **71**, 92, 99, 102, 108–110
Le Tour du Monde, 140, 276
Lê Văn Khôi revolt, 481
Levant, 457
Levant Company, 368
Lewis Powell (assassin), 60
Liao dynasty, 480
Liber Historiae Francorum, 292
Libu, 370
Lichfield, 215
Lieve Pietersz. Verschuier, 392
Life imprisonment, 1, 24, 61
Life imprisonment (England and Wales), 2
Life (magazine), 41
Life unworthy of life, 71
Life without parole, 26
Ligature (medicine), 325
Ligature strangulation, 43, 44
Ligne, 435, 562
Lima, Peru, 220

Lincolnshire, 354
Linen, 403
Lingchi, 463, **476**
Lion, 135
Lipophilic, 87
List of European Union member states, 19
List of execution methods, 145
List of ICD-9 codes, 410
List of Marian Martyrs, 215
List of Mughal emperors, 138
List of regicides of Charles I, 299, 306
List of territorial entities where German is an official language, 178
List of United States death row inmates, 106
Lithuania, 12, 105
Lithuanians, 205
Liu Cixin, 510
Liu Jin, 481
Liu Ziye, 480
Liver, 89, 411
Liverpool, 58
Liverpool (HM Prison), 58
Livilla, 344
Livonian people, 177
Livy, 396
Lizzie Halliday, 100
Locus classicus, 180
Lodi dynasty, 147
Lollards, 207
LOM Ediciones, 236
Londinium, 334
London, 321, 332
London Bridge, 298, 300, 304, 307
Longcase clock, 421
Looting, 11
Lord Chancellor, 302
Lord Curzon, 527
Lord Haw Haw, 58
Lord High Treasurer, 302
Lord Kalvan of Otherwhen, 154
Lord Peter Wimsey, 59
Lorestan Province, 342
Los Nogales, 233
Louisbourg, 459
Louis de Rouvroy, duc de Saint-Simon, 180
Louis Dominique Bourguignon, 185
Louisiana, 80, 176
Louisiana ex rel. Francis v. Resweber, 102
Louisiana State Penitentiary, 100
Louis IX of France, 207
Louis Rousselet, 140, 276
Lucas Cranach the Elder, 455
Lucasville, Ohio, 86
Lucian, 254
Lucius Aemilius Paulus Macedonicus, 144
Lucius Appuleius Saturninus, 508

Ludhiana, 151
Luis Candelas, 329
Luis del Mármol Carvajal, 464
Lundy Island, 300
Lung, 279
Lu Xun, 320
Lu You, 480
Lye, 410
Lynching, 259
Lynching in the United States, 62, 233
Lynchings, 40
Lynda Lyon Block, 101
Lyon, 324
Lysias (Syrian chancellor), 486
Lystra, 509

Macedon, 143
Machine gun, 70
Madhhab, 496
Madliena, 353
Madras, 150
Ma Duanlin, 404
Maecenas, 543
Maggie dela Riva, 100
Magician (paranormal), 487
Magic (paranormal), 5, 25, 217
Magistrate, 338
Maha Bandula, 463
Maharajah, 194
Mahatma Gandhi, 51
Mahmoud Asgari and Ayaz Marhoni, 22, 52
Mahmud Shah Durrani, 153
Mahout, 135
Maiden (beheading), 118
Maids (2015 TV series), 297
Maimonides, 9
Main Intelligence Directorate, 233
Mainspring, 426
Majdanek concentration camp, 104
Majorca, 209
Makkot, 567
Malaysia, 18, 137
Malcolm Bosse, 485
Malik Ambar, 227
Maliki, 496, 498
Malik ibn Anas, 263, 497, 498
Malmö, 356
Malouetine, 79
Malta, 211
Mamertine Prison, 327
Mamluk, 348
Mamoru Takuma, 54
Manasseh of Judah, 455
Manchester, 58
Manchukuo, 324
Mandarin, 477

Mandatory sentencing, 1
Manichaeism, 323
Manicheanism, 274
Manicheans, 205
Manila, 326
Mani (prophet), 274, 323
Manius Aquillius (consul 101 BC), 226
Mankato, Minnesota, 60
Mannequin, 332
Manoharpur, 234
Manslaughter, 49
Mantel clock, 426
Man That You Fear, 510
Mantlepiece, 447
Manuel Martínez Coronado, 72
Manu Smriti, 138
Mao Zedong, 11, 194
Maratha, 139
Maratha Empire, 146
Maratha kingdom, 324
Marcantonio Bragadin, 323
Marcel Ophüls, 324
Marcus Aemilius Lepidus (triumvir), 508
Marcus Licinius Crassus, 226, 537
Marcus Tullius Cicero, 398
Margaret Clitherow, 277
Margaret I of Denmark, 191
Margaret Pole, 8th Countess of Salisbury, 115
Maria Anna of Spain, 64
Maria Barbella, 101
Mariana de Pineda Muñoz, 329
Mariano Gómez, 329
Marie-Joseph Angélique, 218, 536
Marie-Josephte Corriveau, 334, 335
Marilyn Manson, 510
Marine (ocean), 391
Marin Mersenne, 419, 434, 445
Marinus van der Lubbe, 127
Mari, Syria, 370
Mark Antony, 127
Mark Codman, 337
Mark Dean Schwab, 86
Märkisches Museum, 172
Mark Twain, 358
Marmion (poem), 357
Marquis de Condorcet, 446
Marrakesh, 347
Marranos, 63, 208
Marsyas, 321
Martha M. Place, 101
Martial, 127
Martial arts, 514
Martials Epigrams, 127
Martin Hengel, 542
Martinique, 129
Martin Luther, 403

Martín Merino y Gómez, 329
Martyr, 163, 165, 277, 379
Martyrdom in Sikhism, 176
Martyrs of Otranto, 461
Marx Reichlich, 488
Mary Fallin, 109
Mary I of England, 215, 303
Mary Kings Close, 354
Maryland, 108
Mary, Queen of Scots, 115
Mary Surratt, 60
Mashhad, 52, 506
Mass, 414, 417, 429, 435
Massachusetts, 75, 218
Massacre, 25
Massacre at Huế, 193
Mass killing, 25
Mass murder, 478
Mass of the Earth, 436
Matricide, 478
Matthew Hale (New York), 94
Matthew Paris, 299, 300, 314
Matthias Klostermayr, 175, 186
Maud de Braose, 344
Mauritania, 487
Maximian, 281
Max Payne 3, 232
Max Schuler, 447
McAlester, Oklahoma, 86
Mecca, 268
Mechanical equilibrium, 411, 414
Medical ethics, 75
Medical examiner, 75
Medication, 411
Medieval, 142, 205
Mehmed II, 222
Mehmed the Conqueror, 460
Mehmet II, 376
Meiji period, 125, 264
Meir Tobianski, 54
Meleager (general), 143
Melrose Chronicle, 164
Melun, 65
Membrane potential, 411
Menelaus (High Priest), 486
Mercadier, 323
Mercury (element), 410, 427
Meridian arc, 446
Meridian (geography), 446
Merneptah, 370
Mesopotamia, 142
Meşterul Manole, 352
Metal Gear Rising: Revengeance, 298
Methanol, 411
Methods of execution, 375
Methohexital, 87

Metre, 446
Metric system, 436, 446
Metropolitanate of Karlovci, 465
Mexican Drug War, 131
Mexicans, 13
Mexico, 283, 486, 508
Mexico City, 209, 273, 287
Meyrick Hewlett, 480
MGal, 439
Michael Servetus, 214
Michael Szilágyi, 460
Michael VII Doukas, 404
Michelangelo, 252, 319
Michele Angiolillo, 329
Michel Foucault, 313, 320
Michelson interferometer, 442
Michigan, 12
Microgal, 443
Midazolam, 80
Middle Age, 7
Middle Ages, 37, 165, 171, 291, 327
Middle Assyrian period, 201
Middle chronology, 553
Midnapore, 150
Miguel Hidalgo y Costilla, 130
Mildred Harnack, 128
Military justice, 328
Military personnel, 67
Military tribunal, 61
Milk, 475
Millennials, 13
Milliequivalent, 79
Ming Dynasty, 320, 464, 479, 481
Ministry of Justice (Afghanistan), 500
Ministry of Public Security (North Korea), 233
Miorița, 352
Miran Edgar Thompson, 106
Mirror punishment, 171
Mirza Abu Bakr Dughlat, 552
Miscarriage of justice, 2, 27
Mishna, 490
Mishnah, 202, 490
Missionary, 234
Mission Istanbul, 511
Mississippi, 92, 106, 458
Mississippi River, 98
Missouri, 75, 80, 108
Misuse of Drugs Act (Singapore), 27
Mitanni, 372
Mithridates (soldier), 474
Mithridates VI of Pontus, 226
Mitochondria, 411
Moaz al-Kasasbeh, 234
Moctezuma II, 508
Mode locking, 447
Modern Asian Studies, 485

Modestinus, 400
Modesty, 262
Mofsed-e-filarz, 4
Mohammad Mohammad Sadeq al-Sadr, 53
Mohammed ben Abdallah, 222
Moharebeh, 4
Moloch, 487
Molsheim, 183
Moment of inertia, 415
Monarch, 323
Mongol, 138
Mongolia, 70, 340, 343
Monochrom, 195
Monomotapa, 148
Montepulciano, 457
Montmartre, 126
Montreal, 218
Monty Python and the Holy Grail, 296
Monty Pythons Life of Brian, 511
Moon Embracing the Sun, 297
Moors, 458
Moral panic, 7
Moratorium (law), 19, 30
Moravia, 345
Mordecai, 554
Morgue, 187
Morisco, 464
Morisco rebellions in Granada, 464
Moriscos, 208
Morocco, 221, 222, 452
Morris S. Arnold, 459
Mortal Kombat, 298
Moses, 487, 510
Moses Maimonides, 491
Mount Sinai, 456, 487
Mouth-to-mouth resuscitation, 106
Movement (clockwork), 431
Mozaffar ad-Din Shah Qajar, 14
Mozambique, 145
Muath Al-Kasasbeh, 54
Mughal emperor, 136
Mughal emperors, 346
Mughal Empire, 69, 136, 138, 145, 147
Mughals, 145
Muhaddis, 493
Muhammad, 221, 263
Muhammad Ali of Egypt, 457
Muhammad Zia-ul-Haqs Islamization, 502
Multan, 152
Mummy, 285
Munich, 119, 488
Münster Rebellion, 336
Murder, 2, 4, 48, 56, 108, 171
Murder (Abolition of Death Penalty) Act, 58
Murder Act 1751, 330, 337
Murderer, 316, 330

Murder of Becky Watts, 295
Murder of Bernard Oliver, 295
Murder of Jessica Ridgeway, 295
Murder of John Alan West, 58
Murder of Kim Wall, 295
Muscle contraction, 411
Mutiny, 4
Muwatta Imam Malik, 497
Myanmar, 70
Mystras, 460
MythBusters, 195, 370, 531
Mythology, 163
Mytilene, 461

Naboth, 509
Nagasaki, 228
Nagasaki, Nagasaki, 265
Namdhari, 152
Nam Định Province, 463
Namibia, 230
Namibian war of independence, 317
Nanking Massacre, 190, 193
Napoleon, 119
Naraka (Buddhism), 465
Naraka (Hinduism), 465
Narciso López, 329
Narcos, 297
Narmer Palette, 113
Narragansett people, 302
Naruto Shippuden: Ultimate Ninja Storm 3, 298
Nathuram Godse, 51
National Geographic Channel, 256
National Geographic Magazine, 337
Nationalist faction (Spanish Civil War), 317
Nationalist government, 482
National Museum of Crime & Punishment, 76
National Public Radio, 538
Nation state, 9
Nat Turner, 131, 324
Nat Turners slave rebellion, 324
Natural and legal rights, 10
Natural rights, 27
Nausea, 475
Navarre, 328
Nazi crimes against the Polish nation, 11
Nazi Germany, 50, 57, 104, 119, 128
Nazis, 12
Nazism, 41
Neagu Voda, 352
Nebraska, 93
Neck, 45
Necklacing, 231, 232, 234
Necromancy, 487
Neo-Assyrian, 318
Neo-Assyrian Empire, 202, 323, 343, 364, 371

Neo-Nazi ideology and symbols, 269
Neoplatonism, 323
Nepal, 230
Nero, 532
Nerve gas, 411
Nervous system, 118, 410
Nesîmî, 323
Netherlands, 164
Neurology, 95
Neuromuscular-blocking drug, 71, 79
Neuromuscular-blocking drugs, 88
Neuromuscular junction, 79
Neurotoxin, 316, 411
Nevada, 108
Nevada State Prison, 106
Newcastle upon Tyne, 300
New France, 218
Newgate Prison, 57
New Hampshire, 62
New Latin, 412
New Mexico, 108, 274
New Mexico State Penitentiary, 109
New Mexico State Penitentiary riot, 233
New Mexico Territory, 43
New Orleans, 458
Newport Rising, 310
New Testament, 509, 510
Newton (unit), 43
New York Conspiracy of 1741, 219
New York Court of Appeals, 98
New York Daily News, 101
New York Law School, 25
New York Slave Revolt of 1712, 176, 219
New York (state), 71
New York Times, 519
Nezahualcoyotl (tlatoani), 283, 486
Niccolò Barbaro, 377
Nicholas A. M. Rodger, 393
Nicholas Ridley (martyr), 214
Nick Berg, 132
Nickel, 429
Nicolas Jacques Pelletier, 129
Niedererbach, 183
Nigeria, 18, 21, 487, 502
Nikah mutah, 494
Nine million victims, 214
Ninestane Rig, 164
Nineveh, 143
NIST, 431
Nitrogen asphyxiation, 109
Nixs Mate, 337
Nizari, 460
NKVD, 106
Nl:Anna Utenhoven, 191
Nl:Julien Wolbers, 220
Nokogiribiki, 124

Noose, 37
Nordic countries, 129
Norio Nagayama, 22, 54
Norman Chevers, 144
Norna-Gests þáttr, 162
Norsemen, 4
North Berwick witch trials, 217
North Carolina, 80, 108
North Korea, 19, 23, 70, 104
North Pole, 562
North Vietnam, 280
Norway, 129
Norwegian language, 179
Not proven, 1
Novellae Constitutiones, 402
Novorossiya (confederation), 269
Nuclear weapon, 101, 297
Nude, 262
Nun, 545
Nuncio, 224
Nuremberg, 192
Nuremberg Trials, 24, 41, 231

Oberammergau Passion Play, 273
Oberursel (Taunus), 282
Oblate spheroid, 418, 435, 444
Oblation, 205
Occupation of Japan, 54
Occupation of Lithuania by Soviet Union 1940, 105
Oceania, 12
October Revolution, 56
Oda Nobunaga, 124
Odin, 44, 161, 162
Odo I, Count of Blois, 65
Odyssey, 37
Offences against the Person Act 1828, 310
Office of the United Nations High Commissioner for Human Rights, 544
Official Table of Drops, 40
Ohio, 80
Oklahoma, 71, 80, 92, 101, 102
Oklahoma State Penitentiary, 86
Olavinlinna, 351
Old Bailey, 57
Old Believer, 201
Old Norse, 161
Old Prussians, 205, 282
Old Sparky, 103
Old Testament, 5, 334, 509, 510
Oleg Penkovsky, 233
Ole Rømer, 445
Olfert Dapper, 293
Olga Bancic, 128
Oliver Cromwell, 334
Oliver Plunkett, 308

Omaima Nelson, 295
Oman, 70
Omer Vrioni, 556
Omey Island, 126
On Crimes and Punishments, 16
On the Detection and Overthrow of the So-Called Gnosis, 542
Op. cit., 524
Operation Barbarossa, 104
Operation Pastorius, 101
Operation Reinhard, 104
Opioid, 74, 85
Opium, 227, 480, 482
Oral law, 492
Orbital motion, 418
Oregon, 108
Organ (anatomy), 279
Organ donation, 70
Organism, 410
Orgetorix, 205
Orkney, 164
Orkneyinga saga, 161
Orpheus, 297
Osama (film), 511
O Sang-hon, 233
Oscar Wilde, 358
Oscillate, 411
Oscillatory motion, 449
Osiris, 297
Ossuary, 258
Ostracon, 323
Otranto, 461

Öttingen, 63

Otto III of Olomouc, 345
Ottoman Empire, 49, 143, 324, 328, 374, 377, 460
Ottoman Greece, 378
Ottoman invasion of Otranto, 461
Ottomans, 323
Ottoman Turks, 376
Otto René Castillo, 232
Out of phase, 447
Ovambo people, 230
Overseas France, 129
Ovid, 297
Owensboro, Kentucky, 60
Oxford, 57
Oxford English Dictionary, 37, 303
Oxford University, 269
Oxford University Press, 517, 524
Oxygen, 513

Paederasty, 345
Paganism, 323, 356

Pakistan, 18, 21, 352, 487
Pakistan Armed Forces, 234
Palamedes (mythology), 507
Palatine Hill, 542
Palazzo, 358
Pampanga, 273
Pancras of Taormina, 508
Pancuronium bromide, 74, 77
Panthéon, Paris, 420
Papal bull, 205
Pappenheimer family, 375
Papua New Guinea, 166
Parachinar, 234, 503
Parallel Lives, 284
Paralysis, 44, 74
Paralytic, 71, 79
Param has ext link, 359, 361, 362
Parboiled, 281, 307
Pardon, 2, 136
Parenteral nutrition, 284
Parliamentary Assembly of the Council of Europe, 31
Parliament of the United Kingdom, 231
Parole, 2, 61
Parricide, 394
Parricides, 205
Pars pro toto, 325
Partisan (military), 50
Parts per million, 427
Parysatis, 453, 486
Pashtun people, 123
Passion play, 273
Passion Play of Iztapalapa, 273
Passport, 58
Pathfinder (2007 film), 296
Patriarch of Aquileia, 344
Patricide, 397, 478
Patrick Hamilton (martyr), 214
Patrick Wormald, 316
Paul Haupt, 372
Paulicians, 508
Paul Jacobsthal, 126
Paul of Tarsus, 274, 510
Paulo Miki, 265
Paul Revere, 337
Paul the Apostle, 259, 509
Peasant, 280
Pederasts, 211
Pedro Américo, 288
Pedro Bautista, 265
Pedro Berruguete, 327
Pedro II of Aragon, 205
Pedro II of Brazil, 16
Pedro Medina, 103
Pehčevo, 193
Pelagia of Tarsus, 169

Penal code, 16, 268
Penal servitude, 310
Penal transportation, 310
Pendulum, **411**
Pendulum clock, 411, 418, 419, 425, 435
Pendulum (mathematics), 414
Pendulums for divination and dowsing, 449
Penetrating trauma, 364
Pentateuch, 5
Pentobarbital, 73, 74, 78
Pentrich rising, 310
Peoples Court (Germany), 128
Peoples Republic of China, 21, 76
Peraia, Thessaloniki, 188
Perdiccas, 143
Perfusion, 117
Périgueux, 208
Perlachturm, 211, 345
Perleberg, 178
Persecution of Christians, 356
Perseus of Macedon, 144
Persia, 223, 340, 486
Persian language, 453
Perth, Scotland, 300
Perth, Tasmania, 337
Perugia, 323
Peruvian people, 291
Peshawar, 152
Pesticide, 411
Petachiah of Ratisbon, 142
Petechiae, 47
Peter Anthony Allen, 58
Peter Kürten, 127
Peter Mundy, 385
Peter Niers, 174, 545
Peter Stumpp, 177
Petronilla de Meath, 217
Petty treason, 216, 301
Pew Research Center, 505
Pfizer, 73
Phaedriades, 316
Phalaris, 167, 223
Pharaoh, 201
Pharisees, 260
Pharmacokinetics, 85
Philadelphia, 508
Philadelphia, Pennsylvania, 333
Philip Augustus, 207
Philip de Montmorency, Count of Horn, 130
Philip II, Duke of Orléans, 180
Philip III of Spain, 192
Philip II of Spain, 281
Philip IV of France, 323
Philip of Jesus, 265
Philipp Andreas Nemnich, 394
Philippicae, 127

Philippines, 19, 92, 99, 100, 265, 273, 326
Philip V of France, 208
Philosophiæ Naturalis Principia Mathematica, 418
Phobia, 187
Phoenicia, 260
Photojournalism, 101
Physician, 75
Piano wire, 325
Pierre Barbet (physician), 257
Pierre Basile, 323
Pierre Bouguer, 435
Pieter Brueghel the Elder, 183
Pilar Prades, 328
Pilar Prades Santamaría, 329
Pilgrimage of Grace, 334
Pindar, 167, 223
Piracy with violence, 16
Pirate, 332, 391
Pirates, 261, 330
Pisa, 357
Pisa Cathedral, 417
Pisanello, 38
Pistol, 68, 69
Pitch (resin), 221
Pius II, 224
Planet, 418
Plastination, 321
Plautus, 260, 397
Playa Vicente, 232
Plea, 276
Plea bargain, 25
Plesse Castle, 356
PLoS Medicine, 86
Plough, 176
Plutarch, 204, 260, 396, 474
Poena cullei, 205, **394**, 475
Poison, 104, 163, 410
Poisoning, **410**
Poland, 128
Polish–Soviet War, 380
Political corruption, 4
Political crime, 119
Political ideology, 2
Political protest, 25
Political repression, 11
Pöls-Oberkurzheim, 178, 179
Põlva, 351
Polycarp, 203
Polycrates, 260
Pompey, 127
Pompey the Great, 398
Pontius Pilate, 274
Pope, 119
Pope Gregory IX, 205
Popish Plot, 307

Poppo of Treffen, 344
Porridge, 163
Portal:Criminal justice, 2
Portal:Law, 2
Portuguese colonialists, 148
Portuguese Empire, 145
Portuguese Inquisition, 210, 533
Posthumous execution, 207
Post-mortem, 482
Potassium, 74, 79
Potassium chloride, 71, 73, 74, 77, 411
Potassium cyanide, 108
Pothinus, 127
POW, 124
Poznan, 104
Poznań, 534
Prague, 41
Precess, 420
Precipitation (chemistry), 74
Pre-Columbian, 486
Predator (film), 324
Premature burial, **187**, 340
Přemyslid dynasty, 345
Presidency of Hamid Karzai, 500
President of Lithuania, 12
Presumption of innocence, 1
Pre-trial, 1
Prien am Chiemsee, 183
Priest, 277
Priest hunter, 304
Prima facie, 28
Primary standard, 444
Prince of Wales, 300
Principality, 376
Principality of Transylvania (1711–1867), 177
Principia Mathematica (Newton), 435
Prior, 320
Priscus, 344
Prison, 7, 43, 200
Prisoner of conscience, 503
Prisoners of war, 58, 376
Pritzwalk, 178
Privy Council of the United Kingdom, 302
Privy Seal, 302
Probation, 2
Procopius (usurper), 294, 455
Project Gutenberg, 199
Prometheus, 254
Propaganda, 57
Propofol, 87
Prosecutor, 328
Proskynesis, 260
Protestant Reformation, 215
Protestants, 215
Province of Perugia, 333
Prussia, 63, 171, 178

Prussian blue, 105
Psychological torture, 17, 26
Psychological warfare, 280, 378
Ptolemy IV Philopator, 144
Public domain, 133
Public execution, 50, 70, 135, 171
Publius Cornelius Lentulus Sura, 327
PubMed Identifier, 91, 246
Pudukkottai district, 366
Pulley, 163
Pulmonary embolism, 256
Pulse, 417
Punishment, 364
Punjab, 152
Punjab, Pakistan, 503
Puritan, 303
Pyongyang, 106

Qadi, 497
Qaid, 457
Qajar Shahs of Persia, 1794–1925, 14
Qatar, 111, 487
Qazvin Province, 500
Q:Capital punishment, 32
Q factor, 430, 431
Qin dynasty, 290, 480
Qin Er Shi, 480
Qing dynasty, 480, 482
Qin Shi Huang, 347
Qisas, 4
Quake 4, 298
Quartz, 421
Quartz clock, 412, 421, 425, 432
Quartz watch, 430
Quebec, 334
Queen Victoria, 154
Quintus Curtius Rufus, 143
Quintus Tullius Cicero, 399
Quran, 492

Rabbi, 142
Rabbi Akiva, 323
Radiation poisoning, 411
Radius (bone), 256
Ragnar Loðbrók, 161
Rainey Bethea, 60
Rajasinha II of Kandy, 489
Rajm, 487, 492, 496, 501, 502
Rakhine State, 346
Ralph Cifaretto, 297
Ralph Crockett, 305
Ramesses IX, 370
Ramsay Bolton, 324
Ram Sharan Sharma, 303, 315
Rani Lakshmibai, 154
Rape, 4, 25, 52, 504

Raqqa, 234, 268, 504
Rashidun, 493
Ratification, 21
Rational choice theory (criminology), 10
Rattanakosin Kingdom, 226
Raven, 162
Ravished Armenia, 379
Razavi Khorasan Province, 500
Realm, 302
Reason (magazine), 569
Rebellion, 364
Red Hat Cell Block, 100
Red Riding Hood (2011 film), 170
Refectory, 345
Regular army, 119
Regulator clock, 434
Rehoboam, 509
Reichstag fire, 127
Renaissance, 417
Renate von Natzmer, 128
René Descartes, 419
Renyin palace rebellion, 481
Reprieve (organisation), 89
Republican faction (Spanish Civil War), 317
Republic of Macedonia, 193
Republic of Venice, 323, 461, 535
Resistance fighter, 119
Resonance width, 430, 431
Resonant frequency, 430
Responsibility for the death of Jesus, 274
Restoring force, 411, 426, 429
Resurrection, 172
Retentionist, 19
Retributive justice, 298
Retrofitted, 418
Revolt of Horea, Cloşca and Crişan, 177, 375
Revolutionary Association of the Women of Afghanistan, 506
Reyhaneh Jabbari, 53
Rhetorica ad Herennium, 396
Rhodes, 461
Ribe, 191
Richard Bourke, 6th Earl of Mayo, 527
Richard, Count of Acerra, 65
Richard Gwyn (martyr), 306
Richard II, 215
Richard I of England, 323
Richard Mant, 567
Richard Roose, 163
Richard Schiff, 296
Richard Topcliffe, 304
Rictor Norton, 216
Ridda Wars, 221
Riefler escapement, 424, 429
Riegersburg Castle, 179
Rigas Feraios, 462

Right to a fair trial, 1
Right to counsel, 1
Right to life, 17, 26
Rigid body, 415
Ringer Edwards, 266
Río Bravo, Suchitepéquez, 232
Rio de Janeiro, 239
Rio de Janeiro, Brazil, 232
Río de la Plata, 209
River Thames, 332
Robbers, 374
Robbery, 171
Robert Abercromby (missionary), 535
Roberta Frank, 162
Robert A. Heinlein, 510
Robert Alton Harris, 108
Robert Aske (political leader), 334
Robert Blecker Wants Me Dead, 25
Robert Conquest, 11
Robert Devereux, 2nd Earl of Essex, 115
Robert-François Damiens, 291
Robert Heindl, 478
Robert Hooke, 418
Robert Kerr (writer), 139
Robert Knox (sailor), 141
Robert Leslie Stewart, 57
Robert Peel, 310
Robert Robinson (Dissenting minister), 189
Robert the Bruce, 164
Robert van Gulik, 485
Rocket (weapon), 146
Rodrigo Rojas DeNegri, 233
Rohilkhand, 152
Roman Blood, 404
Roman Britain, 334
Roman Catholic, 277
Roman Catholic Church, 215
Roman civil wars, 260
Roman Empire, 5, 143, 203, 260, 275, 316, 454
Roman Forum, 316
Romani people, 104
Roman law, 394
Roman mythology, 275
Romanov Dynasty, 56
Roman Republic, 127, 274, 316
Roman Republic (19th century), 16
Roman triumph, 127
Rome, 275, 316, 491
Romell Broom, 80, 86
Romulus, 396
Ronald Hutton, 163
Ronald Ryan, 49
Roper v. Simmons, 17, 21
Rostra, 127
Roswell P. Flower, 100

Rotation of the Earth, 420, 444
Rotisserie, 378
Round shot, 146
Rousas Rushdoony, 504
Rowan tree, 351
Roxbury, Massachusetts, 218
Royal assent, 231
Royal Commission, 71
Royal Commission on Capital Punishment 1864-1866, 310
Royal families, 160
Royal Society, 445
Rozafa Castle, 352
Ruben Enaje, 273
Rudolf Kühnapfel, 178
Rumāl, 327
Running the gauntlet, 11
Russia, 3
Russian Empire, 56
Russian language, 69
Ruth Bader Ginsburg, 82
Ruth Ellis, 58
Ruth Snyder, 101
Rye, East Sussex, 333

S^2, 439
Sabawi Ibrahim al-Tikriti, 54
Sabine, 275
Sabines, 396
Sabotage, 101
Sachsenhausen concentration camp, 105
Sachsenspiegel, 171, 403
Sacristan, 320
Sadakat Kadri, 263
Saddam Hussein, 53, 132
Sadhu Haridas, 194
Safe room, 358
Safety coffin, 189
Safi of Persia, 227
Saga, 160
Sahih al-Bukhari, 496
Sahih Bukhari, 495
Sahih Muslim, 495, 496
Saigon, 280
Saint Andrew, 274
Saint Barnabas, 510
Saint Bartholomew, 323
Saint Castulus, 191
Saint-Domingue, 459
Saint Dominic, 327
Saint Eskil, 508
Saint Eustace, 169
Saint Jerome, 348
Saint Otteran, 195
Saint Paul, 111
Saint Peter, 274

Saint Sebastian, 163
Saint Stephen, 488, 509
Saint symbolism, 180
Saint Timothy, 508
Saint Vitalis of Milan, 191
Sajida al-Rishawi, 54
Sakineh Mohammadi Ashtiani, 509
Salem witch trials, 277
Saline (medicine), 71
Salix viminalis, 204
Salomon Schweigger, 552
Saltire, 172, 274
Salvador Puig Antich, 328, 329
Sambhaji, 139, 324
Samos, 260
Sam Shockley, 106
Samuel Butler (poet), 445
Samuel Clarke, 303, 312
Samuel Haughton, 41
Samuel Pepys, 330
Samuel Romilly, 309, 315
Samurai, 123, 279
Sandro Botticelli, 491
Sanhedrin, 490, 492, 508
Sanhedrin (tractate), 567
Sanjak of Gelibolu, 461
San Pedro Cutud, 273
San Quentin State Prison, 14, 60, 75, 82, 106, 110
Santaji, 139
Santiago, Chile, 233
Santorio Santorii, 417
Sardar, 342
Sardinia, 316
Sardonicism, 316
Sargon II, 323, 371
Sarin gas attack on the Tokyo subway, 54
Sasanian Empire, 453
Sassanid Empire, 142
Satanism, 7
Sati (practice), 339
Satyr, 321
Saudi Arabia, 18, 21, 23, 111, 267, 487, 503
Saul, 372
Saw (2004 film), 296
Saw 3D, 170
Saw IV, 296
Saxony, 403
Scaffold (execution site), 171, 330
Scalpel, 285
Scalping, 318
Scapegoating, 510
Scaphism, **474**
Scarface (1983 film), 296
Schuler tuning, 447
Schwabenspiegel, 191

Science education, 449
Scientific American, 90, 95
Scientific instrument, 412
Scotland, 176, 217
Scottish people, 300
Sea level, 446
Sebastian Münster, 114
Secondary poisoning, 411
Second Catilinian Conspiracy, 327
Second Optional Protocol to the International Covenant on Civil and Political Rights, 31
Second Punic War, 397
Seconds pendulum, 425, 426, 434, 444, 445
Second Temple of Jerusalem, 510
Secret History (television documentary series), 266
Sect, 32

Şehzade Bayezid, 329

Seishirō Itagaki, 54
Seismometer, 412, 416
Seismometers, 447
Sejanus, 344
Self-defence, 512
Self-defense, 514
Self-immolation, 227, 229
Self-incrimination, 1
Self-published sources, 235
Seljuq dynasty, 142
Semi-trailer truck, 296
Seneca the Elder, 400
Seneca the Younger, 252–254, 260–262, 400, 548
Sengoku period, 124, 264
Sennacherib, 371
Sentence (law), 1, 2
Sentencing guidelines, 1
Senusret I, 201
Separatism, 25
Sepoy, 150
Sepoy Mutiny of 1857, 69
Sepoys, 149
Seppuku, 124, 279, 280
Sepsis, 256
Serbia in the Balkan Wars, 193
Serbian epic poetry, 352
Serbian Revolution, 379
Serbs of Bosnia and Herzegovina, 125
Serfdom, 56
Sergey Solomko, 270
Serial killer, 100, 172, 515
Serial murderer, 101
Seti, 370
Set (mythology), 297

Settara, 152
Seven Sleepers, 356, 357
Seville, 209
Sex offender registration, 2
Sextus Roscius, 398, 404
Sexual assault, 49
Sexually violent predator legislation, 2
Shabbat, 5
Shafii, 263, 498
Shah, 452
Shah Jahan, 138, 346
Shahnameh, 452
Shah Shujah Durrani, 153
Shah Shuja (Mughal), 346
Shalmaneser III, 553
Shaman, 297
Shapur II, 456
Sharia, 268, 495, 505
Shariah, 132
Sharia law, 52, 291, 492, 500
Shattiwaza, 372
Shaun of the Dead, 296
Shen Jiaben, 481
Shenyang, 268
Sheriff, 60, 231
Shia, 495
Shihab al-Din Muhammad al-Nasawi, 537
Shi Jingtang, 480
Shin guntō, 124
Shiraz, 342
Shirley Jackson, 510
Shock (circulatory), 174, 262, 318
Shock (mechanics), 40
Shockumentary, 232
Shōgun (novel), 125
Shoko Asahara, 20, 54
Shooting, 67
Short bowel syndrome, 284
Shortt-synchronome clock, 431, 432
Show trial, 127
Shrub, 395
Shuja Shah, 146
Shuja-ud-Daula, 526
Shunning, 4, 80
Shunzhi Emperor, 464
Shuttarna III, 372
Siam, 136, 137
Sibylline Oracles, 396
Sicily, 167, 223, 374
Siddiq Barmak, 511
Sidon, 370
Siege of Baghdad (1258), 226
Siege of Jerusalem (70), 253, 254
Siege of Lachish, 371
Siege of Missolonghi (1825), 556
Siege of Tripolitsa, 556

Siege of Tyre (332 BC), 260
Sigmund, 162
Sigurd, 162
Sigvatr Þórðarson, 161
Sikh, 152, 165, 176
Simeon of Jerusalem, 274
Simon Fraser, 11th Lord Lovat, 125
Simon the Zealot, 452, 456
Simple gravity pendulum, 412, 414
Simple harmonic motion, 415
Simplified Chinese characters, 476
Sinaai, 183
Sin City (film), 296
Singapore, 18, 19, 27, 56
Sing Sing, 94
Sir Archibald Alison, 1st Baronet, 556
Sir Charles Forster, 1st Baronet, 311
Sir Frederick Pollock, 1st Baronet, 544
Sir Frederick Pollock, 3rd Baronet, 314
Sir Henry Holland, 1st Baronet, 555
Sir Henry Norman, 1st Baronet, 482
Sir Herbert Maxwell, 7th Baronet, 306, 314
Sir Nathaniel Wraxall, 1st Baronet, 356
Sir Robert Graham, 224
Sir Thomas Armstrong, 306
Sisamnes, 323
Sistine Chapel, 491
Skagen, 446
Skald, 160
Skin, 318
Skinning, 318
Skull and crossbones (symbol), 410
Slavery in ancient Rome, 261
Slaves, 205, 261
Slovakia, 367
Slow slicing, 6, 7
Smithfield, London, 300
Smiths Parish, Bermuda, 334
Smolyan, 549
Smyrna, 399
Snake, 117
Snorri Sturluson, 161
Sobekhotep II, 370
Sobibór extermination camp, 104
Soccer-specific stadium, 22
Social policy, 16
Sodium cyanide, 108
Sodium thiopental, 74, 76, 77, 80
Sodomy, 4, 9, 210, 507
Sofia, 49
Sogdianus, 486
Solon, 5
Somalia, 18, 21, 23, 487, 504
Song dynasty, 404, 480
Song of Çelo Mezani, 352
Sophie Scholl, 119, 128

Sophocles, 356
Soraya Manutchehri, 501, 508
Soultzmatt, 63
South Africa, 231, 234, 317
South Asia, 25, 135
South Carolina, 92, 100, 102
South Dakota, 80
Southeast Asia, 25, 135
Southeastern Europe, 352
Southern Min, 477
Southern United States, 233
South Korea, 19
South Slavs, 466
South Sudan, 19, 31
South Vietnamese Army, 280
Soviet partisans, 51
Soviet Union, 51, 68, 101, 105
Spain, 265
Spanish colonization of the Americas, 327
Spanish Inquisition, 208, 450, 515
Spanish language, 325
Spanish Netherlands, 281
Spartacus, 260, 274
Spartacus: War of the Damned, 297
Speed of light, 442
Speedy trial, 1
Spencer Horatio Walpole, 310
Spiezer Schilling, 211
Spinal column, 40
Spinal cord, 14, 118
Spree killer, 22
Spring (device), 426
Square root, 417
Sri Lanka, 19, 22, 141, 145, 489
Sri Vikrama Rajasinha, 141
Stalin era, 11
Standard Chinese, 477
Starvation, 187, 340
State electrician, 97
Stateira (wife of Artaxerxes II), 453
State of Louisiana, 100
State of Palestine, 18
State religion, 4
Stato da Màr, 461
Statute Law (Repeals) Act 1973, 125
Statutory, 298
Stay of execution, 73
St Bartholomew, 319
St Catharines College, Cambridge, 183
St Catherines College, Oxford, 182, 183
St. Columba, 195
Steel, 428, 429
Stefano Pendinelli, 461
Stereoscope, 268
Steven Saylor, 404
St. Feichin, 126

S:The Code of Hammurabi (Harper translation), 553
Stick figure, 542
Stirling, 300
St. Matthews German Evangelical Lutheran Church, 255
Stones, 487
Stoning, 14, 22, **487**, 512
Stoning of Aisha Ibrahim Duhulow, 22
Stoning of Dua Khalil Aswad, 502
Stoning of the Devil, 493
Stop Child Executions Campaign, 21
Stop Stoning Forever Campaign, 506
Stora Hammars I, 160
St. Peter am Perlach, 212, 345
St. Peters Roman Catholic Church, Drogheda, 308
St Pierre and Miquelon, 129
Stralsund, 165
Stranger in a Strange Land, 510
Strangeways Prison, 58
Strangling, 316, 325, **512**, 515
Strangulation, 39, 40, 305, 529
Strappado, 450
Strasbourg, 208
Strasbourg massacre, 208
Struga, 549
Stunt, 187
Sturmabteilung, 127
Stuttgart, 336
Stutthof concentration camp, 39, 40
Styria, 178, 179
Subedar, 149
Subluxation, 46
Sub-Saharan Africa, 31
Substance intoxication, 316
Sudan, 19, 21, 268, 487
Suetonius, 317, 399, 400
Sufentanyl, 85
Suffering, 262
Suffocation, 84
Suffocation in ash, 283, **486**
Sugamo Prison, 54
Sugitani Zenjubō, 124
Suicide, 37, 43, 44, 71, 124, 279
Suicide (book), 350
Suicides, 40
Suicide watch, 43
Sukhmani, 166
Sulfuric acid, 108
Sulla, 127
Sultan, 461
Sultanate of Aceh, 227
Sultan Hashim Ahmed, 53
Sultan of Brunei, 500
Sumer, 347

Summary execution, 40
Sun Hao, 320
Sunnah, 494, 495
Sunni, 495
Superjail, 297
Suppression of dissent, 364
Suppression of Heresy Act 1414, 207
Supreme Commander for the Allied Powers, 54
Supreme Court of India, 51
Supreme Court of Japan, 22
Supreme Court of the United States, 15, 21, 101
Supreme Peoples Court, 77
Surgical, 286
Suriname, 66, 369
Surveying, 439
Susan Sontag, 484
Suspended sentence, 1
Suxamethonium chloride, 79
Sv:Aubry de La Motraye, 377
SWAPO, 317
Sweden, 129
Swedish Empire, 177, 374
Swedish language, 179
Swedish people, 352
Swimming pool, 284
Swindler, 165
Switzerland, 114
Sword, 129
Symmetry (mathematics), 433
Symphorosa, 456
Syria, 268

Tacitus, 190, 253, 261, 274, 334, 532
Tackys War, 220
Taha Yassin Ramadan, 53
Tahvo Putkonen, 115
Taiwan, 19, 70
Taiwanese Romanization System, 477
Taiwan Taoyuan International Airport, 24
Takayuki Fukuda, 22
Takelot II, 201
Takestan, 508
Tale of Ragnars Sons, 161
Taliban, 13, 234, 511
Taliban insurgency, 500
Talleyrand, 446
Tallow, 163
Talmud, 323, 490, 492
Tamar (Genesis), 202
Tamil Nadu, 366
Tanakh, 509, 510
Tang dynasty, 6, 290
Tanit, 503
Tanner Lectures on Human Values, 518
Taphophobia, 187

Tar, 163, 332
Tara Maclay, 324
Târgovişte, 376
Tariq Aziz, 54
Tarpeia, 275
Tarpeian Rock, 275, 316
Tarquinius Superbus, 396
Tarsus (city), 259
Taş Köprü Zade, 222
Tatmadaw, 269
Tau, 254
Tautochrone problem, 419
Ted Bundy, 101
Teheran, 508
Telemachus (Acragas), 167
Television series, 324
Tell-Tale Heart, 297
Template:Criminal procedure (trial), 2
Template talk:Criminal procedure (trial), 2
Templo Mayor, 287
Ten Commandments, 487
Tennessee, 73, 80, 92, 100, 102
Terrorism, 4, 25, 132
Tertullian, 204, 260
Teruhiko Seki, 22
Tetanus, 273
Tete, 148
Teutonic Knights, 282
Texas, 72, 80
Texcoco (altepetl), 283, 486
Thailand, 70, 136, 226
The Adventures of Tom Sawyer, 358
The Ancient Allan, 475
The Atlantic, 544
The Battle of Algiers (film), 119
The Black Cat (short story), 358
The Bridge on the Drina, 379
The Bucharest pogrom, 281
The Building of Skadar, 352
The Canterbury Tales, 517
The Canterville Ghost, 358
The Cask of Amontillado, 358
The Civil War, 284
The Complete Peerage, 523
The Council of Europe, 69
The Crucible, 278
The Crucible (1996 film), 278
The Crucified Soldier, 266
The Dark Forest, 510
The Divine Comedy, 297, 357
The Family of Pascual Duarte, 328
The Five Pains, 290
The Frozen Dead (TV series), 324
The Great Terror, 11, 517
The Green Inferno (film), 296
The History of English Law, 544

The Hitcher (1986 film), 296
The Hitcher (2007 film), 296
The Holocaust, 104
The Independent, 547
The Injustice to Dou E, 566
The Joy Luck Club (novel), 485
The Judgement of Cambyses, 322
The Kite Runner, 510
The Kite Runner (film), 511
The Lancashire Witches, 358
The Lancet, 15, 84, 91
The Last Judgment (Michelangelo), 319
The Latin Library, 542
The Lost World: Jurassic Park, 296
The Lottery, 510, 511
The Lovely Bones, 297
The Newgate Calendar, 59
The New York Times, 70, 91, 153, 188, 523
The Night Attack, 376
Theodore Schurch, 58
Theodor Mommsen, 395
The Old Testament, 509
Theologian, 259
The Pagan Religions of the Ancient British Isles, 163
The Paleface (1948 film), 296
The Pit and the Pendulum, 450
The Punishment of Korah and the Stoning of Moses and Aaron, 491
Therapia, 377
Thermal decomposition, 200
Thermal expansion, 421
Thermopylae, 379
Theron of Acragas, 167
The Sand Pebbles (film), 485
The Silence of the Lambs (novel), 324
The Slovak Spectator, 520
The Sopranos, 297
Thessaloniki, 188
The Steam House, 154
The Stoning of Soraya M., 510, 511
The Straight Dope, 394
The Texas Chain Saw Massacre, 296
The Thaw (2009 film), 296
The Times, 483
The Twelve Caesars, 547
The Twelve Conclusions of the Lollards, 15
The Wind-Up Bird Chronicle, 324
The Winters Tale, 475
Thigh, 318
Thing (assembly), 4
Thiopental, 73
Third Anglo-Mysore War, 149
Third Reich, 127
Third Servile War, 260, 274
Thirty Years War, 374

Thomas Armstrong (English politician), 307
Thomas Cranmer, 214
Thomas de Brantingham, 180
Thomas Edison, 94, 95
Thomas Felton (died 1381), 112
Thomas Ford (martyr), 304
Thomas Francis Wade, 482
Thomas Harris, 324, 485
Thomas Harrison (soldier), 306
Thomas Jefferson, 446
Thomas More, 15
Thomas Pilchard, 303
Thomas Shaw (divine and traveller), 222, 368
Thomas Smart Hughes, 378
Thomas Young (scientist), 445
Thompson v. Oklahoma, 21
Thomson-Houston Electric Company, 94, 97
Thoracic diaphragm, 85
Thornton Abbey, 354
Thracians, 454
Three Moments of an Explosion: Stories, 404
Thucydides, 344
Thuggee, 327
Thurible, 449
Tianjin, 482
Tiber, 317
Tiberius, 316, 400, 559
Tiberius Gracchus, 397
Tibia, 171
Tiglath-Pileser III, 553
Tihar Jail, 51
Timbavati Game Reserve, 513
Timbuktu, 511
Timbuktu (2014 film), 511
Time (magazine), 545
Timothy Brook, 485
Timothy Brook (historian), 484
Timothy Evans, 28
Timurid dynasty, 142, 323
Tiradentes, 49, 288
Titan (mythology), 297
Titian, 322, 323
Titus, 254, 258
Tobago, 220
Toise, 444, 445
Tokugawa Shogunate, 264
Tokyo subway sarin attack, 20
Tokyo Trials, 24
Tom Howard (photographer), 101
Tom Ketchum, 42, 43
Tony Soprano, 297
Torah, 5, 323, 334, 487, 488, 494
Torah Laws, 491
Torf-Einarr, 161
Torr, 430
Torre dei Gualandi, 357

Torso, 364, 454
Torture, 16, 167, 171, 276, 279, 291, 318, 364, 450, 506
Torture murder, 25
Torturous death, 487
Totality principle, 1
Totila, 323
Toulouse, 224
Tour de Nesle Affair, 323
Tower of London, 114, 300
Toxication, 411
Toxicity, 410
Toxicology, 410
Toxic substance, 410
Toyotomi Hideyoshi, 165, 265
Traditional Chinese characters, 476, 477
Trafficking in human beings, 4
Traitor, 330
Traitors, 364
Trajan, 254, 456, 543
Transcendence (philosophy), 484
Transitional Federal Government, 22
Travancore, 150
Treachery Act 1940, 58
Treason, 2, 4, 16, 25, 119, 200, 301, 316, 320
Treason Act 1351, 298, 301
Treason Act 1695, 302
Treason Act 1790, 231, 309
Treason Act 1814, 309, 310
Treason Felony Act 1848, 310
Treaty of The Hague (1720), 374
Treblinka extermination camp, 104
Trial by combat, 4, 64
Trial by ordeal, 136, 191
Triarchy of Negroponte, 461
Tripoli, 222
Tripolitsa Massacre, 220
Triumvir, 508
Tropa de Elite, 232
Tsardom of Russia, 177
Tsutomu Miyazaki, 54
Tubocurarine chloride, 79
Tudor period, 392
Tulayha, 221
Tunica molesta, 203
Tunis, 221
Túpac Amaru II, 291, 292
Turco-Persian, 153
Turi (Pashtun tribe), 234
Turkey, 31
Turkic peoples, 323
Turret clock, 426
Turtle, 117
Tusk, 141
Twelver, 263
Twelve Tables, 203, 454

Twenty-six Martyrs of Japan, 265
Twilight (2008 film), 296
Twitter, 268
Tyburn, 57, 545
Type 56 assault rifle, 69
Tyrant, 167
Tyre, Lebanon, 260, 401

Üç Şerefeli Mosque, 222

Ugarit, 370
Ugolino della Gherardesca, 357
Ukiyo-e, 280
Ukraine, 19
Ulema, 222
Ulna, 256
Ulpian, 203
Umar, 263
Unconsciousness, 74, 512, 514
Unequal justice, 261
UNICEF, 22
Unionists (American), 60
United Arab Emirates, 70, 268, 487
United Nations, 21, 29
United Nations General Assembly, 3
United Nations Human Rights Council, 21
United States, 18, 19, 21, 23, 92
Unit of length, 444
Universal House of Justice, 248
University of Cambridge, 482
University of Miami, 84
Unlawful combatants, 119
UN moratorium on the death penalty, 3, 29
Unsupported attributions, 89, 90
Upright jerker, 37
Ur, 347
Urbain Grandier, 214
Urechye, 531
US Coast and Geodetic Survey, 441
U.S. Court of Appeals for the Ninth Circuit, 108
US Department of State, 166
Use of capital punishment by nation, 4, 16
USSR, 266
Utah, 73, 132
Utah Territory, 132
Utica, Tunisia, 284
Utilitarian, 10
Utopia (book), 15
Uzbekistan, 166

Valdemar Atterdag, 549
Valens, 294, 455
Valerius Maximus, 144, 396, 486
Valknut, 160
Vantaa, 115, 130

Vasile Ursu Nicola, 375
Vasil Levski, 49
Vasily Vereshchagin, 151
Vatican City, 119
Vecuronium bromide, 81
Vellore Mutiny, 150
Venetian Republic, 374
Venezuela, 16
Venice, 210
Venipuncture, 74
Venom, 410
Verdict, 1
Verge escapement, 419
Vermin, 474
Vertebral arteries, 513
Vertebrate trachea, 513
Verulamium, 334
Vestal Virgin, 187, 191, 341
Vestal Virgins, 340
Vesta (mythology), 191, 341
Viceroy of India, 527
Vichy France, 57
Victor Feguer, 61
Victoria and Albert Museum, 321
Victoria (Australia), 49
Victorian morality, 154
Victor Suvorov, 233, 538
Viet Cong, 280
Vietnam, 19, 77, 138, 477
Vietnamese Martyrs, 463
Vietnam War, 193, 280
Viking, 323
Vikings, 44
Vilvoorde, 191, 192
Vincente de Valverde, 228
Vincenzo Gamba, 417
Vincenzo Viviani, 417
Viper, 394
Virginia, 84, 92, 100, 102, 103
Virginity, 504
Virgin Mary, 64
Virgins, 374
Visby, 351
Viscus, 279
Visigoths, 223
Vlad III the Impaler, 375
Vlad the Impaler, 346, 375
Voice of America, 568
Volto Santo of Lucca, 274
Votive offering, 172

Wachtebeke, 183
Waco Horror, 233
Waco, Texas, 233
Wade–Giles, 477
Wadi El Natrun, 323

Waffen SS, 58
Wagons East, 296
Waikato Times, 238
Waist chop, 122, 290
Waldensian, 349
Wallachia, 346, 375
Walter Hadwen, 190
Walter LaGrand, 108
Walter Scott, 357
Walter Stewart, Earl of Atholl, 224
Wanda Klaff, 39
Wandsworth (HM Prison), 58
Wandsworth Prison, 58
Wapping, 332
War, 364
War crime, 2
War crimes, 4, 26, 54
War criminal, 42
War elephant, 135, 143
War in Bosnia and Herzegovina, 125
Warmia, 529
War of Currents, 95
Warren Mears, 324
Warriston, 176
Washington College of Law, 33
Washington, D.C., 60, 101
Washington Post, 34
Washington (state), 80
Wasp, 475
Watban Ibrahim al-Tikriti, 54
Water dropwort, 316
Wayback Machine, 275
Weapon, 325
Weight, 429
Weights and measures, 445
Weimar Republic, 119
Well poisoning, 208
Welsh people, 300
Wends, 282
Wenxian Tongkao, 404
Werner Seelenbinder, 128
West Asia, 25
Western Australia, 16
Western culture, 487
Western world, 135
West Feliciana Parish, Louisiana, 100
West Germany, 119
Westinghouse Electric Corporation, 94
Westminster Abbey, 320
West Slavs, 282
Wheel train (horology), 426
Whig (British political party), 302
White elephant (pachyderm), 136
White Rose, 119, 128
Who breaks a butterfly upon a wheel?, 180
Whoever Did This, 297

Wicker man, 204
Wiedergänger, 192
Wikinews:Category:Death penalty, 32
Wikipedia:Avoid weasel words, 128, 258
Wikipedia:Citation needed, 57, 61, 69, 76, 89, 90, 101, 110, 115, 119, 120, 123, 125, 128, 129, 167, 169, 175, 176, 193, 210, 216, 221, 275, 318, 320, 324, 328, 338, 340, 343, 480, 481, 484, 498, 515
Wikipedia:Citing sources, 9
Wikipedia:Link rot, 186, 315
Wikipedia:No original research, 393
Wikipedia:Please clarify, 7, 220, 480
Wikipedia:Verifiability, 494
Wikisource, 160, 250
Wikt:antiporta, 9
Wikt:draconian, 5
Wiktionary:sagittally, 452
Wiktionary:transversely, 452
Wikt:pivot, 411, 412, 425, 437
Wikt:rack ones brain, 180
Wilgefortis, 274
Wilhelm von Grumbach, 289
William Anderson (naturalist), 285
William Blackstone, 27, 216, 312, 544
William Blake, 66, 369
William Bray (antiquarian), 313
William Dean (priest), 304
William de Marisco, 300
William de Soules, 164
William Hacket, 305
William Harrington (priest), 281
William Harrison Ainsworth, 358
William Henry Drayton, 546
William Irvine (historian), 157
William Joyce, 58
William Kemmler, 97, 98
William Kidd, 331, 332
William Lithgow (traveller and author), 211, 289
William Marwood, 41
William Muir, 517, 527
William Perkins (Puritan), 303
William Sawtrey, 216
William Shepherd (minister), 551
Williamsport, Pennsylvania, 190
William St Clair, 536
William Tebb, 190, 199
William the Silent, 281
William Trickett Smith II, 295
William Tyndale, 214
William Wallace, 296, 300, 303
William Wilberforce, 309
Willie Francis, 102
Willow Rosenberg, 324
Winchester, 333

Witch, 59
Witch (Buffyverse), 324
Witchcraft, 4, 7, 25, 200, 215, 217, 234, 374, 504
Witch trials in the early modern period, 7
Wolfgang Behringer, 534
Wolfsangel, 269
Womens rights, 506
Woodcut, 114, 140, 376
Woodstock, Ontario, 188
World Coalition Against the Death Penalty, 31
World War I, 266
World War II, 15, 18, 54, 57, 101, 105, 130, 193, 231, 266, 370
Worm, 475
Wound, 391
WP:NOTRS, 219, 231
Wrecking ball, 449
Württemberg, 63
WWV (radio station), 443
Wyoming, 73, 108, 324

Xerxes II, 486
Xhosa people, 317
Xinjiang, 483
Xipe Totec, 321
Xunzi (book), 477

Yahu-Bihdi, 323
Yakub Memon, 51
Yale romanization of Cantonese, 477
Yama (Hinduism), 465
Yamen, 482
Yard, 444, 446
Yard arm, 558
Yazidi, 502
Yazidis, 193
Yemen, 21, 70, 111, 487
Yerwada Central Jail, 51
Yggdrasil, 44
Yokohama, 264
York, 161
Yuan Chonghuan, 479, 481
Yuan (currency), 77
Yuan dynasty, 479

Zacapa, 232
Zahhak, 452
Zaida Catalán, 121
Zaman Shah Durrani, 153
Zambia, 12
Zaragoza, 210
Zawidow, 544
Zechariah ben Jehoiada, 509
Zhang Heng, 416
Zhang Xianzhong, 320

Zhao Erfeng, 480
Zhengde Emperor, 320
Ziad al-Karbouly, 54
Zina, 25, 492, 498, 501
Zinc, 428
Ziselmius, 454
Zittau, 173, 403
Zombie, 296
Zoophilia, 490
Zorba The Greek, 511
Zoroastrian, 142
Zulu people, 317
Zurich, 174, 374
Zürich, 211
Zwickau, 373
Zyklon B, 104

ויקיעם, 372

www.ingramcontent.com/pod-product-compliance
Lightning Source LLC
Chambersburg PA
CBHW021412300426
44114CB00010B/472